Jewish Identities in Postcommunist Russia and Ukraine
An Uncertain Ethnicity

Before the USSR collapsed, ethnic identities were imposed by the state. After a discussion of concepts of ethnicity and identity, this book analyzes how and why Jews decided what being Jewish meant to them after the state dissolved and describes the historical evolution of Jewish identities, experiences with anti-Semitism, politics, and migration. Surveys of more than 6,000 Jews in the early and late 1990s reveal that Russian and Ukrainian Jews have a deep sense of their Jewishness but are uncertain what it means. They see little connection between Judaism and being Jewish. Their attitudes toward Judaism, intermarriage, and Jewish nationhood differ dramatically from those of Jews elsewhere. Many think Jews can believe in Christianity and do not condemn marrying non-Jews. This complicates their connections with other Jews and their resettlement in Israel, the United States, and Germany, as well as the rebuilding of public Jewish life in Russia and Ukraine. Nonetheless, some postcommunist Jews are transforming religious-based practices into ethnic traditions and increasingly manifesting their Jewishness in public.

Zvi Gitelman is Professor of Political Science and Preston R. Tisch Professor of Judaic Studies at the University of Michigan, where he has been director of the Center for Russian and East European Studies and of the Frankel Center for Judaic Studies. Gitelman has been awarded fellowships by the Guggenheim, Ford, and Rockefeller Foundations; the Institute for Advanced Study at Princeton; and the Davis Center for Russian and Eurasian Studies at Harvard. He has been a research Fellow at Oxford and a visiting professor at Tel Aviv and Hebrew Universities, Central European University (Budapest), and the Russian State University for the Humanities. Gitelman is a summa cum laude graduate of Columbia University where he also received his doctorate. He is the author or editor of 15 books and more than 100 articles in scholarly journals. His book *A Century of Ambivalence: The Jews of Russia and the Soviet Union since 1881* was translated into Japanese and Russian. His most recent edited volume is *Ethnicity or Religion? The Evolution of Jewish Identities*. Gitelman is a member of the U.S. Holocaust Memorial Museum Council and has been active in many academic and civic organizations.

Jewish Identities in Postcommunist Russia and Ukraine

An Uncertain Ethnicity

ZVI GITELMAN
University of Michigan, Ann Arbor

CAMBRIDGE UNIVERSITY PRESS
Cambridge, New York, Melbourne, Madrid, Cape Town,
Singapore, São Paulo, Delhi, Mexico City

Cambridge University Press
32 Avenue of the Americas, New York, NY 10013-2473, USA

www.cambridge.org
Information on this title: www.cambridge.org/9781107608733

© Zvi Gitelman 2012

This publication is in copyright. Subject to statutory exception
and to the provisions of relevant collective licensing agreements,
no reproduction of any part may take place without the written
permission of Cambridge University Press.

First published 2012

Printed in the United States of America

A catalog record for this publication is available from the British Library.

Library of Congress Cataloging in Publication Data

Gitelman, Zvi Y.
Jewish identities in postcommunist Russia and Ukraine : an uncertain ethnicity / Zvi Gitelman.
   p. cm.
Includes index.
ISBN 978-1-107-02328-4 (hardback)
1. Jews – Russia – Identity.   2. Jews – Ukraine – Identity.   3. Jews – Russia – Politics
and government – 20th century.   4. Jews – Russia – Social conditions – 20th century.
5. Jews – Russia – Politics and government – 21st century.   6. Jews – Russia – Social conditions –
21st century.   7. Jews – Ukraine – Politics and government – 20th century.   8. Jews – Ukraine –
Social conditions – 20th century.   9. Jews – Ukraine – Politics and government – 21st
century.   10. Jews – Ukraine – Social conditions – 21st century.   11. Russia – Ethnic
relations.   12. Ukraine – Ethnic relations.   I. Title.
DS134.86.G58   2012
305.892′4047–dc23   2012010131

ISBN 978-1-107-02328-4 Hardback
ISBN 978-1-107-60873-3 Paperback

Cambridge University Press has no responsibility for the persistence or accuracy of URLs for
external or third-party Internet Web sites referred to in this publication and does not guarantee
that any content on such Web sites is, or will remain, accurate or appropriate.

For our grandchildren
איתן אריאל, דוד יהודה, יקירה שרה,
נתנאל שי, שרה שושנה, ובנימין אלון

Contents

Acknowledgments	*page* ix
Introduction	1
1. Ethnicity and Identity	19
2. The Evolution of Jewish Identities	46
3. Soviet Policies and the Jewish Nationality	79
4. Construing Jewishness in Russia and Ukraine	103
5. Judaism and Jewishness: Religion and Ethnicity in Russia and Ukraine	119
6. Becoming Soviet Jews: Friendship Patterns	158
7. Acting Jewish: Jewish Collectivities or Communities?	176
8. Anti-Semitism and Jewish Identity	195
9. Identity, Israel, and Immigration	234
10. Ethnicity and Marriage	265
11. Politics, Affect, Affiliation, and Alienation	296
Conclusion	326
Appendix A: The Evolution of a Survey	349
Appendix B: Index of Jewishness	354
Index	359

Acknowledgments

What began as a chance meeting with two Soviet sociologists in Moscow in late 1989 resulted in the most ambitious and comprehensive surveys of the outlooks of Jews living in Russia and Ukraine in the 1990s. This book is the culmination of my collaboration with Dr. Valeriy Chervyakov and Professor Vladimir Shapiro. Together we designed surveys of Jews in the former Soviet states, and they supervised their implementation during the course of the 1990s. The data were processed in Moscow and we spent a summer in Ann Arbor analyzing them. I am deeply grateful to both of them, and to Irina and Natasha, for their friendship, hospitality, entrepreneurship, and exhilarating collective efforts in "turning up the virgin soil" of empirical research among post-Soviet Jews.

Over the years many people and institutions have read parts of our study and have thereby contributed to this book. At the University of Michigan, I learned a great deal from my colleagues in the Department of Political Science, John Jackson and Ashutosh Varshney (now at Brown University), and in History, Todd Endelman and Ronald Suny. My old friends and collaborators, Kenneth Goldstein and Lenore Weitzman read parts of the book, providing constructive criticism and useful comments. I could not have written the book without the data analysis and comments by then-students and now Drs. Su-Feng Kuo, Jae-Jae Spoon, and Vsevolod Gunitskiy. Andrea Jones-Roy, Stephanie Ketchum, and Jennifer Miller were also helpful. Patrick O'Mahen, from whom I learned a great deal, did the final data analyses and prepared tables and charts as well as Appendix A. I appreciate the patience, good cheer, and encouragement of all my colleagues who gently guided me into some of the mysteries of data analysis and tactfully suggested that some details of Soviet history and politics, Yiddish linguistics, and arcane rabbinic writings might not be of that much interest to most readers.

Over many years an embarrassingly large number of institutions have provided me with time off from teaching, as well as financial support and congenial settings. They include the Center for Russian and East European Studies, the Frankel Center for Judaic Studies, and the Department of Political Science, all at the University of Michigan; the National Council for Eurasian and East European Research; the Oxford Centre for Hebrew and Jewish Studies; the Institute for Advanced Study at Princeton and the Institute for Advanced Studies at the Hebrew University, Jerusalem; the Annenberg Center for Advanced Jewish Studies (now Herbert D. Katz Center) at the University of Pennsylvania; the Davis Center for Russian and Eurasian Studies, Harvard University; the Budapest Collegium; and the Yitzhak Rabin Center for Israel Studies, Tel Aviv. Our field research was funded in part by the Russian Jewish Congress, Dr. David Egger, the Jewish Community Development Fund, and the Jewish Studies Center, Institute of Sociology, Russian Academy of Sciences.

Many times my wife Marlene patiently awaited my return from several parts of the world and my daily retreats into "working on the book." Her support and forbearance are not visible in the text that follows, but without them it could not have been written.

Introduction

> One can say with confidence that there is no people that talks as much about itself and knows so little about itself as the Jews.... Yet... we find among Jews no serious interest in Jewish culture, no attention paid to their preservation and further development and not the slightest conscious striving for studying the national weltanschauung and national characteristics of the Jewish nation.[1]

When empires or states break up and territorial configurations and political jurisdictions change, people must adjust their formal citizenship, their political allegiances, and, very often, their cultures. They adapt to new circumstances with varying degrees of enthusiasm. Some welcome a break from the past, others cling to past loyalties, and still others merely go along with the new realities.

During the twentieth century, people in the former Russian Empire, East Central, and Southeastern Europe lived through frequent changes in their states and official cultures. For example, a resident of Lemberg in 1918 was a citizen of the Hapsburg or Austro-Hungarian Empire, but by 1920 had become a Polish citizen living in the same city, which was then called Lwow. Nineteen years later, he or she became a Soviet citizen living in Lvov, only to come under Nazi German occupation in 1941, return to Soviet jurisdiction in 1944, and become a citizen of independent Ukraine in 1991, in a city now called Lviv. Similarly, a person living in Austro-Hungarian Czernowitz in 1918 became a Romanian citizen in Cernauti, a Soviet citizen in Chernovtsy, a subject of the Nazis (1941), a Soviet citizen again, and a citizen of independent Ukraine, resident in Chernivtsi. People in Lithuania, Poland, Hungary, Romania,

---

[1] S. Rappoport [An-sky], "Evreiskoe narodnoe tvorchestvo," *Perezhitoe* (St. Petersburg: Brokgauz-Efron, 1908), Vol. 1, 1. Gabriella Safran kindly alerted me to this opening statement by the famous ethnographer and dramatist.

I

Czechoslovakia, and Yugoslavia (the latter two states created after World War I) had similar experiences.

The disintegration of the Soviet Union and other socialist states resulted in similar kinds of dislocations. Fifteen newly independent states emerged from the shards of the USSR, Czechoslovakia became two states, and Yugoslavia fractured into six warring states.

Like other citizens, Jews had to shift their political and cultural allegiances as states and regimes changed. However, although others continued to live in territories they could call their own, Jews remained an ethno-cultural minority everywhere. This status posed special challenges because most had some sort of Jewish identity that had to be reconciled with the shifting allegiances and identities brought about by political and cultural changes.[2]

The collapse of the USSR gave peoples a chance to redefine themselves as they wished. Before then, the state had prescribed what is a nation, who qualified for national status, and who would be relegated to such lower classifications as *natsional'nost'* (ethnic group), tribe, or clan. Soon after the Bolshevik seizure of power in 1917, the authorities decided that Jews were a "nationality" or ethnic group, ignoring the age-old religious character of the Jewish entity. In the 1930s and thereafter, the Soviets discouraged and made very difficult the acquisition and transmission of any kind of Jewish cultural, not to speak of religious, content. However, in the decade following the fall of the Soviet system – the 1990s – Jews, as well as all other peoples of the USSR, could redefine themselves, their religious commitments and civic or political attachments. Nearly two of every five Soviet Jews chose to leave their country, creating the largest Jewish immigration in Israel's history and the largest Jewish immigration to the United States in a century, and increasing the Jewish population of post-1945 Germany approximately tenfold. Those who remained could assert, deny, or remain indifferent to their "Jewishness," meaning a sense of belonging to an entity called the Jews and identification by others as belonging to it. Thus, the years between 1992 and the beginning of the twenty-first century were ones of dramatic opportunities and demographic, social, and psychological change. This book is a study of those changes, their long-term consequences, and what we can learn from the experiences of Jews in the two largest postcommunist states about ethnicity and ethnic identity more generally.

In recent decades, identity has been much discussed among social scientists and humanists. After all, who people think they are influences how they think and act, which in turn affects the thinking and behavior of others. Many categories can be used to answer the questions, "Who am I and who are you?" One can mention a name, a vocation, a geographical designation, or an

---

[2] Marsha Rozenblit, *Reconstructing a National Identity: The Jews of Habsburg Austria during World War I* (New York: Oxford University Press, 2001). See also Hillel Kieval, "Negotiating Czechoslovakia: The Challenges of Jewish Citizenship in a Multiethnic Nation-state," in Richard Cohen, Jonathan Frankel, and Stefani Hoffman, eds., *Insiders and Outsiders: Dilemmas of East European Jewry* (Oxford: Littman Library, 2010).

affiliation such as religion, race, ethnic group, club, or the like. Most people identify with many groups. The social scientist then asks which identity is most important to the person. The usual answer is that it depends on the circumstances.

In the Middle East, in the nineteenth and much of the twentieth centuries, the first answer given to the "who are you?" question might likely have been a religion – Muslim, Christian, Jew. In Europe it was just as likely to have been an ethnic group or nation – English, French, Russian. Many expected these two categories, religion and ethnicity, to fade in importance as modernization proceeded, because they assumed that industrialization, education, and urbanization would produce secularization and that class consciousness would replace ethnic or national affiliation. One would have expected these broad social changes to have occurred most rapidly and thoroughly in the Soviet Union, a state dedicated to industrial-style modernization, the eradication of religion and its replacement by "scientific" thinking, and the amalgamation of ethnic groups and nations into a human whole differentiated only by class – and that only temporarily.

Within Soviet society, the Jewish minority should have been in the forefront of these linear trends, according to Marxist thinkers, including Vladimir Ilyich Lenin, founder of the Soviet state. At the time of the Bolshevik Revolution, Jews were more urbanized than almost every other people of the collapsing Russian Empire; they also had higher rates of literacy and a strong socialist secular movement (the Bund), although the Jewish nationalist movement, Zionism, was quite powerful. Most Jews were still nominally religious – and Orthodox to boot – but there were clear signs of secularization. Secular Hebrew and Yiddish literatures had developed rapidly from the mid-nineteenth century on, and Jews belonged to political and cultural movements that were secular in intent or practice.

The Bolshevik Revolution accelerated these trends, putting the full force of a strong state behind them. For more than seven decades, from 1918 to 1992, Jews and others experienced state-directed economic and educational modernization, campaigns against religion, and a nominal commitment to "friendship of the peoples" – the elimination of prejudice and ethnic competition – as a prelude to a society without ethnic divisions and even ethnic groups. The Soviet experiment in social engineering that ended in 1991 yielded mixed results. It transformed the economy, which was overwhelmingly agricultural in 1917, into a mighty but flawed industrial one; spread literacy from about 20 percent of the population to just about all of it, but restricted access to reading materials; and achieved much in science, technology, and the arts, but lagged behind other countries. Income differentials were far lower than in capitalist societies, but the general standard of living was low. Only old people went to church, mosque, or synagogue, but fewer and fewer believed in Marxist-Leninist doctrine. People of different ethnic groups were marrying each other and seemed to identify above all as Soviet citizens, not as members of particular ethnic groups, but in the late 1980s ethnic riots broke out in Kazakhstan, the

Caucasus, and elsewhere, and in 1991 the USSR fractionated along ethnic fault lines.

By the 1980s the cracks in the façade of Soviet success had become obvious even to its most dedicated supporters. One of them, Mikhail Gorbachev, courageously allowed them to be exposed and tried to patch them up. What began as a reconstruction (perestroika) effort ended with the collapse of the entire structure, its foundations so deeply rotten that it could not stand firm as renovation proceeded.

After the collapse of the Soviet Union, its successor states and societies had to decide how to deal with ethnicity. Should it be resuscitated and encouraged, repressed, or merely tolerated? What did the ex-Soviet nationalities (ethnic groups) want to do? Should states help, discourage, or ignore them? The breakup of the Soviet Union and the shattering of a common political ideology and system forced people to look for other bases of connection, protection, and solidarity. Religion is one obvious alternative. In times of crisis the family is another. If the ethnic group is viewed as an extension of the family, as another ring in the concentric circles of social connection surrounding an individual, then the ethnic group too should be an anchor or haven. One observer of a small ethnic group in the Caucasus remarked that the dissolution of the Soviet Union and the collapse of such values as "the Soviet people" and the collective (she did not mention socialism) made the family and the ethnic group all the more important as sources of stability and identity: "In unstable conditions, a person strives to identify with a group that defends him/her from the difficulties of the new economic times, and helps the person restore integrity and good order [*uporiadochenost'*]."[3]

This study of the reconstitution of post-Soviet Jews focuses on the group that seemed most likely to be postethnic and postreligious. It is based on interviews conducted with 6,664 Jews in Russia and Ukraine over the first post-Soviet decade, the 1990s, as part of the largest empirical study of Jews in the Former Soviet Union. Perestroika and glasnost [openness] made it possible for two Soviet researchers, Professor Vladimir Shapiro and Dr. Valeriy Chervyakov, to meet with me, an American academic, in 1989–90 and plan a study that could not have been carried out while the USSR existed. We were able to implement it several years later in the USSR's two largest European successor states, Russia and Ukraine. When we met in 1989 in Moscow at the founding congress of the Va'ad, the organization formed as an umbrella group for all the nascent Soviet Jewish organizations, we agreed to seize the opportunity to find out what Soviet Jews really thought about themselves. We had many questions. How did they conceive their Jewishness, and how did they come to their understandings of this ancient but elusive identity? What, if anything, were they prepared to do about their Jewishness? Would they be most influenced by Jews elsewhere or by other ethnic groups in their own country? It was far from

---

[3] L. [iudmila] A. [lievna] Delova, *Mezhetnicheskaia sem'ia v polikul'turnom sotsiume* (Maikop: OAO "Poligraf-iug," 2009), 64.

clear whether Jews would be willing to talk to researchers about what had been a touchy, sometimes even dangerous, subject. Even if they were, how would we find them and construct a reasonably representative sample from which we could generalize? Would they give truthful answers or assume we represented a government – theirs or another – or an organization with its own agenda?

Using their experience in Soviet fieldwork and Shapiro's connections with Jewish cultural and academic activists, my colleagues devised a plan to do the research in eight cities, three in Russia and five in Ukraine, that encompass the diversity of the Jewish population of what had just become the *Former* Soviet Union. We hammered out a questionnaire, mostly in the kitchen of Valeriy and Irina Chervyakov in the Ostankino neighborhood in Moscow, pretested it, revised it, and went into the field in 1992/93. Appendix A describes our methods and sample.

We were pleasantly surprised that almost everyone we approached agreed to be interviewed and treated our interviewers warmly and respectfully. The interviewers, mostly middle-aged women with some Jewish background and middle-level education, were trained intensively by Shapiro and Chervyakov. In the Russian and Jewish traditions, the respondents often invited them to share cups of tea and other refreshments. Most interviews lasted about an hour and a half, but some went on for three hours or longer. Respondents took our questions seriously, pondered, and answered in what seemed to us an honest, thoughtful way.

Realizing that this might be a unique opportunity, we touched on every subject we thought relevant to our exploration of what it means to be Jewish. Because our respondents had rarely if ever been asked their opinions by market researchers or social scientists, and they had most certainly never been queried about Jewish matters, they did not suffer from interview fatigue. In fact, when, we routinely promised them anonymity, some were disgruntled because they wanted "the world to know" what they thought.

Because the interviews were anonymous, and also because so many had emigrated or passed away, when we returned to the field five years later in 1997/98, to see what changes had taken place, we were not able to interview the same people with whom we had spoken earlier. However, we constructed our sample in the same way and repeated most of the questions although we did add and drop some questions. We also decided to go beyond the quantitative data and conducted sixty-four extended conversations, eight in each city. Those who were chosen to participate in these interviews represented different types in the sample – men and women, young and old, people involved in Jewish activity and those who were not, and more and less educated. We did not try to structure our samples by "class" or income because by the 1990s, Soviet Jews were about 98 percent urban and at least half had some form of higher education. Moreover, income differentials were small and consumption styles in the USSR could vary only in a narrow range.

To our surprise, when we analyzed the data we found that gender explained almost none of the variation in our findings. There are clear differences among respondents from Russia and those from Ukraine, although city of residence did not consistently account for them. The single most powerful explanatory variable is age. The various age groups display quite different outlooks and behaviors and for good historical reasons.

We did not rely on the surveys alone to make our analyses and draw our conclusions. Shapiro and Chervyakov had lived their whole lives in the Former Soviet Union (FSU) and brought a Jewish and a non-Jewish perspective and life experience to the project. I am an American Jew, who received an extensive Jewish education and has been studying Russian Jews for more than forty years. We have drawn on the Russian and Western literatures on ethnicity, politics, and sociology and placed our case in the broader context of collective ethnic identities and how they are affected by rapid social change.

What Did Not Happen and Why

In recent decades there has been a resurgence of religions and ethnic affirmation worldwide, including in the most developed countries. How should one explain the fact that the overwhelming majority of Americans claim to believe in God? If religion is passé, why do nearly half of Americans claim to attend religious services regularly,[4] especially when other parts of the Western world have become increasingly secularized? In 2004, a study of Britons found that one-third of the young people surveyed described themselves as agnostics or atheists and only 44 percent of Britons said they believed in God, in contrast to the 77 percent who asserted such belief in 1968. Fully 81 percent said that Britain was becoming more secular.[5] Few people in Scandinavia and other European countries claim to attend religious services regularly, and even in traditionally Catholic societies such as Italy and Spain, church doctrines are regularly flouted and people behave as they wish. If being Jewish means adhering to Judaism, the tribal religion of the Jews, what possible meaning could that have for presumably secularized Jews in a militantly atheist state, the USSR?

Ethnicity was also predicted to fade with time. In the nineteenth and twentieth centuries, the heyday of nationalist ideologies and movements, nationalists argued that the nation was the most important social unit and individuals should subjugate themselves to it. Many thought or hoped that the emergence of nations from under imperial dominance would promote democracy by strengthening group and individual rights. At the same time, other theorists, policy makers, and ordinary people looked forward to the day when nations, ethnic groups, and religions would disappear. They saw nationalism as leading to violence and repression. Just when nationalism was all the rage, Karl Marx and others envisioned a world without nations. Indeed, the repression of ethnic and religious minorities by emergent national majorities and the militaristic

---

[4] See Pippa Norris and Ronald Inglehart, *Sacred and Secular: Religion and Politics Worldwide* (New York: Cambridge University Press, 2004).
[5] *The Star* (Johannesburg), December 28, 2004.

nationalism of the Axis powers in World War II demonstrated that nationalism was a two-edged sword.

In theory, the Soviet Union aimed for its own dissolution and the disappearance of nations, religions, and ethnicity. Dedicated to the implementation of the theories of Karl Marx and Friedrich Engels, who looked forward to classless societies and a world without nations, the early Bolsheviks envisioned a worldwide class revolution that would render nationalism irrelevant. Yet Lenin, ever the political pragmatist, realized that ethnicity would persist longer than most Marxists expected. He propounded a dialectical theory whereby nations, especially those that had been oppressed, would have to be liberated and allowed to develop their cultures as a prelude to their eventual decline and disappearance. Thus, the Soviet state encouraged the development of national consciousness, reformed and promoted national cultures, and created political boundaries based on ethnic criteria, all the while paying lip service to the goal of eventual mutual assimilation. At the same time, the USSR selectively repressed ethnic groups and denied them opportunities for cultural and political development that were given to others. At the end of its seventy-four-year run, the Soviet system's record was mixed: it had raised national consciousness to the extent that in 1991 several nations, which had not existed before the 1917 Revolution, became independent states (five Central Asian states and Moldova), and others seized the opportunity to act on pre-Soviet national urges and declared political independence (the Baltic states, Armenia, Georgia, and Ukraine).[6] Yet, under the Soviet system other peoples had lost their traditional homelands, the use of their national languages, and their particular religious character. Their national consciousness and national cultures had been weakened, in some cases to the point where they no longer constituted a distinct ethnic group (Karaites, some peoples of the Caucasus).

Some "nationalities" (in Soviet nomenclature, but more like the Western term "ethnic groups") had no territories in the USSR they could call their own, but had historical, cultural, and religious links to co-ethnics and co-religionists abroad: for instance, Jews, Poles, Koreans, Germans, and Greeks. Because they would not construct states of their own and were by the late twentieth century culturally distant from their co-ethnics, how would these groups fit into the new post-Soviet states? Some wanted to become part of these states, but others were indifferent to the prospect. This freedom to choose affords the external observer the opportunity to observe how ethnicity is reconstituted, by whom, and in what ways. Such observations can tell us much about the nature of ethnicity and the processes of rethinking ethnic affiliation and reconstituting ethnicity.

Jewishness: Ethnicity, Religion, Culture, or Community?

This study of ethnic and religious reconstruction among Jews in the Russian Federation and Ukraine examines the public, collective, and institutional

---

[6] Belarusians, who never had a viable independent state, appeared to be divided between those who wanted to separate themselves from the Russians and those who felt no need to do so.

dimensions of the reconstitution of Jewishness, but focuses on the reformulation of individuals' conceptions of what it means to be a Jew. We aim to cast new light on the meanings of ethnicity in general and on Jewish ethnicity in particular, as well as on the interaction between ethnic groups and the historical, cultural, social, and political environments they inhabit.

Identity is a person's sense of self in relation to others. A conscious identity places a person in a group that has a set of views of the world, values, beliefs, and practices that set it apart from other groups. The group influences how its members perceive the world and think and act in it. Yet if the group loses its religion, culture, institutions, and other ethnic markers, how does this loss affect its members? Ethnic groups are not immutable forces of nature – they can be created and destroyed, emerge and disappear. In the past few centuries, Ukrainians, Palestinians, and Bosnians, for example, have emerged as nations from previously inchoate groups, whereas Sorbs, Transylvanian Germans, and Karaites have nearly faded into the pages of history. Soviet Jews seemed destined to be in the vanguard of the assimilated, as Lenin had remarked approvingly. By the 1950s they had lost much of their cultural distinctiveness, and many nominal Jews preferred to be classified as members of some other nationality. Ironically it was the Soviet state's insistence on classifying all its citizens by nationality, as well as people's perceptions that Jews were "different" and not Russians or Ukrainians, that kept the Jews from assimilating.

What kind of Jewishness resulted from the simultaneous stripping away of culture and religion and the state's insistence that Jews remain Jews? It is an identity without much cultural content, a label as much imposed from outside the group as it is the name of a group that interacts intensively. Nevertheless, a sense of belonging to "the Jews" that most people find very hard to articulate persists even in the absence of any concrete Jewish content. As one young person expressed it,

> I knew we were Jews, and could not understand what it meant, because nobody could explain it to me.... We spoke Russian, ate the same food, wore the same clothes, dad was an officer – everything is the same. I only knew it was something different, not good.... It was a secret of my childhood... something mystical around them [Jews]. There are many of them, they are visible, they are in Moscow, they are in Leningrad, they are everywhere. They are humanitarians [humanists?], they are technicians, they are great scientists and they are illegal.... This was a secret and I had to guess it.[7]

Some residents of Russia and Ukraine who speak Russian, never visit a synagogue or observe a Jewish ritual, know not one word in any Jewish language, are married to non-Jews, and have never been to Israel and are not interested in going there nevertheless "feel" they are Jewish. Why? Is it only because others

---

[7] "Informant 3" (a person refused permission to emigrate in the 1970s, now living in the United States), quoted in Olesya Shayduk-Immerman, "Where Did the Soviet Jewish Movement Move: Research Methodology," paper delivered at the annual meeting of the Association for the Study of Nationalities, Columbia University, April 8–9, 2009.

insist that they are Jews or that they may have suffered because of their Jewish identity? Is the simple – and in most people's view – unfortunate accident of birth to a Jewish parent or parents sufficient to make them Jewish, however others may categorize them? Or does Jewishness, like other ethnicities, have staying power that cannot be accounted for easily by the categories of social analysis? Is attachment to ethnicity – be it positive or negative – not primarily formal and institutional but rather emotional or psychological, making it as difficult to describe in words as love or religious belief? Is a common historical experience sufficient to maintain a distinct identity, so that a group that saw as many as 55 percent of its members (2.7 million out of about 5 million) systematically murdered between 1941 and 1945 is likely to trust its members more than others?

That some Soviet citizens of different nationalities collaborated in the Nazi atrocities of the 1940s and that the Soviet government itself persecuted Jews after World War II may have been sufficient to foster a sense that even when Jews no longer share a faith, they have a common fate. As we shall see, most post-Soviet Jews to this day consider their Jewishness a burden and a disadvantage. Shared misery became for many the nexus of Jewishness. As one interviewee told us, to be Jewish was to "carry throughout your life a heavy burden of punishment for sins you never committed." Another used a Christian metaphor, "to bear your cross until your last breath." Little wonder that

> Jews were almost the main secret of the Soviet Union. Only sexual life was probably concealed more diligently. Both of these could exist only in the form of euphemisms.... Common sense and a sense of propriety pointed out when, where and with whom an intercourse or Jewish origin could be discussed.[8]

Over many centuries the meanings of being Jewish have changed, influenced by the environments inhabited by Jews. For hundreds of years the primary distinctive characteristic of Jews was their religion, Judaism – a tribal, not universal religion. Every person who practiced Judaism, whatever his or her race or residence, was considered a Jew by all Jews and non-Jews. Yet when the winds of nationalism and secularization swept over Jews in Europe and the Americas in the nineteenth century, some Jews shifted their defining characteristic from religion to ethnicity and nationhood. Zionists argued that, because Jews are a nation, like all other nations they should have a state of their own. Bundists[9] maintained that Jews were a diasporic people with a distinctive culture that could be wholly secular. They needed only cultural autonomy within other states, not a state of their own, to meet their ethnic needs, and their political

---

[8] Piotr Vail and Alexandr Genis, "60-e: mir sovetskogo cheloveka," *Sobranie sochinenii*, tom 1 (Ekaterinburg: U-Faktoriya, 2004), 849 quoted (with slight changes) in Shayduk-Immerman, "Where Did the Soviet Jewish Movement Move," 8.

[9] The Jewish Labor Bund (General League of Jewish Workingmen in Lithuania, Poland, and Russia), was founded in 1897. It stood for social democracy, national-cultural autonomy, and the promotion of secular Yiddish culture.

and economic needs would be met by the socialist revolution in which they would participate with other peoples.

Bundists and Zionists did not deny that Judaism could be a core characteristic of Jewishness for individuals and communities, but they asserted that nonbelievers were also Jews because they were members of an ethnic group or nation. Religious Jews had maintained since biblical times that Jews were a distinctive nation – "*hen am levadad yishkon*" [they are a people who dwell apart, observes the non-Jewish prophet Bil'am; Numbers 23:9]. Religious and secular Jews, Zionists and Bundists, Hebraists and Yiddishists, Polish and Persian Jews recognized each other as members of the same group. The definition of Jewishness had not been completely uprooted and replaced, but some were now emphasizing different historic elements of the notion "Jew."

The experience of European and American Jews in the last 250 years does not, as some would have it, show that "Jewish" is an ever-changing category and has no "essential" meaning. I do not accept the premise that all categories are infinitely flexible and changeable, nor do I believe they are immutable. Rather, they are flexible within boundaries that define who is in the group and who is not. In this book I explore what those boundaries have been historically, how they changed in the Soviet Union, and how they have been rethought and redrawn not only in contemporary Russia and Ukraine but also among Jews everywhere, including those in Israel, the Jewish state.

All conceptions of Jews are hybrids of historic elements and environmental influences. For example, American Jews and Greek Jews speak different languages, listen to different Jewish music, and cook Jewish foods differently, but they have in common core, universally shared elements that define being a Jew: sacred texts and language, many historic memories, holidays, some kind of attachment to Israel, and many values. These may change, but slowly. We return to the definitive characteristics of Jewishness in Chapter 2. Secondary characteristics, such as language or dress, are more amenable to change – perhaps it is their very changeability that defines them as secondary. As we see later, post-Soviet Jews define core and secondary characteristics in various and individual ways, because, unlike other Jewish populations, they had no widely accepted authorities, texts, or communal structures to guide them, and thus no communal consensus.[10] How this anomalous situation came about is summarized in Chapter 3.

Another irony of the Soviet Jewish experience should be pointed out. In the 1920s–30s many young Russian and Ukrainian Jews abandoned their Jewish identities, just when the Soviet government was making unprecedented efforts to promote and disseminate Jewish culture, albeit a de-Judaized one that abjured Hebrew and Zionism; it was a secular, Soviet, and socialist Jewish

---

[10] Of course, there are serious boundary disputes among Jews elsewhere. For example, whereas the Reform movement recognizes as Jewish a person who has only a Jewish father, the other movements do not. Yet, the differences are clear, and there are institutions that articulate and defend each position.

Introduction

culture based on Yiddish. Instead, many in the first postrevolutionary generation embraced Soviet socialism's ideals fervently, including the meta-ethnic nature of the socialist society they were helping build that would render ethnicity irrelevant. Asya Balina, who grew up in Baku in the 1930s, described her thirty-two classmates as follows:

> The class was international. There were Azerbaijanis, Armenians, Georgians, Jews. All of us were very close...we were friends and there were never any discussions or even an idea about who you were [by ethnicity].... There is nothing negative I can tell you. I did not feel it [anti-Semitism]. Not in school, in the university, never. I did not feel that I was Jewish.[11]

In equally cosmopolitan Odessa, many young people paid no attention to their ethnicity ("nationality" in Soviet terminology). They were a-national or postnational, and both then and later they were proud of it. Aleksandr Sepino, who grew up in Odessa, remembered that in school "nobody ever talked about nationality; this question almost did not exist." Among his close friends were an Armenian, a Georgian, Jews, and Russians: they "did not distinguish nationality" and "did not have a clue what it is."[12]

It was only after World War II, when all Yiddish cultural institutions were closed and leading Yiddish and Jewish cultural activists were imprisoned or murdered, that consciousness of Jewishness returned. The same Asya Balina, who was so "internationalist" before the war, moved to Moscow after serving as a physician in the army. It was in 1952–53 that she became aware of being Jewish: "Unfortunately, for the first time in my life I found out that I was Jewish, they let me know." She fell victim to the purges of Jews from their work or study places and to the media's portrayal of Jews as unpatriotic parasites and connivers who had insinuated themselves into Russian culture. This was an unexpected, sharp slap in the collective face of a cohort that was more fervent in its Soviet patriotism than any before or after it. They had never known or had forgotten or abandoned Judaism, Bundism, and Zionism and their teachings and practices, and had embraced Soviet values and Russian culture. Now, suddenly, the main meaning of being Jewish was being a pariah. It was not clear what else being Jewish meant, but it was clear that Jewish identity was something to be denied, repressed, renounced, and forgotten; it was an embarrassment. Some found solace in the accomplishments of "great Jews," foreign and domestic, past and present: Karl Marx, Albert Einstein, Isaac Babel, David Oistrakh, or even Olympic high-jumper Valery Brumel. Of Abraham and Rabbi

---

[11] Interviewed in Detroit in 1997, as part of a project on Soviet Jewish veterans of World War II.
[12] Yad Vashem Archives, 03/5171, quoted by Diana Dumitru, "The Friendship of People Tested: Jews and Non-Jews in Occupied Odessa, (1941–1945)," unpublished essay, pages not numbered. Ironically, today, when Odessa has become far less diverse in its ethnic composition, "the so-called Odesan myth proliferates. Its main elements are vibrant multiethnic diversity, the coexistence of 'locals' and 'foreigners,' and apolitical commerce." Vera Skvirskaja, "New Diaspora in a Post-Soviet City: Transformations in Experiences of Belonging in Odesa, Ukraine," *Studies in Ethnicity and Nationalism* 10, 1 (2010), 79.

Akiva, Moses and Maimonides, Queen Esther and Theodor Herzl they knew nothing. Soviet Jews could point to the accomplishments of individual Jews, but of the cultures and civilizations of Jewish communities they knew little. Therefore, many outside the USSR assumed that Soviet Jews had assimilated. After all, whereas more than 90 percent of Russian Jews considered a Jewish language their "mother tongue" [*rodnoi iazyk*] before the Revolution, only 14 percent of Jews cited a Jewish language in the 1979 census and only 11 percent in the last Soviet census in 1989.[13] This lack of Jewish literacy was understandable because there was not a single Jewish school of any kind throughout the length and breadth of the Soviet Union. Neither Yiddish nor Hebrew could be studied, and there was hardly any Jewish cultural expression in any language, including Russian. Judaism seemed to be dying with the older generations.

The error made by those who did not understand Soviet reality was to confuse assimilation with acculturation. True, most Soviet Jews had lost their original culture and had become thoroughly Russianized. Yet they had not – could not – change their identities. They were Russians culturally, but Jews officially, socially, and psychologically. Many felt a permanent tension between who they thought they were and how the state and society classified them. In the nineteenth century a Russian Jew remarked about the would-be assimilationists: "Our best people have done everything in their power to advance a merging in which they saw the most reliable cure for our ills and for the sake of which they were ready even to give up our traditions . . . but what can one do if those with whom one so wants to merge shun the merger?"[14] During the Soviet era some attempted to resolve Russian–Jewish tensions by emigrating to the Jewish state, Israel, beginning in 1971. In the late 1980s, when emigration was peaking, a significant number of people sought a different way of reconciling their Russian culture and residence with their Jewishness – reviving or creating Jewish cultural institutions within the Soviet Union and the states that emerged from it.

Some considered such an attempt quixotic. Many foreign Jews, especially Israelis, were skeptical of the prospects of Jewish "revival" in the FSU, and some even discouraged it because it would drain resources and attention from what they argued was the only viable way of preserving Jews for Jewishness – through aliyah [ascent] to Israel. Others held that the "process of assimilation is not irreversible"[15] and that, in any case, most FSU Jews had acculturated but

---

[13] There was a steady decline in the proportions giving a Jewish language as their native one. In 1926, less than a decade after the Revolution, only one-quarter of the Jews listed Russian as their mother tongue, whereas by 1939, 55 percent did so. After the war, Russian became the dominant language among Jews in Russia, Ukraine, and even the Baltic, Polish, and Romanian territories annexed in 1939–40.

[14] Lev Levanda, quoted in Jonathan Frankel, *Prophecy and Politics* (Cambridge: Cambridge University Press, 1981), 87.

[15] Svetlana Lur'e, "Etnicheskaia samoidentifikatsiia v usloviakh krizisa 'materinskogo' etnosa: opyt armianskoi obshchiny v Sankt-Peterburg, (1989–1993 gg.)." in *Etnicheskii natsionalizm i gosudarstvennoe stroitel'stvo* (Moscow: IV RAN – Natalis, 2001), 273.

not assimilated. If the spark of Jewish identity could be fanned, and Jewishness turned from a negative to a positive, there would be a chance for the kind of ethnic revival that had occurred in the West where multiculturalism, pluralism, and diversity were being hailed and promoted.

There were no autonomous Jewish communal institutions in the Soviet Union after about 1924 and no government-sponsored institutions after 1948. Perestroika in the late 1980s enabled hundreds of grassroots organizations to appear as if from nowhere. State-directed anti-Semitism disappeared as rapidly as Jewish organizations appeared, and unofficial contacts with foreign Jews and others resumed. Jewish newspapers, magazines, and books were published. In just two years (1988–89), 204 Jewish cultural, athletic, and religious organizations sprang up in 77 Soviet cities. This flurry of organizational activity culminated in establishing the umbrella national Jewish organization, Va'ad, in an air of euphoria, excitement, and anticipation in December 1989. By January 1991 there were 283 Jewish organizations in 85 cities. Yet, at the same time there was mass emigration and the USSR itself fell apart. Still, in April 1995, there were 197 Jewish societies and organizations in 76 cities affiliated with the Va'ad. There were twenty-six Jewish periodicals: seven newspapers, seven journals, and twelve informational bulletins. Radio and TV stations aired programs of Jewish content. Jewish theaters, dance troupes, and musical groups formed, and hundreds of schools were established. Kosher restaurants and stores were opened, yeshivot were established. This seemed to be truly *creatio ex nihilo*.

"Although the role of the initiators [of these processes] was significant, the most important aspect of the emigration of 1989–1992 was the personal accounting that each person carried on in his self."[16] The same held regarding Jewish re-identification. There were domestic and foreign "entrepreneurs" who tried to stimulate it and "guide" FSU Jews to their understanding of what it meant to be Jewish, but ultimately the decision whether and how to reconnect to Jewishness was and is a personal one. The period was seen as a "historic chance to become a nation and not simply a collection of people of 'Jewish (by passport) nationality.'"[17]

As might be expected, there was no agreement on the structure and nature of a revived Jewish community and culture. The Soviet experience had muddled understandings of what it meant to be a Jew, divorcing it from religion, making it a nationality, and then destroying even secular Jewish culture. So what was the content under the label "Jew"? As discussed in Chapter 2, this was not a new question. It arose in the French Revolution and has been debated among Jews and non-Jews ever since. Nor was it an issue unique to Jews. Just about every modern nation has confronted it. "By the time of the revolution there was no unanimity among the Russians on how to define their nation. Whereas

---

[16] Arkadii Levin, "Vliianie tretei volny emigratsii v izrail' na izmenenie natsional'nogo samosoznania evreev SSSR i rossii," in G. Branover and R. Ferber, eds., *Evrei v meniaiushchemsia mire: materialy 1-yi mezhdunarodnoi konferentsii, Riga, 28–29 August 1995g.* (Riga, 1996), 142.
[17] Ibid., 143.

at the turn of the 20th century an ethnic definition of the Russians by language and religion had supporters among intellectuals and government officials, only numerically small extreme nationalist groups saw 'blood' as the main element defining nationality."[18] As we see in Chapter 4, Jews in Russia and Ukraine do not include language or religion in their definitions of their people, but do see biological descent – "blood" – as critical to establishing one's Jewishness.

What Does It Mean to Be a Jew?

Chapter 4 addresses what being Jewish means to Russian and Ukrainian Jews. If being Jewish is not fundamentally about Judaism, traditional customs, Jewish languages, or communal participation and activity, what *is* it about? It is not about behaviors but about identification.[19] Most Jews in Russia and Ukraine conceive of their Jewishness as, first, a matter of descent; second, belonging to a nationality; and, third, subjective feelings of belonging to a group. In their view the most fundamental basis of Jewish identity is being born to Jewish parents. Some say that one must be born of a Jewish mother or that "one must be of Jewish origin according to Halakha," but more say that descent from either a Jewish mother or father is sufficient to qualify as Jewish.[20] The important point, as one put it, is "to have Jewish blood for many generations, Jewish genes." Or, as a Russian Jew expressed it, "If you are a Jew by blood, this will define your entire perception of the world [*mirooshchushchenie*]. Whoever you might be, you will nevertheless feel yourself to be Jewish. You cannot escape this."

Second, Jewish identity is understood in the way the Soviet state defined it; that is, as membership in an ethnic group ("nationality"). "I don't understand the question," said one respondent, "what does it mean to be a Russian or a Yakut? A given [*dannost'*] is a given." Yet, this membership goes beyond official designation. The sense of belonging to a distinct group is quite powerful for most respondents. Two-thirds of Russian respondents said in 1992 that "to feel oneself a part of the Jewish people" is what being Jewish is all about. Nearly as many said that "to be proud of the Jewish people is the essence." Research among Roma uncovered the same concept. Being Roma "is somehow in people's blood, in the soul, something inside a person, which cannot perhaps be described in words."[21]

The most frequent way of expressing these kinds of sentiments among our Ukrainian respondents in 1997 was "to feel yourself part of the Jewish people

---

[18] Vera Tolz, *Russia* (London: Arnold, 2001), 203.

[19] Amyot and Sigelman make this very useful distinction in their analysis of American Jewry. Robert Amyot and Lee Sigelman, "Jews without Judaism? Assimilation and Jewish Identity in the United States," *Social Science Quarterly* 77, 1 (March 1996), 178–79.

[20] In 1997, nearly two-thirds of those we interviewed in Russia and Ukraine said the traditional definition of a Jew as someone with a Jewish mother or maternal grandmother ought to be abandoned. The youngest cohort, those most likely not to meet the halakhic criteria of Jewishness, rejected this definition most strongly.

[21] Camilla Nordberg, "Claiming Citizenship: Marginalised Voices on Identity and Belonging," *Citizenship Studies* 10, 5 (November 2006), 533.

Introduction

[*narod*]" or "to feel an inner kinship with Jews, to feel we're one family." Another respondent put it strongly: "When everything relating to Jews and Jewish life in the world, their culture and the Yiddish and Hebrew languages, that which relates to Israel touches my soul – that's what it is to be a Jew." Some found it difficult to express: "this is an internal feeling. It's difficult to transmit [*peredat'*] it." As a British scholar observes, "If there is one necessary and sufficient condition for membership of an ethnic group, it is surely a subjective feeling of belonging, of kinship, of a desire for group continuity and a sense of corporate identity."[22] Indeed, for quite a few post-Soviet Jews, the only necessary and sufficient condition for being Jewish is to feel oneself a Jew or, as one put it, "to feel yourself a Jew in your soul." Others put the same sentiment even more graphically, as we see in Chapter 4. In sum, two-thirds of the respondents chose descent and the feeling of being part of the Jewish people from among nine criteria offered them for establishing Jewish identity. This parallels what Fran Markowitz found among Soviet Jewish immigrants in Brooklyn, New York. "[For them] being a Jew is an immutable biological and social fact, ascribed at birth like sex and eye color. It may or may not include belief in the Jewish religion, but being a Jewish atheist is not considered a contradiction in terms. Being a Jew is self-evident.... [whereas] in American society where one's Jewishness is not self-evident, it is necessary to demonstrate, both to the Gentile world and the Jewish community, that one is a Jew by doing specifically Jewish things."[23] In the FSU one does not have to *do* anything Jewish; one simply *is* Jewish.

Many add a sense of pride to the feeling of belonging. To be a Jew, it was often remarked, is "to be proud of your nationality." An interesting variant on this theme is the statement that "[t]o be a Jew you should be proud of what your ancestors did in the distant past, giving Christianity to the world, love of God, the ability to survive in all circumstances, not to be enslaved and to rise up from the ashes."

Others see few redeeming qualities in bearing the burdens of being Jewish. One expressed the insecurities of being Jewish by defining it this way: "To be a tightrope walker, to tread carefully along the line; in our circumstances it's very complicated." Most others were less equivocal. "In Ukraine," said several, "to be a Jew is to be an outcast" [*izgoem*]. Another respondent said that to be a Jew is "to be discriminated against, to be persecuted and expelled from one place to another." One man put the same idea in a quintessentially Jewish way. He said simply, "[T]o be a Jew? *az okh un vay*" [alack and alas]!

Some mix an element of pride into the sense of suffering. As one put it, to be a Jew is "to belong to a persecuted, hunted and beaten group who suffer because of the ageless existence of Jewishness [*Evreistvo*]. I am proud to be

---

[22] Stephen Miller, "Religious Practice and Jewish Identity in a Sample of London Jews," in Jonathan Webber, ed., *Jewish Identities in the New Europe* (London: Littman Library of Jewish Civilization, 1996), 199.
[23] Fran Markowitz, "Jewish in the USSR, Russian in the USA: Social Context and Ethnic Identity," in Walter Zenner, ed., *Persistence and Flexibility: Anthropological Perspectives on the American Jewish Experience* (Albany: SUNY Press, 1988), 81, 83.

one of them!" Every sixth respondent in 1992/93 and every fourth in the later survey defined Jewishness largely in negative terms. Yet, it is important to note that among the 16–29 year olds, in 1997/98 only 7 percent mentioned anti-Semitism as the defining factor in Jewishness. It is the factor least often mentioned by this age group in both years of the survey.

The responses we received move across the spectrum from negative feelings about being Jewish to indifference or even rejection of the category of "Jewish" – and perhaps of any nationality. Some believe that to be a Jew is to be defined as such by others, usually pejoratively. "As wise people have said, 'a Jew is a person whom an anti-Semite considers a Jew.'" Then comes rejection of ethnicity. "To be a Jew means nothing. You should be a human being [*chelovek*]." "The most important thing is to be a human being, and who you are by nationality is of no importance." "For me this question does not exist. I don't care about it." One person explained, "For me in principle this means nothing" because "we are so assimilated that it makes no difference."

Further along the spectrum, we find a more positive understanding, the equation of Jewisness with decency. Quite a few respondents opined that to be Jewish is to "be a normal decent [*poriadochnyi*] person." This is not the negation of Jewishness but its universalization. Others believe that Jews are ethical, kind, good, helpful, sympathetic, and intelligent ("to be a Jew means to have a smart Jewish head") – presumably, more so than others. Also on the positive side of the affective spectrum is the idea that Jews should know the customs, traditions, history, and languages of their people. As one put it, you "should feel yourself a Jew and little by little become attached to the Jewish religion and history, and do the same for your children." Finally, the most radical and minority position in the Russian/Ukrainian context is the traditional religious one. "To be a Jew is to be a follower of Abraham, a wanderer and alien in this world, but to go in the direction that God commands people, to carry out his commands and to be blessed." Or, "[t]o believe in and trust the God of Abraham, Isaac and Jacob. To have a personal relationship to God and to do his will, to accept calmly and with gratitude all that you encounter in life."

Of all these conceptions, descent, ethnicity and a feeling of belonging are the most frequently articulated. Although Jews who identify as Jews around the world share a subjective sense of belonging, outside the FSU most would point to some cultural content beyond this feeling as that which defines the group. For most Russian and Ukrainian Jews, however, sentiment and biology have largely replaced faith, Jewish law and lore, and Jewish customs as the foundations of the Jewish edifice. Are these sufficient to elicit commitment, activism and intergenerational continuity?

Uncertain Ethnicity: An Overview

After a discussion of the nature of ethnicity generally and the evolution of Jewish identity in particular (Chapters 1 and 2), I survey Soviet policies toward ethnic groups (nationalities) and toward Jews (Chapter 3). By making "Jewish" an ethnic rather than religious category – historically, it had been both – the Soviets tried to give new, if temporary, meaning to the term. I explore the long-term effects of this attempt, concluding that it generally succeeded. In Chapter 4, I examine in detail how Jews in Russia and Ukraine construed Jewishness in the crucial decade after the dissolution of the USSR and the efforts of religious and ethnic entrepreneurs who tried to influence them. The subject of Chapter 5 is the relationship of post-Soviet Jews to religion generally and to Judaism specifically. Chapter 6 examines the friendship patterns of Russian and Ukrainian Jews. Despite the success of secularization, ethnic attachments were not severed by the state, which was committed to "fusion of the nations" or mutual assimilation. We find a marked preference for Jewish friends among our respondents. Does this mean that Jews are committed to their ethnic group per se or just that shared values, experiences, and outlooks are sufficient to create feelings of kinship? In the 1990s, when the political and social climates were favorable to the reconstruction of ethnic institutions and their unfettered activity, something propelled Jews to organize local, regional, and even national institutions in which post-Soviet Jewishness could be expressed. In Chapter 7 I focus on the reconstruction of Jewish life at the beginning of the decade and how Jews related to that effort at the beginning and end of the 1990s.

During the Soviet period the one element that united Jews was the experience of governmental and social anti-Semitism. I show in Chapter 8 that this was the single greatest creator of Jewish identity. As such, it made being Jewish something negative, a misfortune. Yet, strikingly, neither the youngest group of our respondents nor the oldest has been shaped primarily by anti-Semitism. Jews younger than age 30 came to ethnic and social consciousness in the post-Soviet era when being Jewish is neither a stigma nor a reason for persecution. Jews over 60 came to that consciousness when there was still a tolerated secular Soviet Jewish culture and when ethnic discrimination had not yet become government policy.

Some would argue that the most prominent way of expressing Jewishness is to emigrate to the Jewish state, Israel. Chapter 9 discusses what Jews who remained in the FSU thought of emigration and the impact it has had on them. Along with a few other nationalities whose ancestral homelands are beyond the borders of the successor states to the Soviet Union, after 1971 the Soviet regime permitted limited numbers of Jews to "return" to their historic homeland. By the end of the 1980s, they did so in massive numbers; all told, more than 1.6 million Jews emigrated since 1971, about 60 percent of them to Israel. In 1970, there were 2.15 million self-reported Jews in the USSR. By 1989, there were only 1,449,000, and today there are probably no more than a half-million in the post-Soviet states. Yet no single force led to this massive emigration. Its propellants include anti-Semitism, the search for political and economic opportunity, and the desire to live among a majority of Jews.

In Chapter 10, I consider interethnic marriage. Historically, two strong border markers differentiating Jews from others were religion and marriage.

One who practiced a religion other than Judaism or who married a non-Jew was considered to have left the Jewish fold. The first boundary marker holds among the vast majority of Jews today, though post-Soviet Jews are not certain of its validity, as described in Chapter 5. The second border is being eroded all over the world by increasing rates of marriage to non-Jews. Chapter 10 focuses on Russian and Ukrainian Jews' views of marriage to non-Jews and raises the issue of how Jews outside the FSU regard post-Soviet Jewish identities.

The following chapter examines the political views and preferences of Russian and Ukrainian Jews during windows of democratic opportunity. In the early 1990s many people the world over believed that the Soviet Union was on the way to becoming an archipelago of democracies. By 2000 in Russia and about 2006 in Ukraine these beliefs had been challenged by political developments in the two states. However, in the decade of our fieldwork, politics was still an interesting, hopeful, contested arena.

Jewish ethnicity is complicated by its relationship to religion. Jewishness in the Soviet Union was further complicated by its divorce from religion. Therefore I begin with discussions of ethnicity, Jewish ethnicity, and Soviet policies toward ethnicity.

I

Ethnicity and Identity

Things did not turn out as they were supposed to: ethnic groups were supposed to disappear. Marxists, Western liberals, and social scientists agreed on that but for different reasons. For Marxists, the inevitable demise of capitalism would kill off ethnicity. Others banked on economic development and modernization to render irrelevant ethnicity and other "traditional" categories. Many intellectuals and statesmen believed that the era of ethnicity and nationalism, which had brought such violence and bloodshed to humankind, would soon be superseded by rationalism and science. They felt that the nationalism that propelled World War II had been so discredited that all expressions of ethnicity would be looked at suspiciously. Yet, ethnicity persisted and is one of the fundamental cleavages in many European, Asian, and African societies, as well as in parts of the Americas. As the example of Yugoslavia shows, national or ethnic hatreds still cause war, the dismemberment of states, and the killing of one's neighbors, even in a region that suffered so much from ethnic wars just a half-century earlier.

Ethnicity is a relatively recent category. For centuries, religion was the fundamental cleavage in Western and Middle Eastern societies. Religion was intertwined with the state, and hence with political and social power. Wars were fought over religious affiliations and beliefs, status was assigned on the basis of religious affiliation, and some people were killed because of their religious beliefs. In the nineteenth century, after industrialization had stratified societies beyond the lord–peasant structure, Karl Marx had elucidated the idea of social class and its implications, and Charles Dickens and others had portrayed vividly the realities of capitalism, many appreciated the importance of class as a social cleavage. At the same time, the spread of romantic nationalism in entities that later became Germany, Italy, and France and in the Ottoman, Russian, and Austro-Hungarian Empires raised awareness of another category that differentiated people: ethnicity.

Ethnicity cannot be defined as simply as can religion – a system of beliefs and practices assuming a supernatural deity – or as class, the relationship of a group to the means of production (although many consider this Marxist definition to be overly simple).[1] According to a literary scholar, the word "ethnic" is derived from the Greek *ethnikos*, which itself is a translation of the Hebrew *goy*, which was used to define another people "contrastively, and often negatively," as in association with "heathen."[2] In the nineteenth century "ethnic" was defined as "pertaining to a race or nation," but in the United States it retained its connotation of someone "not fully American."[3]

Scholars have attempted to formulate less value-laden definitions of ethnicity to enable its use in social and political research. Anthony D. Smith offers a useful definition of an ethnic group: "We may define the '*ethnie*' or ethnic community as a social group whose members share a sense of common origins, claim a common and distinctive history and destiny, possess one or more distinctive characteristics, and feel a sense of collective uniqueness or solidarity." The most important element is "the myth of a common and unique origin."[4] Ethnic *categories* are established by those outside the group because they perceive the group as having common characteristics, but the people within that category lack the self-consciousness that turns them into ethnic *communities*. A leading Russian scholar, Valeriy Tishkov, argues that an ethnic group defines itself by those characteristics that the group itself considers significant.[5]

The Soviet state identified all Jews in the USSR as Jews by ethnicity ("nationality" in Soviet nomenclature). However, as our research has made clear, European/Ashkenazic Jews of the former USSR do not see themselves as part of the same group as the Jews of the Caucasus and Central Asia, and possibly vice versa. Likely they do not see themselves as sharing a common culture, because religion played an insignificant role in that culture. There are parallels to Evenks, Gypsies,[6] and possibly members of other groups who may be seen

---

[1] Werner Sollors observes, "Terms like 'ethnicity,' 'melting pot,' 'intermarriage'... are all used in a dazzling variety of elusive ways." *Beyond Ethnicity: Consent and Descent in American Culture* (New York: Oxford University Press, 1986), 5.

[2] Ibid., 25.

[3] Ibid.

[4] Anthony D. Smith, *The Ethnic Revival in the Modern World* (Cambridge, 1981), 66. A similar definition is offered by R. A. Schermerhorn, *Comparative Ethnic Relations* (New York: Random House, 1970), 12. The leading Soviet authority on ethnicity for many years, Yuri Bromley, defined "ethnos" as "a historically formed aggregate of people who share common, relatively stable specific features of culture (including language) and psychology, realization of their unity and distinctiveness from other similar aggregates of people as well as the self-nomination [sic]." "On the Typology of Ethnic Communities," in Regina Holloman and Serghei Ariutiunov, eds., *Perspectives on Ethnicity* (The Hague: Mouton, 1978), 18.

[5] V[aleriy] A[leksandrovich] Tishkov, *Rekviem po etnosu* (Moscow: Nauka, 2003), 60. Tishkov is director of the Institute of Ethnology and Anthropology of the Russian Academy of Sciences and served as the Russian minister for nationality affairs in 1992. He has been accused by Russian nationalists of "gathering intelligence... for the United States under the guise of engaging in research." Igor Romanov, "Tishkov under Attack from Eurasians," *Nezavisimaya gazeta*, June 21, 2007, transl. in *Current Digest of the Post-Soviet Press* 59, 25 (July 18, 2007), 9 [translation slightly revised].

[6] These are cited in Tishkov, *Rekviem po etnosu*, 61.

Ethnicity and Identity

by outsiders as belonging to the same ethnos but who do not see themselves that way, usually because they live in different countries. Nationalist mobilizers thus had to persuade members of ethnic groups living in different countries – Jews after the year 70 CE, Poles between 1795 and 1918, Germans and Italians in the nineteenth century, and Ukrainians in the nineteenth and twentieth centuries – that they are one people who ought to unite and have their own state.

Ethnic groups are defined by shared content and boundaries. "Content" may encompass shared interests, shared institutions, or shared culture, but in most cases is shared language, territory, or religion – the "distinctive characteristics" posited by Smith. Boundaries are the demarcation lines drawn to establish who is in the group and who is not.[7] Both insiders and outsiders draw these lines, but may do so differently.[8] "Ethnic identity, like any other identity, is not only a question of knowing who one is subjectively, but also of how one is seen from the outside."[9] The ethnic (or religious) group itself may formally set criteria for membership, just as a state establishes criteria for citizenship. However, boundaries can also be set by custom, etiquette, and prejudice. Behavioral norms ("Jews don't do that kind of thing;" "Real Russians don't act that way"), dress, or other markers, such as the style of hair, may be used to set boundaries. Hair is probably the most easily manipulated body parts and so can be used to signal affiliation. Sikhs do one thing with their hair, Buddhist monks another, and Orthodox Jews yet another, presumably because they are following religious dictates. The *effect*, however, is to signal their membership in a group and mark them off from others. Food taboos, whatever their origin, have the same effect. To maintain boundaries, the ethnic group creates a set of rules on interethnic interaction, which govern such matters as friendship, hostility, or indifference; socializing (especially eating) with members of other groups; allowing others to acquire membership (e.g., through religious conversion) or not;[10] and, most important of all, marrying into other groups or not.

As mentioned earlier, the outsider may also define the group, if only to distinguish it from the group to which he or she belongs. The criteria of the insider and outsider may not coincide. To take a notorious example, the Nuremberg Laws promulgated by the Nazis in 1935 defined as Jews those who had three or four Jewish grandparents, and categorized those with one or two Jewish

---

[7] Stephen Cornell, "The Variable Ties That Bind: Content and Circumstance in Ethnic Processes," *Ethnic and Racial Studies* 19, 2 (April 1996), 265–89.
[8] The seminal work on boundaries is Frederik Barth, *Ethnic Groups and Boundaries: The Social Organization of Cultural Difference* (Boston: Little, Brown, 1964). See also Sun-ki Chai, "A Theory of Ethnic Group Boundaries," *Nations and Nationalism* 2, 2 (July 1996), 282.
[9] George De Vos, quoted in Anya Peterson Royce, *Ethnic Identity* (Bloomington: Indiana University Press (Bloomington: Indiana University Press, 1982), 33.
[10] Muslims and Evangelical Christians encourage people to join their faith; Zoroastrians forbid it; Jews have generally permitted but discouraged it.

grandparents as "of mixed blood." Rabbinic Jewish law (halakha) has for centuries defined a Jew as one born of a Jewish mother or who has converted to the Jewish religion. Thus, according to Jewish law, one can be a Jew with only a single Jewish grandparent (the mother of one's mother) or no Jewish grandparents at all, if conversion has taken place.[11] Needless to say, Jews and Nazis did not recognize the boundaries set by the other. As we see later, boundary issues have become highly controversial among Jews today, and they are not the only ethnic or religious group involved in boundary disputes.[12]

Historically, the most salient cultural content of the Jewish ethnic group was Judaism, a religion whose compass was so wide – at least in what came to be called its Orthodox variant and that prevailed for about 1,700 years – that it shaped mundane behavior (eating, sexual relations, dress, commercial relations, criminal law, etc.) and molded a culture to a far greater extent than Christianity, but perhaps in ways similar to Islam. Although most contemporary forms of Jewishness appropriate the symbols of Judaism, the content of Jewishness is shifting in many instances away from Judaism, but not toward anything substantive, such as language, kinship patterns, or territory. Few Jews outside of Israel speak a Jewish language – it is possible that more Palestinian Arabs than diaspora Jews speak Hebrew; in all diaspora countries the number of marriages between Jews and non-Jews is increasing, thereby weakening kinship; and there are no distinctively Jewish territories outside Israel.

Language, dress, and food taboos are part of what might be called "thick" culture,[13] which encompasses most of life, conditions much individual and collective behavior, and has tangible manifestations (language, customs, foods, clothing). This kind of culture is increasingly rare among non-Orthodox Jews. Yet there is a second kind of culture, one that is a "common and distinct system of understandings and interpretations that constitute normative order and world view and provide strategic and stylistic guides to action."[14] Styles of life, values, and how one reacts to situations distinguish one group – not necessarily ethnic – from another. This is "thin culture." In contrast to thick culture, which is intense, wide in scope, has well-defined content, and is relatively difficult to acquire, thin culture is "relaxed," optional, with shallow

---

[11] Orthodox, Conservative, and Reform Jews disagree on what the conversion process consists of and by whom it can be performed.

[12] Some Lemkos in Poland feel themselves to be Polish and others Ukrainian, and they may disagree on what makes a Lemko. See Chris Hann, "Ethnicity in the New Civil Society: Lemko-Ukrainians in Poland," in Laszlo Kurti and Juliet Langman, eds., *Beyond Borders: Remaking Cultural Identities in the New East and Central Europe* (Boulder, CO: Westview, 1997). Residents of Moldova debate whether they are "really" Romanians or a separate group. An American-born student of South Asian origin told me he could not decide whether to join the campus Indian student group or the Muslim group. He explained that he could not belong to both simultaneously.

[13] William Mishler and Detlef Pollack, "On Culture, Thick and Thin: Toward a Neo-Cultural Synthesis," in Detlef Pollack, Jorg Jacobs, Olaf Muller, and Gert Pickel, eds., *Political Culture in Post-Communist Europe* (London: Ashgate, 2003).

[14] Ibid., 271.

content, and is easily accessible. The crucial question for Jews who do not live in Israel is whether without substantive, manifest thick cultural content, Jewishness becomes merely "symbolic ethnicity," much like the ethnicity of most Polish Americans or Swedish Americans, or whether thin culture is sufficiently substantive and sustainable to preserve a group's distinctiveness on more than a symbolic level.[15]

Social scientists have debated whether ethnicity is "primordial" or "instrumental," "perennial" or "situational." Like many academic debates, this one makes differentiations that may be useful for analytic purposes but often do not exist in reality. Primordialists hold that one's cognizance of ethnicity is acquired at an early age, arises "naturally" and not as a result of purposive calculation, and is an integral part of the self. Ethnicity is a given of social existence: "For virtually every person, in every society, at almost all times, some attachments seem to flow more from a sense of natural – some would say spiritual – affinity than from social interaction."[16] The anthropologist Clifford Geertz asserts that

> congruities of blood, speech, custom ... have an ineffable, and at times overpowering, coerciveness in and of themselves. One is bound to one's kinsman, one's neighbor, one's fellow believer, ipso facto; as the result not merely of personal affection, practical necessity, common interest, or incurred obligation, but at least in great part by virtue of some unaccountable absolute import attributed to the very tie itself.[17]

In contrast, instrumentalists believe that ethnicity is "constructed." Designed to achieve ends such as social or economic advantage, it is not a constant, but is evoked or suppressed by circumstances. In some situations a person will highlight his or her ethnic identity – perhaps it will be salient in an ethnically heterogeneous group – whereas in others it will not be noticed, as when most people in the environment share the same ethnicity. At times, ethnicity is claimed for personal advantage, as when white American students born in South Africa or in Spain check off the categories "African American" or "Hispanic" on applications to college or financial aid, hoping to qualify for affirmative action programs. Valeriy Tishkov tells of a deputy to the legislature who in the early 1990s declared that the inhabitants of three Siberian villages speaking a Koriak dialect were actually "Aliutortsy" (a made-up name) and deserved recognition. In the oil- and gas-rich area of the Khanty-Mansi there appeared new "ethnoses" who tried to lay claim to the region's resources.[18]

---

[15] For an elaboration of this argument, see Zvi Gitelman, "The Decline of the Diaspora Jewish Nation: Boundaries, Content and Jewish Identity," *Jewish Social Studies* 4, 2 (Winter 1998).
[16] Clifford Geertz, "The Integrative Revolution," in Geertz, ed., *Old Societies and New States* (New York: Free Press, 1963), 109.
[17] Ibid.
[18] Tishkov, *Rekviem po etnosu*, 252.

Social scientists generally dismiss the primordial basis of ethnicity. Calling primordialism "a bankrupt concept," Eller and Coughlan assert that social scientists should reject its "social passivity and anti-intellectualism" and replace it with empirical research. Do they mean that social phenomena based on emotion are "anti-intellectual" or that emotions cannot be researched empirically?[19] Ashutosh Varshney takes a middle position: "No one seriously argues any more that ethnic identity is primordial nor that it is devoid of any intrinsic value and used only as a strategic tool."[20]

It seems that most writers lean toward the instrumentalist position, perhaps because of the vogue of seeing just about everything as "constructed."[21] However, if there were no primordial emotions to tap, it would be very hard, if not impossible, for anyone to mobilize ethnicity for social or political purposes. It is doubtful whether Franjo Tudjman in Croatia or Slobodan Milosevic in Serbia, who clearly used national sentiment instrumentally (and perhaps cynically), would have been able to make the transition from communist to nationalist leaders were there not a preexisting primordial ethnic consciousness among Croats and Serbs. Belarussian politicians who tried between 1991 and 1994 to evoke a sense of Belarussian nationalism among the people of that former Soviet republic failed, whereas some of their peers in the Baltic states and Ukraine succeeded. The difference may be due not only to the skills of the respective politicians but also to the fact that Belarussians have weak attachments to their ethnicity, whereas Ukrainians – especially West Ukrainians – and Balts are intensely committed to their groups and cultures. Comparing several nationalities in the Soviet Union, one scholar found that, as the state was breaking up, ethnic elites had the capacity to set political agendas but their appeals did not work unless there was a predisposition among significant

---

[19] Jack Eller and Reed Coughlan, "The Poverty of Primordialism: The Demystification of Ethnic Attachments," *Ethnic and Racial Studies* 16, 2 (1993), 201, excerpted in John Hutchinson and Anthony D. Smith, *Ethnicity* (Oxford: Oxford University Press, 1996), 45. Steven Grosby severely criticized Eller and Coughlan in the same journal, 17, 2 (1994), excerpted in Hutchinson and Smith, *Ethnicity*, 51–56.

[20] Ashutosh Varshney, "Ethnicity and Ethnic Conflict," ch. 12 in Carles Boix and Susan Stokes, eds., *The Oxford Handbook of Comparative Politics* (Oxford: Oxford University Press, 2007), 291.

[21] "Primordialism appears to have come upon bad times. The 'view of the nation as constructed or invented' is... 'currently dominant.' 'Primordialist theory,' claims David Laitin, is 'theoretically discredited.'" Alexander Motyl wisely suggests that defining characteristics be loosened so that "these properties can come together in various ways and to various degrees" and primordialism and instrumentalism or constructivism can be used as complementary, not mutually exclusive, concepts. *Revolutions, Nations, Empires: Conceptual Limits and Theoretical Possibilities* (New York: Columbia University Press, 1999), 83. Motyl also reminds us of the "cyclical nature of social science theorizing" and that "epistemological robustness is far from the only factor involved in deciding the fate, or popularity, of theories." He cites the trajectories in political science of "institutionalism" and "rational choice" as examples, and many more can be adduced in every field. There may not be much more rationality in the changing fashions in academia than in the garment industry. Fashion changes may sell, because what was "out" becomes "in," but wider or narrower lapels, higher or lower hems, or changing colors do not signal incremental gains in knowledge or understanding.

publics to accept them. Grievances evoke a response only if they fit people's individual experiences.[22]

The debate between primordialists and instrumentalists seems more about scoring academic points than describing what actually happens in most cases, although some postmodernists reject the very notion of *wie es eigentlich ist*. As Pierre Van Den Berghe observes, "The primordial-instrumental debate serves little purpose other than to help Ph.D. candidates organize their examination answers.... Both positions are correct."[23] Paul Brass strikes a sensible note when he notes that elites who manipulate ethnicity for their own ends are constrained by the beliefs and values prevailing among those they seek to mobilize, so that they have to simplify, distort, and select the beliefs that are useful to them, as was done by Muslims in south Asia.[24] If we recognize that the "strength and richness" of cultural traditions and traditional institutions vary among groups, we could discern that in some cases ethnic activism arises more from primordial sources and in others from instrumental uses.[25]

Varshney introduces a third concept, constructivism, which he regards as the new conventional wisdom.[26] He draws a distinction between instrumentalism and constructivism, the former being a "radical *short-run* fluidity of identities," whereas constructivism "is about the *long-run* formation, and the consequent *stickiness* of identities.... That identities are constructed does not mean that they do not become internalized and institutionalized, and acquire meaning."[27] The constructivist approach avoids both the premise of primordialism that ethnicity is "instinctual" and difficult to change and the assumption by instrumentalists that ethnicity is highly labile and is often evanescent. Of course, constructivism is itself a "construct" of academic observers and not a conscious activity of most people: "People may believe all sorts of things about their beliefs and behaviors, but there is no reason... to suppose that they are self-consciously engaging in 'social construction.'"[28]

Nations

The term "nation" has also eluded precise definition, although many have tried to specify the characteristics needed to make a group a nation. Some

---

[22] Elise Giuliano, in Dominique Arel and Blair Ruble, eds., *Rebounding Identities: The Politics of Identity in Russia and Ukraine* (Baltimore: Johns Hopkins University Press, 2006).
[23] *The Ethnic Phenomenon* (New York: Elsevier, 1981), 18. A good discussion of the primordial–instrumental debate is George Scott, Jr., "A Resynthesis of the Primordial and Circumstantial Approaches to Ethnic Group Solidarity: Towards an Explanatory Model," *Ethnic and Racial Studies* 13, 2 (April 1990).
[24] Paul Brass, *Ethnicity and Nationalism: Theory and Comparison* (New Delhi: Sage Publications, 1991), 16.
[25] Ibid., 74.
[26] Varshney, "Ethnicity and Ethnic Conflict," 285.
[27] Ibid., 288.
[28] Alexander Motyl, "The Social Construction of Social Construction: Implications for Theories of Nationalism and Identity Formation," *Nationality Papers* 38, 1 (January 2010), 63.

say, "a nation is an ethnic group with a flag." That is, a nation is an ethnic group that has adopted a political agenda, usually striving for autonomy or independent statehood.[29] Max Weber wrote that a "nation is a community which normally tends to produce a state of its own."[30] Joseph Stalin, an ethnic Georgian drawn into the predominantly ethnically Russian Bolshevik wing of the Russian Social-Democratic Labor Party (RSDLP) at the end of the nineteenth century, postulated, in a formula that was to become Bolshevik doctrine for a half-century, that "[a] nation is a historically constituted, stable community of people, formed on the basis of a common language, territory, economic life, and psychological make-up manifested in a common culture."[31] Stalin's work was not an academic exercise. He aimed to discredit the arguments of the Jewish Labor Bund, from 1898–1903 a constituent member of the RSDLP. The Bund advocated national-cultural autonomy for Jews and other ethnic groups in the Russian Empire. Stalin argued that Jews are not a nation and therefore should have no such autonomy. No doubt, Stalin's larger aim was to establish what a nation is so that there would be a firm criterion by which to assess the claims of the many ethnic groups in the Russian Empire to nationhood. Nationhood could confer territorial autonomy on some entities that would enter the future socialist federation, but deny it to those not deemed a "nation."

Stalin's definition proved to be too restrictive. Several groups conventionally recognized as nations or asserting themselves as such were excluded, as were any diasporic people (Jews, Germans) or groups not inhabiting contiguous territories (Kurds). Ironically, Stalin mentioned Ossetians and Abkhazians as people who were not nations, and yet in his native country (Georgia) these two groups demanded national independence, and after a brief war in 2008, Russia recognized them as states. They would disagree with Stalin's postulate that the "national problem in the Caucasus can be solved only by drawing the backward nations and peoples into the common stream of a higher culture."[32]

At the same time, Stalin's definition was too expansive. Might not the people of Paris meet all the criteria for nationhood? They shared a language, territory, economy, and perhaps a "psychological makeup manifested in a common culture," yet no one would call Parisians a "nation." This illustrates the difficulties in defining a nation. Walker Connor rightly says that the terms "state, nation, nation-state and nationalism" are "essential to global politics" but "all four terms are shrouded in ambiguity due to their imprecise, inconsistent, and often

---

[29] Walker Connor defines a nation as a "self-conscious ethnic group" but he sees the group striving for self-determination, which means in almost all cases, statehood. "The Politics of Ethnonationalism," *Journal of International Affairs* 27, 1 (1973), 3.
[30] "The Nation," in John Hutchinson and Anthony D. Smith, eds., *Nationalism* (Oxford: Oxford University Press, 1994), 25.
[31] Stalin, *Marxism and the National and Colonial Question* (New York: International Publishers, n.d.), 8.
[32] Ibid., 49.

totally erroneous usage."[33] Tishkov calls "nation" a "semantic-metaphorical category" that arouses great emotions but that "did not become and cannot become a category of analysis, that is, get a scientific definition. One cannot define a nation; one can only call something a nation."[34] Perhaps the most satisfactory definition of a nation is Rupert Emerson's: "The largest community which, when the chips are down, effectively commands men's loyalty, overriding the claims both of the lesser communities within it and those which cut across it or potentially enfold it within a still greater society... the nation can be called a 'terminal community'... the end point of working solidarity between [among] men."[35] In the same vein, the Royal Institute of International Affairs just before World War II observed that nationalism differs from the feelings that bind together "Londoners, Trade Unionists, cricketers or Wesleyan Methodists" because the nation "is a community, rather than an association; that is, it covers a comprehensive range of human activities instead of being restricted to a single range of human activities."[36]

Even more controversial than the definition is the *origin* of nations. "Modernists" such as Ernest Gellner hold that nations are a product of industrial development and the concomitant need for cultural homogeneity and search for community by people uprooted from previous economic and social roles.[37] Benedict Anderson claims that until the advent of "print capitalism," when newspapers could be cheaply sold and widely distributed, there were no nations because people could not "imagine" those not living in their immediate vicinity; they could identify only with people in their own environs. Only when a person in New York could read about events in San Francisco could he or she identify as part of the same American nation, or "imagined community."[38] In contrast, "perennialists" such as Anthony D. Smith, see modern nations as only larger, updated versions of premodern ties and sentiments that bound ethnic groups together.[39] Some nations existed long before capitalism, printing, and industrialization. Similarly, I argue later that ancient Israelites or Jews met

---

[33] *Ethnonationalism: The Quest for Understanding* (Princeton: Princeton University Press, 1994), 91.

[34] Tishkov, *Rekviem po etnosu*, 157. Tishkov comments, "All known attempts to differentiate with objective criteria among nation, people [*narodnosti*], ethnic and tribal groups are... unproductive" (168).

[35] Rupert Emerson, *From Empire to Nation* (Boston: Beacon Press, 1960), 96–97.

[36] *Nationalism: A Report by a Study Group of Members of the Royal Institute of International Affairs* (London: Oxford University Press, 1939), 329.

[37] Ernest Gellner, *Nations and Nationalism* (Oxford: Blackwell, 1983).

[38] Benedict Anderson, *Imagined Communities: Reflections on the Origins and Spread of Nationalism* (London: Verso, 1983).

[39] See Anthony D. Smith, *The Ethnic Origins of Nations* (Oxford: Blackwell, 1987). Smith's critique of modernists is sharply put in his "The Nation: Invented, Imagined, Reconstructed?" *Millennium: Journal of International Studies* 20, 3 (Winter 1991). "It would be absurd to talk of the intelligentsia 'constructing' Poland *tout court*, let alone 'inventing' the Polish nation." They reformulated the specifically modern conception of "Poland" but built it on premodern myths, tradition, rituals, symbols, and artifacts (364). The same may be said of Zionists, mutatis mutandis, and other national movements.

the criteria for ethnicity and nationhood laid down by most contemporary analysts.[40]

As in the debate about the primordial and instrumental nature of ethnicity, the lines between the modernist and perennialist schools are too sharply drawn to be useful. Some peoples such as Ukrainians, Palestinians, Slovaks, or Macedonians came to think of themselves as nations only in modern times. Others have been nationally self-conscious for centuries. E. J. Hobsbawm, one of the most oft-cited writers on the concept of "nation," concedes that Jews "never ceased to identify themselves, wherever they were, as members of a special people quite distinct from the various brands of non-believers among whom they lived," but he maintains that they did not have "a serious desire for a Jewish political state, let alone a territorial state, until a Jewish nationalism was invented at the very end of the nineteenth century."[41] Therefore, "[i]t is entirely illegitimate to identify the Jewish links with the ancestral land of Israel...or the hope of return there...with the desire to gather all Jews into a modern territorial state situated on the ancient Holy Land."[42]

Hobsbawm is apparently unfamiliar with the Jewish liturgy, such as that of the Ninth (day) of (the month of) Av, which laments the destruction of the two Temples in Jerusalem and makes explicit the link between a territorial Jewish state and religious salvation.[43] Perhaps he considers this evidence not "serious." However, Zionism was only able to capture the allegiance of traditional Jews – which is to say the majority of Jews found in the largest concentrations of Jewish population around 1900 – not because they were exposed to modern nationalist ideas but precisely because a "primordial" Jewish nationalism had wellsprings in Judaism, the Bible, and prayer book. Many more Jews were reading the *siddur* [prayer book] several times a day than were reading Theodor Herzl's *Jewish State*.

Why should it matter whether nations are ancient or recent, "real" or "invented?" Those involved in the debate do not address this question. Hobsbawm's analysis of the Jewish case may hint at agendas that lie behind the positions in the debate. If a nation is ancient, its contemporary claims may carry more weight, whereas a nation born of more recent self-consciousness may be

---

[40] Aviel Roshwald makes the case for the antiquity of the modern Greek, Jewish, Armenian, and Chinese nations in *The Endurance of Nationalism* (Cambridge: Cambridge University Press, 2006). Bruce Routledge warns against overgeneralizing the experiences of groups in the ancient Near East and projecting present concepts on the past. "The Antiquity of the Nation? Critical Reflections from the Ancient Near East," *Nations and Nationalism* 9, 2 (April 2003), 213–33.

[41] E. J. Hobsbawm, *Nations and Nationalism since 1780* (Cambridge: Cambridge University Press, 1990) 47.

[42] Ibid., 47–48.

[43] For example, several poems by Yehudah Ha-Levi (ca. 1080–1140), the Spanish Jewish poet, which lament the loss of Zion and his own distance from it, occupy a central place in that liturgy. It is not stretching a point to understand these poems as yearnings for a political restoration. One of his famous lines, "My heart is in the east and I am at the end of the west," refers to a specific territory.

treated more skeptically. Jews and Palestinians argue about how long each has inhabited the territories they dispute. Some challenge the very existence of "new" nations. A former prime minister of Israel, Golda Meir, is said to have asserted, "There is no such thing as a Palestinian." Many Turks consider Kurds "Mountain Turks." Ukrainians were dismissed by Russians as "Little Russians." In turn, some claim that Rusyns – a branch of the Ukrainian family living in the Carpathian Mountains – are Ukrainians, whereas others insist they have a distinct identity as Rusyns.[44]

Lurking behind these disputes is the question of statehood. If a group is not a nation, but "only" an ethnic group, it may not merit a state of its own. This is why the Zionist movement had to convince Jews and others that Jews are a nation. If not, they would not have had a claim for statehood. The only case that can be made for statehood apart from the existence of a nation is the presence of several ethnic groups or even nations on a contiguous territory where they might be united by a political ideal. For example, Americans have no common origins, race, religion, or original languages. What makes them "American," at least in theory, is fealty to common political principles embodied in the U.S. Constitution. Over time, perhaps, this civic nation called America took on many of the features of ethnic nations, as one language became dominant and Americans developed an attachment to the territory they shared. Yet Americans remain racially, religiously, and culturally diverse, unlike, for example the Polish or Japanese nations. By contrast, the Yugoslav state failed to create a lasting supra-ethnic (national) loyalty to a shared political ideal. The Soviet case falls somewhere between the American and Yugoslav. Russian became a dominant lingua franca, a larger proportion of the population than in Yugoslavia seems to have become committed to the state's political ideals, but the supra-ethnic "Soviet man" was outnumbered by people who thought of themselves as Russians, Ukrainians, Lithuanians, Armenians, and the like. Of course, even the American state was rent asunder in the mid-nineteenth century when regional loyalties and sharp differences over slavery caused the nation to split. Remarkably, and very unusually, it came together again and a common civic ideal seems to have taken firm hold.

Although scholars do not agree on the precise meanings of "ethnic" and "nation," there is some consensus about the nature of ethnicity. First, ethnicity is variable. It varies in stability and intensity. Ethnic groups are not necessarily permanent. They can be created (Palestinians, Ukrainians), and they can decline and disappear (Sorbs, Wends, European Karaites, Transylvanian Germans).[45] West Ukrainians are generally more concerned with their Ukrainian identity than East Ukrainians. Ukrainians in general are generally more concerned with

---

[44] See Paul Magocsi, *The Shaping of a National Identity: Subcarpathian Rus', 1848–1948* (Cambridge, MA: Harvard University Press, 1977).

[45] On the last, see Katherine Verdery, "The Unmaking of an Ethnic Collectivity: Transylvania's Germans," *American Ethnologist* 12, 1 (February 1985), 62–83.

their ethnicity and culture than their neighbors, the Belarussians. Second, ethnicity is defined in relation to others and therefore is a product of interaction rather than being invented in isolation. Some say that, ironically, Zionism spurred the development of a Palestinian national consciousness, although others assert that it predated the Zionist immigrations. Moldovans today debate whether they are Romanians or a distinct nationality or nation. Finally, as we have seen, there is disagreement on how ethnic groups and nations are formed or on why they even exist. The rationale for their existence is presented in a "narrative" that may not be based in fact but is accepted by members of the group. According to some, the narrative *constructs* the group. Be that as it may, ethnic groups are not static; whether they are permanent is also contested.

Farewells to Ethnicity

As noted earlier, many believed that ethnicity was an evanescent feature of premodern and perhaps modernizing societies. Marxists believed that in capitalist societies ethnicity is useful to the bourgeoisie for it can divert the attention of the masses from their economically based deprivations and create ethnic scapegoats on whom they can blame their troubles. It follows that when the economic substructure would be changed radically by revolutions – caused by the rising awareness by workers that the fundamental cleavage in society is class, not ethnicity or religion – ethnicity would no longer have a social use and would "wither away," as would the state itself. "The working men have no country," proclaims the Communist Manifesto, and the seizure of power by the proletariat would cause national tensions to disappear.[46]

Marxists who dismissed ethnicity were later forced to modify their positions. Vladimir Ilyich Lenin, an eminently pragmatic politician as well as a theorist, acknowledged that ethnicity could be used instrumentally to bring down the tsarist order in Russia. He became an "internationalist" rather than a "national nihilist" or "cosmopolitan" such as the Polish Jewish Marxist, Rosa Luxemburg.[47] In 1913, the same year that his comrade Joseph Stalin was commissioned to write on "Marxism and the National Question," Lenin acknowledged that the "national question has now become prominent." He argued that territorial autonomy could be granted to compactly settled ethnic

---

[46] Karl Marx, *The Communist Manifesto* (Chicago: Gateway, 1954), 50. Marx's inconsistencies in his writings on nations and ethnicity are discussed by Walker Connor, *The National Question in Marxist-Leninist Theory and Strategy* (Princeton: Princeton University Press, 1984), ch. 1.

[47] True to her fundamentalist Marxist beliefs, Luxemburg, affiliated with the Social Democratic Party of the Kingdom of Poland and Lithuania, saw no need for Polish independence; in contrast, the Polish Socialist Party understood that independence was the highest priority for the Polish "masses" and combined national restoration with socialism in its program. Born into a Jewish family, Luxemburg was equally contemptuous of Jewish concerns. She wrote to a friend, "Why do you come to me with your special Jewish sorrows? I feel just as sorry for the wretched Indian victims in Putamayo, the negroes in Africa.... I cannot find a special corner in my heart for the ghetto." Quoted in J. P. Nettl, *Rosa Luxemburg* (London: Oxford University Press, 1969), 32.

groups, that states might exist for a while after the revolution, and that ethnicity would also persist for a while and, on purely tactical grounds, could not be ignored. Ultimately, socialism was the only solution to the national question.[48]

Soviet analysts debated how long ethnicity would persist in the socialist society before it became a communist society and would surely no longer exist. The general tendency in the 1960s and later was to modify Stalin's hitherto sacrosanct definition of a nation[49] and to posit that in socialist society a process of *sblizhenie* – rapprochement, a drawing together – of nationalities (ethnic groups) was taking place, as manifested in reduced ethnic tensions, more interethnic marriages, and the "mutual enrichment of languages," a euphemism for the adoption of Russian terms in many non-Russian languages spoken in the USSR. The next historical step would be *sliianie*, the fusion of nationalities into some homogeneous entity. That would surely happen, but it was postponed to an indefinite, seemingly perpetually receding future. In fact, the main ideological textbook, used in all the obligatory courses in Marxism-Leninism in institutions of higher education, acknowledged in 1963 that "nations, and, therefore, national cultures and languages will, of course, continue to exist for a very long time after the victory of communism. But life and the contacts of various peoples will be freed from everything that gives them even the least pretext for enmity and discord, isolation and estrangement, national egoism and exclusiveness."[50] The 1961 Program of the Communist Party, which was supposed to set the agenda for the party in the post-Stalinist period, does not even mention *sliianie* and speaks only of *sblizhenie*.[51] Ironically, the desire for national independence, particularly by the three Baltic states and Ukraine, was one of the causes of the USSR's dissolution.

The second school of thought that saw no future for ethnicity was Western liberalism. In the eighteenth and nineteenth centuries, liberals placed the individual at the center of society and downplayed the importance of social groups. John Stuart Mill made the role of the individual clear in his classic *On Liberty*:

> [I]t is the privilege and proper condition of a human being...to use and interpret experience in his own way. It is for him to find out what part of recorded experience is properly applicable to his own circumstances and character. [Others'] experience may be too narrow, or they may have not interpreted it rightly.... Their interpretation of experience may be correct, but unsuitable to him.[52]

---

[48] N. [sic] Lenin (V. Ulyanov), "Kriticheskie zametki po natsional'nomu voprosu," in *Izbrannye stat'i po natsional'nomu voprosu*, 2nd ed. (Moscow: Gosizdat, 1925), 21–61.

[49] See Grey Hodnett, "What's in a Nation?" *Problems of Communism* 16 (September–October, 1967). Hodnett's analysis was based largely on an extended series of articles in the main Soviet historical journal, *Voprosy istorii*.

[50] *Fundamentals of Marxism-Leninism*, 2nd rev. ed (Moscow: Foreign Languages Publishing House, 1963), 713.

[51] *Program of the Communist Party of the Soviet Union* (New York: Crosscurrents, 1961), 114–18.

[52] John Stuart Mill, *On Liberty* (Indianapolis: Bobbs-Merrill, 1956), 70–71.

Contemporary liberal thinkers are also skeptical of claims that groups make on individuals. John Rawls writes, "A well-ordered democratic society is neither a community nor...an association. It is not united by a comprehensive doctrine, as a church is, nor does it have shared ends."[53] One might infer that ethnic groups or nations could not be compatible with a "well-ordered democratic society," because they "locate the source of individual identity with a 'people,' which is seen as the bearer of sovereignty, the central object of loyalty, and the basis of collective solidarity,"[54] in opposition to a system that places the individual's interests foremost. Indeed, other political theorists criticize the emphasis on the "autonomous person" and maintain that "[e]ach of us moves in an indefinite number of communities, some more inclusive than others, each making different claims on our allegiance, and there is no saying in advance which is *the* society or community whose purposes should govern the disposition of any particular set of our attributes and endowments."[55]

Perhaps the liberal position, growing out of the Enlightenment, overemphasizes rational calculation. Were people to make strictly rational calculations with the guiding principle being self-interest – an assumption that underlies much of "rational choice" thinking in the social sciences – "irrational" sentiments such as patriotism and chauvinism, or even loyalty to a group, might not appear as frequently as they do. I agree with Dominique Schnapper who asserts,

> The feeling of "ethnic" belonging and the passions that it arouses are the direct expression of the natural [n.b.] attachment that men have to the land and to the immediate familial or ethnic collectivity in which they were raised. What is familiar tends to become a value in itself. Patriotism transferred this primordial sentiment on to an inherently abstract historical community and a political organization.... Man is an animal of passions as much as of reason. It was impossible to found the nation simply on the rational and universalist ambition of citizenship. Instead, it was imperative that the nation appeal to those emotions linked to the historical and cultural singularity of each national entity.[56]

The persistence, even increase, of nationalism and ethnic consciousness has forced liberal thinkers to accommodate it to their principles. In his most influential book, *Multicultural Citizenship: A Liberal Theory of Minority Rights*,[57] Will Kymlicka emphasizes that liberal theory grants to ethnic groups the right to preserve their culture and that this right obligates the state in

---

[53] John Rawls, *Political Liberalism* (New York: Columbia University Press, 1993), 40.
[54] Liah Greenfeld, *Nationalism: Five Roads to Modernity* (Cambridge, MA: Harvard University Press, 1992), 3.
[55] Michael Sandel, *Liberalism and the Limits of Justice* (Cambridge: Cambridge University Press, 1982), 146 and 153. I thank Arlene Saxonhouse for steering me toward the works by Rawls and Sandel.
[56] Dominique Schnapper, *Community of Citizens* (New Brunswick, NJ: Transaction, 1998), 129.
[57] Oxford University Press, 1995. See Stephen Deets, "Reconsidering East European Minority Policy: Liberal Theory and European Norms," *East European Politics and Society* 16, 1 (Winter 2002), 31.

Ethnicity and Identity

several ways. Arguing from what he calls a "liberal perspective," Stephen Deets questions why ethnic groups ("national minorities") have rights, whereas other minorities – religious, sexual, political, or physical (disabled) – do not. He argues that the "underlying defense" of the practice of granting group rights to ethnic groups is that "national and ethnic cultures [have] become accepted public goods like clean air and water."[58] That "states have privileged ethnic identity over other types of identity" troubles Deets because it "raises problems of fairness."[59]

One reason ethnicity is so salient may be that violent ethnic conflict is so salient – the Balkans, the Baltics, Rwanda-Burundi, Darfur, Iraq, and Cyprus come to mind – that no one can ignore it. Other kinds of minorities pose no threat to the integrity of states and at most can prick the liberal conscience. Yet liberals have been forced to shift their focus from the individual to the ethnic group if they are to understand and influence the real world.[60]

Liberals proceed from *normative* assumptions to the conclusion that ethnicity should be anachronistic; many social scientists arrive at the same place from *empirical* assumptions and observations. Modernization, a concept popular in the 1950s and 1970s, was seen as a process in which humans asserted increasing control over the environment, which was made possible by the spread of science and rationality.[61] Later this concept was criticized as being politically biased and imprecise[62] (and was abandoned by convinced or intimidated academics). Social scientists defined modernization as a syndrome of related characteristics: economic development, which in most but not all cases meant industrialization; secularization; the assertion of the efficacy of human activity; and the supplanting, in whole or part, of religious, traditional, familial, and ethnic authorities by a single, secular national political authority.[63] Observing the process in Turkey, Daniel Lerner described it as involving "village *versus* town, land *versus* cash, illiteracy *versus* enlightenment, resignation *versus* ambition,

---

[58] Deets, "Reconsidering East European Minority Policy," 33.

[59] Ibid., 52.

[60] Leo Despres got it wrong when he wrote in the early 1980s: "In theory, ethnicity poses a threat to the modern state. But the threat is not serious. Not one of the ethnonationalist ... movements ... over the past twenty years seems to have been successful in establishing a new nation-state. ... Ethnic confrontations are not likely to be sustained nationally. To the extent that these confrontations result in conflict, it will not be prolonged and the consequences probably will not be widespread." "Ethnicity: What Data and Theory Portend for Plural Societies," in Stuart Plattner and David Maybury-Lewis, eds., *The Prospects for Plural Societies* (Washington, DC: American Ethnological Society, 1984), 19. Bangladeshis, Lithuanians, Estonians, Latvians, Serbs, and Croats would not agree.

[61] See, for example, C. E. Black, *The Dynamics of Modernization* (New York: Harper and Row, 1966), 7, and David Apter, *The Politics of Modernization* (Chicago: University of Chicago Press, 1965), introduction.

[62] Some of the criticisms of modernization theory are taken up and refuted – convincingly, in my view – in Myron Weiner and Samuel Huntington, eds., *Understanding Political Development* (Boston: Little Brown, 1987), 444–68.

[63] See Samuel Huntington, "Political Modernization: America vs. Europe," *World Politics* XVIII, 3 (April 1966), and his *Political Order in Changing Societies* (New Haven: Yale University Press, 1968).

piety *versus* excitement." The "basic challenge" posed by modernization was the "infusion of a 'rationalist and positivist spirit.'"[64] As Clifford Geertz put it, a modern society had to be able to innovate, in beliefs as well, without falling apart and to produce technological skills and knowledge.[65]

Modernization theory implied that because ethnicity is based on tradition rather than rationality (the idea of instrumental ethnicity had not yet been developed) and was promoted by ethnic, traditional leaders (separate from national leaders who pushed ethnic or national causes), it had no place in a technologically driven, rational, urbanizing, industrializing society. Instead it was part of traditional, rural, agricultural life, and as that life passed, so would ethnicity. As modes of production would become more alike owing to industrialization, ethnic nuances attached to products would disappear. When rugs would no longer be produced by hand but instead by machine, the products might still be thought of as "Bukharan," "Chinese," "Indian," or "Turkish," but the means of producing them would be the same. Crafts, foods, music, transportation and even art would become international rather than national.

Ethnicity Strikes Back

There is no denying that cultural diffusion and homogenization may erase many of the distinctive cultural patterns, rituals, and other behaviors we associate with ethnic groups. Modern communications may erode difference and produce homogeneity as people see, read, and hear the same things. Indeed, where it was once easy to tell country folk from city slickers by their clothes and speech, today it is much harder to do so in many countries. Jeans seem to have become a near universal folk costume, and American popular music has displaced local music in many parts of the world. Yet precisely because "everyone" dresses in jeans, stares at small hand-held screens while walking, and stops for a Coca-Cola and McDonald's hamburger, some feel the urge to assert their individuality against the crowd. One way of doing so is by "going native," reverting to (or adopting) folkways, dress, foods, dance, music, and, more rarely, language that will establish their identities as different from the rest. Surely this is an instrumental use of ethnicity, but it may come to have deep meaning for the one who employs it.

Ethnicity has proved remarkably resilient, even where it was assumed to have faded: "Some modern ethnic identities have been Phoenix-like, subsiding for decades and then roaring back to life. Scottish, Welsh and Breton nationalism all illustrate [this]."[66] Stephen Van Evera proposes that "ethnic identities

---

[64] Daniel Lerner, *The Passing of Traditional Society* (London: Free Press of Glencoe, 1958), 44, 45.
[65] "Political Religion in the New Nations," in Geertz, *Old Societies and New States*, 62.
[66] Stephen Van Evera, "Primordialism Lives!" in *Symposium: Cumulative Findings in the Study of Ethnic Politics*, APSA-CP (Winter 2001) 20.

harden when mass literacy is achieved" because they can be stored in writing and disseminated to a wide audience: "Identities are often etched into stone when they are printed on paper." He maintains that there are "no clear examples of major mass-literate Eurasian identities that have vanished,"[67] although certainly there are small groups with modest levels of literacy that have been forcibly or willingly fused into larger groups; for example, in addition to groups cited earlier, peoples of the Russian-Canadian-American Far North and Dutch Frisians. Violent conflict also hardens identities; for example, among Israelis and Palestinians, Balkan peoples, Tamils and Sinhalese in Sri Lanka, Pakistanis and Indians, and some Southeast Asian peoples.

Moreover, if modernization is supposed to lessen ethnic consciousness, how can one explain the persistence and even resurgence of militant ethnic mobilization in such modern countries as Canada (Quebec), Spain (Basques and Catalans), Italy (Tyroleans), the United Kingdom (Scotland and Wales), and Belgium (Walloons and Flemings)? These are not recent immigrant groups struggling to resist assimilation, but peoples who have lived for centuries in these countries and who are no less modernized than other citizens. The failure of communism to override national loyalties in the Former Soviet Union, Yugoslavia, and Czechoslovakia – states that encompassed about 325,000,000 people – may be due as much or more to the bankruptcy of their economic and political systems than to the power of ethnic separatist sentiments. Yet these industrialized states fragmented into ethnically defined units when they broke up. One cannot easily dismiss Anthony Smith's assertion: "The political myths of the... modern period have proved... insufficient to the task of welding poly-ethnic states together.... The advance into the future has frequently taken the route of a return to the ethnic past."[68]

Modernization can encourage ethnicity in other ways.[69] Modern communications and transportation increase interactions among groups, heightening consciousness of difference and specificity. Villagers living in an ethnically homogeneous environment become aware of their ethnic identity only when they move away and see people who do not look, dress, speak, or eat as they do. The questions "who am I?" and "who are they?" do not arise in the all-Uzbek village, but they do in Tashkent, where Russians, Tajiks, and others are highly visible. Moreover, ethnic entrepreneurs who wish to mobilize ethnic feelings are better able to do so with modern technology, because it enables them to reach more people with more durable and perhaps rousing messages. Language, folk music, epic tales, and the like can be disseminated widely through print and electronic media. Compare, for example, the single bard who recites hundreds of verses of the national epic, and who may have a small number

---

[67] Ibid.
[68] Anthony D. Smith, *The Ethnic Revival in the Modern World* (Cambridge: Cambridge University Press, 1981), 194.
[69] Many of them are elucidated by Walker Connor in "Nation-Building or Nation-Destroying?" *World Politics* 24, 3 (April 1972), 39–355.

of acolytes who will continue the tradition, to the mythologized story of the nation's origins as presented in a television series or in movies.

Karl Deutsch proposed that a people or nation is defined by communication patterns among its members. A people is a "community of shared meanings," a group that has "interlocking habits of communication.... When we can predict what another person will do, we are more inclined to trust him.... Thus, a people becomes a community of probable mutual trust and mutual favors."[70] (Might this not be a good definition of a family? Again, we encounter a definition of nation that may be too inclusive). The Swiss can communicate effectively with each other, and better with each other than with outsiders, despite their different languages. Function – how a group works – not its characteristics, is what defines a nation. Deutsch saw a nation as a group that shares communication across many areas – emotions, food preferences, recreation – as opposed to a group whose members share a narrow band of interests (e.g., engineers, stamp collectors). Then it develops capabilities for "forming, supporting, and enforcing a common will."[71] Obviously, communication is shared more frequently, easily, and intensively in modern societies with advanced technology than in less developed ones.

In addition, there are arguments for the persistence of, or return to, ethnicity that have little to do with the impact of modernization or the lack of it. Might identification with an ethnic group be an inherent human proclivity similar to identification with a family? True, a family nurtures and protects its members to a greater degree than does any other social group, thereby creating dependence and attachment. Yet the difference between a family and an ethnic (or religious) group may be one of degree, not kind. The ethnic group may be the logical extension of the family into the next concentric circle of human attachments. As Harold Isaacs notes,

> Neither visionary beliefs... nor large-scale industrialization, nor the passage of generations, nor concentrated centralized power, nor massive repression, not elaborate theories, nor structural schemes have... been able to check the survival and the persistence of the many nationalities or tribes of people who live under the Communist system.[72]

People seem to be engaged in the "lunge back to tribal caves" because they are "desperate" to "get behind walls... if only in their minds, in a place where they feel they can belong, and where, grouped with their kind, they can regain some measure of what feels like physical and emotional safety."[73] A study of the German army in World War II concluded, "Primary group ties, of which ethnicity is one, become the irreducible allegiance when other ties are

---

[70] Karl Deutsch, *Nationalism and its Alternatives* (New York: Knopf, 1969), 14. Connor (ibid.) discusses the changing positions that Deutsch took regarding the impact of modernization on ethnicity.
[71] Ibid., 19.
[72] Harold Isaacs, *Idols of the Tribe: Group Identity and Political Change* (New York: Harper Colophon, 1975), 19.
[73] Ibid., 24.

shattered.... The ethnic group has many of the same qualities as the family. An individual may claim membership by ascription often without demonstrating any achieved characteristics.... It is a ready-made support group."[74] Or, as a writer put it in the 1930s, "Attachment to one's own kind or people is a fact, almost an instinctive urge.... Like most instincts or sentiments, it is not invariable; it expands and contracts in response to a need."[75]

Robert Frost wrote, "Home is the place where, when you have to go there, they have to take you in." Perhaps that is true of the ethnic group, albeit to a lesser extent. Van den Berghe sees ethnicity (and race) as "extensions of kinship" and therefore "deeply rooted in our biology and [it] can be expected to persist even in industrial societies, whether capitalist or socialist."[76] At a minimum, if we accept that humans are social animals, ethnicity's persistence can be explained simply as a form of social organization, like the family, that provides a feeling of appreciation by others, the comfort of knowing one is not alone. Agnes Heller, the Hungarian philosopher and sociologist, put it succinctly: What "is now called 'ethnocentrism' is the natural attitude of all cultures toward alien ones."[77] It is culturally richer ("thicker") and more stable than the club or team. One is not traded from one ethnic group to another, and except through migration, it is rare for a person to change his or her ethnic identification.

For many generations, the prevailing ethos in American society discouraged preservation of pre-American ethnic identities imported with the millions of immigrants who populated the new world. Yet, Mary Waters observes, "[American] people cling tenaciously to their ethnic identities."[78] They do so because they seek community; ethnicity allows one "to express ... individuality in a way that does not make you stand out as in any way different from all other kinds of people." By being "ethnic," at least nominally or symbolically, people can simultaneously claim to be unique while finding community and conformity with others.[79] The writer Eva Hoffman, a Jew born in Poland who after World War II emigrated to Canada, then to the United States, and now lives in London, observes that "essential humanity is all very well, but we need the colors of our time and the shelter of a specific place."[80]

---

74 Edward Shils and Morris Janowitz, "Cohesion and Disintegration in the Wehrmacht in World War Two," *Public Opinion Quarterly* 12 (1948), 223. Shils and Janowitz found that the focus of loyalty of the soldier was his unit, not Germany as a whole.
75 Joseph Tenenbaum, *Races, Nations and Jews* (New York: Bloch Publishing Company, 1934), 47.
76 Pierre Van den Berghe, *The Ethnic Phenomenon* (New York: Elsevier, 1981), xi. He is well aware that "this perspective ... conflicts with both the liberal and the socialist views of ethnocentrism and racism as purely cultural products peculiar to certain types of society."
77 "Can Cultures be Compared?" *Dialectical Anthropology* 8 (April 1984), 271, quoted in Sollors, *Beyond Ethnicity*, 27.
78 Mary Waters, *Ethnic Options: Choosing Identities in America* (Berkeley: University of California Press, 1990), 150.
79 Ibid.
80 Eva Hoffman, *Lost in Translation* (New York: Penguin, 1990), 139.

Social scientists did not always see ethnicity as a permanent feature of most societies. When Nathan Glazer and Daniel Patrick Moynihan convened a conference on ethnicity in 1972, they discovered that standard handbooks in sociology had no entries for the term.[81] They observed wryly that when they studied ethnic groups in New York City, which culminated in the publication of *Beyond the Melting Pot*, they were studying "groups that were supposed to be disappearing."[82] Fellow sociologist Edward Shils explained why most social scientists did not deal with ethnicity or nationality: the subject was "associated with patriotism, fanaticism, chauvinism and militarism" and was seen as a "retrograde phenomenon." Moreover, "[n]ationality is simply an extraordinarily difficult subject to study," because "a nationality is a structureless collectivity," although it could not exist "without institutional mechanisms of self-maintenance, self-reproduction, and self-protection."[83]

In the 1960s the salience of ethnic issues in so many parts of the world forced the academy to revise its biases and take up – once again – ethnicity and nationalism as not only legitimate but also important subjects of study. As often happens, the pendulum has since swung too far in the other direction, and books and journals devoted to ethnicity, nations, nationalism, and migration have proliferated exponentially. "Ethnicity truly was in vogue in the 1970s, and new primordialist and even old biological interpretations of the power of descent affiliations became fashionable again."[84]

Identity

Even more popular today in academic work is the study of identity. The term seems ubiquitous in the social sciences and appears with astonishing frequency in literary studies. Identity is "a person's sense of self in relation to others, or... the sense of oneself as simultaneously an individual and a member of a social group."[85] Some believe there is a "fundamental need... for coherence; identities create and express coherence."[86] A conscious identity places a person in a group that has a *weltanschauung*, a set of values and priorities that help set the person's agenda and guide his or her thoughts and actions. The group "sacralizes" this *weltanschauung*, making it "immune to scrutiny and proof against cognitive growth."[87] One critique of the category "identity" argues that

---

[81] Nathan Glazer and Daniel P. Moynihan, eds., *Ethnicity* (Cambridge, MA: Harvard University Press, 1975), 3–4.
[82] Ibid., 5.
[83] Edward Shils, "The Constitution of a Nationality," Foreword to Dominique Schnapper, *Jewish Identities in France [Juifs et Israelites]*, (Chicago: University of Chicago Press, 1983), xix–xi.
[84] Sollors. *Beyond Ethnicity*, 21.
[85] Perry London and Allissa Hirschfeld, "The Psychology of Identity Formation," in David Gordis and Yoav Ben-Horin, eds., *Jewish Identity in America* (Los Angeles: Wilstein Institute, 1991), 33.
[86] George Schofplin, *Nations Identity Power* (New York: New York University Press, 2000), 27.
[87] Ibid.

because those who use it "routinely categorize... it as multiple, fragmented, and fluid [it] should not be conceptualized as 'identity' at all. Identity is too blurred as a category of analysis and as a category of practice; it tends to mean either too much or too little.[88] "Self-understanding" or and "self-conception" are proposed as more useful terms. However, as long as identity is explicitly defined, just because some misuse the term is not a reason not to use it.[89] As Motyl observes, "identity in general and national identity in particular is nothing other than the answer to the question: who am I?"[90]

How people think of themselves in relation to others, how they develop such conceptions, and how those conceptions are affected by state policies and affect policies are very important in politics and social relations.[91] Brubaker and Cooper criticize "the habit of speaking without qualification of 'Albanians' and 'Serbs'... as if they were sharply bounded, internally homogeneous 'groups,'"[92] but the sad fact is that people kill each other only because they bear these labels, even sometimes against their will. Identity choices or self-conceptions matter a great deal in international relations. Whether a state sees itself as Islamic, Christian, Jewish, democratic, or part of the developing world determines its policies.[93] States that see themselves as the saviors of a people or guardians of an idea may be tempted to "save" others, even against their will. Thus, the identity of a state must be of concern to people outside it as well.

Recent writers on identity emphasize that people have no fixed, essential, or permanent identity.[94] In their enthusiasm for the fragmented, unstable, and uncertain, they overlook the fact that who you think you are *at any one point* often determines how you behave and even how you think. Of course, people have multiple identities: they think of themselves as belonging to a gender, class, nation, religion, territory, vocation, and the like. To some extent, "[i]dentity is not a stable, intrinsic, and independent property of a person or a group. We do not 'have' an identity – what we see are simply ways that we are identified (passive) and ways we identify (active)."[95] Yet at any particular moment we deploy an identity; we choose one depending on the social situation and which

---

[88] Rogers Brubaker and Frederick Cooper, "Beyond Identity." *Theory and Society* 28 (1999), 147.
[89] Another critique of "identity" is Mervyn Bendle, "The Crisis of 'Identity' in High Modernity," *British Journal of Sociology* 53, 1 (March 2002), 1–18.
[90] Motyl, "The Social Construction of Social Construction," 69.
[91] Dominique Arel, "Introduction: Theorizing the Politics of Cultural Identities in Russia and Ukraine," in Arel and Blair Ruble, eds., *Rebounding Identities: The Politics of Identity in Russia and Ukraine* (Baltimore: Johns Hopkins University Press, 2006), 2.
[92] Brubaker and Cooper, "Beyond Identity," 28.
[93] See Ted Hopf, *Social Construction of International Politics: Identities and Foreign Policies, Moscow, 1955 and 1999* (Ithaca: Cornell University Press, 2002) and Ronald Grigor Suny, "Provisional Stabilities: The Politics of Identities in Post-Soviet Eurasia," *International Security* 24, 3 (Winter 1999/2000), 139–78.
[94] Stuart Hall, "The Question of Cultural Identity," in Stuart Hall, David Held, and Tony McGrew, eds., *Modernity and its Futures* (Cambridge: Polity Press, 1992), 277.
[95] Zdzislaw Mach, *Symbols, Conflicts and Identity* (Albany: SUNY Press, 1993), 6.

one we see as more important. These identities may be "nested," arranged like a matryoshka doll, one identity within another. They are separable but related, and most often stable. Yet the arrangement of the nested identities may change; at any particular point some are more salient and important than others. A Christian will be more aware of his religious identity in a room full of Muslims than at a ballgame; yet his Christianity is a constant, one that is sometimes more salient and sometimes less so. "Since ethnicity changes situationally, the individual carries a portfolio of ethnic identities that are more or less salient in various situations and vis-à-vis different audiences."[96]

The relative position of one's multiple identities is crucial both for individuals and for groups. The fate of Yugoslavia – created in 1918, dissolved by force in 1941, re-created in 1945, and shattered in 1991 – illustrates how much it matters whether people who inhabit a state think of themselves as members of that state. When enough people were persuaded (or forced to accept) that being Yugoslav was more important than being Serb, Croat, or another ethnicity, Yugoslavia held together. Even if most Serbs, Croats, and Bosnians may never have identified themselves primarily as Yugoslavs, a strong leader was able to keep the country together. Yet after Josip Broz Tito, Yugoslavia's charismatic leader, died and power dissipated, people openly reverted to earlier identities, which were primarily ethnic, not civic. Then the great majority of citizens of Yugoslavia considered themselves Serbs, Croats, Macedonians, Slovenes, Bosnians, or Montenegrins first, and Yugoslavs, second – if at all. The Yugoslav state collapsed because people's shared political identity mattered far less than their distinct ethnic identities.[97]

The Soviet Union is a second example. Despite claims in the 1970s to the contrary, the Soviet regime did not succeed in creating a "new Soviet man" and a new type of ethnos, the *Sovetskii narod*[98] – a meta-ethnic, civic identity. When the center collapsed in 1991, what remained were fifteen states nominally defined by ethnicity. There are people in all the successor states who still define themselves primarily as Soviet – many are older Slavs in the non-Slavic states – but most people in the post-Soviet areas have reverted to ethnic identities or to new civic identities (*Rossianin*, for example) as primary.

In contrast, Canada and the United States, both of which are even more ethnically and religiously diverse than Yugoslavia, have held together for far longer, though challenged by issues of race, ethnic tensions, and threatened separatism. An "essential" (*horibile dictu*!) sense of being Canadian or American

---

[96] David Hollinger, *Postethnic America* (New York: Basic Books, 1995), 16.
[97] There is a huge literature on the breakup of Yugoslavia and the multilateral wars that accompanied it. An article that addresses issues of identity in the Yugoslav conflicts is Gale Stokes, John Lampe, and Dennison Rusinow with Julie Mostov, "Instant History: Understanding the Wars of Yugoslav Succession," *Slavic Review* 55, 1 (Spring 1996).
[98] See E. Bagramov, "The Soviet Nationalities Policy and Bourgeois Falsifications," *International Affairs* (Moscow; June 1978) and M. I. Kulichenko, "Socialism and Ethnic Features of Nations: The Example of the Peoples of the Union of Soviet Socialist Republics," in Regina Holloman and Serghei Ariutiunov, eds., *Perspectives on Ethnicity* (The Hague: Mouton, 1978), 421–28.

has survived, not without difficulty (including a civil war), even into the postmodern age. Of course, the reasons for the collapse of Yugoslavia and the Soviet and Czechoslovak federations, and the survival of the North American nations, are very complex, but these examples should caution us against accepting simplistic generalizations about fragmentation, dissolution, and decentering.[99]

Identity is transmitted by a collective that sets rules of admission and expulsion and establishes the nature and boundaries, sometimes challenged and subverted, of the identity. In addition, external groups – the state or society writ large – play an important role in establishing identities. Richard Jenkins criticizes anthropologists in particular for emphasizing "internal definition and *group identification* at the expense of external definition and *categorization*."[100]

I argue that Jewish identities, although multiple, flexible, and perhaps somewhat incoherent over the long haul of history, have a constant core of elements that define Jewishness normatively and empirically. As Stephen Whitfield writes, Jewish history

> can serve as a warning that the case for contingency and plasticity can be pushed too far.... Even if identity is socially constructed rather than "given," who would transmit or inherit it other than a Jew?... If Jewish culture depended on choices made available to every generation, something as intricately systematic as a culture could not be perpetuated.... The recent scholarly emphasis on social construction obscures the determinacy that governs social persistence.... Practices that may not be rituals and values that may not be invested with theological meaning, plus Judaism, add up to a culture.[101]

People argue over the nature of identity because it seems such an important notion. "Today it seems that everyone claims a right to their own identity... as if it were a necessity of life itself. Identity has taken on the status of a sacred object, an 'intimate concern,' worth fighting and even dying for."[102] This is part of the trend toward individuation in affluent, developed societies. The popularity of spiritualism, healing therapies, psychology, and concepts such as "self-esteem" and "self-fulfillment" exemplify the focus on the self. Individuation runs counter to the early-twentieth-century notion of identifying with a group, usually a class or a nation or a religion, not so much as the result of a conscious choice carefully made but as a result of "objective" circumstances. Earlier, although one could choose to be a Catholic or a Jew, a worker or a capitalist, a Czech or a German, the choice was often made for a person

---

[99] The orthodoxies of postmodern "discourse" are succinctly presented by Stuart Hall, "The Question of Cultural Identity," 274–316.
[100] Richard Jenkins, "Rethinking Ethnicity: Identity, Categorization and Power," *Ethnic and Racial Studies* 17, 2 (April 1994), 219.
[101] Stephen J. Whitfield, "Enigmas of Modern Jewish Identity," *Jewish Social Studies* 8, 2–3 (Winter–Spring 2002), 166.
[102] John Gillis, "Memory and Identity: The History of a Relationship," in Gillis, ed., *Commemorations: The Politics of National Identity* (Princeton: Princeton University Press, 1994), 4.

by birth, place, and other circumstances over which one had little control. Recently, in affluent societies people have had greater latitude in choosing their place of residence, vocation, and even such previously given identities as religion, gender, and class. For example, it has become a cliché that "today all Jews are Jews by choice,"[103] because it is much easier to disaffiliate or affiliate with Judaism or a Jewish community than in the past. Gender, traditionally conceived as a binary category, has been complicated and expanded conceptually. Social mobility and wider access to education in many societies make class and vocation less matters of ascription and more based on achievement. Although group boundaries are more permeable than they were a century ago – classes of people who used to be excluded from positions, areas of residence, and social circles now are accepted there – one's identity remains of practical importance in many instances (citizenship, affirmative action, and other governmental policies) and, perhaps even more, psychologically.

How Identities Change

Identities are neither infinitely malleable nor indefinitely fixed. Millions have changed their political and later their cultural and social identities by migrating to new lands. Countries of immigration usually strive to convert the immigrants' political and ethnic identities from those of the old country to those of the new. A spectrum of identity outcomes and a parallel spectrum of state strategies result from migration. Some immigrants lose their former identities and affiliations completely,[104] others combine them with newly acquired ones and become, for example, "hyphenated Americans,"[105] and still others resist any change. Similarly, although all states encourage acculturation – the acquisition of a new culture – some encourage assimilation, the replacement of the previous culture, loyalty, and identity. Some states develop accommodationist strategies, such as federalism, autonomy, and multiculturalism, which enable people to combine old and new identities. Canada, the Netherlands, Ukraine, and the Russian Federation have done so recently, although they harbor strong rejectionist currents as well. Other states isolate newcomers and prevent their re-identification. Germany, with its citizenship based on *jus sanguinis* and not

---

[103] "In the twentieth century in particular, the history of the Jews can be recounted in terms of the erosion of a stable identity, so that eventually all of them would be described as Jews by choice, and to choose not to be Jews at all would also become an option unscarred by shame or accusations of cowardice or betrayal." Whitfield, "Enigmas of Modern Jewish Identity," 165.

[104] When calling the roll in class years ago, I pronounced a student's name as it should have been in Polish. There was no response. Finally, he said, in a rather hostile tone, "In *America* it's pronounced....."

[105] An interesting case is described by Marian Rubchak, "'God Made Me a Lithuanian': Nationalist Ideology and the Constructions of a North American Diaspora," *Diaspora* 2, 1 (1992), 124. "The feeling of Lithuanianess remained in the minds of American-born Lithuanians although they were no longer Lithuanian Lithuanians." (124).

jus solis, for a long time prevented Turks and others from becoming Germans, but granted immediate citizenship to those of German descent who migrated to Germany, no matter how long they had been detached from the *vaterland*.[106] Saudi Arabia and other Persian Gulf states do not permit guest workers to acquire citizenship, and Japan has generally excluded from citizenship those not ethnically Japanese. The United States, Israel, France, and Great Britain have generally pursued neither accommodationist nor isolating policies, but assimilationist ones. "We will not exclude you as long as you become like us," is the message they send.

Identity shifts are not always well thought out, purposive, permanent, or definitive. Identities can be complex and murky, shifting and internally illogical. Particularly since the bombings of London transport by British-born Muslims in 2005 but also well before, Britons have debated the loyalties and identities of Britons of Pakistani, Middle Eastern, African, and Indian origin. In the 1990s the researcher Jessica Jacobson interviewed young British Pakistanis and found that they had "an extraordinarily wide range of views on what it means to be British and what the chief criteria of Britishness are." She concluded that national identity is malleable, but not "subject to limitless interpretation.... There may be no one set of criteria of Britishness, but there are various sets of criteria."[107]

As mentioned in the Introduction and illustrated by the examples of Lemberg/Lwow/Lvov/Lviv and Czernowitz/Cernauti/Chernovtsy/Chernivtsi, even when people remain in place, they sometimes find that their country has changed. Yet when people's citizenship – their political identity – changed, did their ethnicity also change? David Laitin studied Russian speakers in Estonia who comprised about one-third of the population when that country opted out of the collapsing Soviet Union. He conceives of ethnic identity changes as "tips" and "cascades." At times of social stability (Laitin calls it "equilibrium"), there is no reason to explore new identities. Thus, in Soviet times one could be a resident of Estonia, be ethnically and linguistically Russian, and be a Soviet citizen. However, when people are forced to choose between two identities – say, Russian *or* Estonian rather than Russian *and* Estonian – they "tip" toward one or the other. When "enough" people do so, it sets off a "cascade" whereby individual decisions are transformed into social changes. In the early 1990s, Estonian governments denied citizenship to Russian-speaking residents and discriminated against them in other ways. Under pressure from the European Union and other bodies, Estonia and Latvia adopted more accommodating policies to those not ethnically Estonian/Latvian. In Estonia the result has been a "conglomerate identity" of Russian-speaking residents of Estonia. From Russia's viewpoint, they are part of the Russian diaspora in the "near

---

[106] Rogers Brubaker, *Citizenship and Nationhood in France and Germany* (Cambridge, MA: Harvard University Press, 1992).
[107] Jessica Jacobson, "Perceptions of Britishness," *Nations and Nationalism* 3 (July 1997), 181, 186–87.

abroad," and many Estonians regard them as former colonists. They themselves have to sort out a synthesis between their Russian and Estonian identities.[108] Another researcher concludes, on the basis of surveys in Estonia and Latvia, that although Russians and Estonians have come to share a great deal culturally, "for political actors in both Russia and Estonia it is no longer possible to create a common umbrella identity for Russians in Estonia."[109]

People change identities as their political outlooks, styles of life, vocations, and convictions change. Democrats become Republicans, workers become managers, Baptists become Episcopalians. Some changes are easier to make and occur more frequently than others. Except in the case of migration or when one's parents are of different ethnicities, ethnic identity should be one of the harder identities to change because it is based partly on one's past, though that might be worn lightly and cast aside.

To argue that "identity ... is continuously performed rather than [being] a natural construct"[110] exaggerates the evanescence and instability of identity and poses a false dichotomy between continuous activity and the stability of a natural phenomenon (many of which change too). Instead identities are subject to inertia; they tend to rest in place until agitated by force.[111] Such a force may come from without, when a group or a state pushes individuals to change, or from within, as a person struggles to harmonize multiple identities. The impact of such forces has led some to exaggerate identity's fluidity and claim that "identity is always [sic] project, not settled accomplishment."[112] It seems to me that most people do not wrestle with identity issues very often. They arise

---

[108] David Laitin, *Identity in Formation: The Russian-Speaking Populations in the Near Abroad* (Ithaca: Cornell University Press, 1998).

[109] Triin Vihalemm, "Crystallizing and Emancipating Identities in Post-Communist Estonia," *Nationalities Papers* 35, 3 (July 2007), 497. See also Vihalemm and Anu Masso, "(RE)Construction of Collective Identities after the Dissolution of the Soviet Union: The Case of Estonia," *Nationalities Papers* 35, 1 (March 2007), 71–91.

[110] Alina Curticapean, "'Are You Hungarian or Romanian?' On the Study of National and Ethnic Identity in Central and Eastern Europe," *Nationalities Papers* 35, 3 (July 2007), 412. "*Identity is not something that we have, nor something we achieve, rather identity is performed*" (417 [italics in original]). She cites David Campbell's and Cynthia Weber's work that suggests that "nation-states are not pre-given subjects but subjects in process and that all subjects in process (be they individual or collective) are the *ontological effects of the discursive practices* that are *performatively enacted*" [Italics in original]. Would this be useful to foreign ministers and secretaries of state?

[111] Curticapean (ibid.) proposes that "collective identity be understood as continuously 'performed' rather than 'fixed'" (416). This strikes me as a false dichotomy. At most, collective identity is *continually* (occurring in steady but not uninterrupted succession), not *continuously* (occurring without cessation), changing, at least insofar as its relevance to social life is concerned. Few would argue that collective or individual identities are permanently fixed. The rate at which they change is highly variable. To some they may appear to be fixed and to others in constant flux, but that is in the eye of the beholder.

[112] Craig Calhoun, *Critical Social Theory* (Oxford: Blackwell, 1995), 221. Calhoun claims that "in living we invest ourselves in identities not statically but with an orientation to the future and to action" and therefore identities are not stable. I am not persuaded that most people wrestle regularly with identity issues.

Ethnicity and Identity

only when internal or external challenges appear, and for most people this is not a daily occurrence.

This book deals with a period and place when such challenges *did* appear and were hard to avoid. When the Soviet Union fractured in the late 1980s and early 1990s – it was formally dissolved in December 1991 – nearly 300 million people had to reorient themselves as citizens of new states. In the Soviet system, a distinction had been made between citizenship – "Soviet" – and ethnicity (*natsional'nost'*), which allowed for well over a hundred possibilities.[113] After the dissolution of the USSR, citizenship had to change. Yet did ethnicity change then as well? Was it reconceived after the Soviet period and, if so, how? The titular peoples of the fifteen Soviet republics had ready-made states they could make their own. Ossetians and Abkhazians challenged the integrity of the Georgian Republic; the Nagorno-Karabakh area of Azerbaijan, which erupted in violent clashes between Armenians and Azeris as early as 1988, declared itself independent of Azerbaijan but is unrecognized by any state, including Armenia; and the "Transdniestrian (*Pridnestroi*) Republic" did the same in Moldova and also remains internationally unrecognized. Otherwise, fifteen viable states have emerged from the shards of the USSR.

What about the millions of people of the USSR who had no republics of their own and the roughly 28 million ethnic Russians (as well as other Slavs) who found themselves in the new states? Have they melted into the peoples of the new states, as Marxist-Leninist theory would predict? How have they construed their ethnicity? What is its content and what are its boundaries? Have they created formal organizations or communities to establish and legitimize their presence in the new states? A student of religion and ethnicity in the post-Soviet Russian Federation concludes that "In the hierarchy of factors of self-identification, ethnic affiliation is especially significant. Surveys conducted by the Russian Academy of Sciences Institute of Sociology in 1999 showed that... the overwhelming majority of respondents identified themselves with ethnic communities rather than with their regions or the Russian Federation."[114]

This book analyzes individual- and communal-level Jewish identity conceptualization, referring occasionally to parallel cases. The Jewish case is complicated by a long, complex history of what being Jewish has meant historically and by contemporary conflicts over the meaning of Jewishness.

---

[113] Ashutosh Varshney distinguishes between ethnicity, nation, and nationality. "A nation is a group with a political and territorial home; a nationality is a large ethnic group without such a home (but with cultural rights pertaining to language and sometimes religion); and an ethnic group is a smaller collectivity, different from a nationality but not large enough to be called a nationality." Varshney, "Ethnicity and Ethnic Conflict," 277. In the Soviet context, the difference suggested by Varshney between ethnic group and nationality had few practical consequences. The Soviet term *natsional'nost* is deceptively translated as "nationality," but in English and American usage "nationality" usually connotes citizenship, not ethnicity.

[114] Marietta Stepaniants in Juliet Johnson, Marietta Stepaniants, and Benjamin Forest, *Religion and Identity in Modern Russia* (Aldershot: Ashgate, 2005), 26.

2

The Evolution of Jewish Identities

> "What does it mean to be a Jew? Oh, in my opinion the biggest brains cannot give an answer to that question."
>
> – A resident of Chernivtsi, Ukraine, 1993

> When Dr. Sigmund Freud asked, What remains Jewish in a Jew who is neither religious nor a nationalist and who is ignorant of the Bible's tongue, you managed to mutter the answer he had himself given: much. You did not explain what that meant, since he had been careful enough not to offer explication.
>
> – Norman Manea, 2003[1]

> While every other group is striving for development by asserting its nationality... Let us make clear to the world that we too are a nationality striving for equal rights to life and to self-expression.
>
> – Louis Brandeis[2]

"A word can mean many things to many people; and no word, one may almost conclude, means more things to more people than... the word 'Jew'.... Of all human groupings, there is none wherein the problem of definition has proved to be more difficult than for the Jews."[3] This is how the eminent anthropologist Melville Herskovits concluded a survey of anthropological literature on Jews from the nineteenth to the middle of the twentieth centuries. Not only are Jews difficult to define using conventional terms for different types of groups but also, like many other groups, they redefine themselves with some regularity. Jews confound conventional social science wisdom in two ways: (1) they were probably a nation before "print capitalism," *pace* Benedict Anderson, and

---

[1] Norman Manea, *The Hooligan's Return* (New York: Farrar, Straus and Giroux, 2003), 241.
[2] Louis Brandeis, "The Jewish Problem – How to Solve It," quoted in Victoria Hattam, *In the Shadow of Race: Jews, Latinos and Immigrant Politics in the United States* (Chicago: University of Chicago Press, 2007), 51.
[3] Melville Herskovits, "Who are the Jews?" in Louis Finkelstein, ed., *The Jews*, Vol. 4 (Philadelphia: Jewish Publication Society, 1949), 1153, 1168.

The Evolution of Jewish Identities

(2) they do not fit conventional categories neatly, such as race, nation, ethnic group, or religion. Both peculiarities are partly due to the antiquity of the Jews; relatively modern categories cannot capture them easily. Academics especially need to be reminded that these categories are invented ("constructed"); they do not exist in nature but are designed by humans to make sense of and bring order to social phenomena. Moshe Rosman observes, "The interplay of genealogy, religion, common history and other factors makes classifying the Jews in some conventional category virtually impossible."[4] If a collectivity does not fit neatly into one or another category – pigeonholes marked "race," "ethnic group," "nation," or "religion" – it is not the group that is problematic and lacking but the categories and the larger conceptual system of which they are a part.

Nevertheless, there is the urge to classify in order to understand.[5] That urge is no less strong among members of the group itself than among those who would analyze it. As Michael Meyer notes, "Long before the word became fashionable among psychoanalysts and sociologists, Jews in the modern world were obsessed with the subject of *identity*. They were confronted by the problem that Jewishness seemed to fit none of the usual categories."[6] Perhaps this is because Jews emerged in the ancient Near East, where religion and ethnicity were not differentiated. The distinction between these two categories began to be made in eighteenth-century Western Europe when Jews began to be "emancipated." For the first time, Jews could choose to be Jewish *and* something else (they had long been able to choose not to be Jewish by converting to Christianity). For the last two hundred years or so, Jews and non-Jews have struggled to establish whether they are a race, religion, ethnic group, nation, or a cultural group. This has not been an academic exercise, but one fraught with practical consequences because, as we saw in Chapter 1, identity has attitudinal and behavioral consequences. Perhaps that is why "[f]ew subjects arouse so much passion and misunderstanding as the identity and status of the Jewish people."[7] So what are the Jews? Have they always been the same kind of entity? And why does it matter?

Classic Jewish thinkers disagreed on what made one Jewish. Historian Jacob Katz observed,

> Both the Midrash[8] and philosophers like Yehuda Halevy[9] traced religious and historical differences to the dissimilar character of Jew and non-Jew.... It is irrelevant whether they traced these differences to a biological or racial

---

[4] Moshe Rosman, *How Jewish Is Jewish History?* (Oxford: Littman Library, 2007), 33.
[5] It is instructive that a book that was for many years one of the most popular general histories of the Jews among Jews themselves, Nathan Ausubel's *Pictorial History of the Jews* (New York: Crown, 1953) begins with a discussion of whether Jews are a race, nation, religion, people, etc.
[6] Michael Meyer, *Jewish Identity in the Modern World* (Seattle: University of Washington Press, 1990), 3.
[7] Anthony D. Smith, "The Question of Jewish Identity," in *Studies in Contemporary Jewry* VII (New York: Oxford University Press, 1992), 219.
[8] Ancient rabbinic legal and homiletical interpretations of the Bible.
[9] Spanish Jewish philosopher, poet, and author of a major Jewish philosophical work, the *Kuzari*, who lived from 1075–1141.

source ... or to divergent reactions to a particular historical and metaphysical event.... A qualitative difference was involved for which the individual was not responsible and which he could not change. Hence, the theological divergences were to be traced to a deep-seated, essential distinction of a meta-biological and meta-historical nature between the two camps.[10]

The poet and philosopher Yehuda Ha-Levi, who lived in Spain in the eleventh and twelfth centuries, adopted a Platonic view that people are born with intrinsic characteristics or "fully formed souls," in contrast to Aristotle's assumption that humans acquire culture and character as they develop. According to Ha-Levi, Jews are distinct from other people and transmit their unique characteristics from generation to generation. To deal with the fact that people can become Jews by conversion. Ha-Levi's "essentialist" position postulated that converts are not themselves fully formed Jews and only their descendants may become so[11]: "Any Gentile who joins us sincerely shares our good fortune, but he is not created equal to us. If the Torah were binding on us because God created us, the white and the black man would be equal since He created them all. But the Torah (is binding) because He led us out of Egypt and remained attached to us. For we are the pick of mankind."[12]

In contrast, perhaps the most authoritative Jewish philosopher and religious decisor, Maimonides (1135–1204), defines a Jew as one who accepts the thirteen principles of faith that he postulated. Menachem Kellner observes, "Given that the standard *halakhic* definition of a Jew is a person born of a Jewish mother or properly converted to Judaism (with no reference in the classic discussions to acceptance of 'the principles of faith'), Maimonides's insistence on seeing the issue in theological terms demands an explanation."[13] Kellner argues that for Maimonides,

> there is nothing "essential" about the person him- or herself that makes him or her a Jew. At basis all human beings are the same. What differentiates them, in religious terms, at least, is the doctrines that they accept or reject. It is on the basis of those doctrines (their "software") that they are accepted as Jews and accepted into the world to come.[14]

Thus, the convert is fully Jewish because he or she accepts the postulated beliefs: there is nothing "ethnic" about this conception. So we find Maimonides

---

[10] Jacob Katz, *Tradition and Crisis: Jewish Society at the End of the Middle Ages* (Glencoe, IL: Free Press, 1961), 26. I am indebted to Chaim Waxman for this and the following reference.

[11] Menachem Kellner, *Maimonides on Judaism and the Jewish People* (Albany: SUNY Press, 1991), 4–5. See also Baruch Frydman-Kohl, "Covenant, Conversion, and Chosenness: Maimonides and Halevi on 'Who is a Jew?'" *Judaism* 41 (Winter 1992), 64–79.

[12] *Kuzari*, Book One, proposition 27. Yehuda Ha-Levi, *Kuzari*, in Issak Heinemann, ed., *Three Jewish Philosophers* (New York: Meridian, 1960), 35. The Zohar – a classic work of Jewish mysticism – assumes that the convert possesses a Jewish soul but through some error it wound up in a Gentile body and conversion has liberated it.

[13] Kellner, *Maimonides on Judaism and the Jewish People.*

[14] Ibid., 62–64.

ruling that "a Jew who worshiped idolatry [*avodat kochavim*] is a complete idolater [*mumar lechol haTorah kulah*] and is unlike an Israelite who commits a sin whose punishment is stoning.....Heretics [*Epikorsim*] of Israel are not Israelites for any purpose [*ledavar min hadvarim*] and we do not accept their repentance ever."[15]

The late Jean-Marie Cardinal Lustiger, archbishop of Paris, disagreed. Born to a family of Polish Jewish immigrants to France, Aharon Lustiger converted to Catholicism at age 13 when living with a Catholic woman to whom he had been sent by his parents to escape the Nazis. His mother was murdered in Auschwitz; his father survived the war. Lustiger maintained that he remained a Jew after his religious conversion: "I was born Jewish, and so I remain, even if that is unacceptable to many. For me, the vocation of Israel is bringing light to the goyim. That is my hope, and I believe that Christianity is the means for achieving it." Not surprisingly, Jews rejected this claim. One rabbi commented that "a Jew becoming a Christian does not take up authentic Judaism, but turns his back to it." Another, a former chief rabbi of Israel who had also survived the Holocaust, said that Cardinal Lustiger had "betrayed his people and his faith during the most difficult and darkest of periods." But Lustiger insisted, "To say that I am no longer a Jew is like denying my father and mother, my grandfathers and grandmothers. I am as Jewish as all the other members of my family who were butchered in Auschwitz or in the other camps."[16] Nazis would have agreed with him; Jews did not. It was reported that when Lustiger was ordained as a priest in 1954, "his father watched the ceremony from a seat far in the back."[17]

People also disagree on the issue of continuity and change in the meanings of being Jewish. Traditionalists see Jewish identity as fixed across time and space, whereas modernists maintain that Jewishness is influenced by context. Indeed some postmodernists argue for the total flexibility of Jewishness as a category and its constantly changing content. Those who argue that there are multiple understandings of what it means to be Jewish generally are led to two different conclusions. Postmodernists embrace the "diversity" and indeterminacy behind the label "Jew." They maintain that all conceptions are equally valid[18] and authentic, because there is no such thing as "authenticity," and any assertion of it commits the error of "essentializing." In contrast, those who believe that they know what being Jewish means, and that it admits of little ambiguity, postulate that although empirically various people at various times may hold different conceptions of Jewishness, there is a single normative definition. Any deviation from it must be treated as such and its adherents excluded from the

---

[15] Maimonides, *Sefer HaMada, Hilchot Avodat Kochavim*, 29. The commentary of the *Lekhem Mishneh* tries to qualify this ruling. Ibid.

[16] John Tagliube, "Jean-Marie Lustiger, French Cardinal, Dies at 80," *New York Times*, August 6, 2007.

[17] Ibid.

[18] David Theo Goldberg and Michael Krausz, eds., *Jewish Identity* (Philadelphia: Temple University Press, 1993).

Jewish people, as happened with the Samaritans, Karaites, and Sabbateans. Today, "Hebrew Christians," "Messianic Jews", and "Jews for Jesus" are generally not included in the fold by other Jews.[19] Attempts to exclude Hasidim, Reform, and Reconstructionist Jews failed, possibly because in modern societies Gentile authorities no longer demanded an official, compulsory Jewish community.[20] There were and are ethnic entrepreneurs who seek to "return lost Jews" to the fold, whether they be Ethiopian, Bukharan,[21] Crypto-Jews, post-Soviet Jews, or, simply, assimilated or nonpracticing or non-Orthodox Jews who can be made *lakhzor bitshuvah* (literally, to "return in penitence"). The entrepreneurs usually assume that authenticity resides in the Jewishness they themselves practice and that they are doing a favor both to the deviant Jews and to the Jewish collective by returning those who have strayed back to the flock.

If the problem with traditionalists is denial of historical changes in the content and meaning of Jewishness, "[t]he modernist problem ... is that once the narrow, classical definition of Jewish identity is discarded ... there would appear to be no simple, self-evident, and adequate formula to replace it with."[22] In response, the postmodernist would say there is no classical definition of Jewish identity, and therefore one need not worry about replacing it. An ethnic group cannot have fixed characteristics, because it is forever changing. Like categories such as gender, it is being constantly constructed and deconstructed. Consider these postmodernist assertions. Sarah Abrevaya Stein observes, "All too frequently, the conceptual category 'Jew' is employed as if its meanings were inherent and self-evident.... Scholars of Jewish studies ... are sustained by ill-defined assumptions about the transparency of identity and communal cohesion."[23] Taking the point further, Juliet Steyn asserts, "Jews are a group without a single foundation, a heterogeneous linking of the non-identical."[24] Michael Krausz takes an extreme constructivist position when he writes,

> No essences are to be described at all. Accordingly, there is no essence of the Jewish people as such. Rather, there are people in Jewish positions, or positions that are bestowed as Jewish. Jewishness is understood as a set of characteristic positions in which certain people are cast or ascribed – by themselves and by others.... Jewish

---

[19] An extensive bibliography on Messianic Judaism and Jews for Jesus is provided by Owen Power in H-JUDAIC Digest – 23 Mar 2009 to 24 Mar 2009 (#2009–50), accessed on March 25, 2009.
[20] I thank Nancy Sinkoff for this observation.
[21] Alanna Cooper, "Looking Out for One's Own Identity: Central Asian Jews in the Wake of Communism," in Zvi Gitelman, ed., *New Jewish Identities in Contemporary Europe*, (Budapest: Central European University Press, 2003), 189–210.
[22] Jonathan Webber, *Jewish Identities in the New Europe* (London: Littman Library, 1994), 8.
[23] "Sander Smarts: Gilman's Smart Jews," *Jewish Social Studies* 4, 2 (Winter 1988), 184.
[24] Juliet Steyn, *The Jew: Assumptions of Identity* (London: Cassell, 1999), 18. This author, who makes the usual obeisances to Walter Benjamin, Michel Foucault, Jacques Lacan, and other "icons," as she might say, of postmodernism, is "concerned to inaugurate the possibility of thinking 'singularity' and 'particularity,' but now to be understood as connoting *both* identity and transformation."

history is not of reified entities but of positions or situations. And positions and situations are socially constructed. Thus, the question, What is a Jew? or What is Jewishness are misconceived if they are understood essentialistically [sic] and should be recast as, What characterizes one's being positioned as a Jew or Jewish in various historical circumstances?[25]

"No essences are to be described at all" is in itself a kind of essentialist argument, a form of flat-footed dogmatism. As Alejandro Grimson has argued, a group of people need not share all elements of a culture to identify with each other:

> Heterogeneity and singularity do exist, but within the confines of a relatively coherent distribution of cultural characteristics.... The world is complicated, but the first language of Japanese children is Japanese and not French or Russian, and in childhood, Mexicans do not hear Rumanian music or consider it "natural" to eat lamb cooked Algerian style.... borders do exist.... At times, the cultural and identitary [sic] borders of a group can grow or shrink together.[26]

Even Krausz admits, "While there can be no single correct Jewish history, there may be incorrect Jewish histories, for, as I have allowed, any twentieth-century history of the Jews that ignores or minimizes the Holocaust is incorrect."[27]

There are several arguments against the radical constructivist position:

1. if everything is flexible and situational, terms and identities have *no* meanings, not just shifting meanings. If 2 + 2 sometimes equals 4 and sometimes equals 5, then one cannot make a meaningful statement about 2 + 2, unless one specifies a specific and different meaning to each addition exercise. If being Jewish can mean anything, it means nothing.
2. In practice people need to know who is a Jew and who is not for purposes of admission to synagogues, organizations, the Jewish state, and the like, and they will therefore have at least an implicit "essence" of Jewishness in mind. They need this even for simply identifying themselves and others as Jews/non-Jews. If this were not the case, Jews today would not be passionately debating whether Jewishness is ethnic, cultural, or religious; whether it can be acquired patrilineally and through what kinds of conversion processes; and whether American Jewry is assimilating and losing its Jewishness or merely transforming it. As Charles Liebman stated, "Most Jews in the modern world are uncomfortable if they cannot locate their own Jewish identity in commonly accepted categories. As a result, there has been a continued effort to reinterpret Judaism in

---

[25] "On Being Jewish," in Goldberg and Krausz, *Jewish Identity*, 265.
[26] Alejandro Grimson, "Culture and Identity: Two Different Notions," *Social Identities* 16, 1 (January 2010), 61–77, passim. Grimson relies on arguments made by C. Brumann, "Writing for Culture: Why a Successful Concept Should Not Be Discarded," *Current Anthropology* 40 (February 1999), 1–41.
[27] Ibid., 273.

order to make it, and one's identification with it, comparable to other forms of identity as expressed by other peoples."[28]

Similarly, as Jonathan Webber wrote, "The fact that some manifestations of... identity have become garbled or unrecognizable does not mean that the basic identity has ceased to exist in the popular imagination."[29] Identities represent "the force of belief rather than of fact empirically verifiable by the disinterested observer [although those beliefs about identity can be empirically verified, as I show in this book].... Identities can be weak, strong, confused, disordered or in crisis."[30] Webber continues,

> Classical Jewish identity has in the modern world broken up (if not also broken down) into multiple Jewish identities, some of which indeed trace connections with the more distant past, while others define themselves more directly and explicitly through highly contemporary issues.... Jewish identity seen historically reveals both continuity and discontinuity; where the emphasis is to be placed depends on a person's point of view.[31]

Moshe Rosman similarly concludes,

> Jewish identity and culture have always been contested and under construction to some extent; certainly they have always been in active relationship with the hegemonic culture. If that means, however, that they have no fixed content whatsoever, no defining – yes, I'll say it – *essential* characteristics, how can we identify what in the past is properly the object of the study of Jewish history? If anything can be Jewish, then is anything not Jewish, or is nothing Jewish?[32]

3. Even Krausz admits that "at any given time there are requirements for membership in the group.... One might say that there are essences without essentialism [sic!], although it would be best if we did not speak of essences at all."[33] The fact that the meaning of Jewishness has varied over time and space does not mean that it is a completely open concept. There may have been and are today a range of meanings of Jewishness, but they are bounded. They may have varied more over time and across spaces than they do in the same space and time, although there is variance even there – Jews in a single country at a single time define themselves differently in terms of religion, for example – but historically there have been defining core characteristics. This is not a normative but an empirical observation.

---

[28] Charles Liebman, "Changing Jewish Identity in Israel and the United States," in Stuart Cohen and Milton Shain, eds., *Israel: Culture, Religion and Society, 1948–1998* (Capetown: Jewish Publications, n.d), 36.
[29] Introduction," in Webber, ed., *Jewish Identities in the New Europe*, 2.
[30] Ibid., 5.
[31] Ibid., 3.
[32] Rosman, *How Jewish Is Jewish History?* 98. See also p. 184.
[33] Krausz, 267.

What are these characteristics, and what have been the boundaries within which different understandings of Jewishness have been deployed or have contended? We may be able to derive an "essential" core of Jewishness *inductively* from past understandings and practices that include the following:

1. A preference for Judaism over other religions or a closer identification with it even if one is not religious in either belief or practice. The British cultural commentator Bernard Levin provides a good example. He averred that he was a nonbeliever but "[w]hen I am filling in a form on which there is a space labeled 'Religion,' I don't hesitate, but put Jew.... Am I a Jew? If I do not pray with the Jews, and sing with the Jews, and refuse to eat pork with the Jews, and read books backwards with the Jews, how can I be a Jew? Well, don't forget the form that I filled in."[34]

"Privileging" Judaism over other religions does exclude "Jews for Jesus." There is some ambiguity over whether one who adopts another religion ceases to be a Jew, but in Eastern Europe those who converted to Christianity were definitely read out of the community. In Western Europe, Jews converted to become fully recognized as Europeans, which they assumed, correctly, meant for most people being Christians. There were a few converts who continued to regard themselves as somehow and somewhat Jewish (Heinrich Heine, Benjamin Disraeli), but they were exceptional. The same holds true today. Religion has long been recognized as a nexus of Jewishness.[35]

2. Some kind of attachment or relationship to Israel rather than to another country in which one does not live.
3. A common set of observances, customs, and rituals, however understood, interpreted, and expressed. Even the most radically secular kibbutzim created a Passover seder and haggadah (the text read at the seder).
4. Descent from Jews as the normative case, although with a possibility of acquiring Jewishness (conversion) by those not born to Jewish parents.
5. Mutual recognition and "glances" of understanding ("members of the tribe," *b'nai brith* [sons of the Covenant]). "There is always some kind of imperceptible restraint. Go to a Jewish lodge and bring one non-Jew in, and you find an imperceptible change in the presence of a Goy. You sit up a little straighter; you talk a wee bit more grammatically; you will be a wee bit more polite.... It's the difference between the in-group

---

[34] "The Jews Who Choose," *The Times* (London), October 6, 1995. Strikingly, none of the five letters to the editor reacting to Levin's article even hinted that one could be a Jew without practicing Judaism. *The Times*, October 10, 1995, 19.

[35] Olena Bagno makes the interesting observation that Judaism was and is an integrating force among diaspora Jews, but in the Jewish state it may have become as divisive an issue as an integrating one. Personal communication, January 11, 2012.

and the out-group. It was not a question of friction. What is relevant is a feeling of being at ease."[36] As pointed out in Chapter 1, feelings of kinship and mutual recognition exist as much among humans as among animals.

6. Definition as Jews by others. The Soviet state did this by assigning "nationality" (ethnic identity) to its citizens. The State of Israel does so by recognizing matrilineal Jews, although they may not think of themselves as Jewish. Webber calls them "classificatory Jews."[37] The most common form of external definition is when ordinary people regard someone as a Jew.[38]

Karen Cerulo describes postmodernists as advocating "a shift in analytic focus, deemphasizing observation and deduction and elevating concerns with public discourse."[39] My own preference is for the more difficult task of gathering and analyzing empirical evidence. Ian Lustick has correctly pointed to the preponderance of polemic over empirical research in the writings of many constructivists:

> This ritualized beating of primordialist and essentialist dead horses can be explained in part by lack of theoretical imagination, but also in part because of the difficulties of gathering data suitable for the categories constructivist theory suggests as crucial.... Constructivists... must somehow probe the multiplicity of identities available to individuals, the range of "identity projects" available within a population or across overlapping or intermingled populations, and the relationship of those identities and projects to changeable sets of preferences and changeable institutional circumstances.[40]

In this study I try to discern the conceptions of Jewishness held by Russian and Ukrainian Jews and examine the implications of those conceptions for those who hold them and for those, Jewish and not, who come in contact with them. I do compare these conceptions to those that have prevailed historically and contemporaneously, not to judge or draw up an agenda for changing thought and behavior, but to identify points of commonality and uniqueness or deviance from prevailing norms so that the origins, nature, and consequences of such differences may be explored.

---

[36] Harold Isaacs, *American Jews in Israel* (New York: John Day, 1967), 89. This 1963 interview was with an American immigrant to Israel. Perhaps younger American Jews today would not have the same feelings when encountering members of the "out-group."
[37] Webber, *Jewish Identities in the New Europe*, 17.
[38] As Meyer points out, experiencing anti-Semitism may lead one to negate one's Jewishness or, on the other hand, to affirm it. Meyer, *Jewish Identity in the Modern World*, 33.
[39] Karen Cerulo, "Identity Construction: New Issues, New Directions," *Annual Review of Sociology* 23 (1997).
[40] Ian S. Lustick, "Agent-Based Modeling and Constructivist Identity Theory," in Kanchan Chandra, ed., *Cumulative Findings in the Study of Ethnopolitics*, APSA-CP (Winter 2001), 23.

Why Does it Matter?

How we define the Jews has important real-world consequences and has even been a matter of life or death. If Jews are a religious group and not an ethnic one, they would have no claims to a state and would form no political allegiances other than to the states in which they live. In contrast, if they are a nation, that status would legitimize their claim, at least in the nineteenth century and since, to statehood and territory. Membership in a nation, like membership in a religious group, would promote feelings of mutual responsibility and concern among the members. Yet, if Jews are only a nation, people who practice different religions or no religion should be eligible for inclusion in the nationally defined group. A "Jewish Catholic" or a "Muslim Jew" would not be an oxymoron, as they are widely considered today. Finally, the Nazi conception of Jews as a race, specified in the first Regulation to the Reich Citizenship Law (November 14, 1935) – known as the Nuremberg Law – determined who would live or die in the territories ruled by the Nazis until 1945. Thus, people who had only one Jewish grandparent, were practicing Christians, had no knowledge of or interest in Jewish culture, and considered themselves completely German could have been murdered on the grounds that they were racially Jewish. A prominent refugee from Nazi Germany, the philosopher Hannah Arendt, wrote, "Jews had been able to escape from Judaism into conversion; from Jewishness there was no escape."[41]

In Israel the question "who is a Jew?" has become a contentious sociopolitical and religious issue. Jews are the privileged group in this "ethnic democracy,"[42] in which 20 percent of the population is not Jewish. Moreover, as we see in Chapter 9, Jewish status matters for the acquisition of citizenship by immigrants.

Let us look, then, at the historical evolution of Jewishness. I paint the picture in very broad strokes, with many details omitted, and rely on others' research for this sketch. I do not try to document the meanings of Jewishness at any one time with great precision, but to see whether and to what extent there have been significant shifts in its content or meaning. By doing so I can place in perspective the conceptions of Jewishness held by Jews living in Russia and Ukraine in the 1990s and assess to what extent these conceptions comport with those held by other Jews historically and today.

In the Beginning

There is wide agreement that Judaism cannot be divorced from its ethnic and communal dimensions. Some have called it a "tribal religion" because of the absolute congruence between what we have come to call religion (Judaism)

---

[41] *The Origins of Totalitarianism* (Cleveland: Meridian Books, 1958), 87.
[42] See Sammy Smooha, "The Model of Ethnic Democracy: Israel as a Jewish and Democratic State," *Nations and Nationalism* 8, 4 (October 2002), 475–503.

and ethnicity (Jewishness). Edward Shils explains, "Judaism became a religious community from a plurality of tribal communities. In so doing it became simultaneously a nationality, its religious beliefs referring to the particular territory as a sacred place and assigning particular religious significance to the nationality."[43] Jews saw themselves as a *people* "chosen" by God, not just as a collective on whom God's grace had descended. Unlike Catholicism's relation to, say, Spaniards, Islam's to Libyans, or Buddhism's to Thais, "Judaism is not a case of a religion arising somewhere and then influencing, impregnating, and shaping a people. The people and the religion have grown together," although "even the most orthodox Jewish theologians – as, indeed, also the ancient prophets – would agree that even without faith and practice there was a Jewish people."[44] Perhaps this is because Jewish identity originated in the ancient Near East where religion, kinship, and nationality/ethnicity were fused. In that time and place, there seems to have been no concept of "religion" because it suffused the lives of all peoples to such an extent that it was not a thing apart. There were no atheists or secularists in the ancient world that we know of[45]:

> Although all the ancestors of today's Europeans (like the ancestors of all the world's inhabitants) had what we would call religions, no ancient Indo-European language had a special word for religion, Latin having been the first – which is probably why the great majority of modern European languages have some version of *religio* as their term for it. Probably this was because, precisely since religion was everywhere in the ancient world and no activity was divorced from it, it never struck anyone as a distinct aspect of life calling for a name of its own.[46]

Were the Israelites a Nation?

In 1934 Joseph Tenenbaum wrote,

> It is an irony of fate that one of the oldest living peoples should be subjected to an inquiry or doubt as to its identity. Jews were a nation when there was neither a German nor a French or a British people.... Jews had a literary language of their own, a highly developed culture and literature before the Gauls or the Teutons knew the art of reading or writing. And yet, such is the fate of this strange people that not even the merits of priority can serve the Jewish cause.[47]

---

[43] Edward Shils, "The Constitution of a Nationality," foreword to Dominique Schnapper, *Jewish Identities in France* (Chicago: University of Chicago Press, 1983), xiii.
[44] R. J. Zwi Werblowsky, *Beyond Tradition and Modernity* (London: Athlone Press, 1976), 49.
[45] See Yaron Z. Eliav, "Secularism, Hellenism, and Rabbis in Antiquity," in Zvi Gitelman, ed., *Religion or Ethnicity? The Evolution of Jewish Identities* (New Brunswick, NJ: Rutgers University Press, 2009), 7–23.
[46] Philologos, "Roots of 'Religion,'" *Forward* (New York), May 25, 2007, B4.
[47] Joseph Tenenbaum, *Races, Nations and Jews* (New York: Bloch Publishing Company, 1934), 81.

The Evolution of Jewish Identities

Antiquity helps legitimate political claims to nationhood and statehood. Therefore, the age of the Jewish collective has become a subject not only of historical investigation but also of contemporary political import. We recall the debate, discussed in Chapter 1, between modernists, who see nations as a phenomenon of the industrializing, modernizing epoch, and perennialists, who think of nations as larger, updated expressions of premodern ties and sentiments.[48] Benedict Anderson, aware that Jews (Hebrews/Israelites) existed long before "print capitalism," fits them into his theory by arguing, "The significance of the emergence of Zionism and the birth of Israel is that the former marks the reimagining of an ancient religious community as a nation... while the latter charts an alchemic change from wandering devotee to local patriot."[49] The Hebrew Bible and Jewish liturgy make it clear that no "reimagining" was needed for Jews to "imagine" themselves as a nation.[50] As described in Chapter 1, E. J. Hobsbawm made an argument similar to Anderson's,[51] concluding, "It is entirely illegitimate to identify the Jewish links with the ancestral land of Israel... or the hope of return there when the Messiah came... with the desire to gather all Jews into a modern territorial state situated on the ancient Holy Land."[52] Hobsbawm was apparently unaware of messianic movements that mobilized thousands of Jews to return to their ancestral homeland, the best known being the seventeenth-century movement led by Sabbatai Zvi (although perhaps this was more of a religious than national movement but, again, it is not easy to separate the two).[53]

---

[48] Anthony D. Smith, *The Ethnic Origins of Nations* (Oxford: Blackwell, 1989), 13. Smith wisely suggests that there is more continuity from *ethnie* to nation than modernists say, and more changes in the *ethnie*, wrought by modernization than the perennialists admit. Far too much has been written, and repeated, on the issue of whether nations are modern "constructs" based on politics and territory or entities that existed before modern times and were based on shared symbols and culture. The main points in the debate are covered in Montserrat Guibernau and John Hutchinson, eds., *Understanding Nationalism* (Oxford: Polity, 2001); Anthony D. Smith, *Nationalism* (Oxford: Polity, 2001); and Daniele Conversi, ed., *Ethnonationalism in the Contemporary World* (London: Routledge, 2002), chapters 3–5.

[49] Benedict Anderson, *Imagined Communities: Reflections on the Origins and Spread of Nationalism* (London: Verso, 1991), 149, n.16.

[50] Phrases such as *"amcha beit Yisrael"* [your nation, the house of Israel], *"am Yisrael"* [the people/nation of Israel], and *"Uvanu bakharta m'kol am ve-lashon"* [you have chosen us from among all nations and languages], as well as the word "Israel" itself – and variants on these – abound in the texts. Of course, there are also universalist conceptions in these texts. The coexistence and tensions between national and universalist values are explored in Steven Grosby, "The Biblical 'Nation' as a Problem for Philosophy," *Hebraic Political Studies* 1,1 (Fall 2005), 7–23.

[51] E. J. Hobsbawm, *Nations and Nationalism since 1780* (Cambridge: Cambridge University Press, 1990), 47.

[52] Ibid., 47–48.

[53] See Gershom Scholem, *Sabbatai Sevi: The Mystical Messiah* (Princeton: Princeton University Press, 1973). Scholem, a scholar of Jewish mysticism, warns against "an easy sociological or economic explanation of the Sabbatian success" (3). He interprets the entire story as a religious one and seems to ignore its possible ethno-national character.

Certainly, at the end of the nineteenth century Zionism captured the allegiance of more Jews in the Russian Empire, which had the largest concentration of Jews in the world (more than five million), than any other movement. In 1917 Zionist parties won the national elections to an aborted national Jewish congress; they got more votes to the (also abortive) Constituent Assembly that was supposed to write a constitution for post-tsarist Russia than any other Jewish party; and they were victorious in the majority of local communal (*kehilla*) elections.[54] Zionist success was achieved because as late as the Russian Revolution the majority of Russian Jews were religious (Orthodox) and they did not need to read the Zionist manifesto, *Der Judenstadt*, by the assimilated Austro-Hungarian Jew Theodor Herzl to be persuaded that Jews needed a territorial, sovereign Jewish state. Although the Bund and other socialist movements had gained many Jewish adherents, at the beginning of the twentieth century there was a "primordial" Jewish nationalism, with which the socialists had to contend, whose wellsprings were in Judaism and which had existed for centuries. This was a challenge not only to internationalists such as Vladimir Lenin but also to many founders of the Bund who had no intention of encouraging Jewish nationalism. As one of them put it, "We were for assimilation; we did not even dream of a special Jewish mass movement.... Our task was developing cadres for the Russian revolutionary movement."[55] However, the dreams of the masses were different: "Zionism did not spring into existence *deus ex machina* but was rather an articulation of the millenarian Jewish spiritual yearning for Return, in the political and conceptual terminology of today, notably self-determination."[56]

Moreover, a strong case can be made that ancient Israelites, Egyptians, Armenians, Chinese, perhaps Greeks,[57] and some others constituted nations, even in the modern sense of the term, long before print capitalism and modernity. "Tribal" religions helped establish cultural content and social boundaries, two necessary attributes of an ethnic group[58] that set their adherents apart from others.[59] Some of those groups were also nations, if one accepts the ideal-typical definition of nation offered by Anthony Smith: "a named human population sharing a historic territory, common myths and historical memories, a mass, public culture, a common economy and common legal rights and duties for all

---

[54] Zvi Gitelman, *Jewish Nationality and Soviet Politics* (Princeton: Princeton University Press, 1972), ch. 2.
[55] T. M. Kopelson, "Evreiskoe rabochee dvizhenie kontsa 80-kh i nachala 90-kh godov," quoted in Henry Tobias, "The Bund and Lenin until 1903," *Russian Review* XXXIX, 4 (October 1961), 344–45.
[56] Efraim Karsh, Introduction, in *Israel: The First Hundred Years*, Vol. 1 (London: Frank Cass, 2000), 5.
[57] See Jonathan Hall, *Ethnic Identity in Greek Antiquity* (Cambridge: Cambridge University Press, 1997).
[58] Stephen Cornell, "The Variable Ties That Bind: Content and Circumstance in Ethnic Processes," *Ethnic and Racial Studies* 19, 2 (April 1996).
[59] See John Armstrong, *Nations before Nationalism* (Chapel Hill, NC: University of North Carolina Press, 1982).

The Evolution of Jewish Identities

members."[60] According to Doron Mendels, in the ancient Near East, "many peoples could cope with the idea of being a nation through the preservation of their religion and culture without being within the framework of an independent state of their own."[61]

If a nation is an ethnic group with a political agenda, often aiming to create a state, arguably the ancient Israelites constituted both a nation and a state. Steven Grosby sees the clan (*beit av, mishpakha*) among the ancient Hebrews evolving into a nation when they accepted a legal system that, along with postulating a historically distinctive past, set the boundary differentiating the Hebrews, Israelites, and, later, Jews from others.[62] The Hebrew Bible uses the terms *am* and *goy* to describe the Hebrews – despite the latter's current colloquial usage to describe non-Jews[63] – and the terms "come[s] rather close to the modern definition of 'nation.'"[64] Several scholars have made the argument for ancient Israelite nationhood on the basis of other kinds of evidence, although others argue against it on what seem narrow semantic grounds.[65] One could

---

[60] Anthony D. Smith, "Nations and History," in Guibernau and Hutchinson, eds., *Understanding Nationalism*, 19. Smith persuasively argues that the involvement of all Jewish men in the regular cycle of festivals and the rule of Jewish law over all inhabitants of ancient Israel suffice to meet the criterion of mass participation in the organized community (21).

[61] Doron Mendels, *The Rise and Fall of Jewish Nationalism* (New York: Doubleday, 1992), 15.

[62] Steven Grosby, "The Chosen People of Ancient Israel and the Occident: Why Does Nationality Exist and Survive?" *Nations and Nationalism* 5, 3, 360, 369 and his *Biblical Ideas of Nationality, Ancient and Modern* (Winona Lake, IN: Eisenbrauns, 2002). See also Antonin Causse, *Du Groupe Ethnique a la Communaute Religieuse* (Paris: F. Alcan, 1937).

[63] For example, Valeriy Tishkov states, "The [Biblical] Hebrew *goyim* means non-Jews." *Rekviem po etnosu* (Moscow: Nauka, 2003), 97. In fact, the first time God speaks to Abraham, the putative "father" of the Jewish people, he says "*ve'e-escha le-goy gadol*" [I shall make you a great nation] (Genesis 12:2). In Deuteronomy 26 *goy* is used to refer to the Israelites (v. 5), as is *am* (v. 15, 18,19) and in chapter 27 (v. 1). In Deuteronomy 27:9 Moses and the priests and levites address "all of Israel" and say, "Today you have become an *am*." The term *am* is repeated several times in the following chapters. The Passover haggadah, quoting the biblical text, refers to the Israelites in Egypt as "*goy gadol atzum varav*" [a great nation, powerful and numerous]. The Sabbath afternoon liturgy refers to the Jews as "*goy ekhad ba'aretz*" [one nation in the land]. It is true that in modern Yiddish, and to some extent in Hebrew, *goy* has come to mean non-Jew. In some contexts it has a pejorative connotation (e.g., *shiker vi a goy* [drunk as a non-Jew]), but in others it does not (e.g., *gezunt vi a goy* [healthy or strong as a non-Jew]). These usages reflect Jewish perceptions in Eastern Europe. The term is completely neutral in the common expression, *shabbes goy* (a Gentile who performs tasks forbidden to Jews on the Sabbath). It is sometimes used to criticize a nonobservant Jew, equating him or her with a Gentile (*a goy gomur* [Yiddish, a complete "goy"]).

[64] E. A. Speiser, "'People' and 'Nation' of Israel," *Journal of Biblical Literature* 79 (1960), 160.

[65] For example, Mitchell Cohen, *Zion and State: Nation, Class and the Shaping of Modern Israel* (Oxford: Blackwell, 1987) and Avi Erlich, *Ancient Zionism* (New York: Free Press, 1995). Umut Ozkirimli rejects Israelite nationhood in his critique of Steven Grosby's works. Grosby sees ancient Israel, early Sri Lanka, eighth-century Japan, and medieval Poland as nations because each "exhibited: 1) a self-designating name; 2) a written history; 3) a degree of cultural uniformity, often as a result of and sustained by religion; 4) legal codes; 5) an authoritative center; 6) a conception of bounded territory" (535). Ozkirimli says, inter alia, that the existence of an Israelite legal system and clear distinctions made between Israelites and others do not

plausibly argue that even into the short-lived monarchy, the Israelites were more a confederation of tribes than a nation, if one adapts Rupert Emerson's definition of a nation.[66]

However, for our purposes it is sufficient to note how Jews do not fit neatly in one of the dominant conceptions of nationhood, as a modern construction. Of course, "[t]he huge paradox of Jewish history is that the people who gave the world the model of nationhood, and even nation-statehood, lost it for nearly two millennia and yet survived.... They retained the core identity of a nation through the exercise of collective memory, the usages of religion based upon a specific literature."[67] In sum, as Anthony Smith has argued – and this certainly applies to the Jews – some peoples have a "vivid ethnic legacy" from premodern times.

Among the Hebrews/Israelites/Jews, religion, kinship, and nationality/ethnicity were fused. The convert to Judaism is called *ben Avraham* (son of Abraham) or *bat Sarah* (daughter of Sarah) – the first patriarch and matriarch – not to establish literal biological kinship but to assert membership in a group, one of whose defining characteristics is a putative common ancestry. Kinship could be fictive and symbolic. Contrary to John Locke's assertion that only explicit consent makes one a member of a political society and that "has been the practice of the World from its first beginning to this day,"[68] the Hebraic conception is that membership is conferred by birth (i.e., kinship) or by a fictional kinship conferred on "naturalization" (note the reference to "natural"); that is, conversion. Members of the group are called, significantly, *b'nai* Yisrael [children of Israel].[69]

The traditional conception that Jews form a group that fuses ethnicity and religion is expressed in the phrase, "*Yisrael ve'orayta – khad hu*" [Jews and

prove the existence of a nation: "Who is this 'us' and who is 'them'? Evidence suggests that this distinction was made mostly between 'believers' and 'non-believers,' and not between two 'national' groups." He misses the point that religion and ethnicity were fused, and his argument uses anachronistic terms. After much rhetoric about "contingency, plurality, heterogeneity, ambivalence in the formation of nations" – none of which Grosby or anyone else denies – Ozkirimli lamely says, "Let us admit that there were nations in antiquity, that, say, ancient Israel was indeed a nation. What contribution does this make to our understanding of nations?" (528, 529). Umut Ozkirimli and Steven Grosby, "Nationalism Theory Debate: The Antiquity of Nations?" *Nations and Nationalism* 13, 3 (2007), 525.

[66] "The nation is today the largest community which, when the chips are down, effectively commands men's loyalty, overriding the claims both of the lesser communities within it and those which cut across it or potentially enfold it within a still greater society." Rupert Emerson, *From Empire to Nation* (Boston: Beacon Press, 1960), 95–96.

[67] Adrian Hastings, *The Construction of Nationhood: Ethnicity, Religion and Nationalism* (Cambridge: Cambridge University Press, 1997), 186.

[68] Locke, *Second Treatise*, quoted in Jacqueline Stevens, "The State of the Nation: Naming Names," paper presented to the annual meeting of the American Political Science Association, San Francisco, September, 1996, 21–22.

[69] Stevens argues that "reliance on marriage and birth for membership [in a political community] are not features specific to monarchies, but [are] exercised with special force in republics and democracies." Ibid., 24.

The Evolution of Jewish Identities

the Torah are one]. Judaism is a tribal religion because whoever adheres to it is considered a member of the tribe or people, unlike the universal religions of Christianity and Islam whose adherents are of different peoples or nationalities. In this respect, Jews resemble Hindus, Sikhs,[70] Tibetan Buddhists, the Druze, and the Amish. After the destruction of the Temples,

> However widely the Jews were scattered, they felt themselves members of the Jewish nation.... The Jews... were, both in their own mind and in the eyes of their Gentile surrounding, and before the Roman law, not adherents of a peculiar religion, but members of a nation who carried with them from the land of their origin into every quarter where they established themselves their national religion and their national customs.[71]

In addition to the prohibition against proselytizing in Christian countries, this conception of nationhood might have played some role in making Judaism a nonproselytizing religion. Certainly, Jews and non-Jews knew who and what Jews were. Therefore the *issue* of Jewish identity seems not to have arisen before modern times, although it is clear that the *nature* of that identity shifted over time; even the name given to the people changed from Hebrew to Israelite to Jew (this change, however, is not unusual in the nomenclature of ethnic groups; e.g., colored, Negro, Black, Afro-American, African-American; Hispanic, Chicano, Latino; Ruthenian, Little Russian, Ukrainian).

According to Shaye Cohen, there was no single definition of "Jew" in the Greco-Roman period: "Jewishness was a subjective identity, constructed by the individual him/herself, other Jews, other gentiles, and the state,"[72] much like today. Yet the Hasmoneans gave outsiders access to membership in Judaean society, thereby changing Jewishness from being a function of birth and geography to a function of religion and culture, which one who was not originally a Jew could adopt.[73] Thus, after the destruction of the Jewish state and the center of Judaism in Jerusalem in the year 70 CE, religion – not language, territory, or statehood – became the nexus of Jewishness. (Some might regard a collective memory of a shared language, territory, and state as another nexus). The Talmud has it that Rabbi Yohanan ben Zakai pleaded with the Romans after the destruction of the Temple, "Give me Yavneh and her sages," thereby establishing the independence of Jewish learning and practice from the Temple.

---

[70] See Giorgio Shani, "The Territorialization of Identity: Sikh Nationalism in the Diaspora," *Studies in Ethnicity and Nationalism* 2,1 (2002), 11–19. The "narratives of Sikh identity" regard Sikhs as a "world religion, nation and diaspora" (17). Sikh identity may also be closely tied to territory, namely, the Punjab.

[71] George Foote Moore, *Judaism in the First Centuries of the Christian Era*, Vol. 1 (New York: Schocken, 1971), 224, 233.

[72] Shaye J. D. Cohen, *The Beginnings of Jewishness: Boundaries, Varieties, Uncertainties* (Berkeley: University of California Press, 1999), 3.

[73] Ibid., 137. On rabbinic conceptions of Jewish identity, see also Sacha Stern, *Jewish Identity in Early Rabbinic Writings* (Leiden: E. J. Brill, 1994).

Because it was made portable, unlike other religions that were dependent on a sanctified place and could not survive removal from that place or its destruction, Judaism preserved the Jewish collectivity no matter where its adherents were dispersed.[74] Even before the diaspora, E. A. Speiser asserts, "Yahweh was not specifically traced to a single locality as, say, Enlil is traced to Nippur, or Marduk to Babylon, or Ashur to his homonymous city. Theophanies on sacred mountains are not to be equated with political ties."[75]

If territory was not essential to the definition of Jewishness, however, religion was. Whether in Babylon or Spain, Morocco or Germany, Persia or Poland, Jews felt themselves part of a transnational diaspora, sharing common historical origins, a religious faith and practices, and an aspiration to return to a homeland that was also the center of their religion. This feeling of collective membership was reinforced, or perhaps just "forced," by the segregation of Jews socially and culturally, some of which was self-segregation, and ultimately their confinement to ghettos in Western Europe beginning in the mid-sixteenth century and to the Pale of Settlement in the Russian Empire in the late eighteenth century.

In the rigid European system of medieval estates and categories, Jewish identity was quite clear to both Jews and non-Jews. To avoid any confusion, the church imposed special clothing on Jews that would mark them as such, and Jews were segregated residentially in ghettos in some parts of Europe. In the fifteenth to the seventeenth centuries the only questionable populations were Conversos and New Christians, those who had been Jewish and were now putatively not.[76] In modern times the conception of a fused ethno-religious group was challenged when some societies in Western Europe began to separate religion and ethnicity, although in Eastern Europe and in the Middle East and North Africa under the Ottoman millet system these were still fused in popular perception. In Eastern Europe, too, the family and the community still exercised a powerful hold on thought and behavior, and the sense of difference from others was powerful. As Jews began leaving *shtetlakh* (small market towns) for larger cities, more influences and options appeared.

---

[74] W. D. Davies asserts that "[t]here was before 70 C.E. and immediately after in the early Tannaitic period, no uniformity of territorial doctrine.... Eretz Israel in Judaism... has received different emphases among various groups at different times... there has not been one unchangeable, essential doctrine universally and uniformly recognized by the whole of Judaism." W. D. Davies, *The Territorial Dimension of Judaism* (Berkeley: University of California Press, 1982), 104. Davies believes this conveys a contemporary political message. "The sober 'myth' of Jamnia [Yavneh] has longer and better served the survival of Jews and Judaism... than the more spectacular 'myth' of Masada. In this century, no less than in the first, patient pliability and moderated enthusiasm are more likely to be constructive for Israel and the world than intransigence, however heroic" (143–44).

[75] Speiser, "'People' and 'Nation' of Israel," 158, n.5.

[76] See Miriam Bodian, *Hebrews of the Portuguese Nation* (Bloomington: Indiana University Press, 1997). Michael Meyer notes that "[i]n premodern times the congruity between family and society prevented Jewish identity from becoming a problem." Meyer, *Jewish Identity in the Modern World*, 6.

The Evolution of Jewish Identities

Jewish solidarity and distinctiveness were challenged with the advent of the modern era when, first, the French Revolution and the republic it created, and then other states began to emancipate the Jews. In most cases this process meant removing some, if not all, of the disabilities under which they had labored. Emancipation gave individual Jews access to the larger societies in which they lived and to their cultures and institutions, but by and large denied the Jewish population collective rights. In the oft-quoted words of the Comte de Clermont-Tonnere, "One must refuse everything to the Jews as a nation, and to give them everything as individuals. They should become neither a political body nor an order. They should become individual citizens."[77] As Salo Baron observed, "Jewish identity constituted no problem before the emancipation era,"[78] but emancipation required that Jews decide whether there could be Judaism (religion) without Jewish nationality or ethnicity; still later, they asked whether there could be Jewishness without religion. The discussion was complicated by Jews' dispersal in different cultures where nationality, ethnicity, and even religion were understood differently. Geographic and ideological differences created serious disagreements among those who claimed the same identity.[79]

Non-Jews also faced the question whether there could be Judaism (religion) without Jewish ethnicity, so they would know who would be subject to certain policies and who would not. For example, Russian attitudes toward Jewish converts to Christianity changed during the nineteenth century. In the early years of the century such converts were usually accepted as Christians and hence Russians. In contrast, by the end of the century, those hostile to Jews denied that conversion "changed" the Jew. Gabriella Safran calls this "the change in focus from text to blood,"[80] which ironically is a good characterization of how Soviet Jews have come to define Jewishness today. Perhaps it was the complexity of the issue that caused Karl Lueger to expostulate as he supposedly did that *"wer ist ein Jude, das bestimme ich"*[81] [I decide who is a Jew].

---

[77] *"Il faut tout refuser aux juifs comme nation et tout leur accorder comme individus; il faut qu'ils ne fassent dans l'État ni un corps politique, ni un ordre: il faut qu'ils soient individuellement citoyens."* A translation of the count's speech can be found in Paul Mendes-Flohr and Jehuda Reinharz, eds., *The Jew in the Modern World*, 2nd ed. (New York: Oxford University Press, 1995), 114–15.

[78] Salo Baron, "Problems of Jewish Identity from a Historical Perspective: A Survey," *American Academy for Jewish Research* 46/47, 1 (1980), 33.

[79] Meyer maintains that the Enlightenment, anti-Semitism, and Zionism have shaped modern Jewish identity more than any other forces, but his perspective is largely that of Western Europe where the Enlightenment was more powerful than in the eastern part of the continent. Meyer, *Jewish Identity in the Modern World*, 8.

[80] Gabriella Safran, *Rewriting the Jew: Assimilation Narratives in the Russian Empire* (Stanford: Stanford University Press, 2000). See also Eugene Avrutin, "Returning to Judaism after the 1905 Law on Religious Freedom in Tsarist Russia," *Slavic Review* 65, 1 (Spring 2006), 90–110.

[81] John W. Boyer, "Karl Lueger and the Viennese Jews," *Leo Baeck Institute Year Book* 26 (1981), 128. My thanks to Todd Endelman for this reference. Shlomo Avineri tells me that this statement has been attributed also to the Nazi leaders Joseph Goebbels and Hermann Goering. Goebbels' wife was the stepdaughter of Jewish parents.

Thus, in the modern period, Jews have faced two great ideological challenges: (1) whether their emancipation and the modernization of societies they inhabited demanded a renovation of Judaism and, if so, what it should be; and (2) whether any version of Judaism could be divorced from Jewishness and thus maintain the Jewish people in secularizing and secular contexts. In turn, European societies moved from viewing Jews as a religious group to regarding them as some kind of *ethnos*, although few regarded them as a nation. In Western Europe, by the nineteenth century, few Jews did so either. This shift also meant that anti-Semitism changed from being a Christian, theologically animated hostility to people of another heretical religion to an animus against a people despised for being racially, linguistically, and culturally different.

Jews as a Race

In the nineteenth century, when seeking to define who is a Jew, "Jewish social scientists looked to statistics and images of Jewish bodily traits and forms to prove that at the fundamental physical level Jews constituted a recognizable 'type,' one that set them apart from the people in whose midst they lived, and connected them, despite geographic divisions, with other Jews."[82] Many defined Jews as a race, a popular if ill-defined term in late-nineteenth and early-twentieth-century Europe.[83] French Jewish community leaders referred to Jews as a race even before the rise of the anti-Semitic political movement of the late 1870s, which also used the category. "Racial self-identification allowed Jews to describe themselves in terms that made sense in the academic discourse of the time" and provided a defense against attacks on Judaism and a "way to explain continued distinctiveness."[84] "'Race' now meant more than just a 'lineage' or even a variation of the human species induced by climate or custom. It meant an innate and fixed disparity in the physical and intellectual make-up of different peoples."[85]

---

[82] Mitchell Hart, *Social Science and the Politics of Modern Jewish Identity* (Stanford: Stanford University Press, 2000), 22.

[83] Eric Goldstein explores Jews' changing attitudes toward their racial identity in *The Price of Whiteness: Jews, Race, and American Identity* (Princeton: Princeton University Press, 2006); Matthew Frye Jacobson comments that "[t]he racial odyssey of American Jews from 'white persons' to 'Hebrews' to 'Caucasians' illustrates how historical circumstance, politically driven categorization, and the eye of the beholder all conspire to create distinctions of race that are nonetheless experienced as natural phenomena, above history and above question." *Whiteness of a Different Color* (Cambridge, MA: Harvard University Press, 1998), 199.

[84] Lisa Moses Leff, "Self-Definition and Self-Defense: Jewish Racial Identity in Nineteenth-Century France," *Jewish History* 19 (2005), 8. See also Jay Berkovits, *The Shaping of Jewish Identity in Nineteenth-Century France* (Detroit: Wayne State University Press, 1989). On France more generally, see Herman Lebovics, *True France: The Wars over Cultural Identity, 1900–1945* (Ithaca: Cornell University Press, 1992).

[85] Nicholas Hudson, "From 'Nation' to 'Race': The Origin of Racial Classification in Eighteenth-Century Thought," *Eighteenth-Century Studies* 29, 3 (1996), 258.

Discussing those who used the terms "race" or "blood," Todd Endelman points out that they were "not biological determinists in the main. Their use of the word race was imprecise and often contradictory. By using the word, they wanted to suggest a feeling of community with other Jews, a sense of common historical fate, and a deep emotional bond that transcended religious faith and observance."[86] However, American Zionists and Reform Jews were leery of the classification of Jews as a race by the U.S. Immigration Commission in 1907 and "sought a way ... that would avoid racial classification ... yet sustain Jewish particularity. Both wanted recognition of Jewish difference in nonracial terms."[87] Yet, in early 1918 the scholar Israel Friedlaender asserted, "The Jews have never regarded themselves otherwise than as a sharply distinguished *racial* group, as a community which is knit together not merely by the bodies of faith, but also ties of blood.... The Jews have always *felt* themselves as a separate race, sharply marked off from the rest of mankind"[88] (italics in original). Friedlaender seems to have been using "race," a notoriously vague and contentious term, as we would use "ethnic group" today.[89]

At about that time, Adolf Hitler was also describing Jews as a race, but imputing deep biological meaning to the word. The Nazi appropriation of the concept explains why by the late 1930s Jews were no longer describing themselves as a race – strenuous efforts were made to show that Jews encompassed many "racial types"—but as a people, ethnic group, and so on.[90] A leading American historian of immigration wrote in 1957 that Americans "had ceased to believe in race" after the experience with Nazism and because of the findings of "science."[91] Victoria Hattam asserts that it was a group of American Zionists and Jewish intellectuals who established the concept of "ethnicity" in the United States in the period around World War I.[92] One of the best known

---

[86] Todd Endelman, "Jewish Self-Identification and West European Categories of Belonging from the Enlightenment to World War II," in Zvi Gitelman, ed., *Religion or Ethnicity? The Evolution of Jewish Identities* (New Brunswick, NJ: Rutgers University Press, 2009), 124.

[87] Victoria Hattam, *In the Shadow of Race*, 81. Hattam notes that "[c]lassification of the Jews became a litmus test for securing the boundaries of race" in the 1910 American census and thereafter (83). I owe this reference to Ashutosh Varshney.

[88] "Race and Religion," in Israel Friedlaender, *Past and Present* (Cincinnati: Ark Publishing, 1919), 431–32.

[89] See John Efron, *Defenders of the Race: Jewish Doctors and Race Science in Fin-de-Siecle Europe* (New Haven: Yale University Press, 1994) and Todd Endelman, "Anglo-Jewish Scientists and the Science of Race," *Jewish Social Studies* 11, 1 (Fall 2004), 52–92. See also Hattam, *In the Shadow of Race*, 35–39.

[90] Joseph Tenenbaum quoted approvingly an unidentified author who wrote, "race is nothing but a state of mind," long before contemporary social scientists discovered that race is "socially constructed." In Tenenbaum's view, if "race" means a "peculiar cultural and ethnic constellation, a 'Jewish state of mind,'" the Jews could be called a race. "Unfortunately, the word 'race' is spiked with so much explosive material that it is healthier for the Jewish people to appear what they are – a people *sui generis* instead of a non-existent Jewish race." Tenenbaum, *Races, Nations and Jews*, 44.

[91] Oscar Handlin, *Race and Nationality in American Life*, quoted in Jacobson, *Whiteness*, 134.

[92] Hattam, *In the Shadow of Race*, 45 ff.

twentieth-century writers on race, Ashley Montagu, who was born Israel Ehrenthal to Jewish parents in the East End of London, wrote, "Strictly speaking, a person is a Jew by virtue of his adherence to the Jewish religion. If he is not a member of some organized form of religion, then he is not a Jew."[93] He thus eliminated race, ethnicity, or nationhood as categories into which Jews could fit. In recent decades the concept of "race" has come under intense scrutiny, and not only because of the search for precision in social science. Political and social agendas clearly drive much of the enterprise and have influenced even biological research.[94]

Some Jews who feel uncomfortable with the ideas that Jews are a nation or a race and who do not adhere to Judaism describe themselves as being "of Jewish origin." In many instances, this implies a rejection of a present Jewish identity and signals that their Jewishness is of biological or historical relevance only.[95] The term *Abstammung* was particularly in vogue in the Weimar era as a self-designation for Jews,[96] favored by those who disliked the terms "nation" and "religion." Its popularity can be explained in part by its vagueness. Assimilationists took it in the sense of *Stamm* (compare Bavarians or Saxons), whereas for Zionists *Abstammung* became a synonym for a Jewish *Volk*.[97]

The "marriage" of race and nation bred various exclusivist doctrines, all of them inimical to European Jews and most notoriously, Nazism. Little wonder that Jews, many of whom had once embraced their "racial" distinctiveness, then sought to get rid of it. They have not been entirely successful. Whether driven by political or scientific considerations or both, recent scholarship has arrived at "a growing consensus that 'race' is best understood as a social-historical rather than a biological-genetic phenomenon."[98] If race is a biological category, it can

---

[93] Quoted in Alain Corcos, *The Myth of the Jewish Race: A Biologist's Point of View* (Bethlehem, PA: Lehigh University Press, 2005). Corcos was born in France in 1925 to nonreligious, unaffiliated Jewish parents. The Nazis classified the family as Jews. Corcos does not consider himself Jewish, although his brother does. Alain Corcos defines "race" as a group of people "separated geographically and sexually from other groups for long enough and under sufficient conditions to retain and/or develop an assortment of traits which completely distinguish its members from those of other human groups and which are transmissible by descent" (10).

[94] See, for example, Nicholas Wade, "Race is Seen as Real Guide to Track Roots of Disease," *New York Times*, July 30, 2002 (Science section, pp. 1–2); Nicholas Wade, "2 Scholarly Articles Diverge on Role of Race in Medicine," *New York Times*, March 20, 2003; and Linda Villarosa, "Beyond Black and White in Biology and Medicine," *New York Times*, January 1, 2002. Some useful selections are found in Martin Bulmer and John Solomos, *Racism* (Oxford: Oxford University Press, 1999), section VII, 329–87.

[95] Elias Bickermann, *Das Edikt des Kaisers Caracalla*, cited in Albert I. Baumgarten, "Elias Bickerman on the Hellenizing Reformers: A Case Study of an Unconvincing Case," *Jewish Quarterly Review* 97, 2 (Spring 2007). After moving from Russia to Germany, Bickerman described himself as being of "Jewish origin," although he identified openly and strongly as a Jew.

[96] Michael Brenner, *The Renaissance of Jewish Culture in Weimar Germany* (New Haven: Yale University Press, 1996), 39–42. I owe this reference to Albert Baumgarten of Bar-Ilan University.

[97] Ibid., 228, n.12.

[98] Steven Kaplan, '"If There Are No Races, How Can Jews Be a 'Race'?" *Journal of Modern Jewish Studies* 2, 1 (2003), 81. See note 11 for some of the debates on race.

The Evolution of Jewish Identities

be shown easily that Jews are *not* a race, although many Jews – including some in Russia and Ukraine, as we see later – continue to believe that "continuous descent from the Patriarchs is the sine qua non of Jewish identity."[99] However, if race is a socially and historically constructed category, a good argument could be made that by such definitions, Jews *are* a race. That conversion to Judaism, and thus inclusion in the Jewish collective, is possible, "would appear to be one of the strongest arguments against associating Jewishness with race, [but] the fact that those who convert *from* Judaism are still considered in both the religious and legal sense to be part of the Jewish people, would seem to support just such an association."[100]

That converts from Judaism may still be considered part of the Jewish people evokes three comments. First, not all Jewish authorities agree that converts from Judaism – for example, to Christianity – are still considered Jewish "in both the religious and legal sense" or even ethnically Jewish, as the cases of Cardinal Lustiger and Brother Daniel (Oswald Rufeisen) illustrate.[101] Second, popular classificatory schemes and perceptions are not always logical nor do they follow scientific principles. Third, because of the ambiguity surrounding Jews-as-a-race, and the fact that the idea that race is "socially constructed" is not widely known or accepted outside academic circles, on a practical level it is best to think of Jews as an ethnic group (and/or religious one) rather than as a race.

Categorical Confusion

Analysts have long been frustrated in their attempt to classify Jews. For example, because for nearly two thousand years Jews did not have their own state and were made into a diaspora by the Assyrian, Babylonian, and Roman Empires, Anthony Smith prefers to label Jews a "demotic *ethnie*" rather than a nation, so that they are not put in the same category as, say, the French. An *ethnie* is a "named human population with a shared myth of descent, shared memories and culture and a sense of attachment to a 'homeland.' Such communities are found... from the period of the Bronze age... and they appear in every epoch and continent from antiquity to the modern era.... *Ethnie* are both mutable and durable."[102]

An earlier observer, bothered by the cultural diversity of diaspora Jews, concluded that they are an "artificial nation, a compound of numerous nationalities brought about by a common religion, formed both by a voluntary and

---

[99] Ibid., 85.
[100] Ibid., 89.
[101] The Carmelite monk Brother Daniel was born a Jew (Oswald Rufeisen) in Poland, passed as a *volksdeutsche* during the German occupation and saved Jews in the town of Mir, converted to Catholicism, and came to Israel in the early 1960s, requesting that he be granted citizenship under the Law of Return because he was ethnically Jewish. This became a cause celebre and was dealt with by the Israeli Supreme Court.
[102] Anthony D. Smith, "The Question of Jewish Identity," in Peter Medding, ed., *A New Jewry? Studies in Contemporary Jewry* VIII (Oxford University Press, 1992), 220.

a forced separation from the other nations and by the prohibition of mixed marriages, all of which have been the result of religious principles." Jews are "an artificial nation created by religious rules and ordinances and compounded of numerous racial elements."[103]

Another example of categorical uncertainty is C. Bezalel Sherman's statement that Jews "would seem to be all of these and more": a religious group, a "historical continuum," a "cultural group with peculiar racial traits," and a "people." However, he noted, "Collectively, American Jews regard themselves as first of all a *religious* community"[104] (italics added). Yet, at the same time in the 1960s, sociologists Nathan Glazer and Daniel Patrick Moynihan found that most Jews in New York City had no synagogue or temple affiliation and that what really linked them was a *"sense of common fate"* (italics added). "And yet we know from experience that when asked, 'what is your religion?' even [non-religious and anti-religious Jews] answer, 'Jewish.' They concluded that *"the common fate is defined ultimately by connection to a single religion,* to which everyone is still attached by birth and tradition, if not by action and belief"[105] (italics added). By contrast, a decade after Moynihan and Glazer, two other sociologists asserted that for Jews, "Ties to tradition and minority experience are far more important than common belief, making it *more an ethnic than a religious* collectivity in many respects"[106] (italics added). Steven M. Cohen deduced from a 1997 survey of a thousand American Jews that, "although the Jewish ethnic dimension may still be stronger than its religious counterpart, Jewish *ethnic attachments of all sorts seem to be in decline*" (italics added). Those attachments – expressed through organizational membership, philanthropy, commitment to Israel, and political involvement as Jews – were found to be strongest among the older cohorts.[107]

Another way of understanding the data is that they reflect a turn not so much from ethnicity as from communalism, as well as a movement not so much toward religion as to individual concerns:

> The spirit of religious individualism signals a general decline in survival concerns and the perceived need to ban together for protection.... Religion in contemporary America is conceptualized as expressive behavior that can meet personal

[103] Count Heinrich Coudenhove-Kalergi, *Anti-Semitism throughout the Ages* (London: Hutchinson, 1935), 198.
[104] C. Bezalel Sherman, *The Jew within American Society* (Detroit: Wayne State University Press, 1965), xi, 218.
[105] Nathan Glazer and Daniel Patrick Moynihan, *Beyond the Melting Pot* (Cambridge, MA: MIT Press, 1963), 140–42.
[106] Wade Clark Roof and William McKinney, *American Mainline Religion: Its Changing Shape and Future* (New Brunswick, NJ: Rutgers University Press, 1987) 102. Similar conclusions are reached by Barry Kosmin and Seymour Lachman, *One Nation under God* (New York: Harmony Books, 1993), 121.
[107] "Religiosity and Ethnicity: Jewish Identity Trends in the United States," in Eli Lederhandler, ed., "Who Owns Judaism? Public Religion and Private Faith in America and Israel," *Studies in Contemporary Jewry* XVII (2001), 127.

needs for meaning... as well as the desire for belonging. This reflects two seemingly antithetical qualities: an individualistic pursuit of personal meaning and spirituality and the quest for community and a sense of belonging.[108]

Yet in their comparison of American and Israeli Judaism, Charles Liebman and Steven Cohen point to "familism" as a "key element of the Jewish collective consciousness." Jews see themselves as part of an extended family, "a group into which a person is born and of which the person remains a part regardless of what he or she does."[109]

These seeming contradictions arise as much from the perceptions of the writers as they do from changes in American Jewish self-conceptions. Most of all, they are caused by the ongoing fuzziness of Jewish identity and the ever-blurred boundary between ethnicity and religion. American and other Jews conceive of, describe, and present themselves differently at different times and in different places.

An example of why defining Jews is not just a semantic game but has real-life consequences is the U.S. courts' wrestling with whether Jews are a race or religion so as to determine whether the Civil Rights Act of 1866 applies to them. The Supreme Court has held that the act prohibits discrimination against races or ethnic groups, but not against religious groups. Nevertheless, district courts have held that Jewish religious practices fall under its protection. In deciding on the relationship of ethnicity to race and to religion U.S. courts have taken up such issues as whether ethnicity entails a common culture or a common genetic origin.[110]

In 2009 in another judicial system the British Court of Appeal ruled that Jews are defined by their religious practice, rather than by their birth or ethnicity. Thus, one must engage in personal acts of faith to qualify as a Jew. Therefore, giving priority in Jewish schools to those born to Jewish parents, no matter the degree of religious observance, amounts to racial discrimination. This decision "shocked the country's 300,000 strong Jewish community."[111] It does not help the courts that Jews themselves continue to debate furiously "who is a Jew?"

---

[108] Roberta Rosenberg Farber and Chaim Waxman, "Postmodernity and the Jews," in Farber and Waxman, eds., *Jews in America* (Hanover: Brandeis University Press, 1999), 397, 403.

[109] Charles Liebman and Steven Cohen, *Two Worlds of Judaism* (New Haven: Yale University Press, 1990), 17.

[110] The fascinating complexities are explored in William Kaplowitz, "We Need Inquire Further: Normative Stereotypes, Hasidic Jews, and the Civil Rights Act of 1866," *Michigan Journal of Race and Law* 12 (2007), 537–70.

[111] John Jeffay, "In Major School Case, British Courts Rule on Who is a Jew," *Forward* (New York), July 17, 2009. "The ruling means that Jewish schools of any denomination, whether privately or state funded, will be barred from giving priority to children who are born Jewish or who convert, and instead must consider how the children and their families practice their Judaism."

Nation and Nomenclature

Those who practice Judaism, the Jewish religion, are Jews. Are self-described Jews – or those who are defined by others as such – who practice no religion also Jews? Are Jews who practice a religion other than Judaism still Jews in the eyes of other Jews? Jewish tradition acknowledges as Jews those who do not believe in God or adhere to the tenets and practices of Judaism. Yet most contemporary Jews exclude from the Jewish fold those who actively practice *another* religion. If a nonreligious person can be an ethnic, secular, or cultural Jew, that implies that "Jew" is an ethnic category. As we have argued, this idea is embedded in the founding myths of the Jews. From ancient times, they have conceived of themselves as a "people" or "nation" (*am* or *l'eom*) and have been seen by others as such. Therefore, there should be a quality that in English would connote "Jewishness" – the quality of being Jewish, not necessarily a practitioner of the Jewish religion, but including such a person.

The word "Jewishness" is not in the Microsoft Word program dictionary nor in some older English dictionaries,[112] but it is found in more recent ones. Webster's *Twentieth Century Dictionary* defines "Jewishness" as "the state of being Jewish,"[113] which tells nothing about what being Jewish means, and the *Random House Dictionary*, marginally more helpfully, defines it as "the state or quality of being Jewish."[114] Interestingly, although the *Encyclopedia Judaica* published in the 1970s has no entry for "Jewishness," the later (2007) edition includes the term. The early-twentieth-century *The Jewish Encyclopedia* lists it among "several curious more or less obsolete forms" of adjectives describing the Jewish religion.[115] The uncertainty surrounding the term exists in other languages as well, including Hebrew and Yiddish. *Yahadut* in Hebrew is most often understood as "Judaism," yet there is no consensus on whether the word signifies primarily religion or ethnicity.[116] The same term (*Yahadus*, in Yiddish) is translated from Yiddish simply as "Judaism" in Alexander Harkavy's popular dictionary, and even the Yiddish term *Yiddishkayt* is translated as "Judaism, Jewish faith."[117] However, in Uriel Weinreich's *Modern Yiddish-English, English-Yiddish Dictionary*

---

[112] For example, *Webster's Collegiate Dictionary*, 5th ed. (Springfield, MA: G & C Merriam, 1943).

[113] *Webster's New Twentieth Century Dictionary, Unabridged*, 2nd ed. (New York: Simon and Schuster, 1979), 984.

[114] *The Random House Dictionary of the English Language, College Edition* (New York: Random House, 1968), 719. "Jewry" is defined as "the Jewish people collectively."

[115] Others are "Jewhead (1300), Jewhood (Carlyle)... Jewdom, Jewism, and Jewship, all used for the religious system of the Jews." *The Jewish Encyclopedia*, Vol. VII (New York: Funk and Wagnalls, 1907), 175.

[116] One dictionary lists a word "*Yahadutiyut*," probably the closest equivalent to "Yiddishkayt." Yet it defines it as "the essence of Judaism" [*ikar ha-yahadut*]. Yaacov Chaueka, *Ha-milon Ha-shalem* (Israel: Center for Educational Technology, 1997), 764. I have not heard the word used in conversation.

[117] Alexander Harkavy, *Yiddish-English-Hebrew Dictionary* (New York, 1925), 251, 254.

"Jewishness" in English is rendered as Yiddishkayt in Yiddish, which it defines as "Jewishness, Judaism," with "Jewishness" as the first meaning. Perhaps this reflects Weinreich's secular outlook more than the frequency of popular usage.[118]

Lexicographical confusion about the term "Jewishness" reflects uncertainty not only about nomenclature but also about the very meaning of being Jewish. However, in some languages there are meaningful distinctions among synonyms for Jews. For example, in French the terms *Israelite* and *Juif* mean different things. "Israelite" connotes a member of the Israelite (sic) *faith*, whereas *Juif* implies membership in the Jewish *people*, whether they constitute an ethnic group or a nation. Dominique Schnapper sees "Israelites" as Jews who are "acculturated to the values of French intellectuals, often after two or three generations," whereas "*Juifs*" are practitioners of Judaic rituals and are active in Jewish life.[119] The semantic difference is politically and sociologically loaded. Those who wish to emphasize the purely religious nature of their Jewish affiliation, rejecting any implication that they are members of an ethnic group or nation other than the French, would call themselves "Israelite," whereas others who see their identity as Jews in both religious and ethnic terms would use "*Juif*."

In the United States, the terms "Hebrew," "Jew," and "Israelite" have been used over the years, sometimes interchangeably but more often signaling different conceptions of Jewishness. "Hebrew" was a "racial" category in ship manifests that described immigrants. It was also the favored term of the Reform Jewish movement, whose national congregational body was known from 1873 to 2003 as the Union of American Hebrew Congregations (it is now the Union for Reform Judaism) and whose seminary continues to be called the Hebrew Union College. "Hebrew" may have been a way of signaling a purely religious and historical form of Jewishness while rejecting the more ethnically inflected "Jew" or "Jewish." German and American Reform Judaism rejected the idea that Jews are a nation and opposed Zionism's advocacy of a state for a Jewish nation or people. Orthodox Jews did not hesitate to call their main congregational body the Union of Orthodox Jewish Congregations of America. The Conservative movement, endorsing the idea of Jewish peoplehood, calls its seminary the Jewish Theological Seminary of America. Note that all the movements include "America" in their institutional titles. Perhaps this is merely a locating device, but it may also be signaling fealty to the American state and civic nation.

Like many other Yiddish terms, "Yiddishkayt" is so culturally laden that when translated as "Jewishness," which is the closest single word I can think of, it loses much of its emotional power and multiple connotations. Yet because

---

[118] Uriel Weinreich, *Modern Yiddish-English, English-Yiddish Dictionary* (New York: YIVO Institute and McGraw-Hill, 1968), 174, 587. The order in which the entries are to be read is explained on p. xvi, and it is Jewishness that takes precedence over Judaism.

[119] See Dominique Schnapper, *Juifs et Israelites* (Paris: Gallimard, 1980), 41, 51–52.

of the ambiguity of the term "Yiddishkayt," as exemplified by its different connotations in religious and nonreligious circles, and because it is not widely understood by English speakers, in this book I use "Jewishness" as the complement to Judaism. I mean by "Jewishness" a consciousness of being Jewish, whether perceived as ethnicity, religion, or both. It is an identity whose content is not always easy to specify either by those who claim it describes them and those who do not.

Defining Jewishness in Modern Times

Jews responded in different ways to the opportunities and dangers of emancipation. Their first impulse was to embrace European citizenship and culture, often accompanied by conversion to Christianity. Realizing after some disappointments that legal emancipation did not necessarily bring with it social acceptance, some gave up their "Mosaic" faith to become Christians, in the hope of achieving full integration. As Heinrich Heine famously said after he converted to Christianity, "Baptism was my entry ticket into European civilization."[120] In most cases these were individual acts made to change what was seen as one's problematic status or to "trade up" for better status. Soon an ideology of assimilation developed not only to justify but also to spur this process. Some began to advocate wholesale assimilation – the abandonment of any form of Jewish identity – as the only solution to the "Jewish problem." The assumption was that the Jews had a problem, not those who rejected or persecuted them.

Some attempted to stem the tide of assimilation and conversion by reforming Judaism so that it would be more attractive. The idea was to bring it in line with European – that is, Christian – norms so that one could be European and Jewish too, without having to be Christian. Reform Judaism, established in Germany in the early nineteenth century, dispensed with much of Jewish ritual, substituted the local vernacular for Hebrew in prayers and sermons, adopted clerical attire from Christian denominations, introduced instrumental music and greater decorum into the synagogue (now renamed the "temple"), and emphasized the ethics that Jews and Christians shared rather than the beliefs and practices that differentiated them.[121] Reform Judaism denied that Jews were a nation, declaring, in effect, Berlin as the "New Jerusalem," thus smoothing the way for individual Jews to "become German" or French or English, and the like. Jews could now be Germans, French, Magyars, or Poles "of the Mosaic or Israelite faith." "Jew" signaled ethnicity; "Mosaic" or "Israelite" meant only religion. One Reform leader explained his opposition to Zionism this way: "Zionism makes race and nationality, rather than religion ultimate and essential for Jews. Jews have no lasting claims for a

---

[120] See Todd Endelman, *Jewish Apostasy in the Modern World* (New York: Holmes and Meier, 1987) and his *Radical Assimilation in English Jewish History, 1656–1945* (Bloomington: Indiana University Press, 1990).

[121] On the rise of the Reform movement, see Michael Meyer, *Response to Modernity: A History of the Reform Movement in Judaism* (New York: Oxford University Press, 1988).

separate existence excepting their religious mission."[122] Although individual Reform rabbis began to adhere to Zionism in the late nineteenth century, the movement itself did not give up its anti-national stance until well into the twentieth century. After the Holocaust and the definitive rejection of Jews-as-Germans by the Nazis, Reform Judaism changed course and officially identified itself with Jewish nationhood.

There were five other responses to the challenge of emancipation, aside from conversion to Christianity and reforming Judaism. Appalled by the radical changes in religious belief and practice made by the Reform, which he saw as heresy, Rabbi Moshe Schreiber (1762–1839),[123] leader of Hungarian Orthodoxy based in Bratislava (Pressburg, Poszony), now Slovakia, declared, in a play on a biblical passage, that "*khadash asur min ha-Torah*" [innovation is forbidden by Jewish law].[124] He established the position of what came to be known as Orthodoxy or later ultra-Orthodoxy: Jews should reject emancipation because it would lead to heresy and assimilation. Secular culture and European dress and ways of life were dangers to Judaism and were to be avoided.

The second response was that of Samson Raphael Hirsch (1808–88), who founded a strictly Orthodox community in Frankfurt-am-Main and articulated a variant of Orthodoxy popularly known as *Torah im derekh eretz*: traditional Jewish law and lore but with acceptance of European culture. Hirsch maintained that one did not have to give up European culture – he himself studied at the University of Bonn – to remain a strictly traditional Jew. This ideology was more popular in Western than in Eastern Europe.[125]

Zionism was a third response to emancipation and the lures of assimilation. It was an expression of Jewish nationalism in modern European form. Influenced by the romantic nationalism sweeping Europe in the latter half of the nineteenth century, Zionists postulated that, contrary to Reform's denial of Jewish nationhood, the Jews were first and foremost a nation, albeit a stateless one. Therefore, Jewish nationality was independent of religion. Most early Zionists were not religious and quite a few were antireligious, but a minority of Orthodox rabbis embraced Zionism as compatible with and indeed an integral

---

[122] Henry Berkowitz, "Why I am Not a Zionist" (1899), in Joseph Blau, ed., *Reform Judaism: A Historical Perspective* (New York: Ktav, 1973), 378.
[123] Known as the *Hatam Sofer* (Hebrew) or *Khsam soifer* (Yiddish).
[124] "*Khadash*" (Hebrew) literally means "new." According to biblical law, the first fruit that a tree yields, "new" fruit, may not be eaten and is forbidden.
[125] As far as I know, only two yeshivot (schools of higher rabbinic learning) in the Russian Empire included general studies in their curricula, one in Lida (Belarus) founded by Rabbi Yitzhak Yaacov Reines and the other in Odessa (Ukraine), founded by Khaim Tshernovitz ("Rav Tsair"). A vivid portrait of the Lida yeshiva around 1907 is painted by Ben-Zion Ziv in Emanuel Etkes and Shlomo Tykocinski, eds, *Yeshivot Lita: Pirkei zichronot* (Jerusalem: Zalman Shazar Center for Jewish History, Hebrew University, 2004), 320–23. The Russian government closed Eitz Chaim, the most prestigious yeshiva in the region, located in the small town of Volozhin between Vilna and Minsk, after its leaders refused the government's demand that secular studies be introduced. Rabbi Reines had been a student in that yeshiva.

part of Judaism. Thus, Zionism was acceptable to some religious Jews, and it also provided a modern, a-religious alternative to Judaism for those who wished to identify as Jews but not practice Judaism. Zionism maintained that there was a "Jewish problem" in Europe that could not be solved by modernizing Judaism and the Jews, as the Reform movement believed. Nor was it possible to change European society, as socialists and other political reformers were urging. The only solution to the plight of the Jews was to give them what other nations enjoyed or would soon possess: territory and sovereignty. The Jewish state was to be a haven from persecution and, in the view of some Zionists, a center of renewed Jewish culture, a model society, or a harbinger of the messianic age.

Statehood was the primary goal of Theodor Herzl, a highly acculturated Jew who knew little about Jewish religion or culture. For him the establishment of a haven from persecution was a sufficient *raison d'etre* of the Zionist movement. When the British government broached the idea of giving Jews a territory in Africa, he was prepared to consider it seriously. Other Zionists rejected the idea on the grounds that Jews had no historic or cultural ties to that area, and their view prevailed. This highlights the point that "national movements are motivated by a desire to assure the existence and flourishing of a particular community, to preserve its culture, tradition, and language, rather than merely to seize state power."[126] Not only religious Zionists but also secular ideologues such as Ahad Ha-Am (Asher Ginsberg) were as much concerned with cultural preservation, revival, and development as they were with sovereignty. Ahad Ha-Am warned against the creation of a "Herodian state," one in which Jews were sovereign but where the culture was foreign.[127]

Although both Western and European Jews advanced forms of Zionist ideology,[128] it found its strongest grassroots support in Eastern Europe where assimilation was not an attractive or viable alternative. In that area a fourth solution to the "Jewish problem" – socialism – enjoyed considerable popularity. There a Jewish variant of socialism emerged in the form of the Jewish Labor Bund, founded in 1897, the same year in which the World Zionist Organization was established. Socialists believed that by overthrowing the capitalist order and bringing social, economic, and political equality to the world, their movement would ipso facto solve the "Jewish problem," because it would eliminate all ethnic discrimination. However, their unacculturated and certainly unassimilated working-class constituents pushed leaders of the Bund to demand national-cultural autonomy for Jews and other ethnic groups, even in a socialist society. This demand got them expelled in 1903 from the Russian

---

[126] Yuli Tamir, *Liberal Nationalism* (Princeton: Princeton University Press, 1993), xiii, quoted in Erica Benner, "Is There a Core National Doctrine?" in Maria Kovacs and Petr Lam, eds., *Studies on Nationalism from CEU* (Budapest: Central European University Press, 2004), 63.
[127] See Arthur Hertzberg, ed., *The Zionist Idea* (Cleveland: Meridian, 1960), 247–77 on Ahad Ha-Am, and 102–15 and 398–463 on religious Zionists.
[128] Ibid. See also Walter Laqueur, *A History of Zionism*, (London: Weidenfeld and Nicolson, 1972) and Shlomo Avineri, *The Making of Modern Zionism* (New York: Basic Books, 1978).

The Evolution of Jewish Identities

Social-Democratic Labor Party, which the Bund had helped found, but it also established the Bund's credentials as a plausible secular, socialist but unquestionably Jewish alternative to Judaism and Zionism.[129] Another autonomist but not socialist ideology, represented by a small party, was conceived by the historian Shimon Dubnov.[130]

Yiddishism, related to but distinct from the Bund, was the secular, apolitical movement that promoted Yiddish language and culture as an ethnic and cultural alternative to Judaism as well as to political Zionism. A "Yiddishist" ideology developed.[131] One of its architects, Chaim Zhitlovsky, claimed that the substitution of Yiddish language and culture for religion "succeeded in building a 'spiritual-national home,' purely secular, which can embrace Jews throughout the world." (Whether Zhitlovsky seriously thought that Sephardic Jews would adopt Yiddish, or whether he simply ignored their existence, is not clear, but telling). For Zhitlovsky, Yiddish had become the content of Jewishness: "The Yiddish language form becomes for us ... a fundamental."[132] For the first time, language was identified as the "distinctive characteristic" or "epitome of peoplehood" of the Jews.[133] This ideology was rendered irrelevant by the Nazis' murder of most of the world's Yiddish speakers, the coerced

---

[129] There is no comprehensive history of the Bund in English. A partisan history is Y. Sh. Hertz, ed., *Di geshikhte fun Bund*, 5 volumes (New York: Unser tsait, 1960–81). More balanced but less comprehensive studies include Henry Jack Tobias, *The Jewish Bund in Russia: From Its Origins until 1905* (Stanford: Stanford University Press, 1972); Yoav Gelbard, *Bi-se'arat ha-yamim: ha-"Bund" ha-Rusi be-'itot mahpekhah* (Tel Aviv: Tel Aviv University, 1987); Daniel Blatman, *For Our Freedom and Yours: The Jewish Labour Bund in Poland, 1939–1949* (Portland: Vallentine Mitchell, 2003); Yoav Peled, *Class and Ethnicity in the Pale: The Political Economy of Jewish Workers' Nationalism in Late Imperial Russia* (New York: St. Martin's, 1989); and Robert Brym, *The Jewish Intelligentsia and Russian Marxism: A Sociological Study of Intellectual Radicalism and Ideological Divergence* (New York: Schocken, 1978).

On competing Jewish ideologies in fin-de-siecle Eastern Europe, see Jonathan Frankel, *Prophecy and Politics* (New York: Cambridge University Press, 1981). More recent works dealing with the Bund are Jack Jacobs, ed. *Jewish Politics in Eastern Europe: The Bund at 100* (New York: New York University Press, 2001) and Zvi Gitelman, ed., *The Emergence of Modern Jewish Politics: Bundism and Zionism in Eastern Europe* (Pittsburgh: University of Pittsburgh Press, 2003).

[130] Dubnov's ideas on national autonomy can be found in a collection of his essays edited by Koppel Pinson, *Nationalism and History* (Cleveland: Meridian, 1961). An extensive bibliography of Dubnov's works is in Kristi Groberg and Avraham Greenbaum, eds., *A Missionary for History* (Minneapolis: University of Minnesota, 1998), 137–57.

[131] See Emanuel Goldsmith, *Architects of Yiddishism at the Beginning of the Twentieth Century: A Study in Jewish Cultural History* (Rutherford, NJ: Farleigh Dickinson University Press, 1976) and David Weinberg, *Between Tradition and Modernity: Haim Zhitlowski, Simon Dubnow, Ahad Ha-Am and the Shaping of Modern Jewish Identity* (New York: Holmes and Meier, 1996).

[132] Chaim Jitlovsky, "What is Jewish Secular Culture?" in Joseph Leftwich, ed., *The Way We Think*, Vol. 1 (South Brunswick, NJ: Thomas Yoseloff, 1969), 92, 93, 95.

[133] Weinberg believes that ultimately the secularists of the "transitional generation could not shake their deep-seated belief that the core of Jewishness lay in spiritual and ethical ideas that were eternal and independent of outside influences." op. cit., 13.

and spontaneous demise of Yiddish in the Soviet Union, and its weakness in competition with the dominant languages – English, French, and Spanish – in countries to which Yiddish-speaking Jews immigrated.

These then were conceptions of who and what Jews were in the European and American marketplaces of Jewish identities at the turn of the twentieth century. Of course, the categories were not mutually exclusive. In the Hapsburg Empire Jews defined themselves in several ways simultaneously: as loyal citizens of the empire, Jews by religion, and often German by culture. After World War I, in the new Austria they tried to define themselves as "Austrians by political loyalty, as Germans by cultural affinity, and as Jews in an ethnic sense."[134] Some Jews in Western and Eastern Europe combined socialism or religion with Zionism, or acculturation with religion or with Zionism.

The traditional ethno-religious fusion and Zionism, which, partly for tactical reasons, did not reject that fusion,[135] fared the best into the twenty-first century. All Jewish religious movements today embrace the idea of Jewish ethnicity and nationhood. A Jewish state was established in 1948 and has survived against heavy odds. In contrast, the Holocaust and Stalinist repression bankrupted the idea of secular, Yiddishist autonomism. The idea that socialism would rescue the world from ethnic hostilities and religious and racial discrimination was put paid by ethnic wars that broke out in socialist Yugoslavia and the USSR in the late 1980s and the 1990s. The experience of highly acculturated Jewries in Germany and Hungary, where even the most assimilated and those who had converted to Christianity were subjected to persecution, raised doubts about the efficacy of assimilationism in solving the "Jewish problem."

Generally, ideologies of assimilation and cosmopolitanism have fallen out of fashion and have been overtaken by "identity politics." George Schopflin sees "among the great debates in Europe since the eighteenth century... whether to organise power on the basis of reason or of identity."[136] In recent times, many have found identity to be more attractive than "reason." However, in practice, assimilation remains a powerful and perhaps growing force in many Western societies. It is certainly powerful in the Jewish diaspora. People drop their ancestral culture or religion without thinking much about it, usually in a process over several generations. Rather than being conscious assimilationists, they simply assimilate.[137]

---

[134] Marsha Rozenblit, "Jewish Ethnicity in a New Nation-State," in Michael Brenner and Derek Penslar, eds., *In Search of Jewish Community* (Bloomington: Indiana University Press, 1998), 135. On the identity adjustments made by Jews in the newly independent states of East Central Europe after the war, see Rozenblit, *Reconstructing a National Identity: the Jews of Habsburg Austria during World War I* (New York: Oxford University Press, 2001).

[135] I owe this observation to Professor Sammy Smooha, University of Haifa.

[136] George Schopflin, *Nations Identity Power* (NewYork: NYU Press, 2000), 9. He points out that "the term 'identity politics' is a misnomer, because it implies that there is such a thing as 'non-identity politics.' This is nonsense... because... we all have identities and these influence how we engage in politics" (15).

[137] On assimilation in the United States, see Milton Gordon, *Assimilation in American Life: The Role of Race, Religion, and National Origins* (New York: Oxford University Press, 1964);

This is precisely what the early Bolsheviks thought would and should happen. Nations would disappear under socialism because they were politically constructed. They were maintained by the bourgeoisie in order to divide the proletariat by seducing workers to national loyalties, distracting them from class consciousness and class warfare. Once the bourgeois order had been replaced by a proletarian revolution, nations would have no raison d'etre, and like the state itself, they would "wither away." Vladimir Lenin and his disciple Joseph Stalin thought Jews would be in the forefront of this development.

Yet despite being armed with Marxism, the "science of society," the Bolsheviks were uncertain how to handle ethnicity, which, as Lenin reluctantly realized, was of immense practical significance in the Russian Empire.[138] They also had as much trouble defining the Jews as anyone else. They did agree that Jews were not a nation "for a nation without a territory is unthinkable," and settled on the vague term "caste" to describe the Jews.[139] Nor were Jews a religious group, and there was no connection between religion and ethnicity in this or any other case. As Stalin argued in 1913, Jews were a *natsional'nost'*, a nationality or ethnic group. As such, they were officially recognized by the state. In January 1927, as the first Soviet census was coming to an end, experts and politicians met in Moscow to discuss the official list of nationalities. In the discussion of Jews, ethnographers maintained that "all Jews shared the same tribal origins," but because Georgian Jews, those from Central Asia, Crimean Jews, and Jews living in the Slavic republics spoke different languages, "the ethnographers were unsure how to count them."[140] In the end, among the 172 peoples granted official recognition were 5 geographic groups of Jews. By the next censuses (1937, 1939), all Jews were lumped together. Jews were now listed as a *narodnost'*[141] and individual Jews were required to register officially as members of the Jewish nationality, one of more than a hundred such nationalities in the Union of Soviet Socialist Republics.

Soviet Jews themselves widely accepted the Soviet concept of Jewishness as ethnicity, but not as religion. Official militant atheism and, even more so, urbanization, acculturation, and education made the Jews overwhelmingly secular.

The balance sheet of the Soviet experience regarding the Jews showed that the regime (1) uprooted religion almost entirely but was less successful in eliminating faith or belief (Russian Orthodoxy was left in institutionally far

---

Richard Alba, *Ethnic Identity: The Transformation of White America* (New Haven: Yale University Press, 1990); and Mary C. Waters, *Ethnic Options: Choosing Identities in America* (Berkeley: University of California Press, 1990).

[138] See Richard Pipes, *The Formation of the Soviet Union: Communism and Nationalism* (Cambridge, MA: Harvard University Press, 1997 [1954]).

[139] Lenin's and Stalin's attempts to categorize the Jews are discussed in Zvi Gitelman, *Jewish Nationality and Soviet Politics* (Princeton: Princeton University Press, 1972), 43–44.

[140] Francine Hirsch, *Empire of Nations: Ethnographic Knowledge and the Making of the Soviet Union* (Ithaca, NY: Cornell University Press, 2005), 132.

[141] On the shifting meanings of this term, see ibid., 115–23 and 266–67.

better condition); (2) created a strong sense among Jews that they were part of an ethnic group or nationality, but weakened the sense that Jews are a nation; and (3) destroyed thick culture in all its varieties – religious, Hebraic, and even Yiddish secular. However, because of the Soviet state's rigid adherence to Stalinist definitions of a nation and somewhat mechanical understanding of ethnicity, it did not realize that a thin culture could survive. It helped create a thin Russian-Jewish culture by allowing Jews mobility so that urbanism and education became Jewish markers. At the same time the regime permitted social anti-Semitism and introduced governmental anti-Semitism in the 1940s that, together with the Shoah, which made Jewishness involuntary and ineradicable, created another "ethnic" marker, victimization. Finally, many Jews came to abandon support of the system and lost their eagerness to integrate into it and the society it was revolutionizing. Instead, many became alienated and eventually emigrated. In the next chapter we delineate how this "balance sheet" was drawn up.

3

Soviet Policies and the Jewish Nationality

Ideological desires and practical necessities were continually in tension in Soviet nationality policies. Marxism aimed to eliminate ethnicity and expected that it would start to disappear with the coming of the socialist revolution; however, seventy-four years after its birth, the first socialist state in the world broke up partly because nationalism proved stronger than Marxist-Leninist ideology. The record of the Soviet system regarding the nationalities, like its assessment by outsiders, was mixed. The Soviets constructed but also destroyed nations and cultures and were both applauded and condemned for their efforts.

Soviet policies treated different nationalities differently, and these policies also changed over time. After about 1930, Russians were a favored nationality, whereas Jews, Germans, West Ukrainians, and the Baltic peoples were often regarded with suspicion. John Armstrong observed that some nationalities were treated as "younger brothers" (Ukrainians and Belorussians, some Finnic peoples) and others as colonials (Tatars, Azerbaijanis, Central Asians, Bashkirs).[1] The official and unofficial status of various peoples changed over the period of Soviet rule. In general, the 1920s were the heyday of the development of national cultures and of the social, political, and economic advancement of non-Russian peoples. The apogee of chauvinistic Russian nationalism was reached in the late 1940s through the mid-1950s.[2] Central Asians came into national political prominence – for example, as members of the Communist Party's highest organ, the Politburo – only in the 1960s. The number and proportion of Jews in party and government leadership posts fell steeply in the 1950s and 1960s from the heights reached in the 1920s and early 1930s.

There were also policies toward specific ethnic groups that were out of line with general nationality policies. These general policies stemmed from

---

[1] John Armstrong, "The Ethnic Scene in the Soviet Union: The View of the Dictatorship," in Erich Goldhagen, ed., *Ethnic Minorities in the Soviet Union* (New York: Praeger, 1968), 3–49.

[2] See Frederick Barghoorn, *Soviet Russian Nationalism* (New York: Oxford University Press, 1956).

79

ideological assessments of where in the process of socialist (or social) development the USSR found itself, whereas policies directed at specific ethnic groups were motivated by more pragmatic and immediate concerns. Therefore general theory and specific policy did not jibe easily. For example, while advocating internationalism and the diminution of ethnic consciousness, the government registered each Soviet citizen by nationality and made it nearly impossible for citizens to change this status. An individual's nationality was inscribed on the fifth line of his or her internal identification card, known as a "passport." Because the passport was presented on many occasions in daily life the bearer and the viewer were made aware of the bearer's ethnic affiliation. That affiliation was permanent: it did not depend on where one lived, what language one spoke, one's religion, or how one preferred to be identified. Thus, a resident of Ukraine who spoke only Ukrainian, was an adherent of the Ukrainian Catholic Church, and regarded himself as Ukrainian would nevertheless be registered as Russian if both his parents were registered as Russians. When one's parents were of the same nationality, nationality was fixed according to the ethnicity of the parents and by no other criterion. Only when parents were of different nationalities – say, Russian and Ukrainian – could one choose which of the parental nationalities to adopt. It was not possible to choose a third nationality.

On the collective level, all peoples had their histories rewritten in line with Bolshevik dogmas. The state destroyed religious traditions; selectively purged and adopted literatures; and purged and drove abroad, imprisoned, or executed national leaders. Thus, for example, Ukrainians and Russians were depicted as having age-old friendships sabotaged only by "feudal" or "bourgeois-nationalist elements" who exploited ethnic tensions to protect their class interests. Jews were not considered a diasporic nation; only those who practiced Judaism belonged to the Jewish group, and that was a religious rather than ethnic entity. Nonreligious Jews who lived in different states supposedly had no connection with each other. Jewish history taught in Soviet Yiddish schools started no earlier than the eighteenth century with the "class struggle in the Pale of Settlement."[3]

All religions were discouraged and hounded, but some were considered actively inimical to the Soviet regime and were suppressed. The Russian Orthodox Church was the most tolerated, whereas the Ukrainian Catholic Church (Uniate) was abolished and driven underground because of its links to the Vatican and identification with Ukrainian nationalism.[4] At the urging of

---

[3] See Zvi Gitelman, *Jewish Nationality and Soviet Politics* (Princeton: Princeton University Press,1972), ch. VI; Zvi Halevy (Harry Lipset), *Jewish Schools under Czarism and Communism: A Struggle for Cultural Identity* (New York: Springer, 1976); and Elias Schulman, *A History of Jewish Education in the Soviet Union* (New York, 1971).

[4] On the Russian Orthodox Church, see John Shelton Curtiss, *The Russian Church and the Soviet State* (Boston: Little Brown, 1953); Dimitry Pospielovsky, *The Russian Church under the Soviet Regime, 1917–1982* (Crestwood, NY: St. Vladimir's Orthodox Seminary, 1984), 2 vols; and Harvey Fireside, *Icon and Swastika: The Russian Orthodox Church under Nazi and Soviet Control* (Cambridge, MA: Harvard University Press, 1971).

Soviet Policies and the Jewish Nationality

one of the few "Old Bolsheviks" of Muslim background, Mirza Sultan-Galiev, during the Bolsheviks' militant atheist campaigns in the 1920s they were a little easier on Muslims because they were persuaded that Muslims would resist more violently than others.[5]

In the great purges of 1934–40, almost all the non-Russian political leaders – communists all – were purged, usually on charges of "petit-bourgeois nationalism." The leaders of the Communist Parties of Ukraine, Belorussia,[6] Central Asia, and the Caucasus found that what had been acceptable and even laudable just a few years earlier – seen then as the "construction of socialist nations" – was now considered a political deviation and inadmissible heresy for which they often paid with their lives.[7] In the Ukrainian Communist Party, for example, those who tried to combine the development of Ukrainian culture with socialism in Ukraine – such as Oleksander Shumsky, Mykola Khvylovyi, Mykola Skrypnik, and former members of the Borotbist party – were purged as petit-bourgeois nationalists.

As briefly mentioned earlier, there were several changes in the party line on ethnic matters. In the 1920s, the party encouraged peoples of the Soviet Union to develop their particular cultures. Languages were systematized; alphabets invented or reformed; cultural institutions such as ethnic theaters, newspapers, and journals were encouraged; and non-Russians were helped to enter educational institutions and rise in party, government, and military hierarchies.[8] This policy was called *korenizatsiia*, literally "rooting." To "root" Bolshevik ideology among the non-Russians, the ideology should be presented in the native languages of the peoples, many of whom did not understand Russian well or at all. This was not a matter of merely translating key texts, because the aim was to envelop the people with a comprehensive culture that would express socialist ideas in all possible forms – literature, the media, schools, theaters, and films.

Why would a socialist regime, which looked forward to the demise of ethnicity, encourage ethnic consciousness and culture? Lenin explained the dialectic involved. Peoples who had been oppressed by the tsarist regime felt a strong need to assert themselves and gain cultural and political autonomy. These aims should be accommodated temporarily. Once people were allowed

---

[5] See Gregory Massell, *The Surrogate Proletariat* (Princeton: Princeton University Press, 1974) and Douglas Northrop, *Veiled Empire: Gender and Power in Stalinist Central Asia* (Ithaca: Cornell University Press, 2004).

[6] The territory was known as Belorussia in Soviet times. Since 1991 it has been called Belarus. Its largest ethnic group was called Belorussians in Soviet times and now Belarusians.

[7] On Ukraine, see Robert Sullivant, *Soviet Politics and the Ukraine 1917–1934* (New York: Columbia University Press, 1962); on Belorussia, see Ivan Lubachko, *Belorussia under Soviet Rule 1919–1957* (Lexington: University Press of Kentucky, 1972); on Central Asia, see Alexander Park, *Bolshevism in Turkestan, 1917–1927* (Columbia University Press, 1954), and Northrop, *Veiled Empire*.

[8] See Terry Martin, *The Affirmative Action Empire: Nations and Nationalism in the Soviet Union, 1923–1939* (Ithaca: Cornell University Press, 2001).

to develop their cultures, they would realize that doing so would not solve their fundamental problems, which stemmed from class, not culture. Having satisfied their hunger for ethnic and cultural self-expression, formerly oppressed peoples would then be ready to join the international, interethnic enterprise of world revolution and its realization of socialist goals. In brief, for them to shift their focus from ethnicity, formerly oppressed peoples must be given the chance to realize and express it. Only then would they attain full proletarian and internationalist consciousness.

Joseph Stalin, Lenin's successor, moved decisively away from this kind of reasoning. Just as he halted the New Economic Policy (1921–28), which was designed by Lenin to ease the transition to socialism by retaining temporarily some features of capitalism such as small enterprise, so too did Stalin turn away from *korenizatsiia* and increasingly toward identifying Russians as the "elder brother" in the Soviet family of nations. Stalin, the ethnic Georgian whose given name was Djugashvili, believed the country had entered a new stage, which would lay the foundations of socialism. Agriculture would be collectivized, producing the surplus labor and state control necessary for the unprecedented rapid industrialization that would enable the USSR to defend itself from "capitalist encirclement" and also demonstrate the superior productive capacity of a socialist system. As Stalin said, Russia had been

> beaten by the Turkish beys. She was beaten by the Swedish feudal lords. She was beaten by the Polish and Lithuanian gentry. She was beaten by the British and French capitalists. She was beaten by the Japanese barons. All beat her – because of her backwardness.... Do you want our socialist fatherland to be beaten and to lose its independence? If you do not want this, you must put an end to its backwardness in the shortest possible time and develop a genuine Bolshevik tempo in building up its socialist economy.[9]

He pledged that Russia would not be humiliated again because industrialization would make it strong.

It would take an enormous effort to bring the country, which was economically and culturally backward, from a precapitalist stage of development to socialism. Four of five inhabitants of the Russian Empire were illiterate at the beginning of the twentieth century; the country lagged behind Europe on almost every indicator of economic development. To achieve the common goal of socialist construction would take all the energies and talents of millions of Soviet citizens, leaving hardly any time or resources for the continued development of ethnic cultures. Therefore that part of Lenin's dialectical process would be assumed to have succeeded. It was time to move on to the great common goals that united all inhabitants into a Soviet people and pay less attention to their aims as Georgians, Uzbeks, Tajiks, Poles, Jews, or Ukrainians.

---

[9] "The Tasks of Business Executives: Speech Delivered at the First All-Union Conference of Leading Personnel of Socialist Industry, February 4, 1931," in Joseph Stalin, *Works*, Vol. 13 (Moscow: Foreign Languages Publishing House, 1955), 40–41.

In the 1930s it became increasingly clear that the great common effort to modernize the country would be led by the Russian people, who had achieved the status of "elder brother." In mid-1936 the term *russkii narod* or "the Russian people" reappeared in the media.[10] Just as Stalin had moved away from the idea of a simultaneous world socialist revolution to that of "socialism in one country," so too did he shift the emphasis from proletarian internationalism to the status of the Russians as the primus inter pares among the Soviet peoples. The Soviets continued to pay lip service to world revolution, which was now assumed to take place sequentially rather than simultaneously. In addition, they never abandoned the rhetoric of the equality of all the nationalities. Perhaps this explains the seeming paradox that in December 1932 the system of internal passports was introduced whereby Soviet citizens would have identity cards that included their officially registered nationality.[11] "The practice of fixing nationality in each citizen's internal passport on the basis of parentage rendered an inherently liquid identity into a solid commitment to a single ethnocultural group."[12]

Whether ethnicity is in most cases an "inherently liquid identity" is debatable. Yet if the Soviets were serious about the irrelevance of ethnicity in the present and its eventual disappearance, why give people an ethnic status and remind them and others of it? A possible explanation is that if Russians were to be given preferential status they would first have to be identifiable. It would not be possible to classify all others, who constituted nearly half the Soviet population, as "non-Russians" or "others." Therefore if one group of people were to be registered by nationality, all would have to be. Another possibility is that Stalin and his colleagues so prized control of the population over ideology that they wanted to be sure of each person's ethnicity, in addition to the person's class, education, political allegiance, and culture.

Some have argued that, whatever the intentions of the new policies, by establishing a federal structure in the 1920s and giving boundaries, national symbols, systematized languages, and constitutions to nationalities, the Soviet government created national self-consciousness and the potential for sovereignty among many peoples. These policies were to come back to haunt the government and party in the 1980s as movements arose for cultural rights, autonomy, and eventually independence in the Baltic republics, Ukraine, and elsewhere.[13]

---

[10] See Martin, *Affirmative Action Empire*, 452–61; David Brandenberger, *National Bolshevism: Stalinist Mass Culture and the Formation of Modern Russian National Identity, 1931–1956* (Cambridge, MA: Harvard University Press, 2002), 43–62.

[11] See Sven Gunnar Simonsen, "Inheriting the Soviet Policy Toolbox: Russia's Dilemma over Ascriptive Nationality," *Europe-Asia Studies* 51, 6 (September 1999), 1069–87.

[12] Ronald Suny, "Constructing Primordialism: Old Histories for New Nations," *Journal of Modern History* 73 (December 2001), 867.

[13] See Ronald Grigor Suny, *The Revenge of the Past: Nationalism, Revolution, and the Collapse of the Soviet Union* (Stanford: Stanford University Press, 1993).

In an oft-cited article,[14] Yuri Slezkine claimed that the Soviets consistently promoted group rights to weaken individual rights and pointed out that the Soviet state was the first to institutionalize ethno-territorial federalism (cf. nonethnic federalism in the United States or Germany) and to classify all citizens according to their biological nationalities. One might ask whether Stalin really had to promote group rights to weaken individual rights or whether his regime could have repressed individual rights without making concessions to group rights.

Valeriy Tishkov was asked in the 1990s by a political representative of one of the "small peoples of the far north," as they were labeled in Soviet times, "When can we Nanaitsy call ourselves a nation?" He replied, "From the moment you asked this question, you believe that the Nanainets nation exists." Yet there were not enough supporters of the Nanaiets' national idea for the nation to come into being.[15] Tishkov told this story to buttress his claim that the Soviet system, in the name of "resolving the nationality question," "created" ethnic states (*natsional'nye gosudarstva*) that, in reality, existed only on paper.

In Slezkine's striking metaphor, the Soviet authorities insisted on "separate rooms" in a "communal apartment building." As Ronald Suny reminded us, "At the end of the 1930s the Soviet authorities celebrated the putative 'anniversaries' of the epics of various Soviet peoples... Georgian... Russian... Armenian... and... Kalmyk."[16]

Yet as mentioned earlier, different nationalities were treated differently.[17] One cannot make the argument that the "Belorussian room" was reinforced[18] or that the Jewish, Korean, Polish, or German nationalities were encouraged to maintain a distinct identity. All of the latter were considered nonterritorial minorities, and after the 1920s their cultures and ethnicities did not enjoy official support. Except for the Jews, all were suspected of disloyalty to the Soviet Union as World War II approached (the Jews' turn came after the war). In the late 1930s ethnic groups not living in their titular territories but connected to nations outside the USSR – Germans, Poles, Greeks, Latvians, Estonians,

---

[14] Yuri Slezkine, "The USSR as a Communal Apartment, or How a Socialist State Promoted Ethnic Particularism," *Slavic Review* 53, 2 (Summer 1994), 414–52.

[15] Valeriy Tishkov, *Rekviem po etnosu* (Moscow: Nauka, 2003), 168.

[16] Suny, "Constructing Primordialism," 876.

[17] John Armstrong, "The Ethnic Scene in the Soviet Union: The View of the Dictatorship," in Rachel Denber, ed., *The Soviet Nationality Reader* (Boulder: Westview, 1992), 227–56; (original in Erich Goldhagen, ed., *Ethnic Minorities in the Soviet Union* [New York: Praeger, 1968]).

[18] Nelly Bekus contends that Belorussian mass national consciousness was created by the Soviet government in the 1920s. Before that, such consciousness could be found only among a small elite. "Nationalism and Socialism; 'Phase D' in the Belarusian Nation-Building," *Nationalities Papers* 38, 6 (November 2010), 829-846. By the 1950s, such consciousness had diminished, and most Belarusians have remained quite indifferent to their ethnicity.

Iranians, and Afghans – were arrested and deported. About 187,000 Koreans were deported from their homes in the Soviet Far East to Kazakhstan in Central Asia. Germans were uprooted and also deported to Central Asia, and a disproportionate number of ethnic Poles were sent to labor camps. Several of the Caucasus and Karelian peoples disappeared from the census as they were judged to have assimilated into other, larger peoples. Alphabets that had previously been Latin or Arabic were changed to Cyrillic, the alphabet of Russian. Languages such as Belorussian, Ukrainian, or Yiddish were deemphasized in favor of Russian. Schools in those languages were closed down. Russian became a compulsory second language in the non-Russian republics. A larger proportion of Russians entered the "cadres" of the state and Communist Party.[19] Many ethnically defined soviets and regions were merged with others and "internationalized." Research institutes that focused on a single ethnic culture were closed. These actions were surely more important than celebrations of putative ethnic anniversaries.

Already in 1936 a lead editorial in *Pravda* declared that all peoples of the USSR "are equal Soviet patriots. But the first among equals is the Russian people whose role...has been exclusively great."[20] During World War II, Russian national sentiments were mobilized to rally a population that had suffered through the collectivization of agriculture and the Great Purges and could be expected to nurse resentments of the Soviet system. Some nationalities were particularly disaffected, especially the Ukrainians, who had experienced a severe famine in 1932–33 that some believed was deliberately engineered against their nation.[21] Yet even thousands of ethnic Russians defected to armies commanded by General Vlasov and fought alongside their Nazi sponsors, as they saw it, against the Stalinist system. Stalin understood that defense of Russia was a stronger motivation for opposing the Nazis than the defense of socialism. On March 15, 1944, the "Internationale" was replaced as the national anthem by the "Hymn of the Soviet Union." The words of the first paragraph, written by Sergei Mikhalkov, convey the intended message effectively:

> Unbreakable union of freeborn republics
> **Great Russia** (*velikaya Rus'*) welded forever to stand!
> Created in struggle by will of the people
> United and mighty, our Soviet land!

---

[19] See Martin, *The Affirmative Action Empire*, ch. 10.
[20] "RSFSR," *Pravda* 31 (February 1, 1936), 1, quoted in Martin, ibid., 452.
[21] The issue is discussed in, inter alia, Hiroaki Kuromiya, "The Great Famine: The Issue of Intentionality," in James Mace, "Is the Ukrainian Genocide a Myth?"; David Saunders, "The Starvation of Ukrainians in 1933: By-Product or Genocide?" all in Lubomyr Lucyuk, *Holodomor* (Kingston, Ontario: Kashtan, 2008). See also the debate between Michael Ellman in "The Role of Leadership Perceptions and Intent in the Soviet Famine of 1931–1934," *Europe-Asia Studies* 57, 6 (2005), 823–41, and R. W. Davies and Stephen Wheatcroft, "Stalin and the Soviet Famine of 1932–33: A Reply to Ellman," *Europe-Asia Studies* 58, 4 (2006), 625–33.

The Soviet press reflected this turn to Russian patriotism.[22] It hailed pre-Soviet military heroes such as Marshalls Kutuzov and Suvorov[23] and identified Russians as the "main fighters" against fascism.[24] In subtle ways, the adjective "Russian" began to replace "Soviet."

In 1943 Stalin made an agreement with the Russian Orthodox Church, a pillar of Russian national identity – as his post-Soviet successors have appreciated – giving it greater freedom than at any time since the Revolution, in return for its support of the Soviet, and specifically, Russian war effort.[25] At the conclusion of the war, on May 24, 1945, in his final toast in the Kremlin to the victorious Soviet officer corps, Generalissimo Stalin said,

> I would like to raise this toast to the health of the Soviet people, and first of all, of the Russian people... because it is the most outstanding nation of all the nations who belong to the Soviet Union... because it earned in this war general recognition as the leading force of the Soviet Union among all the peoples of our country.... It has a clear mind, steadfast character, and patience.... The trust of the Russian people in the Soviet Government turned out to be the decisive force that guaranteed the historic victory over the enemy of humanity – fascism. Thanks to the Russian people for that trust! To the health of the Russian people![26]

From this toast made specifically to the Russian people, one can infer that some non-Russian peoples had been disloyal or at least ambivalent in their support of the war effort. Note also that Stalin praised the Russian people for ultimately "trusting" the Soviet government, implying that this trust could not be taken for granted. No doubt, Stalin, "the father of all the peoples," was correct in both judgments.

The equation of "Soviet" with "Russian" had an unanticipated consequence: as the line blurred, ethnic Russians were less sure which traditions, customs, and practices were distinctly Russian and which were of Soviet origin. Today substantial proportions of Russian youth are unfamiliar with Russian customs and traditions.[27] Much has been written about the attempt to reestablish

---

[22] See, for example, Nikolai Tikhonov, "*My – Russkie!*" Izvestiia, April 14, 1943. He asserts that the Germans will never defeat the "Russians," rather than the Soviets.

[23] N. Podorozhnie, "Veliki Russkii polkovodets," Izvestiia, April 28, 1943, 3 (about Kutuzov). See also "*Dokumenty Russkoi slavy,*" Izvestiia, July 1, 1943 (about Suvorov).

[24] Aleksandr Fadeev, "Velikii Russkii narod – peredovoi borets protiv fashizma," Izvestiia, May 11, 1943, 2. See also Leonid Leonov, "Slava Rossii," Izvestiia, July 10, 1943, 2. Fadeev and Leonov were prominent Soviet writers.

[25] See the sources cited in note 4.

[26] Quoted in Arkady Vaksberg, *Stalin against the Jews* (New York: Alfred A. Knopf, 1994), 141–42.

[27] M. V. Savva, *Etnicheskii status* (Krasnodar: Kubanskii gosudartsvennyi universitet, 1997) reports that 20 percent of Russian youth surveyed in the Russian Federation (in a survey called "Social Development of Soviet Youth") and 24 percent of Ukrainian youth – but only 10 percent of Tatar youth – said they do not know the customs and traditions of their ethnos. Between 64 percent (Ukrainians) and 74 to 76 percent of Russians and Tatars say they "don't

Russian national identity and culture in the post-Soviet era and differentiate it from what was distinctively Soviet.

Official Russian and Soviet Conceptions of Jewishness

The tsarist Russian regime, which had no clear or consistent policy toward the non-Russian peoples over whom it ruled,[28] regarded Jews primarily as a religious group. The tsars' Soviet successors reversed the emphasis on religion and classified Jews as a nationality. Before and after the Revolution, Bolsheviks were rather loose in their use of terms such as *natsiia*, *natsional'nost'*, and *narodnost'*,[29] but they agreed that Jews did not constitute a nation. In 1903, in the course of polemics against the Jewish Labor Bund,[30] Lenin, then leader of the Bolshevik faction of the Russian Social-Democratic Labor Party, specifically asserted that the Jews were not a nation: "The idea of a Jewish nationality runs counter to the interests of the Jewish proletariat, for it fosters among them, directly or indirectly, a spirit hostile to assimilation, a spirit of the 'ghetto.'"[31]

---

know them very well" (34). A parallel survey in Kirgizia showed that Russians there also have a weak knowledge of their own customs and traditions, unlike the Kirgiz.

[28] The Russian legal corpus "was astonishingly imprecise and confused throughout the imperial period, with categories and definitions assuming merely formal, not descriptive, significance. The status of the Jews was characteristically convoluted." Michael Stanislawski, *Tsar Nicholas I and the Jews* (Philadelphia: Jewish Publication Society, 1983), 8.

[29] In *Etnicheskie i etno-sotsial'nye kategorii* (Moscow: Institute of Ethnography and Anthropology, Russian Academy of Sciences, 1995), V. I. Kozlov, a leading Soviet ethnographer, made the following distinctions: "*Narod*" is equivalent to "people" (English) or *volk* (German). "This term is used in Russian... to indicate a large group of people who are connected primarily by their place of birth or origin, as distinguished from a simple mass or crowd, or the population of an entire state (for example, the 'Indian *narod*')" (68). In Soviet usage, Kozlov writes, *narod* means those "strata and classes" who "participate one way or another in the accomplishment of progressive development" in a particular historical era. In the 1970s the term "*Sovetskii narod*" was used to mean the meta-ethnic Soviet people, but that term fell into disuse in the early 1990s when the concept of a "multinational Russian [*Rossiiskii*] *narod* came into use." Kozlov explains that "*natsional'nost'*" is the equivalent of "nationality in English, *nationalitet* in German" (82). The term is used in two senses in Russian. It is used for all the *narodnosti* (ethnic entities) inhabiting a place, except for tribes; thus the "*natsional'nosti* of the Soviet Union." In the political-legal sense it refers only to ethnoses that have some form of national-territorial autonomy. *Natsional'nost'* also signifies that a person belongs to a certain entity. "In the west it usually signifies belonging to a political entity." Actually, "in the west" belonging to a political entity is more accurately described as "citizenship," for which the term in Russian would be *grazhdanstvo*. Finally, a nation ("*natsiia*") is "a type of ethnos characteristic of a developed class society" (88).

[30] Its official name was *Algemeiner bund fun yidishe arbeter in Poiln, Rusland un Liteh* – the General Alliance of Jewish Workers in Poland, Russia, and Lithuania. Founded in 1897, a year later the Bund helped found the Russian Social-Democratic Labor Party, from which it was expelled in 1903 for demanding national-cultural autonomy for ethnic groups and advocating that the party be federated along ethnic lines. On the evolution of the Bund's name, see Y. Sh. Hertz, ed., *Di geshikhte fun Bund*, Vol. 1 (New York: Unzer tsayt, 1960), 115–20.

[31] *Iskra* 51, October 22, 1903.

A decade later, Joseph Stalin, the Georgian who had become the Bolsheviks' leading spokesman on ethnic issues, made his debut with a pamphlet titled "Marxism and the National Question." In it Stalin postulated, "A nation is a historically evolved, stable community of language, territory, economic life, and psychological make-up manifested in a community of culture."[32] Furthermore, "[i]t is only when all these characteristics are present that we have a nation [*natsiia*]."[33] Because Jews around the world did not have a common territory, language, or economy, obviously they were not a nation:

> If there is anything common to them left it is their religion, their common origin and certain relics of national character.... But how can it be seriously maintained that petrified religious rites and fading psychological relics affect the "fate" of these Jews more powerfully than the living social, economic and cultural environment that surrounds them? And it is only on this assumption that it is generally possible to speak of the Jews as a single nation.[34]

Moreover, Stalin wrote, somewhat contradicting himself, "The Jewish nation [sic] is coming to an end, and therefore there is nobody to demand national autonomy for. The Jews are being assimilated."[35] In addition, Jews were showing the way to other peoples by becoming so fully integrated with others that they were losing their specific national characteristics.

Yet, in 1918, shortly after the Russian Revolution, someone decided to classify the Jews of Soviet Russia as a "*natsional'nost'*." They were not to be regarded as a nation (*natsiia*), but they were to be admitted to the long list of peoples whom the Soviet authorities acknowledged as nationalities or ethnic groups. To my knowledge no one has uncovered any discussion that led to this decision. It is not clear why Lenin and Stalin decided to acknowledge the persistent ethnicity of the group that they confidently predicted was well on the way to disappearing.

As discussed in Chapter 2, in January 1927, as the first Soviet census was coming to an end, experts and politicians met in Moscow to discuss the official list of nationalities. In the discussion of Jews, ethnographers maintained that "all Jews shared the same tribal origins," but because Georgian Jews, those from Central Asia, Crimean Jews, and Jews living in the Slavic republics spoke different languages, "the ethnographers were unsure how to count them."[36]

---

[32] Joseph Stalin, *Marxism and the National and Colonial Question* (New York: International Publishers, n.d.), 8. Stalin's definition of nation guided Soviet policy until the 1960s when it was questioned by Polish and Soviet scholars. See Jerzy Wiatr in *Z Pola Walki* IX, 3 (1967), 87, and the series of "discussion" articles in *Voprosy istorii* in 1966 and 1967. The discussions are analyzed by Grey Hodnett, "The Debate over Soviet Federalism," *Soviet Studies* XVIII, 4 (1967) and in his "What's in a Nation?" Problems of Communism 16 (September–October, 1967).

[33] Ibid., 9.

[34] Ibid., 10.

[35] Ibid., 35.

[36] Francine Hirsch, *Empire of Nations: Ethnographic Knowledge and the Making of the Soviet Union* (Ithaca, NY: Cornell University Press, 2005), 132.

In the end, among the 172 peoples granted official recognition were 5 geographic groups of Jews. By the next two censuses (1937, 1939), all Jews were lumped together and were listed as a *narodnost'*.[37] Shortly after Stalin's death in 1953, the *Great Soviet Encyclopedia* changed the terminology from *narodnost'* to "ethnographic group," which, according to some, implied that the subethnic groups of Jews spread across the USSR's territory were part of the same people.[38]

In the mid-1920s, when the Soviet government tried to establish Jewish agricultural colonies in Jewish districts (*raiony*) and announced the plan to create a Jewish Autonomous Region (Oblast') in Birobidzhan (Siberia), some Jewish activists began to speak of the "creation of a Jewish nation" in the USSR, because this territorial base would facilitate their sharing a common language. In 1927 Abram Bragin, a former member of a Zionist party, argued, "The significance of our work is that we are laying the foundation for the national self-determination of the Jewish nation, as set forth in the policy of the Communist Party and the Leninist conception of the problem."[39] Esther Frumkin, a former Bundist who had become a leading activist in the Jewish Sections of the Communist Party but who died a prisoner in a labor camp in 1943, similarly reasoned as follows:

> Among all the peoples (*felker*) and tribes (*shvotim*) to whom October has opened new possibilities is also the extraterritorial Jewish people (*folk*). This is not yet a nation in the strict scientific sense of the word because it has neither territory nor common economy. But naturally, in the *practical* policy of the party and of Soviet power nations, peoples (*felker*), tribes are all treated as separate national units which have equal rights to national development.... Under the dictatorship of the proletariat the possibility of consolidating itself as a nation (*natsie*) opens up to the Jewish people (*folk*).[40]

To the astonishment of the delegates to a conference of the organization (Komzet in Russian, Gezerd in Yiddish) created in 1924 to settle Jews on the land, the Russian Mikhail Kalinin, the "*Starosta* of the Soviet Union" (chairman of the council of the Supreme Soviet) stated flatly that "it is completely natural that the Jewish population, a lively [people], its masses quite cultured, politically and socially tempered in the constant struggle for its existence – also discovers itself, also strives to find its national place in the Soviet Union."[41]

---

[37] On the shifting meanings of this term, see ibid., 115–23 and 266–67.

[38] A detailed comparison of how Jews were described in the second and third editions of the *Encyclopedia* is found in L. Dymerskskaya-Tsigel'man and M. Kipnis, "Voprosy etnicheskogo opredeleniia evreev v sovetskikh entsiklopediakh do serediny 80-kh godov," *Vestnik evreiskogo universiteta v Moskve* 2, 15 (1997), 82–113.

[39] *Ershter alfarbandisher tsuzamenfor fun 'GEZERD: stenografisher baricht* (Moscow: 1927), 28–29, quoted in Zvi Gitelman, *Jewish Nationality and Soviet Politics* (Princeton: Princeton University Press, 1972), 412.

[40] *Alfarbandisher baratung fun di idishe sektsies* (Moscow: Shul un bukh,1927).

[41] *Ershter alfarbandisher tsuzamenfor*, 38.

Seemingly disparaging the Marxist-Leninist ideal of assimilation, Kalinin told the delegates,

> The Jewish people faces the great task of preserving its own nationality, and to this end a large part of the Jewish population must be transformed into an economically stable, agriculturally compact group which should number at least hundreds of thousands. Only under such conditions can the Jewish masses hope for the future existence of their nationality.[42]

Within a few years, such ideas would be roundly condemned as bourgeois-nationalist, reactionary, and Zionist and those who expressed them would be subject to severe punishment.

The Cold War and the "Black Years" of Soviet Jewry

After World War II, the trend toward elevating the Russians above all other peoples was accelerated. As the Cold War developed, the Soviet Union proclaimed Russian superiority over the West in all fields; it even claimed that Russians had invented *beizbol* (baseball) in Siberia long before Alexander Cartwright or Abner Doubleday. Hostility to the West led to the denigration of Western culture and political systems. Those who had any contact whatever with people in Western countries were suspected of treason. Even mild praise of any aspect of Western technology, economies, or culture was considered seditious. Those who served with Soviet forces in occupied Germany or Austria were strictly forbidden from contact with their Allied counterparts.

Of all the Soviet peoples, Jews were the most likely to have connections to people in the West. Between 1881 to 1912, 1,889,000 Jews had emigrated from the Russian Empire, 84 percent of them to the United States, 8.5 percent to England, 2.2 percent to Canada, and 2.1 percent to Palestine.[43] Ties between these migrants and their relatives in the empire and the Soviet Union were eroded by time and disrupted by World War II; however, immediately after the war those in the West wanted to reconnect with their Soviet relatives to find out whether they had survived. Yet the Soviet authorities regarded any contact between Western and Soviet families as treasonable.

In January 1948, Solomon Mikhoels, the most famous Yiddish actor and director in the country, was called to Minsk in connection with the award of some Stalin prizes to cultural figures. The official announcement later said he "died in tragic circumstances" there, although in fact he was murdered and his

---

[42] Ibid., 41.
[43] D. S. Pasmanik, *Sud'by evreiskago naroda* (Moscow: Safrut, 1917), 145. Samuel Joseph, *Jewish Immigration to the United States*, Vol. LIX (New York: Columbia University Studies in History, Economics and Public Law, 1914), 101. For the period 1881–1910, Joseph counts 1,119,059 Jewish immigrants from the Russian Empire to the United States. The discrepancy between his figures and Pasmanik's is due not only to the two additional years included by Pasmanik but also to the fact that before 1899 immigrants were classified by country of birth or residence, not nationality or ethnicity, so that figures for the years before that are necessarily estimates.

death was staged to look like a traffic accident. Mikhoels' death signaled the start of the massive repression of Yiddish culture and Jewish national expression. Beginning in 1948, the Soviet government closed all remaining Jewish institutions, except for a small number of synagogues. The Jewish Anti-Fascist Committee was dissolved and its leading members arrested.[44] Its newspaper was closed, as was the surviving Yiddish publishing house. From 1948–53 several hundred Jewish cultural figures – writers, actors, artists, sculptors, musicians, journalists, and editors – were arrested, and many were sentenced to ten years at hard labor on charges of "bourgeois nationalism," slander of Soviet Union (for asserting that anti-Semitism existed there), or espionage on behalf of the West.

The repression of Yiddish culture directly affected only a minority of Jews, the majority having been acculturated to Russian. However, many more were affected by a broader campaign that was launched against "cosmopolitanism" in the arts, literature, music, philosophy, and scholarship. Jews were singled out as "rootless" cosmopolitans, meaning they were unpatriotic and had no attachment to the Soviet motherland. Many were removed from their posts and expelled from professional organizations and from the Communist Party. The general public understood very well that an official campaign against the Jews had originated at the very top and that it was open season on the "rootless cosmopolitans." In July 1952, twenty-five prominent Jewish cultural figures were tried, and on August 12, about a score – including some of the most famous Yiddish writers – were executed. They were charged with trying to sever the Crimea from the USSR in order to establish a Zionist republic there "to serve as a base for American imperialism," espionage for foreign states, and "bourgeois nationalist activity and anti-Soviet propaganda." Relatives of those executed, who did not know of their fate, were imprisoned and exiled.

As part of a drive against corruption, many Jews were accused of theft of state property, embezzlement, currency speculation, economic sabotage, bribery, and other economic crimes. The press widely publicized their misdeeds, reinforcing stereotypes about the sharp business practices and fundamental dishonesty of Jews. After a major "economic crimes" trial involving Jews in Kiev in November 1952, three Jewish defendants were executed. A newspaper editorial commented that "all those khains and yaroshetskys, greensteins... perses... and kaplans, and polyakovs... arouse the profound loathing of the people."[45]

---

[44] See Shimon Redlich, *War, Holocaust and Stalinism: A Documented Study of the Jewish Anti-Fascist Committee in the USSR* (Luxembourg: Harwood Academic Publishers, 1995); for transcripts of the trials of the JAFC members, see Joshua Rubenstein and Vladimir P. Naumov, eds. and transl., *Stalin's Secret Pogrom: The Postwar Inquisition of the Jewish Anti-Fascist Committee* (New Haven: Yale University Press, 2001). On the period more generally, see Yehoshua Gilboa, *The Black Years of Soviet Jewry, 1939–1953* (Boston: Little Brown, 1971).

[45] Quoted in Gilboa, ibid., p. 291. All the names appeared in lowercase letters, implying types, not individuals.

The final, and perhaps most ominous, blow came in an article in *Pravda* on January 13, 1953, which announced the arrest of a "group of saboteur-doctors." Most had obviously Jewish names. Several were linked to the American Jewish Joint Distribution Committee, which was said to have been "established by American intelligence" to spy on and terrorize the USSR and other countries. Others were said "to be old agents of British intelligence." These "monsters in human form" were accused of having murdered medically two leading Soviet politicians, Andrei Zhdanov and Alexander Shcherbakov, and of planning to murder several leading military figures. A *Pravda* editorial thundered, "The Soviet people wrathfully and indignantly condemn the criminal band of murderers and their foreign masters. They will crush like loathsome vermin the despised hirelings"; it warned that, "to end sabotage it is necessary to put an end to gullibility in our ranks," signaling a new campaign of "vigilance" and rooting out "enemies of the people."[46] Such a campaign was a logical concomitant of the Cold War, then at its height. Jews, with their Western connections, were obvious candidates for the role of spies and collaborators with Western imperialists.

Nationwide, Jewish medical personnel were demoted or fired, and some people avoided them as potential "poisoners" and murders. An ominous rumor spread in punitive labor camps and beyond that barracks were being constructed in Siberia on such a scale that it could only mean the deportation of the bulk of the Jewish population. Even children and teens were affected by the campaign. Raisa Palatnik was then in the ninth grade. She recalled that the "Doctors' Plot" made her acutely aware of her nationality: "It was scary to leave the classroom and go into the hallway because from all sides you heard, 'You Yids, you poisoned Gorky, you wanted to poison Stalin, you poisoned all our great leaders,' and the atmosphere was very tense. Even the teachers allowed themselves such remarks."[47]

Jews were now second-class citizens and even a potential fifth column. The percentage of Jews in the party Central Committee was reduced from 10 percent (1939) to 2 percent (1952). In the republics Jews disappeared from the upper echelons of the party. Their numbers in government posts declined drastically, especially in those dealing with foreign, security, and military affairs. Whereas in 1937 there were forty-seven Jews in the Supreme Soviet, the highest legislative organ, in 1946 there were only thirteen, and in 1950 only eight.[48]

The Thaw

In 1954 the popular Soviet Jewish writer Ilya Ehrenburg published a novel whose title, *The Thaw*, gave its name to an era. The ice of Stalinism began to

---

[46] Quoted in ibid., 296.
[47] Quoted in Irina Kirk, *Profiles in Russian Resistance* (New York: Quadrangle, 1975), 166.
[48] Binyamin Pinkus, *Yehudai Russiya u-Brit Hamoetzot* (Beer Sheva: Ben Gurion University, 1986), 316.

break up. Terror was curbed, political prisoners were released, and the reins guiding cultural expression were relaxed. The Jews' situation improved somewhat: although they were no longer singled out as potential traitors, the "glass ceiling" on their vocational and educational possibilities did not crack very much. Not a single Jewish school or state-supported Yiddish theater reopened, although a few Yiddish books were published each year beginning in the late 1950s. In 1961, a Yiddish journal, *Sovetish haimland* [Soviet Homeland], was published, initially in a press run of 50,000 copies, soon to decline by half. However, because there were no Yiddish schools to teach the language, the journal could be read only by older generations, and many copies were sent abroad. Nor did any synagogues reopen, although in 1957 a yeshiva was opened in Moscow, only to be closed shortly thereafter. These were symbolic gestures, designed as much for a foreign audience as for the putative Soviet beneficiaries.

In 1957 Nikita Khrushchev, who emerged as the primary leader of the party and state after an intraparty struggle, launched a campaign against religion. It had a unique effect on Jews, even though the vast majority were not religious. Christianity or Islam were "universal religions," not tied to any particular national group, and so attacks on them were not directed to any one nationality. Only one religion – Judaism, a "tribal" religion – was practiced by a specific group. Therefore, attacks on Judaism, some of them very crude and accompanied by caricatures that the Nazis could have produced,[49] were interpreted by Jews, and probably by some non-Jews, as attacks against the Jews. Similarly, many perceived Soviet condemnation of Zionism and the State of Israel, which accelerated after the June 1967 war in which the Soviet client states, Egypt and Syria, were defeated within a week, as directed at Jews generally. Soviet media, like others, were not always careful to distinguish between Zionists and Jews, deepening Jews' sense of alienation. They were very uncomfortable as they witnessed their own country supporting states that were pledged to eliminate the Jewish state, just as the Germans had tried to destroy the Jewish people during World War II. The intensification of Soviet criticism of Zionism as "racism" and "imperialism" and, most galling, the analogies drawn between Zionism and Nazism hurt many Jews deeply. The cultural crackdown following the 1966 arrest of writers Yuli Daniel (son of a writer who had written on Jewish themes) and Andrei Sinyavsky (who had taken the Jewish-sounding pseudonym "Abram Tertz") was taken to mean that there were severe limits to cultural expression in the post-Khrushchev era (Leonid Brezhnev had ousted and succeeded him in 1964). The Soviet-led invasion of reformist Czechoslovakia in August 1968 made it clear that political relaxation, let alone reform, was unlikely.

---

[49] See, particularly, Trofim Kichko, *Iudaizm bez prikraz* [Judaism without Embellishment] (Kiev: Academy of Sciences, 1963). The book was so widely condemned in the West that Soviet authorities were forced to criticize it and withdraw it from circulation, although its author continued to publish and received state awards.

In the late 1960s too political, cultural, religious, and ethnic dissident movements emerged in the USSR. Among them were Lithuanian Catholics, Crimean Tatars who wanted to return from exile, Ukrainians demanding greater cultural freedom, those who wanted the USSR to return to pre-Stalinist "Leninist norms," and those who wanted to go further and move toward Western-style democracy. A Jewish movement began then, spreading from the Baltic capitals of Riga and Vilnius to Moscow, Kiev, Leningrad, and beyond. At first Jewish dissidents demanded Jewish cultural opportunities, but after the June 1967 war, they gave up on internal reform and demanded the right to emigrate to Israel as their "national homeland."[50] Soviet authorities had not allowed free emigration since the mid-1920s; providing that right would be both embarrassing and dangerous. Emigration would refute the Soviet claim to being the best society ever devised, and emigrants would carry information with them that the authorities did not want conveyed abroad. Moreover, if one group were allowed to leave that might open the floodgates to a mass emigration that neither the Soviet economy nor polity could tolerate.[51] Faced with internal dissent complemented by support in the West for the demand to emigrate,[52] Soviet leaders decided reluctantly to permit some limited, controlled emigration.

In March 1971 the first significant group of emigrants left for Israel. Soviet leaders had gravely underestimated the depth of Jewish alienation, nor did they understand the dynamics of migration, whereby the first immigrants would draw others in their wake because they were related or were friends, or simply because the first to go would report back that they had made the right move and it would be good to join them. As the number of those requesting exit visas grew, the Soviet leadership reconsidered its decision.[53] In 1979, the peak of emigration was reached, with more than 51,000 Jews leaving the USSR. Following the Soviet invasion of Afghanistan at the end of that year and the rapid cooling of Soviet–Western relations as a result, Brezhnev and his colleagues tried to shut off emigration as a sign of displeasure with the West, which had pushed for free emigration. The right to free emigration/immigration had been

---

[50] On the Jewish dissident movement before 1967, see Yaacov Ro'i, *The Struggle for Soviet Jewish Emigration, 1948–1967* (New York: Cambridge University Press, 1991) and Benjamin Pinkus, *Tehiyah u-tekumah le'umit:ha-Tsiyonut veha-tenu'ah ha-Tsiyonit bi-Verit-ha-Mo'atsot, 1947–1987* (Sdeh Boker, Israel: Ben-Gurion University, 1993). There is no comprehensive study yet of the Jewish movement for emigration.

[51] See Zvi Gitelman, "Moscow and the Soviet Jews: A Parting of the Ways," *Problems of Communism* XXIX, 1 (January-February, 1980), 18–34.

[52] On the American movement to aid Soviet Jewry, see Frederick Lazin, *The Struggle for Soviet Jewry in American Politics: Israel versus the American Jewish Establishment* (Lanham, MD: Lexington Books, 2005); Stuart Altshuler, *From Exodus to Freedom: A History of the Soviet Jewry Movement* (Lanham, MD: Lexington Books, 2005); Henry Feingold, *"Silent No More": Saving the Jews of Russia, the American Jewish Effort, 1967–1989* (Syracuse: Syracuse University Press, 2007); and Gal Beckerman, *When They Come for Us, We'll Be Gone: The Epic Struggle to Save Soviet Jewry* (New York: Houghton Mifflin Harcourt, 2010).

[53] For details, see Zvi Gitelman, *A Century of Ambivalence: The Jews of Russia and the Soviet Union, 1881 to the Present*, 2nd ed. (Bloomington: Indiana University Press, 2001), ch. 6.

included in "Basket Three" of the 1975 Helsinki agreements, which the Soviet Union had signed, but Soviet leaders saw it as something easily manipulated to signal how they felt about Western policies or actions.

During the 1980s, Jewish emigration was severely restricted. About 11,000 applicants were refused permission to leave at one time or another, which only spurred foreign efforts on behalf of these "refuseniks." In the late 1980s, after Mikhail Gorbachev became leader of the Communist Party, he initiated domestic reforms that were grouped under the rubrics of perestroika [reconstruction] and glasnost [openness] and that were designed to revive a moribund system. In parallel, Gorbachev sought successfully to open a new era in Soviet–Western relations. Just as Brezhnev had closed down emigration to defy the West, Gorbachev relaxed the restrictions to accommodate Western concerns and satisfy domestic Jewish demands. In the fall of 1989 a massive wave of emigration began, propelled ironically by Jews' fears that the Soviet system was collapsing and that the anarchy that might result would unleash anti-Jewish activity. In 1990, an astounding 213,042 Jews emigrated, with 181,759 going to Israel. In the following year, 179,720 Jews emigrated, of whom 145,005 went to Israel.[54]

After the Fall

There were more than three million Jews in the USSR in 1939. The annexation of eastern Poland (1939), the Baltic States (1940), and Bessarabia and Bukovina (1940) increased the number to about five million. After World War II, during which more than two million Soviet Jews had been murdered by the Germans and their local accomplices, and a generation of potential fathers was greatly diminished, the first census (1959) enumerated 2,268,000 Jews. Two decades later the number fell to 1,811,000, and in the last Soviet census, in January 1989, 1,445,000 Jews were counted.[55] Post-Soviet censuses show that in 2005, there were about 233,600 Jews in Russia, 104,300 in Ukraine, and 27,800 in Belarus.[56] In all, there are probably about 450,000 Jews left in all of the FSU, with the large majority in Russia and Ukraine.

Massive emigration, combined with very low birth rates, high mortality rates, and ever-increasing marriages to non-Jews, severely reduced the size of

---

[54] Yoel Florsheim, "Immigration to Israel from the Soviet Union in 1991," *Jews and Jewish Topics in the Soviet Union and Eastern Europe* 3, 19 (Winter 1992); see also reports of HIAS, the organization responsible for Jewish immigrants to the United States.

[55] Soviet census takers were instructed to ask for a person's nationality but were not permitted to ask for documentation. A citizen was free to name any nationality. Thus, there could be a substantial discrepancy between those who were registered in their passports as Jews and those who declared themselves as such. Yet, unlike the passport inscription, the declaration on the census had no consequences for the individual.

[56] See Mark Tolts, "Post-Soviet Jewish Demography, 1989–2004," in Zvi Gitelman and Yaacov Ro'i, eds., *Revolution, Repression and Revival* (Lanham, MD: Rowman & Littlefield, 2007), 285.

the Jewish population in the FSU. The ratio of Jewish deaths to Jewish births reached 10:1 in 1996 – 9,953 Jewish deaths were recorded, more than ten times the number of births to a Jewish mother[57] – and later worsened. In 1988, 48 percent of Jewish women and 58 percent of Jewish men marrying in the USSR, married non-Jews; in the Russian Republic the respective percentages were in the 70s and 60s. In 1993 in Russia, only 363 children were born to parents who were both Jewish; three years later only 289 children had two Jewish parents.[58] In the 1980s, for every 100 Jews there were an additional 60 non-Jews in "Jewish" households; in the 1990s that ratio increased to 80 non-Jews for every 100 Jews.

This drastically diminished population enjoys greater cultural and religious freedom than at any time in seven decades of communist rule. All ethnic groups in Russia and Ukraine have much greater latitude than ever in choosing, individually and collectively, whether and how to identify and express themselves. When the meta-ethnic, supranational ideology of Communism proved too weak to hold the union of republics together, no single political or social ideology replaced it. Tentative but significant steps were taken toward democracy in Russia and Ukraine, but with the ascendancy of Vladimir Putin to the presidency in Russia in 2000, democratization was halted or reversed. The media and economy are controlled increasingly by the government, and no sustainable political parties have emerged to contest power seriously. In Ukraine, the "Orange Revolution" of 2004–5 promised to firm up a democratic political system, but the ineptitude of the leadership and deep cleavages in society and in politics have prevented the promise from being fulfilled.

Absent an attractive political-ideological alternative to Soviet communism, in the late 1980s and thereafter many turned to nationalism and religion as guides to social and personal behavior and to the direction the state should take. This was not a sharp, radical turn because, beginning in the late 1960s, official Soviet thinking on nationality issues had moved away from two earlier doctrines: the supremacy of Russians was not emphasized after the death of Stalin and the drive toward amalgamation of all peoples was postponed. The party acknowledged that two distinct processes would take place on the road to a world without nations. First was *sblizhenie*, or rapprochement, drawing the Soviet nationalities together and reducing ethnic tensions to the point of disappearance. In practice, *sblizhenie* meant slow, subtle Russianization of the non-Russians.[59] As noted earlier, it was to be accomplished by the "mutual enrichment of languages," which really meant the infiltration of Russian terms and forms into non-Russian languages. Non-Russians would learn the Russian

---

[57] Ibid.
[58] Mark Tolts, "Recent Jewish Emigration and Population Decline in Russia," *Jews in Eastern Europe*, 1, 35 (Spring 1998), 21.
[59] Vernon Aspaturian drew a useful distinction between "Russianization," which entailed acculturation, and "Russification" which meant assimilation. See Allen Kassof, ed., *Prospects for Soviet Society* (New York: Praeger, 1968), 159–164.

language, although ethnic Russians living in the national republics would not have to learn the languages of the titular nationalities.[60] Second, interethnic marriages would blur ethnic identities and complicate ethnic affiliations. In the future, at some unspecified time, *sblizhenie* would eventuate in *sliianie*, the fusion of all peoples into an ethnically undifferentiated *Sovetskii narod* (Soviet people).[61] The language of this people was not specified.

In reality, however, sometimes ethnic consciousness led to conflicts. In the late 1980s riots broke out in Kazakhstan, when Kazakhs, one of the most Russianized of the larger Soviet nationalities, demonstrated against the appointment of a Russian as first secretary of the Kazakh Communist Party. Armenians and Azerbaijanis clashed violently over control of Nagorno-Karabakh, an Armenian-populated enclave in Azerbaijan. The three Baltic peoples set off national demonstrations for "sovereignty" within the USSR that quickly developed into demands for independence. Similar demands were made in Armenia and Moldavia. Pressures for adjusting the relationship between the federal state and the republics in favor of the latter became irresistible. Mikhail Gorbachev was contemplating the negotiation of a "union treaty" that would change these relations when opponents of change tried to unseat him in a coup d'etat in August 1991. The coup failed but the USSR fell apart in December of that year as one republic after another declared independence. The bond of communism that had seemingly united these linguistically, religiously, and economically disparate components of the Soviet federation had been torn asunder. What ideology or common values and beliefs could replace it?

Some hoped, naively, that the removal of an authoritarian system would result automatically in its replacement by a democratic one. Yet democracies, like any other political system, have to be implanted and nurtured carefully and consciously. They will survive and thrive only in cultural environments conducive to their principles. Weimar Germany and Iraq after 2003 are two of many failures to create stable democracies simply by implanting institutions associated with democratic governance. In the FSU, democracy could not be created ex nihilo, and some republics have not moved toward democracy in the two decades after the fall of communism.[62]

---

[60] Michael Bruchis, "The Language Policy of the CPSU and the Linguistic Situation in Soviet Moldavia," *Soviet Studies* 36, 1 (January 1984), 108–26; S. I. Bruk and M. N. Guboglo, "The Converging Nations in the USSR and the Main Trends in the Development of Bilingualism," in I. R. Grigulevich and V. Kozlov, eds., *Ethnocultural Processes and National Problems in the Modern World* (Moscow: Progress Publishers, 1979), 51–89.

[61] On the "Sovetskii narod," see E. Bagramov, "The Soviet Nationalities Policy and Bourgeois Falsifications," *International Affairs* (Moscow), June 1978; M. I. Kulichenko, "Socialism and the Ethnic Features of Nations: The Example of the Peoples of the Union of Soviet Socialist Republics," in Regina Holloman and Serghei Arutiunov, eds., *Perspectives on Ethnicity*, (The Hague: Mouton, 1978), 426–27; M.I. Kulichenko, *Natsional'nye otnosheniia v SSSR i tendentsii ikh razvitiia* (Moscow: Mysl, 1972); and Iu. V. Bromlei, ed., *Sovremennye etnicheskie protsessy v SSSR* (Moscow: Nauka 1977).

[62] This is especially true of the Central Asian republics, but Belarus and Russia, after initial starts toward democracy, drew back.

Because a major propellant of the USSR's dissolution was national assertiveness, it was likely that some forms of nationalism would unite the peoples of the newly established states. Moreover, as a highly emotional force, nationalism had an advantage over other kinds of ideologies. It takes time to explain political ideology and programs to people who must then think them over before declaring allegiance to one or another party, and even more time for firm allegiances to ideologies and institutions to emerge; however, it takes little time and not much thinking to say, "Our people [Serbs, Croats, Armenians, Azerbaijanis, Estonians, Ukrainians, Maronite Christians, Afrikaners] are in danger, and we must defend ourselves." Or, "Our people's greatness has been suppressed by hostile nations; let us show them who we are and what we can do." National and religious symbols evoke emotions that in turn drive action. Responses to intellectual or ideological appeals are usually slower and less passionate.

To prevent the initial force of nationalist appeals from dissipating, in the post-Soviet period local residents and foreign ethnic and religious entrepreneurs have made conscious attempts to revive individual ethnic identities and reconstruct ethnic communities. Those entrepreneurs see themselves as helping to correct historical injustices, return what is rightfully theirs to those who have been deprived, and augment the numbers in their particular groups. This activism is ethnicity "constructed," but it is based on the assumption that there are primordial sentiments that can be mobilized.

The preferred "solutions" to the problem of re-identification vary from group to group and sometimes over time within a group. South Koreans, while encouraging the revival of Korean language and culture among their kinsfolk in the FSU, do not encourage Soviet Koreans to emigrate to Korea. Israelis advocate the immigration of Jews to Israel, although organizations in the Jewish diaspora sometimes prefer that efforts be made to revive Jewish culture and communities in situ. Germany began by encouraging emigration of ethnic Germans from the USSR, but in recent years has fostered a revival of German culture and identities in the FSU and no longer advocates mass emigration to the *heimat*.

The states that emerged from the shards of the USSR pursue different policies toward ethnicity. The Baltic states seek to make the autochthonous ethnicity dominant in politics and culture. Only pressure from the European Union, which all have joined, prevented them from relegating Slavs to second-class citizenship. The Central Asian states have informally reduced Slavic influence and presence. Georgia has refused to accommodate Ossetian and Abkhaz separatism, and Russia and Georgia fought a brief war in 2008 ostensibly over the political status of these areas. Moldova has granted autonomy to the Gagauz, a Christian Orthodox Turkic people, but has rejected the legitimacy of the Slav-dominated "Transdniester Republic" alongside Moldova. Moldovans also debate whether they are Romanians and share the same language, or if there is a distinct Moldovan people with its own language. Belarusians have moved from national and ethnic assertion before 1994 to self-abnegation during the dictatorship of Alexander Lukashenko.

Even Russians are searching for an identity separate from that of the imperial center of the Soviet Union. The Russian Orthodox Church has attempted to reestablish itself as a pillar of Russianness, thus re-creating a link between ethnicity and religion, which exists in neighboring Poland and Lithuania (Catholicism). Russia and Ukraine have declared themselves civic, rather than ethnic, states. The Russian Federation's structure is based to a small extent on ethnicity (more so on territorial divisions). Its inhabitants are all described as *Rossiiskii*, meaning something like "of Russia," rather than *Russkii*, which means ethnically Russian, even though about 80 percent of *Rossianie*, or residents of the Russian Federation, are *Russkie*, ethnically Russian. Ukraine is pledged to give equality to its Russian and other minorities, despite pressures from some nationalists, particularly in West Ukraine, to adopt a more Ukrainocentric posture.

Ethnicity and Identity after Communism

In the first chapter we discussed the nature of identity and how it changes. Simply put, identity is an answer to the question, "Who am I?" The answer goes a long way to determining how a person feels about certain issues and with which group he or she will identify. People who define themselves as Muslim and Palestinian will obviously have very different views on a range of issues than those who see themselves as Jewish and Israeli. Even when people share one important identity, such as being Irish, their different religious affiliations – Catholic and Protestant – may drive them to emphasize what differentiates them rather than what they have in common. Yet "[i]dentity only becomes an issue when it is in crisis, when something assumed to be fixed, coherent and stable is displaced by the experience of doubt and uncertainty."[63]

One important change resulting from the collapse of the Soviet Union is that its successor states no longer classify citizens by nationality. Yet in many cases these citizens are forced to define themselves ethnically, politically, or in terms of religion and class. Among those are the nearly 30 million Russians living outside the Russian Federation since 1991 who must decide whether to stay or move to Russia; Uzbeks wrestling with their relationship to Islam and to other Central Asian states, Turkey, Russia, and the Far East; and Jews, Germans, and Poles pondering their place in the independent states that were part of the USSR. Not only they but also their co-ethnics or co-religionists elsewhere are challenged to define what their relationships are. The immigration of large

---

[63] Kobena Mercer, "Welcome to the Jungle," in Jonathan Rutherford, ed., *Identity* (London: Lawrence and Wishart, 1990), quoted in Stuart Hall, "The Question of Cultural Identity," in Stuart Hall, David Held, and Tony McGrew, eds., *Modernity and its Futures* (Cambridge: Polity Press, 1992), 275.

numbers of Germans and Jews compelled Germany and Israel to deal with the status and identities of the emigrants and decide what responsibilities the state has toward them. More than a million Jews and their non-Jewish relatives have left the Former Soviet Union since 1989, resettling mainly in Israel, the United States, and Germany. Conflicting or competing notions of Jewishness confront each other in a very concrete way and create or exacerbate a social, cultural, and religious issue.[64]

Therefore the question of what and who is a Jew is not an abstract or purely academic one but a matter of practical policy, with profound personal and collective consequences. It becomes important to know whether "Jewish" is a fixed or flexible category, one that has always had the same meaning or has changed over time, because this has clear implications for admission to or exclusion from Jewish communities, the granting of political and social rights by the Jewish state, and social recognition by others. As a largely diasporic people, Jews have developed different conceptions of Jewishness in different places and different times. As Fran Markowitz observes, "While the media may have brought all peoples throughout the world closer together, geographical mobility and ethnic dispersal have had the opposite effect, resulting in symbolic breakdowns between people claiming the same identity."[65]

Advance and Retreat

Developments in Jewish life parallel the general course of developments in Russia and Ukraine since the end of communism. Russia began its post-Soviet era with bold experiments in economics and politics. None succeeded. The "wild capitalism" that marked the presidency of Boris Yeltsin yielded to Vladimir Putin's reassertion of government control of what Bolsheviks used to call the "commanding heights" of the economy. The oligarchs of the Yeltsin era were brought to heel, and the government has consistently expanded its control of the crucial petroleum and natural gas industries. It has also increased its control of all forms of media. Political parties never had a chance to establish clear ideologies nor build stable constituencies, and they have ceased to play a meaningful role in Russian politics.

In Ukraine, corruption and illegality vitiated moves toward a market economy. Foreign investors were leery of what appeared to be a poorly regulated economy and unstable politics. The somewhat authoritarian and corrupt leadership of presidents Leonid Kravchuk and Leonid Kuchma was unseated by

---

[64] See Zvi Gitelman, *Immigration, Identity and Israeli Politics: The Resettlement and Impact of Recent Immigrants from the Former USSR* (Los Angeles: Wilstein Institute, 1995); Moshe Sicron and Elazar Leshem, *Dioknah shel aliyah* (Jerusalem: Magnes Press, 1998); and Moshe Lissak and Elazar Leshem, eds., *M'Rusiyah l'Yisrael* (Tel Aviv: Hakibutz hameukhad, 2001).

[65] Fran Markowitz, "Jewish in the USSR, Russian in the USA: Social Context and Ethnic Identity," in Walter Zenner, ed., *Persistence and Flexibility: Anthropological Perspectives on the American Jewish Experience* (Albany: SUNY Press, 1988), 92.

the Orange Revolution following challenges to the manipulated 2004 national election results and the rise of Viktor Yushchenko to the presidency. Yet that "revolution" petered out as a result of constant factional fighting within Ukraine's leadership and Yushchenko's failure to implement economic or political reforms. In 2010, the more conservative and Russian-oriented Victor Yanukovich was elected president. Nevertheless, in both Russia and Ukraine there has not been a full retreat to authoritarianism, certainly not to the comprehensive and repressive state control that existed in the Soviet period.

As is detailed in Chapter 7, Jewish public life has also flowered and declined. In the late 1980s and early 1990s it seemed that there would be an ethnic revival in much of the FSU and that Jews would be part of it. Israel and the Jewish diaspora rushed to the aid of a Jewish population that had not had organizations, schools, leaders, funds, religious institutions, and even its own language for at least a half-century. There were willing and seemingly able potential leaders among Soviet Jews, as well as a constituency whose size and aspirations were not fully known but which displayed strong interest in creating or re-creating some forms of Jewish life. Indeed, as we have seen, local and national organizations quickly formed and provided inspiration, social services, a sense of community, and pride to thousands and perhaps hundreds of thousands. Ironically, the movement was weakened by immigration to Israel. Most Western Jewish communities pay lip service to aliyah ("going up" or settling in Israel) but the majority of the *olim* from England and the United States are Orthodox, although they are a minority in those communities. For a small group of Soviet Jews, aliyah had become an ideal in the 1970s, and almost all of those who emigrated before 1974–75 went to Israel. After that time and until 1989, Soviet Jews who left their country went overwhelmingly to the United States and other Western countries, as discussed in Chapter 9. Then the United States curtailed Soviet immigration just at the time that many Jews perceived a threat from a weakened state that could not protect them against nationalism, anti-Semitism, and religious fanaticism. Israel took them in unconditionally, and so they headed there, sometimes reluctantly. As in all migrations, the young were overrepresented, thus sapping Soviet and post-Soviet Jewry of much of its demographic strength, talent, and potential. The mass movement to Israel also drew the most Jewishly committed people away from their birthplaces.

Just as institutional change in politics and economics has been insufficient to transform Russia and Ukraine into democratic polities and well-functioning market economies, so has the emergence of public Jewish organizations not produced a well-functioning Jewish communal life. Some of the same problems found in Jewish life elsewhere – oligarchic rule, wealth as the main criterion for nominal leadership, the failure of that leadership to arouse genuine support, factionalism, and organizational decay – have appeared in the FSU. For some, leadership positions have become vehicles to gain domestic and international respectability, social prestige, access to other "leaders," invitations to international meetings, and other perquisites, rather than responsibilities assumed to truly develop and enhance Jewish culture and social life. Like Russia and Ukraine, the Jewish collectivities within them have not fully fulfilled the hopes of those who expected the downfall of communism would bring revolutionary change.

4

Construing Jewishness in Russia and Ukraine

What does being Jewish mean to post-Soviet Jews in Russia and Ukraine? Are they a religious community, a nation, or an ethnic group? What does it take to be a Jew, and a "good Jew" at that? To ascertain what components of Jewishness are deemed crucial by Russian/Ukrainian Jews, we presented the 3,000 respondents in each "wave" of our surveys with a list of eighteen items and asked which are "necessary," "desirable," or "not important" for a person to consider him- or herself a Jew.

Table 4.1 shows that most answers focus on a sense of pride and belonging, on emotions rather than knowledge, and that beliefs and knowledge are not considered important to being a Jew. Specifically, about half the respondents chose "being proud of," not hiding and "defending" one's Jewishness, and remembering the Holocaust as necessary to Jewishness. Almost none believed that religious mandates – such as keeping the Sabbath or the dietary laws, attending synagogue, or circumcising male sons – are an integral part of being Jewish. Fewer than 2 percent saw marrying a Jew and less than 5 percent considered belief in God to be vital components of Jewish identity.[1] Although there was a strong consensus that Judaism has preserved the Jews as a nation, even among those who were not religious, many rejected the notion that to be Jewish one had to practice Judaism.

Post-Soviet Jews do not consider the items relating to the tenets of Judaism essential to being a "genuine Jew." For them the most essential ingredients of Jewishness are matters of feeling and memory – being proud of one's ethnicity and defending it and, increasingly, remembering the

---

[1] Very similar results were obtained in surveys of Jewish identity in the Volga region and in St. Petersburg. See Solomon Krapivenski, "Jewish Identity of Russian Jews in the Volga Region: A Sociological Survey," *Jews in Eastern Europe* 2, 27 (Fall 1995), and Marina Kogan, "The Identity of St. Petersburg Jews in the Early 1990s, A Time of Mass Emigration," *Jews in Eastern Europe*, 3, 28 (Winter 1995). See also Rozalina Ryvkina, *Evrei v postsovetskoi Rossii – Kto oni?* (Moscow: URSS, 1996).

TABLE 4.1. *Components Essential to Jewishness as Understood by Jews in Russia and Ukraine (percentages)*

	Russia '92	Russia '97	Ukraine '92	Ukraine '97
Be proud of one's nationality	33.3	22.9	29.4	31.4
Defend Jewish honor and dignity	27.1	17.3	21.4	19.7
Not hide one's Jewishness	0.5	20.8	0.7	13.6
Remember the Holocaust	7.3	15.1	15.5	21.5
Know Jewish history	5.0	2.8	3.0	2.1
Marry a Jew	1.8	1.1	1.1	0.8
Know Jewish traditions	3.2	1.4	0.2	1.4
Help other Jews	7.1	4.3	6.6	6.4
Feel a tie to Israel	4.2	4.3	5.7	2.8
Believe in God	2.7	4.2	3.9	5.4
Know the basics of Judaism	1.0	0.7	0.2	0.3
Circumcise one's son	0.2	0.1	0.2	0.1
Observe kashrut	0.0	0.0	0.0	0.1
Observe the Sabbath	0.0	0.3	0.3	0.4
Attend synagogue	0.0	0.1	0.2	0.1
Know a Jewish language	2.2	1.2	1.6	0.4
Share Zionist ideals	0.2	0.2	0.3	0.2
Give children Jewish education	1.2	0.8	2.0	1.3
Don't know, no answer	3.1	2.4	0.7	0.4

Holocaust. The increase in the importance given to remembering the Holocaust from the first to the second wave of interviews is undoubtedly due to efforts made by local and foreign Jews to bring greater knowledge of this catastrophe to the FSU, where the Soviet government, while never denying the Holocaust, suppressed knowledge of it or submerged it into the larger story of massive, prolonged Soviet suffering at the hands of the Nazis and their allies.[2] From 1992 to 1997 Holocaust memorial centers were established, books on the subject were published, and survivors told their stories. In Russia the proportion characterizing "defending Jewish honor and dignity" as necessary or desirable declined over the 1990s possibly because in 1992 there was more visible grassroots anti-Semitism – the militantly anti-Semitic Russian nationalist organization *Pamyat'* was active and highly visible – but five years later Jews were a less visible target of ethnic animosity; instead "peoples of Caucasian nationality" had become the favorite ethnic whipping boys.

In sum, in the 1990s the dominant conception of Jewishness held by people in Russia and Ukraine who considered themselves Jews or were registered as such by the Soviet authorities was that it is, in Soviet terms, a nationality. Jewishness is secular and ethnic, has little to do with Judaism, and is based on biological

---

[2] On the Soviet attitude toward the Holocaust, see my chapter in Zvi Gitelman, ed., *Bitter Legacy: Confronting the Holocaust in the Soviet Union* (Bloomington: Indiana University Press, 1997).

descent and an ineffable feeling of belonging – not on language, territory, customs, or behaviors. Interestingly, Jews' conceptions are quite similar to the ideas of Ukrainian identity as expressed in a national survey in Ukraine in 1998. The main things that "make someone a Ukrainian" are, in order of priority, "consciousness of oneself as a Ukrainian," Ukrainian ancestors, and citizenship in the Ukrainian state. Language and knowledge of Ukrainian history are far less important.[3] Thus Ukrainians and Jews seem to have developed similar conceptions of ethnicity during the Soviet period.[4]

Let us look more closely at the components of Jewishness as understood in Russia and Ukraine.

Jewishness Is Secular
Judaism has little to do with being Jewish, although there is uncertainty as to whether one can practice another religion and still be a Jew. Few respondents claimed to know much about Judaism; one-quarter to one-third said they know nothing at all about it. This lack of knowledge is not surprising, given the status of Judaism under the Soviets, but what may be significant is that there was no increase from 1992/93 to 1997/98 in the proportion claiming to know about the basics of Judaism, despite the activity of religious organizations during that time.

We then asked respondents whether they felt they *should* know more about Judaism. At most, only slightly more than one-quarter of respondents (Ukraine, 1993) thought it necessary. The number of people who felt they should know the fundamentals of Judaism actually declined over time in both countries. Yet the respondents were not dismissive of Judaism because about half or more said it is "desirable," if not "necessary," for them to know about it. Moreover, a slight majority in both interview waves and countries agreed with the statement that Judaism preserved the Jewish people over the centuries; thus post-Soviet Jews are not fighting against religion, as some Jews did in the 1920s and 1930s. That 20–30 percent said they felt it "not at all necessary" to know about Judaism is meaningful because it indicates not whether people think they ought to *practice* Judaism to be considered genuinely Jewish, but simply whether they ought to *know* about it. The respondents made a distinction between the value of knowledge about customs and traditions versus knowledge of religion: in the first survey 30 (Russia) to 43 (Ukraine) percent felt it necessary to know about customs, although the percentage that felt it necessary to know about

---

[3] Andrew Wilson, "Elements of a Theory of Ukrainian Ethno-National Identities," *Nations and Nationalism*, 8, 1 (2002), 44.

[4] The early twentieth-century American Jewish thinker Horace Kallen asserted, "Men may change their clothes, their politics, their wives, their religions, their philosophies to a greater or lesser extent: they cannot change their grandfathers. Jews or Poles or Anglo-Saxons, in order to cease being Jews or Poles or Anglo-Saxons would have to cease to be. The selfhood which is inalienable in them ... is ancestrally determined." "Democracy versus the Melting Pot," *Nation*, February 25, 1915, 220, quoted in Victoria Hattam, *In the Shadow of Race: Jews, Latinos and Immigrant Politics in the United States* (Chicago: University of Chicago Press, 2007), 60.

TABLE 4.2. *"Do You Believe in God?" (percentages)*

	Russia '92	Russia '97	Ukraine '92	Ukraine '97
Yes, I believe in God	18.3	22.8	24.2	31.0
I am inclined to such belief	23.9	25.3	29.7	24.4
I am not inclined to such belief	19.1	17.2	18.3	17.1
I do not believe in God	31.1	28.3	23.2	22.1
Don't know, no answer	6.4	7.6	4.8	5.5

religion declined over the five years. Knowledge of traditions is thus rated more important than knowledge of Judaism.

These responses do not mean that post-Soviet Jews are without faith. Rather, they are without religion. In other words, substantial proportions believe in God, but even those who believe do not draw a connection to behavior or even beliefs prescribed by Judaism. A young Ukrainian Jew explained, "Believing is something spiritual, something completely not understandable.... It doesn't obligate you to anything... but religiosity is simply a religious person... who is obligated to carry out certain things."[5]

Among Russian and Ukrainian Jews, Judaism as organized religion plays no role as a "façade for ethnicity." It was the Soviet state that defined and even constricted their ethnicity, Soviet society that reinforced it, and an ineffable sense of consanguinity that sealed it. A deity is present in the "inner life" of a surprising number of post-Soviet Jews, but religion is not, strange as that may sound to Western ears. Contrary to official Soviet hopes and expectations, belief in God was not eliminated, but Soviet citizens largely discarded religion as systematic theology, doctrines, and practices. A fair number of those we interviewed are people of faith, but very few practice religion in the conventional sense. Table 4.2 shows the answers to our straightforward question, "Do you believe in God?"

In Russia nearly half and in Ukraine slightly more than half the respondents either believed in God or were "inclined to" such belief. Fewer than one-third in Russia and fewer than one-quarter in Ukraine definitely did *not* believe in God. A 1990 survey of the general population in four large Russian regions found that 30 percent affirmed a belief in God and 16 percent declared themselves "convinced" atheists.[6] Interestingly, among Russian Jews there was a slight increase in the proportion of believers from 1992 to 1997, whereas the results in Ukraine were more ambiguous, showing perhaps that some migrated from the category of those "inclined" to faith to the group of unhesitating believers.

Interestingly, both among the general population of Russia (and some areas of Ukraine) as well as among Jews, the oldest and youngest were the most

---

[5] Rebecca Golbert, "Constructing Self: Ukrainian Jewish Youth in the Making," unpublished doctoral dissertation, St. Cross College, Oxford University, 2001, 217.
[6] L. Byzov and S. Filatov, "Religia i politika v obshchestvennom soznanii sovetskogo naroda," in S. B. Filatov and D. E. Furman, eds., *Religiia i demokratiia* (Moscow: Progress, 1993), 12.

inclined to theistic belief. The authors of the Russian study cited earlier maintain that Russian religiosity has two sources: traditional religious upbringing, which is what explains the beliefs of people over age 60, and what they call "avant-gardism," the desire by young people to be associated with Western civilization, which they perceive as standing for "democracy, human rights, the market, multiparty systems," and religion.[7] We cannot tell whether this is true of the Jewish respondents or whether their greater inclination to belief is caused by their being targeted by religious entrepreneurs or "missionaries" – or some other reason. We did find in both Russia and Ukraine and in both years that people under 30 and over 70 had the highest proportions of those "inclined" to belief and of those whose belief is unequivocal.

However, belief in God does not imply the practice of Judaism. Having faith does not imply following God-dictated commandments (*mitzvot*), nor that one sees God as intervening in human history, two major premises of Judaism. Bearing in mind that Orthodox Judaism was historically dominant in the lands of the FSU, it is striking that ritual observance is not dramatically greater among believers who prefer Judaism to other religions than among nonbelievers or those who do not name Judaism as their preferred faith. Most of those defining themselves as religious do not think they are obligated to keep the Sabbath and Jewish dietary laws (kashrut). Perhaps this is because more respondents preferred Reform Judaism than any other variety, though only one-third of them did so. Still, it is remarkable that in the year preceding the 1992 survey in Russia, only about half the *religious* people fasted on Yom Kippur or participated in a Passover seder, rituals generally observed by Reform Jews. Significantly, in 1997 in Russia the proportion of religious people fasting on Yom Kippur increased only slightly, but nearly three-quarters participated in a seder, probably because the seder gained in popularity as a communal event. In Ukraine, larger proportions (two-thirds to three-quarters) of religious Jews fasted on Yom Kippur, but only about 60 percent participated in a seder.[8] Only slightly more than one-third of those whom we call religious observed the Sabbath in either country, and less than one-quarter said they observe the dietary laws. Overall, in Russia in 1992 only 14 percent said they observed Shabbat and 10 percent said they observed kashrut.[9] In all, only half of those affirming Judaism observed the religious laws about which we inquired and one-quarter did not observe them at all. Clearly, the term "religious Jews"

---

[7] Ibid., 14–20. The "traditionalist" believers have no such attachment to Western values. In fact, they display more authoritarian outlooks than others. They prefer strong government and have positive views of Lenin, the Bolshevik Revolution, and the Communist Party.

[8] It is not clear why this should be so. Perhaps in the 1990s the communal seder was not as popular or widely available in Ukraine as in Russia.

[9] It is difficult to explain the substantial increase in observance of these two rituals in Russia over the five years. It may be that "observing Shabbat and kashrut" may mean to respondents that occasionally they might engage in a ritual such as lighting Sabbath candles or eating kosher food; this kind of behavior may well take place in communal settings and at the kinds of events that increased substantially in the 1990s.

does not necessarily describe people who adhere to traditional behavioral norms.

Jewishness Is an Ethnic Matter

Russian and Ukrainian Jews accept without question the Soviet conception of Jews as a nationality. This is how they were identified on the fifth line [*piataia grafa*] of their internal "passports" or identity cards in the USSR until independent Ukraine and then the Russian Federation (1997) abolished the nationality line.[10] Producing this document several times a day, the Soviet citizen was reminded of his or her "nationality" – and reminded others of it – very often.

Our respondents are uncertain about the Zionist conception of Jews as a *nation*. They have a parochial conception of Jewish nationality. They feel much closer to Russian non-Jews in their own city than to Georgian or Mountain Jews. They are uncertain as to whether even Belorussian and Ukrainian Jews, from whence most Russian Jews derive, are part of the same group. In Russia, two-thirds of those interviewed in 1992/93 said they feel "spiritually and culturally" closer to the Russians of their city than to Georgian, Bukharan (Central Asian), or Mountain Jews, and 46 percent said they feel closer to local Russians than to Jews in Belarus or Ukraine.[11] The feeling of distance from Jews elsewhere increased somewhat in 1997/98, either because the most nationally minded Jews had emigrated or because the breakup of the USSR increased the psychological distance among Jews (and others) in its independent parts. In contrast to Russian Jews, more Ukrainian Jews feel affinity for Russian Jews than they do for local Russians, and they feel greater affinity for local Russians than for Ukrainians. Like Russian Jews, they are distant from non-Ashkenazic Jews, although less so than Russian Jews. Other measures also indicate that Jews in Ukraine have a more powerful sense of Jewish kinship and affinity than Jews in Russia.

Jewishness Is Biological

Beliefs held by post-Soviet Jews about how one is or becomes Jewish run contrary to Jewish norms and halakha. For them, Jewishness is an inherited trait; for most it is sufficient to inherit it from one parent, and it does not matter which one (in contrast to halakha). Conversion to Judaism does not necessarily bring entry into the Jewish collectivity, which is also contrary to Jewish norms according to which conversion confers membership both in the religion and

---

[10] A good study of the debates around the abolition of mandatory nationality registration is Sven Gunnar Simonsen, "Between Minority Rights and Civil Liberties: Russia's Discourse over 'Nationality' Registration and the Internal Passport," *Nationalities Papers* 33, 2 (June 2005), 211–29. Simonsen finds that in the twenty-one ethnically defined republics of the Russian Federation there was strong sentiment, especially among political elites, for keeping the ethnic registration. He quotes a few Jewish activists as favoring it as well. We report the views of our respondents on this issue in Chapter 11.

[11] Twenty percent feel equally close to both, and 16 percent feel closer to the non-Russian Jews.

the people (*"amaich ami ve-elohayich elohay"* – your people/nation are my people/nation, and your God is my God, says Ruth, the archetypical convert in Jewish tradition). This makes sense: if Judaism is not an essential ingredient of Jewishness, why should acquisition of the former confer the latter? One respondent defined ethnicity so independently of religion that for her practicing Judaism does not make one a Jew (contrary to Jewish tradition, which admits any practitioner of Judaism to the Jewish people).[12] "I can be a French person and practice Judaism, but that does not make me a Jew," she maintained.

Jewishness Is Based on Feeling

In this respect, as well as in their idea that Jewishness is a matter of "blood" or inheritance, Russian and Ukrainian Jews echo nineteenth-century West European Jewish ideas:

> Rabbi Cesar Seligmann told his Frankfurt congregants: "It is not Jewish conviction, not Jewish doctrine, not the Jewish creed that is the leading, the primary, the inspirational; rather it is Jewish sentiment, the instinctive, call it what you will, call it the community of blood, call it tribal consciousness [*Stammesgefuhl*], call it the ethnic soul... but best of all call it the Jewish heart."[13]

Jewishness was much more primordial than instrumental until the possibility of emigration appeared in the 1970s; then in the 1990s Jewishness provided access to social services sponsored by Jewish agencies. Yet most respondents described the sense of being Jewish as innate and nearly ineffable. A woman in Kiev, in her eighties, said she is not particularly proud to be Jewish and years ago might have preferred to be registered in her passport as something else; she observed no Jewish holidays and was not at all active in Jewish public activities. Yet she said, "There must be something hidden deep inside which is very hard to characterize. For example, when I hear Jewish songs, they touch something deep inside of me, even though I grew up in a Russian environment. We didn't observe any special traditions or anything. And even so something touches me." Two-thirds of 1992 Russian respondents said that "to feel oneself a part of the Jewish people" is what being Jewish is all about, and nearly as many that "to be proud of the Jewish people" is the essence. The most frequent way of expressing these sentiments among Ukrainian respondents in 1997 was "to feel yourself part of the Jewish people [*narod*]" or "to feel an inner kinship with Jews, to feel we're one family." Another respondent put it strongly, "When everything relating to Jews and Jewish life in the world, their culture and the Yiddish and Hebrew languages, that which relates to Israel touches my soul – that's what it is to be a Jew." Some found this feeling difficult to express: "This is an internal feeling. It's difficult to express [*peredat'*] it."

[12] See Zvi Zohar and Avraham Sagi, *Giyur vezehut Yehudit* (Jerusalem: Mosad Bialik and Machon Hartman, 1994).
[13] Quoted in Todd Endelman, "Jewish Self-Identification and West European Categories of Belonging from the Enlightenment to World War II," 124.

As a British sociologist observes, "If there is one necessary and sufficient condition for membership of an ethnic group, it is surely a subjective feeling of belonging, of kinship, of a desire for group continuity and a sense of corporate identity."[14] For quite a few, the only necessary and sufficient condition for being Jewish is to feel oneself a Jew or, as one put it, "to feel yourself a Jew in your soul." A resident of Kharkov, where we found the lowest levels of Jewish commitment, described his reaction to a Jewish seminar he attended: "A euphoria enveloped me because nowhere and never before, in no group and not in my student days did people understand me so well and I understand them.... This is – mine! I felt it! Explain it? Explain it exactly? I don't know, I can't.... Maybe it's a mentality.... People find it simpler to find a point of contact with each other."

Two-thirds of the respondents chose descent and the feeling of being part of the Jewish people from among nine criteria offered them for establishing Jewish identity. This parallels what Fran Markowitz found among Soviet Jewish immigrants in Brooklyn, New York:

> Being a Jew is an immutable biological and social fact, ascribed at birth like sex and eye color. It may or may not include belief in the Jewish religion, but being a Jewish atheist is not considered a contradiction in terms. Being a Jew is self-evident....[whereas] In American society where one's Jewishness is not self-evident, it is necessary to demonstrate, both to the Gentile world and the Jewish community, that one is a Jew by doing specifically Jewish things.[15]

In the FSU one does not have to *do* anything Jewish; one simply *is* Jewish.

Manifestating Jewishness in Private and Public

Some analysts of American religion believe that Americans increasingly "privatize" religion and that it is "anchored in the personal realms. Custom and tradition play less of a role in what an individual believes, religious feelings become...more a matter of choice or preference.... Each person has a different 'version' of religious reality."[16] They see this privatization as the product of a culture in which satisfaction of individual wants is a dominant motif, personal achievement and self-interest are important goals, and finding oneself is a "central quest." However, when religion is fused with ethnicity, it is more difficult

---

[14] Stephen Miller, "Religious Practice and Jewish Identity in a Sample of London Jews," in Jonathan Webber, ed., *New Jewish Identities* (London: Littman Library, 1994), 199.
[15] Fran Markowitz, "Jewish in the USSR, Russian in the USA: Social Context and Ethnic Identity," in Walter Zenner, ed., *Persistence and Flexibility: Anthropological Perspectives on the American Jewish Experience* (Albany: SUNY Press, 1988), 81, 83.
[16] Wade Clark Roof and William McKinney, *American Mainline Religion* (New Brunswick, NJ: Rutgers University Press, 1987), 32.

to discard custom and tradition because, although they may be less relevant to religious faith, they are crucial to ethnic self-consciousness and expression. True, among American Jews, "New Age" religions, (pseudo) kabbalah, and mysticism enjoy some popularity, indicating that the trend toward the privatization of religion has affected them. However, it is difficult to privatize the ethnic dimension of Jewishness. Noting that of six religious groups studied, Jews rank lowest in attendance at services and in the proportion agreeing that religion is very important in their lives, Roof and McKinney conclude, "Ties to tradition and minority experience are far more important than common belief for [Jews], *making it more an ethnic than a religious collectivity in many respects*"[17] [italics added].

Indeed, in many Western countries, Jewishness is expressed publicly, through affiliation with organizations and institutions and through philanthropy. One prominent American rabbi decries what he sees as a trend to move even the previously home-centered Jewish observances out into the public sphere, in this case the synagogue:

> The Passover seder has been moved out of the home into the social hall, words read by the rabbi, melodies sung by the cantor, food prepared by the caterer.... The succah does not adjoin the walls of the private home but only those of the temple. We are socialists in our religious possessions. Nothing is privately owned. The lulav and ethrog are owned by the temple. The siddur, machzor, Bible, prayer-shawl, and skullcap are all public property.[18]

These observations do not apply to Soviet Jewry.

In the Soviet Union "public declarations of Jewishness [were] not made.... Jewish holidays are celebrated within the confines of one's home, in private, with family."[19] Organizational affiliation, Jewish philanthropy, and the public observance of Jewish rites and holidays were impossible in the Soviet state. Soviet Jews were forced to "individualize" whatever faith they had because there were no public forums and collective institutions through which faith could be expressed, developed, and transmitted; there was not a single Jewish organization to belong to nor, aside from a few synagogues, was there an opportunity to give money to Jewish institutions or causes. In addition, for much of the Soviet period it was safest not to manifest one's Jewishness in any way. Small wonder that post-Soviet Jewish identity is one

---

[17] Ibid., 102.
[18] Harold Schulweis, "The Role of the Synagogue in Jewish Identity," in Gordis and Ben-Horin, *Jewish Identity*, 160. Lulav and ethrog are the palm branches and citron used on the Sukkot holiday; *siddur* is the prayerbook, and *machzor* is the prayerbook used on holidays.
[19] Markowitz in Zenner, ibid., 85.

that requires little public manifestation, proclamation, ritual, or observance of customs or the use of a language, symbolic affirmation. Jewishness is a feeling, a sense one has and shares with others, but silently for the most part – except for holiday celebrations that have moved into public spaces in the post-Soviet era. To be a good Jew one need not march in a parade, attend a rally, go to synagogue, participate in a festive meal, have a Jewish name, hang a mezuzah on one's door, or wear a *kippah* or a "*chai*" or *Magen David* around one's neck.

Some respondents said that the choice to publicly manifest one's Jewishness "depends on the person" and his or her preferences. A Ekaterinburg respondent observed, "It seems to me that if the activity is directed to people who are also Jewish, then of course one may want to discuss it... let's say, speaking about common traditions. But if it's simply to show off [*gorditsiia*] among one's comrades, who are not Jewish, it seems simply silly to me." A Muscovite opined, "I think it [Jewishness] is more an internal matter.... You should not exhibit anything. If it's interesting to him and he wants to somehow splash it around [*vyplesnust'*], then fine [*radi Boga*]. But there can be no talk here about obligation [*dolshenstvovaniia*]." An Odessite remarked, somewhat testily,

> Just to shout it from every corner.... Imagine if a man stands there and shouts, "I am a Jew!" Well... and so what? He will not be a better person for it [*ot etogo on luchshe ne stanet*]. He might even be worse! It's insulting [*obidno*] to someone else. Sometimes people shout that they are Jewish. Then they do something bad and then others think: "Aha, if that Jew does something bad, the whole Jewish people must be like that."

To sum it up, a St. Petersburg respondent said pithily, "One should not demonstrate one's Jewishness. What for? Just feel that you are a Jew. But to show it off is unnecessary."

For some, Jewishness means possessing certain traits, although they are not essential components of Jewishness. Urbanity, education, a penchant for intellectuality, "decency," and tight-knit families are among those traits. An oft-repeated theme is that Jews have been socialized to study and work harder so that they can overcome the barriers placed in their paths. Another common idea is that Jewish families are tighter knit and more caring, and that women are better treated in them. A Kievan felt that "Jewish mothers are more caring. They care more about their children, they watch over them more carefully.... Some people say that Jewish husbands are more devoted, more caring, more sympathetic, but I think that's all in the past. Nowadays everyone is the same – that's been my experience." A middle-aged Jewish woman from Odessa, married to a Russian, asserted, "There is a difference in the way they [Jews] relate to the old, to their children, to each other. The Jewish families are more tender and affectionate to their children, more caring than the Russian families. They are also more caring and respectful to the old than the Russian families."

Crossing Boundaries

An important way in which post-Soviet notions of Jewishness differ from Jewishness elsewhere is a willingness to cross two major boundaries long essential to the definition of Jewishness and that still hold for most Jews: practicing a faith other than Judaism and marrying non-Jews. When Judaism was the defining hallmark of Jewishness, conversion was the definitive step out of the Jewish fold. Maimonides (1135–1204), perhaps the most influential Jewish religious philosopher and religious decisor [*posek*], ruled that "a Jew who worshiped other gods [lit., "*avad avodat kochavim*,"] is considered a worshiper of other gods in all respects... and so the heretics [*epikorsim*] of Israel are not Israelites in any respect and one does not accept their repentance."[20]

The separation of religion from ethnicity raised the theoretical possibility of Jews still being Jewish while practicing another religion. However, the Brother Daniel case in Israel in the 1960s demonstrated that the impossibility of Jewish ethnicity coexisting with active non-Jewish faith still held. A recent study in the United States among "moderately affiliated Jews" found that the taboo on practicing a faith other than Judaism still obtains, even while the stricture on intermarriage is weakening. In the United States Jewishness is often defined by the fact that it is not Christianity: "The only way to lose this Jewish birthright is to choose a different religion for oneself."[21]

Today there is considerable uncertainty among Jews in the FSU about whether one can practice another faith and still being Jewish, as we see in Chapter 10.

Conclusion

The Jewish identity of Russian and Ukrainian Jews is stronger than many might expect, but is problematic in three ways. First, it may be the product of a Soviet environment that no longer exists. Ethnic identities are often reformulated in changing contexts, and "Jewish identities in general are to be understood as constructs in response to the circumstances."[22] The Soviet context was unique, not replicated even in allied socialist countries, which did not register nationality in citizens' identity documents; in some socialist countries, Jewishness was defined as a religious, rather than ethnic, category. In the USSR, state-imposed identity and governmental and grassroots

---

[20] Maimonides, *Mishneh Tora, Sefer Hamada, Hilchot avodat kochavim*, ch. 2, section 5.
[21] Steven M. Cohen and Arnold M. Eisen, *The Jew Within: Self, Family, and Community in America* (Bloomington: Indiana University Press, 2000), 23.
[22] Webber, "Modern Jewish Identities," in *Jewish Identities in the New Europe*, 82.

anti-Semitism combined to maintain boundaries between Jews and others long after "thick" Jewish content had disappeared. Russia and Ukraine no longer impose an official ethnic identity, and none of the successor states to the USSR pursues an anti-Semitic policy. Popular anti-Semitism, which may wax and wane, may be the last barrier to assimilation. Some of the ingredients of Soviet Jewish identity have been changed, though descent and feelings of kinship remain.

There are no longer any restrictions on infusing a largely hollow Jewish identity with Jewish content of all kinds. Yet only a minority is beginning to participate in public Jewish activities, educate their children Jewishly, and explore Jewish traditions and cultures. Moreover, it is precisely those most interested in Jewish content who are most likely to emigrate. In Israel their Jewishness takes on new content – language, territory, national traditions, patriotism – and in the United States or Germany they have the option of adopting the local normative modes of Jewishness. Yet the historically unique Jewish identity created in the USSR may not survive the demise of the conditions that created it. It may not be transferable to future generations and may not survive in the current generation, although other forms of Jewish identity may replace it even on native soil.

Second, the conceptions of being Jewish held by the great majority of Russian and Ukrainian Jews are so different from those prevailing in most of the diaspora and in Israel that sensitive questions of mutual recognition inevitably arise. A significant portion of post-Soviet Jewry do not accept the criteria for admission to the Jewish club that are set in the Jewish world. Thus the gatekeepers of the Jewish club, whoever they may be – this is one of the most contentious issues in world Jewry today – have three choices when FSU Jews present themselves for admission. The gatekeepers can abandon the rules altogether and adopt the suggestion of some of our respondents that "whoever thinks he or she is a Jew, is a Jew." By doing so they would be abandoning any admission criteria and would have to include "Jews for Jesus" or anyone else declaring themselves a Jew, perhaps pleasing those for whom essentialism is a cardinal sin but emptying the category "Jew" of any meaning at all.[23] Another option is for the gatekeepers to modify the rules for admission, but if they do so extensively the rules can become so loose as to be inoperative or meaningless.

---

[23] Rebecca Golbert criticizes scholars for "their applications of certain fixed external criteria to measure the self-identification of Jews" and for "ignor[ing] the local frameworks for self-definition and cultural continuity and the multi-linear processes of social and political change which have affected them." She performs an important service in pointing out that there are subtle ways in which Jewish identity was expressed and transmitted in the Soviet Union, but in her zeal to establish a new paradigm she ignores the questions of multigenerational viability and external validation or recognition of the peculiarly Soviet – or, Russian, Ukrainian, etc. – identity that evolved. Rebecca Golbert, "In Search of a Meaningful Framework for the Study of Post-Soviet Jewish Identities, with Special Emphasis on the Case of Ukraine," *East European Jewish Affairs* 28, 1 (Summer 1998), 15.

Or they can stick to the rules they have evolved and turn away many who seek admission. Those rejected may form their own, competing Jewish club, or they may turn away from the gates altogether and seek membership elsewhere.[24]

Third, the challenge of developing a viable Jewish identity in Russia and Ukraine is formidable because it involves constructing a secular Jewish identity. In the United States Amyot and Sigelman find that "[r]eligious devotion... is the main pillar of Jewish identity... although close interpersonal relations with other Jews also play an important role." To the extent that American Jews reject "ethno-religion" they also renounce their ethnic heritage.[25] Yet this is not the issue in Russia and Ukraine. One must assume that for the foreseeable future most Jewish identities in the European parts of the Former Soviet Union will be secular and that interpersonal relations with other Jews will decline along with the sheer number of Jews – unless Jewish communities develop further. Secular Jews have long struggled with the problem of maintaining ethnicity divorced from religion and its symbols. A secular Yiddish educator observed that when the "secular ship" floats on the "Jewish sea," one permeated by religion, "it turns out that one floats empty, with no ballast. And a terrible similarity appears between secularism and simple assimilation."[26] Some secular Jews substituted ethics for religion, others the Yiddish language and culture, and still others a modern Jewish state. All reverted to symbolism emanating from religious sources, although they tried to infuse the symbols with new emphases. As one of the ideologists of secular Yiddishism put it, "if the Jewish Passover is kept because a people liberated itself from slavery and went out to seek a land in which to live its own life freely – though the whole story of the Exodus from Egypt is perhaps only a legend – the festival is of... great human significance.... Of course... there must be no supernatural elements introduced into the observance, nothing of confessional faith."[27] A Hungarian

---

[24] Ronald Suny argues that two different ideas of nation-making should be distinguished. "In the first, the nation exists even when people argue about what it is; in time they will get it right. In the second, the nation is precisely that cultural and political space where people create and recreate their sense of who they are. Like culture, it is an arena of contestation, an argument about membership and boundaries, of authenticity. It is in the debate that the nation exists and is created and recreated." Comment at conference on "A Century of Modern Jewish Politics: The Bund and Zionism in Poland and Eastern Europe," Frankel Center for Judaic Studies, University of Michigan, February 15–16, 1998. The second notion is compelling, but it is hard to see how people can be admitted or barred from a "cultural and political space." The nation is surely an "arena of contestation," but the contestants must agree on some boundaries for the arena itself.

[25] Robert Amyot and Lee Sigelman, "Jews without Judaism? Assimilation and Jewish Identity in the United States," *Social Science Quarterly*, 77, 1 (March 1996), 187–88. See also Bruce Philips, "Accounting for Jewish Secularism: Is a New Cultural Identity Emerging?" Contemporary Jewry, 30 (2010), 63–85.

[26] Yudl Mark, "Yidishkayt un veltlikhkayt in un arum undzere shuln," in Shloime Bercovich et al., eds. *Shul-Pinkes* (Chicago: Sholem Aleichem Folk Institute, 1948), 14.

[27] Chaim Jitlovsky, "What is Jewish Secular Culture?" in Joseph Leftwich, ed., *The Way We Think*, Vol. 1 (South Brunswick, NJ: Thomas Yoseloff, 1969), 95.

Jew explained the dilemma this way: "We do not want to practice religion itself but we want to belong.... It is incredibly difficult, we are Negroes without the color."[28]

Almost from the establishment of the state, Israelis have discussed *toda'a Yehudit* [Jewish consciousness] and the Jewish identity of the nonreligious population. Israeli educators continue to wrestle with the problem of how to convey Jewish history, literatures, values, and traditions to nonreligious students. In the United States, where the basis of East European secularism, Yiddish, yielded to English, Jews have maintained Judaism as the expression of ethnicity. One sociologist asserts, "Jewish self-definition is that of a religious group but few Jews are believers in any significant way. As one Reform rabbi has stated the problem, 'Prayer is still the pretext, but the justification of the act, the real purpose, is now achievement of community, the sense of belonging.'"[29] In Britain, too, "a feeling of belonging, rather than belief in God, is the driving force behind synagogue attendance."[30]

In the Soviet Union, because religious forms were unacceptable they did not serve the same purpose as in the United States or Britain. Secular, socialist, Soviet forms devised by the Jewish Sections of the Communist Party were seen as ersatz and never replaced Judaism-based symbols and rituals. Nevertheless, secular Jewish identity in the Soviet Union was powerful because it was maintained by a combination of official designation, anti-Semitism, and a feeling of apartness, especially after the 1930s. Today, some of these elements of identity are gone. Is grassroots anti-Semitism the last basis of Jewish identity? In addition to its being a completely negative cause of such identity, can one now escape anti-Semitism because the boundaries of ethnicity have become permeable and blurred as a result of intermarriage?

Our data clearly show that the youngest cohort, those between 16 and 29, differ significantly from their elders. Along with those over 60 or 70, they are least embarrassed by their Jewishness. They are the least aware of or threatened by anti-Semitism and most inclined to participate in Jewish public activities. Yet they are also the least opposed to intermarriage and among the most inclined to consider emigration. If their attitudes remain the same as they proceed through the life cycle, it is hard to know whether they will lead to a sustained revival of Jewish life in Russia and Ukraine or further demographic erosion – or possibly both simultaneously.

Moreover, because those most active in Jewish public life are most likely to emigrate, the viability of communal life is called into question. Future emigration levels depend on three variables that are impossible to predict: (1) political

---

[28] Andras Kovacs, "Antisemitism and Jewish Identity in Postcommunist Hungary," in Randolph Braham, ed., *Anti-Semitism and the Treatment of the Holocaust in Postcommunist Eastern Europe* (New York: Rosenthal Institute for Holocaust Studies, CUNY and Columbia University Press, 1994) 138.
[29] Paul Ritterband, "Modern Times," unpublished paper, March 22–23, 1991.
[30] Stephen Miller, 200.

and economic situations in Russia and Ukraine; (2) the situation in Israel and the Middle East; and (3) immigration policies of Germany, the United States, and other Western countries.

For those who stay in Russia and Ukraine, we expect to see greater and more rapid changes in behavior than in attitudes and beliefs. More people attend Jewish events more regularly, although not in great numbers. Perhaps exposure to ethnic entrepreneurs and local and foreign Jewish organizations will have the effect of changing not only behavioral habits but also values and beliefs.

Not surprisingly, there is a good deal of inconsistency and diversity in conceptions of Jewishness among Russian and Ukrainian Jews. Scholars long ago demonstrated that there are often logical inconsistencies in people's attitudes, let alone between attitudes and behaviors. Moreover, in the FSU, where there was no Jewish education that would promote norms based on classic and shared premises, but instead only informal socialization to understandings of Jewishness, there are bound to be diversity and lack of uniformity or consensus. Informal socialization was carried out in the family and within peer groups and was a result of life experiences. Because there was a fair degree of variance in all three, not to speak of regional variations, people were bound to form quite different conceptions of Jewishness – what it is, how it is acquired, and how it is transmitted. These conceptions might not have much in common with conceptions across space (those held by other Soviet Jews) and across time (those held traditionally).

The interesting question becomes what new understandings will emerge. Is "thin culture" or "symbolic ethnicity" transferable across generations? How far can something that is already thin be stretched across generations before it breaks entirely? In other words, can Jewishness survive without Judaism? As Henry Feingold has written, "The survival dilemma posed by secular modernity is whether the corporate communal character at the heart of Judaism can accommodate the individuation that is the quintessence of modern secular life. It is whether Jewishness can become again a living culture without its primary religious ingredient, Judaism, from which it has become separated."[31] Secular Jewishness as it emerged just a century ago was based on a common language (Yiddish), territorial concentration of Jews (the Pale, ethnic neighborhoods), a high degree of concentration in certain professions (needle trades, artisanal trades, commerce, and trade), and a strong sense of being part of a distinct Jewish entity. Jews were kept distinct by anti-Semitism or – for immigrants – by their cultural apartness, and by their sense of cultural superiority in many countries (Lithuania, Russia, Romania). In others they strove to the "higher culture" as they perceived it (France, England, Germany, the United States). Today, Yiddish and Hebrew are little used or even posited as ideals, Jewish neighborhoods no longer contain as high a proportion of the Jewish population or do not exist, and the Jewish working class has disappeared

---

[31] *Lest Memory Cease* (1996) 8.

and with it Jewish dominance in certain trades. No states with significant Jewish populations pursue anti-Semitic policies. Everywhere the vast majority of Jews have acculturated to the majority culture or, as in the Baltic Republics and Ukraine, to the culture of another non-Jewish people. Thus, the bases of secular Jewishness have eroded or disappeared. In such conditions, can there be a viable, transferable secular Jewish life? "Classical Jewish identity has... broken up (if not also broken down) into multiple Jewish identities, some of which... trace connections with the more distant past, while others [as in the FSU] define themselves more directly and explicitly through highly contemporary issues." Thus, if the classical definition of Jewish identity is discarded, as Jonathan Webber notes, "there would appear to be no simple, self-evident, and adequate formula to replace it with."[32] For some this might not be problematic but when the decision of who and what Jews are is left to others, this not only cedes the sovereignty of a people to outsiders but, as Jews have learned, also may lead to catastrophic results.

---

[32] Webber, "Modern Jewish Identities," 8.

5

Judaism and Jewishness

Religion and Ethnicity in Russia and Ukraine

As we saw in the first chapter, the nature of ethnicity is not a settled matter. Ian Lustick found more polemic than empirical research in the writings of many "constructivists" on ethnicity. I follow his advice in probing "the multiplicity of identities available to individuals, the range of 'identity projects' available within a population or across overlapping or intermingled populations, and the relationship of those identities and projects to changeable sets of preferences and changeable institutional circumstances."[1]

This chapter explores what Russian and Ukrainian Jews mean when they say someone is Jewish and how strong their Jewish identity is relative to other identities they claim. Being Jewish means something different to them from what it means to Jews elsewhere, and I examine the implications of these variations in Jewishness. Because the Jewish world is drawing closer together through increased travel and communications, migration, population shrinkage, and concentration in fewer places – about eleven million of the world's thirteen million Jews live in Israel and the United States – different conceptions of Jewishness (which are also present in a single society) now confront each other. This confrontation raises the boundary issue of who is in the group and who not and affects policies related to conversion to Judaism, the Israeli Law of Return, access to restituted Jewish properties in Eastern Europe, eligibility for marriage in some cases, and admission to communal institutions such as Jewish Community Centers and Jewish schools. For example, administrators of Jewish schools must decide whether to admit "patrilineal Jewish children" (i.e., those who have a Jewish father and a non-Jewish mother). Reform temples now admit non-Jews with Jewish spouses to membership and do not demand

---

[1] Ian S. Lustick "Agent-Based Modeling and Constructivist Identity Theory," in Kanchan Chandra, ed., *Cumulative Findings in the Study of Ethnopolitics*, APSA-CP (Winter 2001), 23.

that they convert to Judaism.² Conceptions of Jewishness determine who is eligible for immigration to Israel under the Law of Return (of Jews to their "homeland") and whom Jewish immigration agencies will help resettle in the United States or Canada.³

A second issue is the relationship of Jews to the states and societies in which they live. If Jews see themselves as an ethnic group, and the state accommodates ethnicity by formal recognition and provision of goods and services, Jews can become collective political actors. However, in Hungary, in 2005 Jews chose to retain their traditionally religious identity and rejected the ethnic status offered by the government, along with the rights and privileges accorded to ethnic groups.⁴ In the Canadian census, Jews can be listed by both religion and ethnicity, so that one individual can list his or her ethnicity as Jewish and religion as something other than Judaism, and another can list religion as Jewish and ethnicity as something other than Jewish. In Germany, Jews are eligible for assistance granted to Jewish communities only if they are members of those communities. Because membership is determined by halakha (rabbinic law), those who have only a Jewish father but not a Jewish mother and have not converted to Judaism are not admitted. These are just some of the many issues entwined in the study of Jewish identity that have important policy implications.

---

² In his presidential sermon to the 68th General Assembly of the Union for Reform Judaism in 2005 (formerly the Union of American Hebrew Congregations), Rabbi Eric Yoffie spoke of the need for "welcoming non-Jewish spouses" into Reform temples. Citing Alexander Schindler, who had pushed for Reform Judaism to recognize as Jews those who had a Jewish father but not a Jewish mother, Yoffie talked of welcoming the intermarried "into our synagogues, our families, and our homes. We would do this in the hope that the non-Jewish partners would ultimately convert to Judaism; and if not, that they would commit themselves to raising their children as Jews." http://urj.org/yoffie/biennialsermon05, p. 5, accessed March 12, 2009. "Raising children as Jewish," a Catholic concept, does not confer Jewish status on those so "raised," according to Orthodox and Conservative Jewish practice. Yoffie noted "the decline in the number of non-Jewish spouses who convert to Judaism" and mused that "by making non-Jews feel comfortable and accepted in our congregations, we have sent the message that we do not care if they convert. But that is not our message." Ibid., 6.

Kathryn Kahn, director of the Department of Outreach and Membership of the Union of Reform Judaism, writes that "all Reform congregations welcome IF [inter-faith] couples but congregations vary in their policies about official membership for the person who is not Jewish.... Most of our congregations offer membership to the non-Jewish spouse individually and some do not. We're Reform and every congregation is autonomous." E-mail message to Zvi Gitelman, March 12, 2009.

³ A recent issue of *Sh'ma: A Journal of Jewish Responsibility*, was devoted to this topic. See 41/678, March 2011.

⁴ The Federation of Hungarian Jewish Communities (MAZsIHISZ) claimed "there was no precedent for the Hungarian Jewish Community to define itself as a national minority. Their chief concern was that the plan would result in 'the separation of Jews from Hungarians.'" Advocates of classifying Jews as an ethnic minority were unable to gather 1,000 signatures needed to have the idea considered by the government. Andras Kovacs and Aletta Forras-Biro, *Jewish Life in Hungary: Achievements, Challenges and Priorities since the Collapse of Communism*, Institute for Jewish Policy Research Report, September 2011, 11.

Grasping the Shifting Content of Jewishness in Russia and Ukraine

How states or Jewish law define Jews is one thing; how Jews define themselves may be quite another. As the sociologist Egon Mayer pointed out, "What's been left out in most [studies of American Jewish identity] is the subjective self-understanding of Jews: what Jews think about each other, what they think about Judaism."[5] This certainly applies as well to post-Soviet Jews, because only in the 1990s did it become possible to investigate their opinions, outlooks, and self-understandings. Another analyst of American Jewry wrote that studies of Jewish identity have emphasized "objective, readily countable behaviors, without attending to subjective experience, meaning and motivation. Thus, there is a wealth of data about who lights candles and how often people have visited Israel; while much less is known... about why people do what they do or feel what they feel about Jewishness."[6]

For decades only sporadic and impressionistic information was available about how Soviet Jews thought about their Jewishness and how they expressed it behaviorally. At least outwardly, most Jews in the Former Soviet Union changed the contents of their Jewish identities several times in the twentieth century. In the 1920s and 1930s most moved from the traditional religious, modern Zionist, or Yiddishist bases of Jewish identity of the prerevolutionary period to a predominantly Russian and Soviet culture and identity; only a minority adhered to the newly constructed secular, socialist Soviet Yiddish identity. Jews married non-Jews at unprecedented rates. Only the introduction of internal passports in the early 1930s and the official registration of nationality prevented many Jews from assimilating; that is, becoming Russians in all ways. Ironically, the very state that preached assimilation of all peoples as the solution to the "national [Jewish] question" kept people from assimilating and losing their ethnicity by identifying them by nationality on their internal identification documents (passports): the internationalist Soviet state kept Jews at least nominally and consciously Jewish, against the will of many who hoped to become Russian.

The content of Jewish identity changed again in the 1940s and 1950s when the Holocaust and Stalinist anti-Semitism shattered illusions of acceptance and assimilation. Because there was no longer any positive cultural content left in Jewishness, Jews identified themselves as "invalids of the fifth category"[7]: Jewishness was seen as a form of disability. For most Ashkenazic Jews, Jewish identity became an amalgam of four elements: state-imposed identity (nationality = Jewish), social anti-Semitism, consciousness of the Holocaust, and awareness of Israel. Only the last element had a positive affect, and after 1967 it became more salient. After 1988 the possibility of reconstructing Jewish life in

---

[5] "Secularism among America's Jews: Insights from the American Jewish Identity Survey, 2001," paper presented to the Association for Jewish Studies, Washington, DC, December 2001, 5.
[6] Bethamie Horowitz, "Connections and Journeys: Shifting Identities among American Jews," *Contemporary Jewry* 19 (1998), 71.
[7] A play on the fifth line of the internal passport, designating nationality.

the FSU challenged Jews to redefine themselves yet again.[8] Yet, in our 1997/98 survey, described in Appendix A, 52 to 54 percent maintained that the greatest impact on the formation of their national consciousness was exerted by negative experiences.

Religion and Ethnicity

Ethnic and religious identities are more closely associated in some groups than in others; in some cases religion and ethnicity are practically coterminous, whereas in others they have little relationship to each other. "Tribal" religions are associated exclusively with one people, ethnic group, or nation. A tribal religion is one in which a faith is appropriated by a specific closed community (ethnic or otherwise; e.g., a cult) as uniquely its own or where access to it is determined by membership in such a community.[9] Hindus, Jews, Sikhs,[10] the Amish, Bulgarian Pomaks,[11] and increasingly, Bosnians[12] are people whose religion and ethnicity are nearly coterminous. Among these groups, one could say that religion defines ethnicity. It is impossible to separate Hinduism as a

---

[8] See Zvi Gitelman, *A Century of Ambivalence: The Jews of Russia and the Soviet Union, 1881 to the Present*, 2nd ed. (Bloomington, IN: Indiana University Press, 2001), and Gitelman, "The Evolution of Jewish Culture and Jewish Identity in the Soviet Union," in Yaacov Ro'i and Avi Beker, eds., *Jewish Culture and Identity in the Soviet Union* (New York: New York University Press, 1991).

[9] See Judith Nagata, "Particularism and Universalism in Religious and Ethnic Identities: Malay Islam and Other Cases," in Stuart Plattner and David Maybury-Lewis, eds., *The Prospects for Plural Societies* (Washington, DC: American Ethnological Society, 1984), 122–135.

[10] There is a "narrative" that "identifies the Sikhs as followers of a universal world religion, such as Islam or Christianity." A second "narrative identifies the Sikhs as a nation with definite physical boundaries, those of the Indian state of Punjab." From this perspective, "[n]ot everyone can be a Sikh; one is born into an *ethnie*, or ethnically-defined community." A third narrative focuses on the Sikh diaspora (more than 1 million people out of a total of 16–17 million Sikhs) and on a return to the Punjabi "homeland." Giorgio Shani, "The Territorialization of Identity: Sikh Nationalism in the Diaspora," *Studies in Ethnicity and Nationalism* 2, 1 (2002), 11–19.

[11] See Maria Todorova, "Identity (Trans)formation among Pomaks in Bulgaria," in Laszlo Kurti and Juliet Langman, eds., *Beyond Borders* (Boulder: Westview, 1997), 63–82.

[12] The last case illustrates how the content or substance of ethnicity can shift over time. Bosnians speak Serbo-Croatian, but since the violent breakup of Yugoslavia they have tried to develop a distinctly "Bosnian" language. Bosnians are, in the main, Slavs converted to Islam by Ottoman conquerors. They differ from their Serb and Croat neighbors only by religion. In the 1990s this ethnic marker became much more prominent because of the multilateral wars among Serbs, Croats, and Bosnians. Of course, "Bosnian" has acquired a more salient political content since the declaration of political independence in 1991. The Yugoslav government introduced a category called "ethnic Muslims" in the 1961 census. In 1964, a Sarajevo (Bosnia) journal, *Pregled*, asserted, "The overwhelming majority of the Bosnian-Hercegovinian Moslems have made clear their feeling of belonging to the Moslem community as an ethnic, and not religious, group." Quoted in Paul Shoup, *Communism and the Yugoslav National Question* (New York: Columbia University Press, 1968), 216.

religion from Hindus as a people, and anyone who practices Judaism is considered to be ethnically Jewish. The Amish, who are defined by their religious practices, nevertheless fit most definitions of ethnicity very well. They began as a sect in a universal religion, but "tribalized" their religion and became "closed communities in which membership is acquired only by birth."

In the middle of the spectrum of relationships between religion and ethnicity are peoples closely associated with a particular religion but who admit to membership people of other religions. Most Slovaks are Catholic, although there are Lutheran Slovaks who are regarded as no less Slovak than the Catholics. Today, almost all Poles are Catholic, and Polish nationalists have insisted that *"Polak to jest Katolik"* [a Pole is a Catholic] – although this was not always true in the past and there are still some Polish Protestants. Religion and ethnicity can be used to buttress each other in other ways. After World War II, Mennonite, Lutheran, and Catholic advocates rallied Soviet ethnic Germans to both church and nation after the Stalinist regime deported Germans from the German Autonomous Soviet Socialist Republic in 1941.[13]

Many European peoples came to be identified with a particular religion after their national identity was fairly well established. In other cases, certainly the Jews, the religion was already present when the people became a nation: "The people and the religion have grown together, the religion not only proclaiming beliefs and dictating behaviour which the people adopt, but imposing these very beliefs specifically on that particular people as its vocation, life-giving purpose and guarantee of existence."[14] As we discussed earlier, "Jewish" became an unclear category after religion and ethnicity became distinct categories and were separated.

At the other end of the spectrum from tribal religions are the universal religions, Christianity and Islam, which are not confined to any ethnic group, race, nation, or state. In fact, "certainly Christianity, at least as understood by Paul, exists in tension with nationality."[15] Unlike Judaism and Hinduism, Christianity and Islam actively seek new adherents among all peoples and have used force to bring into the fold those who do not yet accept the faith. However, universal religions sometimes become very closely identified with ethnic or national entities. Some states mandate a particular religion as a prerequisite to citizenship. To be a Saudi one must be a Muslim. In other instances, there is no formal relationship between ethnicity and religion, but it is assumed by members of the group as well as those outside it. The adherents of national

---

[13] D. V. Grigoiev, *Etnopoliticheskie protsessy v nemetskoi obshchine Respubliki Bashkortostan* (Ufa: RIO BashGU, 2005), 127.
[14] R. J. Zwi Werblowsky, *Beyond Tradition and Modernity* (London: Athlone Press, 1976), 49.
[15] Steven Grosby, "Nationality and Religion," in Montserrat Guibernau and John Hutchinson, eds., *Understanding Nationalism* (Cambridge: Polity, 2001), 107.

Christian churches, such as the Serbian, Greek. or Bulgarian Orthodox, are, respectively, Serbs, Greeks, and Bulgarians almost exclusively.[16] Conversely, if one is Polish,[17] Spanish,[18] Italian, Mexican, or Argentinian, one is assumed to be at least nominally Catholic. Finally, there are states with official religions but whose populations are highly secular. Although few attend church services in Denmark and Sweden where Lutheranism is the official religion, if pressed Danes and Swedes will identify with Christian, specifically Lutheran, customs and values, considering them part of the national culture.[19] Uzbeks, Tajiks, Turkmen, Kirghiz, and Kazakhs are routinely described as Muslims, although because of Soviet influence, many, including the leaders of their now independent states, rejected religion. Complementing this situation are instances where religion expresses national identity or provides a substitute for it. The Church of England "rarely hesitated to claim that it embodied the Englishness of English Religion."[20] In the early twentieth century "in the absence of a nationalist party, religion gave rise to a form of surrogate nationalism in Scotland as well as Wales."[21]

On the other hand, to say one is Canadian or American, or even German, Hungarian, or Dutch, does not evoke a religious identity, because in these countries there are either many religions to which citizens adhere or there are at least two dominant religions, and ethnicity does not coincide exclusively with any one religion.[22]

By contrast, among Hebrews/Israelites/Jews, religion and ethnicity were fused. In biblical accounts, ancient Near Eastern peoples are identified by three markers: ancestry – there is a mythical "father" of most, but not all, peoples; territory; and specific gods. Language or political systems do not stand out as

---

[16] "A Serbian orthodox priest living in London told me that he would have to have very compelling reasons indeed before he would baptize a non-Serb into the Serbian orthodox church." Stella Alexander, "Religion and National Identity in Yugoslavia," in Stuart Mews, ed., *Religion and National Identity* (Oxford: Blackwell, 1982), 592.

[17] Zdislaw Mach suggests that Catholicism is so salient in Polish national consciousness because Poles have fought for independence against peoples whose religions differ from theirs (Turks, Mongols, Russians, Swedes, and Germans). This is not true of the Habsburgs, one of the three empires that carved Poland up beginning in 1772. *Symbols, Conflict, and Identity* (Albany: SUNY Press, 1993), 147.

[18] A kind of national Catholicism emerged in medieval Spain. During the Spanish civil war those who sided with Francisco Franco often emphasized that "Spain is essentially identical with the Christian religion.... Therefore, between the Spanish nation and Catholicism there exists a profound and essential identity." Manuel Garcia Morente, quoted in Frances Lannon, "Modern Spain and a National Catholicism," in Mews, *Religion and National Identity*, 587.

[19] Philip Zuckerman, *Society without God* (New York: New York University Press, 2008).

[20] Keith Robbins, "Religion and Identity in Modern British History," in Mews, *Religion and National Identity*, 468.

[21] D.W. Bebbington, "National Feeling in Wales and Scotland," in ibid., 503.

[22] Of course, there have been attempts to identify the United States, for example, as a "Christian country," a statement made by a religious leader that aroused some discussion during the 2000 presidential campaign. Controversy over whether the United States is a Christian country, in any but a demographic sense, goes back to the founding of the republic.

markers of identity. Thus, in Genesis 15, God promises a land to Abraham, the founder of a religion and a nation simultaneously. Here one finds four elements: a religion, a common ancestor ("children of Abraham," later the "children of Israel"), a nation, and a specific territory. Similarly, Edomites, Moabites, Ammonites, Amalekites, Egyptians, and the Philistines are identified by "religious" markers. The Bible imputes specific ancestry to some of them, and each seems to have its own religion.

Religions became identified not only with a people but also with a state when a ruler adopted a religion and made it mandatory for his subjects. When Emperor Constantine adopted Christianity in the fourth century CE, the entire Roman Empire was at least nominally Christianized. Other examples are King Bulan of the Khazars adopting Judaism in the eighth or ninth century,[23] Vladimir in Kiev adopting Greek Orthodoxy, and Mieszko in Poland adopting Catholicism in the tenth century.[24]

A tribal religion does not guarantee the survival of an ethnic group because it must be disseminated beyond an elite, adapt, and have meaning in new conditions.[25] Over time, religions that offered personal salvation began to gain ascendance over those based on what we call ethnicity. This is analogous to what happened in former communist states: once the old (secular) religion crumbled, having been perceived as irrelevant mumbo-jumbo, states fell apart because that "secular religion" was what kept them together. Alternatives that arose were either personalistic salvation religions, such as evangelical Christianity, Islam, and a variety of cults,[26] or secular collectivist, salvationist nationalism, the functional equivalent of religion.[27]

Public rites and liturgies blur the line between ethnicity and religion and create a sense of community that fuses the two. Religious taboos, such as intermarriage and food taboos, and commonly observed rituals reinforce ethnicity because they strengthen the boundaries necessary for the existence of an ethnic group.[28] Religious salvation and ethnic destiny are sometimes joined. After Poland lost its sovereignty, Polish romantic literature of the nineteenth century used the imagery of the "Christ among nations" to explain both Poland's martyrdom and its eventual resurrection and mission to the world. In the nineteenth and twentieth centuries, American evangelicals believed "that every nation has

---

[23] He adopted Judaism after considering Islam and Christianity. Whether Judaism was imposed on all his subjects or on just the elite is a matter of scholarly controversy. See D. M. Dunlop, *The History of the Jewish Khazars* (Princeton: Princeton University Press, 1954).
[24] Some argue that, although the leaders of the Khazars followed the ruler in accepting Judaism, the masses did not. Similarly, pagan religious practices often persist – for example, in Siberia, the United States, or Africa – after they have been supposedly superseded by other religions. Sometimes, as in the Christmas tree, they are incorporated into the new religion.
[25] Anthony D. Smith, *The Ethnic Origins of Nations* (Oxford: Blackwell, 1986), 121.
[26] In Ukraine charismatic figures founded cults. In Russia Hare Krishna and Aum Shinrikyo, a notorious Japanese cult, seemed for a time to have many followers.
[27] Carleton J. H. Hayes, *Nationalism: A Religion* (New York: Macmillan, 1960).
[28] Fredrik Barth, *Ethnic Groups and Boundaries* (Boston: Little Brown, 1969).

a particular role to play in God's scheme of things, and that the role assigned to America is something quite special and distinct from that assigned to other nations."[29] The Jewish tradition imputes a religious meaning to the liberation from Egyptian bondage that might otherwise be seen as a national struggle for liberation or as a revolt of slaves. In sum, religion, like ethnicity, provides a sense of belonging to a protective and supportive group, satisfies what seems to be a widespread spiritual longing, and provides another binding tie for the community.

Long after universalistic Christianity was imposed on an ethnically diverse empire, religion and ethnicity were decoupled in modern times when democracy made all citizens equal irrespective of creed. This destroyed the traditional hierarchy where one religion was the state religion and the others were "tolerated," at best, as with Joseph II's Toleration Edict in Austria. The separation of church and state extended this decoupling so that the state is no longer fused with religion. Furthermore, modern liberalism went beyond individual rights to promote group recognition and rights. Unlike the Ottoman Empire, which organized its subjects in a millet system of religious groupings, states began to recognize not only religious but also linguistic and territorial groups (i.e., ethnic groups). The granting of collective or group rights is still much discussed in many multiethnic societies such as India, Israel, Canada, the United States, and Russia and in social science literature.[30]

Another impetus to the disaggregation of ethnicity and religion is some people's tendency to seek personal salvation in religion, not just communal affirmation. The two need not contradict each other and are often complementary, but those who find their spiritual needs satisfied in an intensely personalistic religion may not feel a need for ethnic affiliation or may see their primary community as a religious group that has no ethnic coloration.

Finally, religious belief and affiliation are eroded by secularization, a process that gained force several centuries ago in Europe and has spread in a much more limited way to other parts of the world. Many Europeans consider religion unimportant, as church attendance figures and opinion surveys attest. The answer to "who am I?" is less and less likely to be in religious terms, and ethnicity often supersedes religious identification. Around 1917 most Central Asians and most Middle Easterners would have given "Muslim" or the name of a clan as the first response to that question. By the 1940s or 1950s that answer had changed to Tajik, Uzbek, Turkmen, Syrian, or Iraqi. The growth of individualism and relativism, the decline of universal ideologies and normative institutions, and the rise of consumerism are other developments that have weakened the power of religion.

---

[29] Richard Carwardine, "The Know-Nothing Party, the Protestant Evangelical Community and American National Identity," in Mews, *Religion and National Identity*, 450.
[30] One of the more prolific writers on the subject is Will Kymlicka. See, especially, his works: *The Rights of Minority Cultures* (New York: Oxford University Press, 1995); *Multicultural Citizenship* (New York: Oxford University Press, 1995); and *Ethnicity and Group Rights* (New York: New York University Press, 1997).

Judaism and Jewishness

Chapter 2 examined some of the consequences of secularization for Jews and Jewish identity and the responses to the challenges and opportunities of emancipation. Some argued that Jews were a religious group only and that their ethnicity should be coterminous with their newfound citizenship in the modern state. Others, especially those who were subjects more than citizens, insisted that Jews were an ethnic group with its own culture that has national aspirations, whether political or cultural autonomy or statehood. What that culture was and what should be its language were matters of great debate.

Judaism and Jewishness in Russia/USSR/Russia

As noted in Chapter 3, the tsarist regime regarded Jews primarily as a religious group. The implication was that if Jews became Orthodox Christians they could become Russians. By the late nineteenth century, however, anti-Semites were denying that conversion to Christianity "changed" the Jew. As in Western Europe, racial considerations began to drive anti-Semitism, even though theological anti-Semitism remained strong. The tsars' Soviet successors reversed the emphasis on religion, but in their own way accepted the "change to blood" when they classified Jews as a nationality, despite their strenuous denials since 1903 that Jews constituted a nation.[31] The Bolsheviks assumed that *natsional'nost'* or ethnicity was biologically inherited, but they never accepted the invidious distinctions that "race science" in Europe had made. For them, neither language, culture, area of residence, subjective identification, nor religion determined *natsional'nost'*. In Soviet theory and practice religion was irrelevant. A Jew could become Russian Orthodox in religion but never Russian by ethnicity (unless one of his or her parents was Russian – then "Russian" could be chosen as one's registered nationality). A Jewish atheist represented no contradiction because religion and ethnicity had nothing to do with each other. Thus, to be a Jew in the Soviet Union and its successor states is to be a member of an ethnic group (nationality), with no implications for religious affiliation or lack thereof.

This total separation of religion and Jewish ethnicity was unprecedented, but has been largely accepted by Russian and Ukrainian Jews. This separation is difficult for most European, American, and even Israeli Jews to understand, and it is what makes FSU Jewry different from much of the rest of world Jewry.[32]

---

[31] Basing himself on Karl Kautsky, Lenin ruled, "The Jews have ceased to be a nation, for a nation without a territory is unthinkable." He pointed out that "modern scientific investigation" had demonstrated that Jews are not a "race." Lenin criticized the Zionist idea that Jews are a nation because it would impede Jews' participation in the class struggle: "The idea of a Jewish nationality runs counter to the interests of the Jewish proletariat, for it fosters among them, directly or indirectly, a spirit hostile to assimilation, the spirit of the 'ghetto.'" *Iskra*, 51, October 22, 1903.

[32] "For most Anglophones and especially for most Americans today, expressions such as 'Jewish Christian,' 'Jewish convert," or 'baptized Jew' are contradictions in terms: a Jew who converts to Christianity is usually perceived at once as ceasing to be a Jew (though such a person can

Against this background this chapter examines the nature of religious belief and affiliation among Jews in Russia and Ukraine in the 1990s. It focuses on the levels and nature of religious belief among Jews and the connections they see between Jewish ethnicity and Jewish religion. This analysis can help measure the impact of seven decades of Soviet socialization to atheism and assess how Jews in the FSU attempt to reconstruct their own identities and Jewish communities. Are these identities and communities likely to be completely secular, or will Judaism be revived in some form and incorporated into evolving identities and communities? To what extent will Russian and Ukrainian Jews' conceptions of Jewishness conform to those held by other Jews?

Soviet Atheism and Institutional Religion

Karl Marx's famous postulate that "religion is the opiate of the masses" is the ideological basis of the antireligious animus of socialist movements. Socialists saw religion as an integral part of the capitalist system, used by capitalists to divert workers' attention from their miserable condition and to delay their uprising against the bosses. It followed that the struggle against capitalism necessitated a battle against religion. However, the degree of antireligious militancy varied among socialist movements and communist regimes. The variation is explained by the degree to which religions were part of the presocialist state structures, the strength of religious commitment among the people, and perhaps attitudes toward religion held by leaders of the regimes. In the Russian Empire, the Orthodox Church was an integral part of a system that did not separate church and state. As Minister of Education Count S. S. Uvarov put it in 1832, the "best guarantees of Russia's strength and greatness" were the "conservative principles of Orthodoxy, autocracy and [Russian] nationality."[33] Little wonder, then, that the Bolsheviks thought it necessary to destroy religion as part of their struggle against the *ancien regime*.[34]

The Bolsheviks' attack on all religions and their institutions was particularly strong in the mid-1920s, and again in 1929–39 and 1957–64.[35] At other times, the party and state maintained an official antireligious posture, which

---

be 'of Jewish origin'). In Russian, these phrases are differently valenced. All the common terms for 'Jew,' both the neutral *evrei* and the derogatory *zhid*, refer to nationality, ethnicity, or race, rather than religion.... For a Russophone, a person can as easily be a 'Jewish Christian,' as a 'Polish Catholic,' or a 'Black Baptist.'" Gabriella Safran, *Rewriting the Jew: Assimilation Narratives in the Russian Empire* (Stanford: Stanford University Press, 2000), 148.

[33] Quoted in Michael Florinsky, *Russia: A History and an Interpretation*, Vol. II (New York: Macmillan, 1961), 797.

[34] The following section draws on Zvi Gitelman, Valery Chervyakov, and Vladimir Shapiro, "Religion and Ethnicity: Judaism in the Ethnic Consciousness of Contemporary Russian Jews," *Ethnic and Racial Studies* 20, 2 (April 1997) 280–305.

[35] Documents on the suppression of religion are found in Boleslaw Szczesniak, ed., *The Russian Revolution and Religion* (Notre Dame: University of Notre Dame Press, 1959).

eased during World War II, but campaigns against religion were milder and routinized, much as religious ritual often becomes. The Soviet constitution guaranteed both freedom of religion and freedom of antireligious propaganda, but prohibited teaching religion to anyone under age 18. Because the state promoted and funded antireligious propaganda and because the crucial period for religious socialization is childhood, the system was effectively inimical to religious interests. The Soviet state invested untold sums in antireligious agitation and propaganda; the number of antireligious books, pamphlets, magazines, and placards produced probably ran into the millions. Religious practices were ridiculed and even "put on trial."[36] The authorities created organizations of militant atheists, such as the League of the Godless. School curricula promoted antireligious teachings. Even at institutions of higher learning courses in atheism were required of all students, whatever their field of study.[37] Nevertheless, "atheism never achieved its goal of 'educating conscious militant atheists....' Instead of being a real conviction, atheism was a formality, 'an element of communist pseudoreligion.'" This explains the sharp decline in the proportion of people calling themselves atheists after 1991.[38]

Although Judaism was certainly not part of the tsarist establishment, it was still attacked after the Revolution. The Bolsheviks could hardly tolerate the religion of a minority, Judaism, while attacking Christianity, the religion of the majority. Among Jews before the Revolution there were antireligious elements, notably the Bund, a Marxist socialist movement that was usually careful to attack the clergy rather than religion itself. When the Bolsheviks dissolved the Bund in 1921, some of its leaders joined the Communist Party and became active in its Jewish Sections, or *Evsektsii*. They brought with them the Bundist hostility to religion, but now had a license from the state and party to pursue an atheist line enforced by state power. The Jewish communists, very few in number before 1919, realized that religion still exerted a powerful hold "on the Jewish street" and were determined to establish a monopoly of power there. They threw themselves enthusiastically into the antireligious campaigns of the early 1920s, hoping to prove that though they were latecomers to Bolshevism, they were as committed to the cause as others. By the mid-1920s, more than 600 synagogues were closed, Jewish religious schools were abolished, and most clergy were forced to take up other vocations and deprived of civic rights.

---

[36] Jewish holidays, *hadorim* (religious primary schools), and rituals such as circumcision or keeping kosher were subjected to "public trials" and crude satire. See Zvi Gitelman, *Jewish Nationality and Soviet Politics* (Princeton: Princeton University Press, 1972) ch. 3; Anna Shternshis, *Soviet and Kosher: Jewish Popular Culture in the Soviet Union, 1923–1939* (Bloomington, IN: Indiana University Press, 2006).

[37] A concise but comprehensive overview of Soviet measures to promote atheism, with an overview of types of atheism, is by Robert Triomphe, "Aspects de l'Atheisme Sovietique Officiel," Centre de Recherches sur L'U.R.S.S. et les Pays de L'Est, *Annuaire de L'U.R.S.S. 1965* (Paris: Editions du Centre National de la Recherche Scientifique), 5–88.

[38] Kimmo Kaariainen, *Religion in Russia after the Collapse of Communism* (Lewiston, NY: Edward Mellen Press, 1998), 60, 62.

In the 1930s, many were arrested and deported.[39] In that decade, too, the League of Militant Atheists pressed atheism as policy across a broad front. Higher educational institutions were purged of believers in 1929, and by 1931 there were eighty-four "atheist universities." By 1930, 800 million pages of antireligious propaganda had been printed.[40]

A study of Russian Orthodoxy and Catholicism in ten postcommunist societies tried to ascertain whether processes of modernization-cum-secularization account for the decline in religious belief, church membership, and religious practices or whether this decline was caused by seven decades of atheistic socialization. Using mass surveys from the early 1990s, the researchers concluded that secular (sic) trends probably explain more of the decline in religion than communist propaganda in Catholic countries, but that state atheism might have been more effective in Orthodox societies.[41]

Indeed, urbanization and education probably did more to weaken religions than government campaigns.[42] As Jews streamed out of the ruined and impoverished *shtetlakh* and sought education and employment in the larger cities of the old Pale of Settlement and the expanding industrial centers of Russia, they abandoned their old ways of life. They gave up Yiddish for Russian, no longer practiced Jewish customs and traditions, abandoned religion, adopted new foods and clothing styles, and increasingly married non-Jews. By 1939, about 87 percent of the Jews were urban dwellers, of whom 46 percent lived in cities with more than a half-million inhabitants. Some 55 percent declared Russian as their mother tongue, up from 26 percent in 1926.[43] In the aborted 1937 census, 53 percent of the Soviet population over 16 years old identified themselves as religious, compared to only 17 percent of Jews. In Leningrad oblast' in 1937 there were 846 working churches and more than 2,000 priests. Nearly 133,000 people had attended morning services at Easter 1934, and over 30,000 were young people.[44] But "[i]n the late 1930s self-identification as religious was 3–4 times less among Jews than among Christians and Moslems. This...may

---

[39] See Zvi Gitelman, *Jewish Nationality and Soviet Politics*, 298–317.
[40] Philip Walters, "A Survey of Soviet Religious Policy," in Sabrina Petra Ramet, ed., *Religious Policy in the Soviet Union* (Cambridge: Cambridge University Press, 1993).
[41] In both kinds of societies church attendance levels cannot be accounted for either by modernization or the effects of state atheism. Ariana Need and Geoffrey Evans, "Analysing Patterns of Religious Participation in Post-Communist Eastern Europe," *British Journal of Sociology* 52, 2 (June 2001), 229–48.
[42] Of course, the generations that had matured before the Revolution sometimes combined Jewish and Soviet practices, but their descendants observed fewer Jewish rituals and customs. See, for example, a study of Jews in the Vitebsk area by Arkadii Zel'tser, *Evrei sovetskoi provintsii: Vitebsk i mestechki 1917–1941* (Moscow: Rosspen, 2006). Zel'tser also believes that urbanization and industrialization spurred secularization more than Soviet campaigns against religion (266).
[43] Mordechai Altshuler, ed., *Distribution of the Jewish Population of the USSR 1939* (Jerusalem: Centre for Research and Documentation of East European Jewry, 1993), 5.
[44] Sarah Davies, *Popular Opinion in Stalin's Russia* (Cambridge: Cambridge University Press, 1997), 74–75.

be a direct result of the fact that Jews were urban-dwellers, with a large proportion of them living in big cities."[45] Moreover, three-quarters of those Jews who identified themselves as religious were over 50 years old. Only 2 to 3 percent of the 16–29 year olds identified themselves as religious.[46] Thus, by the 1930s religion seemed to be dying among Soviet Jews.

During the campaigns against religion in 1957–64 initiated by First Secretary of the Soviet Communist Party Nikita Khrushchev, many synagogues were closed, leaving fewer than 100 operating by the 1970s.[47] Except for a token yeshiva in Moscow, which operated sporadically, there were no Jewish religious schools of any kind anywhere in the USSR. The prerevolutionary generation that had some knowledge of Judaism was nearly gone. Only the few religious people among the *Zapadniki*, those from the Western periphery of the country (the Baltic states, areas formerly in eastern Poland, and Bessarabia/Bukovina) who had become Soviet citizens in 1939–40, could transmit knowledge of Judaism, a high-risk enterprise. In Central Asia and Georgia there were proportionally more Jews who observed the traditions, but most were not religiously well educated. By the 1980s, one of the strongest religious taboos, marriage with non-Jews, was being violated by more than half the Jewish population. It could be expected that religious belief and practice would be exceedingly rare, especially among the European (Ashkenazi) Jews.

Yet Soviet campaigns against religion did not succeed in eliminating belief: militant atheism succeeded more in destroying *knowledge of religion* than in eliminating *faith*.[48] There is some survey evidence that as people grew disenchanted with Marxism-Leninism in the 1980s, there was a parallel rise in professed belief in God, although only about one in five declared such belief or were uncertain about it.[49] By the time the USSR broke apart in 1991, 45 percent of ethnic Russians said they believed in God, and by 1998, 60 percent did so.[50] A 1990 survey of the general population in four large Russian regions found 30 percent affirming a belief in God and 16 percent declaring themselves "convinced" atheists.[51] Other surveys of the late 1990s and 2000 found up to

---

[45] Mordechai Altshuler, "Religion in the Soviet Union in the Late 1930s in the Light of Statistics," *Jews and Jewish Topics in the Soviet Union and Eastern Europe* 1, 14 (Spring 1991), 25.
[46] Ibid., 26.
[47] According to the (Soviet) Council for Religious Affairs, the number of registered synagogues fell from 135 in 1958 to 92 in 1964. Felix Corley, "Judaism in the Former Soviet Union: Three Snapshots," *East European Jewish Affairs* 52, 1 (1995), 77.
[48] For a useful survey of the Soviet state's policy toward religion, see Philip Walters in Ramet, *Religious Policy in the Soviet Union*, 14.
[49] Yuri Arutiunian, "Changing Values of Russians from Brezhnev to Gorbachev," *Journal of Soviet Nationalities* 11, 2 (Summer 1991), 12. The data are from surveys in 1988 in six Soviet cities.
[50] VTsIOM survey cited in Andrew Greeley, *Religion in Europe at the End of the Second Millennium* (New Brunswick, NJ: Transaction, 2003), 108.
[51] L. Byzov and S. Filatov, "Religia i politika v obshchestvennom soznanii sovetskogo naroda," in S. B. Filatov and D. E. Furman, eds., *Religiia i demokratiia* (Moscow: Progress, 1993), 12.

TABLE 5.1. *Religious Distribution in Russian Federation (percent of the population)*

	1991	1993	1996	1999	2002
Believers	22	32	34	40	44
Unsure	28	28	30	30	29
Unbelievers	7	30	24	22	20
Atheists	35	5	6	5	5
Don't know	7	4	6	2	2

Source: Dmitri Furman and Kimmo Kaariainen, "Religioznaya stabilizatsiia: otnosheniya k religii v sovremennoi Rossii, *Svobodnaya Mysl*, 7, 1533 (2003), 25, cited in James Warhola and Alex Lehning, "Political Order, Identity, and Security in Multinational, Multi-religious Russia," *Nationalities Papers* 35, 5 (November 2007), 934.

60 percent of Russians claiming to be believers, but very few went to church regularly or observed religious rituals.[52] In three surveys between 1991 and 1998, the period of our own surveys, between 21 and 24 percent of respondents said they had not believed in God during the Soviet period but did so "now." "In other words, at least one-fifth of all Russians (or one-third of former atheists) have abandoned atheism since the collapse of communism. This proportion is higher than in any other formerly communist Eastern European country."[53] Although survey results vary widely and are not to be taken too literally, Table 5.1 shows the results of reliable surveys of religiosity in Russia that have tracked the increase in belief, based on national samples. It finds a precipitous drop in the number of self-proclaimed "atheists," a widely used and politically correct term in Soviet times, and a doubling in eleven years of the proportion of self-described believers, a post-Soviet politically correct term.

Whatever the meaning of these figures, all agree that, for historical and political reasons, in the FSU there is enormous ignorance of the tenets and practices of all faiths. This has led to confusion of doctrines, beliefs, and symbols. Religious instruction is available, many more clergy are being trained, and religious publications and media programs are quite common, but it will take years to overcome the ignorance created by the Soviets.

Empirical data support this conclusion. Shortly after the fall of communism, a national survey in Russia found 47 percent of the population describing themselves as "Orthodox," but only 10 percent said they attended church services and only 2 to 3 percent prayed regularly and claimed to "strive to live up to the standards of Christian morality in their everyday lives." Only about half those who identified as "believers" said they firmly believed Jesus had existed; nearly 30 percent rated religion as "not very important" or completely

[52] Kimmo Kaariainen and Dmitri Furman, eds., *Starye tserkvi novye veruiushchie* (Moscow-St. Petersburg, Letnii Sad, 2000), 15, 21–24.
[53] Alexey Krindatch, "Patterns of Religious Change in Postsoviet Russia: Major Trends from 1998 to 2003," *Religion State and Society* 32, 2 (June 2004), 127.

unimportant" in their lives.⁵⁴ A 2002 survey by VTSiOM, a leading public opinion polling organization, found two-thirds of the population of the Russian Federation claimed adherence to a religious confession, 58 percent said they were Orthodox believers, and about 31 percent described themselves as atheists. Yet "[o]f those who said that they believe in God, 60 percent said that they had never read any biblical text. Of those who claimed to be Orthodox believers, 42 percent said that they had never been in an Orthodox church, while another 31 percent said that they went to church 'not more than once a year.'"⁵⁵ In a 2005 survey, nearly half the respondents who identified themselves as believers said they never attended church services or did so, on average, less than once a year; 69 percent had never taken communion or had done so years earlier.⁵⁶

Thus, religious affiliation is largely nominal, perhaps a means of identifying more with a people and a culture than of expressing theological conviction. A churchman noted that nominal Orthodoxy was "not piety but a means of national self-identification."⁵⁷ Indeed, in the postcommunist period the Russian Orthodox Church (ROC) has pushed hard to be closely identified with Russian ethnicity. In 1997, a law was passed that prevented the registration, and therefore property acquisition, of any but the four "traditional" religions in Russia: Orthodoxy, Buddhism, Islam, and Judaism. Metropolitan Kirill, chairman of the Moscow Patriarchate's Department of External Church Relations, asserted that every ethnic Russian is "Orthodox by birth." Therefore, any attempt by other Christian or non-Christian groups to proselytize among Russians should be viewed as a criminal act.⁵⁸ When the Vatican raised four administrative areas in Russia to the level of an archdiocese, the late Patriarch Aleksei II issued a strong condemnation⁵⁹; he also vigorously opposed the Pope's visit to neighboring Ukraine. Catholic priests have been denied visas to Russia.

Russian Orthodoxy has come to be closely identified with the Russian Federation. The ROC has demanded that religious instruction be given in state

---

54 Dmitri Furman and Kimmo Kaariainen, *Religioznost' v Rossii: v 90-e gody XX-nachale XXI veka* (Moscow: Institut Evropy, Ogin TD, 2006), 53.
55 RFE/RL, Newsline, Part I, August 27, 2002.
56 Furman and Kaariainen, *Religioznost' v Rossii*, 56. The authors conducted surveys at four points in the 1990s and then in 2002 and 2005. They included 1,600–2,000 respondents but no information is given on their regional or demographic distribution.
57 Abbot Innokenty (Pavlov), "The Recent Past and the Possible Future," *Segodnya*, May 7, 1994, transl. in *Current Digest of the Soviet Press* XLVI, 18 (June 1, 1994), 10–11.
58 Aleksandr Soldatov, "God Forbid!" *Moskovskiye novosti*, December 18–24, 2001, 1, 21, transl. in *Current Digest of the Post-Soviet Press* 53, 50 (January 9, 2002), 15–16. On the relationship of Russian Orthodoxy and Russian identity, see Natalia Dinello, "Religion and National Identity of Russians," in William Swatos, ed., *Politics and Religion in Central and Eastern Europe* (Westport, CT: Praeger, 1994), 83–104; and Dmitri Pospielovsky, "Some Remarks on the Contemporary Russian Nationalism and Religious Revival," *Canadian Review of Studies in Nationalism* XI, 1 (Spring 1984), 71–102.
59 Aleksandr Korolyov, "Vatican Hurls Challenge to Eastern Orthodoxy," *Trud*, February 14, 2002, transl. in *Current Digest of the Post-Soviet Press* 54, 7 (March 13, 2002), 5.

schools and the media be subject to church censorship, though neither of these demands were instituted.[60] Both Boris Yeltsin and Vladimir Putin endorsed religious belief and practice, though both had been Soviet officials and Communist Party members. They allocated large sums to the reconstruction of churches and other religious activities. Russian Orthodoxy has come to be closely identified with the Russian Federation. By 2005, 54 percent of respondents in a national survey rated the Russian Orthodox religion as "very good" and another 41 percent as "good." Corresponding percentages were 41 percent for Catholicism, 38 percent for Judaism, and 25 percent for Baptists. More than 70 percent said they "completely" or "mostly" trusted the Russian Orthodox Church, and 84 percent of all respondents, regardless of their attitudes toward religion, agreed that "Russians are Orthodox in their souls."[61] Thus, like the Serbian, Bulgarian, Greek, and other Orthodox churches in their respective countries, the ROC is perceived as being an integral part of Russian *national* identity.

The religious scene in Ukraine is more complicated. The Orthodox Church is split between those affiliated with the Moscow patriarchate and a Kiev patriarchate. In addition, the Greek Catholic (Uniate) church, which follows an Orthodox ritual but maintains allegiance to the Pope, is strong in West Ukraine. In national surveys taken in 1994–98, about one-third of the respondents said they were not members of any church, between 26 and 34 percent said they identified with the Moscow Patriarchate, and fewer than 10 percent identified with another church. More than 60 percent said they either completely trusted in God or were inclined to trust more than distrust God.[62] There was no linear trend in either church affiliation or in trust in God.

Religion and Ethnicity, Judaism and Jewishness

As we have seen, most Jews in the United States and the United Kingdom associate Jewishness with Judaism. Even avowed Jewish agnostics or atheists find it difficult to dissociate the two. Secular Jewish movements, such as the Bund, territorialists, and Yiddishists, have all but disappeared,[63] although in

---

[60] In 2003 the Russian Ministry of Education permitted religious education on school grounds outside the regular curriculum. It could take place only with the consent of the children and at the request of their parents. Yelena Yakovleva, "Religious Organizations Receive Access to Secular Schools," *Rossiiskaya gazeta*, August 13, 2003, 1, transl. in *Current Digest of the Post-Soviet Press* 55, 32 (September 10, 2003), 14.

[61] Furman and Kaariainen, *Religioznost' v Rossii*, 41. According to the authors, "Russian" and "Orthodox" are becoming synonymous – as they were in prerevolutionary times.

[62] N. Panina and E. Golovokha, *Tendencies in the Development of Ukrainian Society (1994–1998): Sociological Indicators* (Kyiv: Institute of Sociology, Ukrainian Academy of Sciences, 1999), 95.

[63] The reasons for this are discussed in Zvi Gitelman, "A Century of Jewish Politics in Eastern Europe," in Gitelman, ed., *The Emergence of Modern Jewish Politics: Zionism and Bundism in Eastern Europe* (Pittsburgh: University of Pittsburgh Press, 2003), 3–19. Reasons for the demise of the Bund in several countries are explored in David Slucki, "The Jewish Labor Bund after

Judaism and Jewishness

recent years an international secular humanist movement has attracted some Jews. Some analysts claim there is a significant and growing proportion of American Jews who are in some way "secular," though what that means is not at all clear.[64] In Israel, the only Jewish state in the world, Jews can base their Jewish identity (often assumed to be the equivalent of Israeli identity) on territory, language, and citizenship in an ethnically defined state.[65] Certainly, most of the founders of Israel were secular and even antireligious Jews. Yet Israeli civic culture draws heavily on Judaism,[66] and it has proved impossible to eliminate Judaism from public life – and not just because of the political power wielded by the Orthodox minority, as is often asserted. In surveys conducted among Israelis in the 1990s, 60 percent of respondents said they "firmly believe in the existence of God or a supreme power that guides the world. Even among the nonobservant, one fifth hold these beliefs."[67] Belief in a deity is not the same as adherence to Judaism, but nearly 40 percent of the respondents defined themselves as "strictly observant" of Judaism (14%) or "observant to a great extent" (24%). Another 41 percent described themselves as "somewhat observant," leaving only 21 percent claiming to be "totally

---

the Holocaust: A Comparative History," unpublished PhD dissertation, Monash University (Australia), 2010.

[64] According to the American Jewish Identity Survey of 2001, "more than 40% of America's Jewish adults (who identify as Jewish-by-religion) describe their outlook as 'secular' or 'somewhat secular.' That figure increases significantly when the ... Jewish population [is] defined to include those who see themselves as having no religion but describe themselves as being of Jewish parentage or Jewish upbringing." Egon Mayer, Barry Kosmin, and Ariela Keysar, *American Jewish Identity Survey 2001* (New York: Graduate Center of the City University of New York), 37. Yet, the same survey found that about 17 percent of the "core" Jewish population "hold beliefs that can be described as atheist or agnostic" (40). In addition, "just [sic] 53% [of the "secular"] agree (strongly or somewhat) with the proposition about God's existence [i.e., that God exists]. Of all who agreed (strongly or somewhat) with the proposition: *God exists*, just 19% described their outlook as secular and 14% as somewhat secular" (41). Thus, "secular" and "atheist" or "agnostic" do not seem to mean the same things. To say, then, that 40 percent of Jews have a secular outlook does not mean they do not believe in God. In fact, it is not at all clear what secular means either to the researchers or certainly to the respondents. Given that the information was gathered in a seven-minute telephone interview (14), it is not surprising that the meaning of "secular" could not be explored.

[65] There is much discussion about Israel as an "ethnic democracy," which, like Estonia, Slovakia, Latvia, and Malaysia, favors one ethnic group and yet manages to maintain a democratic political order. See, for example, Sammy Smooha, "Minority Status in an Ethnic Democracy: The Status of the Arab Minority in Israel," *Ethnic and Racial Studies* 13, 3 (July 1990), 389–414; Yoav Peled, "Ethnic Democracy and the Legal Construction of Citizenship: Arab Citizens of the Jewish State," *American Political Science Review* 86, 2 (June 1992), 432–443; Oren Yiftachel, "The Concept of 'Ethnic Democracy' and its Applicability to the Case of Israel," *Ethnic and Racial Studies* 15,1 (January 1992), 125–136.

[66] See Charles Liebman, *Civil Religion in Israel* (Berkeley: University of California Press, 1983). See also Boas Evron, *Jewish State or Israeli Nation* (Bloomington: Indiana University Press, 1995).

[67] Charles Liebman and Elihu Katz, eds., *The Jewishness of Israelis: Responses to the Guttman Report* (Albany: SUNY Press, 1997), 25.

non-observant."⁶⁸ Nearly four of five Israelis attend a Passover seder, although that observance can be construed as simply a festive meal with family and friends. Yet 70 percent always fast on Yom Kippur, an intensely personal, religious holiday that does not commemorate a historical event of national import, and they join in at least some of the prayers.⁶⁹ As Gershon Shaked observed, "Alongside a culture based on faith and mitzvah [commandment] observance, a Jewish culture has been created in Israel that is based on . . . tradition but is not a religious culture."⁷⁰

The key word is "tradition." Judaism is the source of the form and content of most Jewish traditions. Even when traditions are observed not out of religious conviction but to express communal solidarity, or out of nostalgia, or because they are esthetically pleasing or simply enjoyable, Judaism is invoked. This presents committed secularists with a problem: How can one "act Jewishly" without seeming to enact Judaism?

Religion after Communism

Postcommunist states dropped antireligious policies and allowed religious revivalists, many from outside the Former Soviet Union, to reconstruct religious institutions and undertake religious education. American evangelical Christians, Islamic teachers from the Middle East, and rabbis and other Judaic advocates have been able to reach out to "lost brothers and sisters" and bring them back into the fold. Yet, as noted, the Russian Orthodox Church, threatened by the need to compete in the marketplace of religious ideas and beliefs, succeeded in limiting the number of non-Orthodox churches that could operate legally in the Russian Federation. Uzbekistan's President Islam Karimov, fearful of Islamic fundamentalism, launched a vigorous campaign to rein in militant Islam. To discourage proselytism, foreign clergy are not given visas for longer than thirty days. An American military presence was welcomed in Uzbekistan in the fall of 2001 as part of a joint effort against the Taliban and Islamic militants, although Uzbek–American relations deteriorated significantly in 2006 and thereafter.

Soviet repression of Judaism had more far-reaching consequences for Jews than advocacy of militant atheism had for Orthodox Christians or Muslims. Because Judaic religious traditions are the means of preserving and transmitting the historical experience of a people that, for a long time, had no territorial or governmental basis for doing so, enforced atheism in effect tore people away from their historic and ethnic roots. This is why renewed interest in Jewishness should logically imply some interest in Judaism. National traditions, rituals, and customs grounded in Judaism cannot be ignored by those curious about

---

[68] Ibid., 1.
[69] Ibid., 11.
[70] Ibid., 159.

Judaism and Jewishness

their Jewish ethnicity – certainly not by those committed to infusing it with meaning and content.

Jewish religious entrepreneurs have been virtually unimpeded in their attempts to reach potential adherents.[71] By the late 1990s, about 40 full-time Jewish day schools and 120 Sunday schools had been established, many of them with a religious character. Synagogue buildings that had been sequestered by the Soviet state for other uses were returned to many newly formed Jewish communities. Religious articles, kosher food, matzo, and religious texts are freely available, whereas in the 1960s to 1980s they had to be smuggled into the USSR. Successive presidents of Russia and Ukraine have publicly embraced Jewish religious leaders and have appeared at Jewish holiday celebrations and synagogue dedications.

Yet, in the European FSU very few observe religious practices. Post-Soviet Jews do not use religious affiliation or forms to express their ethnicity or even religiosity. The modest religious revival is largely institutional and does not come from within, but is funded and promoted from without, largely by the right-wing Orthodox, especially the Hasidic Chabad-Lubavitch and Karlin-Stolin[72] groups, and by the Progressive (Reform) movement. Two movements more in the center of the Jewish religious spectrum, the Modern Orthodox and Conservative/Masorti, are largely absent from the scene. Although there are said to be seventy-five Reform congregations in the FSU, most are small and very few have rabbis.[73] There is no facility in the FSU for training Reform rabbis. A few natives of the FSU have returned after some rabbinical training at the Leo Baeck Progressive seminary in London, but in contrast to the Hasidim, as a Reform rabbi put it, "We don't have people that are prepared to go to some god-forsaken [sic!] place like Siberia."[74]

Nearly all the Orthodox rabbis are from the two Hasidic groups: Chabad-Lubavitch and Karlin-Stolin. Many are natives of the FSU who emigrated and received their rabbinical training in Israel and the United States. Unlike rabbis from other groups, they appear to be willing to stay in the FSU indefinitely.

---

[71] From time to time Russian authorities have denied visas to foreign-born rabbis and clergy of other faiths.

[72] Karlin, once an independent community alongside Pinsk in the Polesie region of what is today southern Belarus, was absorbed into Pinsk. Stolin is a town southeast of Pinsk, near the Ukrainian border. The rabbinic Hasidic dynasty of Stolin was established by Asher (1760–1828), son of "Aaron the Great," leader of the Karliner Hasidic dynasty.

[73] A Moscow woman born in 1922 told an interviewer why she could not take Reform Judaism seriously: "This is not real religion! I heard they can even have a woman rabbi, who can wear pants! This is not real Judaism. My parents would not have approved. No, they are for young people, but not for me." Anna Shternshis, "Kaddish in a Church: Perceptions of Orthodox Christianity among Moscow Elderly Jews in the Early Twenty-First Century," *Russian Review* 66 (April 2007), 285.

[74] Rabbi Arnold Hirsch of the UAHC in *Moment* magazine, quoted in the *Detroit Jewish News*, October 20, 2000. One would have thought that it is precisely to "God-forsaken" places that rabbis would want to go.

Chabad-Lubavitch[75] has been engaged in outreach to Jews all over the world for the last half-century or so. Although its headquarters are in Brooklyn, New York, it sees the FSU as its "home grounds" because the movement was founded in the eighteenth century in what is now Belarus, and its last leader, Menachem Mendel Schneerson (1902–94), was born in Ukraine.[76] Chabad-Lubavitch, at least some of whose adherents believe that Schneerson, the last "rebbe," is the messiah,[77] is very active in the FSU but does not collaborate with larger communal organizations nor does it cooperate with existing religious communities, a pattern it follows outside the FSU as well. Yet Chabad-Lubavitch has become the government's favored religious Jewish movement. When U.S. President George W. Bush visited Russia in May 2002, he "compressed a scheduled half-hour of Kremlin sight-seeing into a seven-minute blur," but extended a twenty-minute tour of St. Petersburg's Choral Synagogue by more than a half-hour. The *New York Times* commented, "The visit was... another in a string of honors that Mr. Putin accorded Russia's Lubavitcher Hasidim... [who have] all but assumed the mantle of Jewish revival in Mr. Putin's Kremlin."[78]

In Ukraine, Yaakov Bleich, an American-born Karlin-Stolin Hasid, has been a major force in the revival of Jewish life and in representing the Jewish community to the broader Ukrainian population. Closely associated with former president Leonid Kuchma and less so with former president Viktor Yushchenko, Bleich has learned Russian and Ukrainian and makes frequent media appearances. He has established a large religious comprehensive school in Kiev and oversees Karlin-Stolin activities in other cities. Predictably, Chabad-Lubavitch installed one of its own in the second large synagogue in Kiev, which was given to them after the building had been a puppet theater for many

[75] Lubavitch is the Belarusian town where the founder of the movement, Shneur Zalman, born in the small hamlet of Liady, established the movement. "Chabad" is the Hebrew acronym for "*Khochma, bina, da'at*" [wisdom, understanding, knowledge], which the movement adopted as its name.
[76] His father-in-law, Yosef Yitzhak Schneerson, was expelled from the Soviet Union in 1929, but maintained contact with the dwindling number of his followers until his death in 1950. These contacts were expanded by his successor.
[77] A prominent Jewish historian, himself an Orthodox rabbi, has severely criticized the messianic cult that developed in the late twentieth century around the "*Rebbe*," or leader of the group, as being a serious deviation from Orthodox Judaism. See David Berger, *The Rebbe, the Messiah and the Scandal of Orthodox Indifference* (London: Littman Library, 2001).
[78] Michael Wines, "Visiting Synagogue, Bush Praises Russian Religious Tolerance," *New York Times*, May 27, 2002. Earlier, Putin had spent an hour and a half with Lubavitch rabbis from fifteen Russian cities. He thanked them "for their energetic participation in the process of integrating Russia into the international economic space. He particularly singled out Berel Lazar's recent appeal to the US president to repeal the Jackson-Vanik Amendment." Oksana Alekseyeva, "Rabbis Come to President for Advice," *Kommersant*, March 20, 2002, transl. in *Current Digest of Post-Soviet Press* 54, 12, April 17, 2002. The president of the Lubavitch-controlled Federation of Jewish Communities of Russia was Israeli diamond and real estate magnate, Levi Levayev, born in Uzbekistan.

years. A second "chief rabbi" of Ukraine, this one affiliated with Chabad, was appointed.

However, all this activity has **not** brought about a religious revival among the Jews of the FSU. True, many of those who become observant tend to emigrate, making it inherently difficult to gauge the extent of religious observance and belief at any particular time. Nevertheless, at no point can one see very many people coming to synagogues, adhering to Jewish rituals, or studying religious texts – the norms of traditional Jewish religious behavior. There are some very large religious schools, but the majority of children and parents are not observant. It is safe to say that the Jews of Russia and Ukraine, even those who have become active in Jewish life, remain overwhelmingly nonobservant religiously.[79]

Is Judaism "Good for the Jews"?

In 1993, just two years after Lithuania led the way out of the USSR, a comprehensive survey was conducted of the estimated 6,500 Jews then living in Lithuania. More than 4,000 Jews in over 1,600 households were interviewed, mostly by phone.[80] Although 83 percent of the respondents identified themselves as Jews "by nationality," only 40 percent said they were Jewish by religion (7% identified as Christian[81] and 53% said they "had no religion"). This finding "strongly suggests that many Jews do not consider religion the basis of their identity, but rather think of it as 'peoplehood' – that is, on the basis of historical and cultural considerations."[82] Only among those 65 and older did a bare majority consider themselves Jewish by religion. There is a "consistent increase from the oldest to the youngest group in the percentage professing no religion."[83] Clearly, the Soviets succeeded in their drive to weaken religion while preserving ethnicity.

Unsurprisingly, few of our Russian and Ukrainian respondents claimed to know much about Judaism; one-quarter to one-third said they know nothing at all about it. More surprising is that the proportion claiming to know about the basics of Judaism did not increase from 1992/93 to 1997/98, despite the activity of religious organizations during that time (though only 9 to 15 percent said they have no familiarity at all with Jewish customs and traditions).

---

[79] One estimate, which probably errs on the high side, is that of 233,439 Jews enumerated in the 2002 Russian census, about 30,000 (ca. 13%) are "religious." Sergei Filatov and Roman Lunkin, "Statistics on Religion in Russia: The Reality behind the Figures," *Religion, State and Society* 34, 1 (March 2006), 34.

[80] Sidney Goldstein and Alice Goldstein, *Lithuanian Jewry 1993: A Demographic and Sociocultural Profile* (Jerusalem: Avraham Harman Institute of Contemporary Jewry, Hebrew University, 1997), 4.

[81] Ten percent of them identified as Jews by nationality. Ibid., 16.

[82] Ibid., 14.

[83] Ibid., 15.

Despite considerable investments of money and personnel, religious organizations established in Russia and Ukraine since the late 1980s seem to have had only a modest influence on the life of the local Jewish population, one that is weaker than the influence that nonreligious Jewish organizations had. In 1997, in Russia only 14 percent said the religious institutions had "significant" influence, and in Ukraine 25 percent said so. Yet one of four Russian Jews and one of three Ukrainian Jews rated *non*religious organizations as having significant influence.

Along with weak knowledge of traditions, we found clear expressions of positive attitudes toward reestablishing those traditions. Every third respondent in Russia asserted that Jewish traditions are "close" to him or her. Large majorities in Russia and Ukraine considered it "obligatory" or "desirable" to know more about them. However, this may be nothing more than lip service because in Ukraine in 1993, 63 percent did not attend a single lecture or seminar on Jewish history, religion, or traditions; that was true of more than 70 percent in Ukraine in 1997 and in Russia in both years. Of course, before the late 1980s, very few would have been able to attend such an event, so that even modest attendance rates represent a new feature of Russian/Ukrainian Jewish life. Interestingly, the percentage of those who attended synagogue or a prayer service during the year was higher, ranging from 45 to 66 percent. No doubt, "attendance" includes such communal festivities as Purim and Hanukkah parties and Passover seders that are often celebrated in synagogue buildings. After all, the most direct and chief means of identification with Jewishness is to observe traditions connected with significant dates on the Jewish calendar: "A Jew is never as affirmed in his Jewishness as at those times when the Jews of the whole world engage in one and the same ritual act, as for example, at the Passover seder or on Yom Kippur."[84]

Religion, Tradition, and Holiday Observances

Before the Revolution and in the *shtetlakh* of the former Pale for some years after it, major holidays were observed in the traditional way. Older Soviet Jews remember well these holiday celebrations, which took place mostly in the homes of their grandparents. It was dangerous politically and socially then for a young *Komsomolets* (member of the Communist youth organization) to be seen in synagogue. Their parents were usually less strictly observant than their grandparents, but some still selectively observed what had then become conceived as "traditions" rather than "commandments," as one Jewish veteran of World War II recalled:

> My parents were not religious, but they observed Jewish traditions. Grandma and grandpa were religious. God knows what would happen if one of us was caught

---

[84] Milton Steinberg, *Osnovy Iudaizma* (Jerusalem: Biblioteka Aliya, 1989), 155. This is a Russian translation of Steinberg's *Basic Judaism* (New York: Harcourt Brace, 1947).

with non-kosher food! We always celebrated Passover at our grandmother's. She had a very large room where the family could gather. She had three daughters and six sons. There were very many of us grandchildren. Our grandpa would sit on a pillow and hide the matzo under it. We were then supposed to search for it. I also remember the holidays of Simhas Torah, Purim, Yom Kippur, Rosh Hashanah very well. Our parents always observed fasting periods. There was also one holiday named Sukkos. I even remember the songs that were sung during the holiday.[85]

Sometimes, even committed communists would accommodate their parents' religious ways. A Jewish woman who grew up in Proskurov, now Khmel'nitsky,[86] in Ukraine, remembered her father as a "devout Communist" who joined the party in 1924:

As a Communist, he wasn't religious. However, he showed tolerance toward religious people.... He had a very good relationship with my grandmother who came to our house for all the religious holidays.... My father respected my grandmother's religiosity. We kept special kosher dishes for my grandmother. Those dishes were always stored in a special place and when my grandmother came she would eat only out of her dishes because she considered our dishes not kosher, she wouldn't use them.[87]

As time went on, the number of holidays and rituals or customs observed dwindled, but the sons and daughters of prerevolutionary religious Jews still kept some traditions, mostly those having to do with food, at least until the late 1930s or World War II. Another Jewish veteran reminisced, "We usually celebrated Pesach. I remember how my parents made raisin wine and other delicacies for Pesach. That was before the war, of course. After the war, they stopped celebrating altogether."[88] The son of parents born in a Ukrainian *shtetlakh*, himself now about 70, recalled,

We celebrated Shabbat every Saturday, even though my family wasn't religious. Even if we didn't have meat all week, we'd buy a piece of veal or chicken for Shabbat. All that was cooked in a bouillon. And then we cooked the beans separately and then we added them to the bouillon. [This is a description of the traditional Jewish Sabbath food, *cholent*.] And it was a must to have wine. We didn't quite observe the laws about not working on Shabbat, but it certainly was a holiday. My father used to visit relatives. He visited his mother and his brothers. It was a holiday.

---

[85] Interview with Piotr Bograd, June 19, 1999, Soviet Jewish WWII Veterans Project, Frankel Center for Judaic Studies, University of Michigan.
[86] Bohdan Khmelnytsky was a leader of the Ukrainian uprising against the Poles in 1648. He was transformed from a nationalist into a class hero by the Soviets. Among Jews, he is remembered as the leader of a movement that killed tens of thousands of Jews.
[87] Interview with Sara Naftulovna Kaplan, December 9, 2001, in the Soviet Veterans Project.
[88] Interview with Miron Glaykhengauz, July 10, 1998, in the Soviet Veterans Project, ibid.

Note how the special holiday foods loom very large in the memories of people whose parents or grandparents observed the holidays. Genya Hochman, born in Ukraine, remembered,

> I remember all the holidays, starting from Shavuot, then the New Year, then Yom Kippur, then Sukkot, then... Purim and Hanukkah. Our momma prepared all manner of wonderful things for the holidays. For Shavuot, everything was made out of custard; for Hanukkah, there would be *latkes*; for Purim, *homentashn*. Our mother told us the histories of the holidays, and they usually included some sort of a major Jewish tragedy. My mother was more inclined toward all this than my father.[89]

As Hochman observes, in the 1920s, it became increasingly common for one spouse to observe Jewish traditions and customs while the other abandoned them, but we have no systematic evidence as to what role gender might have played in observance of ritual. Age also affected observance, and there were often tensions between young militant atheists and their religious grandparents:

> I had a grandmother who was religious and she wanted me and my cousin to believe in God. She was such a beautiful, kind, and gentle old woman. And my cousin used to tell her, "There is no God!" And I used to tell him, "Why don't you have pity on her and tell her there is a God? Look how tortured she feels because of this! I tell her there is a God, even though I know there isn't. Please, don't make her feel bad." But he was stubborn. "No, and that's that."[90]

A woman who eventually emigrated to the United States and became an adherent of Chabad recalls that as a *Komsomolka* she used to reprove her grandmother who lit candles every Friday night: "Why are you doing this? Don't you know there is no God?" The grandmother would reply gently, "*povolie, povolie*" [easy, easy now]. Her father ate pork and her mother did not, so each parent had a separate set of dishes.[91]

In the 1930s, religious observance could be construed as "bourgeois nationalism," and many Jews, like other Soviet citizens, either abandoned religious ritual or observed it secretly. A Kievan born in the mid-1920s recalled, "In my childhood I remember celebrating Passover... secretly, because things like that were persecuted, we used to buy matzo, but we did it quietly so no one would know where and how we go it. We used to bake matzo too."

The chain of tradition was weakened but not broken by the war, although in the "black years," 1948–53, when government-inspired anti-Semitism raged, it was quite risky to observe any Jewish customs and traditions, except perhaps in Georgia and Central Asia.[92] By the time of the post-Stalinist relaxation, many

---

[89] Interview, March 24, 1998.
[90] Interview in Kiev with a 76-year-old woman.
[91] Interview with Irina Chernomordik, Ann Arbor, MI, October 7, 1995.
[92] In Kutaisi, Georgia, in 1952, the year of the "Doctors' Plot" when Jewish doctors were accused of poisoning Soviet leaders, the authorities tried to expropriate a synagogue but a mass sit-in by the community, some 20,000 strong, blocked their way and the authorities retreated. Until

of the members of the prerevolutionary generation had died, and the purges and the war had ruptured family and communal continuity. Still, some tried to mark major Jewish holidays as best they knew how: "We... celebrated Jewish new year [Rosh Hashanah]... by saying 'Happy New Year' to each other and having tea and a holiday meal."

Over the course of nearly a century we observe a shift from religious observance to commemoration of traditions, from the public to the private sphere, from communal gatherings for prayer to family get-togethers, and from the observance of a national-religious holiday to the reaffirmation of family bonds. This affirmation was both horizontal, bringing together the living, and vertical, linking the living to generations past and making these observances a gesture to the continuity of family and people or nation, if not to religion.

New-Old Traditions in the Post-Soviet Era

In the post-Soviet period there has been a huge upsurge in the number of religious congregations and organizations, although the number of registered Jewish congregations has fluctuated somewhat. In 2004, 256 Jewish religious organizations were registered with the authorities, many in reclaimed former synagogues that had been turned to other uses by the Soviets. Along with the emergence of a public Jewish religious presence, a new mode of holiday celebration caught on quickly. At the initiative of ethnic and religious entrepreneurs and facilitated by the disappearance of sanctions for religious observance or ethnic assertiveness, holiday observances moved out of the home and into the community center, synagogue, or rented space in theaters, auditoriums, and restaurants. Many rituals were reintroduced, and several generations learned or relearned the texts and ceremonies their ancestors knew intimately.

Yet, observance of important *mitzvot* (commandments) remained minimal. Our surveys show that nine of ten Jews in Russia and Ukraine did not observe the Jewish dietary laws (kashrut), despite the activities of religious emissaries and the lowering of technical barriers to such observance. Data collected by Vladimir Shapiro in St. Petersburg in 2004 show that Jews there observed holidays *less frequently* than the Russian or Ukrainian Jews generally had in the 1990s. Our surveys show that between 1992 and 1997 the proportion who "never" attended synagogue rose from 56 to 63 percent.[93] Only 5 percent in the 1990s (average of all four samples) said they attended synagogue regularly, less than half the percentage of American Jews.[94] Roughly one of every six or

---

the 1940s Sabbath observance was universal in the Georgian communities. See Zvi Gitelman, *A Century of Ambivalence*, ch. 7.

[93] In St. Petersburg, 6 percent in 1992 and 4 percent in 1997 said they "regularly" attended synagogue services, whereas 40 percent (1992) and 33 percent (1997) did so "occasionally."

[94] Ekaterinburg had no synagogue at the time of the surveys, and no resident of that city claimed to attend synagogue services regularly. According to NORC's General Social Survey in the 1980s, 13 percent of American Jews attended synagogue services regularly, 39 percent

TABLE 5.2. *Percentage of Respondents Observing Jewish Holidays in the Previous Year*

	Russia 1992	Ukraine 1992/93	Russia 1997	Ukraine 1997/98	St. Petersburg 2004
No holiday observed	37	21 (.001)	39	24 (.001)	39*
Passover	46	66 (.001)	54	68 (.001)	31*
Passover seder	18	31 (.001)	26	30 (.01)	25
Rosh Hashanah	30	51 (.001)	33	52 (.001)	26*
Yom Kippur	22	42 (.001)	24	35 (.001)	19*
Fast on Yom Kippur	11	27 (.001)	12	18 (.001)	11
Hanukkah	22	15	32	38 (.001)	28*
Purim	23	36 (.001)	33	38 (.01)	25*
N	1,300	2,000	1,317	1,984	1,050

*Regular observance over the past "several years."

Note: Numbers in parentheses are the *p*-values of difference-of-proportion tests used to determine that a greater percentage of Ukrainians observed a particular holiday than their Russian counterparts. The two sets of national surveys are paired by year.

seven respondents – among the young, one of every four to six – "regularly" celebrated Jewish holidays, and another 20 to 25 percent observed them "from time to time" (see Table 5.2).

As among American and Israeli Jews, the most popular holiday was Passover, although the level of claimed observance in the FSU is, not surprisingly, far lower. In the 1990 National Jewish Population Survey in the United States, 86 percent of "entirely Jewish" families and 62 percent of "mixed Jewish-Gentile" families claimed to attend a Passover seder "sometimes, usually, or always." In Israel, in 1979, 99 percent (!) of a national sample claimed to attend a Passover seder, and in another national survey in 1991, 78 percent said they "always" attended one.[95] In contrast, nearly one-third of respondents in Russia claimed to observe it regularly and another 28 percent, occasionally – which means, in almost all cases, attending a Passover seder and, possibly, eating matzo during some part of the eight-day holiday. In Ukraine, Passover observance was higher. More than half said they observed the holiday in 1992, and slightly less than half did so in 1997.

Observance of the High Holidays – Rosh Hashanah and Yom Kippur – was also substantially greater in Ukraine than in Russia; more than one-third claimed observance in Ukraine compared to only about one-fifth in Russia.

attended occasionally and 48 percent did so less often. Cited in Wade Clark Roof and William McKinney, *American Mainline Religion: Its Changing Shape and Future* (New Brunswick, NJ: Rutgers University Press, 1987), 97.

[95] The 1979 Israeli figure is from Peri Kedem, "Dimensions of Jewish Religiosity in Israel," in Zvi Sobel and Benjamin Beit-Hallahmi, eds., *Jewishness and Judaism in Contemporary Israel* (Albany: SUNY Press, 1991), 253. The datum for 1991 is from Shlomit Levy, Hannah Levinsohn, and Elihu Katz, *Beliefs, Observances and Social Interactions among Israeli Jews: Highlights* (Jerusalem: Louis Guttmann Institute of Applied Social Research, 1993), 8.

Judaism and Jewishness

That holiday observance was substantially greater in Ukraine than in Russia, with only a small exception (Hanukkah 1993), is probably another manifestation of Ukrainian Jews' greater closeness to *shtetl* life and the influence of *Zapadniki*, the less acculturated Jews who became Soviet citizens in 1939–40.[96] In the five-year interval between surveys, holiday observance did *not* increase substantially, except for the two minor holidays, Purim and Hanukkah. No doubt, that increase was due to the "new tradition" of celebrating these two joyous holidays with festive communal meals, carnivals, plays, and other "fun" activities.

A fairly typical example of the evolution of Jewish identity as a result of increased Jewish communal activity in the FSU is the Ekaterinburg woman who discovered she was Jewish when she was in the second grade and described it as a "terrible discovery... one of the greatest shocks in my life." She cried and screamed and said did not want to be Jewish because of what she had heard from her schoolmates about Jews. In the 1990s she became positive toward her ethnicity, partly because of all she learned through local Jewish organizations. At the age of 35, she learned about Jewish holidays from her daughter, and both attended all the holiday celebrations sponsored by the Jewish Agency for Israel or Menorah, a local Jewish organization. These consisted of "some entertainment followed by a discotheque for young people." In this instance, "outreach" worked.

A young man in Lviv, who discovered he had a maternal Jewish grandmother when he was 18, began to observe "all holidays, all *Shabbatot* and *havdalas* [sic]." He did so at the Jewish Youth Club and never at home because his Ukrainian father – his mother is registered as Russian – "is somehow negative about everything that has to do with my ties to Jewishness, so no Jewish holidays are celebrated at my home." No doubt there are others who found it awkward to perform Jewish rituals at home and more convenient and exhilarating to do so in a communal setting. This is especially true of joyous holidays such as Hanukkah and Purim.

The communitarian rather than the theological dimension of Hanukkah and Purim is what draws relatively large numbers, just as elsewhere.[97] A 29-year-old woman in Ekaterinburg, who was "proud of looking Jewish" and wore a Star of David, was raised by her Yiddish-speaking grandparents. Yet except for eating *homentashn*[98] on Purim and matzo on Passover, sent to them from Leningrad,

---

[96] That more than twice as many people claim to observe Passover as attend a seder probably means that at home they have matzo during the holiday, perhaps alongside bread and other forbidden foods. Observing Yom Kippur without fasting probably involves attending services, however briefly, especially if one has lost a parent or other close relative, because *Yizkor*, the memorial prayer for the dead, is recited then.

[97] In the United States Hanukkah has become a major holiday, even an industry, because it has been represented as the Jewish equivalent of Christmas. In their earnest desire to be "fair to all" and as enthusiastic multiculturalists, Americans have elevated the status of Hanukkah, invented Kwanza, and, of course, commercialized them.

[98] A traditional triangular shaped pastry, usually filled with jam or prune filling.

they observed no holidays at home. After the breakup of the USSR, she still observed no holidays at home, but as an active member of the local Jewish Cultural Society and its "management team," she celebrated them with the Society and learned their significance and traditions. Of course, when speaking of holiday observance among FSU Jews we are aware that ceremonial or ritual observance is inaccessible to most because they don't know the rituals. The theological meaning and religious significance of the holidays, even for those who observe them, are not very salient or are absent altogether. Nevertheless, participation in such events is a strong expression of ethnic solidarity and personal connections with the past, present, and future of the Jewish people. As an employee of a Ukrainian national Jewish organization put it,

> I am not a religious person, but I believe that it's valuable to try and preserve traditions as much as possible. So...I try to attend a synagogue for Jewish holidays or celebrate those holidays with my own people, observing all the rules traditional for each holiday. *I do that in order to preserve the traditions and not for religious reasons....* I am in a holiday mood on Jewish holidays and that's it.... For some holidays I go to the synagogue, but others just celebrate among friends and family. *We don't read any prayers ourselves, because we don't know how to do it well. But I believe that we do enough in order to feel part of the Jewish people. And I feel that that's quite enough for such Jews as we are* [italics added].

What then of religious *belief* among Jews in the FSU, as distinct from observing customs and performing rituals that may or may not be infused with religious significance? Decades ago, philosopher Martin Buber expressed some doubts about the extent and depth of religious belief among Jews. Buber's words apply not only to post-Soviet but also to most of the rest of world Jewry:

> Where is there among Jews a divine fervor that would drive them from the purposive busyness of our society into...a life that bears witness to God, that...transmutes Him from an abstract truth into a reality? To be sure, today, too, there [are]...all sorts of adherences: adherence out of loyalty...out of pride...out of inertia.... But where is there...a community dominated not by Jewish inertia (called "tradition")...but by...an elemental God-consciousness? As for inner reality, Jewish religiosity is a memory, perhaps also a hope, but it is not a presence.[99]

Researchers of religion in the Russian Federation reach a similar conclusion in regard to many of its peoples and their associated faiths. "Most Russians, Jews, Tuvinians, Tatars or Adygei will recognize their links with a historical faith, but most will not feel any religious obligations as a result. Attending

---

[99] Martin Buber, "Judaism and the Jews," in his *On Judaism* (New York: Schocken, 1967), 12–13.

service and subscribing to creeds are not basic characteristics of people identifying themselves as adherents of traditional religions (though of course there are some)."[100]

Among many Jews worldwide, even those who attend synagogue services, Judaism serves to express their ethnicity, not theological conviction. Compared to other religious groups, in most countries for which data are available Jews rank among the least ritually observant and the most skeptical of religious doctrines, including the existence of God. For many Jews, religion has become, as Will Herberg put it, a "haven for ethnicity." For some, it is not even ethnicity but a culture or style of life.

Surveys taken in the United States support this conclusion. Pollster George Gallup concluded that "religion is a relatively low priority for American Jews." A 1989 U.S. survey found that "[i]n the mid-1980s, 40 percent of the general American populace claimed attendance at religious services on a weekly basis, compared with less than half that percentage of American Jews."[101] Nearly one-third of Jews viewed religion as *not* very important in their lives, in contrast to only 14 percent of the general population. One in five Jews was skeptical about their belief in God, whereas more than 90 percent of the American population affirmed such a belief.[102]

A recent comprehensive survey of British Jews concluded, "For most Jews, religious observance is a means of identifying with the Jewish community, rather than an expression of religious faith." Nearly half those surveyed define themselves as "secular" (26%) or "just Jewish" (18%) with no religious identity. Interestingly, "the level of belief or faith in God (which is relatively low for most respondents) does not vary greatly between the [self-defined] Secular, Just Jewish, Progressive and Traditional Jews."[103]

By contrast, among Russian and Ukrainian Jews, the Jewish religion plays no role as a "façade for ethnicity." For many, religion is an intensely private matter, requiring no public manifestations and, in many cases, not following religious doctrines and rules.

This privatization of religion is increasingly the case in the United States,[104] where as a sociologist of religion writes,

> A history of separation of church and state, a pluralistic religious order, a heritage emphasizing personal autonomy and voluntarism, and a consumer culture have all encouraged a deep personal type of religion.... *Believing* [is] disjointed from

---

[100] Filatov and Luknin, "Statistics on Religion," 47.
[101] Jack Wertheimer, *A People Divided* (New York: Basic Books, 1993), 63.
[102] Ibid.
[103] Stephen Miller, Marlena Schmool, and Antony Lerman, *Social and Political Attitudes of British Jews: Some Key Findings of the JPR Survey* (London: Institute for Jewish Policy Research, February 1996), 3, 10.
[104] Wade Clark Roof and William McKinney, *American Mainline Religion*, 7. They point to "the greater privatism of the modern era, or the tendency toward highly individualized religious psychology without the benefits of strong supportive attachments to believing communities."

belonging, it amounts to a "portable" faith – one that a believer can keep in the inner life... having little contact with a religious institution or ascribed group.[105]

Judaism is a tribal religion and when attachments to the tribe weaken, as they have in pluralist, accepting America, so does observance of tribal customs and rituals. As Americans increasingly concentrate on individual well-being, spirituality becomes more important than manifesting membership in the tribe. Not surprisingly, one aspect of Judaism that is directed toward intense individual experience, kabbalah, has become more fashionable among Jews (and non-Jews). The emergence of New Age religions is another manifestation of the search for personal spiritual experience rather than religion as experienced communally.

However, the sources of privatization of faith in the FSU are different from those in the United States. It was not an individualistic orientation, which was anathema to the Soviets, but rather a prohibition on the public display of religion and, in the Jewish case, after 1948 even of secular Jewishness, that drove faith inward and decoupled it from religion, its institutions, and doctrines.

Has the religious education introduced to the FSU since the early 1990s affected young people's religious beliefs and behavior? In 2004, in his partial replication of our study in St. Petersburg, Vladimir Shapiro found that one-quarter of the oldest cohort and almost half of the 16–19 year olds interviewed said they believe in God.[106] Among our Russian respondents there was a slight increase in the proportion of believers from 1992 to 1997, whereas results in Ukraine were more ambiguous, showing perhaps that some migrated from the category of those inclined to faith to the group of unhesitating believers. We do not have sufficient information on the effect of Jewish education on FSU young people. A study in Kharkiv compared the views of 12- and 15-year-olds in a general school and those in a school that, although not a religious one, included the study of Hebrew, Jewish history, and culture in its curriculum. Nearly half the students in the general school declared a belief in God, compared to only one-third of those in the Jewish-curriculum school. There were also more believers among the 12-year-olds than among the 15-year-olds in the general school.[107] Some students in the Jewish-curriculum school resisted efforts to convince them to believe in God. Said one, "I know a lot about God because in our Judaica lessons they 'tell us tales' [*traviat baiki*] about God. But this in no way influences my life, because I don't take it seriously."[108] Not a single younger child in the Jewish-curriculum school identified as a practicing

---

[105] Wade Clark Roof, *A Generation of Seekers* (New York: Harper Collins, 1993), 194, 200.
[106] Vladimir Shapiro, *Jews of St. Petersburg Today and Tomorrow*, Final Report (Moscow-St. Petersburg: Jewish Research Center, 2004), 17.
[107] V. N. Pavlenko, "Sootnoshenie formirovania etnicheskoi i religioznoi identichnosti," in *Identichnost' i tolerantnost'* (Moscow: Institute of Ethnology and Anthropology, Russian Academy of Science, 2002), 53.
[108] Ibid., 59,

Jew. Among the older group, 23 percent said they practiced Judaism. There was a strong decline in both religious belief and ethnic self-identification in the *general* school between the 12- and 15- year-olds, whereas the opposite was observed in the Jewish-curriculum school. The older children identified more with Jews as an ethnic group and with the Jewish religion, and the proportion of atheists fell from 29 to 9 percent.[109] Children of mixed ethnicity had a particular problem. In the general school one girl pointed out, "I am a half Jew. They say that Jews don't cross themselves; God does not allow it. The Ukrainians say that one should cross oneself. I don't really know what to do."

Further analysis of the surveys convinced the researchers that the Jewish-curriculum school had influenced its pupils to be more ethnically and religiously committed. One wonders what the researchers would have found in Sha'alvim, the other Jewish school in Kharkiv, which is an Orthodox Jewish school with dormitories for boys and girls.[110]

As noted, Russian and Ukrainian Jews who believe in God do not necessarily observe the commandments and rituals of Judaism. The same absence of a connection between professed belief and ritual observance has been found among Jewish immigrants from the FSU in the United States, so this seems to be a "disconnect" among Russian-speaking Jews irrespective of their environment.[111] Indeed there are parallels among Russian Orthodox Christians: very few "believers" actually observe basic practices such as church attendance.[112] One analysis concludes that "the Orthodox religiosity of Russians today is so amorphous, so organizationally, dogmatically and ideologically unstructured, that any criteria for measuring it and any figures obtained about it are essentially imprecise."[113] Other analysts of Russian Orthodoxy and Islam in the FSU write of "the persistent gap between high levels of belief and negligible levels of religious practice among Russian citizens."[114] They offer

---

[109] Ibid., 63–64.

[110] See Zvi Gitelman, "Do Jewish Schools Make a Difference in the Former Soviet Union?" *East European Jewish Affairs* 37, 4 (December 2007), 377–98. Revised in Alex Pomson, ed., *Jewish Day Schools, Jewish Communities: A Reconsideration* (Oxford: Littman Library, 2009); Russian version in Elena Nosenko-Shtein, ed., *Izrail' glazami "russkikh": kul'tura i identichnost': Sbornik nauchnykh trudov* (Moscow: Natalis, 2008).

[111] Rasma Karklins, "Determinants of Ethnic Identification in the USSR: The Soviet Jewish Case," *Ethnic and Racial Studies* 10, 1 (January 1987), 31. Karklins uses data from the "Soviet Interview Project," which included 2,424 "respondents with a Jewish nationality identification" who came to the United States in 1979–82. See p. 28. She observes that "the self-conception as a 'religious' Jew widens for younger age cohorts. This suggests that Jewish religious identity in the USSR is decreasingly purely religious and increasingly a form of ethnic affiliation with Jewish traditions" (34).

[112] Furman and Kaariainen, *Religioznost' v Rossii*, 58, table 33.

[113] Filatov and Lunkin, "Statistics on Religion in Russia," 43.

[114] Juliet Johnson and Benjamin Forest, "Preface," in Juliet Johnson, Marietta Stepaniants and Forest, *Religion and Identity in Modern Russia* (Aldershot: Ashgate, 2005), xi.

three explanations for the belief–practice gap: (1) "belief is individual and natural, while practice is community-based and learned" so when community was destroyed under the Soviets, practice withered; (2) "espousing the traditional religion of one's ethnic group became an important part of Russian citizens' self-identifications in the inevitable search for meaning after the fall of communism"; and (3) traditional religions survived the Soviet era and "provided symbolic continuity with an idealized past, a sense of continuity that many Russian citizens sought and needed after their country, government, economy and corresponding worldview collapsed."[115]

All three explanations are plausible in relation to Judaism and Jewishness, although the levels of belief and practice reported by Jewish respondents are lower than among Russian Orthodox and Muslims. Moreover, bearing in mind that Orthodox Judaism, the most ritually demanding form of Judaism, was historically dominant in the lands of the FSU, it is striking that though believers who prefer Judaism to other religions claim substantially higher levels of ritual observance than those who do not believe in God (or who do, but prefer a religion other than Judaism), their levels of observance are significantly lower than among religious Jews in Israel or in the rest of the Jewish diaspora (see Table 5.3). As Anna Shternshis observes, "Even those... exposed to Jewish tradition in their childhood have failed to reconnect with it."[116] Religious Jews in Russia and Ukraine are far more observant than nonreligious Jews. Yet only a minority of those who believe in God **and** are most attracted to Judaism claim to observe the Sabbath – and because we did not specify what that entails, it may mean a minimal symbolic ritual rather than adhering to all the extensive rituals and laws of Sabbath observance.

Religious Jews in Ukraine are considerably more Sabbath-observant than those in Russia – in 1992, only 11 of 79 religious Russian Jews asserted they were regular Sabbath observers – though the difference narrowed considerably between the early and late 1990s. During the 1990s, religious Jews in Russia went from less Sabbath observance than their Ukrainian counterparts to similar levels of observance. The percentage of regular Sabbath observers among those who did not meet our criteria of "religious Jews" (believing in God, preferring and feeling "close to" Judaism) also increased over the period between the surveys by 40 to 50 percent. Therefore the overall level of "regular" Sabbath observance did increase in both countries over the five-year interval ($p = <.01$ in a difference of proportions test). However, self-reported levels of Sabbath observance were still lower than among Orthodox Jews, and perhaps Conservative Jews, in other countries.[117]

---

[115] Ibid., 19, 21.
[116] Shternshis, "Kaddish in a Church," 293.
[117] In the United States, only 12 percent of temple-affiliated Reform Jews, only 15 percent of affiliated Conservatives – but 60 percent of affiliated Orthodox – defined themselves as "Shomer Shabbat" (Sabbath observant). Steven M. Cohen, "Assessing the Vitality of Conservative Judaism in North America," in Jack Wertheimer, ed., *Jews in the Center: Conservative Synagogues and their Members* (New Brunswick, NJ: Rutgers University Press, 2000), 25.

TABLE 5.3. *Self-Declared Religiosity and Ritual Observance*

		Regular Observance	Occasional Observance	Do Not Ever Observe	N
Russia 1992	Religious Jews	13.9	30.4	55.7	79
	Other Jews	1.3	9.2	89.5	1,221
	N	27	136	1,137	1,300
Russia 1997	Religious Jews	33.0	36.1	30.9	97
	Other Jews	2.2	12.1	85.7	1,220
	N	59	183	1,075	1,317
Ukraine 1992/93	Religious Jews	34.1	38.9	27.0	185
	Other Jews	2.8	15.9	81.4	1,815
	N	113	360	1,527	2,000
Ukraine 1997/98	Religious Jews	37.9	34.9	27.7	206
	Other Jews	4.3	16.4	79.2	1,794
	N	156	366	1,478	1,984
St. Petersburg 2004	Religious Jews	26.8	35.7	37.5	938
	Other Jews	2.1	14.3	83.6	112
	N	50	174	826	1,050

Which *denomination* of Judaism did respondents find most attractive? We asked this question only in the second wave of interviews (1997/98).[118] In both Russia and Ukraine, nearly 60 percent could not designate such a denomination, 23 percent named Reform or Progressive Judaism, and about 10 percent named Orthodoxy, either in its Hasidic or Mitnagdic[119] forms, as most attractive. Only 4 percent named Conservative Judaism, which hardly has a presence in the FSU. In 2004 in St. Petersburg, Reform again was most popular, although only about 10 percent chose it.

One of those who saw Reform ("Progressive") Judaism as most attractive did so because it allowed "more freedom, flexibility, tolerance toward other religions." Some considered Orthodoxy "fanatical" and "stagnant," with "too many rules, which are no longer necessary." One respondent opined, "Orthodox Judaism implies a ghetto, while Reform Judaism permits one to live within society."

In contrast, some adherents of Orthodoxy in Russia saw Reform as lacking in tradition and as "an interest club rather than a religion." Several respondents condemned Reform: "Reform Judaism leads to the self-destruction of

---

[118] We did not think that in the early 1990s Russian and Ukrainian Jews were familiar enough with the denominations within Judaism to give informed responses about them. Indeed, even in the late 1990s, most could not name a denomination that appealed to them.

[119] Mitnagdim (misnagdim) are those who opposed Hasidism, a movement that arose in Podolia (now Ukraine) in the eighteenth century. Hasidim were actually banned ("put in *herem*") by the leading rabbinic sage of the time, the Vilna Gaon (1720–97) but have always been included in Judaism (unlike Samaritans or Karaites). See Allan Nadler, *The Faith of the Mithnagdim: Rabbinic Responses to Hasidic Rapture* (Baltimore: Johns Hopkins University Press, 1997).

Judaism... that which reforms is no longer Judaism." Orthodoxy is "the religion as formulated by Moses and Abraham, and all deviations [from it] are bad." "Reform Jews do not believe in God, don't follow the commandments. Their children are not Jews; they assimilate."

Several people were critical of both Reform and Orthodoxy. "Orthodox Jews are too religious, while Reformists are flighty – everything is fluid and changing." Another put it this way: "Reformists make Judaism simple and convenient, which robs it of important things; the Orthodox are sometimes too strict in carrying out some rituals."

As one would expect, those identifying with Orthodoxy observe more traditions than the Reform, attend synagogue more frequently, and are more likely to fast on Yom Kippur.

Can a Jew Be a Christian?

Earlier we asserted that the two boundary lines most clearly drawn by Jews to define them against others were strictures against practicing a faith other than Judaism and marrying a non-Jew. In the FSU, the boundaries between Judaism and Christianity are blurring for many people, although for some respondents the boundaries were still quite marked: "As far as I know, a Jew is a Jew because he professes Judaism. As soon as he ceases to do so, he ceases to be a Jew!" Or as someone from Odessa put it, quoting his *landsman* Isaac Babel, "a Jew who rides horses has become a Russian, not a Jew.... A Jew is a person who feels Jewish. If he crosses over to another religion that means he no longer feels Jewish and doesn't want to be one." A Kievan accepted the idea that one does not have to be religious to be Jewish – "You can be a good Jew without being religious" – but maintained that if a Jew adopts another religion "he ceases to be a Jew because, even if one is not religious Jewishly, one must respect the traditions." Zhanna P., born in Moscow and now in Israel, said, "A Jew who is an atheist – this is normal. But to convert to another religion – this is betrayal of your people."

With just as much certainty, a Muscovite who said she was unsure how to define a Jew asserted, "There is a difference between a Jew-by-nationality [*Evrei*] and a Jew-by-religion [*Iudei*]. So a Jew can take on a different religion."[120] Many found it hard to answer this question. "It's hard to say... it's a personal matter, how one feels inside." A resident of Lviv said, "In principle, no [a Jew cannot be a Christian]. But I meet people who are so convinced... they believe in Jesus Christ... well, let each person decide for

---

[120] In interviews with seventy-nine Moscow Jews in 2001–2, Anna Shternshis' informants emphasized "that Christianity and Judaism essentially represent the same philosophies and religious doctrines and that, therefore, synagogues and churches can serve religious needs equally for the same people. Yet when my respondents go to church, they create their own rituals, which suit their understanding of Judaism, Christianity and personal observances." Anna Shternshis, "Kaddish in a Church," 284.

TABLE 5.4. *Jews and Religious Preference: Which Religious Doctrine Do You Find Most Attractive? (percent)*

	Russia 1992	Russia 1997	Ukraine 1992/93	Ukraine 1997/98	St. Petersburg 2004
None	36.3	44.1	38.5	36.6	35.4
Christianity	13.2	13.7	10.2	15.5	20.1
Islam	0	0	.1	.1	.3
Judaism	33.2	26.7	37.6	32.4	27.0
Other	4.4	5.4	0	2.9	7.0
Don't know/ no answer	13.0	10.2	9.6	12.6	10.2
N	1,300	1,317	2,000	1,984	1,050

himself." A few responded that whereas they were previously uncommitted to any religion, they had become convinced that "Judaism is the religion that is closer to me." A person from Kharkiv explained, "After the seminar of Aish Hatorah[121] I thought to myself, if I'm going to be a believer, then I'll be a Jew and nothing other.... It's stupid, in my opinion, simply ridiculous for a Jew to take on another faith."

Asked which religion was most attractive to them, respondents gave the answers summarized in Table 5.4. "No religion" is always preferred to any particular religion. For Jews attracted to *any* religion, Judaism is the choice of two to two-and-a-half times as many as are attracted to Christianity, the second most attractive religion. Still, more than 10 percent see Christianity as most attractive – and an astonishing 20 percent in St. Petersburg in 2004, in contrast to 11 to 13 percent in the 1990s.[122] The number of those who could not answer the question is quite high, indicating at least that Judaism is not a clear choice for them. Ryvkina and Brym in their 1993 survey of Jews in three cities, and Ryvkina in 1995 (four Russian cities), reported even higher percentages of respondents identifying as Christians.[123] Another survey found as many as one-quarter of Jews interviewed identifying themselves as Christians of various denominations and 23 percent as atheists or belonging to no religion. Only 8 percent said they belong to the Jewish faith.[124]

Some of the attraction to Christianity may be due to the efforts of groups such as "Jews for Jesus" that have been active in the FSU and preach that ethnic

---

[121] An organization based in the United States that is active in religious "outreach" to Jews.
[122] Shapiro, *Jews of St. Petersburg Today and Tomorrow*. There is no obvious reason for this increase. Perhaps it reflects a presumed greater incidence of interethnic marriage among 2004 respondents than among those of the 1990s. The proportion attracted to Judaism remains the same as in 1997 (28%), although in 1992 it was higher (37%).
[123] Robert Brym and Rozalina Ryvkina, "Russian Jewry Today: A Sociological Profile," *Sociological Papers* 5, 1 (1996), 16, 32; Ryvkina, *Kak zhivut evrei v Rossii?* (Moscow, 2005), 212–13.
[124] L. M. Vorontsova and S. B. Filatov, "Religioznost' – demokratichnost' – avtoritarnost'," *Polis*, 3, 147, quoted in Filatov and Lunkin, "Statistics on Religion," 37.

Jews can be "fulfilled" by believing in the divinity of another ethnic Jew, Jesus. This doctrine is rejected by all denominations of Judaism, but is more plausible to Jews disconnected from the articles of their faith for several generations.

Judith Deutsch Kornblatt, who studied Russian Jews who have converted to Christianity,[125] found the following:

> Although I began my series of in-depth interviews of so-called Russian Jewish Christians with the assumption that entrance into the Church would make Jews feel more *Russian*, I heard over and over that the experience actually increased their sense of *Jewish* identity.... Their hereditary chosenness as Jews takes on added meaning in the Church, as these Russian Jews find a positive, if conflicted, new and internal identity.[126]

In Russia and Ukraine, in both the early and late 1990s, only 30 to 39 percent were prepared to condemn Jews who "convert to Christianity," only 4 percent condoned conversion, and 60 percent said they would neither condone nor condemn Jews who become Christians. As one St. Petersburg member of Betar, a Zionist organization, put it in another context, "A Jew who practices a religion other than Judaism is not a bad Jew – it's his choice.... If you want to believe in Jesus Christ, believe, please, who forbids you to do so?" A woman in Chernivtsi said in no uncertain terms, "Of course a Jew can practice any religion they want; they certainly have the right to do that. I even know some Jews who go to church. What still makes them Jewish is the inscription in their passport, but by faith they are Russian Orthodox." What makes Jews a nation, which this woman thought they are, are religion (sic), traditions, and customs. We should not be surprised at logical contradictions in the positions taken by people who are asked about entangled issues and terms such as religion, nationality, citizenship, and the connections among them.[127]

Nor can one ignore the influence that life histories have on people's views of these complicated issues. A Kievan woman, whose father was Jewish but whose

---

[125] Judith Deutsch Kornblatt, *Doubly Chosen: Jewish Identity, the Soviet Intelligentsia, and the Russian Orthodox Church* (Madison: University of Wisconsin Press, 2004).

[126] Judith Deutsch Kornblatt, "Jewish Identity and the Orthodox Church in Late Soviet Russia," in Zvi Gitelman, Barry Kosmin, and Andras Kovacs, eds., *New Jewish Identities in Contemporary Europe*, (Budapest: Central European University Press, 2003), 171–188. See also her chapter, "Jewish Converts to Orthodoxy in the Contemporary Period," in Gitelman, ed., *Jewish Life after the USSR* (Bloomington: Indiana University Press, 2003), 209–223. On the relationship between Christianity and Judaism in the Russian context, see Z. A. Krakhmal'nikova, *Russkaia ideiia i Evrei* (Moscow: Nauka, 1994) and L. Arie, "Evrei i tserkov," in A. P. Bessmerrtnyi and S. B. Filatov, eds., *Religiia i demokratiia* (Moscow: Progress/Kultura, 1993). See also Anna Shternshis, "Kaddish in a Church."

[127] In a "National Conversation on American Pluralism and Identity," participants advanced logically contradictory ideas about American national identity. Richard Merelman, Greg Streich, and Paul Martin, "Unity and Diversity in American Political Culture: An Exploratory Study of the National Conversation on American Pluralism and Identity," *Political Psychology* 19, 4 (1998), 800. A classic study of inconsistency in attitudes is Philip Converse, "The Nature of Belief Systems in Mass Publics," in David Apter, *Ideology & Discontent* (London: Free Press of Glencoe, 1964) 206–261.

mother was Russian, is married to an Arab. When she was 17 or 18 she learned that her mother's mother was Jewish; she began considering herself Jewish and then at the time of the survey was raising her four children as religious Jews: "I observe all Jewish holidays with my children... completely, with all the rules and prayers." She believed that Jews are "God's chosen people" Yet, when asked whether a Jew can practice another religion, she replied, "Certainly. Because all Christians are Jews, the First Christians were Jews.... First was Moses and then was Jesus Christ on the same territory."

A very different example of separating Judaism from Jewishness is provided by the woman quoted earlier who defined ethnicity so independently of religion that for her practicing Judaism does **not** make one a Jew (contrary to Jewish tradition, which admits any convert to Judaism as part of the Jewish people).[128] The American Jewish historian Jonathan Sarna contrasts an earlier day in U.S. Jewish history, when Jewish cultural identity was determined "largely by... *descent*," with the present when "religious and ethnic loyalties are commonly matters of choice. Identity, to a considerable degree, is based on *consent*." He worries that "Jewishness by consent [conversion]... is something completely revocable, purely a matter of choice.... Jewishness by consent implies a marital metaphor: committed today, perhaps divorced tomorrow." He concludes, "There is an urgent need for a vigorous new emphasis on Jewish communalism and peoplehood for converts."[129]

Summary

Despite trying mightily, the Soviet system did not eliminate people's faith in God or a Supreme Being, although there are far fewer believers in the FSU than in the United States, which has the highest proportion of religious believers in the Western world.[130] Soviet repression of religious education, practice, and of religious teachers and functionaries had its effect. Buddhists, Muslims, Jews, and Christians in the FSU are often greatly ignorant of the practices and doctrines of their nominal religions. Some "new religions" have attracted followers, although this might be a transient phenomenon. The challenge to

---

[128] See Zvi Zohar and Avraham Sagi, *Giyur ve-zehut Yehudit* (Jerusalem: Mosad Bialik and Machon Hartman, 1994). A young Czech Jew expressed the same idea when he denied that converts are Jewish. "For them, Judaism is a list of 613 commandments, and so they act it out from their head and not their heart. For me, it's tradition; the history of my family, my ancestors, people with the same experience." Pavel Kral in Eli Valley, "Guess Who's Coming to Seder," *Pozor* 5 (May 1996), 29, quoted in Leah Markowitz, unpublished paper on Czech Jewry.

[129] Jonathan Sarna, "Committed Today, Divorced Tomorrow," *JTS Magazine* 7, 2 (Winter 1998), 12.

[130] Gallup polls consistently find that more 90 percent of Americans say they believe in God. The proportions are far lower in Scandinavia, Britain, and Canada. See Barry Kosmin and Seymour Lachman, *One Nation under God* (New York: Harmony Books, 1993), 8–9.

established institutional religions is to restore the link between faith and observance, between inner conviction and outward behavior, between a deity and its institutional embodiment or representative. Two students of Russian Orthodoxy conclude, "It is difficult to imagine not only a rise in traditional religiosity in the future but even its preservation on its present modest levels. 'Beneath the surface' [*v glubinie*] not only is there no religious revival but quite the opposite is happening – a gradual diminution in the small and marginal group of people who one can call minimally 'genuine' Orthodox believers."[131]

However, among Jews observance became more popular in the decade after communism to the extent that it was enjoyable and provided reaffirmation and even creation of community. As in the United States, "fun" and food-centered activities were much more popular than demanding and onerous ones, such as keeping Shabbat, fasting, following sexual prohibitions, and keeping kosher.[132]

Yet rituals and customs whose origins lie in religion can be used as the basis for a secular ethnic culture. For many years, avowed secularists in Yiddish-speaking secularist circles sponsored third seders, gatherings at which nonkosher food would be served in conjunction with a secular Jewish cultural program. A study among members of the United Synagogue in London – of whom only 10 percent defined themselves as Orthodox and two-thirds labeled themselves "traditional" – found that outside the "Orthodox fringe," belief and traditional observance "seem to be virtually independent of each other."[133] In the USSR, where Jewish practices were discouraged or forbidden even if they were not being observed out of religious motivations, and where there were powerful incentives to acculturate and even assimilate where possible, most rituals and customs fell into disuse. For FSU Jews neither language, territory, nor dress, which sometimes define other peoples of the Russian Federation and Ukraine, will become the "epitome of their peoplehood" that some posit as essential to an ethnic group.[134] In this, FSU Jews may come to resemble diaspora and Israeli Jewry more than they do now. As Werblowsky comments, "The fact that Judaism is the religion of a people – not in the sense of being a religion that happens to have been adopted by a certain people, but an essential dimension of its national identity – renders a (temporary?) retreat into secular

---

[131] *Starye tserkvi novye veruiushchie*, 41.
[132] Keeping the Jewish dietary laws is very difficult in almost all formerly socialist countries. Only 4 to 9 percent of our respondents claim to keep kosher, and we do not know what that means to them.
[133] Stephen Miller, "Religious Practice and Jewish Identity in a Sample of London Jews," in Jonathan Webber, *Jewish Identities in the New Europe* (London: Littman Library, 1994), 198. The "Orthodox fringe" seems to be the 10 percent among United Synagogue members who said they observed the Sabbath. Though the United Synagogue is an organization of Orthodox synagogues, two-thirds of the sample defined themselves as "traditional (not strictly Orthodox)," 4 percent said they were secular, 16 percent said they were "just Jewish" and 3 percent said they were Progressive or Reform (194–95).
[134] R. A. Schermerhorn, *Comparative Ethnic Relations* (New York: Random House, 1970) 12.

forms possible."[135] The word in parentheses is all important: it alerts us to the problem of the viability of secular Judaism, to which we return later. In any case Jews in the FSU will be set apart from other Jews, at least for the near future, by the fact that nearly half accept marriage to non-Jews and that a majority accepts the notion of Jews practicing a faith other than Judaism.

---

[135] Werblowsky, *Beyond Tradition and Modernity*, 51. He observes, "From the religious point of view, there is the danger of cultivating the religious heritage as a kind of national or ethnic folklore, valuable because it helps to safeguard a sense of historic continuity. It has been said of nineteenth century *Kulturprotestantismus* that what it cultivates is not Protestantism but a pious reverence of Protestantism's past" (50).

6

Becoming Soviet Jews

Friendship Patterns

Attempting to explain the paradox of resurgent nationalism in an era of globalization, some argue that it is precisely globalization that drives people to a search for a distinctive identity. Most people seem to need a sense of belonging to a collective. Aside from the family, the state, nation, or ethnic group, religious, social, and political movements provide alternative communities linked by bonds of sentiment and shared goals.[1]

In the Former Soviet Union, it was the collapse of the Soviet state, far more than globalization, that threw open Soviet concepts of nations and nationalities for reconsideration. Contrary to some expectations, however, this reexamination did not lead to redrawing state boundaries. The sometimes peculiar territorial divisions created by the Soviet government in Central Asia and the Caucasus have remained in place, although particularly in the latter states some areas are disputed (e.g., Nagorno-Karabakh, Chechnya-Ingushetia, Ossetia, and Abkhazia). "Peoples" created by the Soviet state have not changed their status, and more surprisingly, those whom the Soviets repressed have mounted only modest campaigns of revival, with Chechens the major exception. True, Baltic peoples, West Ukrainians, and a few others have attempted to reinvigorate threatened languages and cultures, but other peoples – Belarusians, Siberian peoples, and nonterritorial peoples such as Koreans, Poles, and Germans – have made only modest attempts at self-assertion and cultural revival. Of course, there are Ukrainians who are indifferent to their ethnicity and Belarusians who are passionate about it, Moldovans who would be just as happy to be considered Romanians, and Poles living in Belarus and Ukraine who wish to reclaim Catholicism and Polish culture. But all in all, in contrast to what happened after the breakup of the Ottoman, Austro-Hungarian, and

---

[1] See, for example, Montserrat Guibernau, *Nations without States: Political Communities in a Global Age* (Cambridge: Polity Press, 1999) and Harold Isaacs, "Basic Group Identity: Idols of the Tribe," in Nathan Glazer and Daniel Moynihan, eds. *Ethnicity* (Cambridge, MA: Harvard University Press, 1975), 29–52.

Russian Empires after World War I, there has been no radical realignment of states nor, with some Central Asian exceptions, intensive efforts by new national elites at imposing new identities and loyalties on the masses.

Soviet leaders aspired to transform the cultures of widely disparate peoples, not only their economies and polities. They engineered massive, radical social and cultural change, affecting just about every group, albeit differently. Yet, attachments to religion, pre-Soviet ethnicity, folkways, and languages persisted, many in altered forms. For example, clans persisted in Central Asia, if somewhat clandestinely. "By driving these behaviors and identities underground, the state infuse[d] clan divisions with explosive potential" because as clan divisions became less visible they were less available to state control. The attempt by state authorities to control the exchange of social, economic, or political goods "willy-nilly provided a mechanism for clan divisions to reproduce themselves. Underground networks allowed access to scarce goods in the all-pervasive 'gray market' that developed under Soviet rule. Kin-based networks... provided such access across much of the Soviet southern tier."[2]

Jews were not organized in clans and their kinship networks were thin, although these networks survived among Central Asian Jews. Even though the usual agencies of ethnic socialization – schools, religious institutions, an ethnic language, ethnic associations, and kin-based economic networks[3] – did not exist for Soviet Jews after World War II, there were several stimulants of Jewish consciousness – positive and negative, strong and weak:

1. Childhood socialization
2. Association with other Jews as friends
3. Activity of ethnic entrepreneurs
4. Physical appearance (*vneshnost'*) that led others to identify them as Jewish
5. Anti-Semitism and other life experiences

The first three can be regarded as positive stimuli and the last two as negative. This chapter focuses on socialization and friendship, and the next one deals with ethnic entrepreneurs. External stimuli of Jewish consciousness, including anti-Semitism, are dealt with in Chapter 8.

One might suppose that people whose Jewishness derives from positive stimuli would be more likely to join Jewish groups and manifest their Jewishness publicly than those who had negative experiences and would therefore try to hide their Jewishness. Yet some Jews feel compelled to openly combat anti-Semitism, and doing so becomes their only visible, formal Jewish connection. In other countries, organizations that fight anti-Semitism (in the United States,

---

[2] Edward Schatz, *Modern Clan Politics: The Power of 'Blood' in Kazakhstan and Beyond* (Seattle: University of Washington Press, 2004), xxii–xxiii.
[3] These did exist at the margins of Soviet society in the illegal "second economy." Certain higher educational institutions, laboratories, and places of work became known after the 1940s as places that accepted or rejected Jews.

the Anti-Defamation League and American Jewish Committee) appeal to a wide spectrum of Jews, some of whom engage in few other Jewish activities. Anti-Semitism is the "lowest common denominator" of Jewish consciousness and activity.

Soviet Aims, Soviet Realities

The Soviet system aimed to create a "new Soviet man" whose primary allegiance would be to the political ideals of Marxism-Leninism (at one time, Marxism-Leninism-*Stalinism*) and only secondarily to his own ethnic group ("nationality"). The Soviet regime succeeded in part – probably more among Jews than among most other nationalities – but by 1991 fealty to the Soviet ideal had eroded to such a point that many ethnic allegiances were stronger claimants on loyalty. Perhaps there was so much disillusionment with the economic and political systems that even had the entire population been Russian the system would still have collapsed.

Beginning in the late 1960s, a debate of sorts went on among Soviet scholars and especially politicians. Some argued that the Soviet peoples were proceeding on the road to *sliianie* (fusion, mutual assimilation), whereas others emphasized the persistence and viability of ethnic consciousness even in socialist societies. Communist Party Secretary Leonid Brezhnev proudly asserted, "Leninist nationality policy... can truly be put on the same level as the achievements in the construction of a new society in the USSR such as industrialization, collectivization, and the cultural revolution."[4] The official line was that "the Soviet people is a fundamentally new social and international community of people" based on "friendship, complete equality, multi-faceted fraternal cooperation, and mutual... assistance."[5] This "Soviet people" (*Sovetskii narod*) was "not a nation or an ethnic category, but a new historical form of social and international unity of people of different nations."[6] As such, it represented a long step forward on the road to the merger of nationalities. Others acknowledged that "objective conditions" for *sblizhenie* (rapprochement among ethnic groups) and perhaps even *sliianie* had been created, but cautioned that ethnic relations were dependent "in increasing measure on subjective factors."[7] They argued that it was necessary to shift from studying the "results of national processes and relations" to "discovering the internal mechanism of such phenomena." This would require empirical studies of ethnic relations, rather than citation of

---

[4] L. I. Brezhenev, *Leninskim kursom*, Vol. 4 (Moscow: Politizdat, 1974), 50.
[5] P. N. Fedoseev et al., *Lenin and the National Question* (Moscow: Progress, 1977), 327, 334.
[6] P. N. Fedoseev, *Izvestiia AN Kirghiz SSR* (Frunze), 6 (1975), 22, quoted in M. I. Kulichenko et al., *Osnovnye napravleniia izucheniia natsional'nykh otnoshenii v SSSR* (Moscow: Nauka, 1979), 65–66. E. A. Bagramov engages in a relatively frank discussion of the concept of "Soviet people" in "Chto oznachaet poniatie 'Sovetskii narod'?" in *Otklik* 6 (Moscow: Molodaia gvardiia, 1989), 67–74.
[7] Kulichenko et al., *Osnovnye napravleniia izucheniia natsional'nykh otnoshenii v SSSR*, 96.

communist leaders' hortatory declarations about those relations.[8] Such studies were carried out in the USSR, although their design and, especially, reporting were very much politically constrained. Studies of ethnic relations based on interviews with Soviet émigrés were less constrained, although they too had their limitations.[9]

Ethnic tensions did not cause the breakup of the USSR, but did contribute to it. It became crystal clear that ethnic consciousness had survived the "emergence of the Soviet *narod*," but the cultural content and political and social implications of that consciousness remained for the peoples of the former USSR – including Jews – to define for themselves.

The Soviet state imposed ethnic identity (the "fifth paragraph" on internal passports), while state/societal anti-Semitism spurred Jewish acculturation but stemmed assimilation. As noted, practically every form of Jewish culture, like that of some other peoples, was suppressed: first, in its traditional religious and Zionist expressions, and later even in the secular, socialist Soviet Yiddish mode created in the 1920s, which gradually weakened in the 1930s and was killed off in 1948–53.[10] Yet, while forced to *acculturate*, largely to Russian culture, Jews were not permitted to *assimilate*; that is, become Russians (or any other nationality). They were forced to abandon their culture (which many were happy to do), but prevented from changing their identities. For most Jews Jewish identity became a matter of consciousness without culture, and a negative one at that.

Why and how did Jewish identity persist, in the absence of possibilities for Jewish affiliation? If it had been imposed by state and society but held no intrinsic value for those nominally Jewish, why after the dissolution of the Soviet Union did Jews not abandon any formal affiliation? Why did some Jews publicly declare their affiliation with their ethnic group or nation and join

---

[8] Ibid., 26. On debates in communist countries between those who believed that leadership views ipso facto reflected public opinion and those who called for empirical research to gauge how people felt, see Walter Connor and Zvi Gitelman, eds., *Public Opinion in European Socialist Systems* (Greenwood, CT: Praeger Publishers, 1977).

[9] See, for example, Zvi Gitelman, "Are Nations Merging in the USSR?" *Problems of Communism* XXXII, 5 (September–October 1983); Juozas Kazlas, "Social Distance among Ethnic Groups," in Edward Allworth, ed., *Nationality Group Survival in Multi-Ethnic States* (New York: Praeger, 1977), 228–252.; and Rasma Karklins, *Ethnic Relations in the USSR* (Boston: Allen and Unwin, 1986). Studies based on émigrés might be biased because émigrés may be more ethnically conscious than others. This would not apply to the post-1989 emigration. Some Soviet studies are Iurii Ariutiunian, *Sotsial'noe i natsional'noe, Opyt etnosotsiologicheskikh issledovanii po materialam Tatarskoi ASSR* (Moscow: Nauka, 1973); Iurii Ariutiunian and L. M. Drobizheva, "Etnosotsiologicheskie issledovaniia v SSR," *Sotsiologicheskie issledovaniia* 1 (1981); and L. M. Drobizheva and A. A. Susokolov, "Mezhetnicheskie otnosheniia i etnokulturnye protsessy (po materialam etnosotsiologicheskikh issledovanii u narodov SSSR)," *Sovetskaia etnografiia*, 3 (1981). An interesting though uneven analysis is found in Natalia Daragan, "Soviet Ethnography and the 'Jewish Question,'" *Jews in Eastern Europe* 1, 35 (Spring 1998).

[10] See Zvi Gitelman, *A Century of Ambivalence: The Jews of Russia and the Soviet Union, 1881 to the Present* (Bloomington, IN: Indiana University Press, 2001).

or participate in Jewish organizations? "Groupness does not survive merely by definition; rather, it survives (if and when it does) because of identifiable mechanisms of identity reproduction. Consequently, if such mechanisms are disrupted or changed, we can expect concurrent changes in the shape, meaning and salience of associated group identities."[11] Obviously, "mechanisms of identity reproduction" had changed radically under the Soviets. Judaism (religion) and language (Yiddish, Hebrew) had become marginal components of Jewish identity. Customs and traditions based on religion, such as the observance of Jewish holidays, had to be abandoned or maintained in private and even in secret, like Central Asian clan affiliations. The chronic shortage of housing eroded ethnic residential compactness because people took apartments anywhere they could get them. Yet some traditional values, however secularized and transformed, persisted: respect for education, although no longer *Jewish* education; close family ties; and relatively powerful roles for women in the family.

Yet perhaps these shared values were not what drew people together. Rather, it was the unspoken recognition by Jews that they and their ancestors had shared experiences, making them a "community of fate," and that they were identified by others as members of the same group. In many cases this recognition was reinforced by shared values and social positions. There is some precedent for this kind of Jewish identity, a Jewishness without Judaism. Spanish Jews in the fifteenth century who, under pressure from the Catholic Church, converted to Christianity "occupied a cultural gray area regardless of their official status. They often continued to associate with their Jewish relatives." In the seventeenth century when any vestige of Jewish religious practice had been extirpated by the Inquisition, the "New Christians...relied heavily on genealogical essentialism to define and articulate their sense of difference." Their descent, not their beliefs and practices, was held up as their defining characteristic, just as post-Soviet Jews do.[12]

Todd Endelman writes that, although many of the legal and social barriers separating West European Jews from others broke down in the nineteenth and twentieth centuries, the Jews remained socially segregated:

> While acculturation was well advanced by the turn of the century, integration into non-Jewish social circles and voluntary associations was not. During the nineteenth century, Jews in Western and Central Europe gained access to institutions and organizations that had excluded them in the past: legislatures, municipal councils, the military, the professions, fraternal groups, elite secondary schools, universities, clubs and casinos, charities, athletic and recreational associations.... [But] Jews remained a people apart in terms of their most fundamental social ties. Most married Jews, formed their closest friendships with other Jews, relaxed and felt most comfortable in the homes of Jewish friends and relatives. In recalling his...youth in...Erwin Blumenfeld recalled that his freethinking, atheist parents contentedly lived within "invisible walls," associating exclusively

---

[11] Schatz, *Modern Clan Politics*, xx.
[12] David Graizbord, "Religion and Ethnicity among 'Men of the Nation': Toward a Realistic Interpretation," *Jewish Social Studies* 15, 1 (Fall 2008), 49–50.

with other Jews, and "were probably not even aware of it themselves." Very rarely "a stray goy happened to find his way into our house," and when one did, "we had no idea how to behave."[13]

Similarly the scholar and Zionist Gershom Scholem noted that despite his father's allegiance to liberal integrationism, "no Christian ever set foot in our home," not even members of organizations in which his father was active.[14]

The vocational profile of the Soviet Jewish population changed dramatically, as it did among other peoples. During the great industrialization drives of the 1930s, about half of all Jewish wage and salary earners were manual laborers, at least double the proportion in 1926; however, by 1939 a significant number of these manual workers had advanced through education to white-collar positions.[15] This trend accelerated after the war. Being in the same social stratum also contributed to the sense of commonality among Jews.

When Jews realize that they share experiences, values, attitudes, behaviors, and a place in society (formal and informal) this recognition facilitates friendship; having many Jewish friends, in turn, strengthens Jewish consciousness and perhaps confidence. These dynamics were observed in a 2001 study of the Jews of Manchester, England:

> Time after time, respondents mentioned feeling comfortable in the presence of other Jews. Generally Jews seemed to be a part of and also separate from wider society. Interviewees referred to humour, a distinctive Jewish cuisine and the importance of food, a way of talking about and looking at life, a body language that was easily understood, and above all a sense of understanding of what it means to be a Jew in Britain. Not having to explain and feeling empathetic with the other person or group helps to cement a sense of belonging.... It is ... easier to interact with others in situations in which one is unquestioningly accepted.[16]

Let us consider the roles played by family background, upbringing, and friendships in forming Soviet and post-Soviet Jewish identities. Had we conducted our studies in the western periphery of the USSR, especially those parts annexed in 1939–40, we would have found that many respondents had parents and grandparents who spoke Yiddish and Hebrew, had been members of Jewish political and cultural movements, or had been religiously observant. In the absence of formal Jewish institutions, the family undoubtedly would have been the major agency of socialization to Jewishness. Soviet "heartlanders" who are third- and fourth-generation "homo Soveticus" were more remote from such Jewishly knowledgeable ancestors. By the 1989 census, only 11 percent of Soviet Jews declared a Jewish language as their native one. Only a small

---

[13] Quoted in Todd Endelman, "Jewish Self-Identification and West European Categories of Belonging: From the Enlightenment to World War II," in Zvi Gitelman, ed., *Religion or Ethnicity: The Evolution of Jewish Identities* (New Brunswick, NJ: Rutgers University Press, 2009), 115.
[14] Quoted in ibid.
[15] Solomon Schwarz, *The Jews in the Soviet Union* (Syracuse: Syracuse University Press, 1951), 169–70.
[16] Ernest Schlesinger, *Creating Community and Accumulating Social Capital: Jews Associating with other Jews in Manchester* (London: Institute for Jewish Policy Research, no. 2, 2003), 20.

number of elderly Jews were familiar with the prayers and rituals of Judaism. Religious schools were shut down in the 1920s, and the last Yiddish school closed before or shortly after World War II; Hebrew was not taught in any Soviet school, save in two university graduate programs and in the Institute of the Peoples of Asia and Africa. How then could Soviet Jews gain a sense of their Jewishness and of the culture, history, and customs of their nationality?

In our surveys, the age of the respondent had an effect on the age at which they first felt Jewish. Half of our respondents said they first felt themselves to be Jewish when they were 8 years old or older. Older respondents felt their Jewishness earlier in life, possibly because they had more chances to hear Yiddish, see Jewish practices, and be aware of open anti-Semitism. Moroever, more of them had Jewish parents so that the Jewish component of their identity might have emerged earlier.

As I discuss in Chapter 8, those who felt negative emotions when they discovered their Jewishness vastly outnumbered those who had positive feelings, but the age of the respondent had an effect on whether this discovery was positive or negative. As might be expected, the oldest group was most inclined to remember their earliest Jewish awareness positively. Those who remembered it most negatively were between ages 50 and 59 at the time of interview. Little wonder – they were born between 1933 and 1948, and their formative years were spent under the shadows of war and "high Stalinism," the worst times to be Jewish.

We inquired (in 1997 only) about the "biggest influence on the formation of your ethnic consciousness." Respondents could choose such positive elements as music, food, books, holiday celebrations, and religious rituals, as well as negative stimuli, such as anti-Semitism. Two-thirds of the Russian respondents and nearly half of those in Ukraine identified anti-Semitism as the primary influence.

However, when asked to name *who* had the greatest influence on their ethnic consciousness, the most cited influence was a family member. Mothers were reported slightly more often than fathers as the major influence, with grandparents ranking third. Most parents told their children in general terms what "Jewish" means and explained very little about it. Few avoided the subject altogether but, according to our 1997/98 interviewees, only about one in five explained in detail the meaning of being Jewish. In adulthood, friends had considerably more influence on ethnic consciousness than spouses – Jewish or not – or relatives.[17]

Respondents' childhood homes had few ritual or Jewish objects and few Jewish traditions were observed there. When we asked in more general terms about the "Jewish atmosphere" in their childhood homes, the modal response was "very little," though about one-third described it as palpable. About one

---

[17] Between 41 and 52 percent of respondents identify mothers as the major influence on their identity formation, and 37 to 44 percent name fathers. Grandparents are named by 22 to 33 percent.

in five people averred there was no Jewish atmosphere at all in their childhood homes. Yet, strong majorities remembered Jewish foods (unspecified) being served at home, and almost as many recalled hearing Jewish music. Passover, which has been characterized as involving "food, family and fun," was the most observed holiday, though only symbolically, with few of the highly detailed prescriptions and proscriptions attached to it surviving beyond the 1930s. The general picture is one of highly Russified homes with traces of prerevolutionary Jewish culture.

When asked about the national traditions closest to them, about one-third of 1992/93 respondents pointed to Jewish traditions, whereas 34 to 41 percent named "Jewish traditions and those of another nation." By 1997, the proportion naming Jewish traditions alone had fallen to 26 to 27 percent and that claiming "Jewish and other" was slightly more than 40 percent. In both years and countries, at least two-thirds of the respondents cited Jewish traditions as being among those "closest" to them.

"Some of My Best Friends Are Jews"

A defining characteristic of an ethnic group is that members share a sense of solidarity and recognize each other as part of the group. People in a multinational environment will generally pick out co-ethnics as friends, at least initially. "Similarity breeds connection,"[18] whereas the mere existence of difference – whether in skin color, body shape, language, religion, sexual orientation, or ethnicity – arouses suspicion and often hostility. As discussed in Chapter 1, Pierre Van den Berghe has argued that ethnicity has a biological basis. Kin are preferred to non-kin and close kin to distant. Ethnicity, as Van den Berghe sees it, is an extension of kinship.[19]

A survey of empirical works on networks of many types concludes that ties between similar individuals are tighter and last longer than those between dissimilar people. "Homophily... the principle that a contact between similar people occurs at a higher rate than among dissimilar people,"[20] an assumption made as far back as Plato and Aristotle, has been confirmed by many empirical studies in the United States and Germany. "An extensive experimental literature in social psychology established that attitude, belief and value similarity lead to attraction and interaction."[21] Robert Putnam found, somewhat to his chagrin, that in the United States, "[i]n the short run... immigration and ethnic diversity tend to reduce social solidarity and

---

[18] Miller McPherson, Lynn Smith-Lovin, and James Cook, "Birds of a Feather: Homophily in Social Networks," *Annual Review of Sociology* V, 27 (2001), 415.
[19] Pierre Van den Berghe, "A Socio-Biological Perspective," in John Hutchinson and Anthony D. Smith, eds., *Nationalism* (Oxford: Oxford University Press, 1994), 96–102.
[20] McPherson, Smith-Lovin and Cook, "Birds of a Feather," 416.
[21] Ibid., 428.

social capital. People living in ethnically diverse neighborhoods are less trustful of others (including those of their own race), less altruistic and cooperative, and have fewer friends."[22] Controlling carefully for variables such as economic level of the residents, Putnam concludes, "Many Americans today are uncomfortable with diversity."[23] His "hunch is that at the end we shall see that the challenge is best met not by making 'them' like 'us,' but rather by creating a new, more capacious sense of 'we,' a reconstruction of diversity that does not bleach out ethnic specificities but creates overarching identities that ensure that those specificities do not trigger the allergic, hunker down reaction."[24]

Reconceptualizing diversity might work in the United States, but it patently failed in Yugoslavia, the Soviet Union, Czechoslovakia, Belgium, and several African countries. Attempts to create a meta-ethnic "we" and establish "Yugoslavism" or "Sovietism" as the prime focus of loyalty failed. Nor have Hutus, Tutsis, and many other ethnic groups in Africa transferred their tribal loyalties to the states in which they live. Even in largely binational states such as Belgium, Czechoslovakia, or Canada political elites have had a hard time maintaining a supranational state (they failed in Czechoslovakia). Israel has not managed to integrate the 20 percent of its population who are Arabs. The British and French today debate whether it is possible to make their Muslim "thems" more like their settled populations and whether local Muslims really share a "capacious sense of 'we.'"

Many ethnic groups have both historical and current reasons for distrusting those not in their group. In addition, they often feel more secure in dealing commercially with "their own," placing greater trust in them than in outsiders.[25] Yet, some research in the Russian Federation has shown that among several (but certainly not all) nationalities, "[h]igh ingroup trust is no barrier to faith in others. In fact, we found most people to be inclusionary – displaying confidence both in their own and in the major outgroup."[26]

---

[22] Robert Putnam, "*E Pluribus Unum*: Diversity and Community in the Twenty-first Century, the 2006 Johan Skytte Prize Lecture," *Scandinavian Political Studies* 30, 2 (June 2007), 137–74.
[23] "We have tried to test every conceivable artifactual explanation for our core finding, and yet the pattern persists. Many Americans today are uncomfortable with diversity." Ibid., 158.
[24] Ibid., 158.
[25] One example is how Iranian Jews in Los Angeles lost a great deal of money when they lent large sums to a fellow Iranian Jew who seemed to repay them handsomely, but actually lost most of the money. "One of the most telling aspects of the ... affair ... is not how much money was lost or to whom, but how easily community members handed over their life savings as unsecured credit. It is the result ... of an Old World value system in which financial dealings are kept within the proverbial ethnic family, and a promise from an upstanding businessman is considered strong enough collateral to lend ... tens of millions of dollars." Rebecca Spence, "Iranian Jews Hurt by One of Their Own," *Forward*, February 6, 2009, 1. The same may be said of the "New World" phenomenon of fellow Jews investing huge sums with Bernard Madoff in New York only to see their investments totally wiped out, as became clear in 2008–09.
[26] Donna Bahry, Mikhail Kosolapov, Polina Kozyreva, and Rick Wilson, "Ethnicity and Trust: Evidence from Russia," *American Political Science Review* 99, 4 (November 2005), 529.

This was not always the case for Jews living in modern Europe and the Americas. When they were socially shunned and considered by the majority as "not our kind of people," Jews formed fraternal associations to find friendship and mutual support. Thus, B'nai Brith (Sons of the Covenant) was established in nineteenth-century Europe and then formed branches all over the world. Similarly, even in the open society of the United States, such fraternal orders as B'nai Zion, Free Sons of Israel, and the Independent Order of Sons of Abraham; hundreds of *landsmanshaftn* (organizations of people from the same town in Europe);[27] and Jewish fraternities and sororities were established as social settings in which Jews could feel comfortable. These institutions served, in turn, to reinforce a sense of commonality and community. Striking measures of the acceptance of Jews in American society are the disappearance of the fraternal orders, the acceptance of non-Jews as members of Jewish Community Centers (largely to keep them financially viable), and the admission of Jews to social and athletic clubs from which they were once excluded.

Jews' tendency to establish social ties with each other more than with non-Jews can be observed in other countries as well. In national surveys of Jews in Great Britain (1995, n = 2,180, by mail) and South Africa (1998, n = 1,000, face-to-face), 41 percent of British Jews and 56 percent of South African Jews stated that all or nearly all of their close friends were Jewish:

> 17 percent of British Jews have no or very few Jewish friends compared with only 2 percent of South Africans.... The South African friendship networks are more concentrated and the concomitant high level of social segregation is evident. In contrast, British Jews...hav[e] broader social circles.... Within the South African sample, age was found to have no effect on the likelihood of being closer to or more distant from Jewish friends. However, there was a strong age divide within the British sample; those over the age of sixty were more likely than other age groups to have closer Jewish social circles.[28]

In a rigidly segregated society such as South Africa, it is not surprising that ethnic groups are isolated from each other. Britain is less socially segregated, although class, ethnic, and religious distinctions are stronger than in the United States. Curiously, no national U.S. Jewish population survey has reported on friendship patterns. The decline of prejudice in American society and the ongoing acculturation of North American Jews have lowered social barriers, which has had an impact on friendship patterns. Among U.S. Conservative Jews, "[w]hereas 78 percent of the parents report most of their friends

---

[27] On the history of the *landsmanshaftn*, see Daniel Soyer, *Jewish Immigrant Associations and American Identity in New York, 1880–1939* (Detroit: Wayne State University Press, 2001) and Michael Weisser, *A Brotherhood of Memory: Jewish Landsmanshaftn in the New World* (New York: Basic Books, 1985).

[28] Jacqueline Goldberg, "Social Identity in British and South African Jewry," in Zvi Gitelman, Barry Kosmin, and Andras Kovacs, eds. *New Jewish Identities: Contemporary Europe and Beyond* (Budapest: Central European University Press, 2003), 15–16.

are Jewish, this applies to only 36 percent of the younger generation. Conversely, only 4 percent of the older generation have few or no Jewish friends compared with 19 percent of the children." In parallel, older Conservative Jews see anti-Semitism as a problem to a significantly greater degree than younger Jews do.[29]

Nevertheless, in Europe at least, the tendency to choose friends from one's own ethnic group has survived the loss of ethnic markers and many other manifestations of ethnic consciousness. Of course, from earliest times Jews (like many others) designated themselves "the chosen people" and were recognized by others (the biblical prophet Bil'am, for example) as a "people that dwelt apart" [*am le'vadad yishkon*]. On the one hand, Jews have been faulted for being "clannish." On the other, they have been excluded from certain residential areas, professions, and social clubs and forced into physical and social ghettos. At the same time, non-Jews have perceived Jewish opposition to marrying non-Jews and the very formation of Jewish social frameworks as driven by Jews' insistence on remaining not just distinct, but aloof.

In tsarist Russia, Jews were physically separated in the Pale of Settlement, and even the privileged minority (3 percent) who lived beyond it was not generally accepted in Russian society. After the 1917 Revolution, all social barriers were supposed to fall along with the legal disabilities that had been imposed on non-Russian ethnic and religious groups. Many Jews were eager to believe that social acceptance would follow automatically the achievement of juridical equality. In the 1920s and 1930s, it appeared to many younger people that Jews had indeed gained social acceptance. A woman I interviewed in connection with a project on World War II observed,

> I did not consider myself to be of any nationality. I simply thought that I was a Soviet human being. We did not have either religion or conversations about nationality in Baku. The city was absolutely international and I considered myself to be simply a Soviet person. . . . [30]

After the war, when the government launched its campaigns against Yiddish culture, "rootless cosmopolitans," and the Jewish doctors accused of murdering Soviet leaders, the myth of "friendship of the peoples" could no longer be sustained. From the late 1940s on Jews became a distrusted and often despised group, barred from the higher echelons of Soviet society and suspected of disloyalty. At the same time, they enthusiastically embraced Russian culture and felt themselves Russian in that sense. Small wonder that in Russia and Ukraine, about 60 percent of our respondents described their national self-consciousness and lifestyles as a mixture of Jewish and Russian

---

[29] Jack Wertheimer, ed., *Jews in the Center* (New Brunswick, NJ: Rutgers University Press, 2000), 245–46.
[30] Asya Balina, interviewed in Detroit, 1997.

(rarely Ukrainian) elements, with the Russian prevailing in most instances. One-quarter defined their lifestyles as "mostly Jewish."[31]

Despite their attachment to Russian culture and hybrid ethnic consciousness, our respondents' closest friends are mostly Jews. When asked to recall the nationality of their three closest friends in the FSU, 58 percent of respondents in Russia (1992) and 71 percent in Ukraine (1992) mentioned a Jew first, compared to 55 percent of émigrés surveyed in Israel[32] and 89 percent of émigrés surveyed in Chicago.[33] In our study this tendency is somewhat weaker in the youngest cohort (ages 18–29) and weakens overall by 1997, but it is still marked. The overwhelming majority of respondents reject the *idea* that one should choose friends of one's own nationality, but in practice they seem to do just that. There is an obvious contradiction between principle and practice. Perhaps they *wish* that the principle had governed social relations in the world the Soviets purportedly constructed, but in life itself ethnicity turns out to be thicker than ideology.

Friendship Networks and Jewish Involvement

Anecdotal evidence suggests that, even without formal institutionalized ties, some Jews (and other nationalities) formed networks of economic and social cooperation in the Soviet period. When in the late 1940s and the following decades, many places of employment and departments in higher educational institutions were closed to Jews, some Jews in a position to do so would hire their own, although others would refuse lest they be accused of "turning the place into a synagogue."

The "mechanisms of identity reproduction" changed from prerevolutionary times, with anti-Semitism being a relative constant, but some primordial identification with one's own may have been powerful enough to maintain Jewish identity among those who had not completely embraced proletarian internationalism and did not insist on being "Soviet people" only. In the 1960s and 1970s, when cultural and political dissident movements appeared, so did a movement of Jewish assertiveness. Although its goals varied somewhat over time and from area to area – revival of Jewish culture, Judaism, and Hebrew in the USSR and emigration to Israel were all goals of greater and lesser salience in 1965–91 – the common denominator was the postulate that being Jewish was not something to be ashamed of, that it bore positive cultural content.

---

[31] The data reflect a slight decline in the proportion asserting a largely Jewish consciousness (28%) in 1992. In Ukraine, the percentages asserting a largely Jewish consciousness are slightly higher than in Russia, 33 percent in 1993 and 29 percent in 1997.

[32] From a survey of 808 Soviet immigrants in Israel, in Zvi Gitelman, *Immigration, Identity and Israeli Politics: The Resettlement and Impact of Recent Immigrants from the Former USSR* (Los Angeles: Wilstein Institute, 1995).

[33] From a 1990 survey of some 500 Soviet immigrants in Chicago, in Zvi Gitelman, *Becoming American Jews: Resettlement and Acculturation of Soviet Jewish Immigration in Chicago*, unpublished manuscript.

Even outside Jewish activist circles, as the data make clear, post-Soviet Jews disproportionately chose other Jews as friends. There is no difference between men and women in this regard, although Russian and Ukrainian Jews do differ somewhat on friendship issues and in ways we have come to expect. Even Russian Jews who have a high number of Jewish friends feel closer to Russians in their cities than they do to Jews of Belarus and Ukraine, and certainly of the Caucasus and Central Asia. By comparison, Ukrainian Jews feel much closer to Russian Jews than they do to Russians (6%) or Ukrainians (3%) in their localities. This is another manifestation of Ukrainian Jews' greater closeness to Jews in general.

Why is there is such a high proportion of Jews among our respondents' friends? If friendship develops among co-ethnics, it reinforces feelings of closeness and consanguinity. In turn, these feelings produce trust, a rare and prized commodity in Soviet society where most people presented themselves publicly quite differently from the way they actually felt and thought. Throughout the Stalinist period one could never know who was reporting to the police and who could be trusted.[34] "Clan cleavages persist because... trust lies at the heart of this attachment."[35] If a person has two trusted Jewish friends who do not know each other, it is highly likely that he or she will bring those two together. They, in turn, will introduce their trusted friends into the circle and the circles will become concentric.

Expansion of friendship circles is also spurred by membership in a common organization. We found that friendship plays a role in attracting people to public Jewish activity. However, the path of causality is not clear. Does the tendency to associate with Jews explain why some Jews attached themselves to Jewish institutions and became active in Jewish affairs, or does such activity itself lead to more friendship with Jews? Do friendships spur public and private Jewish involvement, or does such involvement create those friendships? Or is mutual reinforcement at work so that, whatever the initial cause of association with Jews, it results in further such association?

People with mostly Jewish friends are indeed twice as likely as those whose friends are not mostly Jewish to be members of Jewish organizations. The same is true of attendance at Jewish events: 21 percent of those whose friends are mostly Jewish frequently attend Jewish events, compared to only 9 percent of those whose friends are mostly Russian and 13 percent whose friends are both Russian and Jewish. Those with mostly Jewish friends are also more likely to have Jewish objects in their homes, observe Jewish holidays, and look askance

---

[34] Vivid illustrations can be found in much memoir literature. See, for example, Nadezhda Mandelshtam, *Hope against Hope* (New York: Atheneum, 1970) and *Hope Abandoned* (New York: Atheneum, 1974). Mandelshtam's husband was the great Russian Jewish poet, Osip Mandelshtam, who was arrested in 1933 and again in 1938. He died that year in a labor camp. He was done in by someone in his circle who reported to the police on a ditty Mandelshtam had composed, but never published, about Stalin. See also Orlando Figes, *The Whisperers: Private Life in Stalin's Russia* (New York: Metropolitan Books, 2007).

[35] Schatz, *Modern Clan Politics*, 12.

at Jews who convert to Christianity. Russian and Ukrainian Jews preferred Jews as friends *before* the possibilities of Jewish activism may have spurred such friendships, but once shared public Jewish activity became possible, more contacts with Jews occurred, which increased the likelihood that one's friends would be Jewish. Thus, the pattern of causation is *spiral*: those with more Jewish friends tend to participate in public Jewish life, which reinforces their inclination to choose friends who are Jewish.

Not surprisingly, those with many Jewish friends are more likely to have a Jewish spouse and to oppose intermarriage. These people are also more inclined to agree that "sooner or later, all Jews should return to their homeland [Israel]," – but not to emigrate to Israel themselves (except in Ukraine in 1992) – and to feel closer than others to Israelis. They are also more inclined to believe that Jews all over the world constitute a single nation. Thus, *Jewish friendships are not accidental, but are produced by more intensive Jewish consciousness and involvement.*

In Russia and Ukraine (1997) those whose ethnic consciousness was Jewish, rather than Russian, Ukrainian, or "cosmopolitan," were more likely to have Jewish friends. What is the logic of this relationship? Does having Jewish friends increase Jewish consciousness, or does that consciousness incline one to seek out Jews as friends? It seems more likely that Jewish consciousness precedes the establishment of a largely Jewish friendship network because, given the small number of Jews in the general population, it is unlikely that one would randomly have many Jewish friends. Rather, heightened ethnic consciousness leads one to seek out co-ethnic friends. Again, a spiral causation mechanism is work: the more Jewish friends one has, the more one's Jewish consciousness develops.

Ethnic consciousness is often heightened by exposure to those of a different ethnicity. The Uzbek villager may realize that he is an Uzbek only when he leaves his ethnically homogeneous *aul* and moves to Tashkent, where he encounters Tajiks, Russians, and others for the first time. At that point he realizes that he differs from them in being Uzbek. However, almost none of our respondents had experienced a totally or even a largely Jewish environment and most were acutely aware of their minority status, of their being different, often from early childhood.

Figure 6.1 illustrates the proclivity of Jews to have other Jews as friends. It displays the answers to two questions: What is the nationality of *most* of your friends, and what is the nationality of your *closest* friend? Jews predominate among respondents' friends; a very high proportion of their single "closest" friend are Jews.[36] We can also see that in the five years between surveys, the ethnocentric nature of friendships declined somewhat, especially in

---

[36] Rozalia Ryvkina's surveys came up with roughly similar results. In 1995 in four Russian cities, 48 percent of her interviewees said "about half" of their friends were Jewish and another 25 percent said the "majority" were Jewish. The figures for a survey in 2004 in Moscow are lower (40% and 18%). *Kak zhivut Evrei v Rossii* (Moscow, 2005), table 3.13, p. 77.

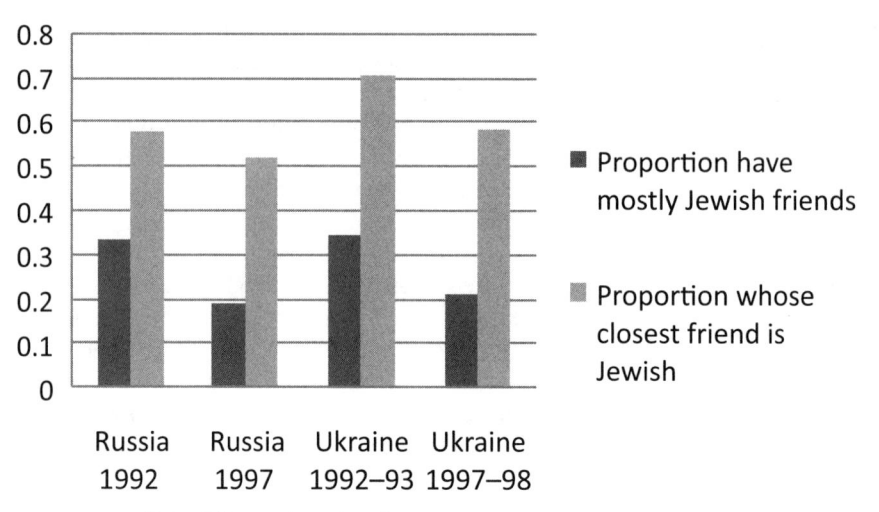

FIGURE 6.1. Friendship and Nationality.

Ukraine. Again, mass emigration is the most likely explanation for the change because it removed more than a million Jews from the population, thus reducing the chances that one would befriend a Jew. It is also likely to have carried off some of the most ethnically conscious and committed Jews. Those left in Russia and Ukraine would be less likely – and less able – to seek out Jews as friends.

As mentioned earlier, women and men display the same pattern of friendship preferences,[37] and differences by age are much more marked. In both countries and in both surveys, the older one is, the more likely one is to have Jewish friends. Many of those over 60 grew up in Jewish environments, such as *shtetlakh*, and some attended Soviet Jewish schools. They are more likely to have formed their earliest friendships with other Jews. They experienced the traumas of World War II and post-war Stalinist anti-Semitism, which makes it more likely that fellow Jews will understand their apprehensions, reactions, and behavior more than others. The youngest respondents are more likely to have grown up in ethnically mixed families, not to have been involved with Jewish observances or culture, and to have experienced less discrimination as Jews for two reasons: by the time they entered higher education or the workforce governmental anti-Semitism had disappeared, and in the circles in which they mix, young and educated residents of the largest cities are less likely to encounter anti-Semitism than their (great) grandparents did when growing up in working-class and less urbanized environments. The young can therefore feel just as comfortable with non-Jews as with their coethnics.

---

[37] The correlations between preferences for Jews and gender are very low: Russia 1992: -.0044; Russia 1997: -.0201;Ukraine 1992/93: -.0061; Ukraine 1997/98: .0064.

Analyzing the data more closely, we uncover a pattern that may reflect the tension between adherence to the principle that one should not choose friends on the basis of ethnicity and the real-world proclivity for friendships with "one's own." When asked about the nationality of their closest friends, and "mostly Jews" is counterposed to "mixed, various," only about one-third of all respondents said that *most* of their friends are Jewish. The modal reply was "mixed, various." If this is accurate, it means that Jews do not form friendships exclusively with a single nationality, not even their own. Yet, except in Russia in 1997, Jews are the nationality most often mentioned as friends. Perhaps respondents were reluctant to answer "mostly Jews" because that would contradict their assertion that one should not choose friends on the basis of their ethnicity. However, when ethnicity of friends is asked for in a more concrete and specific way – "what is the nationality of your closest friend, of the second closest, and the third? " – quite a different picture emerges. The proportion of Jewish friends reported rises substantially. Moreover, the "closest" friends turn out to be Jewish in almost all instances. One may surmise from Figure 6.1 that respondents hesitate to admit that a disproportionately high number of their friends are Jewish, but when pressed to specify the nationality of the individuals closest to them, it becomes clear that well over half of their closest friends are Jews. In Russia and Ukraine respondents had more Jews than Russians among their closest friends but by the late 1990s, the proportion of non-Jews rose.

These findings have important implications. The less ethnocentric friendship patterns of the young make it more difficult to build Jewish communal institutions based largely on ethnic culture and solidarity rather than religion. Young people may be less attracted to places and activities whose distinctive characteristic is the presence of other Jews. In the United States, Jewish Community Centers not only welcome non-Jews, as noted earlier, but find it harder to retain and attract Jewish members to their health clubs. As social boundaries have weakened, there is no obvious reason that one should sweat with other Jews rather than with a more ethnically diverse group. Cost, convenience, and the facilities available become more important considerations. In the FSU, for some indeterminate time, ethnic institutions that did not exist under the Soviets are attracting people because of their novelty and the new opportunities to "discover" people like oneself. What the staying power of such institutions will be remains to be seen.

Are the Jews a Single Nation?

In contrast to Jews elsewhere, FSU Jews do not extrapolate their preference for Jewish friends to a sense of kinship with Jews the world over or even in non-European parts of the FSU. In a London study, 88 percent agreed with the proposition that "an unbreakable bond unites Jews all over the world."[38] In

---

[38] Jacqueline Goldberg, "Social Identity in British and South African Jewry," 199. The wording of the proposition may have biased responses toward assent.

contrast, in 1992/3, only 41 percent in Russia and 51 percent in Ukraine agreed with the statement that "Jews all over the world constitute a single people;" in Russia about the same percentage disagreed with the statement, compared to 39 percent in Ukraine, with the rest unsure.[39] Five years later, the proportions agreeing to the proposition had fallen slightly to 38 percent in Russia and 48 percent in Ukraine.

In response to this statement, many respondents said that the presence of different groups in Israel – reference is most frequently made to Moroccan and Ethiopian Jews – "prove" that Jews are not a single people. A Russian woman who visited Israel observed, "I saw this in Israel – it's Pinsk, Minsk, and others, and Moscow and Leningrad, these are totally different people! Absolutely!" A Kievan remarked that not even FSU Jews constitute a single people: "Georgian Jews are more Georgians, Jews from Bukhara are more Uzbeks, it's difficult to tell them apart." These responses echo the sentiments of a seventeenth-century Sephardic Jew: "A Portuguese Jew from Bordeaux and a German Jew from Metz... appear to be two entirely different beings."[40]

In Russia, two-thirds of those interviewed in 1992/93 said they felt "spiritually and culturally" closer to the Russians of their city than to Georgian, Bukharan, or Mountain Jews, and 46 percent said they felt closer to local Russians than to Jews in Belarus or Ukraine. The Soviet categorization of Jews throughout the USSR under the same rubric – some censuses differentiated among Ashkenazi, Georgian, Central Asian ("Bukharan"), and Tat (Mountain) Jews, but passports did not – did not produce strong feelings of consanguinity. Where Ashkenazi and indigenous Jews resided in the same city, such as Tashkent and Samarkand (Uzbekistan), Tbilisi (Georgia), Baku (Azerbaijan), or Makhachkala (Dagestan), they had separate synagogues, perhaps because the order of prayer (*nusach*) is different. More tellingly, they tended to reside apart, and there seems to have been little marriage between Ashkenazi and local Jews.

So does culture prevail over ethnicity, in contrast to our conclusion from observed friendship patterns? The contradiction disappears when we realize that many Russian Jews simply do not consider the Georgian or Central Asian Jews as members of the same ethnic group as they, despite Soviet officialdom having classified them as such. Those non-Ashkenazic Jews may be too different in appearance, foods, traditions, and language to be considered part of the same *natsional'nost'*. It is harder to understand why Russian Jews would feel distant from Jews in Belarus and Ukraine, when just three or four generations ago their ancestors were most likely to have lived there[41] and contemporary Belarusian

---

[39] There is a sharp difference between responses in Kharkiv, where less than one-third agreed that Jews are a single nation in 1993, and Chernivtsi, where 69 percent did so. Differences among the Russian cities were not dramatic.
[40] Isaac de Pinto, quoted in Graisbord, 50.
[41] All of contemporary Belarus and most of Ukraine were in the Pale of Settlement to which Jews were confined from 1795 to about 1915 (de facto) or 1917 (de jure). Only about 3 percent of the Jewish population lived in Russia proper before the 1917 Revolution.

and Ukrainian Jews are mostly culturally Russian. Perhaps there is an element of social snobbism here: Russian Jews, especially those from the "two capitals" Moscow and St. Petersburg, regard Jews of Belarus and Ukraine as provincials, but look up to the ethnic Russian intelligentsia of their own cities as the kind of people they would like to be. In any case, there are likely cross-currents at work here, as could be expected from a group that carries a non-Russian label but whose culture is Russian.

The distance perceived between Russian Jews and those elsewhere increased somewhat in 1997/98, either because the most conscious Jews emigrated or the breakup of the USSR increased the psychological distance among Jews (and others) in its newly independent parts. As noted, in contrast to Russian Jews, more Ukrainian Jews feel affinity for Russian Jews than they do for local Russians, and they feel greater affinity for local Russians than for Ukrainians. Ukrainian Jews are more attached to their co-ethnics and less attached to the titular nationality of the country of their residence. Like Russian Jews, they are distant from non-Ashkenazic Jews, though less so than Russian Jews. Ukrainian Jews are more weakly attached to Ukrainian than to Russian culture.

The socialist vision of a world without nations inspired many, especially members of oppressed minorities, but ultimately failed to bring about the demise of ethnicity – though ethnic cultures and consciousnesses were profoundly affected by seven decades of Soviet socialization. Religions were suppressed but ethnicities were sometimes invented, sometimes encouraged, sometimes repressed. Many peoples happily accepted the idea that they were "nationalities" or "nations." The messages were mixed: ultimate fusion while encouraging ethnic cultures; "drawing together" of nations while making sure that every citizen was identified by ethnicity; and equality of peoples while some were "more equal" than others. As we have seen, even the policies pursued toward one small nationality, the Jews, lurched from one position to another, though the repression of their religious culture was consistent. Through it all, a sense of belonging to the Jewish entity persisted, although many Jews saw it as "the cross we have to bear." Perhaps making a virtue of necessity, Jews, while clinging to the myth of the irrelevance of ethnicity, made friends largely with other Jews. "*Dos pintele Yid*," the small Jewish spark of attachment, was hard to extinguish. With the fall of the Soviet system in 1991, attempts were made to fan the spark gently so that more conventional content would be restored to the inflexible category "Jewish." Could one assemble individual Jewish atoms into nuclei of what might ultimately become functioning Jewish communities?

7

Acting Jewish

Jewish Collectivities or Communities?

In many Western countries, the degree of ethnic belonging and commitment is measured by organizational affiliation and donations to ethnic institutions. A "good Jew" is one who belongs to many Jewish organizations and donates money to Jewish causes. In the USSR neither of these external expressions of commitment to Jews, Jewishness, or Judaism was available. There were no Jewish organizations, nor was there any possibility of contributing labor, talents, or funds to Jewish causes or organizations.[1] There was no such thing as synagogue membership, though a board of twenty [*dvatsatka*] was responsible to the state authorities for the operations of each synagogue.[2] There were no Jewish organizations at all – national, republic, regional, or local, including state-sponsored institutions – from 1948 to 1988.

Some see being involved in "a dense network of personal interactions with other Jews" as the behavior, aside from religious practice, that precludes assimilation.[3] Yet during the Soviet period, society was run by the state from above, not organized from below; all activity not sponsored by the government was considered subversive. Of course, such activity existed – as in the "second economy," in patron–client relationships that were criticized as "family circles," and "connections" [*sviazy, znakomstvo*] that greased the wheels of

---

[1] Even when "Jewish organizations" existed, such as GEZERD/OZET (the Society for the Settlement of Working Jews on the Land, 1925–38), the Jewish Anti-Fascist Committee (1942–48), or (stretching a point) the Anti-Zionist Committee of the Soviet Public (1983–94), membership was not restricted to Jews, and the organizations were state sponsored and largely state funded. The minor exceptions were the possibility of donating funds for the upkeep – never the construction – of synagogues or, in some years, of cemeteries. Shortly after World War II, local Jews did gather funds to put up monuments to Holocaust victims.
[2] Details on how synagogues operated and funds raised for them and their ancillary functions can be found in Mordechai Altshuler, *Yahadut ba-makhbesh ha-Sovyeti: ben dat le-zehut Yehudit bi-Verit ha-Mo'atsot, 1941–1964* (Jerusalem: Zalman Shazar Center, 2007).
[3] Robert Amyot and Lee Sigelman, "Jews without Judaism? Assimilation and Jewish Identity in the United States," *Social Science Quarterly* 77, 1 (March 1996).

the clumsy, complicated machinery of the Soviet state – but it was constantly criticized and occasionally disrupted.

Why and how did at least some Soviet Jews remain sufficiently attached to their ethnicity to affiliate with or participate in the activities of Jewish organizations when they emerged in the late 1980s and thereafter? What do our surveys tell us about the types and motivations of Jews drawn to public Jewish activity? A national survey taken in 2001 found only 5 percent of Russians participating in public organizations and 73 percent saying they had no interest in ever participating.[4] After such a long period of state-controlled public activity, one could not expect the immediate emergence of, especially, *Jewish* organizations and activists in the FSU. A 1993 survey of a thousand Jews in Moscow, Kiev, and Minsk found only 6 percent participating in Jewish organizations and only 5 percent claiming membership in them.[5]

In contrast, among our respondents in Ukraine in 1998, 15 percent claimed to take an active part in local Jewish organizations, one-third said they sometimes attended these organizations' functions, and another 19 percent availed themselves of their services. Given how recently such organizations had emerged, it is striking that about two-thirds of those questioned had some contact with them. True, only 15 percent were "active," but this compares quite favorably with the proportions of Jews active in such organizations in other countries, even where they are long established and where organizational activity is seen as a civic virtue. For example, in the 1990 U.S. National Jewish Population Survey, of the "core Jewish population,"[6] 72 percent "indicated that they were not members of any Jewish organization, and only 13 percent belonged to two or more groups. Membership in Jewish organizations was even lower among noncore respondents: only 5 percent belonged to any Jewish organization, and most of these were members of only one group."[7] Only one-third of those in the core population said they belonged to a synagogue or temple, compared to only 3 percent outside the core.[8] A decade later, in a much criticized follow-up survey, 46 percent claimed to belong to a synagogue or temple, 21 percent to a Jewish Community Center, and 28 percent to "other Jewish organizations."[9]

---

[4] Radio Free Europe/Radio Liberty, News Report, July 2, 2001.
[5] Robert Brym and Rozalina Ryvkina, "Russian Jewry Today: A Sociological Profile," *Sociological Papers* 5, 1 (1996), 25.
[6] "All those professing to be currently Jewish by religion, ethnic or cultural identity, or birth and not reporting any other religious affiliation. This population is the one which most Jewish communal agencies recognize as their clientele." Sidney Goldstein, "Profile of American Jewry: Insights from the 1990 National Jewish Population Survey," *American Jewish Year Book 1992* (New York: American Jewish Committee, 1992), 77–176.
[7] Ibid., 139.
[8] Ibid., 138.
[9] *The National Jewish Population Survey 2000–01: Strength, Challenge and Diversity in the American Jewish Population* (New York: United Jewish Communities, January 2004), 7.

Most of our respondents (two-thirds in Russia, three-quarters in Ukraine) were *aware* of the existence of at least one Jewish organization. Such awareness increased modestly between 1992/93 and 1997/98. By 2004 in St. Petersburg, awareness of and participation in Jewish organizations had risen again, especially among younger people.[10] Similarly, the proportion of people claiming membership in Jewish organizations rose from 1995 to 2004 in a study conducted in the earlier year in four Russian cities and in the later year in Moscow alone.[11]

I examine four correlates of Jewish public activism – demographic, family background, identification and social environment, and attitudes and beliefs – in the following sections.

The Demographics of Activism

A somewhat larger proportion of Russian and Ukrainian Jews attended Jewish public events at the beginning of the 1990s (about 40%), when these were still novel, than did at the end of the decade (about 30+%). By the end of the decade, perhaps the novelty had worn off or many of the people most likely to attend had emigrated. In the late 1990s, nearly half the Russian Jews surveyed and two of five Ukrainian Jews said they "never" attended Jewish cultural events (we combined answers regarding concerts, lectures, exhibits, and theater performances). The proportions of those who attended "often," "rarely," or "sometimes" remained quite stable. In both years, the proportion of Russian Jews who "never" attended a Jewish cultural event was higher than among Ukrainian Jews.

Residents of Kiev attended events more frequently than those of Kharkiv, Odessa, and Lviv, and those in Chernivtsi attended most frequently. As a capital, Kiev may have more such events than the provincial cities. However, in Russia there was more activism in Ekaterinburg than in Moscow, despite its much smaller Jewish population. Neither in Russia nor Ukraine does the size of the city and its Jewish population correlate positively with the level of Jewish activism in it. There are at least four possible explanations for why some cities had higher levels of activism: higher levels of Jewish consciousness; more attractive Jewish organizations (personnel, facilities, budgets);

---

[10] According to Vladimir Shapiro's study, about one-quarter of those between 16 and 30 were either employees, members of, or participants in Jewish organizations, whereas about 13 percent of those over 40 were thus involved. "Involvement" could include being the recipient of an organization's services.

[11] Rozalina Ryvkina, *Kak zhivut evrei v Rossii?* (Moscow, 2005) Table 7.1, p. 181. In both years, one thousand people were interviewed. The 1995 interviews were conducted in Moscow, Rostov-on-Don, Ekaterinburg, and Khabarovsk. The 2004 interviews were conducted in Moscow only. The methods employed in the study are explained on pp. 60–63 and 430–42. As in our surveys, the youngest (18–29) and oldest (65 and older) cohorts participated more frequently than others. Overall, Ryvkina found, 19 percent of Moscow respondents claimed membership in a Jewish organization.

more effective leadership and mobilization; and a more civically active general population.

Who attends events with some regularity? In 1992 in Russia, nearly twice as high a proportion of men as women said they attended Jewish cultural events frequently. By 1997 that disparity was gone. In general, there were almost no differences between men and women in their attendance at Jewish events, membership in Jewish organizations, or participation in their activities. Men attended synagogues slightly more, as might be expected,[12] but only 7 percent claimed to attend synagogue services "frequently."

Age is the most powerful correlate of participation. Strikingly, those between 16 and 29 attended Jewish cultural events more frequently than any other age group, with nearly one-quarter claiming to attend "frequently." The next largest group was the oldest, those 60 and over. Those between 30 and 59 attended least frequently. The same pattern was found by Rozalina Ryvkina in her studies of Russian Jews.[13] The reasons for this may be that the young find such activities useful for meeting other Jews of their age, whereas the pensioners not only have the same kind of social need but also the leisure to attend these events, and they are recipients of organizational assistance. Curiously, the youngest group attended synagogues most frequently, although even among them half never or rarely attended.[14] Interestingly in 1992, the oldest group in Russia was the least likely to attend events. Young people are more apt to try new things than the elderly, and in 1992 Jewish cultural and organizational activity may have still been regarded as potentially dangerous by a cohort socialized under Stalin. By 1997, Jewish public life had become legitimated. Moreover, programs geared to the elderly, especially the provision of medical or legal assistance and meals, had been developed in the five-year interim.

Those who felt more positive about being Jewish attended Jewish events more frequently than others. The strength of the "Jewish atmosphere" in one's childhood home, an unquantifiable measure, is a weak but positive predictor of activism. People who never attended Jewish events were most likely not to have celebrated any Jewish holidays or have felt any Jewish atmosphere in their childhood homes. Respondents with non-Jewish or partially Jewish spouses attended Jewish events less frequently than those with Jewish spouses. Thus, personal experience, upbringing, and ethnicity of one's spouse affect participation in Jewish events.

Regarding membership in organizations, in 1992/93 there was a pattern similar to that for attending events, with the exception that the oldest cohort

---

[12] According to halakha, women are exempt from obligations that are time-bound, such as prayers that have to be said at specific times. Thus, traditionally women saw synagogue attendance as an option rather than as an obligation. Although very few post-Soviet Jews adhere to halakha, traditional gender-based patterns of behavior may persist.

[13] See note 22.

[14] In Ryvkina's studies, 99 percent in 1995 and 89 percent in 2004 never or rarely attended synagogues. Table 5.4, p. 123.

TABLE 7.1. *Percentage of Members in Jewish Organizations, by City*

Russia	Moscow	St. Petersburg	Ekaterinburg			Countrywide	N
1992	20.4	10.9	17.0			16.1	1,300
1997	10.0	7.9	14.5			10.3	1,317
N	1,009	1,004	604				2,617

Ukraine	Kiev	Kharkiv	Odessa	Lviv	Chernivtsi	Countrywide	N
1992–93	26.6	21.7	9.5	34.5	30.8	24.4	2,000
1997–98	15.4	8.6	8.8	22.7	22.0	14.5	1,984
N	984	1,000	800	600	600		3,984

had somewhat higher levels of membership than the youngest. In both the early and late 1990s, the proportion of members was higher in Ukraine than in Russia. The proportion claiming membership declined significantly in both countries between 1992/3 and 1997/98. The exception to the decline was the youngest cohort in Russia. Again, it may be that when Jewish organizations and public activities first emerged, people were drawn to them out of curiosity. Once the novelty had worn off, interest and participation declined. Moreover, those most likely to participate in the early 1990s may have emigrated shortly thereafter. As we shall see later, there is a correlation between participation in Jewish public life and the propensity to emigrate. The decline in *membership* over time may be explained by the same considerations that account for the diminution in *participation*.

The middle generations, those between 30 and 60, were least involved in Jewish activities likely because they have family and work obligations that limit *any* sort of civic activity. They were also socialized in the Leonid Brezhnev period (1964–82) when Jewish activity meant dissidence and danger. The youngest cohort came of age in post-Soviet times and does not have the fears of their parents and grandparents. It is certainly a "new generation that knew not Joseph" (Stalin). The oldest group, even in Soviet times, took the lowest risks when engaging in religious or Jewish cultural activities because the authorities paid less attention to their behavior than to that of younger people. Moreover, especially if they or their parents came from the smaller towns of the former Pale of Settlement, they had more early experience of Jewish religious and cultural life than younger Jews. As a result the middle cohorts may be a *dor hamidbar*, a generation of the wilderness transiting from one environment to another, whose members are unlikely to be very active in public Jewish life.

There is no great variation in organizational membership among residents of the three Russian cities (see Table 7.1). In Ukraine, however, in 1997 the proportion of organization members was highest in the two West Ukrainian cities – Lviv and Chernivtsi – which were both outside the USSR until 1939–40. More than one-fifth of the respondents in those cities claimed to be members of Jewish organizations, whereas in Odessa and Kharkiv only 9 percent did so. In Kiev, the capital of Ukraine and the center of national Jewish organizations, more than 15 percent claimed membership. These differences among cities may be due to variations in leadership and resources. The vibrant prewar Jewish life in Lviv and Chernivtsi may be relevant, although most Jews living today in those cities came from elsewhere.

Note that in both years of the survey, membership was higher in Ukraine than in Russia, and the proportion of members declined between the early and late 1990s in both countries. Membership may be higher in Ukraine because our sample includes four "provincial" cities, whereas the Russian sample includes only one. There may be a tendency, similar to that in the United States, for Jews in smaller cities to affiliate at a higher rate than those in larger cities. In the FSU, as in other countries, Jews in smaller cities feel both more isolated and more obligated to band together. Social psychologists discern a great deal of social detachment, even alienation, in the metropolis where people are estranged from each other and communication is socially difficult. The abundance of all kinds of information complicates the selection of that which is most important and needed by the recipient of the information.

Finally, in both years and both countries, people married to Jews were most likely to participate in Jewish activities and belong to Jewish organizations, those with partly Jewish spouses less so, and those with non-Jewish spouses least of all. For example, in Russia (1992) 46% of those with non-Jewish spouses never attended Jewish events, compared to only 29% of those with Jewish spouses. In Russia in 1997, those married to Jews were twice as likely to attend events frequently as those not and were more likely to attend synagogue services (70% of those married to non-Jews never attended a synagogue), but the impact of spouse's ethnicity on organizational membership was weaker.

Family Background and Activism

The degree to which one's childhood home was Jewishly observant or active had a slight positive impact on one's present Jewish activism, but the influence of childhood socialization was generally not great. This may be because under Soviet rule socialization to Jewish activity and observance could not have been very intensive in most instances. However, those in whose childhood homes "*all* holidays" were observed were more likely to attend synagogue, although the influence of childhood observance on attendance at non-religious Jewish events was weaker. They were also somewhat more likely to be members of Jewish organizations.

We developed indices of ethnic self-consciousness, Jewish aspirations, positive or negative feelings toward being Jewish, and the presence of Jewish artifacts and observances in daily life, as well as measures of the ethnic character of respondents' friendship circles. All of these operate in the expected way regarding participation in Jewish events and membership in Jewish organizations. Those who attend Jewish events are more likely to identify most strongly as Jews, feel themselves spiritually closer to Jews than to Russians or Ukrainians, have higher Jewish aspirations (e.g., wish to learn more about Jewish history and languages, customs and traditions, and Jewish culture), are more positive about their Jewishness, and have more Jewish artifacts at home. The closer one feels to Jews, rather than to Russians or Ukrainians, the more likely one is to participate in Jewish affairs and belong to Jewish groups. One-third of those with high Jewish aspirations attend Jewish events often, compared to only 3 percent of those with low aspirations (Russia, 1997). All these associations are logical and expected.

One could conceive of some Jews being religiously observant but not participating in Jewish civic affairs, and vice versa; such patterns exist in the United States.[15] However, in Russia, Jewish activism tends to be across the board: it tends not to be "specialized." People who observe customs and traditions are the most active in cultural and social spheres. This may change as Jews become more sophisticated and selective about the ways they choose to express their Jewishness.

Do Ethnic Entrepreneurs Make a Difference?

The activity of Soviet Jewish ethnic entrepreneurs, who emerged first in the Baltic, then in Moscow and Leningrad, and somewhat later in Ukraine, Belarus, and the Russian provinces, was aided and complemented by the State of Israel and world Jewry. They established Jewish schools, newspapers, and local cultural and welfare organizations.[16] The agendas of the local ethnic entrepreneurs and their foreign supporters sometimes diverged, but as long as the local activists were greatly disadvantaged in their struggle against "Soviet power," foreigners supported them financially, politically, and – importantly – morally, though sometimes selectively and with reservations.[17] It is difficult to assess

---

[15] A study of leaders of the Jewish Council on Public Affairs, an American civic body, showed that they "are also more Jewishly educated, more ritually active, and more committed to being Jewish (by their own testimony) than are members of the American Jewish public." Steven M. Cohen with the assistance of Judith Schor, "Religion and the Public Square: Attitudes of American Jews in Comparative Perspective," unpublished paper, CUNY Graduate Center, June 2000. Nevertheless, there are many American Jews who express their Jewishness largely in the civic or in the religious sphere and not equally in both.

[16] On this process, and for case studies of two Jewish communities, see Zvi Gitelman, "Jewish Communal Reconstruction in the Former Soviet Union," in Peter Medding, ed., *Values, Interests and Identity, Studies in Contemporary Jewry*, XI (New York: Oxford University Press, 1995), 136–56.

[17] Some former Soviet activists have charged that Israeli officials, and American and European organizations that subordinated themselves to Israeli offices, actively supported only those whose agendas were the same as Israel's, mainly emigration to Israel. Israeli officials were not enthusiastic about supporting Jewish activists who included the reform of the Soviet system on their agendas. The story from the point of view of a key Israeli official is told in Nehemiah Levanon, *Hakod – 'Nativ'* (Tel Aviv: Am Oved 1995). Another Israeli view of the later period is Baruch Gur-Gurevich, *Shearim petukhim* (Jerusalem: Jewish Agency, 1996).

the impact of these efforts to bring back Soviet Jews to ethnic and/or religious consciousness and activity.

Israeli officials at first ignored and even discouraged attempts to revive Jewish culture and public life in the Soviet Union and its successor states. They regarded these efforts as futile and insisted that the only place for Jews was Israel, the Jewish state. In 1990 the Jewish Agency for Israel, a quasi-governmental body, adopted the following goals for its activities in the USSR:

> "1. Strengthening Jewish identity;
> 2. Educating for the centrality of the State of Israel in the life of the Jewish people [*am*];
> 3. Strengthening the Zionist movement;
> 4. Encouraging immigration to Israel [*aliyah*]."[18]

Even the goal of "strengthening Jewish identity" was posited not as an end in itself but as leading to emigration to Israel.

However, by the late 1990s, both domestic and foreign activists had adopted a dual agenda of promoting cultural and religious revival within the USSR and allowing unfettered emigration, though different groups had different emphases. Israeli officials came to realize that involvement in local Jewish activities and the acquisition of Jewish education would be as likely to lead to immigration to Israel as it would to activism and participation in public Jewish life in the USSR and its successor states.

The collapse of the Soviet system led to the most massive Jewish emigration in Soviet history. Unlike most would-be Soviet and post-Soviet emigrants, Jews had a "homeland," Israel, which would accept them as immigrants unconditionally, and they also enjoyed nearly automatic refugee status in the United States. Although American policy became more restrictive after 1989, Germany continued to treat Jews from the Former Soviet Union as refugees until January 2005 when it adopted a more restrictive policy. All told, from 1989 through 2004, more than a million Jews and their non-Jewish first-degree relatives emigrated from the FSU, about two-thirds of them going to Israel.

The Federal Republic of Germany also pursued the dual agenda of reviving German culture in the FSU and permitting the "return" of ethnic Germans, but, unlike Israel, it is now more interested in having the ethnic Germans remain in their FSU homes than in encouraging their immigration. Most of the Armenian diaspora adopted a similar position in the Soviet period, when Armenians, along with Germans and Jews, were selectively allowed to emigrate; however, some Armenians abroad feared that emigration would weaken the Armenian Soviet republic.[19]

---

[18] Gur-Gurevitch, *Shearim petukhim*, 75. Gur-Gurevitch was in charge of the *Sochnut's* activities in the USSR at this point.

[19] An interesting comparison among government policies toward their respective diasporas in the FSU is made by Seunghyun Seo, "A Comparative Study of the Korean, German, and Polish

From the late 1980s to at least 1996, when the Russian Jewish Congress was founded, ethnic revivalists depended heavily on foreign sponsors for political, cultural, and financial support. Jewish communities had been destroyed in the 1920s, and unlike the Russian Orthodox Church or the republics of titular Soviet nationalities, Jews did not even have shell institutions that could serve as receptacles for new content. In 1988, at the Extraordinary Nineteenth Conference of the Communist Party of the Soviet Union, Mikhail Gorbachev stated that "members of peoples living outside the borders of their own national state, or peoples not having such a state, should have the opportunity to satisfy their national and cultural needs... through relations with other members of their peoples... and through the establishment of national-cultural centers."[20] That same year, in the favorable atmosphere created by Gorbachev's glasnost and perestroika, the Jewish Cultural Association was established. A year later, Jewish activists established an umbrella organization for Soviet Jewry, the Va'ad. From its inception, the Va'ad had no significant independent funding. Some Soviet Jews felt that foreign support for it came with strings attached. The breakup of the USSR led to the breakup of the Va'ad, although some small Russian and Ukrainian organizations survived.[21]

Several Russian Jewish "oligarchs" freed the Jewish communities of Russia from foreign dependence to some extent by establishing the Russian Jewish Congress (RJC) in 1996. The following year it had a budget of more than $15 million, all generated within the Russian Federation. According to a former president of the Congress it raised and distributed $43.5 million between 1996 and 2000.[22] The brief arrest in June 2000 of Vladimir Gusinsky, president and chief sponsor of the RJC, raised doubts about its viability under President Putin, and in the next few years, Putin marginalized or drove out of the country most of the RJC's leadership. In its place, he found a willing partner in the Chabad-Lubavitch movement, which shielded him from any suspicion of anti-Semitism, as suggested in Chapter 5. A Federation of Jewish Communities of Russia (FEOR) was established under Chabad auspices. Putin demonstrated his endorsement of the new organization by appearing at Jewish holiday events sponsored by FEOR. Although there already were two "chief rabbis" in Russia – the Birobidzhan-born Adolf Shaevich who had served in Moscow's Choral Synagogue in the Soviet period, and the Swiss citizen, Pinchas Goldschmidt – FEOR "elected" Berl Lazar as Chief Rabbi of the Russian Federation. Lazar and FEOR constantly assured the world and

Diasporas in the Russian Far East & Central Asia and the Results of Repatriation to Their Homelands," *Asian Social Science* 6, 4 (April 2010), 61–70.

[20] *Pravda*, July 5, 1988, quoted in Ted Friedgut, "The Problematics of Jewish Community Development in Contemporary Russia," in Zvi Gitelman and Yaacov Ro'i, eds., *Revolution, Repression and Revival: The Soviet Jewish Experience* (Lanham, MD: Rowman & Littlefield, 2007), 247.

[21] Details of the gradual breakup of the Va'ad are found in Eugene Satanovsky, "Organized National Life of Russian Jews in the Late Soviet and Post-Soviet Era: A View from Moscow," *Jewish Political Studies Review* 14, 1–2 (Spring 2002).

[22] The sums allotted to Russian Jewish Congress programs, 1996–2000, are found in ibid., Appendices 1 and 2.

especially world Jewry that President Putin was "good for the Jews" and good for Russia because his authoritarianism at least guarded against the resurgence of communism and of Russian nationalist anti-Semitism. As Ted Friedgut put it, "In return for...public patronage, FEOR and, indeed the entire Jewish establishment, are expected to project a consistently positive image of Russia at all levels, particularly for the consumption of Jewish communities and elites outside Russia. This they do by demonstrating that Jewish religious and social life in Russia is now normal and free and that anti-Semitism in Russia is marginal and diminishing."[23]

These tactics worked very well for Chabad, Putin, and his successor as president, Dmitrii Medvedev. The great majority of local rabbis in Russia (each is known as a "chief rabbi" for some reason) are Chabad-affiliated. This seems to be the case also in Moldova, Latvia, Kazakhstan, and Uzbekistan, although not in Ukraine and Lithuania. In addition to its impressive ability to mobilize funds, Chabad has an asset no other Jewish organization possesses: a seemingly ever renewable cadre of unquestioning adherents, willing to settle permanently in remote unattractive locations and work for their cause for little material compensation. There are said to be permanent Chabad rabbis in 105 FSU locales, and "circuit-riding" *shlukhim* [emissaries] serving another 321 places.[24] Chabad also claims to sponsor seventy-one day schools and sixty kindergartens in the Russian Federation.[25]

In Ukraine, there are said to be 250 Jewish organizations under various auspices, 14 Jewish kindergartens, 14 day schools, and 74 supplementary schools.[26] I concluded in Chapter 5 that this enormous activity has not resulted in a religious revival among Russian or Ukrainian Jews. However, because a high proportion of those who do become religious leave the country, either temporarily or permanently, there may be more people attracted to Judaism than one can observe at any single time in the FSU.[27]

"Jewish Public Life is Local"

One must agree with Ted Friedgut: "Jewish institutions in Russia do not as yet have deep roots and the stability provided by tradition."[28] This is certainly true at regional and national levels, although there is more activity, encompassing many more people, at the local level. Yet, even in 1997, almost

---

[23] Ibid., 252.
[24] Jonathan Mark, "Chabad's Global Warming," *The Jewish Week* (New York), December 2, 2005.
[25] Federation of Jewish Communities of the CIS, Annual Report, 2005.
[26] Religious Information Service of Ukraine, February 23, 2006.
[27] The director of a religious dormitory school in Pinsk, Belarus, and Rabbi Yaacov Bleich, chief rabbi of Ukraine, seem to measure the success of their schools, sponsored by the Karlin-Stolin Hasidic movement, by the proportion of students who go to Israel. Based on personal conversations and observations.
[28] Friedgut, "The Problematics of Jewish Community Development in Contemporary Russia," 265.

a decade after Jewish activity had begun in many localities, from the Baltic to Vladivostok, one-third of the Russian Jews and one-quarter in Ukraine said they were completely unaware of any Jewish organization in their city.

Many respondents felt that Jewish life in their cities was still weak, though the proportion who think it is active increased from the first to the second wave. Very few were aware of the existence of the Va'ad (by the end of the decade a skeleton organization) or of Hillel (which had begun its activities toward the end of the decade). The best known organizations were foreign – the Jewish Agency for Israel and the American Jewish Joint Distribution Committee (the Joint).

In the late 1990s, more than half the respondents in Ukraine and nearly two-thirds in Russia judged that religious Jewish organizations had little or no influence on Jewish life in their cities. They attributed somewhat more influence to social, nonreligious organizations: one-quarter in Russia and more than one-third in Ukraine thought those organizations had made a noticeable impact on Jewish life, but 48 percent in Ukraine and 54 percent in Russia thought their impact was minimal or nonexistent. The kinds of communal activity seen as most beneficial were those involving assistance to the elderly and needy. Educational and cultural activities, such as lectures, courses, and libraries, were also valued. Synagogues, supplementary religious schools, and matchmaking were regarded as unimportant.

Sensing the desire for welfare services, Chabad seems to have shifted its focus from drawing people to religion to providing welfare and human services, especially meals for the poor and elderly. In so doing it began to act as a parallel organization to the Joint, which reported spending $70 million in 2004 in the FSU – reaching 2,980 locales and providing "essential relief to some 240,000 impoverished and socially isolated elderly Jews."[29] The Joint works through a network of seventy-four local "Hesed" (welfare) centers, staffed by local people who were thereby activated to train and work in Jewish communal service. These efforts were curtailed in 2008 by the sharp decline in the value of the American dollar, the currency in which the Joint raises nearly all of its funds, and concomitant cuts in staff and services.

Most respondents (two-thirds in Russia, three-quarters in Ukraine) were aware of the existence of at least one Jewish organization; such awareness rose modestly in the course of the 1990s (see Table 7.2). Knowledge about Jewish organizations was about 1.2 times lower in Moscow, the Russian capital, than in the other Russian cities, despite the fact that the central offices of national organizations and those of foreign Jewish organizations are found there. Indeed, the greatest awareness of Jewish organizations was in Ekaterinburg, the city with the smallest Jewish community in our sample, as noted earlier.

There is a similar tendency in Ukraine, where the level of information among residents of the smaller and peripheral cities (Lviv, Chernivtsi) was 1.2–1.3

---

[29] American Jewish Joint Distribution Committee, *Year Book 2004: JDC in the Former Soviet Union* (New York: JDC, 2004).

TABLE 7.2. *Awareness of Jewish Organizations, Russian Cities 1997–98 (percent)*

	Moscow	Petersburg	Ekaterinburg	Russia
Not familiar	40.3	29.8	26.3	33.0
Have heard of organizations, but not attended events	13.8	15.3	16.1	14.9
Have used services of organizations	9.0	31.0	5.3	16.6
Have attended events, but not a member	26.9	24.0	41.4	29.2
I am a member and participant	10.2	8.1	14.5	10.4
Other	3.5	1.6	0.0	2.0
N	500	500	314	1,314

times higher than that of those who live in the large urban centers with much larger Jewish populations (Kharkiv, Odessa). The Ukrainian capital, Kiev, is exceptional. Here the level of awareness of Jewish organizational activity was high, second only to Chernivtsi (see Table 7.3).

Few Jews in Russia and Ukraine were unaware of *any* Jewish organizational activity, except in Moscow where an unusually high 40 percent were unaware of it. Perhaps as the capital and center of commercial, cultural, and political life, Moscow offers its residents a wider variety of activities than any other city. Jewish organizations must compete with better endowed and long-standing institutions for the attention and affiliation of Muscovites. In addition, Muscovite Jews may be confused or put off by the multiplicity of Jewish

TABLE 7.3. *Awareness of Jewish Organizations in the Ukraine (percent)*

	Kiev	Kharkiv	Odessa	Lviv	Chernivtsi	Ukraine
Not aware	19.6	35.0	35.0	23.0	14.3	26.3
Heard of organization, but not attended events	14.8	19.6	17.8	21.0	13.0	17.3
Used services of organizations	20.4	26.6	15.5	12.0	12.3	18.5
Have attended events, but not an activist	43.6	20.4	29.0	28.7	46.0	33.0
I am a member and participant	15.4	8.6	8.5	22.7	22.0	14.4
Other	0.8	1.6	1.8	0.7	0.3	1.1
N	500	500	300	300	300	1900

TABLE 7.4. *Respondents' Knowledge of Jewish Organizations in Russia in 1997* (percent)

	Know Well	Do Not Know Very Well	Don't Know at All
Jewish Agency	20.1	36.4	43.5
Joint Distribution Committee	12.5	31.5	56.0
Chabad-Lubavitch	8.7	26.9	64.5
Russian Jewish Congress	4.8	17.4	77.8
Jewish National-Cultural Autonomy	3.9	14.8	81.3
Va'ad of Russia	3.9	12.9	83.1
Congress of Jewish Religious Organizations	2.1	10.3	87.5
Hillel	4.6	4.6	90.8

N = 1,300

organizations – local, national, and international. Unsure of where their interests might lie and unclear about the character of Jewish organizations, Moscow Jews may simply give a metaphorical shrug and, rather than put time and effort into investigating these organizations, dismiss them all and turn their attention to the more familiar. In the United States, smaller Jewish communities are generally better organized and have higher rates of affiliation than larger communities, New York being an example of one with low levels of affiliation. In large cities Jews can be anonymous and avoid pressures to affiliate and associate with other Jews. They may feel more secure in their numbers and social position, whereas those in smaller Jewish communities may feel a greater need for vigilance in defense of their interests and compelled to unite and consolidate their social, political, and economic assets.

Neither gender nor education differentiated among respondents' awareness of Jewish organizations. The key explanatory variable, again, was age. In Russia those completely unaware of Jewish organizations were concentrated in the older age group. Whereas only 21 percent of the youngest cohort (ages 16-29) were unaware, among the oldest (70 and over) 38 percent were ignorant of the organizations. The relationship between age and knowledge is linear – ignorance of the organizations increases with age.

In Ukraine there were similar tendencies, although not as consistent. For example, the 30–39 year olds had the lowest level of information, but if one compares the polar opposite groups, the level of information among those over 70 was considerably less than that among the 16–29 year olds.

Closer examination reveals that knowledge of the organizations was very superficial. The overwhelming majority of respondents said they had only a vague idea or none at all of the nature of the organizations (see Tables 7.4 and 7.5).

TABLE 7.5. *Respondents' Knowledge of Jewish Organizations in Ukraine in 1998 (percent)*

	Know well	Do Not Know Very Well	Don't Know at All
Jewish Agency	23.7	43.8	32.6
Joint Distribution Committee	15.9	37.6	46.6
Ukrainian Society of Jewish Culture	12.1	29.9	58.1
Chabad-Lubavitch	5.6	14.6	79.8
Jewish Council of Ukraine	3.6	10.1	86.3
All-Ukrainian Jewish Congress	2.7	12.2	85.1
Va'ad of Ukraine	1.9	5.3	92.9
Union of Jewish Religious Organizations, Ukraine	1.4	6.0	92.6
Hillel	2.3	2.2	95.5

N = 1,900

It is noteworthy that in Russia and Ukraine people were better informed about *foreign* Jewish organizations than about local or national ones. The best known organization was the Jewish Agency (*Sochnut*). Every fifth respondent in Russia and every fourth in Ukraine said they "know well" this Israel-based organization. The Joint ranked second: one of every eight people in Russia and just about one in six in Ukraine claimed good knowledge of the Joint and its activities. All other organizations, with the exception of Chabad-Lubavitch in Russia and the Society for Jewish Culture in Ukraine, had far lower ratings than the *Sochnut* or Joint. Residents of the two capitals, Moscow and Kiev, were more knowledgeable about both the *Sochnut* and Joint than those in the provincial cities. Hillel was least known because it began its activities in late 1994 and had full-scale operations in only four cities of the FSU, though there were nascent programs in fourteen other cities. In addition, Hillel serves college students and young adults (up to about age 25) so older people were not likely to know of it.

The young were the best informed about the *Sochnut*, perhaps because they are the focus of its efforts to promote immigration to Israel, and it sponsors youth groups and activities toward that end. Knowledge of the *Sochnut* decreased with age.

Categories of Involvement

To analyze the data further, we divided Russian and Ukrainian Jews involved in local Jewish communities into four categories: activists, visitors, clients, and interested parties. The first group, "activists," consists of formal members, functionaries, and regular participants in some Jewish organization. A small part of this group might be thought of as "professional Jews" or "Jewish civil servants." They are the nucleus of Jewish national organizational life.

The second category comprises those who have participated, with varying degrees of frequency, in holiday, memorial, cultural, or educational events sponsored by Jewish organizations. They are the audience, standing on the periphery of the nucleus. We call them "passive participants" or "visitors." The third group consists of people who come into contact with Jewish organizations as consumers of their services (social, medical, legal, or other aid, assistance in preparing for emigration, etc.). They are "clients." Finally, there is a group of people, whom we designate "interested parties." They do not attend Jewish activities, but have heard or read about their activities and have some knowledge of these organizations.

Activists

The parameters of the group that forms the nuclei of Jewish organizations in Russia and Ukraine hardly changed in the five-year interval between surveys: there was no increase in the proportion of activists. In both periods, one in ten Russian Jews and one in seven Ukrainian Jews could be considered activists. Perhaps this stability – some would call it stagnation – is explained by the unique feature of Jewish life in the FSU; that is, the continuous flow of migrants. Although some activists may have found that Jewish communal activity fulfilled their Jewish aspirations and, in some instances, provided them with a livelihood, others who came in constant contact with foreign Jews were persuaded that a fully Jewish life could be led only in Israel or in a diaspora Jewish community, or they may have perceived greater personal and economic opportunities elsewhere than in Russia or Ukraine.

There were significant differences among the cities in the proportion of activists. The general rule is that the smaller the city and its Jewish population, the higher the proportion of activists. Thus, in Ekaterinburg the proportion of activists was 1.5 times larger than in Moscow and 1.8 times larger than in St. Petersburg. Similarly, the activist core in Lviv and Chernivtsi was almost 1.5 times larger than in Kiev and 2.6 times more than in Kharkov and Odessa. In smaller communities there are greater opportunities for office holding, and one should not dismiss the possibility of a greater sense of efficacy in smaller populations, as the political science literature suggests.

Once again we find inconsequential differences between the behavior of men and women. Age explains much more. Significantly, the youngest cohort in Russia contained the largest proportion of activists (17.3%). More than one-third of these activists were students in various institutions. In the next cohort (30–39) the proportion of activists dropped by half. It then fell steadily as one went up the scale of age – in the 60–69 year old group (half of them pensioners) only 8 percent could be considered activists. Strikingly, in the oldest group (70 and older), among whom 90 percent are pensioners, the proportion of activists was twice that in the 60–69 year old cohort and 1.4 times as great as in the sample as a whole. Perhaps the most Jewishly knowledgeable and committed people were in the very oldest group, and they were eager to bring their assets to cultural and religious activities. Of course, as retirees they had the time to do so.

The relation between age and Jewish activism in Ukraine only partially resembles that in Russia. In the youngest group, one-third of whom were students, the level of activism (16.4%) was only about 1.2 times higher than among all Ukrainian Jews. As in Russia, activism declined sharply in the next cohort – it was three times less frequent among 30–39 year olds. However, in contrast to Russia, in the rest of the age categories the level of activism intensified. The two oldest groups[30] displayed more activism than the youngest cohort. Among the oldest, every fourth person was an activist. So, contrary to what one might suppose, we discovered that *the oldest and the youngest people are the most active in Jewish public life.* The middle generations were preoccupied with earning a living and were socialized to public *in*activity in the Soviet period in any case.

Curiously, neither income nor education seems to affect activism, with the exception of the poorest people in Russia (those who live from payday to payday) who are half as active as the Jewish population in Russia as a whole. In both republics there is hardly any difference between those with general secondary education and those with higher education.

The "intensity" of ethnicity matters for activism. "Pure Jews" (those with two Jewish parents) in Russia and Ukraine are more active in Jewish public life than part-Jews. Jews married to non-Jews, especially those whose spouses have no Jewish background at all, are less active than those married to Jews. Similarly, those whose self-described national consciousness is "primarily Jewish" are more likely to be active in Jewish life than those whose consciousness is "both Jewish and not Jewish," and they are twice as active as those who feel themselves to be predominantly not Jewish. Among Ukrainian Jews these differences are nearly twice as great.

Passive Participants

Nearly 30 percent of the Jews in Russia were passive participants in Jewish public life, their proportion remaining the same over five years. The ratio of activists to passive participants was about 1:3 in all Russian cities. In comparison, in Ukraine the number of passive participants grew from the first to the second wave. Every third Ukrainian Jew could be considered a passive participant (only slightly more than in Russia), but the ratio of activists to passive participants was lower (1:2.3). There was more local variance in Ukraine than in Russia: the ratio of activists to participants ranged from 1:1.3 in Lviv to 1:3.4 in Odessa. In Chernivtsi and Kiev about 40 percent of the sample were passive participants. In the other three Ukrainian cities the proportion of passive participants ranged from 20 to 25 percent.

---

[30] Fifty-four per cent of the 60–69 year olds are retired, as are 86 percent of those over 70.

Age is again a decisive factor. The youngest group constituted 40 percent of the passive participants in Russia and half those in Ukraine. The proportion of passive participants declined with age and was smallest among the oldest group in both Russia and Ukraine.

Unlike what we found among the activists, the ethnicity of a spouse, level of education, and gender have no effect on *passive* participation. Whether one is a full Jew or part-Jew makes little (Russia) or no (Ukraine) difference for one's passive participation in Jewish life. *To be an activist requires a strong commitment to Jewishness, but to be a passive participant does not.*

Clients

Clients constituted a small group – in Russia only one-sixth of the sample and in Ukraine about one-fifth. However, it is important to note the increase in this category between the two waves. In Ukraine it nearly doubled and in Russia it increased 1.3 times. This increase reflects the aging, and perhaps concomitant impoverishment, of the Jewish population. It may also arise from an increasing awareness among the elderly and disadvantaged that assistance is available from local welfare organizations ("Hesed" societies) and from international organizations such as the Joint.

There is considerable regional variation in the proportion of clients. In St. Petersburg, whose welfare organizations are staffed by remarkably talented and dedicated people and which has served as a model city for others in this respect, the proportion of clients increased 1.6 times over five years, whereas in Moscow and Ekaterinburg there was a slight *decline* in clients during the same period. Put another way, the proportion of clients was 3.4 and 5.8 times greater in St. Petersburg than in Moscow and Ekaterinburg, respectively. In Ukraine there were similar variations, with Kharkiv, and to a lesser extent, Kiev, having larger proportions of clients than in the other cities. However, unlike in Russia, the client category expanded over five years in each of the cities, though with varying intensity, perhaps as a consequence of the failure of Ukraine's economy to improve in the mid-1990s. The proportion of clients in Kharkiv and Kiev doubled in the 1992–97 period and increased almost as much in the other cities.

Who are these clients? The elderly, of course – in Russia, more than one-quarter of the oldest group are clients, five times as many as among the youngest group. In Ukraine, one-third of those 70 and older are clients. Women outnumbered men among the clients in Russia and Ukraine, unlike among activists and passive participants.[31] This may be due to the greater number of widows than of widowers. Needless to say, those with the lowest incomes are overrepresented among the clients.

Interested Parties: The Reserve Forces of Jewish Communities

Those who never participate in public Jewish functions but have some interest in or have heard or read about Jewish organizations and institutions were

---

[31] The number of elderly women is greater than that of men in that age group.

a small group, one-seventh of the Russian and one-sixth of the Ukrainian samples. Nevertheless, some of them might at any time move into the other categories, and their ranks might be replenished by people who previously had no information about or interest in Jewish affairs. The proportion of this group grew both in Russia and Ukraine between the surveys.

Emigration and Activism

Because Russia and Ukraine have by far the largest Jewish populations of the post-Soviet states – although the most reliable estimates are that there remain less than a half-million Jews in these two states, whereas in 1989 there were 570,400 in Russia and 486,300 in Ukraine[32] – they have the best prospects for reconstructing Jewish public life. Ukraine and the Russian Federation have taken the path of civic rather than ethnic states, and there has been no governmental anti-Semitism in either country since they became independent. Both dropped the nationality paragraph from their internal passports. Like others, Jews are free to define who and what they are and how they manifest that identity – in language, religion, territory, and place in the political, economic, and social hierarchies. Jews in Russia and Ukraine can try to assimilate and become Russians or Ukrainians; they can remain indifferent to their ethnicity, neither rejecting nor acting on it; they can deploy it and participate in Jewish communal life while also expressing Jewish identities at home; or they can emigrate.

It is ironic that those most involved in post-Soviet Jewish life are the most likely to emigrate, causing a tension between rebuilding viable Jewish communities and migrating to Israel. The more people who leave for Israel – or any other destination – the less likely it is that Jewish life in the FSU will be viable or at least vibrant. Among those surveyed, people who think that Israel is the "historic homeland of the Jewish people" were more inclined to attend Jewish events and synagogue services and belong to Jewish organizations than those who did not see Israel this way. We asked respondents whether or not they planned to leave Russia and Ukraine and, if so, where they planned to go. When one looks at indices of Jewish activism and emigration plans, one finds that *the clearer and more definite one's plans to emigrate, the higher the level of local Jewish activism*. Thus, in Russia (1997) the proportion of activists was more than twice as great among those who resolutely decided to emigrate "in the near future" than among those who had absolutely no intention of leaving.

In the 1990s, those who attended Jewish events most frequently and who intended to emigrate were twice as likely to emigrate to Israel than to the United States or Germany. Understandably, people who said that the desire "to live a full Jewish life" played a significant role in their emigration plans were more culturally active than those who said such considerations were not significant. The Israel-bound were also more likely to belong to Jewish organizations. One wonders about causality. Did people who intended to go to Israel participate

---

[32] *Natsional'nyi sostav naseleniia* SSSR (Moscow: Finansy i statistiki, 1991), 9, 78.

in Jewish life to prepare for life there, or did those who were exposed to Jewish culture and activity conclude that Israel is the best place to live Jewishly? Was Jewish activism mostly a preparatory course for emigration? Or was it preparation for emigration for many but also an end in itself for a crucial minority who remained as the small but stable core of communities that will be in flux in the foreseeable future? These questions became somewhat moot as emigration from the FSU tailed off sharply after 2001, as I discuss later.

In most migrations, people of child-bearing age migrate in greater proportions than older ones, and this is true of the Russian-speaking Jewish emigration. By 2005, the median age of those who came to Israel from the USSR and its successor states was 36.8 years, about 13 years lower than that of Jews in the USSR in 1989 **before** the mass migration.[33] Jewish communities in Russia and Ukraine will be increasingly aged, small, and with a high and growing proportion of part-Jews. The group we call "clients" of Jewish organizations was small in the late 1990s, but it is important to remember the increase in this category between the two waves. Their participation in the welfare activities of Jewish local, national, and international organizations has become one of the most salient forms of Jewish public life. The rapid spread of Hesed organizations that serve the poor, elderly, and disabled is testimony to the changing nature of the Jewish population in the FSU. On the other hand, the greater participation of young people in Jewish public life, although it may be a first step in a journey outward, may provide temporary or longer term vigor to communities that seem to be simultaneously reviving and declining. Like so much else about post-Soviet life, the condition and future of Russian and Ukrainian Jewry are unclear.

---

[33] Mark Tolts, "Post-Soviet Jewish Population in the Contemporary World: A Study of Demographic Transition in the Course of Mass Migration," paper presented at the European Population Conference, Barcelona, Spain, July 2008, 9.

8

Anti-Semitism and Jewish Identity

> "But was it not a mistake on God's part to settle the Jews in Russia, where they would have been tormented as if in hell? And what would be the harm if the Jews were to live in Switzerland, where they would be surrounded by first-class lakes, mountain air and nothing but Frenchmen? Everyone makes mistakes, even God."
> Isaac Babel, "How it was Done in Odessa"

> "Strange as it may sound, there are children who love their cruel stepmothers.... The Jews love the same Russia that is so cruel to them."
> Fyodor Sologub, "The Fatherland for All"

> "There is no solution to the Jewish problem.... It is impossible not to remain a Jew.... It is impossible to get rid of one's past by wishing it away.... We must simply recognize the fact... that the Jewish minority is not universally popular, and we must recognize the consequences that follow from that."
> Leo Strauss, "Why We Remain Jews"

Anti-Semitism is the lowest common denominator of Jewish identity. No matter what their attachments to Jewishness and Judaism, all people designated as Jews, if only by others, must react to animus against Jews, however differently. Anti-Semitism can preserve a sense of Jewish belonging among those who wish to get rid of it. For those who wish Jews to remain Jews, the trick is to calibrate an optimal amount of anti-Semitism that will preserve Jewishness without escalating into anti-Jewish discrimination and attacks. This is, of course, impossible. A Hungarian Jew wrote early in the twentieth century: "Let murders, torture and deprivation of rights cease. Anti-Semitism can remain in place. It has a certain utility, as do all clashes; it helps like every criticism and competition.... Were there no anti-Semitism, it would be necessary to invent it for the good of the Jew."[1] A quarter-century after Lajos Biro wrote these words, anti-Semitism ceased to be "functional."

---

[1] Lajos Biro, *A zsidok utja* (Vienna, 1921) translated into Hebrew as "Netiv hayehudim," in Guy Miron and Anna Szalai, *Yehudim al parshat derachim* (Ramat Gan, Israel: Bar Ilan University Press, 2008), 178.

We have seen that most Russian and Ukrainian Jews associate the discovery of their Jewishness with negative feelings. This is because in the USSR it was often anti-Semitism that provoked awareness that one is a Jew, demonstrating that identity is shaped not only by oneself but also by others.[2] Jean-Paul Sartre famously observed, "The Jew is one whom other men consider a Jew: that is the simple truth from which we must start."[3]

In this chapter we survey the history of anti-Semitism in the Russian Empire and the USSR to establish what traditions have influenced attitudes toward Jews today. We then examine both how non-Jews in Russia and Ukraine view Jews today and the reactions of our respondents to the ways in which they are regarded and treated. We conclude by tracing the consequences of anti-Semitism for contemporary Jewish identities in Russia and Ukraine.

It turns out that Jewish identities of the oldest and youngest Jews we interviewed are shaped the least by anti-Semitism, but for different reasons. The oldest people had positive pre-Soviet and early Soviet memories of a vibrant Jewish culture and had reason to be proud of being Jewish. The youngest matured after the successor states of the USSR had abandoned anti-Semitism "from above" and when fears and hatreds of other peoples had pushed anti-Semitism lower on the scale of ethnic prejudices. In addition to Soviet policies and popular attitudes, the Holocaust, which killed about 2.7 million Jews who were Soviet citizens in 1941, shapes the fears and feelings of contemporary Russian and Ukrainian Jews. Anti-Semitism is likely to diminish as the major influence on Jewish identity, but whether Jewish affiliation will develop based on positive features, such as an attractive Jewish culture and religion, is uncertain.

Modern European Anti-Semitism

In order to differentiate themselves from minorities, some people establish and insist on the identities of members of racial, ethnic and religious minorities, against their will. Jews have often been forced to identify as Jews when they did not wish to do so. Especially where anti-Semitism is widespread, some Jews have sought to hide their Jewishness, only to be reminded of it by anti-Semites who are determined to maintain the distinction between Jews and others.[4]

---

[2] Richard Jenkins expresses this as the difference between "identification," which is done by the individual, and "categorization," which is done by others. Richard Jenkins, "Rethinking Ethnicity: Identity, Categorization and Power," *Ethnic and Racial Studies* 17, 2 (April 1994), 202.

[3] Jean-Paul Sartre, *Anti-Semite and Jew* (New York: Schocken Books, 1948), 67–68.

[4] The literature on anti-Semitism is voluminous. On anti-Semitism in antiquity and its relation to religion, see Gavin Langmuir, *History, Religion, Antisemitism* (Berkeley: University of California Press, 1990); on medieval anti-Semitism, see Langmuir, *Toward a Definition of Antisemitism* (Berkeley: University of California Press, 1990); on modern anti-Semitism, see Jacob Katz, *From Prejudice to Destruction: Antisemitism, 1700–1933* (Cambridge, MA: Harvard University Press, 1980) [this work focuses on Central Europe]; Peter Pulzer, *The Rise of Political Antisemitism in Germany and Austria* (London: Peter Halban, 1988); and Shmuel Almog, *Nationalism and Antisemitism in Modern Europe, 1815–1945* (Oxford: Pergamon, 1990); and on contemporary

After emancipation from the ghettos, many Jews in Western Europe preferred to think of themselves as Germans, French, English, and the like, but others insisted that they be identified as Jews. In March 1912, a German Jew, Moritz Goldstein, observed, "Among ourselves we have the impression that we speak as Germans to Germans.... But though we may... feel totally German, the others feel us to be totally un-German.... They detect in us something 'Asiatic' and miss the German spirit."[5] My late colleague, Alfred G. Meyer, grew up in Nazi Germany; he recalled, "When I was growing up, I was German – or thought I was. The attitude of my fellow Germans, and, later, the laws of the Nazi state, impressed on me the realization that they considered me alien and undesirable.... Being Jewish thus became a stigma that made me feel a trace of shame.... From earliest youth, I knew I was different from the people in my street and in my school."[6] The Nazi regime stamped the identity cards of German Jews with the letter "J" (for *Jude*), adding the name "Israel" to each Jewish male and "Sarah" to each Jewish female. In the USSR, as we have noted, Jews were identified as such on the fifth line of their internal passports, an identification document each Soviet citizen received at age 16. This policy was not motivated by anti-Semitism, but was part of the classification scheme of more than 100 groups, including Jews, as nationalities or ethnic groups recognized by the state.[7] With the advent of official anti-Semitic policies in the late 1940s, some Soviet Jews began to think of themselves as "invalids of the fifth category," a pun on the designation of war invalids according to the severity of their disabilities and that nationality was noted on the fifth line of the internal passport.

Anti-Semitism has a long history in the territories of the Former Soviet Union.[8] Until the late eighteenth century, Jews were legally barred from living in the Russian Empire. Much of the animus against Jews stemmed from Christian beliefs that the Jews had killed Christ. Tsarina Elizabeth, who ruled from 1741 to 1762, responded to merchants pleading with her to allow Jews to trade there by writing, "From the enemies of Christ I wish neither gain nor profit."[9] Only the annexation of eastern Poland with its large Jewish population in the late eighteenth century forced the tsars to admit Jews to the Russian Empire;

---

anti-Semitism, see, inter alia, Bernard Lewis, *Semites and Antisemites* (New York: Norton, 1987); Michael Curtis, ed., *Antisemitism in the Contemporary World* (Boulder, CO: Westview, 1986), Alvin Rosenfeld, ed., *Resurgent Antisemitism* (Bloomington: Indiana University Press, 2012)..

[5] *Der Kunstwart*, quoted in Paul Mendes-Flohr, *German Jews: A Dual Identity* (New Haven: Yale University Press, 1999), 46.

[6] Alfred G. Meyer, *My Life as a Fish* (privately published, 2000), 316, 501.

[7] On the debates regarding classification of peoples, see Francine Hirsch, "The Soviet Union as a Work-in-Progress: Ethnographers and the Category Nationality in the 1926, 1937, and 1939 Censuses," *Slavic Review* 56, 2 (Summer 1997).

[8] On the history of anti-Semitism in Russia, see Savelii Dudakov, *Istoriia odnogo mifa. Ocherki russkoi literatury XIX-XX vv*. (Moscow: Nauka, 1993) and Shimon Markish's discussion of this and other works in "Historical and Literary Sources of Russian Antisemitism," *Shvut* 1-2, 17-18 (1995), 415-23.

[9] Quoted in Zvi Gitelman, *A Century of Ambivalence: The Jews of Russia and the Soviet Union, 1881 to the Present*, 2nd ed. (Bloomington: Indiana University Press, 2001), xii.

however, they were almost immediately confined to those territories where they already lived, which were declared a "Pale of Settlement."[10] Jews could not live "beyond the Pale." Over time, as John Klier observed, "Russian Judeophobia was largely transformed from a simple, primitive hatred based on a view of the Jews as deicides into a set of more sophisticated, modern myths, encompassing a view of the Jews as participants in a conspiracy directed against the very basis of Christian civilization."[11] By the late nineteenth century discrimination against Jews had been generalized to what might be called racist or ethnic discrimination, what Gabriella Safran has called "the change in focus from text to blood."[12] As Hannah Arendt, a refugee from Nazism, wrote, "Jews had been able to escape from Judaism into conversion; from Jewishness there was no escape."[13]

During the nineteenth and early twentieth centuries, Russian governments imposed restrictions on Jews, such as a *numerus clausus* in education and the professions, a quota system that restricted the number of Jews. Beginning in 1827 Jewish communities had to deliver annually a government-determined number of Jewish boys to the military where they would serve twenty-five years; sometimes they were taken for pre-military training for some years before their service would start. Jews were barred from the civil service and officer rank in the military. Church and state cooperated in attempting to convert Jews to Christianity.[14]

The Russian Empire became notorious as the site of pogroms, attacks on Jews by mobs of local people. In 1881–82, after the assassination of Tsar Alexander II, a wave of pogroms washed over Ukraine and swept away Jewish dreams of acceptance and integration into the larger society. "A few hundred lives were lost and there was great material damage, but the psychological impact was greater than the physical one. As Pauline Wengeroff observed, in 1881 'the sun which had risen on Jewish life in the fifties suddenly set.... Anti-Semitism erupted; the Jews were forced back into the ghetto. Without

---

[10] See John Doyle Klier, *Russia Gathers Her Jews* (Dekalb, IL: Northern Illinois University Press, 1986).
[11] Ibid., xviii.
[12] Gabriella Safran, *Rewriting the Jew: Assimilation Narratives in the Russian Empire* (Stanford: Stanford University Press, 2000).
[13] Hannah Arendt, *The Origins of Totalitarianism* (Cleveland: Meridian, 1962), 87.
[14] On tsarist Russia's policies toward Jews, see Michael Stanislawski, *Tsar Nicholas I and the Jews* (Philadelphia: Jewish Publication Society, 1983); Hans Rogger, *Jewish Policies and Right-Wing Politics in Imperial Russia* (Berkeley: University of California Press, 1986); John Klier, *Imperial Russia's Jewish Question, 1855–1881* (New York: Cambridge University Press, 1995); Heinz Dietrich Lowe, *Tsars and Jews: Reform, Reaction and Antisemitism in Imperial Russia, 1772–1917* (Chur, PA: Harwood Academic Publishers, 1994); Louis Greenberg, *The Jews in Russia* (New York: Schocken Books, 1976); Simon Dubnow, *History of the Jews in Russia and Poland*, Vol. III (Philadelphia: Jewish Publication Society, 1920); Alexander Tager, *The Decay of Czarism* (Philadelphia: Jewish Publication Society, 1935); and Salo Baron, *The Russian Jew under Tsars and Soviets* (New York: Macmillan, 1964)

ceremony, the gateways to education were closed.'"[15] In 1903, forty-five Jews were killed in a pogrom in the Bessarabian (now Moldovan) city of Kishinev (today Chisinau), arousing protests in Western Europe and the United States.[16] In the turbulent year of 1905, pogroms broke out once again when Russia was at war against the Japanese and the government was putting down an attempted revolution.

Most observers saw attacks on the Jews as government-inspired. Historian Simon Dubnow commented on the pogroms of 1905:

> The participants in the "patriotic demonstration" – consisting mostly of the scum of society, of detectives and police officials in plain clothes – would emerge ... carrying the portrait of the Tzar under the shadow of the national flag, singing the national hymn and shouting, "Hurrah, beat the Zhyds! ["Kikes," Jews] The Zhyds are eager for liberty. They go against our Tzar to put a Zhyd in his place." These "patriotic" demonstrators would be accompanied by police and Cossack patrols (or soldiers), ostensibly to preserve order, but in reality to enable the hooligans to attack and maltreat the Jews and prevent the victims from defending themselves. As soon as the Jews assembled for self-defense, they would be driven off by the police and troops. Thereupon, the "patriotic" demonstrators ... would break up into small bands and disperse all over the city, invading Jewish houses and stores, ruin, plunder, beat, and sometimes slaughter entire families.[17]

Recent scholarship has concluded that the pogroms were not planned or inspired by the government, but were spontaneous outbursts, often fanned by the Russian Orthodox Church – Easter was the most dangerous period of the year for Russian Jews.[18] Most observers at the time and scholars today agree that the government did little to prevent the pogroms, interceding only when matters threatened to get out of hand and possibly spill over into demonstrations against the regime itself.

---

[15] Zvi Gitelman, *A Century of Ambivalence*, 10.

[16] On the Kishinev pogrom, see Edward Judge, *Easter in Kishinev* (New York: New York University Press, 1995). On the effect of anti-Semitism in Russia on U.S.–Russian relations, see V. V. Engel, '*Evreiskii vopros' v Russko-Amerikanskikh otnosheniiakh* (Moscow: Nauka, 1998) and Naomi W. Cohen, *Jacob H. Schiff: A Study in American Jewish Leadership* (Hanover, NH: University Press of New England, 1999).

[17] Simon Dubnow, *History of the Jews in Russia and Poland*, 128–29.

[18] See I. Michael Aronson, *Troubled Waters: The Origins of the 1881 Anti-Jewish Pogroms in Russia* (Pittsburgh: University of Pittsburgh Press, 1990) and John Klier and Shlomo Lambrozo, eds. *Pogroms: Anti-Jewish Violence in Modern Russian History* (New York: Cambridge University Press, 1992). John Klier argued that, contrary to popular beliefs among Jews, the Russian Orthodox Church did not make conversion of Jews a high priority and that, despite the Beilis trial, the blood libel (that Jews murdered Christian children to obtain their blood for ritual purposes) was not a significant theme in Orthodox theology or folk belief until the modern period. It became embedded in Orthodox belief in the nineteenth century among both clergy and laypeople. See Klier, "State Policy and the Conversion of Jews in Imperial Russia," in R. Geraci and M. Khodarkovsky, eds., *Of Religion and Empire: Missions, Conversion and Tolerance in Russia* (Ithaca: Cornell University Press, 2001).

Anti-Semitism became an issue in Russia's relations with England, France, and the United States and is also thought to have propelled much of the massive emigration from the 1880s to the eve of World War I.[19] From 1881 to 1912, about 1.9 million Russian Jews emigrated.[20] Much of this migration may have been driven by economic forces,[21] and later by the desire to reunite families, but many thought that Russian anti-Semitism, much of it inspired by the state, was driving Jews away.

From Reform to Repression: The Early Soviet Period

When tsarism fell in 1917, policies that discriminated against Jews were abandoned, although in the course of the Russian civil war another wave of pogroms engulfed the western parts of the country: "The pogroms of 1917–21 far surpassed earlier pogroms in their brutality; nearly sixty thousand Jews were killed,"[22] mostly by the White opponents of Bolshevism and Ukrainian nationalists.[23] The Provisional Government (February/March to October/November 1917) declared civil rights and equality for all inhabitants of the former empire, and the Bolsheviks who seized power from that government affirmed these principles. The Bolshevik regime, while militantly opposing Judaism, Zionism, and traditional Jewish culture, including Hebrew, opened the doors to individual Jewish advancement wider than any other European country. It was also the first government in the world to financially support Jewish cultural institutions such as schools, theaters, magazines, research institutes, and book publishing – as long as that culture was Soviet, socialist, secular, and expressed in Yiddish.[24] For the first fifteen years or so of Soviet rule, Jews

---

[19] See Valeriy Engel, "'Evreiskii vopros' v Russko-Amerikanskikh otnosheniiakh nachala XX veka," in I. Krupnik, ed., *Istoricheskie sud'by Evreev v Rossii i SSSR: Nachalo dialoga* (Moscow: Evreiskoe istoricheskoe obshchestvo, 1992), 146–54, and Engel's previously cited book, '*Evreiiskii vopros*'. On the consequences for emigration of the pogroms, see Ronald Sanders, *Shores of Refuge* (New York: Henry Holt, 1988), part five.

[20] D. S. Pasmanik, *Sud'by evreiskago naroda* (Moscow: Safrut, 1917), 145; Samuel Joseph, *Jewish Immigration to the United States* (New York: Columbia University Studies in History, Economics and Public Law, 1914), 101.

[21] See Eli Lederhandler, *Jewish Immigrants and American Capitalism, 1880–1920* (New York: Cambridge University Press, 2009).

[22] Shlomo Lambroza, "Jewish Responses to Pogroms in Late Imperial Russia," in Jehuda Reinharz, ed., *Living with Antisemitism: Modern Jewish Responses* (Hanover, NH: University Press of New England, 1987), 274.

[23] On the pogroms of this period, see E. Tsherikover, *Antisemitizm un pogromen in Ukraine 1917–1918* (Berlin: Yidisher literarisher farlag, 1923); Tsherikover, *Di ukrainer pogromen in yor 1919* (New York, YIVO Institute, 1965); N. Gergel, "Di pogromen in Ukraine in di yorn 1918–21," in Yaacov Lestchinsky, ed., *Shriftn far ekonomik un statistik* (Berlin: YIVO, 1928); A. D. Rozental, *Megilat ha-tevakh*, 3 vols. (Jerusalem, 1927–31); and Elias Heifetz, *The Slaughter of the Jews in Ukraine in 1919* (New York: Seltzer, 1921). *Kniga pogromov* (Moscow: Rosspen, 2007) is a collection of documents totaling nearly 1,000 pages.

[24] For details, see Zvi Gitelman, *Jewish Nationality and Soviet Politics* (Princeton: Princeton University Press, 1972).

had free access to all forms of higher education and to all areas of the state-run economy. Whereas Jews could not even be policemen under the tsarist regime, under the Soviets Jews served as heads of the secret police, high military and government officers, editors of important newspapers and journals, and high-ranking administrators of research institutes and other academic institutions. A Jew served as foreign minister as late as 1939, another as chief political commissar of the Soviet army. There were Jews on the Politburo, the Communist Party's highest body, and Jewish ministers of the Soviet government, ambassadors, and occupants of leading positions in many fields that had been completely closed to Jews before 1917. The Soviet government actively condemned anti-Semitism in the 1920s, sponsoring lectures and publications that linked it to the despised bourgeoisie and to the ignorant, "backward" elements among the working classes. At times, newspapers exposed anti-Semitic incidents on the factory floor. However, by the mid-1930s the government abandoned its efforts to curb anti-Semitism, as Soviet policy shifted from genuine "proletarian internationalism" to an emphasis on the Russians as the leading nationality in the USSR; Jews became less visible in positions of power.

By the late 1940s, the government was pursuing a clear policy of discriminating against Jews. It seems that popular anti-Semitism "was deeply engrained, and was given an added impetus during the terror [of the 1930s]," when people complained that the Jews had too much social and political power.[25] Valeriy Tishkov claims that anti-Semitism existed "largely at the governmental level,"[26] but there were substantial manifestations of it in the grass roots. It is not altogether clear why there was a radical change in official policy. Some have speculated about Joseph Stalin's increasing paranoia and fear of internal enemies and the West,[27] with which he identified the Jews; others point to rising Russian nationalism,[28] spurred by the war, or to the German occupation when large parts of the USSR were flooded with anti-Semitic propaganda. Whatever its cause, the turn to anti-Semitic policies was visible to all.

Between 1948 and Stalin's death in 1953 – the "black years of Soviet Jewry" – the state destroyed the remnants of Soviet Yiddish culture, closing all Yiddish publishing houses, theaters, and schools. It mounted an "anti-cosmopolitan" campaign, removing thousands of Jews from responsible positions in the arts, science, government, and the economy. About twenty leading Jewish cultural figures, along with a few who still occupied important governmental positions, were shot as "enemies of the people" on August 20, 1952. In January 1953, the "Doctors' Plot" was "uncovered," wherein a group of Jewish doctors in the Kremlin – "murderers in white coats" – were accused of plotting

---

[25] Sarah Davies, *Popular Opinion in Stalin's Russia* (Cambridge: Cambridge University Press, 1997), 85.
[26] Valeriy Tishkov, *Rekviem po etnosu* (Moscow: Nauka, 2003), 331.
[27] For example, Robert C. Tucker, "The Dictator and Totalitarianism," *World Politics* 17, 4 (July, 1965), 555–83. See also the second volume of his biography of Stalin, *Stalin in Power* (New York: Norton, 1990).
[28] Frederick Barghoorn, *Soviet Russian Nationalism* (New York: Oxford University Press, 1956).

on behalf of Western Jewish organizations and governments to poison high Soviet officials. It was rumored that large numbers of Jews would be deported to labor camps. The Jewish population was terrified, but a month after Stalin died in March 1953,[29] the newspapers announced that the "Doctors' Plot" had been fabricated and the surviving physicians were released. However, the idea that Jews were not trustworthy Soviet citizens and therefore their access to higher education and to responsible positions should be restricted continued to guide Soviet policy until the late 1980s.

The Late Soviet Years 1961–1991: Discrimination and Emigration

In the 1960s a series of government campaigns had negative consequences for Jews.[30] During the campaign against financial "speculation" a greatly disproportionate number of Jews were executed for "economic crimes."[31] Government campaigns against religion took on an anti-Semitic caste: when they attacked the universal religions, Islam and Christianity, no particular ethnic group was targeted, but because Judaism is a tribal religion practiced by only one people, attacks on Judaism were construed as attacks on Jews.[32] After the June 1967 war in the Middle East, in which the Soviet Union was embarrassed by Israel's defeat of its Arab clients, Soviet authorities mounted a sustained anti-Zionist campaign that was to last two decades. Jews were equated with Zionists in many publications and by many Soviet citizens. Hostility toward the State of Israel was easily transferred to Soviet Jews. This represented a reversal of Soviet policy; in 1948 the USSR had supported establishment of the State

---

[29] See Yehoshua Gilboa, *The Black Years of Soviet Jewry* (Boston: Little, Brown, 1971). See also Yakov Rapoport, *The Doctors' Plot of 1953* (Cambridge, MA: Harvard University Press, 1991) and Zinovii Sheinis, *Provokatsiia veka* (Moscow: PIK, 1992). A more narrowly focused study is Irina Issakyan, "Blood and Soil of the Soviet Academy: Politically Institutionalized Anti-Semitism in the Moscow Academic Circles of the Brezhnev Era through the Life Stories of Russian Academic Emigres," *Nationalities Papers* 36, 5 (November 2008), 833–60. For the most detailed account, based on recent research in Russian archives, see Gennadi Kostyrchenko, *V plenu u krasnogo faraona* (Moscow: Mezhdunarodnye otnosheniia, 1994), 289–361. An English translation is *Out of the Shadows* (Amherst, NY: Prometheus, 1995). On the purge and execution of the cultural leaders, see Joshua Rubenstein and Vladimir Naumov, *Stalin's Secret Pogrom: The Postwar Inquisition of the Jewish Anti-Fascist Committee* (New Haven: Yale University Press, 2001). The transcript of the trial of members of the JAFC is in V. P. Naumov, ed., *Nepravednyi sud: poslednii Stalinskii rasstrel* (Moscow: Nauka, 1994). Kostyrchenko (152) calculates that 110 people were sentenced to prison terms of various lengths and 10 to death by shooting in trials that were associated with the main trial of leaders of the Jewish Anti-Fascist Committee.

[30] A well-annotated documentary collection is Benjamin Pinkus, *The Soviet Government and the Jews, 1948–1967* (New York: Cambridge University Press, 1984).

[31] Evgeniia Evel'son, *Sudebnye protsessy po ekonomicheskim delam v SSSR* (London: Overseas Publications Interchange, 1986).

[32] See, for example, Trofim Kichko, *Iudaizm bez prikraz*, published by the Ukrainian Academy of Sciences. Its use of Nazi imagery and its unfounded accusations against Jews and Judaism brought worldwide condemnation, as noted earlier.

of Israel, although this support was motivated not by sympathy for Zionism but by a desire to drive the British out of the Middle East and the hope that the Jewish state would pursue a socialist, pro-Soviet policy. Some Soviet Jews, particularly war veterans, seeing the USSR's support for the establishment of Israel, volunteered to fight for Israel in its struggle for independence. Needless to say, the prospective volunteers' requests were noted but not fulfilled.[33] Ironically, the anti-Zionism campaign after 1967 played a large role in increasing Soviet Jews' interest in Israel, many of whom had eagerly welcomed its establishment in 1948, coming as it did so soon after the Holocaust.

In the late nineteenth century, Vladimir Medem, who grew up in a family of Jewish origin that had converted to Christianity, observed, "No matter how hard one... tried to forget one's former Jewishness, the outside world refused to allow it." In his Christianized home, "A sort of code was developed which only the family could understand. Instead of using the word 'Jew,' they said 'Italian,' or 'our kind.'... My Jewish origin was a burden. It was a shame, a degradation, a sort of secret disease about which no one should know."[34]

More than a half-century later, Alla Rusinek recalled her school experience. She described her dread each year when on the first day of school the teacher asked each child to announce his or her name, nationality, and father's occupation:

> She asks my nationality and then it begins. The whole class suddenly becomes very quiet. Some look at me steadily. Others avoid my eyes. I have to say this word... which sounds so unpleasant. Why? There is really nothing wrong with its sound, *Yev-rei-ka* [Jewish girl]. But I never heard the word except when people are cursing somebody.... Every time I try to overcome my feelings, but each year the word comes out in a whisper: *Yev-rei-ka*.[35]

Emil (born Samuil) Draitser recalled that when he was in first grade in Odessa,

> I passionately dream[t] that my surname will change by some miracle.... Why can't it end, not in *-er*, identifying it as Jewish, but in *-ev*, as many Russian ethnic names end? That would be a normal surname, that is, a good one.... Let me have, if not an ethnic Russian surname, at least a Ukrainian one, with the characteristic *-enko* ending. If I were not Draitser but Draitserenko, my stomach wouldn't ache every time I wait for names to be pronounced during the roll call.[36]

---

[33] See Yaacov Ro'i, *The Struggle for Soviet Jewish Emigration, 1948–1967* (New York: Cambridge University Press, 1991) and Binyamin Pinkus, *Tehiya u-tekumah le'umit: HaTsiyonut ve-hatenuah haTsiyonit biVrit ha-Moetsot, 1947–1987* (Beer-Sheva: Ben Gurion University Press, 1993).
[34] Quoted in Lucy Dawidowicz, *The Golden Tradition* (New York: Schocken Books, 1984), 428.
[35] Alla Rusinek, *Like a Song, Like a Dream* (New York: Charles Scribner's Sons, 1973), 20.
[36] Emil Draitser, *Shush! Growing up Jewish under Stalin* (Berkeley: University of California Press, 2008), 49.

This feeling of being marginal and despised eroded the fierce loyalty that many Soviet Jews had to their state and some had to its ideology. A sense of alienation and rejection replaced that loyalty[37] and led to thoughts of either assimilation or emigration, neither of which could be done easily.[38]

However, in March 1971 Soviet policy took a turn, allowing limited, controlled emigration for Jews and some others. Soviet authorities probably did not realize the depth and breadth of Jewish alienation from the system, and the emigration grew to surprisingly large dimensions.[39] By the end of the 1970s about 200,000 Jews had emigrated, most of them resettling in Israel. As a result of growing tensions between the USSR and the United States following the Soviet invasion of Afghanistan in December 1979, emigration was sharply curtailed, only to pick up again during the era of Mikhail Gorbachev's perestroika and rapprochement with the West.

Attitudes toward Jews in Russia

None of the successor states to the Soviet Union has pursued anti-Semitic policies, although the Russian government has not curbed anti-Semitic agitation nor has it passed significant legislation against anti-Semitic incitement.[40] When Boris Yeltsin became Russia's first post-Soviet president in 1991, about 40 anti-Semitic journals were being published, but eight years later there were more than 300.[41] Some claim that Yeltsin followed a "systematic policy of non-interference" with anti-Semitic and other manifestations of ethnic intolerance because he did not want to antagonize political constituencies.[42] "Although he relied to a certain extent on individual Jewish advisors, Yeltsin never actively defended Jews against Russian extremists, and several prominent politicians, such as Krasnodar governor Nikolai Kondratenko, used blatantly anti-Semitic rhetoric in political campaigns.[43] In 2002 one commentator claimed, "The

---

[37] See Zvi Gitelman, "Glasnost, Perestroika and Antisemitism," *Foreign Affairs* 70, 2 (Spring 1991), 141–59.

[38] Significantly, William Korey's book on Soviet Jews is entitled *The Soviet Cage*, (New York: Viking, 1973).

[39] On Soviet emigration policy, see Boris Morozov, ed., *Documents on Soviet Jewish Emigration* (London: Frank Cass, 1999) and Vladimir Khanin, ed., *Documents on Ukrainian Jewish Identity and Emigration, 1944–1990* (London: Frank Cass, 2003).

[40] A succinct survey of the Russian Federation's formal policies toward national groups is R. Abdulatipov, V. Mikhailov, and A. Chikhanovskii, *Natsional'naya politika Rossiiskoi Federatsii: ot kontseptsii k realizatsii* (Moscow: Slavianskii dialog, 1997).

[41] A comprehensive survey of anti-Semitic movements, their leaderships, memberships, platforms, and publications is found in Viacheslav Likhachev, *Antisemitizm kak chast' ideologii pravoradikal'nykh politicheskiikh techenii sovremennoi Rossii* (Moscow: Panorama, 1999).

[42] Tishkov, who served under President Boris Yeltsin as minister for nationality affairs, comments that popular anti-Semitism should be carefully monitored and combated through publicity and education about the consequences of discrimination and intolerance. *Rekviem po etnosu*, 332ff.

[43] Virginie Coulloudon, "Broken Promises: Antisemitism under Yeltsin," paper presented to a conference on post-Soviet Jewry, Davis Center for Russian Studies, Harvard University, February 1999.

State Duma remains a hotbed of antisemitism and racism," especially among the communist deputies and those from the Liberal Democratic Party. "In 2001, hate literature was openly sold in the State Duma, including David Duke's 'The Jewish Question through the Eyes of an American,' and several anti-Semitic newspapers." In addition, many judges treated "antisemitic and racist violence... with kid gloves."[44]

Nearly one-quarter of the 1,000 Jews surveyed in 1993 in Moscow, Kiev, and Minsk by Robert Brym and his colleagues claimed that their respective states were responsible for manifestations of anti-Semitism. Although Brym acknowledged that some individual state officials "presumably continue to discriminate against Jews," he also noted that "[b]laming state authorities for blocking their mobility and making their professional lives unsatisfying is probably a sort of historical reflex for some Jews."[45]

Yeltsin's successor, Vladimir Putin, appeared at many public Jewish events, especially those sponsored by Chabad-Lubavitch, with whom he made a political alliance against other leaders in the Jewish community. When a young woman was injured in 2002 by an anti-Semitic road sign that blew up when she attempted to take it down, Putin awarded her the Order of Courage. While not mentioning anti-Semitism specifically, Putin condemned the "bacillus of chauvinism." In July 2002 he signed a law granting courts and other government agencies the authority to curb "extremism," including incitement to ethnic hostility.[46]

Of course, these actions did not cause popular anti-Semitism to disappear or even necessarily wane. There is considerable disagreement among scholars on the level of anti-Semitic sentiments among the Russian population. On the basis of a 1990 survey of a national sample in the European USSR, James Gibson and Raymond Duch concluded that "the level of anti-Semitism in the European USSR is not particularly high." However, they cautioned, "At one level, it is ill-advised to ask how much anti-Semitism exists in a society – anti-Semitism is a continuum, but more importantly it is a propensity. It is difficult indeed to pinpoint a specific percentage and claim that figure as the estimate of the size of the anti-Semitic portion of the population."[47] Robert Brym maintained that

---

[44] Prepared Statement of Micah Naftalin, in "Intolerance in Contemporary Russia," Briefing of the Commission on Security and Cooperation in Europe, U.S. House of Representatives, 107th Congress, 2nd Session, October 15, 2002, 27.

[45] Robert Brym, *The Jews of Moscow, Kiev and Minsk: Identity, Antisemitism, Emigration* (New York: New York University Press, 1994), 53.

[46] Aleksandr Arkhangelsky and Yekaterina Grigoryeva, "Russia Doesn't Have a Civil Society, but It Does Have True Citizens," *Izvestia*, July 26, 2002 and Andrei Krasnov, "President Signs Law on Combating Extremism," *Kommersant*, July 29, 2002, both transl. in *Current Digest of the Post-Soviet Press* 54, 30 (August 21, 2002), 1. In the same month, courts shut down two newspapers for inciting ethnic hatred, including anti-Semitism.

[47] "Attitudes toward Jews in the Soviet Political Culture," *Journal of Soviet Nationalities* II, 1 (Spring 1991), 91. The literature on post-Soviet anti-Semitism, based on empirical data of one sort or another, includes Vl. Khanin, "Young People of East Ukraine: Value Orientation and

the level of anti-Semitic sentiment depends to a considerable extent on whether political elites evoke and mobilize it. President Yeltsin had not done so in the 1990s, yet "[a]nti-Semitism remains part of Russia's cultural repertoire, ready to be invoked under the right political circumstances."[48] In that decade there was a considerable volume of virulently or subtly anti-Semitic literature, some of it purporting to be scholarly, which was quite popular in certain intellectual circles.[49]

A 1990 survey in four regions where Russian Orthodoxy was traditionally dominant found that those who identified as Orthodox believers had the least favorable attitude toward Jews, with Baptists – who generally rank very low in the eyes of other Christians – having the most favorable views. Among seven nationalities, only Azerbaijanis and Armenians were viewed less favorably than Jews by the Russian Orthodox, whereas among "general Christian" believers four nationalities were ranked lower than Jews. Even nonbelievers ranked Judaism very low, with only Islam ranking lower.[50] This survey thus found a pronounced animus against Judaism, as well as stronger negative

---

Antisemitism," *Jews in Eastern Europe* 25, 3 (Winter 1994), 52–63; L. Gudkov and A. Levinson, "Izmeneniia v otnoshenii k evreiam naseleniia respublik na territorii byvshego SSSR," *Vestnik Evreiskogo Moskoskogo universiteta* 4 (1993), 4–39; L. Gudkov and A. Levinson, *Attitudes toward Jews in the Soviet Union* (New York: American Jewish Committee, 1992); V. Kelner and D. Eliashevich, "Antisemitism and Opposition to it in Leningrad, 1988–90," *Jews and Jewish Topics in the Soviet Union and Eastern Europe* 12 (Fall 1990), 35–49; N. Iukhneva, "Ethnic Minorities in Post-Communist St. Petersburg," *Jews in Eastern Europe* 24 (Summer 1994), 5–14.

Different interpretations of survey data from Russia are found in James Gibson and Raymond Duch, "Attitudes toward Jews and the Soviet Political Culture," *Journal of the Soviet Nationalities*, 2 (1992), 77–117; Gibson and Duch, "Anti-Semitic Attitudes of the Mass Public: Estimates and Explanations Based on a Survey of Moscow Oblast," *Public Opinion Quarterly* 56 (1992), 1–28; Robert Brym and Andrei Degtyarev, "Anti-Semitism in Moscow: Results of an October 1992 Survey," *Slavic Review* 52, 1 (1993); James Gibson, "Understandings of Antisemitism in Russia;" Vicki Hesli et al., "Social Distance from Jews in Russia and Ukraine"; and the exchange between Gibson and Brym, all in *Slavic Review* 53, 3 (Fall 1994); and Robert Brym, "Antisemitism in Moscow on the Eve of the 1993 Duma Election," *East European Jewish Affairs* 24, 1 (Summer 1994), 31–38. A more recent study is Brym's, "Russian Anti-Semitism, 1996–2000," in Zvi Gitelman, ed., *Jewish Life after the Soviet Union* (Bloomington: Indiana University Press, 2003), 99–116.

On attitudes toward Jews in Ukraine, see N. V. Panina and E. Golovakha, "Interethnic Relations and Ethnic Tolerance in the Ukraine," *Jews and Jewish Topics in the Soviet Union and Eastern Europe* 14 (Spring 1991), 27–30 and N. V. Panina and E. I. Golovakha, "Jewish Cultural Activity in the Ukraine: Public Opinions and the Attitudes of Local Authorities," *Jews and Jewish Topics* 2, 18 (Summer 1992).

[48] "Russian Anti-Semitism," in Gitelman, *Jewish Life after the Soviet Union*, 111.
[49] See Vadim Rossman, *Russian Intellectual Antisemitism in the Post-Communist Era* (Lincoln: University of Nebraska Press, for the Vidal Sassoon International Center for the Study of Antisemitism, Hebrew University of Jerusalem, 2002).
[50] L. Byzov and S. Filatov, "Religiia i politika v obshchestvennom soznanii sovetskogo naroda," in S. B. Filatov and D. E. Furman, eds., *Religiia i demokratiia* (Moscow: Progress, 1993), 32.

feelings toward Caucasian and Central Asian peoples.[51] Other research has found no direct connection between religious affiliation and dislike of Jews, though those who attend church services frequently are twice as likely to display xenophobia and hostility toward Jews than those who do not. This relationship between church attendance and anti-Jewish sentiment may be due to the fact that mainly older and poorly educated people attend services regularly.[52]

One writer acknowledged that the Russian Orthodox Church (ROC) maintains its traditionally anti-Jewish attitudes that "Jews... introduce an alien spirit into Orthodoxy.... 'A baptized kike is a forgiven thief' [*zhid kreshcheni, vor proshcheni*] says folk wisdom."[53] In 1995 Father George Chistiakov, a Russian Orthodox clergyman, characterized the ROC as "xenophobic, closed, and highly intolerant of other faiths and the West in general" and noted that anti-Semitism "is accepted quite broadly" within it. He quoted "an ideologue of the new 'Russian' idea: The Jews became one of the most active forces in the destruction of the values of Russian civilization."[54] Father Chistiakov also cited an "'Orthodox' polemicist" who said, "Simple laymen complain that it is difficult for them to go to confession to a Jew-priest. It is another psychology, another mentality.... For this reason many good Russian people are turning to paganism and abandoning the church."[55]

The national surveys of the All-Russian Center for Research on Public Opinion (VTsIOM) in 1990, 1992, and 1997 concluded that "the general mass attitude toward Jews can be characterized as the predominance of positive, or at least tolerant, views... not substantially different from attitudes toward any other ethnic group in Russia."[56] The core of "aggressive, convinced anti-Semites that existed in the early 1990s has not expanded, and represents 6–7% of the Russian population. Contiguous to this group is one which displays unsystematic or inconsistent anti-Semitic views and which constitutes 15–18% of the population." Another group, some 25–30% of the population, showed anti-Semitic attitudes only occasionally.[57] Some analysts in Russia believe these data show a basic tolerance of Jews in Russia, but Brym points out that hostile

---

[51] The other peoples compared to Jews were Lithuanians, Germans, Poles – all Europeans – and Turkmen, Azerbaijanis, and Armenians. The other religions listed, aside from Judaism, were Russian Orthodoxy, Catholicism, Baptism, Old Believers, Islam, and "eastern cults."

[52] L. Gudkov, "Antisemitizm v Rossii, 1990–1997," *Vestnik Evreiskogo universiteta v Moskve* 2, 18, (1998), 14.

[53] L. Arie [Leonid Alekseevich Nikitin], "Evrei i tserkov," in Filatov and Furman, *Religiia i demokratiia*, 107.

[54] *Russkaya tsivilizatsiia* (Moscow, 1995), quoted by Father Georgii Chistiakov in Juliet Johnson, Marietta Stepaniants, and Benjamin Forest, eds., *Religion and Identity in Modern Russia* (Aldershot: Ashgate, 2005), 57. The person quoted is Oleg Platonov.

[55] Ibid., 58.

[56] L. Gudkov, "Parametry antisemitizma. Otnoshenie k Evreiam v Rossii, 1990–1997," *Monitoring obshchestvennogo mneniia* 2 (1998), 36.

[57] "Kak v Rossii otnosiatsia k evreiam," *Inostranets* 26 (1998), 20.

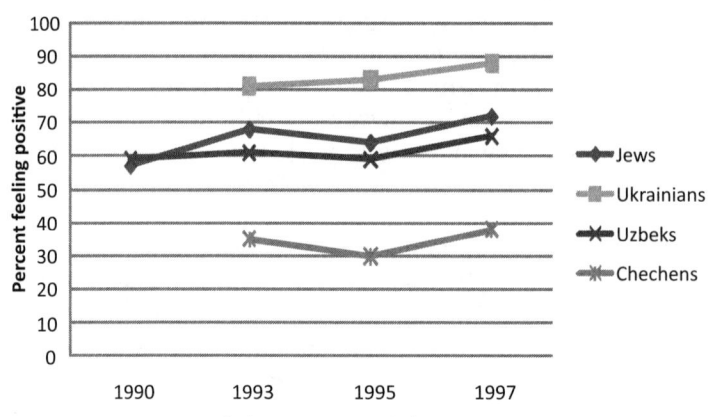

FIGURE 8.1. Positive feelings toward different groups.

attitudes toward Jews are considerably more frequently observed in Russia than in Canada or the United States.[58] Moreover, VTsIOM data from 1997 show that there was "a certain rise in anti-Jewish moods and joining up with the most ideological anti-Semites."[59] Still, VTsIOM surveys in the 1990s show a modest but steady trend toward more positive views of Jews by the population of the Russian Federation, as can be seen in Figure 8.1.

Those most likely to have an animus against Jews are older, less educated men who live in small and medium-sized cities; earn mid-level incomes; and have no Jewish close relatives, acquaintances, co-workers, or neighbors.[60] Sixty percent of these people say they have never encountered a Jew in their social circles. Politically, they are most likely to identify with the Communist Party or the Liberal Democratic Party led by Vladimir Zhirinovsky who, though apparently of at least partially Jewish origin, has made anti-Semitic remarks in public on more than one occasion. Interestingly, non-Russians (excluding Tatars and Germans) in the Russian Federation – especially people of the titular nationality living in one of its ethnically defined regions – express a generalized hostile attitude toward Jews significantly more often than do ethnic Russians. This may be due to their insecure status and tendency to xenophobia.[61] Broad strata of the population hold images of Jews as educated and cultured, averse to physical labor, and enjoying a higher standard of living than others.[62]

Like the VTsIOM findings, another Russian dataset found attitudes toward Jews, Ukrainians, Chechens, and Russians to be quite stable between 1995/96

---

[58] *The Jews of Moscow*, 45.
[59] L. Gudkov, "Parametry antisemitizma," 36–37.
[60] L. Gudkov, "Attitudes towards Jews in Post-Soviet Russia," in Zvi Gitelman and Yaacov Ro'i, eds., *Revolution, Repression and Revival* (Lanham, MD: Rowman & Littlefield, 2007), 203.
[61] Gudkov, "Antisemitizm v Rossii, 1990–1997," 11, 13. See table 8.2, p. 212, for comparisons of negative feelings toward nationalities during the 1991–97 period.
[62] Ibid., 20.

and 1999/2000.[63] Not surprisingly, on a "feeling thermometer,"[64] people were "warmest" toward Russians; the next warmest to Orthodox Christians; followed by Ukrainians, Muslims, and Jews – who got nearly identical scores – and, trailing far behind, Chechens.[65] Attitudes toward Jews were more polarized than those toward other groups. In both surveys, of those who expressed feelings about Jews (about one-third of those asked did not reply), about 18 to 20 percent felt either very warmly or very coldly toward Jews, and about one-third were completely neutral (giving them a thermometer rating of 50).[66] The data[67] show modal scores for Jews at the midway point on the "thermometer" during both waves of their survey. Therefore, results were not skewed by a small group at either extreme. Overall, although there are significant minorities in Russia who have strong negative or positive feelings about Jews, the balance of the population has no strong feelings toward them.

Finally, a "representative national survey" conducted in Russia in 2005[68] found that "religious intolerance is strong and widespread in Russia." Muslims and Russian Orthodox are highly intolerant of Jews (as a religious group) and of Western religions. Nearly one in four Russians would deny Jews at least seven or even eight of eight religious freedoms. The only freedom that slightly more than half the Muslims and Orthodox would grant Jews is to "do charitable work."

Attitudes toward Jews holding political power are more complex. On the one hand, the idea of Jewish individuals in high government positions does not ruffle the feathers of the great majority of the Russian population. In 1997,[69] a VTsIOM poll asked respondents if there were a great many Jews in powerful positions among Russia's leaders.[70] About one-quarter agreed and thought the situation undesirable. However, 60 percent either disagreed with the premise, were favorable toward the idea of Jews in positions of power, or

---

[63] I am grateful to Professors Timothy Colton and William Zimmerman, who supervised the studies, for allowing me access to the data, and to Prof. Jae-Jae Spoon for creating the graphs. Colton and Zimmerman were principal and co-principal Investigators in the 1995–96 Russian election study, replicated in 2000.

[64] Respondents were asked to express the degree of warmth they felt toward each group.

[65] About 35 percent expressed extreme hostility to Chechens in both years (the "first Chechen war" lasted from 1994 to 1996 and the second began in 1999). Surprisingly, about 10 percent felt very warm toward Chechens (Russians protesting government policy? People of Caucasian and Muslim origin resentful of their treatment by the government and ordinary people?).

[66] Modal scores for Jews, both as an ethnic and religious group, are at the midway point on the thermometer, so results are not being skewed by a small group at either extreme. Modal scores for Muslims and Ukrainians are also at the mid-point, whereas the modal score for Chechens is at zero and for Russians and Orthodox Christians it is at 100, the warmest feeling on the scale. These observations apply to both years of the survey.

[67] $N = 2,400$.

[68] Vyacheslav Karpov and Elena Lisovskaya, "The Landscape of Interfaith Intolerance in Post-Atheist Russia," *Nationalities Papers* 35, 5 (November 2007), 881 ff.

[69] Specifically, 14 percent disagreed with the notion that there were many Jews in government, 18 percent agreed but did not see anything wrong with it, and 28 percent did not attach any importance to the number of Jews close to the country's leadership.

[70] Gudkov, "Attitudes towards Jews in Post-Soviet Russia," 207.

did not attach any specific importance to having Jews in influential positions in government. As Lev Gudkov observes, "The demands made by extreme nationalists to limit access to significant resources or positions for one or other ethno-national group... are shared by a relative minority."[71] However, the closer that Jews get to power-holding institutions, the greater the rise in objections. Thus, one of five respondents supported introducing ethnic quotas for teachers or employees in the mass media but more than *half* advocated such quotas for government positions.

During the early Soviet period Jews were disproportionately represented in positions of state power,[72] which made a lasting impression on all. Although the proportion of Jews in leading positions declined drastically after World War II, an image of "Jews in control" persisted. When Boris Yeltsin was president (1991–99), there was a large, sudden inflow of Jews to governmental positions. After Vladimir Putin and then Dmitri Medvedev succeeded Yeltsin, the number of Jews in high echelons dropped significantly, probably because Putin had made his career in the security services, where there were very few Jews after the late 1940s.

At the turn of the twenty-first century, Russians were more antipathetic toward peoples of the Caucasus and to Muslims than to Jews, and there was little opposition to non-Russians holding positions of power and responsibility in the Russian Federation. What can be said about attitudes toward ethnic minorities in Ukraine?

Attitudes toward Jews in Ukraine

Some expected ethnic violence to break out in Ukraine when the country declared independence in 1991, but it did not happen. In 1990, a survey of Kiev residents found little Russophobia or anti-Semitism,[73] and a study of social tensions in Russia and Ukraine after the breakup of the USSR discovered no highly visible ethnic tensions. "Nevertheless... opinion surveys uncover a high level of anxiety among the population about the *possibilities* of inter-ethnic conflicts; in all surveys related to the question of which issues bother people the most, the possibility of inter-national conflict occupied one of the leading and stress-related positions"[74] [italics added]. It seems that in the early

---

[71] Ibid., 208.
[72] See Chapter 10.
[73] "Although 13% of the Ukrainians and 9% of the Russians indicated that they would not allow Jews into Kiev, overall on the scale of social distance the Jews occupied fourth place (after Ukrainians, Russians, and Belarusians) in national acceptability among the 23 groups included in the survey." N. V. Panina and E. I. Golovakha, "Inter-Ethnic Relations and Ethnic Tolerance in the Ukraine," *Jews and Jewish Topics in the Soviet Union and Eastern Europe* 1, 14 (Spring 1991), 28. However, only one-quarter of the respondents would wish to have a Jew as a family member and 41 percent as a close friend. See table 1, p. 29.
[74] E. I. Golovakha and N. V. Panina, *Sotsial'noe bezumie: Istoriia, teoriia, i sovremennaya praktika* (Kiev: Abris, 1994), 106.

1990s the *perception* of serious ethnic tensions in Ukraine was greater than the reality.

In April 1992, a national sample of Ukrainians (n = 1,752) was asked about attitudes toward nationalities. They had more positive attitudes about eastern Slavs (Ukrainians in Ukraine and in the diaspora, Russians, Belarusians, and Poles) than about any other group and were most negatively disposed toward "outsiders" such as Gypsies, "Negroes," Arabs, Vietnamese, Georgians, and Crimean Tatars. They ranked Jews (presumably most of the respondents were thinking of indigenous Jews) closer to foreigners, such as Hungarians, Americans, Germans, French, Romanians, and Japanese, than to Slavs in Ukraine or the diaspora.

One can track attitudes of the population of Ukraine over time through the annual "monitoring" surveys conducted by the Institute of Sociology of the Ukrainian Academy of Sciences. About 1,800 residents of Ukraine are surveyed annually in a "three stage, stratified, random [national sample] with a quota screening at the last stage," which makes regional comparisons possible.[75] Table 8.1 summarizes the relative ethnic distance that residents of Ukraine feel from several of the twenty-three noted nationalities over several years.[76]

Analyzing the results, Golovakha and Panina note that respondents are not unanimous in considering even Ukrainians as members of the family (perhaps these are non-Ukrainian respondents), and no nationality enjoys complete toleration. They characterize the general stance of the Ukrainian population to people of other nationalities as "guarded," which prevents ethnic conflict because people are aware that it could break out.[77] Because the overall index of toleration in Ukraine is 4.63 on a 7-point scale, the Ukrainian population as a whole falls on the *in*tolerant end of the spectrum, at least with regard to the nationalities named.

Residents of small towns and rural areas put the greatest distance between themselves and Jews because for them Jews are "strange" and remote. Thus, in Kiev the score given to Jews is 3.44, and in other large cities (with populations higher than 250,000) the average score is 3.67. In small towns, however, they score 4.25 and in villages, 4.56.[78] The authors note that residents of the large cities are the most tolerant toward *all* groups. Men and women are no different in their levels of tolerance, but the younger and more educated a person is, the more tolerant he or she is likely to be. Russians and Ukrainians rank the

---

[75] N. Panina, *Ukrainske suspil'stvo 1992–2006* (Kiev: Institute of Sociology, Ukrainian Academy of Sciences, 2006), 6.
[76] Unfortunately, the results are not broken down by nationality of respondent, age, gender, or region of residence. Moreover, the results for each nationality are reported in a peculiar way, which is not explained, so that it is difficult to discern whether the figures represent the proportion of people who answered in the affirmative to questions such as "Would you be willing to have a [nationality] as a member of your family?"
[77] Ibid., 110.
[78] Ibid., 111. These results are significant at the 0.005 level and among extreme groups at the 0.001 level.

TABLE 8.1. *Bogardus[a] Average Attitude Scores of Ukrainians toward Selected Ethnic Groups: 1992–2006*

		1992	1994	1998	2002	2006
Slavs	Diaspora Ukrainians	3.5	NA	3.9	3.5	3.2
	Russians	2.5	2.3	2.0	3.3	3.0
	Belarusians	2.5	2.7	2.5	4.2	4.1
	Poles	3.8	4.4	4.6	5.0	5.0
Non-Slavs	Americans	4.3	4.4	4.7	5.4	5.7
	Georgians	NA	4.9	5.1	5.4	5.5
	Germans	5.0	4.5	4.8	5.2	5.3
	Gypsies	5.5	5.1	5.4	6.0	6.1
	Jews	4.2	3.8	3.9	5.1	5.2
N		1,752	1,800	1,800	1,800	1,800

[a] In the Bogardus scales of ethnic difference, in the first six numbered columns we see the percentage of respondents who gave the particular answer (e.g., "I would agree to having Jews as residents to Ukraine") but who did not explicitly agree to having them as part of the family, as close friends, neighbors, or colleagues. The researchers assume that agreeing to having Jews as residents subsumes agreement to having them as visitors and that agreeing to having them as family members subsumes agreement to all the rest of the categories, though they admit there could be some anomalies – for example, where one agrees to having a Jew as a neighbor but not as a co-worker. The higher the score, the *less* tolerant respondents are. The rest of the columns show ratings on a scale that assumes if one agrees to have a member of a group as a family member, one would agree to have them as a neighbor, colleague, etc.

Note: Scores are on a scale of 1–7 with lower numbers indicating higher tolerance for a group.

Sources: 1992 numbers are from Golovakha and Panina; all others, from Ukrainian Academy of the Sciences.

national groups in precisely the same way.[79] However, on a scale of 0–100, where 0 is the most tolerant, Ukrainians, with a score of 62, are a bit less tolerant than Russians, who score 59.[80] As one would expect, West Ukrainians are the most kindly disposed to other Ukrainians, including diaspora Ukrainians, and the least kindly disposed to Russians. Because most Jews in West Ukraine speak Russian as their native language, although many are also fluent in Ukrainian, some Ukrainians lump them together with Russians as "foreigners" and see them as culturally threatening. This helps explain many of our findings from respondents in Lvov/Lviv.[81]

---

[79] Ibid., 114.

[80] Ibid., 115. Golovakha and Panina speculate that this may be due to the deeper rural roots and present-day residence of Ukrainians. However, when they compare Russians and Ukrainians with higher education, Russians score 51, on average, and Ukrainians 59. When comparing Russians with higher education who were raised in large cities with Ukrainians with the same two characteristics, Russians score 45 and Ukrainians 64, so the gap between the two nationalities *widens* in this highly educated urban-socialized group. There are only thirty-five Russians and thirty-three Ukrainians in this group, but the results are significant at the 0.01 level.

[81] Somewhat parallel data from Russia show a rise in acceptance of Jews from 1990 to 1997. In 1997, the percentages of a national sample willing to have Jews in various roles were as follows:

Since Ukraine has become independent, its citizens have put more distance between themselves and other nationalities, except for Ukrainians living abroad. In 1994, of the nine nationalities listed, five were more distant than Jews, compared to only three (Americans, Georgians, and Gypsies) in 2006.[82] Even closely associated Slavic peoples, Belarusians and Russians, were much less desired in 2006 than in 1994: the percentage willing to have Belarusians in the family dropped from 32.4 to 9.8, and for Russians it fell from 40.6 to 29.9.[83] Nevertheless, anti-Russian and anti-Jewish expressions, especially in the western part of the country, remained marginalized even in the turbulent politics of 2004 and thereafter.[84]

In summary, in Ukraine the overt anti-Semitism of the Soviet years was replaced in the 1990s by a general tolerance for Jews, especially among the educated, cosmopolitan classes in larger cities. However, surveys have shown increasing distance between Jews and ethnic Ukrainians and Russians, signaling underlying ethnic anxiety. Although anti-Semitism has receded, it is still alive. Economic and political dislocation, such as Ukraine has experienced in recent years, may be conducive to the revival of anti-Jewish sentiments.

Jewish Perceptions of Anti-Semitism

Having sketched the distributions of anti-Semitic sentiment in Russia and Ukraine in the 1990s, I turn to the role it plays in the formation of individuals' Jewish identities. How did Jews react to others' perceptions and expressions? Even if encounters with anti-Semitism were rare or occasional, and had not occurred recently, they may have left a deep psychological mark. As Sartre observed of highly assimilated Jews, "some day they must learn the truth: sometimes from the smiles of those who surround them, sometimes from rumor or insult. The later the discovery, the more violent the shock. Suddenly they perceive that others know something about them that they don't know.... They feel themselves separated, cut off from the society."[85]

Especially when Jews have little knowledge of Jewish culture and do not practice the Jewish faith or observe Jewish customs, labels largely devoid

---

as a neighbor, 88; as a close family member, 55; as a boss, 62; as a business partner, 64; and as a co-worker, 84. Gudkov, *Antisemitizm v Rossii*, 25.

[82] Another finding that invites speculation is why Americans, so popular in neighboring Poland, but not so in neighboring Russia, should be so consistently unpopular in Ukraine.

[83] Another survey, conducted in 2004, of "representative samples within the major ethnic populations of Ukraine," also "suggests that over half of Ukraine's citizens lack both a sense of attachment and a reservoir of tolerance," and this is especially true of Ukrainians and Russians. Holly Hansen and Vicki Hesli, "National Identity: Civic, Ethnic, Hybrid, and Atomised Individuals," *Europe-Asia Studies* 61, 1 (January 2009), 5, 8.

[84] On radical anti-Semitism and its ideologists, see Liudmilla Dymerskaya-Tsigelman and Leonid Finberg, *Antisemitism of the Ukrainian Radical Nationalists: Ideology and Policy* (Jerusalem: Vidal Sassoon International Center for the Study of Antisemitism, Hebrew University, 1999).

[85] Sartre, *Anti-Semite and Jew*, 75.

of content take on greater importance to the one labeled – and libeled. In the absence of positive cultural content or even sentiment, associating Jewishness with anti-Semitic expressions can produce a Jewish consciousness that is largely negative, a feeling that being Jewish is a curse that should somehow be removed. More than a few Soviet Jews reported that even the word "Jew" was avoided in their households because it was considered embarrassing and pejorative. Instead, they used euphemisms such as "Abyssinians" or "Orientals" or "ours."[86] Social scientists have long commented on *selbsthass*, self-hatred, which is especially frequent among minorities and is well known among Jews. It leads to alterations of one's comportment, language, culture, name, and even physiognomy in attempts to change one's outward appearance and hence perceived identity.[87] The Soviet practice of registering citizens by their nationality foreclosed such "passing" or hiding, although some managed to lose their identity documents and acquire "better" ones, or they bribed officials and used other illegal means to appear officially, at least, as non-Jews – often arousing the antipathy of both Jews and others by doing so.

Of course, one can be critical of one's own group without being motivated by *selbsthass*. In the 1992/93 survey we asked Russian and Ukrainian Jews to characterize Jews as compared to other peoples using adjectives such as gentle, obliging; cunning, clever, able; prudent, niggardly, hardworking; insolent, well-mannered; cowardly; kind, sympathetic; haughty, arrogant. We then coded responses into negative, neutral, mildly positive, and positive descriptions of Jews. One would expect that members of an ethnic group would have a high opinion of their group. Yet, only about 40 percent of all respondents characterized Jews positively, and between 11 and 14 percent did so negatively. We scored one of five respondents as neutral and 26 to 31 percent as mildly positive. There were no significant differences between Russian and Ukrainian Jews or by age groups. The picture that emerges shows neither uncritical adulation nor deep self-hatred, but a moderately positive attitude toward one's own group.

It would be interesting to compare "pure" Jews with "part-Jews" in this regard, but we do not have sufficient numbers for a statistical analysis. However, we do have some responses that offer clues to how "life is lived on the hyphen" between being Jewish and Russian. A respondent's remarks about her

---

[86] Some German Jews had done the same earlier. "Ernst Lissauer... recalled that in his parents' Berlin house they would not use the word *Jude* if young girls were present and instead would replace it with 'Armenian' or 'Abyssinian.'" Todd Endelman, "Jewish Self-Identification and West European Categories of Belonging from the Enlightenment to World War II," in Zvi Gitelman, ed. *Religion or Ethnicity? The Evolution of Jewish Identities* (New Brunswick, NJ: Rutgers University Press, 2009), 119.

[87] Theodor Lessing, *Der judische Selbsthass* (Berlin: Judischer Verlag, 1930); Hans Meyer, *Outsiders* (Cambridge, MA: MIT Press, 1982), ch. 22; and Sander Gilman, *Jewish Self-Hatred: Anti-Semitism and the Hidden Language of the Jews* (Baltimore: Johns Hopkins University Press, 1986).

Anti-Semitism and Jewish Identity

daughter, the child of a Jewish mother and a Russian father, brings forth some of the popular images about Jews, both negative and positive:

> My daughter turned out Russian, although she too values some Jewish qualities, like brain power, talent, hard work. On the other hand, she finds some other Jewish traits negative, like their tendency to yell, their perceived stinginess.... My daughter used to consider herself Russian when she was younger, but I believe that now she may be leaning a bit towards feeling Jewish.... My grandchildren probably don't even know that they are Jewish. Their father and grandfather, my husband, are Russian, we don't usually talk about such things.

Within the same family, people may differ in their attitudes toward their visibility as Jews. A middle-aged Moscow Jew, married to a Russian, noted that his parents had very Jewish-sounding names and patronymics, which he kept, but his sons are changing them to more Russian-sounding ones:

> My grandparents didn't change their names – no way! They were religious. I kept my [Jewish-sounding] last name out of respect for my father who died in the war with Japan. But my sons are changing theirs. In general, I don't mind.... When they got married, they change their last name to their wife's. I believe that's normal. Here, in Russia, you can expect anything to happen. So since my sons are already Russian, let them have Russian last names.[88]

As these comments indicate, in the FSU people are quite sensitive to the importance of establishing their own nationality, as well as those of their fellow citizens. For that reason we asked our respondents when and how they first became aware of being Jewish, whether people could tell at first glance that they were Jewish, and about the role anti-Semitism played in their consciousness of being Jewish.

"Proud of Being Jewish?" Anti-Semitism and the Formation of Jewish Identity

Most people became aware they are Jewish at a relatively early age, although perhaps later than Jews in other countries. In Russia, one-quarter (1997) to nearly one-third (1992) became aware of their Jewishness before the age of 7 and about half by the time they were 9. In Ukraine, Jewish awareness came earlier for more of our respondents. In both countries, only slightly more than 10 percent came to Jewish awareness in adulthood (age 18 and over).[89]

---

[88] Interview in Moscow, 1998. A resident of Kiev, now in his 60s, told us, without irony: "When I was born my name was Solomon Srul'evich. During the war, because of anti-Semitic reactions such a name and patronymic might cause, my mother had my name and patronymic officially changed to Aleksandr Izrailevich." (Of course, every Soviet person would recognize "Izrailevich" as a distinctly Jewish patronymic. "Srul" is a Yiddish contraction of Yisroel or Izrail').

[89] Interestingly, in both countries respondents in the first wave became aware of their ethnicity somewhat earlier than those in the second wave. This finding is in line with the greater Jewish awareness and involvement observed in 1992/93 than in 1997/98.

Strikingly, most people associate becoming aware of their Jewish identity with negative feelings. We asked an open-ended question – "What were the circumstances in which you became aware of your Jewishness?" – and coded the responses as having positive, negative, or neutral valences. In Russia in 1992, 45 percent associated negative emotions with their awareness of being Jewish, and 54 percent did so in 1997. In Ukraine, the figures were 60 percent and 52 percent. Some typical responses were as follows: "I was the only Jewish girl in the class; the teacher and pupils acted toward me not with hostility but as toward someone strange; this influenced me a great deal." "I glanced for the first time at the class register under the rubric 'nationality' and discovered that all the others had the proud 'R' [Russian] next to their name while only I had the slimy 'E' [*Evrei*, Jew]." A young woman from Chernivtsi claimed that she and a Jewish boy poured acid on the teacher's roll book to erase their nationality. Others reported getting into fights in school when called "Yids" [*zhidy*] or claimed that anti-Semitic teachers singled them out for derision or gave them unjustifiably lower grades. A Muscovite now living in the United States recalled how her mother prepared her for the first day of school:

> My Jewish education at home came down to one incident. When I was six and about to go to my first day in kindergarten, my mother told me: "You should keep in mind that you are Jewish, so all the other kids will hate you." That was all the warning I got. "And you must hate them, too," she added. She did not explain why or for what reason.... I can't say I always strictly followed her advice. But it made a big impression on me.[90]

Only one-quarter to one-third of respondents identified the circumstances in which they learned their nationality as positive (the rest were coded neutral; that is, either without any emotional connotation or with a mix of positive and negative emotions). Here are two comments from older respondents: "Grandmother lit the candles every Friday night, took me to synagogue on holidays and explained their significance. Thanks to that I felt myself a Jew from early childhood." And, "My parents were both musicians and they frequently played Jewish melodies on the violin at home, and that went into my soul from early childhood."

Younger people had different kinds of positive Jewish associations, mostly post-Soviet. "All my friends were Russian, I never really felt myself to be Jewish until I went to a summer camp run by the Jewish Agency." Or, "We had a student party and two of my friends, a Russian and an Armenian, embarrassed me: 'You are only formally a Jew, you don't have the slightest idea of what it's all about.' Then I began to read books about Jewish history and tradition and started to teach myself Hebrew. That made me a Jew."

[90] Helena Mandel, "From the Jewish Underground to Bankruptcy Law," in Dennis Shasha and Marina Shron, eds., *Red Blues: Voices from the Last Wave of Russian Immigrants* (New York: Holmes and Meier, 2002), 63.

Anti-Semitism and Jewish Identity

In almost all age groups, Jewish identity was more often formed in negative circumstances than in positive ones. In Russia (1997), among 30–39 year olds (those born in 1959–68) negative circumstances were 2.3 times more frequent than positive, and among the 60–69 year olds (born 1929–38) they were 3.4 times more frequent. Yet among those over 70 (born in 1928 or earlier), negative circumstances were cited only 1.1 times more frequently, probably because this cohort was exposed to more positive expressions of Jewishness while growing up in the 1920s, when many Jewish traditions were still observed and even nontraditional Jews attended Yiddish schools, read Yiddish newspapers and books, and felt equal to others. In Ukraine, those who became aware of their Jewish identity up until about 1929 – when proletarian internationalism was still the watchword in ethnic relations and secular Yiddish culture was encouraged – reported a more positive emotional association than those born during the Stalinist or later Soviet periods, when emphasis had shifted to the preeminence of the Russian people and Yiddish culture was regarded as outmoded and even subversive. Twenty-eight percent of the entire sample reported positive associations with Jewishness, but for the two oldest cohorts it was 41 percent and 56 percent, respectively. For example, Emil Draitser, born in 1938 in Odessa, grew up very much ashamed of his Jewishness, but his parents, a worker and a housewife, did not hesitate to speak Yiddish, observed Jewish holidays, and looked down on Russians and Ukrainians whom they referred to sometimes as *khazeirim* and *shikeirim* [swine and drunkards].[91]

When we examine what respondents feel is needed to be a "real Jew," we can see a steady rise from the younger to the older age groups in the need to be proud of one's Jewishness, to "defend the honor of the Jewish people," and to demonstrate one's Jewishness openly. In other words, except for the oldest group, the older the group the more acute the feeling that Jewishness needs to be explained and defended.

Like the oldest cohort, the youngest (16–29 year olds) group associates Jewishness with more positive feelings, although for different reasons. They came to social and ethnic awareness largely in the post-Soviet period when Jewishness had lost some of its stigma. Thus, Russian Jews born in 1969–82 were 1.5 times more likely to have discovered their identity in positive circumstances (34% did) than the next oldest cohort, the 30–39 year olds. "Only" 32 percent of the youngest respondents attached negative feelings to the discovery of their Jewishness; that is, half the proportion among their parents and partly their grandparents (the 50–69 year olds). Moreover, we observe a change from 1992/93 to 1997/98. In the earlier survey, negative circumstances prevailed over positive ones by a 2:1 ratio in the youngest group: that was the smallest ratio among all age cohorts. In contrast, in the later survey the proportion of those in the youngest group reporting negative circumstances declined slightly

---

[91] Draitser, *Shush!*, passim. One of his mother's closest friends was Russian. "'Take[h] a leytyshe kristlekhe,' she says. 'She's truly a decent Christian. There are scoundrel Jews and there are decent Russians. I have to admit that'" (280).

(by 2.3%). More importantly, the proportion of positive emotional valences attached to the discovery of ethnicity *rose* by a factor of more than two. More than one-quarter of the respondents in Russia (1997) associated feeling Jewish with positive emotions, whereas only 11 percent did so in 1992. The change was similar in Ukraine, where even in the first wave nearly one-third associated positive emotions with Jewish identity, probably because Ukrainian Jews are closer to traditional Jewish culture and also because they may perceive themselves as culturally superior to Ukrainians, if not to Russians. *Clearly, there have been changes in the social environment. Being Jewish has attained a new respectability.*

Yet, the level of positive association among the youngest is still slightly *lower* than that expressed by the oldest cohort and significantly lower than that expressed by those socialized in the early Bolshevik period. This is because the youngest people were more likely to report neutral or undefined feelings regarding their ethnicity than all cohorts except the very oldest. This suggests not only that Jewishness has lost some of its stigma but also that the salience of ethnicity has declined among young people, especially because a higher proportion of them are the children of mixed marriages. It may also be that ethnicity is not foremost among the concerns of young people. As one respondents said when asked about intermarriage, "Young people care about love and not about nationality."

The age at which one became aware of Jewish identity influences whether it will have positive or negative associations. In Ukraine, those who became aware of Jewishness before they were 6 years old associate their ethnicity with more positive emotions than do others. Their sense of being Jewish was produced at home, within the family. However, if one discovers Jewishness later on, it is likely to be because some playmate or neighbor has hurled an ethnic slur or because classmates – or even a teacher – have subtly or directly made it clear that to be Jewish is "not a good thing." The 9- or 10-year-old child is more likely to discover his or her Jewishness on the street or in school than in the warm embrace of the family. Here is how a 19-year-old college student from Kiev recalled his discovery that he was Jewish:

> In my elementary school class there was a small, scrawny boy whose mother must have been from the Ukrainian countryside. So one time he and I were playing at the school playground.... At some point the boy asked me, "How come you have such a Jewish nose?" I shrugged my shoulders and said, "What does 'Jewish' mean?" And he said, "Well, are you Jewish?" I first told him, "I don't know." But to myself I thought, "Maybe, it's some kind of disease? How strange. Maybe it's a symptom of a disease? But I didn't have any diseases." And then I asked him, "What is that?" And he said, "The thing is that the Jews are very bad people, they are mean to everyone, they are just terrible." When I got home, I told my mother this and, of course, got very angry. She told me, and I remember this to this day, that that boy had the brainpower of a chicken and that I shouldn't listen to him, that a lot of famous people were Jewish, that they never wished harm on anyone, and that that boy was mean and would grow up to be a bad

person.... I was about eight years old at that time.... The strange thing also was that I didn't become curious after this incident about who the Jews really were and didn't find out anything about Jews until much later.

Russian Jews who first became aware of their ethnicity at age 9 or 10 were more than four (1997) or seven (1992) times as likely to recall negative feelings, whereas among those who learned they were Jewish before they were 6 years old, the proportion of those with negative associations was "only" one-and-a-half to two times as great as those with positive associations. In Ukraine, in both years, there is a near-linear increase in negative associations with Jewishness as the age of awareness rises. Half of those who became aware that they were Jewish before the age of 6 have positive associations, compared to only 16 to 17 percent of those who did so in adolescence or adulthood.[92] Discovering one's Jewishness between ages 9 or 10 and 18 is most often the result of insults and unpleasant incidents. However, once a person is a young adult, the discovery of Jewish identity may be the result of positive encounters with people or literature.

It is not altogether clear whether the difference between the youngest cohort who feel more positive about their ethnicity and older ones who are more negative reflects a life-cycle or generational phenomenon. That is, will younger people come to have even less positive feelings about their Jewishness as they go through life, or has the change from a Soviet regime "imprinted" new and more positive feelings about Jewishness among them? If there is no revival of state-sponsored and popular anti-Semitism in Russia and Ukraine, the change in feelings about being Jewish may be long-lasting, a generational shift. Yet the fact remains that in both waves and in both countries, nearly half the respondents associate feeling Jewish with negative emotions.

Moving beyond the formative years of Jewish consciousness, we asked, "During the course of your life, were you more often proud or ashamed to be a Jew?" More people reported mixed feelings than either unadulterated shame or pride. The modal response in Russia and Ukraine in both years was "both" or "neither."[93] Those older than 50 and younger than 30, the generations that came to consciousness before and after the worst times for Soviet Jews, were decisively more proud to be Jewish than the other age groups. In Ukraine (1993) the only group who felt "more ashamed than proud" to be Jewish during their lives came to consciousness in 1954–64, the immediate post-Stalinist and Khrushchev era. The only group whose modal response is to have been more proud than ashamed was the 16–19 year olds (n = 67). Only among those over 60 (n = 793) were more people "proud" (184) than

---

[92] Interestingly, in 1997, the proportion of those who became aware of their nationality when they were 18 or older and had a positive emotional association with that was twice as great as in 1993 (34% vs. 17%). This may be the result of Jewish cultural and religious activity in Ukraine following Ukrainian independence.

[93] There are no consistent differences among residents of different cities on the question of pride or shame in being Jewish.

"ashamed" (129). Residents of Chernivtsi and Lviv, incorporated into the USSR only in 1939–40, were least likely to have been ashamed of being Jewish. Older people in those cities had lived in Poland and Romania when official and societal anti-Semitism were strong, but they could look back with pride and, in some cases, nostalgia to the vibrancy and intensity of Jewish religious, cultural, and social life. They seem to have passed on some of this feeling to their children and grandchildren. Moreover, today they live in areas where they may feel themselves culturally superior to local Ukrainians and people of other nationalities, because the proportion of Russians (who represent the "highest" culture) is very low there.[94]

Although *discovering* one was Jewish was often accompanied by shame and embarrassment, in the early 1990s, the proportion of those proud of being Jewish in Russia and Ukraine was slightly greater than those embarrassed by it.[95] By the late 1990s, the proportion claiming to be proud was nearly *three* times that who felt ashamed of their Jewishness.[96] What had changed in five years to increase pride in Jewishness? This is difficult to answer. Massive emigration might have removed those most ashamed of their Jewishness (i.e., those who sought to escape their perceived disability of being Jewish). It is equally plausible that those proud of being Jewish were more likely to emigrate, especially because the great majority in the 1990s were headed for Israel. In fact, in the second wave in Russia among those who said they intended to emigrate, 26 percent claimed to be more often proud than ashamed to be Jewish, whereas 17 percent said they were more often ashamed. However, the difference is not great, and we cannot know what the distribution of pride and shame is among those who actually emigrated during the five-year period between the surveys. A more likely explanation is that by the late 1990s disabilities suffered by Jews had been largely removed and it was no longer as "shameful" to be Jewish.

In Russia only a minority said they had no particular feelings associated with being Jewish. The majority of respondents were either proud or ashamed of their ethnicity or at times felt pride and at others felt shame. Thus, Russian Jews are highly conscious of being Jewish, even when neither Judaism nor Jewish culture influences the way they lead their lives. Moreover, they are quite sensitive to the fact that other people see them as Jews and even recognize them as Jews simply by appearance. Nearly half of all respondents said that strangers could "usually" tell that they are Jewish "at first glance," whereas only a fifth said "usually not." Some who felt recognizably Jewish claimed that this had not exposed them to anti-Semitism, whereas others believed their "Jewish appearance" made them vulnerable to it. The Kiev student who described his

---

[94] According to the 1989 census, in Lviv oblast, Russians were only 7.2 percent of the population, whereas Ukrainians were 90.4 percent; in Chernivtsi oblast, Russians were only 6.7 percent, with Ukrainians being most numerous, followed by Romanians and Moldavians. I calculated these percentages on the basis of figures in *Natsional'nyi sostav naseleniia SSSR* (Moscow: Finansy i statistika, 1991), 84, 86.
[95] Twenty-five percent versus 18 percent in Russia and 23 percent versus 19 percent in Ukraine.
[96] Twenty-seven percent versus 10 percent in Russia and 29 percent versus 10 percent in Ukraine.

discovery of Jewishness when a Ukrainian classmate commented on his "Jewish nose" and who called himself "cosmopolitan" and "disdained the very concept of 'nationality,'" stated, "I never experienced even a hint of anti-Semitism in spite of my obviously Jewish appearance." Yet, he then observed, "When I was called a kike or just was insulted in a milder way because of my nationality, it wasn't because people were looking at my passport. As the saying goes, 'They don't hit you because of your passport, but because of your mug [face]!'"[97]

Are those who think they look Jewish more sensitive to anti-Semitism? Several respondents commented on their "non-Jewish appearance" and speculated that this limited their exposure to anti-Semitic remarks. Indeed, our data show clearly that those in Russia who feel people recognize them as Jews report more anti-Semitic experiences. In Ukraine there are very similar relationships between appearance and encounters with anti-Semitism.[98]

The youngest respondents were least likely to feel they are recognizable as Jews, and the oldest were most likely to perceive themselves as recognizably Jewish. Again, the difference coincides with the difference in sensitivity to anti-Semitism. Or are younger people less recognizably Jewish because they are more the products of interethnic marriages and so they look less typically Jewish and have fewer mannerisms identified as Jewish? Both hypotheses may be valid.

The Role of Anti-Semitism in Jewish Consciousness

In the absence of substantial cultural content, state-determined identity and anti-Semitism "from above" and "below" were very important components of one's Jewishness in the Soviet Union. In effect the Soviet state decided *"wer ist ein Jude."* Inscribing Jewish nationality on one's passport made Jewish identity official and well nigh inescapable.

Ethnic discrimination against any group makes its members more aware of their common interest; nothing mobilizes Jews' identification with other Jews as effectively as anti-Semitism. As has been remarked, even those Jews who do not belong to a "community of **faith**" belong to a "community of **fate**." Lack of faith or religious practice, ignorance of Jewish culture and traditions, and disinterest in matters Jewish do not preclude Jews from being considered as such, either by fellow Jews or non-Jews. The salience of anti-Semitism in Jewish identity would presumably be magnified among Jews who carry only light cultural Jewish baggage and do not practice Judaism – that is, Soviet Jews.

We asked, "What was the major factor contributing to the formation of your ethnic consciousness?" As Figure 8.2 makes clear, anti-Semitism was the single most influential factor in evoking consciousness of being Jewish.

---

[97] Several of the people we interviewed in depth quoted this well-known saying, *"nie po pasportu no po morde"* [they slug you not because of your mug but because of your passport].

[98] The Spearman correlation between the abuse and being recognized often as a Jew is .2151, a modest but quite clear correlation. The correlation between appearance and experiencing anti-Semitism in the street is .2565.

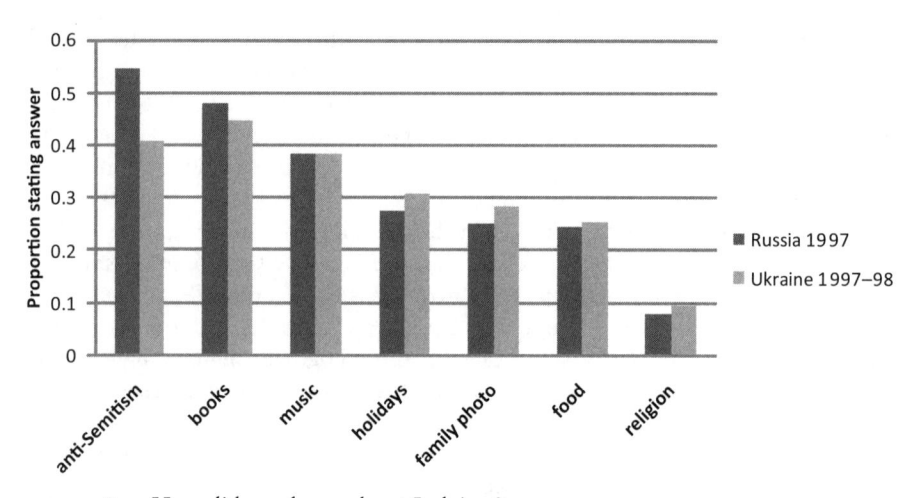

FIGURE 8.2. How did you learn about Judaism?
Note: This question was not asked in the first wave. Respondents could choose more than one answer.

In Russia and Ukraine those who experienced anti-Semitism more often – whether in the form of disparaging remarks, denial of opportunities, or even violent attacks – described their ethnic consciousness as more Jewish than those who encountered it rarely or hardly at all. In both countries, those with two Jewish parents were somewhat more likely than those of mixed ethnic origin to mention anti-Semitism.[99] Consistent with other findings, anti-Semitism plays the smallest role in forming the ethnic consciousness of the youngest age group. Thus, in Russia (1997), one-third of the 16–29 year olds mentioned anti-Semitism as helping form their national consciousness (in Ukraine, 29%), compared to 65 percent of the 50–59 year olds, 63 percent of the 60–69 year olds, and 57 percent of those 70 and older (in Ukraine, the respective figures are 47%, 48%, and 35%). The relatively low percentage of the over-70 group in Ukraine who mentioned anti-Semitism – although some members of this age group lived through the pogroms of 1918–21 and all lived through World War II and postwar Stalinist anti-Semitism – may be due to their intense "positive" Jewish experiences through exposure to traditions, Yiddish schooling, and to parents and grandparents who may have been religious and spoke Yiddish, cooked Jewish foods, and read Jewish books. Indeed, this cohort mentions ethnic foods, holiday observances, and even religious traditions more frequently than any other. In contrast, among the three youngest groups (16–49), more than half cite books and literature, because they have less memory of living traditions and had less direct instruction in ethnic folkways or religion. At the same

---

[99] "We find that respondents who have been socialised in the religion of their ethnic group, who have experienced past discrimination, *and who have parents from the same ethnic group*, all have a higher attachment to their ethnic identity." [italics added] Holly Hansen and Vicki Hesli, "National Identity: Civic, Ethnic, Hybrid, and Atomised Individuals," *Europe-Asia Studies*, 61, 1 (January 2009), 12.

time, they have been exposed to the ethnic and religious entrepreneurs of the 1990s. Their consciousness was formed through more vicarious and cognitive processes, whereas among the older people it was shaped more directly and experientially.[100]

In Russia anti-Semitism is identified most often as contributing to the formation of Jewish consciousness, and in Ukraine it is mentioned second.[101] Contrary to popular images of Ukraine as a hotbed of anti-Semitism, in the late 1990s anti-Semitism was more salient to Russian than Ukrainian Jews. This is because of the proliferation in Russia of anti-Semitic publications; the formation and demonstrativeness of anti-Semitic groups and parties such as Russian National Unity, the National-Bolshevik Party, the Russian All-People Party, and an assortment of skinhead groups; and the presence of conservative elements in the Russian Orthodox Church.[102] Such activities were less visible in Ukraine and seemed mostly confined to its western region.

When anti-Semitism plays a large role in the formation of one's Jewish consciousness, one is somewhat more likely to be ashamed than proud of being Jewish. Yet if we add together the six positive factors in the formation of Jewish identity – books and other literature, music and plays, national holiday observances, family photos and letters, cuisine, and observance of Jewish rituals and customs – these outweigh the influence of the one negative influence, anti-Semitism. Russian Jews cited the six positive factors three times more often than the negative; the youngest cited positive factors almost six times as often.[103] Thus anti-Semitism played a large – perhaps the largest – role in the formation of Soviet Jewish consciousness, but that role diminished in the post-Soviet period.

Encounters with Anti-Semitism

Collective memory of anti-Semitism may have as much influence, or even more, than personal experiences. Stories passed on in the family and cues from more subtle messages may create impressions, beliefs, and stereotypes so

---

[100] There is little difference by city in our results. Anti-Semitism is mentioned least often by residents of Odessa (31%) and most often by those who live in Kharkiv (46%) and Kiev (44%).

[101] Brym's analysis of his survey, from which he developed a 20-item index of Jewishness, concludes that five factors explain most of the variation in Jewishness, and anti-Semitism ranks only fourth on the list: "The single most important determinant of Jewishness is the degree to which one was exposed to Jewish culture during one's upbringing" (33). The major difference between his conclusion and ours likely stems from the fact that we asked respondents directly what factors influenced their "Jewish consciousness," whereas Brym's conclusion is based on correlations of responses to discrete questions that he then subjects to multiple regression analysis (29–33).

[102] For documentation, see Union of Councils for Jews in the Former Soviet Union, *Antisemitism in the Former Soviet Union: Report 1995–1997* (Washington, DC: Union of Councils, 1997) and their volumes titled *Antisemitism, Xenophobia and Religious Persecution in Russia's Regions* (Washington, DC: Union of Councils, 1999, 2001, and 2002).

[103] Respondents were replying not to an open question but to a list in which anti-Semitism was the only negative item, although it would be hard to think of others.

that it becomes "well known" that this or that group has a propensity to anti-Semitism. But some respondents have had personal experiences that shaped their views of other groups. An elderly woman from Chernivtsi expressed her outrage that Ukrainians erected a monument in Lviv to Semen Petliura, head of the Ukrainian Rada during the civil war period. She recalled how as an infant she nearly died in a pogrom. A teenager in Ekaterinburg knew that his grandmother's family was killed in a prerevolutionary pogrom and that the grandmother was beaten so badly that her lungs were permanently damaged.

Do contemporary Russian and Ukrainian Jews experience anti-Semitism directly? Almost no one denies that anti-Semitism exists, but in Rozalina Ryvkina's surveys, many more believe it has diminished since Soviet times than think it has increased.[104]

Some of our respondents have not experienced anti-Semitism. A poet living in St. Petersburg, who is very conflicted about his Jewishness and considers himself a "cosmopolitan," was annoyed by questions of anti-Semitism and denied its existence – while remembering in vivid detail anti-Semitic incidents from his childhood. In a rambling, disconnected way, he tried to understand the reasons for anti-Semitism and attributed it partly to Jews themselves:

> I believe that for the moment there is no anti-Semitism! That is, those every-day expressions of anti-Semitism which do happen are based on nothing!... There was this magazine... where they'd list especially horrible examples of anti-Semitic acts... incidents such as, "In Kishinev, Abram Yosifovich Blumkin was approached by three young people who said, 'You kike!' and spat on the ground at his feet." Here we have people being stabbed on the streets and *they* think the earth is going to fall apart because someone spat at the ground at his feet! I believe that for the moment, there is no anti-Semitism as such. Anti-Semitism is only a problem when it's at the state level. The period of state-sponsored anti-Semitism in our country... must have started in about 1926 and lasted until 1985. But then it ended!

> And of course there were reasons for historical anti-Semitism – starting with medieval ghettos and with the Jews feeling contempt for all others.... And then... Jews weren't allowed to be craftsmen. So they went into lending money for interest. That, of course, had the effect of increasing anti-Semitism with a new force. Who likes money-lenders? And then in Russia they didn't let the Jews live outside of the Pale of Settlement. So all the Jews started becoming merchants or getting higher education.... And then I still remember from my own father's example how Jews were treated in the army.... The Jews were hated there.... My father... had the rank of a captain.... But... he had the knowledge and the experience of a colonel. They just wouldn't let him be promoted.... But among the so-called electoral masses, I don't think there was anti-Semitism, although if I said that in front of my mother, she'd have a fit. But in my memory there was huge hatred towards the communists, no matter what "nationality" they were. There was hatred of the people from Caucasus, which now is even more vicious.... Well, of course, there was slight anti-Semitism which has always been there.... I was

---

[104] Rozalina Ryvkina, *Kak zhivut Evreii v Rossii?* (Moscow, 2005), 274, table 10.2.

going through a calendar recently and discovered this amazing thing: I saw that there was a holiday commemorating all the victims of fascism. Three days later there was another holiday commemorating the Jewish victims of fascism! Why not the Gypsies? Or the French? That's why they don't like Jews. Of course, the Jews had a much greater Holocaust than others, but as my Russian nationalist friend rightly says, you can't extrapolate the Holocaust to all times.... It's the over-emphasis of the Jewish tragedy and the Jewish untouchableness.

Others remembered vividly both spontaneous and official or institutional anti-Semitism during the Soviet period. Highly educated professionals remembered with some bitterness how their non-Jewish colleagues were permitted to travel abroad but they were not. Many are the stories of difficulties Jews experienced in being admitted into desirable institutions of higher education or obtaining employment in certain fields and institutions. A young man in Kiev, whose mother had difficulties being accepted by the Ukrainian Institute of Foreign Languages, although she had graduated from high school with honors, recalled:

When I was applying to the Kiev Polytechnic Institute, they flunked me at the oral math exam, even though I knew mathematics very well. My high school friend, who back in third grade used to say things like, "He is a nice guy, even though he is Jewish"... was applying to the same institute and got an "A" for his oral math exam, even though he didn't know math well at all. So when he learned that I got a D, he wanted to go back and beat up the professors who flunked me; I had to hold him in order to stop him from doing that. Then I went to Moscow to apply to an electronics institute and met about 15 other Jews from Kiev who, just like me, weren't accepted into any colleges in Kiev. There was one department at that Moscow institute which was accepting Jews.

A man who grew up in orphanages and military schools recounted numerous fights with peers who despised him for being a Jew. Some never referred to him by name but only as "Jew." Although he qualified as a ship-building engineer in the 1960s, he recalled,

I had difficulties getting a job after I graduated from the Leningrad Ship-Building Institute because of my being Jewish. I wasn't accepted into many organizations at that time, and the people who recommended me told me openly that that was because I was Jewish.... But, as it turned out, it was all for the better, because I ended up getting a job at a place where I later became a chief engineer and a big shot, even though it wasn't one of the more prestigious ship-building industry places, but just a place which built yachts. One time... they offered me a promotion.... I told them, "Before offering me that promotion, you better find out at the Regional Party Bureau whether they would approve of that, because I am Jewish." So they told me, "Oh, no, you are working in manufacturing; here you wouldn't have any problems with that." But I said, "Well, why don't you talk to the Party Bureau first anyway, and then let me know." And when the Secretary of the Plant's Party Organization came back, he said, "You were right.... They indeed told us there [at the Regional Party Bureau] that we don't need any more

Jews, because several Jews have already been accepted, and if we promote any more, there would be too many."

A woman born in Georgia, now living in St. Petersburg, recalled the following story:

> A group of musicians was supposed to go to the Baltic republics to perform a piece by a contemporary Georgian composer, Machivar'yani. When they were discussing in the Ministry of Culture who should perform his piece [my Jewish brother or a Georgian musician], Machivar'yani said, "I don't need a name, I need a good musician." To which the officials replied, "Do you really need a Jewish thorn in a Georgian bouquet?" And I remembered that phrase forever. They did ask the Georgian musician to practice for that performance, but when Machivar'yani heard him at a recital, he said categorically, "I don't care about thorns or roses. All I care about is music." And at that point my brother was given the opportunity to perform that piece. He had only two weeks to practice.... When he performed it, it was a huge success and he made the greatest impression.... At some point when he was supposed to go to Moscow for the Tchaikovsky competition, there were some problems because... Georgia was sending a Jew to that competition. He did very well in that competition, but wasn't allowed to go on to the Soviet-wide competition, they say, because of his being Jewish. When he talked to his teacher, a music conservatory professor, the professor said, "Why don't you change your last name to a Georgian one? Get the label off yourself," to which my brother said, "I was born a Jew and I will die a Jew."

She mused, "The cause of anti-Semitism is that we [the Jews] are too different from others. It's still a mystery to me that the one who is considered to be God by such a large portion of the world population, was a Jew himself, but yet became the reason for others to dislike the Jews."

Most interviewees focused on discrimination that harmed their life chances, but a few mentioned being deprived of access to Jewish culture. A Muscovite observed, "I am 35 years old and I got an opportunity to learn about Jewish culture and Jewish history only about five or six years ago. Before that I didn't have such an opportunity. I read Leon Feuchtwanger,[105] I went to some Jewish concerts whenever they took place, but I didn't any sources of information to be able to understand what being Jewish meant. And I think that was the case with a whole generation."

The post-Soviet quest for knowledge of Jewish history, culture and, to a lesser extent, religion, has been driven in large part by the sense of having been capriciously and unjustly denied access to them under the Soviet regime. What that regime could not deny them, although it tried to do so, was the knowledge

---

[105] German Jewish writer (1884–1958) whose novel *Jud Suess* (1925) was used by the Nazis as the basis for a notorious anti-Semitic film. His trip to the USSR in 1937 resulted in his book, *Moskau 1937*, which included an interview with Stalin. His novel depicting a Jewish family in the early years of Nazi rule and other historical novels were published in the Soviet Union and became popular sources of Jewish "historical knowledge."

that their people had been singled out for total annihilation by the Nazi armies that had invaded the Soviet Union in 1941. So many European Soviet Jews were personally affected by the Holocaust that, even if their knowledge of it was fragmentary and gained largely from friends and relatives, it could not but play a role in defining what it means to be a Jew.

The Holocaust and Jewish Consciousness

The Holocaust has become an important part of Jewish consciousness in Israel and the Jewish diaspora.[106] Although some debate whether this is desirable and what are its consequences, most Jews seem to believe that remembering the genocide and drawing lessons from it are an important part of being Jewish. In the Soviet Union, by contrast, the Holocaust was never denied, but neither was it singled out for special attention. It was subsumed – some would say submerged – under the general story of the death of some 26 million Soviet citizens during World War II. This was likely a deliberate decision by Soviet policy makers not to "divide the dead," not to make a "Jewish affair" out of a more general tragedy – although only Jews and Roma/Gypsies were singled out for systematic, thorough annihilation. Soviet authorities wanted to prevent the Holocaust from spurring Jewish consciousness and activity.[107]

About 2,711,000 Jews who were Soviet citizens in 1941 died during the war.[108] This figure likely includes an estimated 85,000 Jewish prisoners of war[109] and approximately 180,000 Jews who died in battle. Given that about 26,700,000 Soviet citizens died in World War II, Jewish losses would be more than 10 percent of the Soviet total, although Jews were only 2.5 percent of the population at the beginning of the war. Even if we accept a lower estimate of about two million Soviet Jews murdered by the Nazis (excluding combatants

---

[106] The myth has been propagated that there was a "silence" about the Holocaust in popular literature and the arts until after the trial of Adolf Eichmann in Israel in 1961. See Peter Novick, *The Holocaust in American Life* (Boston: Houghton Mifflin, 1999). Those making this assertion ignore the Yiddish and Hebrew presses, which apparently they cannot read, that were full of memoirs, discussions, and analyses of the Shoah at a time when a significant proportion of American, Canadian, and West European Jews read those media. Growing up in the Bronx, New York, in the 1950s and 1960s, I was certainly aware of the Holocaust, both because of the "survivors" (we called them "refugees" then) I encountered often and because it was discussed in my Jewish day school and in books I read. As a second grader in a Jewish school in 1947 I was given a Hebrew book about a boy in the Warsaw ghetto. Lately, several academics in Jewish studies have "discovered" that the Holocaust was not ignored in the American media in the 1950s. For example, Hasia Diner, *We Remember with Reverence and Love: American Jews and the Myth of Silence after the Holocaust, 1945–1962* (New York: New York University Press, 2009).

[107] See Zvi Gitelman, *Bitter Legacy: Confronting the Holocaust in the Soviet Union* (Bloomington: Indiana University Press, 1997), ch. 1.

[108] Mark Kupovetsky, "Estimation of Jewish Losses in the USSR during World War II," *Jews in Eastern Europe* 2, 24 (Summer 1994), 34.

[109] The estimate is by S. Krakowski, "The Fate of the Jewish POWs of the Soviet and Polish Armies," in A. Cohen, Y. Cochavi, and Y. Gelber, eds., *The Shoah and the War* (New York: Peter Lang, 1992), 229–30.

and POWs),[110] Soviet Jews would still constitute one-third of the total number of European Jewish victims of Nazism.[111]

Some in the USSR asserted that "the Jews fought the war in Tashkent" (i.e., they avoided military service and took refuge beyond the German-occupied territories). In truth, about 350,000–500,000 Soviet Jewish men and women fought in the Soviet armed forces. Since the early 1990s, many books and pamphlets have been published on Soviet Jewish participation in the war. Scholarly literature and newspaper and magazine articles on the Holocaust have appeared in Russia, Belarus, Ukraine, and the Baltic states.[112] Veterans of the war especially resent Soviet silence about the Holocaust and the absence of information on Soviet Jewish combatants, propelling the post-Soviet outpouring of works, most of them nonscholarly, on these subjects.[113] As in the rest of the Western world, in recent years the Holocaust in the FSU has been commemorated in

---

[110] Mordechai Altshuler asserts that "estimates of the number of Jewish Holocaust victims in the Soviet Union fluctuate between 2.5 million and 3.3 million." *Soviet Jewry since the Second World War* (New York: Greenwood Press, 1987), 4. A later assessment is Yitzhak Arad, "The Holocaust of Soviet Jewry in the Occupied Territories of the Soviet Union," *Yad Vashem Studies XXI* (Jerusalem: Yad Vashem, 1991) 47. According to Arad, "Out of a total of 2,750,000–2,900,000 Jews... under German rule in the occupied territories of the Soviet Union... very few had survived.... To the victims of Soviet Jewry in World War Two we should add between 120,000 and 180,000 Jews who fell... while serving in the Soviet Army, as well as about 80,000–85,000 shot in POW camps. Together with other Soviet citizens, tens of thousands of Soviet Jews died due to hard living conditions, shellings and bombings." In a later publication, Arad calculates that between 946,000 and 996,000 Jews were murdered in the pre-1939 Soviet boundaries and between 1,561,000 and 1,628,000 in the annexed territories, for a total of between 2,509,000 and 2,624,500 victims. Yizhak Arad, *Toldot haShoah: Brit haMoetsot veHashtakhim haMesupakhim*, Vol. 2 (Jerusalem: Yad Vashem, 2004), 1005–14.

[111] A detailed, meticulous working out of the number of Jews killed in Ukraine is Alexander Kruglov's "Jewish Losses in Ukraine, 1941–1944," in Ray Brandon and Wendy Lower, eds., *The Shoah in Ukraine* (Bloomington: Indiana University Press, 2008), 272–90.

[112] See Leonid Smilovitskii, "Historiography of the Holocaust in Belorussia: 1996–1998," *Shvut* 7, 23 (1998), for a review of much of the Russian-language literature in that period. See also Smilovitskii, *Katastrofa evreev v Belorusii 1941–1944* (no publisher, 2000); V. Levin and D. Meltser, *Chernaia kniga s krasnymi stranitsami* (Baltimore, 1996). To my knowledge, the most systematic treatment of the Holocaust in the USSR to appear in Russian is Ilya Altman, *Zhertvy nenavisti: kholokost v SSSR 1941–1945 gg.* (Moscow: Fonda 'Kovcheg,' 2002). An American work with much relevant material is Amir Weiner, *Making Sense of War* (Princeton: Princeton University Press, 2001).

[113] Some examples are Iakov Shepetinskii, *Prigovor* (Tel Aviv, 2002); Itshak (Mihkail) Iuzhuk and Ruven Iuzhuk, *Darovano vyzhit* (Pinsk: KUIP, 2002); Andrei Plotkin, *Podvigov ne sovershal* (Moscow: Fond "Kholokost," 2000); Ruven Evilevich, *Ia ne damsia tebe, drakon!* (Jerusalem, 1995); David Stavitskii, *Epizody* (New York, 1998); Grigorii Brazilier, *Razbuzhennie vospominania* (New York, 1997); V. L. Tamarkin, *Eto bylo ne vo sne* ((Moscow-Jerusalem: Zhag-VM, 2002); Mosei Rechester, *My srazhalis protiv natsizma, 1941–1945* (New York, 1982); Sergei Berkner, *Zhizn' i borba Belostotskogo getto* (Moscow: Fond "Kholokost," 2001); Abram Rubenchik, *Pravda o Minskom getto* (Tel Aviv, 1999); O. Arkadieva et al., *Na perekrestkakh sudeb* (Minsk: Chetyre chetverti, 2001); I. M. Shaikin et al., *Rasskazhi synu svoemu*, 2 vols. (Kiev, 1998); E. Levin and I. Spektor-Makarova, *Voiny doma iakova* (Yalta: Adonis, 2001); and B. E. Volovel'skaya and Ts. N. Segal, *Odna na vsekh pobeda: Samarskie evrei na frontakh Velikoi Otechestvennoi* (Samara, 1995).

exhibitions, museums, conferences, and symposia. Attempts have been made to introduce it into school curricula and, in the Baltic states, even into the education of military recruits.

Nearly three-quarters of our respondents said the Holocaust had a "strong influence" on the development of their Jewish consciousness. As might be expected, however, there is a steady decline from generation to generation in the influence of the Holocaust. Among the oldest, those who for the most part experienced the Holocaust, five of six said it greatly or somewhat influenced their Jewish consciousness, in contrast to only half among those under thirty. The oldest generations have personal memory of the Holocaust, but the youngest groups are more influenced by information that has appeared in the public arena in the post-Soviet period.

Nine of ten respondents in 1993 in Ukraine said remembering the Holocaust is crucial to being a "genuine Jew," whereas less than two-thirds of those younger than 30 shared this view. Yet only 7 percent of the youngest group thought it is neither necessary nor desirable to keep the Holocaust in mind to be a "genuine Jew."[114] The statement that the Holocaust had a "strong influence" on one's ethnic consciousness was made more frequently in the late 1990s than in the first survey. The most likely explanation for this seemingly paradoxical change is the increased availability of information on the subject.

When asked to rate eighteen items as "essential," "desirable" or "of no significance" to being considered a "genuine Jew," "remembering the tragedy of the Holocaust" ranked high.[115] The place of the Holocaust in the consciousness of Ukrainian Jews is slightly greater, probably because all of Ukraine fell under the Nazi occupation whereas only the western regions of the Russian Republic did so.

Many believe anti-Semitism continues to be a real threat and that another Holocaust is not unimaginable. Indeed, anti-Semitism is the most frequently mentioned reason given by Russian Jewish respondents for *others* emigrating, although in Ukraine only 15 percent in 1997 and 24 percent in 1992 cited it as the main reason.

The Consequences of Anti-Semitism

Encounters with prejudice heighten consciousness of one's identity, affect relationships with and attitudes toward others, and can shape feelings about one's country and society. Jews have long argued about how to deal with anti-Semitism: Is the best course of action to try to disappear as Jews, thus not

---

[114] Similarly, in Ukraine (1993) the older one is, the more the Holocaust was reported to have influenced one's Jewish self-consciousness. Even among those under 30, only 7 percent said it did not influence their Jewish consciousness at all. The great majority saw the Holocaust as their own personal tragedy. Nearly two-thirds of all respondents thought the Holocaust could happen again.
[115] It ranked third among Russian and Ukrainian Jews in the first survey, and third among Ukrainian Jews and fifth among Russian Jews in the second survey.

"provoking" anti-Semitism, or to confront it, either with force or by trying to educate people away from it, or both? They have debated whether "Esau hates Jacob" is an eternal verity that cannot be changed or whether modernization, education, the replacement of religion and superstition by rationality and science, and the growing appreciation of human rights will change attitudes and behaviors.

The emigration of about 1.6 million Soviet Jews has been propelled by many forces, from mundane economic considerations to abstract notions of what constitutes "civilized" societies, from familial ties to a desire for cultural, political, or religious freedom. Alienation from the Soviet state and one's fellow citizens also played a significant role in driving people to leave the land of their birth and of their ancestors.

Not surprisingly, Soviet Jewish activists struggling in the 1960s and 1970s for the right to emigrate to Israel claimed to have encountered anti-Semitism frequently. Some who got to Israel were interviewed there between 1968 and 1972. About four out of five reported suffering from anti-Semitism as children.[116] Nearly half said they had not experienced governmental anti-Semitism (in education and work), but two-thirds claimed to have been the targets of grassroots anti-Semitism. In a survey of rank-and-file immigrants at about the same time (n = 2,008) only 29 percent said they had *no* experience of anti-Semitism.[117] There may be some bias involved, because Israeli and Jewish media often portrayed Soviet Jews as victims of anti-Semitic persecution, which was presented as the main reason for their emigration.

Among our respondents, experiences with anti-Semitism also correlated with their intention to leave the country. In Russia and Ukraine, in both waves, respondents who scored higher on the "index of anti-Semitism" were more intent on leaving than those who scored lower. Those who thought pogroms were possible were more likely to intend to emigrate.

We did not inquire directly about anti-Semitic experiences over the life course. Rather, we questioned respondents about their experiences with anti-Semitism in the year preceding the interview – in public places, such as the street or while standing in line; in more private venues such as a communal apartment or an apartment house courtyard; at work; or in a governmental office or other institution. The responses were then compiled into an index. It is striking that in all the Russian and Ukrainian cities, reported experiences with anti-Semitism declined during the 1990s (see Figure 8.3).

---

[116] "Survey of Soviet Repatriates, the Hebrew University, 1972," quoted in Benjamin Pinkus, "Soviet Jewry and the Six-Day War," *Shvut* 7, 23 (1998), 73. No details on the survey are given.

[117] Binyamin Pinkus, *Tehiya u'tekumah le'umit: Hatsiyonut ve-hatnuah ha-tsiyonit bivrit hamoetsot, 1947–1987* (Beer-Sheva: Ben Gurion University Press, 1993), 116–17, 553. Here Pinkus mentions that 200 Zionist activists were interviewed in the survey cited in the previous note.

Anti-Semitism and Jewish Identity

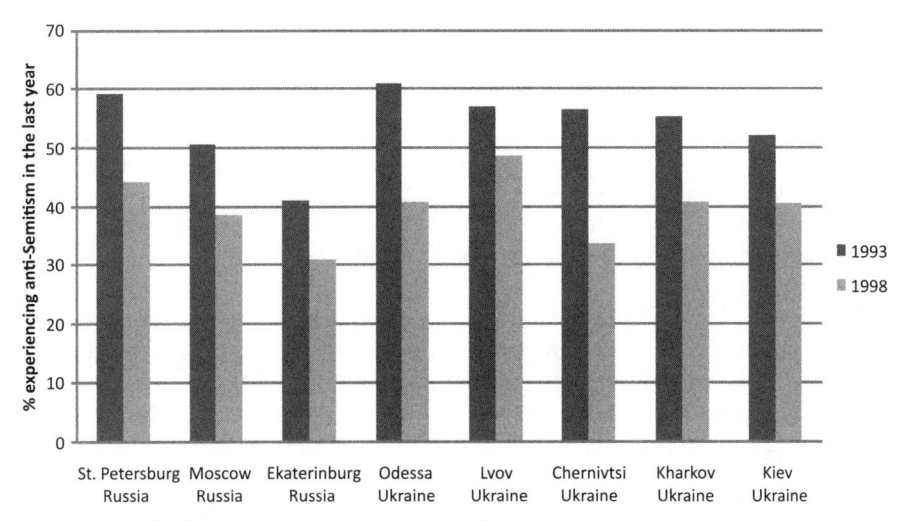

FIGURE 8.3. Decline in anti-Semitism during the 1990s.

People encountered anti-Semitism most frequently in public places.[118] Anti-Semitism was most often encountered in Odessa and Lviv, but even there, claims to have felt anti-Semitism "often" declined by half over the 1990s.

People expressed their sense that things changed for the better; Ryvkina's surveys uncovered the same trend.[119] In 1992, about two of every five Russian Jews asserted that anti-Jewish feelings had increased in their cities during the past year, but in 1997 only about one of ten felt that way. In Ukraine, when describing changes in the level of anti-Semitism over the preceding year, nearly 20 percent of respondents in 1993 said that it had grown stronger, one-quarter said it had diminished, and nearly half said the level of anti-Semitism had remained the same.[120] By 1997, there was a dramatic decline in perceptions of anti-Jewish sentiments. Only 6 percent felt that they had become stronger, and 40 percent reported a weakening of anti-Semitism.[121] Lviv residents stood

---

[118] This is also the case with ethnic discrimination against minorities in Moldova. When questioned about "unpleasant feelings due to your nationality," people reported they were most frequently experienced in public places. Among Russians and "others," 21 percent said they had such unpleasant feelings in the past one to two years "often" or "always," compared to 9 percent of Ukrainians. "Others," who may have included a fair number of Jews, report feelings of unpleasantness more than any other ethnic group in encounters in official institutions, at work, or with neighbors. M. N. Guboglo, *Etnicheskaia mobilizatsiia i mezhetnicheskaia integratsiia* (Moscow: Russian Academy of Sciences, 1999), 333–34.

[119] Ryvkina, *Kak zhivut Evreii v Rossii?* 277, table 10.5. She surmises that the decrease in Jews' concerns about anti-Semitism mirrors feelings of increased personal security in Russia, across all national groups, from the early to the mid-1990s (279).

[120] The rest, nearly 6 percent, either had no opinion or denied that anti-Semitism had ever existed in their town.

[121] The proportion of those who said that the level of anti-Jewish sentiment had remained constant dropped slightly (from 49.3% to 44%).

out from the rest in their perception that anti-Semitism was a rising threat. In 1993, two-thirds declared that anti-Semitism had gotten worse in the past year, whereas only 20 percent of the entire Ukrainian Jewish sample thought so. Lviv residents were also more anxious about the possibility of pogroms. The level of anxiety in Lviv about trends in anti-Semitism was more than three times that expressed in Odessa, the next "most anxious" city, and nearly eight times that expressed by people in Chernivtsi. Yet even in Lviv, in 1997 twice as many people thought anti-Semitism had declined rather than increased in the previous year.

What explains the widespread decline in the recall of anti-Semitic encounters in the mid-1990s? Ongoing emigration may have removed a disproportionate number of those particularly sensitive to anti-Semitism. Moreover, the relative stabilization of Russian and Ukrainian societies, compared to the seemingly anarchic period immediately after the breakup of the USSR, eased social tensions somewhat, although economic crises and political volatility provided fertile ground for ethnic resentments and violence. However, in Russia ethnically directed resentments, fueled by wars against the Chechens, were increasingly expressed regarding "people of Caucasian appearance." In Ukraine, contrary to some expectations, no major tensions surfaced between Russians and Ukrainians. Presidents Kravchuk and Kuchma, for all their failings, managed to project an idea of a multiethnic civic state that would not drive Russian culture and Russian-speaking people out of positions of power and influence.

Nevertheless, people were skeptical of the ability of Jewish organizations to deal with anti-Semitism or of the effectiveness of government efforts to combat it. In Russia 57 percent and in Ukraine 67 percent said the organizations were incapable of handling this problem. Few thought the respective governments had made "considerable" efforts to combat anti-Semitism. Still, by 1997/98, most people were not very concerned about anti-Semitism.

Anti-Semitism and Jewish Identity in Twenty-First-Century Russia and Ukraine

In Soviet times, particularly after 1945, state and societal anti-Semitism propped up a weakening Jewish identity among most Ashkenazic Jews of the USSR. Ironically, the Leninist-Stalinist state, ostensibly aiming for the mutual assimilation of peoples and the disappearance of ethnicity and religion, categorized Jews as a nationality and affixed that label to individuals, many of whom would have been happier to be considered "Russians." Presented with unprecedented opportunities for educational, vocational, social, and political mobility, Soviet Jews were, as Leninists would put it, in the vanguard of the internationalists. Their mobility was stopped cold by anti-Semitism. Thus, the Soviet state preserved Jewish consciousness and a Jewish collectivity for decades after they might have weakened, even to the point of extinction. Stalinist policies defeated Leninist aspirations, as well as those of many Jews.

No Soviet successor state has pursued anti-Semitic policies, although there is no guarantee these policies will not return, especially in authoritarian and incompletely democratized states such as the majority of post-Soviet states. Social anti-Semitism is by no means gone, as the data we have adduced demonstrate, and it can surge in periods of instability and crisis, although there seem to be numerous, more attractive scapegoats available, especially as the Jewish population declines. About one-fifth of the Russian population appears to display attitudes that can reasonably be construed as anti-Semitic. Whether this is many or few depends on the spatial and temporal angles from which one views this proportion: it is a larger group than in most, but not all, Western democracies, yet it may be smaller than the proportion of anti-Semites in other former communist states[122] and in the Russian Empire or the Soviet Union. What gives one pause is that anti-Semitic attitudes seem to be as widespread – or more so – among the young as among people raised in the Soviet Union.

Barring a radical change in state policies or a shift in popular attitudes, anti-Semitism will probably play a diminished role in Jewish identity in Russia and Ukraine. Access to Jewish culture and religion, Jewish education, and increased interaction with Jews in other parts of the world will give Jewish identity more positive content. As boundaries erode – steep rates of intermarriage are one indicator of that – the place of content in Jewish ethnic identity could increase. Anti-Semitism is a weak reed on which to lean commitment and identity. As we have seen, when anti-Semitism plays a major role in Jewish identity, that identity is often negative and will be gotten rid of at the first opportunity. If Jewish identity rests on anti-Semitism, *az okh und vay* [alack and alas], as Russian Jews would have said years ago.

---

[122] For Poland and other countries in Eastern Europe, see Zvi Gitelman, "Collective Memory and Contemporary Polish-Jewish Relations," in Joshua Zimmerman, ed., *Contested Memories: Poles and Jews during the Holocaust and its Aftermath* (New Brunswick, NJ: Rutgers University Press, 2003), 271–90, and the literature cited therein. See also Andras Kovacs, *The Stranger at Hand: Antisemitic Prejudices in Post-Communist Hungary* (Leiden, Boston: Brill, 2011) and the literature cited therein.

9

Identity, Israel, and Immigration

> *Izverivshis' v blazhennom obshchem rae*
> *po prezhnie mechtaniia liubia*
> *Evrei emigriruiut v Izrail'*
> *chtob russkimi pochustvovat' sebiia*[1]
> [We stopped believing in the blessed paradise
> But we still love our dreams
> Jews are emigrating to Israel
> In order to feel themselves Russian]
>
> Igor Guberman

Their tribal religion, Judaism, was the nexus that bound most Jews in most times and places to each other. That is no longer true among post-Soviet Jews, as the evidence in Chapter 5 indicates, and no secular cultural content has replaced it. Since the boundaries between Jews and others are eroding, it would be logical to expect Jews to disappear as an ethnic entity in post-Soviet states. Yet, we found that at least in the decade following the collapse of the Soviet state, Jews retained a strong sense of distinctive identity. As Chapter 6 makes clear, Jews continue to prefer co-ethnics over non-Jews when choosing their friends. However, our cohort analyses indicate that this preference diminishes over time and, in light of the shrinking Jewish population, will be hard to maintain.

Many of those committed to the continuity of the Jewish entity debate whether it has a future in Russia and Ukraine. Those who conclude that it has no future urge post-Soviet Jews to emigrate to the Jewish state, Israel, thereby preserving their ethnicity and strengthening Israel's Jewish population. Something of a self-fulfilling prophecy ensues: the more Jews leave the FSU, the less likely is the rebirth of an organized, active Jewish community

---

[1] Igor Guberman, quoted in Leonid Stolovich, "Fenomen russkogo evreistva," in G. Branover and R. Ferber, eds., *Evrei v meniaiushchemsia mire: Materialy 2-iy mezhdunarodnoi konferentsii, Riga, 25–27 Avgusta 1997 g.* (Riga, 1998), 133.

there – and the more that those trying to rebuild Jewish education, culture, and communal life conclude they would be better off as Jews in Israel or in large Jewish communities outside their native countries.

Whether to emigrate is a highly personal decision, but it has ramifications both for sending and receiving countries and societies. Thus, Jews who go to Israel will enrich their Jewish lives, weaken the Jewish community in their home country, and enhance the likelihood of Jewish survival in the world. In this chapter we explore the dimensions and dynamics of Jewish emigration from the FSU, how it was viewed by potential émigrés of the 1990s, and why it declined precipitously in the first decade of the twenty-first century.

The History and Politics of Jewish Emigration from the USSR

It used to be thought that peoples' search for better economic opportunities propelled most migrations. However, recent analyses demonstrate that not only labor markets but also religious and ethnic ties, ideologies, family ties, and the regulation of emigration and immigration by states affect the decisions of potential migrants.[2] In the USSR, the state played a very large role in determining the volume and direction of internal and external migration.

The Soviet state prohibited emigration from about 1924 until 1971 for several reasons. First, mass emigration would have raised doubts about the Soviet state's claim to be the best social, political, and economic system ever devised by humankind. Second, especially after the devastating loss of 26 million citizens in World War II, there were serious manpower shortages that emigration would exacerbate. Third, every émigré was seen as a potential bearer of hatred of the Soviet system and confidential information about it that would be exploited by the country's enemies. Émigrés might tell of airplane or rail accidents, or of crimes – all rarely reported by Soviet media until the late 1980s. Officials therefore often viewed émigrés as traitors.

By contrast, the Zionist movement envisioned diaspora Jews as returning to their historical homeland voluntarily, motivated by ideological conviction. A major goal of the Zionist movement was *kibutz galuyot*, the "ingathering of the exiles" who were expelled from Palestine after the Roman conquest of 70 CE. Just as pre-Zionist settlers in the Holy Land had been motivated by religious conviction, so would "modern, enlightened" Jews come back to rebuild a Jewish commonwealth.

However, the Holocaust convinced many non-Zionists as well that a Jewish state was necessary for their own survival and that of the Jewish people. After World War II many came to Israel as refugees from persecution in Islamic lands and Europe. Although Zionists did see the Jewish state playing a role as a haven for persecuted Jews, these refugees generally had a lower social status

---

[2] See, for example, Stephen Castles and Mark Miller, *The Age of Migration: International Population Movements in the Modern World* (London: Macmillan, 1993) and Saskia Sassen, *Guests and Aliens* (New York: New Press, 1999).

than those who settled in Palestine not out of self-interest – and often against it – but as "pioneers" prepared to sacrifice for a collective cause. As assimilation eroded the Jewish populations of the Americas and Europe, however, Zionists began to appreciate another motivation for aliyah: the desire to preserve and live a Jewish life. This desire had always been part of classic Zionist ideology, but did not have to be made explicit as long as Jews in North Africa, the Middle East, and Eastern Europe retained their Jewish identities, sometimes *faute de mieux*.

After the Holocaust, Israel became one of the pillars of Jewish identification in most parts of what Zionists saw as the diaspora. Jews around the world, including the USSR, felt enormous pride when the State of Israel was established in 1948. The nation that had been traumatically humiliated and partly annihilated during the Holocaust had reestablished itself as a sovereign entity capable of defending and rehabilitating its people. This is why elderly Jews in the FSU, who are themselves unlikely to emigrate, have a strong emotional connection to Israel, quite aside from family ties. They witnessed the Holocaust and the creation of Israel and drew a connection between them. Even the wife of Marshall Kliment Voroshilov, one of Stalin's closest comrades, who was born Golda Gorbman but who was characterized as a "fanatic Bolshevik-internationalist," was moved to remark on the establishment of Israel in 1948, "Well, and now we [sic] have a homeland [*rodina*]."³ Although Jews generally avoided synagogues because they were regarded as bastions of backwardness and "nests of speculators," about 10,000 people attended a special service in 1948 at Moscow's choral synagogue to mark the declaration of Israeli statehood, and similar services were held in other cities. The mood of many Jews is captured in a letter sent at this time to the Jewish Anti-Fascist Committee:

> Now when the struggle is not about life but about death, when the war [in Israel] is becoming ever more cruel, when the blood of our brothers and sisters is flowing, when Arab fascist bands supported by Anglo-American imperialism want to choke and drown in blood the heroic Jewish people, we, Soviet Jews, cannot remain silent and sit waiting. We must actively assist the... heroes to achieve victory – fight shoulder to shoulder with our brothers. This is our holy duty.⁴

Five hundred Jews in the small Ukrainian town of Zhmerinka wrote to the editorial board of *Pravda*, the Communist Party's central newspaper, requesting permission for "all Jewish residents of the town" to go to Israel "to build there

---

[3] "*Vot teper' u nas est' rodina.*" Quoted in Gennadi Kostyrchenko, *V plenu u krasnogo faraona* (Moscow: Mezhdunarodnye otnosheniia, 1991), 112.

[4] Quoted in ibid., 113. According to Kostyrchenko, the two-time Hero of the Soviet Union, Col. (later General) D. A. Dragunsky, came to the Jewish Anti-Fascist Committee to discuss sending a special Jewish division to Palestine (112 note). This seems doubtful in light of Dragunsky's political orthodoxy. He became a member of the Party Control Commission and in 1983 chaired the Soviet Public Committee against Zionism.

Identity, Israel, and Immigration

the kind of life we have here."[5] Veterans of the Soviet armed forces volunteered to fight in Israel's War of Independence. Needless to say, none were permitted to do so and many were arrested a short time later.

In the years after the June 1967 war between Israel and the Arab states, the luster of Israel was dimmed in the eyes of some diaspora Jews by Israel's policies in the territories it captured and later by controversies over Israeli definitions of "who is a Jew," the Orthodox monopoly of religious life of Israel, and a series of wars. Moreover, the generations who witnessed what they perceived as the miraculous emergence of a Jewish state after nearly 2,000 years of statelessness were passing from the scene. Those born after 1948 tend to take the existence of such a state for granted. In the United States, ties were lessening to Israel: "Since the early 1980s... American Jews had become decreasingly attached to Israel... grew less enamored of Israelis, less interested in Israel, and less active in supporting Israel."[6] Studies of British Jewry showed the same trends.[7] In Hungary, a national survey of Jews in 1999 (n = 2,015) showed the same decline in attachment to Israel from older to younger groups.[8]

In the Soviet Union where there were no Jewish or Zionist organizations Zionism was defined officially as a racist, imperialist ideology. After 1967 Israel was regarded as a pariah state (which had profoundly embarrassed the USSR by ignominiously defeating its Arab clients). Thus it could hardly play the same role among Jews as a source of pride, at least not publicly, as it did in the West. There was no Jewish community to combat the official line on Israel, no fund-raising or political support was possible, nor, except in rare instances, could Soviet Jews visit Israel after 1967. Nevertheless, many Soviet Jews were proud of Israel's existence and survival, its ability to defend itself, and the scientific, agricultural, and social accomplishments of the young state, about which some information filtered through. As one person we interviewed put it, somewhat ironically, "I used to be proud that Marx was a Jew. Now I'm proud of the creation of a Jewish state."

Soviet Jews were impressed with Israel's 1967 victory and depressed by their country's economic, military, and diplomatic support of Israel's enemies, some

---

[5] Translated in Shimon Redlich, ed., *War, Holocaust and Stalinism* (Luxembourg: Harwood Academic Publishers, 1995), 384–85. Other such petitions may be found in the same volume.

[6] Steven M. Cohen," Changing Conceptions of Jewish Collectivity among Young Adult Jews and Their Implications for Jewish Education: A Dual Research Project," unpublished paper, Research Unit, Dept. of Jewish-Zionist Education, August 25, 2002, 12–13.

[7] Stephen Miller, Marlena Schmool, and Antony Lerman, *Social and Political Attitudes of British Jews: Some Key Findings of the JPR Survey* (London: Institute for Jewish Policy Research, 1996), 8–9.

[8] Andras Kovacs, *Zsidok es Zsidosag a mai Magyarorszagon*, (Budapest, 2002), 15. I wish to thank Professor Kovacs for supplying an English translation. South African Jews, long noted for their Zionism, expressed strong attachments to Israel (54%) in a 1998 survey (n = 1,000). Barry Kosmin, Jacqueline Goldberg, Milton Shain, and Shirley Bruk, *Jews of the 'New South Africa': Highlights of the 1998 National Survey of South African Jews* (London: Institute for Jewish Policy Research, No. 3, September 1999), 15

of whom had pledged to destroy the Jewish state.[9] When the USSR and all its socialist allies except Romania broke relations with Israel in 1967 and there were campaigns against Zionism in the media, workplaces, and schools, many Soviet Jews interpreted the campaigns as anti-Semitism – and during the period of glasnost in the late 1980s several Soviet commentators were able to agree with this assessment. Jews felt increasingly uncomfortable in their native land. Israel's accelerated economic development and international political support after 1967, halted temporarily after the October 1973 Yom Kippur War, and Soviet condemnation of Israel, played a significant role in pulling Soviet Jews toward Israel and pushing them out of the USSR.[10]

Russian and Ukrainian Jews relate to Israel primarily as a place to live, not as a state to be supported politically and philanthropically from afar. This relationship is almost diametrically opposite from that of American and West European Jews, among whom only a small minority even considers emigrating to Israel, but far more actively and passively support Israel. These Western Jews are Zionists who mostly do not make aliyah, whereas the Russian and Ukrainian Jews make aliyah but are mostly not Zionists.

Russian and Ukrainian Jews support aliyah because immigration to Israel could resolve the tension between being Jewish officially and socially and being Russian culturally. Soviet Jews were designated as Jews by the state and society but had little Jewish culture; russianized culturally for the most part, they were denied the status of being Russian. Thus, they were in some sense Jewish and in another Russian in a state that did not brook multiple and complex identities.

Israel in the Eyes of Russian and Ukrainian Jews

Do people who choose to remain in Russia or Ukraine do so because they have negative impressions of Israel? Apparently not. Russian and Ukrainian Jews have generally positive attitudes toward Israel – although these have lessened – that are born not of classic Zionist ideals but of a perception that Israel is a fairly prosperous country that offers Jews security (our surveys were taken between the first and second Palestinian *intifadas*, after the Gulf War, and at a time when the Oslo peace process raised hopes for a settlement of the Palestinian–Israeli conflict). Almost no one surveyed in Russia or Ukraine in either year picked "subscribing to the ideals of Zionism" as one of the crucial

---

[9] On the reaction of Soviet Jews to the 1967 war, see Zvi Gitelman, "The Psychological and Political Consequences of the Six-Day War in the U.S.S.R.," in Eli Lederhandler, ed., *The Six-Day War and World Jewry* (Bethesda: University Press of Maryland, 2000), 249–68. See also Yaacov Ro'i and Boris Morozov, eds., *The Soviet Union and the June 1967 Six Day War* (Washington, DC: Woodrow Wilson Center Press, 2008).

[10] On Soviet Jewish attitudes toward Israel before 1967, see Yaacov Ro'i, *The Struggle for Soviet Jewish Emigration, 1948–1967* (Cambridge: Cambridge University Press, 1991) and Binyamin Pinkus, *Tehiya u-tekumah leumit: ha-Tsiyonut veha-Tenuah ha-Tsiyonit biVrit Hamoetsot* (Beer-Sheva: Ben-Gurion University Press, 1993).

components that define one as a "genuine Jew." Yet, large majorities averred that to be such a Jew it would be either "necessary" or "desirable" to "feel oneself close to Israel and worry about its fate."

However, the importance of Israel dropped considerably between the first and second surveys. Thus, in 1992/93, 46 to 47 percent of respondents in Russia and Ukraine felt it was "necessary" to feel close to Israel and be concerned about it, but in 1997/98, only one-quarter of Russian respondents and 29 percent of those in Ukraine thought so. The decline in the salience of Israel and in positive affect toward it may be due to the fact that those more enthusiastic about Israel had already moved there. Or, perhaps the same mild disillusionment with Israel that occurred in Western Jewish communities may have happened among post-Soviet Jews. There may be additional reasons. For example, some post-Soviet Jews may have been put off by negative reports from those who emigrated to Israel, heavy-handed tactics by Israeli emissaries intent on promoting aliyah, and Israeli policies regarding non-Jewish family members of immigrants that affected Russian and Ukrainian Jews more than American and British ones. Still, even in the second stage of the survey, more than three-quarters of respondents felt that to qualify as a "genuine" Jew, it is "desirable" to be close to Israel.[11]

The Soviet government began to permit controlled, limited emigration in 1971–72 because it saw this policy as a relatively cheap way of placating those in the West who were agitating for free emigration of Jews and others.[12] Officials could relax or tighten emigration policies to signal pleasure or displeasure with the West. Emigration was limited to two or three nationalities and therefore would not take on mass proportions.

Connections to Israel were strengthened greatly by immigration of friends and family to the Jewish state. Between 1951 and 1991 the Soviets permitted about 1.8 million Jews to emigrate, the great majority after 1971, and especially after 1989. About two-thirds went to Israel and most of the rest to the United States. About 550,000 ethnic Germans also left, almost all of them for the "capitalist" Federal Republic of Germany rather than the "socialist" German Democratic Republic. About 100,000 Armenians and Greeks and

---

[11] It is interesting that in the 2002 "Annual Survey of American Jewish Opinion" sponsored by the American Jewish Committee, involving 1,008 American Jews interviewed by telephone, only 5 percent said that "support for Israel" was the most important quality of their Jewish identity. "Being part of the Jewish people" ranked first with 41 percent. See http://ajc.org./IntheMedia/Publications.asp.

[12] As early as 1955, the German government had made representations to the Soviets on behalf of Soviet Germans who wished to migrate to the historic *vaterland*. Later, these pressures were accelerated when the Soviets began to pursue détente with the West. Germany became the USSR's largest trading partner outside the Council for Mutual Economic Assistance (Soviet-allied states), and the United States was the "other superpower." D. V. Grigoriev, *Etnopoliticheskie protsessy v nemetskoi obshchine Respubliki Bashkortosan* (Ufa: IO BashGU, 2005), 121–22.

smaller numbers of Evangelical Christians were permitted to emigrate,[13] almost all on the grounds of family reunification.

The Soviets soon realized that emigration feeds on itself and that "chain migration," whereby one émigré pulls another in his or her wake because they are linked by family, friendship, or social connections, meant that a steady stream of people would be applying to leave. The government attempted to curb emigration by imposing education taxes on would-be émigrés, whereby they would have to reimburse the state for the cost of their higher education, or by simply refusing to issue exit visas (permission to leave). This deterred some from even applying for an exit visa, because after doing so, it was likely that they would be dismissed from their jobs, expelled from school, and socially shunned. The plight of "refuseniks"[14] – those who had applied to leave but were denied exit visas – aroused international attention. A sea change in the international system allowed nonstate actors, interest groups, multinational corporations, ethnic and religious groups, and international organizations to play larger, more effective advocacy roles in the international arena. Because of increasing education and the greater reach of mass media ordinary people became more involved in world affairs and more questioning of authority, and they developed a stronger sense of political efficacy.[15] Technology made the transmission of political messages more rapid and effective in penetrating the Iron Curtain.

The high levels of education and urbanity of Western and Soviet Jews made both groups likely candidates for political involvement. Western Jews felt guilty, rightly or wrongly, for not having saved more European Jews during the Holocaust and shame at their political impotence in the 1930s. The inspiration of the American civil rights movement, the Russian origins of so many Western and Israeli Jews, and traditions of cross-boundary solidarity played a role in mobilizing world Jewry on behalf of Soviet Jewish emigration. Soviet Jewry emerged as the single most consensual issue among Jews when support for Israel, the great mobilizing force among diaspora Jews until the late 1970s, began to dissipate over disagreements about Israeli policies.[16] Soviet

---

[13] Figures are from Valeriy Tishkov, *Rekviem po etnosu* (Moscow: Nauka, 2003), 459. See also Sidney Heitman et al., "German and Jewish Migration from the Former Soviet Union to Germany: Background, Trends and Implications," *Journal of Ethnic and Migration Studies* 26, 4 (October 2000), 635–52.

[14] "*Otkazniki*" in Russian; "*Seruvnikim*" in Hebrew. There were 11,000 "refuseniks" at the peak period of refusal.

[15] James Rosenau, *Turbulence in World Politics* (Princeton: Princeton University Press, 1990).

[16] On the movement for Soviet Jewish emigration, see Murray Friedman and Albert Chernin, *A Second Exodus: The American Movement to Free Soviet Jews* (Hanover, NH: Brandeis University Press, 1999); Fred Lazin, *The Struggle for Soviet Jewry in American Politics: Israel versus the American Jewish Establishment* (Lanham, MD: Lexington Books, 2005); Stuart Altshuler, *From Exodus to Freedom: A History of the Soviet Jewry Movement* (Lanham, MD: Rowman & Littlefield, 2005); Henry Feingold, *"Silent No More": Saving the Jews of Russia, the American Jewish effort, 1967–1989* (Syracuse: Syracuse University Press, 2007); and Gal

Jewish activists took the lead. Like other national and cultural dissidents, they defied a sclerotic regime, using the new international arena and new technology to protect themselves to the extent possible.

Western governments supported the right of free emigration for several reasons. Like Jews, some felt guilt for the Holocaust and their immigration policies of the time that effectively condemned hundreds of thousands to death. Conservatives happily joined what they saw as a campaign directed against the "evil empire." Liberals joined what was a genuine human rights issue. U.S. President Jimmy Carter had struggled successfully to make human rights a legitimate concern not only of international bodies but also of individual governments. Nearly all Jewish organizations were advocating on behalf of Soviet Jewry, so elected officials could only gain by supporting it.

Soviet responses to demands to relax emigration restrictions were inconsistent – at times accommodating and at times rejecting. What explains the shifts in Soviet policy? Most observers see them mainly as a function of East–West relations: when the USSR wished to ingratiate itself with the West, particularly the United States, it opened the emigration pipeline. To show its displeasure, it closed it. A curve representing the state of Soviet-American relations and one showing the flow of emigrants would parallel each other. No doubt, some domestic considerations influenced Soviet policy as well, although in my view they were of secondary importance. Laurie Salitan argued that 1976–79 was a period of tension in U.S.-Soviet relations and yet there was a high volume of emigration. I view tensions over Angola, the Horn of Africa, stalled SALT negotiations, and Sino-American detente as irritants, not major conflicts. By contrast, the 1979 Soviet invasion of Afghanistan, which was followed by a steep drop in emigration, was a major downturn in the superpower relationship. Renewed emigration under Mikhail Gorbachev, Salitan argues, was the outcome of his commitment to the rule of law.[17] I am less impressed by Gorbachev's commitment to the rule of law than by his strong desire to win Western support for his political and, especially, economic policies.

In my view, Robert Brym's statistical analysis showing no correlation between U.S.-Soviet relations and emigration is flawed because he takes the volume of trade between the two countries as the sole measure of their relations. Many factors affect the volume of trade, not least of which are economic calculations. Trade is not simply a function of political relations, and it measures them too crudely. Brym argued that in the 1970s the Soviets permitted Jewish emigration because they were worried by an oversupply of highly educated personnel; by the 1980s there were labor shortages, so emigration was

---

Beckerman, *When They Come for Us We'll be Gone: The Epic Struggle to Save Soviet Jewry* (New York: Houghton Mifflin Harcourt, 2010).

[17] Laurie Salitan, "Domestic Pressures and the Politics of Exit: Trends in Soviet Emigration Policy," *Political Science Quarterly* 104, 4 (1989–90). Salitan elaborates her argument in *Politics and Nationality in Contemporary Soviet-Jewish Emigration, 1968–89* (London: Macmillan, l992). My assessment of her argument is in *Political Science Quarterly*, 107, 4 (Winter 1992/93).

curtailed. This argument is more plausible, but the evidence cited is somewhat sparse.[18]

Published documents from FSU archives appear to support my understanding of what determined Soviet emigration policy. In a Politburo meeting on March 20, 1973, party leader Leonid Brezhnev urged his colleagues not to enforce the education tax. He reprimanded Yuri Andropov, head of the KGB at the time, for delaying implementation of a decision to suspend collection of the tax. Brezhnev told his colleagues,

> The Zionists are screaming, [Senator Henry] Jackson bases himself on this, and [Henry] Kissinger goes to [Soviet ambassador Mikhail] Dobrynin and says we understand, this is an internal matter, we cannot interfere, we also have laws. At the same time he says: help us somehow, [President Richard] Nixon can't pass a bill [on his own], he has to work with senators. Who needs this million?[19]
> ....There is a group of Republicans who aim to stop the improvement of relations between the USSR and USA. Nixon is for it... but many senators are opposed [just] because we extract payment from the Jews.[20]

Brezhnev then went on to raise the possibilities of opening a Jewish school and a Jewish theater in Moscow. He reminisced about the 1930s when he and a friend had stumbled into a concert of Jewish music in Dnepropetrovsk where the crowd – "100 percent Jews except for me, my friend and our spouses" – clapped enthusiastically for "some Aunt Sonia" who was singing. If a Jewish theater opened in Moscow, Brezhnev mused, Jews would flock to hear their Aunt Sonias and "this will bring income to our budget." Brezhnev seems to have thought this income would make up for the loss incurred by dropping the education tax. He commented, "You can count on a million, they'll give you a million, even though they don't earn that much."[21]

It turned out that the "million" was close to the number of Soviet and post-Soviet Jews who left from 1971 and thereafter. They constitute the single largest immigration in Israeli history. The great irony is that they came from a state that militantly opposed Zionism throughout its history, condemning it as racism; allowed no Zionist emissaries, publications, or films; banned the study

---

[18] Robert Brym, "Soviet Jewish Emigration: A Statistical Test of Two Theories," *Soviet Jewish Affairs* 18, 3 (1988), and his "The Changing Rate of Jewish Emigration from the USSR: Some Lessons from the l970s," *Soviet Jewish Affairs* 15, 2 (May l985). Even more speculative – and erroneous – arguments are made by John Scherer who opines that the "Soviets probably decided to issue an approximate number of visas by five-year periods and made annual adjustments depending on the political situation and on the number of visas required to fulfill the Plan. The large number of visas issued in 1979 (before the invasion of Afghanistan) was due to a desire to fulfill the plan.... If emigration does not rise in 1986 [it did not], it probably will not rise during the decade" [it did, and to unparalleled heights]. John Scherer, "A Note on Soviet Jewish Emigration, 1971–84," *Soviet Jewish Affairs* 15, 2 (May 1985).

[19] A figure of 1,561,375 rubles collected from the "education tax" had been reported to the meeting.

[20] Boris Morozov, *Evreiskaya emigratsiia v svetle novykh dokumentov* (Tel Aviv: Tel Aviv University Press, 1988), Document 45, 164–67.

[21] Ibid., 167.

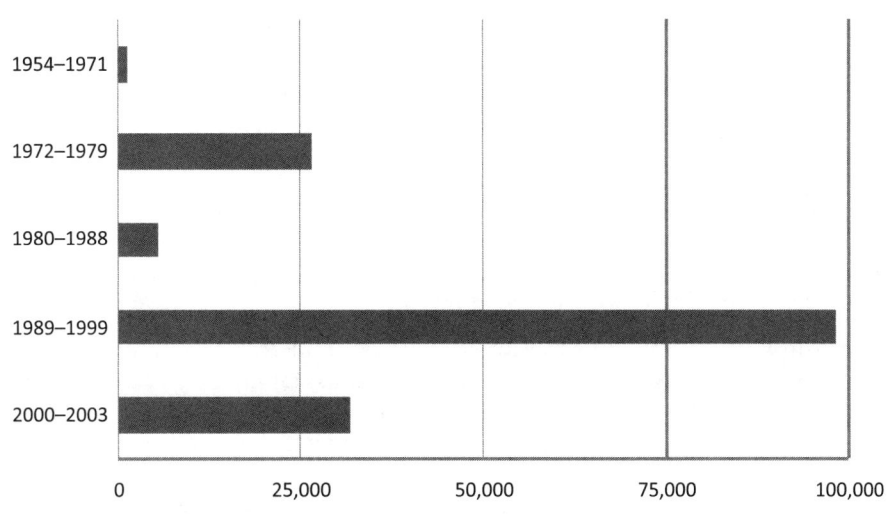

Period	Value
1954–1971	~1,300
1972–1979	~26,000
1980–1988	~5,350
1989–1999	~100,000
2000–2003	~30,000

FIGURE 9.1. USSR mean number of annual Jewish emigrants.

of Hebrew, the only language to be so treated; severely curbed the practice of Judaism; severed diplomatic relations with Israel in 1967 and did not restore them for more than two decades; and trained, supplied, and supported groups and states committed to the destruction of Israel. Yet, by the end of 2002, more than a million Jews had left their native lands: about 1.1 million of them (including their non-Jewish relatives) had come to Israel; at least 350,000 – possibly as many as a half-million – had resettled in the United States; and about 200,000 had emigrated to Germany.[22]

This was by no means a regular, even flow of people from one country to another. There were peaks and valleys in the Jewish emigration from the USSR, just as there were among Germans, Armenians, Evangelicals, and others permitted to leave at one time or another. Between 1954 and 1971 (inclusive), 23,465 Jews left, an average of 1,304 a year. After the Soviet government's decision to allow controlled, selective immigration, 211,444 Jews left between 1972 and 1979, almost all for Israel, for an average of more than 26,000 a year. The peak year was 1979, during which 51,320 left. However, in December of that year Soviet troops marched into Afghanistan, ending détente and leading to a sharp curtailment in the number allowed to leave. Between 1980 and 1988, only 48,151 Jews emigrated, an average of 5,350 a year. The largest wave of emigration began in 1989 and tailed off early in the twenty-first century. We can see the trends in Figure 9.1.

---

[22] About 350,000 Soviets came to the United States as refugees and used HIAS's services – the great majority were probably Jews – but according to the State Department, about 597,000 refugees and immigrants came from the Former Soviet Union. It is impossible to determine how many of the immigrants to the United States are Jews. Data are from Mark Tolts, "Post-Soviet Aliyah and Jewish Demographic Transformation," paper presented at the 15th World Congress of Jewish Studies, August 2–6, 2009, Jerusalem, Israel, table 1.

In the twenty-first century, the number of post-Soviet Jews emigrating to Israel plummeted from an average of 45,000 a year between 1997 and 2000, to about 11,000 in 2001–7, a drop of about 75 percent. The average number emigrating to the United States dropped from 8,500 a year in 1997–2001 to about 1,500 thereafter through 2007. The annual average going to Germany declined from about 15,000 (1995–2005) to less than a thousand after Germany changed its immigration policy in 2005.

Motivations for Emigration and Immigration

What drove the immigrants to leave their native lands?[23] Were they motivated by Jewish consciousness, economic considerations, family ties, anti-Semitism, or other forces? Many Israelis consider the first mass Soviet immigration (March 1971–74), a "Zionist," ideologically motivated immigration, whereas they perceive the massive immigration that began in 1989 as nonideological, driven by economic, political, and family considerations. Like many popular notions, there is more than a grain of truth in it, but it is overly simple. True, many Zionists who had fought for the right to emigrate to the Jewish state seized their first opportunity and came to Israel in the 1970s, along with those strongly motivated by religion. In my interviews with 148 Soviet immigrants in Israel in 1972, nearly two-thirds cited variations on Zionist themes as their primary motivation for aliyah, whereas about 10 percent cited family reasons or political alienation, and others talked about the desire to live among Jews, to escape anti-Semitism, or to improve their economic situation. However, when I interviewed the same individuals in 1975, only one of eight cited Zionism as their primary motivation for having come to Israel. In an earlier work I suggested two explanations for this change:

> Either Zionist rhetoric was seen as the "appropriate" response in 1972 and was no longer perceived that way in 1975, or it was an authentic response in 1972, but after living several years in the Zionist state it had lost much of its meaning,

---

[23] In 1997/98 we asked, "What country do you consider your Homeland [*rodina*], with a capital 'H'?" Understandably, only 10 percent in Russia and 13 percent in Ukraine named Israel; 78 percent in Russia named Russia. However, in Ukraine, only 55 percent named Ukraine and 20 percent cited the USSR. (This is discussed more fully in Chapter 10). As an immigrant in Israel observed, the question of "homeland" is a difficult one. He was born in Odessa, moved to Kazakhstan at age 24, and lived there for twenty-three years before moving to Kirov (Viatka) in Russia where he spent another twenty years before emigrating to Israel: "Earlier I might have said in the words of the song, 'My Address – The Soviet Union.' But now? I don't want to consider Ukraine my homeland [*rodina*], though formally I should; Kazakhstan? I really can't, though there is some basis to it; Russia – there's no reason to. So what will be?" People with less itinerant lives also displayed ambivalence when answering this question. Among the comments it elicited were the following: "I consider myself a citizen of the world, but I love Russia;" "Russia, but not with a capital letter"; "Russia, for now"; "Russia, unfortunately;" "Territorially – Russia, but in general, none." One discussion of diasporas where "one sees the tips of many icebergs," according to the author, is James Clifford, "Diasporas," *Cultural Anthropology*, 9, 3 (1994), 302–38.

since the ideal ha[d] been fulfilled on the personal level and people [had forgotten] how much it [had] meant to them outside of Israel. The humdrum of daily life tends to obscure abstract ideals, and one's concerns tend to be more prosaic.[24]

Moreover, Israel had begun to lose some cachet after the 1973 Yom Kippur War with Egypt and Syria, and the very word "Zionism" began to be intoned cynically in some Israeli circles.

This first wave of about 175,000 immigrants to Israel was demographically unrepresentative of Soviet Jewry. A disproportionate number came from the western periphery of the USSR and from Georgia: between 1968 and 1976, one-quarter of the Israeli immigrants came from Georgia, where in 1970 only 2.5 percent of the Jewish population resided. One-third of this aliyah came from territories annexed by the USSR in 1939–40: Latvia and Lithuania, Bessarabia and Bukovina (currently in Moldova and Ukraine, respectively, but until 1940 part of Romania), and eastern Poland. Together, the Jews of these areas probably made up no more than 10 percent of the total Jewish population in 1970. Only about 40 percent of the immigrants came from Russia, Belorussia, and Ukraine, where 81 percent of the 1970 Jewish population resided.

Religion and tradition, not modern political Zionism alone, motivated Georgian Jews. The pull of immigration to Israel was stronger than the push of emigration from the Soviet Union. *Zapadniki* (Westerners), those who had become Soviet citizens as a result of the annexations in 1939–40, were far less acculturated to Russian or local cultures than those living under Soviet rule since 1917 or 1921. They had strong memories of and commitments to Hebrew, Yiddish, and Zionism.

Georgian Jews were not fleeing the Soviet Union, where they suffered little discrimination and thought of themselves as well off, as much as expressing their traditional values, including both a religiously inflected yearning for Zion and a commitment to close-knit, hierarchical families. Thus, when the head of a family decided to emigrate, many would follow.[25]

After the 1973 war, when Israel's security and economic situation deteriorated drastically, émigrés from the Soviet Union increasingly "dropped out" at the Vienna transit point[26] and opted to settle in the United States and other Western countries as refugees. This wave of immigrants came largely from the three Slavic republics: Russia, Ukraine, and Belorussia (now Belarus). From 1975 to 1989 (inclusive), 69 percent of the émigrés did not settle in Israel, with the trend increasing every year. In 1988, nine of ten émigrés resettled in the United States. After 1976, about 85 percent of those coming to America came from Russia and Ukraine, and about 90 percent of those leaving Moscow,

---

[24] Zvi Gitelman, *Becoming Israelis: Political Resocialization of Soviet and American immigrants* (New York: Praeger, 1982), 222.
[25] The interviews that I conducted in 1972–75 included few Georgian Jews.
[26] There were no direct flights to Israel from the USSR. Emigres went by train to Vienna and from there flew to Israel. Those who did not want to go to Israel were generally transferred to Italy and after a few months were permitted to enter the United States as refugees.

Leningrad, Kiev, and Odessa – where Jews were most acculturated – chose the United States, not Israel, as their destination. In contrast, those from cities incorporated late into the USSR were less likely to go to America. For example, in 1974, 55 percent of those leaving Moscow and Leningrad went to the United States, compared to only one-third of those leaving Lviv, formerly in Poland, and 3 percent of those departing Chernivtsi, formerly in Romania. Fewer than 10 percent of those who left Vilnius (Vilna, Wilno) and Kaunas (Kovno) [Lithuania] went to America in 1974, compared to 51 percent of Kievans and 58 percent of Kharkivites (both in Ukraine).[27] Thus there was a direct relationship between involvement in Jewish culture and the propensity to immigrate to Israel. The Jews of the Slavic republics, many of them third-generation Soviet citizens who had been cut off from Jewish culture for decades, had little reason to go to Israel. They sought political and cultural freedom, economic opportunity, and social equality – in the West.

However, because every Soviet citizen left the USSR on Israeli visas, those who did not want to settle in Israel became a bone of contention between the Israeli government and the Jewish Agency, on one hand, and the American Jewish community, on the other. Frustrated by the low numbers of immigrants to Israel in general and embarrassed by the tens of thousands of Soviet Jews who chose *not* to go to Israel, Israelis charged that American Jewish organizations were seducing immigrants to justify their staffs and budgets. In turn, most of the American Jewish community declared their support for freedom of choice for the émigrés and rejected the kind of Zionism-by-coercion that Israelis seemed to advocate. According to one executive of an American Jewish community, "The entire framework of Jewish organizational life was... caught up in this policy conflict," especially because Soviet Jewish emigration and resettlement in the United States "would represent the single largest investment of resources, and the most extensive mobilization of personnel and institutions, since the days following the end of World War II."[28]

The direction of emigration was abruptly reversed in October 1989 when the United States, perhaps under Israeli pressure, announced a change in policy limiting Soviet immigration to 50,000 a year, of whom presumably 40,000 would be Jews. The effect of the policy change was immediate. In 1989, 59,024 Soviet immigrants had settled elsewhere than Israel, almost all in the United States, but in 1990, 97 percent of the largest single emigration in Russian Jewish history went to Israel, abruptly reversing a decade-long trend.

The composition of this later wave of immigration differed from that of earlier waves. These were not "born again" Zionists, but panicky refugees who viewed with dismay the economic deterioration of the USSR, growing

---

[27] Calculated from data in Zvi Alexander, "Netunim statistiyim shel ha'yetsia," *Hainteligentsia hayehudit bivrih"m* 4 (June 1990); and Z. Alexander, "Jewish Emigration from the USSR in 1980," *Soviet Jewish Affairs* 11, 2 (1981).
[28] Steven Windmueller, "The 'Noshrim' War: Dropping Out," in Murray Friedman and Albert Chernin, eds., *A Second Exodus* (Hanover: Brandeis University Press, 1999), 170–71.

ethnic strife, and the emergence of public, virulent, grassroots anti-Semitism.[29] They went to whatever country would take them.

The Waning of Emigration

The push to leave the FSU weakened as economic conditions in Russia and Ukraine improved and social and political stability was achieved, at whatever cost, in the first decade of the twenty-first century. The number admitted to the United States fell steadily during the 1990s to about 5,000 in the year 2000. After the 2001 terrorist attacks in the United States, tighter immigration procedures choked off migration. In 2005, only 1,600 Jews from the FSU were admitted, and in 2006 less than a thousand resettled in the United States. Those with no first-degree relatives in the United States have little chance of admission, except if they have highly desirable skills or win the "green card" lottery. Political instability and a seemingly never ending struggle with the Palestinians, along with nuclear threats from Iran, made Israel less attractive. In 2007, fewer than 7,000 immigrants came to Israel from the FSU. Although Germany welcomed Jewish immigrants to "make up" for what it had done to its native Jews after 1933, some Russian and Ukrainian Jews would not consider going there,[30] as one interviewee told us:

> If I were to emigrate, then the calling of my soul would be to immigrate to Israel. I'd possibly consider America. But never Germany, because the Germans... even though it may be irrational, I still remember the war very well, the results of it, the concentration camps.... And in my heart I haven't forgiven them. So I wouldn't be able to live among them.... So many of my own people were killed. All of my mother's brothers were killed! All of my father's brothers were killed.

Nevertheless, between 2002 and 2004 more emigrants went to Germany than to Israel, and Germany temporarily became the top-ranking receiving country. However, in 2004 the number of Jews and their non-Jewish relatives who immigrated to Germany dropped to 11,200. In January 2005, to reduce the burden on its welfare system, Germany passed a new immigration law requiring all immigrants to meet certain educational and language requirements. The number of Jewish immigrants to Germany fell to 1,100 in 2006, as compared to an average of 15,000 annually between 1995 and 2005.[31] All in all, by about 2007 emigration from Russia and Ukraine had slowed to a trickle.

---

[29] For an analysis, see Zvi Gitelman, "Glasnost, Perestroika and Antisemitism," *Foreign Affairs* 70, 2 (Spring 1991).
[30] The story of a decorated Soviet Jewish war veteran now living in Hamburg and regretting his decision to emigrate to Germany is told in *Evreiskii kamerton/Novosti nedelii*, June 7, 2001.
[31] Data compiled from publications of the National Conference on Soviet Jewry, HIAS, the Jewish Agency, and German publications.

TABLE 9.1. *Total Jewish Populations of Russia, the Ukraine, and the Soviet Union (in thousands) and Percentage of Total Soviet Jewish Population*

	Russia	Ukraine	USSR
1897	317 (6%)	2,156 (41%)	5,216* (100%)
1926	525 (20)	1,574 (59)	2,672
1939	957 (32)	1,533 (51)	3,028
1959	875 (39)	840 (37)	2,268
1970	808 (38)	777 (36)	2,151
1979	700 (39)	634 (35)	1,811
1989	537 (37)	486 (34)	1,451
2001/02**	259	104	N/A

* In the Russian Empire.
** In the national censuses of Russia and the Ukraine, respectively, nationality was determined by self-declaration.
Sources: Solomon Schwarz, *The Jews in the Soviet Union* (Syracuse, 1951); Mordechai Altshuler, *Soviet Jewry since the Second World War* (New York, 1987); and idem, *Distribution of the Jewish Population of the USSR, 1939* (Jerusalem, 1993). Data from the questionable 1937 census have become available but are not included here because they are only partial results. See Akademiia Nauk SSSR, *Vsesoiuznaya perepis naseleniia 1937 g.* (Moscow, 1991), 83, 85, 94.

The Jews of Russia and Ukraine: Immigration and Identity

In 1897, the Russian Empire had the largest concentration of Jews in the world. After 1917, Russia and Ukraine had the two largest Jewish populations in the Soviet Union, making up 79 percent of the total Jewish population of the USSR in 1926 and 71 percent in 1989. At the beginning of the twenty-first century, there were about 5.4 million Jews in Israel, about 5.3 million in the United States, and only about 400,000 "core Jews" in the territories of the Former Soviet Union.

As Table 9.1 shows, the proportion of the Jewish population living in Ukraine declined over time and that in Russia increased. Since World War II, the proportion living in each republic has been about the same, with 2 to 4 percent more living in Russia. This increased percentage may be because more Jews left Ukraine than left Russia. From 1970 through 1997, more than 422,000 Jews emigrated from Ukraine, compared to 308,500 Jews who left Russia.[32] The greater emigration from Ukraine has several explanations:

---

[32] I am grateful to Dail Stolow, then with HIAS, for supplying me with data on Soviet Jewish immigration to the United States. In 1990, there were 31,283 immigrants to the United States, but HIAS did not issue a statistical report for that year, so I do not know the distribution of the immigrants by republic of origin. The emigration and immigration data in this chapter are derived mainly from the following sources: Yoel Florsheim, "Jewish Emigration to Israel and the United States from the Former Soviet Union, 1992," *Jews in Eastern Europe* 3, 32 (Winter 1993); Yoel Florsheim, "Emigration of Jews from the Soviet Union in 1989," *Jews and Jewish Topics in the Soviet Union and Eastern Europe* 2, 12 (Fall 1990); Israel, Central Statistical Bureau,

the Chernobyl nuclear catastrophe of 1986,[33] looser attachments of Jews to Ukraine than to Russia, Ukraine's unfavorable economic and political situation compared to Russia's, greater economic opportunities in the major Russian cities than in Ukraine, or, simply that a larger initial emigration from Ukraine created the chain that pulled a similar higher proportion of later emigrants.[34]

Identity and Immigration

How does personal identity relate to immigration, if at all? How did ideological and tangible connections that Russian and Ukrainian Jews have to Israel affect their plans for emigration?

Our survey data were collected at the beginning and the end of the unprecedented massive Jewish emigration wave that swept over the Former Soviet Union during the 1990s. This timing allows us to use statistical analysis to assess the changing motivations behind emigration at the height of the wave during the early 1990s and as the emigration began to trail off in 1997–8, in addition to comparing motivations among prospective emigrants from Ukraine and Russia.

As we have seen, many Jews from the USSR and its successor states ultimately chose to immigrate to countries other than Israel. Is there a relationship between a person's Jewish identity, their likelihood of emigration, and their choice to go to Israel? First we examine the pull of Israel. Potential emigrants had a wide variety of reasons for wanting to leave the FSU and go to Israel. Some of these reasons were purely economic and familial, and others were related more deeply to a person's identity. Although anti-Semitism may play a major role in pushing Jews to migrate, there are more positive reasons that draw people to Israel, such as a strong sense of Jewish identity or ideological or religious belief.

Monthly Bulletin of Statistics; Nunu Magor, *Haolim miBrih'm vehanoshrim shehigiu leArha'b–skira demografit hashvaatit (1.1.74–30.6.79)* (Jerusalem: Ministry of Immigrant Absorption, July 1980); Z. Alexander, "Jewish Emigration from the USSR in 1980," *Soviet Jewish Affairs* 11, 2 (1991); David Prital, ed., *Yehudai Brit ha-Moetsot*, 1–14 (Jerusalem: Hebrew University, 1984–91); Z. Alexander, "Mediniyut ha-aliyah shel Brit Ha-Moetsot (1968–1978)," *Behinot* 8–9 (1977–78); HIAS, *Statistical Abstracts*; Joseph Edelman, "Soviet Jews in the United States: A Profile," *American Jewish Yearbook 1977* (New York: American Jewish Committee, 1976); and Steven Gold, "Soviet Jews in the United States," *American Jewish Yearbook 1994* (New York: American Jewish Committee, 1994).

    Mark Tolts observed that immigrants from the Russian Federation were the most numerous only in 1991 and 1994, "but in 1989–90 and 1995–1998 more immigrants arrived from Ukraine." Mark Tolts, "Russian Jewish Migration in the Post-Soviet Era," *Revue Europeene des Migrations Internationales* 16, 3 (2000) 188.

[33] In fact, areas of Eastern Belarus such as Gomel and Mogilev, were harder hit by radiation than was northern Ukraine. Nevertheless, residents of Ukraine could not be sure they would be unaffected.

[34] For a discussion of these issues, see Zvi Gitelman, "Native Land, Promised Land, New Land: Jewish Emigration from Russian and Ukraine," in Zvi Gitelman, Lubomyr Hajda, John-Paul Himka, and Roman Solchanyk, eds., *Cultures and Nations of Central and Eastern Europe* (Cambridge, MA: Harvard Ukrainian Research Institute, 2000), 137–64.

Tangible connections to Israel, such as family or friends living in the country, may pull in potential immigrants. We incorporate these sets of motivations into estimating four regressions that predict a person's probability of emigration.

The Propellants of Immigration

Once emigration assumed substantial proportions, it created its own dynamic and swept up people who had previously had no thought of leaving. "Shall I be the last Jewish woman in Kiev?!" said one. When asked to explain why he was emigrating, another Ukrainian Jew told us simply, "Everyone is leaving – and I'm leaving." How should we understand the correlates and motivations of aliyah beyond fashionability or mass hysteria? We discuss four forces that could propel immigration.

Anti-Semitism: We chose to analyze anti-Semitism as a separate variable to understand its impact on specific elements of Jewish identity. To measure the variable, we constructed an index of anti-Semitism based on two questions asked across all four surveys. The first question asked respondents to consider the level of anti-Semitism they faced in public in the past year. The three-tiered response options ranged from "none," which the survey scored "0," to "often," which was scored a "2." For purposes of measurement, we scored "don't know" answers as "1," which is the equivalent of responding "sometimes." The second question asked respondents whether or not they faced anti-Semitism at work in the past year and had the same response categories. Combining the two questions resulted in a 5-point scale of increasing experiences of anti-Semitism. Because we predict that anti-Semitism acts to push Jews in the former Soviet republics to emigrate, this scale should correlate positively with the likelihood of emigration.

Objective Connections to Israel: Until the 1970s, few Soviet Jews had personal connections or other relationships with Israel. If such connections had existed earlier, they were forgotten, suppressed, or ignored, sometimes for political reasons. In other cases, World War II and the Iron Curtain had cut families and friends off from each other. Suddenly, in the 1970s–1990s massive immigration created a triangular "imagined community" linking Russians in Israel and the United States with Jews in the FSU. About one-third of our respondents had close relatives in Israel, and larger proportions had more distant relatives and close friends in both Israel and the United States. These connections spur tourism, business, cultural contacts, and future immigration. The emigrations to Israel and the United States serve as magnets to Jews in Russia and Ukraine, as well as to Russian and Ukrainian businesspeople, cultural figures, and even politicians. Of course, family situations change and the role they play in emigration decisions changes as well. Following are fairly typical observations, the first from a 56-year-old woman in Odessa and the second from a man in his early sixties who lives in Lviv:

> Of course I have thought about emigrating! Everyone thinks about emigrating! It's being discussed a lot in the Jewish circles. But that doesn't depend just on

me. There was a period of time in 1975 when we almost left, but some family circumstances got in our way. My father-in-law was very ill then, so we couldn't leave. But some of my close relatives did leave then, like my cousin.... I have two grown-up sons (23 and 25 years old). If they decide to emigrate somewhere, I'll go with them.... The most realistic place to emigrate to nowadays is Israel. It's the Jewish historical homeland; it's the country where a Jew will be welcomed as a Jew!... In 1975 we probably would have gone to America, but now the most realistic place to be able to emigrate to is Israel.

The man from Lviv is married to a Ukrainian, and their son went to Israel with *his* Ukrainian wife, but according to the father, the son "is becoming more and more Jewish." The father explained his thinking about emigration as follows:

I have always thought about it! At first, it was related to the opportunity to realize myself better in another country. And it didn't necessarily have to be Israel.... But... now it has to do with my children.... So now they are in Israel. And that's why I am going there.... I am returning to my homeland! This is not emigration, it's repatriation! As I told you before, I have discovered myself as a Jew, so for me, it's not just going after my children, as is the case for my wife. For me it's also a matter of ideology.

We see here the complexity of family calculations and what are perceived of as Jewish motivations, the importance for parents of children's decisions, and the contradictions in some people's rationale for leaving. Another woman explained her thinking this way:

About 10 years ago when the times became tougher and my children had grown up, I started thinking about it [emigrating].... By now I don't want to leave, because I understand... that the language would be difficult for me, moving would be difficult, changing my surroundings would be difficult. I am not a healthy person. So changing the climate would also be difficult. Of course, if my children will decide to leave, I'd probably go with them.

We believe that connections to Israel tend to pull Jews toward a decision to emigrate. The first set of connections are objective, involving relatives and friends living abroad, as well as any trips to Israel the respondent may have made. All four surveys in Russia and Ukraine asked respondents two questions regarding any family and one regarding friends they have in Israel, as well as a question inquiring about any travel to the country. The proportion of respondents who *visited* Israel doubled over five years, rising to 25 percent in Russia and 20 percent in Ukraine. Many, perhaps most, of the travelers to Israel went to visit relatives. Combining the two questions on family, which ask individuals whether they have close or distant relatives in Israel, resulted in a 4-point scale of familial connections. Individuals with no family in Israel scored a "0", individuals with distant family scored "1," individuals with close family scored "2," and those with both close and distant relatives scored "3." Along similar lines, a question asking respondents about friends in Israel generated a dichotomous response. Finally, the surveys tracked the number of times respondents had been to Israel, in which we scored "0," "1," and

"2 or more" visits. Combining responses to these questions created a 6-point additive scale in which the variable asking about family made up the lion's share of possible variation (3 of 6 points), which seems theoretically defensible in light of the importance of family to many individuals. We predict this scale will correlate positively with the potential for emigration.

Because the immigration to Israel has been more than two and a half times as great as that to the United States, personal connections with the United States were weaker than with Israel: 16 to 27 percent of respondents said they had close relatives in the United States, compared to 29 to 47 percent who had such relatives in Israel.[35]

Subjective Connections to Israel: In addition to objective connections, Jews also have feelings about Israel and its people.[36] To tap into these attitudes we constructed a 9-point scale of subjective connections to Israel based on three questions. The first two questions addressed individuals' attitudes toward the concept of Israel as a Jewish state. First, we asked respondents how central "defending the state of Israel" is for a Jew and coded their responses from 0–3 in order of ascending importance. A second question measured the Zionist postulate of the "ingathering of the exiles." This concept holds that all Jews should, and would, eventually be gathered back into the ancestral homeland, the Land of Israel, although they should also be loyal citizens of whatever state they lived in.[37] Interviewers asked individuals to rate the importance of this concept on a 0–3 scale in ascending importance. A final question asked about respondents' attitudes toward Israelis themselves, with answer options ranging from "they are people just like anyone else" to "they are of my

---

[35] The proportions having distant relatives and close friends in the United States are much smaller than those having such connections to Israel.

[36] Feelings about Israelis as people are connected to attitudes toward Israel, of course, but are distinguishable from them. We found that most respondents felt somewhat warm toward Israelis but this feeling cooled over the five years between the surveys. In the second survey almost half of all respondents in both countries said, "I feel no blood tie, but a deep sympathy," whereas about one-quarter said they had no special feelings about Israelis and another quarter said they felt a strong blood tie to them. In the early 1990s fewer than 2 percent said they had no special feelings about Israelis. This drastic shift might be due to what residents of Russia and Ukraine had heard from those who emigrated to Israel or to other reasons.

[37] Erich Gruen asserts that in the Hellenistic period and later "Diaspora Jews did not bewail their fate and pine away for the homeland. Nor, by contrast, did they ignore the homeland and reckon the Book as surrogate for the Temple.... Palestine mattered, and it mattered in a territorial sense, but not as a required residence." Erich Gruen, "Diaspora and Homeland," in Howard Wettstein, ed., *Diasporas and Exiles: Varieties of Jewish Identity* (Berkeley: University of California Press, 2002), 36. Jewish law demands that Jews be loyal to the states in which they lived. Jeremiah (29:7), witness to the first exile, adjures, "Seek the peace of the city to which I have caused you to be carried away, and pray to the Lord on its behalf." In "Ethics of the Fathers" (ch. 3, mishna 2), a work compiled probably from the 5th to the 3rd centuries BCE, Rabbi Hanania is quoted as saying, "Pray for the welfare of the state, because were it not for the fear it inspires, every man would swallow his neighbor alive." Perhaps, like Hobbes, Rabbi Hanania meant states in general, but prayers for the government became standard parts of the synagogue service.

blood." We predict this index will correlate positively with the propensity to emigrate.

Jewishness: To measure the observance of Jewish practices and involvement in Jewish affairs, we constructed a 40-point scale based on a dozen questions regarding religious practice, holiday observance, and involvement in Jewish organizations.[38] This scale should correlate positively with the likelihood of emigration. In sum, we think all of the scales regarding Jewishness and connections to Israel should have positive relationships with emigration. The secondary questions, however, are which scales will have the largest effect in which country at which point in the emigration wave.

Demographic Factors: Additional environmental factors act as lubricants that may reinforce or counteract the influence of connections to Israel, Jewishness, and anti-Semitism on a person's decision to emigrate. The most salient demographic factor is age. The objective circumstances of the elderly make emigration difficult. Old age is generally associated with deep economic and familial roots in the existing community, comfort with or at least resignation to the status quo, and health problems that make travel and adapting to a new community considerably more difficult than for members of the younger generation. All other things being equal, we expect that advanced age should act as an anchor weighing down other impulses to emigrate.[39]

Another major potential factor in migration is one's economic situation. We used two specifications of financial well-being to test a pair of potential mechanisms through which income may influence emigration. First, a direct hypothesis states that increasing amounts of wealth lead to increasing means to emigrate, which should lead to a positive correlation between income and a decision to emigrate. An alternative mechanism accounts for differing levels of comfort and predicts that individuals with a middle level of income would be the most likely to emigrate. Poor people *want* to emigrate, but do not have the means to do so, whereas rich ones have the means, but because of their comfort and assets are less likely to emigrate. Measuring relative wealth is quite difficult in Russia and the Ukraine, especially in the early 1990s, because of the relatively low differences among official salaries under the communist regime and the instability of local currencies. Therefore we recorded respondents' self-reports of how well off they were based on an ascending 6-point scale of their ability to afford necessities, pay bills, and save money. For the first income hypothesis, we used this scale as a variable, which we expected to correlate positively with immigration. To test the second specification, we recentered the scale of zero (from -3 to 3), squared it, and multiplied it by -1. The resulting parabolic scale leaves middle-income individuals with higher scores and those

---

[38] Residents of Lviv and Chernivtsi consistently scored the highest in Ukraine, and those of Kharkiv the lowest. Parallel to these are scores on the index of identification with Israel. On this 5-point scale, 69 percent of Chernivtsi residents and 57 per cent of Lviv residents scored "high," but only 35 percent of Kharkivites did so.

[39] Our respondents' ages ranged from 18 to 97.

on the extremes with lower scores. We predict this scale will relate positively to the propensity to emigrate.

Finally, we controlled for a person's gender and education. We used a dichotomous variable to control for gender (males = 1; females = 0). A 6-point self-reported scale served to measure education, with "1" indicating no formal education and "6" indicating a postgraduate degree.

Measuring the Likelihood to Emigrate: To determine the probability of emigration, we used as the dependent variable the responses to the question from the four surveys asking respondents if they intended to emigrate. For simplicity's sake and to develop interpretable results, responses indicating a desire or precise plans to emigrate scored "1," whereas those who did not know or indicated a general unwillingness to emigrate scored "0." The proper form of regression to use under these circumstances of a dichotomous variable is probit analysis. (For technical details regarding methodology and results see the Appendix to this chapter).

Results: Of our variables, all of the directly "Jewish" variables and age consistently show effects distinct from zero across both countries and time. (The precise regression coefficients are in Appendix A). To provide an intuitive interpretation of the influences of the statistically significant variables, we charted their effects in Figure 9.2. One of the benefits of regression analysis is that the charts in this figure control for the simultaneous impact of all other variables that we have tested, so we can be fairly confident the relationships we show do not mask each other.

The left panels show Russia and the right panels show Ukraine. Each pair of panels from top to bottom shows the effects of a different variable. The vertical axis shows the probability of being a likely emigrant, whereas the horizontal axis shows levels of the variable of interest, with lower quantities at the left and higher quantities at the right.

Glancing at Figure 9.2, even before analyzing the influences of specific variables, four trends become clear. First, Russian Jews have a lower baseline propensity to emigrate than Ukrainian Jews across all variables and survey years. Second, the baseline likelihood of emigration is lower in 1997/98 than in 1992/93. This observation is in line with the basic data on emigration presented in Figure 9.1: 1992/93 was near the start of the massive wave of Jewish emigration during the decade after the fall of the USSR, whereas 1997/98 was close to the endpoint of the wave. Third, despite the different *baseline* probability of emigration, each variable seems to have quite similar *effects* across the two countries. A variable that has a positive effect in Ukraine has a positive effect in Russia of roughly the same magnitude. Finally, on a related point, the strength of the influence of almost all variables – with the one notable exception of subjective attachments to Israel in Ukraine – seems to wane over time; it is stronger in 1992/3 than in 1997/98 (as shown by the gap between the bars on most charts). This feature also seems consistent with the declining numbers of emigrants in the late 1990s. Those who had been influenced already had

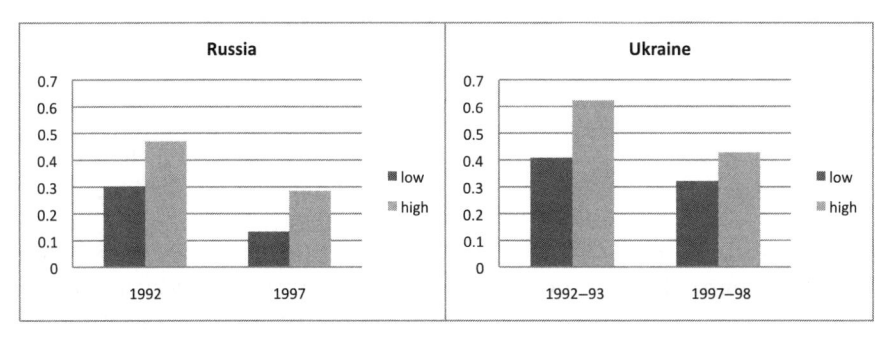

Index of Jewish Identification

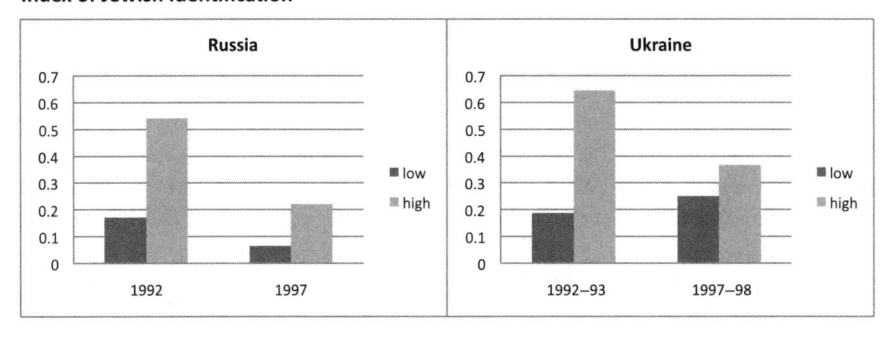

Russia

	1992	1997
low	0.30	0.13
high	0.48	0.29

Ukraine

	1992–93	1997–98
low	0.41	0.33
high	0.63	0.44

Age (second row — unlabeled, likely Identification continued)

Russia

	1992	1997
low	0.18	0.07
high	0.54	0.22

Ukraine

	1992–93	1997–98
low	0.19	0.26
high	0.65	0.37

Age

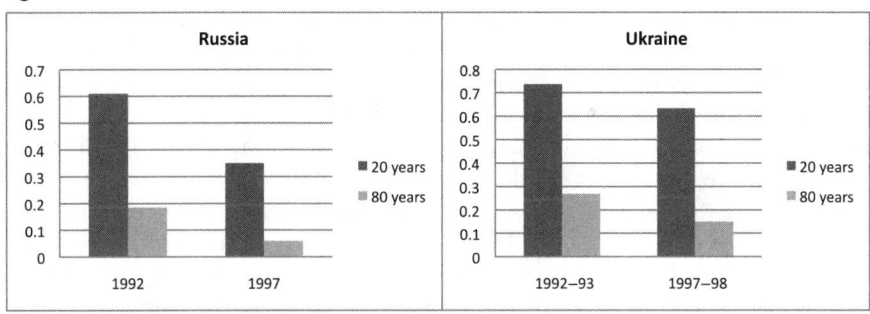

Russia

	1992	1997
20 years	0.61	0.36
80 years	0.19	0.06

Ukraine

	1992–93	1997–98
20 years	0.74	0.65
80 years	0.28	0.15

Vertical axis represents the probability of the respondent being a likely emigrant

FIGURE 9.2. Factors influencing the decision to emigrate.

departed, whereas those with similar attributes who stayed became a large part of the population and muted the effects of the variables.

Each of the variables shown in Figure 9.2 has the predicted effect, although the magnitude across variables and across time varies considerably. The one variable that is not "Jewish specific" is age and has a highly negative correlation with emigration potential in all four surveys, although this correlation is slightly weaker in the second survey in Russia. With all other variables held at their medians, a hypothetical 20-year-old Russian Jew had a 61 percent chance of emigrating, whereas an 85-year old had a mere 16 percent chance. In 1997, that 46-point gap had eroded slightly to 35 percent. The gaps in Ukraine are roughly 50 percentage points in both years.

Overall, in 1997/98, 59 percent of Ukrainian Jews said they do not intend to leave, as did three-quarters of Russian Jews. Yet more than half (58%) of those under 30 in Ukraine and more than one-third (38%) in Russia said they intended to leave or were already in the process of doing so. The elderly are the least likely to ever leave. In fact, by 2004, in a survey taken in St. Petersburg, the great majority declared they would not leave, although about one-quarter of those under 30 said they intended to leave "in principle, but do not know when." This has obvious and critical implications for the future of Jewish communities in Russia and Ukraine. The remaining Jews will be even more disproportionately elderly than in the 1990s; social services, institutions, and organizations have to be oriented to their needs and preferences.

Returning to Figure 9.2, anti-Semitism had a moderate and fairly consistent effect in Russia across both waves, but declined slightly in importance in Ukraine in the second wave. Ceteris paribus, a Russian Jew experiencing no anti-Semitism in 1992 was 17 percentage points less likely to emigrate than one experiencing high levels of anti-Semitism, with a similar 15-point gap in 1997. In Ukraine the corresponding gaps were 22 points and 11 points, respectively.

Although they all have substantive influences, there are several distinctions among the more specifically "Jewish" variables. The primary difference shows up between the predictive strength of attachments to Israel and a general sense of Jewishness. As discussed earlier, Zionists – for whom the State of Israel is central to Jewishness – certainly tend to identify high on the scale of Jewishness, but not all strongly identifying Jews have attachments to Israel. In Figure 9.2, we see that the influences of these two variables diverge across the two waves of the surveys, with that of Jewishness dropping considerably from 1992/93 to 1997/98. In Russia, the median respondent with the lowest level of Jewish identity was 37 percentage points less likely to emigrate than a respondent on the high end of the scale in 1992. In 1997, the difference dropped to 16 points. In Ukraine, the same gap dropped from 46 points to 12.

In contrast, objective and subjective attachments to Israel tended to have a reasonably consistent positive influence across both waves of the survey. Their influence waned only slightly in Russia and Ukraine – and actually increased for subjective connections in the Ukraine – across the two surveys. Regarding *objective* connections, the median Ukrainian respondent who had not visited Israel and had no family or friends there was 27 percentage points less likely to emigrate in 1992/93 than one who had traveled to Israel several times and had numerous connections with family and friends there; the gap declined moderately to 17 points in 1997/98. The corresponding differences for Russia were 21 and 18 points. For *subjective* connections, the median 1992/93 Ukrainian respondent who perceived no special connection with Israelis or attached no particular importance to Israel was 32 percentage points less likely to express a desire to emigrate than his or her counterpart who saw Israelis as "my people" and set large store in Israel as the ancestral homeland of the Jews that needed to be defended at all costs. That gap actually increased to 42 points in the 1997/98 wave. In slight contrast, the influence of subjective feelings toward Israel declined in Russia during the same time period, with the corresponding gaps being 51 and 33 points, respectively. Still, the decline was less in both absolute and relative terms than the decline of influence of the Jewishness variable.

What explains these differences? Most of the Zionists, who had high levels of Jewish identity and connections in Israel, formed the core of Jewish emigration from the former Soviet republics in the 1990s, which would explain the large influence of both Jewishness and Israel connections on the likelihood of emigration. However, by the end of the 1990s, most of the Zionists had left, and a corresponding larger percentage of remaining individuals with high levels of Jewish consciousness did not embrace the centrality of Israel in Jewish experience. As a result, the Jewish variable lost a large portion of its predictive power, whereas the variables measuring connections to Israel retained theirs.

Finally, based on this logic, we would expect a sharp slowdown in emigration after the wave of individuals with strong spiritual and objective connections to Israel had left. The data in Figure 9.1 show a threefold reduction from 1990s levels of emigration during the first decade of the twenty-first century, thereby supporting our contentions. The percentage of Russian respondents seriously considering emigration dropped from 39.2 to 24.2 percent from the first to the second wave of the survey; in Ukraine the proportion fell from 52.4 percent to 40.8 percent.

Whither Immigration?

Having described the decision to emigrate from former Soviet States, we examine why potential émigrés chose their destination countries. During the 1960s and 1970s the destination of Jewish emigration from the USSR was Israel, but during the 1970s and 1980s the flow shifted from Israel to the United States. That immigration was abruptly curtailed in 1990 by U.S. limits on immigrants from the USSR, and so Germany became the country of choice until early in the twenty-first century.

To empirically describe the dynamics of Jewish immigration, we analyzed the subsample of individuals in our four surveys who considered themselves likely to emigrate, as defined by the measure of emigration developed in our first set of analyses. This resulted in a sample ranging from slightly more than 300 in the 1997 Russian survey to roughly 1,000 in the 1992/93 Ukrainian survey. Because Israel was the first choice for Jewish immigrants in the first postcommunist decade, we developed a dichotomous dependent variable scoring individuals who chose Israel as their first-choice destination as a "1" and all other choices as "0."

Connections with Potential Destination Countries

Logically, many variables that pull emigrants out of the former USSR seem likely to pull immigrants *toward* a particular destination country as well. Therefore, we did not include in our analysis anti-Semitism, which functions as a push variable, nor age, which functions to keep respondents in the FSU. The variables we measured to develop individual objective and subjective attachments to Israel obviously should correlate positively with choosing Israel as one's preferred destination. In contrast, a person who has connections to another potential country should have a lower probability of immigrating to Israel. Conveniently, the surveys asked the same questions regarding respondents' connections in the United States as they did of Israel. As a result, we developed an identical 6-point scale measuring emigrants' family, friend, and travel connections to the United States. This scale should correlate negatively with individuals' propensity to emigrate to Israel.

A third variable that should have a positive impact on choosing Israel is increasing scores on the Jewish index. Although the importance of a person's identification as a Jew to the decision to emigrate declined in both Russia and Ukraine over time, the *choice* of destination is a different proposition. It seems plausible that, all other things being equal, a "strongly Jewish" person who has already decided to leave the former USSR would be more likely to choose Israel as a destination.

Wealth and Education

A second set of economic variables should have had a negative impact on choosing Israel. Individuals with high incomes realized that they may have had a better chance to get into the generally high-performing economies (in comparison with Israel) of Germany and the United States. Those with higher educations may have similar motivations. We tested these suppositions with the "well-being" and "education" indexes from the probability-of-emigration analysis.

Results

Figure 9.3 displays the impacts of each of six variables on choosing Israel.[40] The vertical bars show the effect each variable has on the probability that Russian/Ukrainian emigrants will choose Israel as their destination, with all other variables held constant at their median value. The left bars show the probability of choosing Israel with the variable of interest at its low level, whereas the right bar shows the probability of choosing Israel at the variable's maximum.

Looking at all four panels of the graph, the first noticeable result is that the variables have broadly similar effects across both space and time: the same factors that would motivate a Russian Jewish emigrant to choose Israel in 1992 would also motivate a Ukrainian Jewish emigrant to do so in 1998. Each

---

[40] The Appendix shows the raw coefficients of the independent variables.

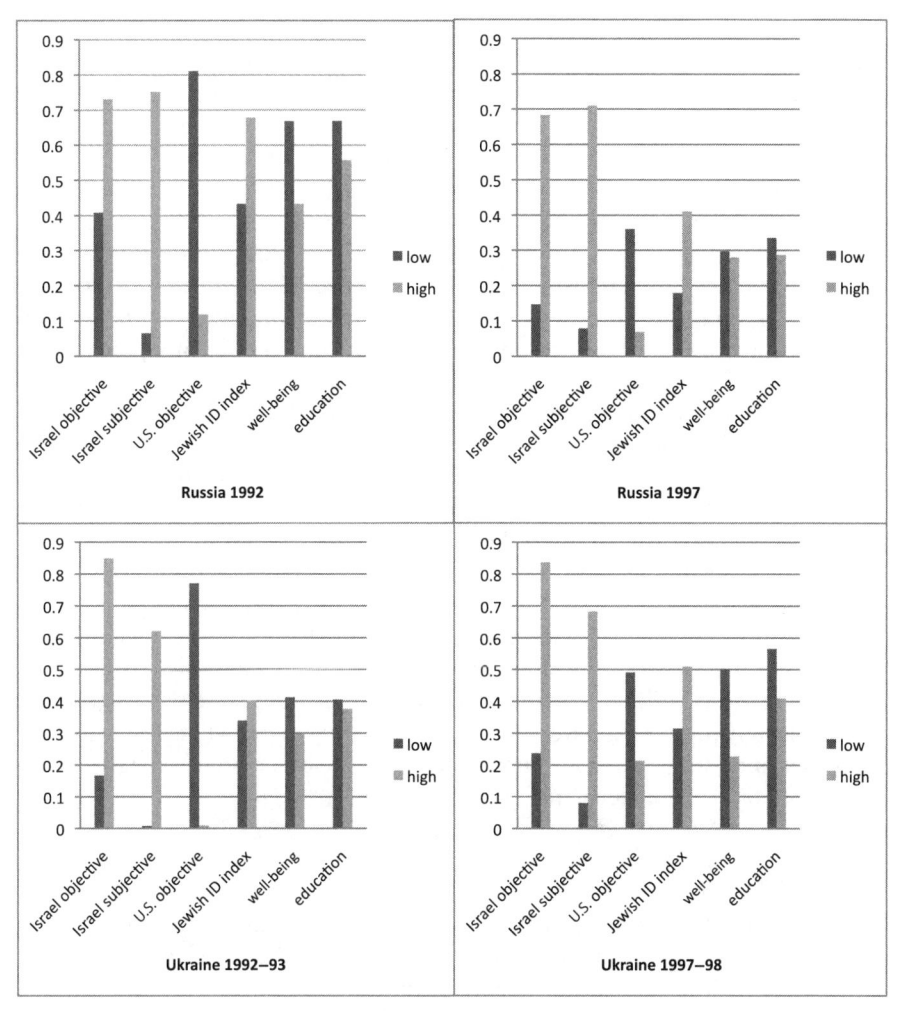

Vertical axis represents the probability of a likely emigrant choosing Israel as their destination of immigration

FIGURE 9.3. Factors influencing migrants' choice of country.

variable also performs in the predicted direction. The strongest performing variables by far are indices measuring a prospective immigrant's attachments to Israel and the United States. For example, the median Ukrainian Jewish emigrant in 1992 with no family or friends in Israel had a 17 percent chance of choosing Israel as his or her ultimate destination, whereas one who had traveled to Israel and had relatives and friends there had a 84 percent chance of picking Israel – a gap of 67 percentage points. The effects of the subjective index have a similarly large magnitude; those with high subjective attachments to Israel were 60 to 70 percentage points more likely to pick Israel as their preferred destination than those with low subjective attachments.

In contrast, attachments to the United States drastically decreased the predicted probability of choosing Israel. The 1992/93 surveys reported a roughly 70-percentage-point decline in immigration intention between those with no objective connections to the United States and those with the maximum number of connections. The second wave showed a lower, but still substantial 30-point gap.

The influences of the other variables are considerably more muted, but are still broadly in line with our predictions. In all four studies, increasing identification as a Jew leads to substantially increased chances of choosing Israel as a final destination. Although no individual regression attains conventional levels of statistical significance, the fact that all four coefficients point in the same direction supports our prediction.

In 1992, for example, a Russian Jew who identified strongly as a Jew was 28 percentage points more likely to choose Israel, whereas the gap in 1997 was 30 points. The one exception is Ukraine in 1992/93, which shows the gap between the strongly identifying Jews and the others as less than 3 percentage points (from 42 to 39). This is more likely a statistical aberration than anything else, because in 1997/98 the gap is 15 points in the expected direction.

The better off and more educated a person, the *less* likely the person is to go to Israel. Although well-being and education show statistical significance only at the 0.1 level in two and three out of four estimations, respectively, the broad pattern still supports our predictions. In sum, attachments to Israel unsurprisingly predict a greater chance of emigrating there, whereas increases in socioeconomic status serve as mild inducements to look elsewhere, particularly the United States and Germany.

Conclusion

Since the time of the biblical Abraham, Jews have migrated frequently. In modern times, large masses of Jews emigrated from the Russian Empire and, unexpectedly, from the Soviet Union. Domestic and foreign demands forced the Soviet leadership to permit controlled Jewish emigration to Israel and other countries. The Soviets then used emigration as a bargaining chip with Western governments. After the collapse of the USSR and the end of most restrictions on emigration, the trickle of emigration became a decade-long flood as Jews flocked to Israel, the United States, and later Germany at the rate of more than 100,000 a year from 1989 to 1999. Stricter immigration laws in the United States and Germany, economic stabilization in Russia and Ukraine, and the sharp decrease in the remaining Jewish population all combined to slow the flow to a steady stream of roughly 30,000 a year in the first decade of the second millennium.

Emigrants in the 1990s divided into those who went to Israel and those who went elsewhere – primarily the United States and Germany. As in past great migrations, anti-Semitism played a consistent role in pushing Jews to emigrate, but the lures of relatives and friends in Israel and the United States played

Identity, Israel, and Immigration

a larger role in their decisions to leave their countries of birth and go to a particular country. Economic and educational considerations played a weaker role in pushing people to emigrate, and a small to moderate role in giving better off and more highly educated migrants more immigration choices. Economic considerations varied according to changes in the economies of sending and host countries. In 1997, Russian and Ukrainian Jews saw Israel as a place where one could fulfill one's professional aspirations better than in Russia or, especially, Ukraine, and where there was a higher standard of living than in the former Soviet republics. We inquired about respondents' perceptions of professional possibilities only in 1997; no doubt, in 1992 we would have gotten an even more favorable picture of Israel. Yet by 2004, in St. Petersburg – and likely in other cities – more than one-third of respondents thought that one could make a better career in Russia than in Israel, obviously reacting to the boom in the Russian economy, although slightly more thought that the prospects for making a good career were equal in each.

By far the biggest and most consistent predictor of both a person's decision to emigrate *and* whether to immigrate to Israel, and not elsewhere, was subjective emotional and religious attachment to Israel. Those who identified with Israelis as "my people" and believed that living in Israel is at the core of being Jewish were five or even ten times as likely to choose to emigrate and then choose Israel as their destination than Jews with low emotional attachments to the State of Israel. This factor maintained its predictive power across the decade and the two ex-Soviet republics. For hundreds of thousands of Russian and Ukrainian Jews, the collapse of the USSR and the opening of its borders provided an opportunity to connect to their Jewishness in a wholly new way. At the same time, the movement out of the FSU of more than a million people, many of them highly educated and relatively young, casts doubt on the demographic viability of the Jewish population there and on the prospects for Jewish communal reconstruction and the revival of Jewish culture. The massive emigration may mark the closing of a relatively brief but important chapter in the convoluted story of the Jewish people, or it may help sustain Jewish life in the FSU by reconnecting Jews there to world Jewry and to their historic religion and cultures.

Appendix

In this chapter some methodological details have been glossed over and some relevant details omitted to present a more straightforward story. This appendix has two objectives. First, it provides standardized regression tables for those looking for coefficients, standard errors, and chi-squared tests. Second, it presents a more detailed, yet simple discussion about regression techniques to give some background on possibly unfamiliar techniques.

The first major empirical question this chapter addresses is the motivations underlying the decisions of individual Russian and Ukrainian Jews to emigrate. Two challenges are to determine precisely what constitutes a decision to

TABLE A9.1. *Are You Considering Living in Another Country/Emigrating?*

	Russia 1992	Russia 1997	Ukraine 1992–93	Ukraine 1997–98
Never	195	331	204	278
No intention, but possible	595	667	749	896
Don't know	33	26	31	40
Yes, but when?	349	220	647	530
Yes – I'm leaving in 2–3 years	77	44	249	155
Yes – I've applied for a visa	26	15	73	63
Yes – I'm waiting for papers	25	14	47	22
Total N	1300	1314	2000	1984

emigrate and how best to operationalize that decision as the dependent variable. The third challenge is to select the most suitable regression technique for the value structure of the final dependent variable. Two factors went into these decisions: achieving conceptual "correctness" and creating readily interpretable results. These two considerations often operated at cross-purposes, forcing a set of compromises.

The question on which the dependent variable is based asks respondents about their likelihood of choosing to emigrate. Responses on a 5-step scale ranged from "never" to respondents who were just waiting for their papers. As shown in Table A9.1, we included "don't know" answers as being a middle ground between those seriously considering emigration and those who are fairly sure they would not consider emigration. The placement of "don't know answers" is somewhat controversial, but its placement or exclusion of "don't know" respondents in our scale makes no substantive difference to our results.

The most precise way to use the answers to this question as a dependent variable would be to leave them as is and create a 6-step ordinal scale of increasing likelihood to emigrate. From there, two regression techniques are possible. First, we could simply use standard ordinary least squares (OLS) regression, which has the advantage of easily interpreted coefficients. However, the data are ordinal in nature, which makes the selection of OLS technically undesirable. Although ordinal data with large numbers of categories tend to behave like continuous data, having six categories forms a borderline case. Alternatively, we could employ ordered probit analysis, which is the most technically correct way. Ordinary probit analysis, used with a binary-value dependent variable, allows us to determine the probability that a respondent is in one group or another when the groups are either ordinal (e.g., emigrating or not) or even categorical (e.g., immigrating to Israel or the United States). With ordinal data, here a 6-point scale of increasing likelihood to emigrate, we can determine the multiple cut-points in the probability distribution dividing each ordinal value. Simple addition and subtraction (usually handled by computer) then give us the probability of answering, "I'll never emigrate," "I'll emigrate in a few years," or any other response on the ordinal scale. However, because of the multiple ordinal categories and the nonlinear relationships among the

TABLE A9.2. *Predicting Emigration Intentions in Russia and the Ukraine*

	Russia 1992	Russia 1997	Ukraine 1992/93	Ukraine 1997/98
Anti-Semitism	.111 (.036)	.136 (.045)	.137 (.027)	.071 (.034)
Objective connections to Israel	.094 (.028)	.063 (.029)	.114 (.024)	.077 (.021)
Subjective feelings toward Israel	.190 (.024)	.154 (.021)	.095 (.018)	.142 (.015)
Jewish identification index	.030 (.007)	.021 (.007)	.036 (.005)	.010 (.005)
Age	−.020 (.002)	−.020 (.003)	−.021 (.002)	−.023 (.002)
Gender	.100 (.079)	−.016 (.086)	.077 (.063)	.182 (.060)
Well-being	−.078 (.048)	.093 (.051)	.003 (.052)	−.285 (.079)
Well-being^2	.020 (.024)	−.036 (.019)	−.003 (.028)	.048 (.023)
Education	.016 (.034)	.026 (.038)	.018 (.024)	−.028 (.025)
Constant	−.920 (.270)	−1.384 (.292)	−.242 (.231)	.723 (.306)
Pseudo R-squared	.1465	.1473	.1358	.1271
Chi square	249.24	202.92	366.64	331.18
N	1267	1285	1950	1941

variables, interpreting coefficients and even providing readily intuitive graphical representation of the data are quite tricky.

We elected to take an alternative route that we feel faithfully represents the nature of the data while allowing us to provide the straightforward graphics of Figures 9.2 and 9.3. We transformed the 6-point ordinal scale into a 2-point scale and drew the dividing line between those likely to emigrate and those not likely to leave between those who said they did not know if they would leave and those who said "yes" in any form. The most serious criticism of this decision is that it discards usable data. We agree, but we also believe our decision is justified by the binary choice that emigration represents at its core – a respondent will either emigrate or not – which limits the utility of a 5-point scale. Second, critics can quibble with our decision to include in the "likely to emigrate" pool those people who answered "yes" but did not know when they would leave. Talk is cheap, and it requires more motivation to actually apply for a visa and make plans to emigrate. This criticism has some validity, but there seems even less theoretical merit in including someone who says they want to emigrate – even at a cheap-talk level – in the camp that clearly does not want to emigrate.

Finally, examining Table A9.1 shows that the individuals who say they want to emigrate, but do not know when, have declined as a percentage of those surveyed, like the other likely emigrants in our classification. In contrast, the three categories we deemed as unlikely to emigrate all remained the same or increased as a percentage of respondents. These behavioral similarities seem to justify our choice.

TABLE A9.3. *Likelihood of Choosing Israel as a Destination for Emigrating Russian and Ukrainian Jews*

	Russia 1992	Russia 1997	Ukraine 1992/93	Ukraine 1997/98
Objective connections to Israel	.142 (.048)	.248 (.058)	.333 (.039)	.283 (.036)
Subjective feelings toward Israel	.244 (.040)	.237 (.043)	.305 (.036)	.209 (.026)
Objective connections to the U.S.	−.345 (.051)	−.213 (.063)	−.521 (.047)	−.129 (.045)
Jewish identity index	.018 (.012)	.022 (.015)	.004 (.008)	.014 (.009)
Well-being	−.121 (.074)	−.009 (.069)	−.078 (.015)	−.149 (.057)
Education	−.049 (.055)	−.052 (.077)	−.015 (.036)	−.079 (.039)
Constant	−.943 (.392)	−1.837 (.400)	−1.891 (.282)	−1.332 (.198)
Pseudo R-squared	.1780	.2210	.2865	.2069
Chi square	117.18	89.15	396.55	220.18
N	477	291	1010	768

Also, for those interested, we display in Table A9.2 the raw coefficients from which we derived the graphics in Figure 9.2.

The other major empirical question discussed in Chapter 9 is the choice of destination country. Obviously, this limited our sample size to those we have determined as likely to emigrate, but confronted us with one major methodological question: Should we use a multiple-category dependent variable listing each country that migrants wanted to live in, or should we choose a binary categorical variable listing Israel as one value and all other countries as another? One problem with listing all desired destination countries as separate values was that it complicates the analysis and representation of the results because the data would be categorical and not ordinal. As a result, the proper regression analysis technique is multinomial probit (or logit), which essentially estimates different binary probit equations for each possible result of the equation (e.g., Israel vs. not Israel, United States vs. not United States). Instead, we chose the simpler binary probit approach, which divided our sample into those who wanted to go to Israel and those who had set their sights on other countries. The central place of Israel for many Jews, its focus as the destination of the majority of Soviet immigrants, and the applicability of many of our variables to Israel dictated the choice. Exploratory attempts at multinomial logit analysis also showed no factors that systemically influenced whether one would go to Germany or the United States. This combination of factors made it easier to decide to use the more intuitive and conducive-to-graphics approach of binary probit analysis. Table A9.3 .shows the raw coefficients that generated Figure 8.3.

10

Ethnicity and Marriage

"Every Jew should feel himself bound, even though the duty involves the sacrifice of precious affections, to avoid acts... [that] weaken the ancestral religion. Every Jew who contemplates marriage outside the pale must regard himself as paving the way to a disruption which would be the final, as it would be the culminating, disaster in the history of his people."[1]

"Victoria Yeon Sun Lim... was married last evening to Peter Jay Sheren.... The Rev. William P. Billow Jr., an Episcopal priest, performed the couple's legally recognized ceremony at the Washington National Cathedral. On Friday, the couple had a Jewish ceremony... and on October 7... had a traditional Korean cultural wedding ceremony... in Seoul."[2]

"The interfaith ceremony was conducted by Rabbi James Ponet and the Rev. William Shillady. Ms. [Chelsea] Clinton is Methodist, and Mr. [Marc] Mezvinsky is Jewish. It included elements from both traditions: friends and family read the Seven Blessings, which are typically recited at traditional Jewish weddings following the vows and exchange of rings."[3]

Some Jews strengthen their Jewish consciousness and fill it with cultural content, intentionally or not, by migrating to Israel or elsewhere. Others distance themselves from the Jewish collective by marrying non-Jews. Although some have rationalized intermarriage as expanding the gene pool or bringing new people into the Jewish fold and thereby increasing the number of Jews in the world,[4] a number declining almost everywhere outside Israel, every study –

---

[1] Morris Joseph (1848–1930), *Judaism as Life and Creed*, quoted in J. H. Hertz, *The Pentateuch and Haftorahs* (London: Soncino, 1952), 774.
[2] *New York Times*, October 28, 2007.
[3] "Chelsea Clinton's Wedding: 'Royalty' in Rhinebeck," *New York Times*, August 1, 2010.
[4] Barry Kosmin, for example is quoted as saying that intermarriage "is not a disaster" because "[a]ll we hear is the negative side of assimilation. There are a lot more people out there with a Jewish connection." The rising rate of intermarriage could mean more ties with and support from other ethnic groups, he suggested. Steve Lipman, "The Intermarriage Dividend?"

some even by those making these arguments – concludes that Jews who marry non-Jews are less likely to identify with Jewish organizations and participate in Jewish activities. Their children are less likely even to identify as Jews.

In this chapter we examine the historical development of Jewish views of marriage to non-Jews and trace marriage patterns and ethnicity in the USSR and its successor states. We then turn to the views of our respondents on interethnic marriage and suggest possible consequences of those views.

The Evolution of Jewish Views toward Marriage and Intermarriage

Time was when two "red lines" marked the boundary of Jewishness: belief in and practice of a religion other than Judaism, and marriage to a non-Jew. A Jew who practiced Christianity, for example, or who "married out" was literally regarded as "out," someone who might still be Jewish according to Jewish law and in his or her self-perception but who had effectively crossed the boundary line into the non-Jewish world. Thus far, the first "red line" holds – *pace* Brother Daniel and Cardinal Lustiger. Jews who practice a religion other than Judaism are considered not heretics but no longer Jews. Ironically, traditional rabbinic law (halakha) considers the apostate Jew still a Jew for many purposes, yet members of even the most liberal religious Jewish sect do not consider them so. The more ambiguous cases of "Jews for Jesus" or "messianic Jews" or "Hebrew Christians" have not been accepted into any Jewish fold.[5]

The Jewish Week (New York), August 5, 2009. One study concludes that intermarried and "in-married" families do not differ much in their beliefs and practices when one controls for the Jewish education and background of the Jewish partner. Leonard Saxe, Fern Chertok, and Benjamin Phillips, *It's Not Just Who Stands under the Chuppah: Jewish Identity and Intermarriage* (Waltham, MA: Cohen Center for Jewish Studies and Steinhardt Social Research Institute, Brandeis University, 2008). Still, the authors found, even when controlling for the Jewish partner's religious upbringing, that 71 percent of in-married couples but only 51 percent of intermarried couples said they were raising their children as Jews. Another researcher, Steven Cohen, challenged the meaning of "raised Jewish" and pointed out that according to the 2000–01 National Jewish Population Survey, only 13 percent of the children of an intermarriage now identify as Jews. Sue Fishkoff, "Intermarriage Debate," *Detroit Jewish News*, January 24, 2008. Another study of Jewish/non-Jewish marriages in the United States found that only 14 percent of the households practiced Judaism largely or exclusively. The most common pattern (31%) was a "dual religion" household. The "nominal identity" of the children of mixed marriages yielded the following: just under one-fifth were raised as Jews, one-third were raised as Christians only, one-fourth were raised as Christians and Jews, and one-fourth were raised with no religion. Bruce Phillips, *Re-Examining Intermarriage: Trends, Textures, Strategies* (New York: American Jewish Committee 1994).

[5] Carol Harris-Shapiro, *Messianic Jews: A Rabbi's Journey through Religious Change in America* (Boston: Beacon Press, 1999). She studied a messianic Jewish sect. She admits that, "Even today, the ineradicable distinction between Christianity and Judaism is a crucial boundary marker for American Jews" (2). Yet, she claims that messianic Jews have gained partial acceptance "even by those organizations most set against the Messianic Jewish movement" (168). She concludes, "Ritual boundaries are eroding as philoJudaic Christians and Messianic believers do Jewish practices with Christological content and Jews in intermarried families blend Jewish and

Ethnicity and Marriage

This boundary line is drawn to maintain the uniqueness of Judaism and, in regard to Christianity, sometimes out of revulsion against a religion whose practitioners persecuted and reviled Jews for centuries.

In recent times, maintaining the other boundary marker – opposition to marriages to people of a different religion or ethnicity – is often interpreted as bigotry or even racism. There may be something to this assertion, but many who oppose interethnic marriage are anxious to preserve their distinctiveness and ensure that it is not diluted by the entry of nonmembers.

Those who wish to enter a community are asked to undergo an identity transformation, such as acquiring citizenship or undergoing a religious conversion, which will confer official membership on them. In some cases, membership may be acquired with relative ease, but in others it cannot be acquired even through a rite of passage. For example, in Canada one can become a citizen relatively easily, but Saudi Arabia does not recognize naturalization as a means of acquiring citizenship; Japan and Switzerland make it difficult. Israel, the Baltic States, Germany, and some other countries grant citizenship easily to those who can demonstrate kinship or blood ties to the dominant ethnic group; those lacking such ties are admitted to citizenship after lengthier and more complicated processes. Some religions actively seek converts, at times to the point of forcibly bringing them into the religion (Christianity, Islam), others remain indifferent to proselytizing, and still others are reluctant to accept converts (Orthodox Judaism) or even refuse to do so (Zoroastrians).

Some of the same kinds of differences can be observed in the matter of marrying someone outside the group. Catholicism tolerates marriage to a non-Catholic as long as the children of such a union will be raised as Catholics. But Judaism forbids marriages to those not of the faith, as does Islam in more complicated ways.[6] Small groups, more vulnerable to dilution and disappearance, may be particularly attentive to the identities and beliefs of potential marriage partners outside the group. They may deal with the issue either by relaxing admission criteria, thereby increasing the group's size at the risk of blurring its distinctiveness and the commitment of its members, or they may insist on strict tests of admission to safeguard distinctiveness, presumed commitment, and "purity."[7] Leaders of the Jewish community have taken both

---

Christian ritual" (185). However, note that she herself identifies those "rituals" as distinctly Jewish and distinctly Christian. "Chrismukkah" is a flippant term for rituals or practices drawn from both religions, but there is no such holiday.

[6] Muslims are enjoined from marrying polytheists. A Muslim man can marry a "kitabiyya," a monotheist, provided he gets express permission to do so. There are many nuances and differences on these issues among groups of Muslims. I thank Sarah Islam and Khurum Saddiqi for enlightening me on some of these points.

[7] A major issue in American Jewry is the 1983 decision by the Reform branch of Judaism to confer Jewish status on children who have one Jewish parent, whether father or mother. Since the time of the Mishna (ca. 200 CE) Jewish status has been determined by one's mother, possibly because the Roman invasion of Palestine made paternity less certain but it was easier to determine the mother of a child. See Shaye J. D. Cohen, *The Beginnings of Jewishness: Boundaries, Varieties, Uncertainties* (Berkeley: University of California Press, 1999). The Orthodox and Conservative

approaches. The former head of the World Jewish Congress, argued in 2010 that "[i]ntermarriage can... be an opportunity for a stronger embrace of Jewish identity.... Intermarriage is not a calamity but an opportunity for both a Jewish and non-Jewish partner to learn."[8] At the same time, the Israeli rabbinate announced that it would no longer automatically accept conversions presided over by foreign Orthodox rabbis (it does not recognize conversions done by non-Orthodox rabbis). An editorial in an American Jewish newspaper mused on the tension between the "warm embrace" Jews extended to Congresswoman Gabrielle Giffords, who had been shot in January 2011, who had a non-Jewish mother and had never converted formally, and "the uncomfortable reality that... rising rates of intermarriage and ambiguous identities are leading to *fewer* Jewish families and *weaker* communal ties."[9]

Intermarriage in Jewish History

An important way in which those called successively Hebrews, Israelites, and Jews established their identities and marked themselves off from others was by prohibiting marriage to people outside the group. In the Bible, even when the Hebrews were but a nuclear family – Abraham, Sarah, and their son Isaac had accepted the new faith, but neither Abraham's other wife, Hagar, nor her son Ishmael seemed to have done so – Abraham, the founder of the group, adjures the steward of his household "not to take a wife for my son from among the Canaanite daughters among whom I dwell, but go to my land and birthplace and take a wife [from there] for my son Isaac."[10] In turn, Isaac's wife, Rebecca,

---

branches of Judaism continue to adhere to matrilineally determined Jewish status and therefore do not recognize as Jews the children of non-Jewish mothers. Interestingly, Canadian Reform Judaism and the Progressive movement in Britain do not recognize "patrilineal Jews," those who have Jewish fathers only. Reform rabbis have debated whether to officiate at marriages of Jews to non-Jews. "Among Reform rabbis... the tide has been shifting steadily for years to the point where those who do not officiate at intermarriages feel great pressure to do so – mostly from their own congregations." Sue Fishkoff, "Reform Revisit Intermarriage Debate," Jewish Telegraphic Agency, March 11, 2008.

It seems that earlier in Israelite history the offspring of non-Jewish mothers – the sons of Joseph and Moses, for example – were considered Israelites. Medieval Jewish commentators and many of their successors assert that the non-Jewish wives were somehow converted to the Israelite faith, although the biblical text does not say so, nor is any conversion process discussed.

According to Christine Hayes, "Ezra and Nehemiah describe foreign women as a threat to the moral purity of Israelites; nevertheless, their opposition to intermarriage is animated by – and explicitly attributed to – a view of foreign women as threatening the genealogical purity of Israel." Christine E. Hayes, *Gentile Impurities and Jewish Identities: Intermarriage and Conversion from the Bible to the Talmud* (New York: Oxford University Press, 2002), 7.

[8] Edgar M. Bronfman, "Opening our Tent," *Forward*, December 17, 2010.
[9] "Who Isn't a Jew?" *Forward*, February 4, 2011 [italics in the original].
[10] Genesis 24: 3–4. Hayes argues that there were "two competing definitions of Jewish identity (moral-religious [which allowed for conversion by acceptance of Israelite doctrines] versus genealogical [which did not]." Hayes, *Gentile Impurities and Jewish Identities*. The rabbis of the Talmud adopted the first definition.

Ethnicity and Marriage

expresses her disdain for the local women, and perhaps at her behest, Isaac tells *his* son Jacob, "do not take a wife from among the Canaanite women" but from the daughters of Laban, his mother's brother.[11] Esau, Jacob's disinherited twin brother, aware that his father dislikes the local Canaanite women, takes a daughter of Ishmael, among others, as a wife. The message is that one must marry within the group, in this case an extended family. Those who marry outside it are putting themselves beyond the group. This is not, however, put in the form of a commandment or decree.

For our purposes, the historical accuracy of the story is irrelevant; what is important is that for thousands of years, millions of Jews read this biblical account and, for the most part, treated it as a model for their own behavior. As the rabbis taught, "*ma'aseh avot siman lebanim*" [the deeds of the [fore]fathers are a model for their descendants].

The pattern established by the patriarchs evolved into a stricture on intermarriage, reinforced many times in biblical and postbiblical accounts. Israelite men were severely punished for having sexual relations with Midianite women.[12] When they entered Canaan and encountered many nations, the Israelites were warned, "Do not marry them, do not give your daughter to their sons nor shall you take their sons for your daughters." The explicit reason given for this prohibition is that "[t]hey [non-Israelites] will remove your children from me and will worship other gods [so that] God shall be angry with you and annihilate you quickly."[13] Because at this point religion was the primary marker distinguishing the Israelites from others, one can say that the prohibition on intermarriage was also designed to define, distinguish, and preserve the group.

This prohibition of intermarriage may be seen as part of a broader biblical emphasis on distinctions and separation. In Genesis, chaos is overcome by separating light from dark, the waters above from waters beneath, day from night. With no reasons given, biblical law prohibits plowing with different kinds of animals, mixing seeds in sowing, or using flax and linen in garments. The Israelites are told "[t]o separate [*lehavdil*] between the impure [*tameh*] and pure [*tahor*], between the animal that can be eaten and that which cannot."[14] As a recent writer observes, "If separation is salvation, throughout the Bible un-separation means disaster."[15]

Despite the strictures on intermarriage, the third king of Israel, Solomon, the "wisest of men," married the daughter of an Egyptian pharaoh and brought

---

[11] Genesis 27: 46 and 28: 1–2.
[12] Numbers 25.
[13] Deuteronomy 6: 3–4.
[14] Leviticus 11: 47.
[15] David Gelernter, "Judaism beyond Words," *Commentary* (May 2002), 33. Later, men and women were separated in the Temple and by extension in synagogues. A formal ceremony called "separation" [*havdalah*] marks the end of the Sabbath, separating the workaday week from sanctified time. The ceremony explicitly mentions the separation of "holy and ordinary, light and dark, *Israel and the nations*, the seventh day and the six days of creation."

her to Jerusalem.[16] Indeed, he "loved many foreign women [*nochriyot*], and Pharaoh's daughter, Moabites, Ammonites, Edomites, Sidonites, Hittites. From those peoples whom *Adonai* had commanded the children of Israel 'Do not mingle with them and they shall not mingle with you because they will turn your hearts to their gods' – to them Solomon cleaved and loved them."[17]

These royal dalliances found parallels among the people. Ordinary folk worshiped "strange gods" and married people who did not share their religion. The Book of Ruth, whose heroine accepted the Jewish faith and is regarded as the model convert to Judaism, records without comment the fact that her Israelite husband and his brother had married Moabite women.[18] Ezra, leader of the Jewish exiles in Babylonia who returned to the Land of Israel under the aegis of Persian rulers in the late sixth century BCE, was told that they had intermarried with local peoples during the exile. "When I heard this," Ezra is quoted, "I shred my garment and coat, tore some hair from my head and beard, and sat alone, desolate [*meshomem*]."[19] Ezra's contemporary, Nehemiah, explicitly ties intermarriage to acculturation and assimilation: "I saw that the Jews had married Ashdodian, Ammonite and Moabite women. And their children half the time speak Ashdodian and don't know how to speak Jewish [*Yehudit*]."[20] He does not view this behavior with equanimity: "I fought them, cursed them and hit some of them, tearing their hair out, and made them swear not to give their sons to their [the heathens'] daughters nor to take their daughters for their sons or for themselves."[21]

The original prohibition on intermarriage applied only to seven Canaanite nations, but was extended in the Hasmonean period to all non-Jews. Shaye Cohen explains that with the destruction of the First Temple the Judeans "sensed that their survival depended upon their ideological (or religious) and social separation from the outside world" and therefore prohibited intermarriage.[22] "The rabbis of the Talmud were the first to develop a sustained and detailed exegesis justifying the prohibition of intermarriage."[23]

Thus, we have a record of prohibitions on intermarriage and their violation. Ironically, Christian rulers and ecclesiastical authorities also forbade their

---

[16] I Kings 2: 1, 3.
[17] I Kings 11: 1.
[18] Ruth I: 4. The medieval commentator, Avraham Ibn Ezra, remarks that the women "must have converted to Judaism," though Ruth does so only long afterward. Her sister-in-law Orpah remained in Moab rather than accompany her mother-in-law, Naomi, back to Bethlehem in Judea.
[19] Ezra 9: 3. See also Nehemiah 10: 31.
[20] Nehemiah 13: 23–24. There is a rather graphic discussion of prohibited sexual relations between Jews and heathens in Talmud Bavli 36a.
[21] Nehemiah 13: 25.
[22] The same motivation apparently is at work in the strict prohibition among the Druze of marriage to non-Druze.
[23] Cohen, *The Beginnings of Jewishness*, 261–62. See also Sacha Stern, *Jewish Identity in Early Rabbinic Writings* (Leiden: E. J. Brill, 1994), 159.

communities from marrying Jews.[24] Over the centuries, as social situations varied, marriages of Jews to others occurred with greater or lesser frequency. When Jews were ghettoized and despised, interethnic/interreligious marriages were less likely. When emancipated and mixing with the larger society, Jews entered such liaisons more frequently. In most German states, marriage between Jews and Christians was not permitted. However, when the German Empire introduced civil marriage in 1875, it permitted Jewish–Christian marriages.[25] Indeed, in Germany, Austria, and Hungary before World War II, about one-quarter of the Jews were married to non-Jews.[26] Similarly in the 1950s, about one-quarter of Jews marrying in Switzerland and the Netherlands married non-Jews.[27]

Yet, most Jews continued to regard marrying out as putting a person outside the Jewish collectivity. It was widely believed that parents of children who married out mourned them ritually (sat *shiva* for them), as if to declare that as far as they were concerned their child had died.[28] This was actually not common practice,[29] but the fact that it was widely believed indicates how seriously intermarriage was regarded, especially because in the United States

---

[24] See James Parkes, *The Conflict of Church and Synagogue* (Philadelphia: Jewish Publication Society, 1934).

[25] Mordechai Breuer, *Modernity within Tradition: The Social History of Orthodox Jewry in Imperial Germany* (New York: Columbia University Press, 1992), 252. Todd Endelman kindly supplied this reference.

[26] Calculated on the basis of figures found in Uriah Zevi Engelman, "Sources of Jewish Statistics," in Louis Finkelstein, ed., *The Jews: Their History, Culture and Religion*, Vol. IV (Philadelphia: Jewish Publication Society, 1949), 1191.

[27] *Encyclopedia Judaica*, Vol. 12(Jerusalem: Keter, n.d.), 166.

[28] In the "Tevye" stories of the greatest Yiddish writer, Sholem Aleichem, this happens when Tevye's daughter Khave marries a non-Jew. It is interesting to compare the original story with the 1939 Yiddish film, *Tevye*, starring Maurice Schwartz, and then with the American retelling of the tale in the play, "Fiddler on the Roof." One can observe a softening of the condemnation of intermarriage, to the point where in the American version Tevye may come across as irrational and old-fashioned and Khave is regarded much more sympathetically. The different treatments reflect the times and audiences.

[29] Thus, for example, Arnold Dashevsky and Zachary Heller wrote in 2008, "The Jewish folk response to the outmarriage of a child, transmitted as a tradition, was for the parents to recite the kaddish, a memorial prayer for the dead, and to observe the customary period of mourning [*shiv'a*] as if the child were indeed dead. While this practice is **not** sanctioned by Jewish religious law, this folk custom suggests quite dramatically that intermarriage was traditionally regarded as a serious taboo." *Intermarriage and Jewish Journeys in the United States* (Newton Centre, MA: National Center for Jewish Policy Studies at Hebrew College, 2008), 39. I inquired about the supposed custom on the List-serv H-Judaic. The upshot of the twenty or so replies I received seems to be that there was a rabbinic controversy about whether one sits *shiva* for a converted child that dates back at least to Rabeinu Gershom (tenth to eleventh centuries). Apparently, it is not done today, though at least two people attested that it was done by people they knew. That this "custom" is reported in film and fiction may not reflect practice but only a heightened dramatization of the story that the writer (e.g., Sholem Aleichem) wishes to tell. In light of the several responses that report "hearing about" sitting *shiva* in their own families or in their communities, this too could be the result of attempts to dramatize the trauma. It is interesting that this is much more widely believed than personally witnessed.

and elsewhere, until about the 1960s, it was often accompanied by conversion to Christianity.

A scholar of Polish Jews observes that a Jewish convert to Christianity in the interwar period "became wholly excluded, even ethnically from the old group, while in the eyes of Christians, a member of the new group would be included religiously, though remaining Jewish ethnically. The latter border was completely impassable from this side."[30] The following scene, described by a Jew who observed it in 1929 as a boy, illustrates dramatically how traumatic conversion/intermarriage was. In the town of Slawatycze (Lublin area) in the late 1920s the daughter of a rabbi fell in love with a Polish policeman. She converted to Catholicism in order to marry him:

> On the Sunday of her *shmad* [conversion], Catholics... paraded down the main street....carrying icons... and singing hymns.... The young girl sat erect, and with a defiant smirk waved from her carriage to the townspeople. Her poor parents followed the carriage, crying and screaming and beating their heads to a bloody pulp on the sides of the wagon pleading with their daughter not to go through with this woeful deed.... After this shameful tragedy, the girl's family secluded themselves and never went out of the house. Her three sisters never married, neither did their cousins in the nearby town. No one would marry them.[31]

Intermarriage in a Secular State: Personal Happiness and Preservation of the People

"Around 1930, most Jews in the world (about 65 percent) lived in countries where the rate of out-marriage was below 5 percent of all currently marrying Jewish individuals.... No country had a Jewish community experiencing an out-marriage rate of 35 percent or higher."[32] However, by 1980, about a third of Jews worldwide were marrying non-Jews. Jews have found it difficult to oppose interfaith/interethnic marriages in societies that (nominally) stand for equality and condemn ethnic, religious, and racial prejudice. Loyalty to the collective has not been an effective argument against romantic love, which became the primary reason for marriage in modern societies. One American sociologist claims, "The stigma has moved from the Jews who marry out to those who oppose intermarriage."[33] Therefore, opponents of intermarriage often argue that, although there is nothing ethically wrong with such marriages,

---

[30] Annamaria Orla-Bukowska, "Maintaining Borders, Crossing Borders: Social Relationships in the Shtetl," in Antony Polonsky, ed., *Polin* 17 (2004), 178.
[31] Henry L. Gitelman, "I Am Drenched in the Dew of My Childhood: A Memoir," privately published, Montreal, October 1997. Gitelman does not mention sitting *shiva* or saying kaddish.
[32] Sergio Della Pergola, "Jewish Out-Marriage: A Global Perspective," in Shulamit Reinharz and Sergio Della Pergola, eds., *Jewish Intermarriage around the World* (New Brunswick, NJ: Transaction, 2009), 26.
[33] Sylvia Barack Fishman, *Jewish and Something Else: A Study of Mixed-Marriage Families* (New York: American Jewish Committee, 2001), paraphrased in Gerald Cromer, *The Quintessential*

cultural differences between the partners and between their respective families make for less happy marriages.[34] That is, although such unions might not be inherently objectionable, they are less likely to "work." Some point to higher divorce rates among the intermarried, and others cite anecdotal evidence. A study of American Jews in the 1980s gathered information from demographic surveys conducted by nine local Jewish community federations over seven years. It concluded, "The most significant facilitator of divorce... is intermarriage." Parallel to findings relating to marriages between people belonging to different Christian denominations, this study found that in Jewish marriages to non-Jews the divorce rate was 32 percent, compared to a divorce rate of 17 percent among those married to Jews.[35]

Still others have argued against intermarriage on the grounds that it will lead to the disappearance of the Jewish people. One contemporary rabbi writes, "Throughout Jewish history, far more Jews have succumbed to the blandishment of assimilation through mixed marriages, than have been victims of all Holocaust executions, expulsions, and pogroms combined. Persecutions notwithstanding, were it not for mixed marriages and assimilation, there would be today well over one hundred million Jews in the world, not twelve million."[36] A contemporary statement combines several of these arguments:

> Children of intermarriages are statistically less likely to identify with Judaism than children raised by Jewish parents, so intermarriage weakens the Jewish people. Therefore, Jews across the spectrum oppose intermarriage in order to prevent this weakening. A large part of Jewish observance and identity centers on the home, family, and community. Religion is a part of daily life, in areas as diverse as making a blessing before wearing new clothes for the first time to thanking G-d before and after meals. Special occasions such as Shabbat and holidays carry special customs and observances. A home made by a Jew and a non-Jew is much less likely to be a "Jewish home." Where children are involved, they are most likely to grow up with a positive Jewish identity when they see both parents Jewishly connected. Also, for many people, a difference in religion is an added stress on a relationship. For this reason, many Jewish parents discourage

Dilemma: American Jewish Responses to Intermarriage (Ramat Gan, Israel: Bar Ilan University, 2004), 47.

[34] "In addition, intermarriages can pose personal problems for the partners involved. If a marriage works, it is often because the marriage partners have a great deal in common. They can share things with each other, and this can maintain a marriage beyond the time of physical infatuation. Partners of an intermarriage, though, may not always have that much to share. After all, members of different religions generally come from different backgrounds and environments. They have known different influences and have been directed towards different goals. Therefore, if a Jew and a gentile marry, they will probably have less in common than two Jews or two gentiles. Consequently, they may find themselves eventually incompatible. Furthermore, relations between the marriage partners and their respective in-laws are likely to be strained – a situation that will not help the marriage." See http://www.russianjews.org/philosophy/q33.asp.

[35] Barry Kosmin, Nava Lerer, and Egon Mayer, *Intermarriage, Divorce and Remarriage among American Jews, 1982–87*, North American Jewish Data Bank, Family Research Series, No. 1 (August 1989), 1–5, 39. Barry Kosmin kindly supplied this essay.

[36] Rabbi Daniel Schur, at http://www.mnemotrix.com/heights.schur16.html.

intermarriage in their children in an honest attempt to help their children find long-term happiness.[37]

Studies in the United States have demonstrated that children of interfaith or interethnic marriages generally have weaker Jewish identities than children with two Jewish parents.[38] In 1995, the Leadership Council of Conservative Judaism in America adopted an official statement on intermarriage: acknowledging that intermarriage was widespread, it pointed out that children of such marriages were unlikely to be raised as Jews, but that while intermarriage is "not a celebration for the Jewish community," it could be mitigated through "outreach" that would lead to the conversion of the non-Jewish partner or at least to the intensification of the Jewish identity and affiliation of the Jewish partner.[39] As the president of the Union of American Hebrew Congregations (Reform) put it, "We believe in boundaries.... Absolutely. But a boundary by definition is a barrier, and... while barriers have their place, bridges are always more important."[40] The Reform movement's acceptance in 1983 as Jews of people whose father, but not mother, is Jewish pushed the boundary of Jewishness way beyond where it used to be, if only for those who accept this accommodation to the reality of intermarriage. Some Reform temples proudly proclaim that they are unconcerned with who is Jewish and who is not. As an advertisement for a Detroit temple put it, "We're a Jewish-Italian-Korean family....What we look for in a temple [is]... a place where everyone is

---

[37] See http://www.faqs.org/faqs/judaism/FAQ/05-Worship/section-23.html.
[38] See, for example, Bruce Phillips, "Assimilation, Transformation, and the Long Range Impact of Intermarriage," *Contemporary Jewry* 25 (2005), 50–79.
[39] "In the past, intermarriage, (that is, marriage between a Jew and a non-Jew who has not converted) was viewed psychologically as an act of rebellion, a rejection of Judaism. Jews who intermarried were essentially excommunicated. But now, intermarriage is often the result of living in an open society, welcoming and encouraging individual differences rather than group responsibility and norms.... Some 33% to 50% of North American Jews are intermarrying.... The majority of the Jewish partners cease to practice Jewish traditions, and often do not provide their children with a Jewish education or experience. If our children end up marrying non-Jews, we should not reject them. Rather, we should continue to give our love and thereby retain a measure of influence in their lives, Jewishly and otherwise.... However, the marriage between a Jew and non-Jew is not a celebration for the Jewish community. We therefore reach out to the couple with the hope that the non-Jewish partner will move closer to Judaism and ultimately choose to convert. Since we know that over 70% of children of intermarried couples are not being raised as Jews, thus further diminishing the Jewish people, we want to encourage the Jewish partner to maintain his/her Jewish identity, and raise their children as Jews. The unprecedented nature of the situation leaves us groping between what works for us individually and what is good for Klal Yisrael. In the face of the challenge, the Conservative Movement has formulated the following position: **We subscribe to a three-tiered approach to intermarriage: beginning with attempts at PREVENTION, then the promotion of CONVERSION, and finally, when prevention and conversion fail to occur,** *keruv* [outreach] **to the mixed family**" [italics in original]. From http://www.rabassembly.org/info/intermar.
[40] Quoted in Cromer, *The Quintessential Dilemma*, 42.

Ethnicity and Marriage

treated the same... Jewish or non-Jewish – nobody knows the difference, or cares."[41]

In Bay City, Michigan, Reform Congregation Anshei Chesed included the following in its Article on Membership: "Any member marrying out of the pale of Jewish religion forfeits his membership."[42] That was in 1885. More than a century later, in 1996, so widespread was marriage between Reform Jews and non-Jews that trustees of the (Reform) Union of American Hebrew Congregations (now Union of Reform Judaism) considered a resolution asking Reform rabbis to abandon a statement adopted twenty-three years earlier opposing their officiating at marriages between Jews and non-Jews.[43] A decade later Reform rabbis were still debating the issue.[44] And as the wedding of Chelsea Clinton and Marc Mezvinsky in 2010 showed, some Reform rabbis have no compunctions about performing a wedding ceremony that contained elements of Judaism and Christianity.

American and British Jews have debated whether to invest in "outreach" to intermarried couples to bring them closer to Judaism or whether resources would be better invested in "inreach," increasing the Jewish knowledge and commitment of those who are unambiguously Jewish and not intermarried.[45] The Reform movement and increasingly the Conservative movement have embraced outreach. Not only is intermarriage more prevalent among non-Orthodox Jews than in the past but also fewer of the partners convert to the faith of the other. Very few Jews seem to convert to Christianity, as some did decades ago, and more Christians, however nominal, seem not to convert to Judaism. This has given rise to more mixed or blended families. As might be expected in the United States, commercial enterprises have been quicker than religious institutions to respond to this relatively new phenomenon. Holiday greeting cards that blend Christmas and Hanukkah are sold in the tens of thousands. A company calling itself "Chrismukkah" pitches its products as follows:

> Chrismukkah is the way millions of people experience the December holidays together... with elements of both Christmas and Hanukkah. While you won't

---

[41] "Shir Shalom... A Place Where Everyone is Treated the Same," advertisement in the *Detroit Jewish News*, August 30, 1996 [italics added]. The Simon family apparently consists of a Jewish father, Italian mother, and two Korean children.

[42] Quoted in Rela Geffen Monson, "What is Jewish about the Constitutional Documents of American Jewry?" in Daniel Elazar, Jonathan Sarna, and Rela Monson, eds., *A Double Bond: The Constitutional Documents of American Jewry* (Lanham, MD: University Press of America, 1992), 66.

[43] Gustav Niebuhr, "A Proposal on Rabbis' Role in Interfaith Weddings Splits Reform Judaism," *New York Times*, December 14, 1996, 9. A decade later the president of the Union for Reform Judaism called for Reform synagogues to increase their efforts to convert non-Jews married to Jews. Michael Luo, "Reform Jews Hope to Unmix Mixed Marriages," *New York Times*, February 12, 2006.

[44] Steve Lipman, "Intermarriage Seen Roiling Reform Ranks," *The Jewish Week*, June 15, 2007.

[45] See, for example, Rachel Fletcher, "Intermarriage – The Trend that Won't Stop," *Jewish Chronicle* (London), May 25, 2007, 4–5.

find Chrismukkah on the calendar, it's as real as you make it.... Chrismukkah is a state of mind for the season... a multi-cultural mish-mash of the cherished holiday rituals we grew up with. Chrismukkah is a way intermarried families of Christians and Jews can share the holidays. Chrismukkah has no dogma or rules. It's customization to suit the individual celebrant and their extended family.[46]

Another company advertises "a tree-shaped menorah, ideal for those who also celebrate Christmas."[47]

Here we see the eradication of boundaries and the synthesis of lightly worn Judaism and Christianity. In its antinomianism, the message conveys the individuation – some would say narcissism and egoism – of American life. The collective's needs and interests take a distant back seat to what suits the individual celebrant. In regard to marriage, concern with its communal consequences "is antithetical to the individualistic pursuit of personal happiness and satisfaction typical to a postmodern consciousness. Within traditional Judaism, however, recognizing and responding to the connection between personal action and communal well-being are accepted as fundamental necessities to ensure the continuity of the Jewish people and therefore are incumbent upon all Jews."[48]

American Jewish religious leaders may still condemn or counsel against intermarriage, but the masses do not seem to be listening: "According to the 2005 December Dilemma Survey, released by InterfaithFamly.com, most interfaith families will celebrate both holidays... two-thirds said they'll keep their celebrations separate."[49] The differences are still maintained, but as in "the Jewish Catholic Family School," they coexist literally under a single roof.[50] In an open society that increasingly stresses inclusion (while at the same time celebrating diversity and multiculturalism!) the erasure of boundaries seems logical. For example, more and more weddings incorporate several religious traditions in a single marriage ceremony. One marriage announcement described a religious ceremony conducted by "a pastor of Kahila, a nondenominational religious group" that would also "include Jewish religious and Mexican cultural traditions."[51] In another wedding an Episcopal priest performed the "couple's legally recognized ceremony at the Washington National Cathedral," but that

---

[46] See www.chrismukkah.com and Leslie Kaufman, "On Web, Season's Greetings Are Sent in One Size Fits All," *New York Times*, December 7, 1999. In 2006 a book by Ron Gompertz was published with the title *Chrismukkah: Everything You Need to Know to Celebrate the Hybrid Holiday* (New York: Stewart, Tabori and Chang, 2006).

[47] Marianne Rohrlich, "Personal Shopper," *New York Times*, November 29, 2007, D10.

[48] Roberta Rosenberg Farber and Chaim Waxman, "Postmodernity and the Jews," in *Jews in America* (Hanover: Brandeis University Press, 1999), 400.

[49] Cathy O'Donnell, "This Year, Interfaith Families Straddle 2 Holidays in 1 Day," *Ann Arbor News*, December 25, 2005, B1.

[50] Ibid.

[51] *New York Times*, December 30, 2007 (marriage of Tali Sedgwick and Adam Walden).

Ethnicity and Marriage

was preceded by a "Jewish ceremony" at a restaurant and an earlier "traditional Korean cultural wedding ceremony at the Korea House in Seoul."[52]

Even traditional Jews – many of whom have intermarried relatives – seem increasingly to regard intermarriage not as betrayal or defiance but as weakness and the inevitable consequence of Jewish indifference and Gentile acceptance. Therefore some offer a variant of this advice: "The Jewish community must turn away from the prior outlook of rejecting the partner of interfaith marriage to the contemporary view of embracing a gentler, more nurturing environment for them in order to strengthen communal continuity and personal identity."[53]

Intermarriage in the Soviet Union

In the Soviet Union the state assumed the task of erasing age-old ethnic and religious distinctions. At the same time it constructed territorial units that were ethnically defined and insisted on identifying each of its citizens by his or her ethnicity, thereby preserving and even promoting ethnic identification. Still, the Soviet push for secularization was notable. "The media and arts presented interethnic marriages as a sign of progress and of the younger generation's liberation from outdated views."[54] A well-known work in 1926 on the "revolutionizing" of the *shtetl* includes a story of love and marriage between a Jewish woman and a non-Jewish man (in Russian).[55] A Yiddish poem about a Jewish girl who went to fight in the civil war and came home with a Russian boy celebrates the irrelevance of the matchmaker [*shadkhn*] and rabbi, and the triumph of interethnic love:

> *Mame, frey zikh haynt in tsveyen,*
> *Nokh a kind kh'hob dikh gebrakht,*
> *Zest dem bokher mit der peye*
> *Mit oygn, shvartse vi di nakht*
> *-vu zhe hostu im genumen*
> *un vos iz er far a mench?*
> *O'nit keyn shadkhn, nit keyn mume*
> *un keyn rov hot undz gebensht!*
> [Mama, today you have a double joy
>   Because I've brought you another child
>   See this fellow with the wave in his hair
>   With eyes as dark as the night.

---

[52] *New York Times*, October 28, 2007 (marriage of Victoria Lim and Peter Sheren). Hindu and Jewish ceremonies were combined in another wedding ("Gandhi-Hoffman") reported in the *Detroit Jewish News*, August 30, 1996.
[53] Dashevsky and Heller, *Intermarriage and Jewish Journeys in the United States*, 50.
[54] Mordechai Altshuler, *Soviet Jewry on the Eve of the Holocaust: A Social and Demographic Profile* (Jerusalem: Hebrew University and Yad Vashem, 1998), 70.
[55] V. Tan Bogoraz, *Evreiskoe mestechko v revoliutsii* (Moscow: Gosizdat, 1926), 84. I am indebted to Anna Shternshis for this reference.

'Where did you get him
And what kind of person is he?'
Without a matchmaker, without an "auntie"
And no rabbi blessed us!⁵⁶]

An American visitor to the USSR in the early 1930s described heated discussions in a Jewish collective farm about Feygele's impending marriage to a Tatar. "'Suppose there will be children, what are they going to be: Tatars or Jews?' 'If there will be children – and I am sure there will be – 'replied Leah, 'they will be simply Soviet citizens, like the rest of the children in the Soviet Union.'"⁵⁷ The visitor asked whether intermarriage would "play havoc with your Jewish culture." The reply did not exactly answer the question: "Jews in Russia are gradually disappearing as a religious unit, but they are getting stronger and stronger as a cultural unit."⁵⁸ A Soviet Yiddish author, Chaim Gildin, depicts a Jewish father's reaction to his son's marriage to a Ukrainian. In response to the wedding invitation, he laments, "What do they really want of me? I'm not a Communist, I'm not a convert, I'm not an apostate.... I raised myself a *kaddish* and now I've got a wedding with a *shikse*."⁵⁹ When he grudgingly goes to the wedding, he sits "blinking his old eyes, dimmed by moisture, with mute pain burning in them... over his son's nuptials."⁶⁰ Yet, as Mordechai Altshuler observes, "Most Jews came to terms with intermarriage – some in mute pain, some by force of habit, and some out of acceptance of the new winds that were blowing. Mixed marriages no longer caused a rupture with the family and the Jewish community, as before the Revolution."⁶¹

Toward Sblizhenie *and* Sliianie: *Interethnic Marriage in the USSR*

Soviet authorities encouraged interethnic marriage because it was a means of drawing together peoples (*sblizhenie*) and a step toward their fusion (*sliianie*) into a united people unmarked and undifferentiated by ethnicity. "In our country every sixth family includes people of different nationalities. This is one of

---

⁵⁶ "Gitele fun Komsomol," *Yungvald* 2 (1925), 10–11 (my translation). This material was also kindly supplied by Anna Shternshis who points out, "There are definitely more intermarriage stories in Russian than in Yiddish. It is in fact hard to find one: most Yiddish stories are about friendship between children (Jews and gentiles), joint work, but not going out or marrying. The same is true about Yiddish songs of the period – they like to get married without the rabbi, but to a Jew. However, working together with a non-Jew is fine." Personal communication, May 29, 2002.
⁵⁷ Leon Dennen, *Where the Ghetto Ends: Jews in Soviet Russia* (New York: Alfred King, 1934), 88–89.
⁵⁸ Ibid., 91.
⁵⁹ Chaim Gildin, *Ongreif* (Kharkov, 1934) quoted in Altshuler, *Soviet Jewry on the Eve of the Holocaust*, 73. Kaddish is the prayer said for the dead by their children, among others. Here it refers to the son who will presumably say kaddish for his father after the latter's death. "*Shikseh*" is a mildly derogatory Yiddish word, derived from Hebrew, for a non-Jewish woman.
⁶⁰ Ibid.
⁶¹ Ibid., 73.

Ethnicity and Marriage

the clear manifestations of friendly inter-national relations established in the country during the period of Soviet power."[62]

Jews began to marry non-Jews with a frequency never seen before the Revolution, not because the state advocated it, but because taboos against intermarriage had weakened along with the erosion of religious commitment and geographic concentration. In 1926, about 3 percent of Jewish marriages in Belorussia, 5 percent in Ukraine, but 17 (women) to 25 (men) percent of Jewish marriages in Russia (the RSFSR) were to non-Jews. By 1936, the rates had climbed to 11–13 percent in Belorussia, 15 percent in Ukraine, and, in a large leap, to 37–42 percent in the RSFSR.[63] Altshuler calculates that in the 1930s, the number of mixed marriages among Jews almost trebled; in that decade more than one-third of Jewish marriages were to non-Jews.[64] On the basis of fragmentary data from various parts of the Soviet Union, he estimates that "for every 100 marriages in the Soviet Union involving at least one Jewish partner through the mid-1970s, between 40 and 50 were mixed."[65] Anna Shternshis notes that attitudes toward intermarriage varied widely among the 225 elderly Jews who lived in the USSR before World War II whom she interviewed: "They insisted that choosing a Jewish partner was a matter of instinct rather than of principle, and very few were able to present any rational justification for this choice. The desire 'not to upset my parents' was the only explicit argument given by people of this generation (mostly from women)."[66] She asserts that "this was the first and last generation to have such an attitude." After the war, some Jewish women, if not Jewish men, were reluctant to marry non-Jews because grassroots anti-Semitism had surfaced and they worried that being part of a non-Jewish family would expose them to it. "The interviews suggest that anti-Semitism was largely responsible for the relatively high level of endogamous marriage among Soviet Jews" in the late 1940s–1950s.[67]

Intermarriage after the Breakup of the Soviet Union

After the end of the USSR, intermarriage rates among Jews skyrocketed, partly because mass emigration had shrunk the "marriage market," making it statistically ever less likely that Jews will marry Jews.[68] According to Mark Tolts,

---

[62] A. A. Susokolov, *Mezhnatsional'nye braki v SSR* (Moscow: Mysl', 1987), 3.
[63] Altshuler, *Soviet Jewry on the Eve of the Holocaust*, 74, table 4.2.
[64] Ibid., 75.
[65] Mordechai Altshuler, *Soviet Jewry since the Second World War* (New York: Greenwood Press, 1987), 29. See also Zvi Gitelman, "Correlates, Causes and Consequences of Jewish Fertility in the USSR," in Paul Ritterband, ed., *Modern Jewish Fertility* (Leiden: E. J. Brill, 1981), 33–63.
[66] Anna Shternshis, "Choosing a Spouse in the USSR: Gender Differences and the Jewish Ethnic Factor," *Jews in Russia and Eastern Europe* 2, 51 (Winter 2003), 13.
[67] Ibid., 29–30.
[68] Interestingly, the opposite tendency was observed among the Adygei people in the early and mid-1990s and was explained as due to the rise of Adygei ethnic consciousness. L. [iudmila] A. [lievna] Delova, *Mezhetnicheskaia sem'ia v polikul'turnom sotsiume* (Maikop: OAO "Poligraf-iug," 2009), 47–48. The Adygei are a people, sometimes included in the broader

On the eve of the start of the mass emigration in 1988, the frequency of mixed marriages among all marriages involving Jews was: in Russia – 73.2 percent for males and 62.8 percent for females (a relative increase of 23 and 46 percent respectively, as compared to 1978); in Ukraine – 54.1 percent for males and 44.7 percent for females (an increase of 21 and 31 percent); and in Belarus – 48.3 percent for males and 39.9 percent for females (the increase being 26 and 53 percent). In 1990 in Latvia this indicator was 59.9 percent for males and 49.1 percent for females (a relative increase of 13 and 38 percent respectively, as compared to 1980...).[69]

Overall, at the end of the Soviet period nearly 60 percent of Jewish men and half the Jewish women were marrying non-Jews. The proportion of mixed marriages was highest in the Russian Federation. Russian Jewry was less traditional and perhaps less ethnically distinct or committed to group preservation than Jews in Georgia and Central Asia, where religious forms were preserved far longer, or in the former Pale areas of Belarus and Ukraine and the more recently Sovietized Baltic and Moldavian republics.

In Lithuania in 1993, 41 percent of all Jews surveyed were in ethnically mixed marriages. The percentage of mixed marriages increased from 28 percent among couples where the husband was 65 or older to slightly more than half among couples in which the husband was between 25 and 44. Among the small number of couples where the husband was under 25, 78 percent were in an interethnic marriage.[70] Men were more likely to marry non-Jewish women than Jewish women were to marry non-Jewish men.[71] As a result of the emigration of the 1990s, and the much smaller number of Jews left outside Russia, intermarriage rates in other post-Soviet states surpassed those noted in Russia at the end of the 1980s: "By 1996... the frequency of mixed marriages among all marriages in Latvia involving Jews was 85.9 percent for males and 82.8 percent for females, and in Ukraine this indicator was 81.6 and 73.7 percent, respectively – levels... much higher than those of the Russia's Jews in 1988."[72]

---

category of Circassians, who live in the northwest Caucasus in Krasnodar krai of the Russian Federation.

[69] Mark Tolts, "Demography of the Jews in the Former Soviet Union: Yesterday and Today," in Zvi Gitelman, ed., *Jewish Life after the USSR: A Community in Transition* (Bloomington: Indiana University Press, 2003), 173-208.

[70] Sidney Goldstein and Alice Goldstein, *Lithuanian Jewry 1993: A Demographic and Sociocultural Profile* (Jerusalem: Avraham Harman Institute of Contemporary Jewry, Hebrew University, 1997), 55.

[71] The Goldsteins speculate that "[t]he greater freedom given men, their wider range of interaction with the larger society through education and work, the looser controls exercised over sons than daughters and possibly even the *halachic* view that Jewish descent is decided by the religious identity of the mother all help to explain the sex differential" (57). This is likely more applicable to those who married in the pre-Soviet era (before 1940). In the Soviet period practically all Jewish women were in the labor force and had equal access to education.

[72] Tolts, op. cit., 185, ibid.

On the basis of the 1994 Russian "micro-census," Tolts estimated that "among all currently married Jews in Russia, 63 percent of males and 44 percent of females had spouses from another ethnic group, an increase of five and four percentage points since 1989, respectively."[73] As a result, "[i]n 1998 in the Russian Federation the proportion of children born to mixed couples among all children born to Jewish mothers reached 74 percent."[74] In other words, three out of four children born in 1998 who were Jewish according to halakha (Jewish law), had non-Jewish fathers.

These trends can be observed outside the FSU as well, though not as dramatically. In the United States the 1990 National Jewish Population Survey found that 52 percent of Jews who had married since 1985 had married non-Jews, although further analysis reduced the figure to 47 percent. The next national Jewish survey (2000–1) found that "[s]ince 1985, the rate of increase in intermarriages has slowed as intermarriage levels have stabilized in the mid-40% range." Among Jews who married between 1985–90, the intermarriage rate was 43 percent.[75]

In September 2000, a national study by the American Jewish Committee found that 56 percent of Jews said they would *not* be pained if their children married a gentile; about three-quarters said that rabbis should officiate at Jewish-gentile marriages; and only a quarter agreed that the gentile partner should be encouraged to convert to Judaism.[76] Among the Orthodox, 84 percent said they would be pained if their child married a gentile, and about the same proportion opposed rabbinic participation in a mixed marriage. A survey of a large cohort of Conservative Jews found that two-thirds thought it was "OK for Jews to marry people of other religions," though among their parents, 86 percent agreed that, "A Jew should marry someone who is also Jewish."[77] In contrast, in a sample of United Synagogue members in London there was near unanimity that "a Jew should marry someone who is Jewish."[78]

In Russia there seems to be little opposition among the general public to interethnic marriage, though it may be "politically incorrect" to express opposition to it. VTsIOM surveys in the 1990s show that respondents in Russia were fairly indifferent toward marrying Jews (see Table 10.1).

---

[73] Ibid.
[74] Ibid., 187.
[75] *The National Jewish Population Survey 2000–01* (New York: United Jewish Communities), 16.
[76] American Jewish Committee, *2000 Annual Survey of American Jewish Opinion* (New York: American Jewish Committee, 2000), 3–4.
[77] Jack Wertheimer, ed., *Jews in the Center: Conservative Synagogues and their Members* (New Brunswick: Rutgers University Press, 2000), 246. Of course, it is likely that a higher proportion of respondents would agree to the statement that Jews should marry other Jews than would disagree with "it is OK for Jews to marry people of other religions," because there is a tendency to agree with the statement presented.
[78] Stephen Miller, "Religious Practice and Jewish Identity in a Sample of London Jews," in Jonathan Webber, *Jewish Identities in the New Europe* (London: Littman Library, 1994), Miller, 199.

TABLE 10.1. *Attitudes toward Marriages with Jewish Individuals, November 1999 (percent)*

I feel that nationality has no significance in marriage	71
Jews should marry non-Jews	5
Not permissible	4
Difficulty in responding	20
N = 2,400	

Source: VTsIOM surveys.

As situations become more personal, however, people are more disapproving of relations with Jews. In Table 10.2 we see the results of a sequence of surveys[79] that asked how a respondent would react if a close relative were to marry a Jew. A plurality of respondents in each of the three waves (1990, 1992, and 1997) said that they had no objections. However, in each wave roughly 30 percent said that they "would not want that to happen" – a much larger rate of disapproval than in response to a general question about interethnic marriage.

Opposition to interethnic marriage comes not only from the Jewish family. A Jewish woman from Yalta, married to a Russian, described how each of their families reacted when she and her spouse started seeing each other:

> My mother had warned me! At first she was very unhappy that I was marrying that man.... As a person he was wonderful! My mother liked him the most of all the sons-in-law. But she still used to say that one must marry someone of their own nationality, because we have seen anti-Semitism and we know that it exists. And then there are relatives ... on the other side.... My husband's father didn't accept our marriage. So my husband basically disowned his own father. And even changed his last name! He took my last name to replace his own from which, according to him, he had suffered all his youth. [Her husband's last name means "pea," and he was no doubt the subject of teasing.] So instead of congratulating us on our marriage, my husband's father said to my husband, "Aren't there enough Russian girls for you?" I remembered that insulting remark for the rest of my life and never forgave him for it.... At my age I am coming to a realization that one should preferably marry one of her own, although it's very complicated; there should also be feelings for one another, etc.

A 1997 opinion poll in Russia found only about one of ten respondents agreeing that a person should marry a member of his or her own nationality. Three-quarters of respondents were in favor of mixed marriages, irrespective of the age of the respondents. However, in December 2002, 46 percent said that they would be unhappy were a close relative to *marry a Jew* (35% were indifferent, 14% would approve, and 5% did not know). This seemingly drastic shift toward a negative attitude is explained by Lev Gudkov as the result of the high tensions in Russian society caused by the financial crisis of 1998–99, intense criticism of the (mostly Jewish) "oligarchs," the rise of open ethnic

---

[79] 1990: n = 1,700; 1992: n = 1,700 1997: n = 1,500.

TABLE 10.2. *How Would You React if a Jew Were to Become the Husband of a Close Relative? (percent)*

	1990	1992	1997
Have no objections	48	45	55
Would not want that to happen	28	29	30
Unable to give a specific response	24	26	15
N	1,700	1,700	1,500

hostilities as a result of the Chechen wars, and "aggression, frustration and social depression."[80]

Interethnic marriage should be less acceptable to Jews than to the general population because of the lingering effects of historic taboos. Nevertheless, post-Soviet Jews' levels of acceptance are higher than those of Jews in other countries, even though intermarriage is increasingly acceptable to American Jews, as we have seen. Robert Brym's and Rozalia Ryvkina's 1993 survey of a thousand Jews in Moscow, Kiev, and Minsk found that "only 26 per cent said that it was important for Jews to marry other Jews."[81] Among our respondents, only 36 to 43 percent agreed in 1997 that a Jew should [*sleduet*] choose a spouse of the same nationality, a decline from 1992 in Ukraine, where slightly more than half agreed with the proposition, but not in Russia where the proportion remained the same.[82] In Russia and in Ukraine more than half the 1997 respondents agreed that "it does not matter" whether one chooses a spouse of one's own nationality, compared to only one-quarter of Russian and 43 percent of Ukrainian Jews in 1992. In 2004 in St. Petersburg, about two of three Jewish respondents in a city-wide survey said that someone married to a non-Jew could be considered a "genuine Jew."[83] Thus acceptance of intermarriage has grown quickly in the FSU.

Rare is the person who says, as a 23-year-old man from Chernivtsi did, that Jews should marry other Jews to preserve Jewish culture through the generations. More typical are the sentiments of a woman of exactly his age and from the same city. Love, she said, "is a great feeling and it doesn't check

---

[80] Lev Gudkov, "Attitudes toward Jews in Post-Soviet Russia and the Problem of Anti-Semitism," in Zvi Gitelman and Yaacov Ro'i, eds., *Revolution, Repression and Revival* (Lanham, MD: Rowman Littlefield, 2007), 207.

[81] Robert Brym and Rozalia Ryvkina, *The Jews of Moscow, Kiev and Minsk* (London: Macmillan, 1994), 26. Only 69 percent of the sample said they were registered as Jews in their passports (22–23). One can reasonably assume that if a higher proportion of registered Jews had been interviewed, the proportion opposed to intermarriage would have been higher.

[82] In 1992, 53 to 55 percent agreed that one should marry a Jew. The decline over five years reflects the increase in intermarriage and the greater proportion of endogamous marriages among émigrés.

[83] Data from the 2004 St. Petersburg survey sponsored by the American Jewish Joint Distribution Committee and carried out by Prof. Vladimir Shapiro. I wish to thank Jonathan Porath, then of the Joint, and Vladimir Shapiro for making the data available to me.

one's passport before it comes. Young people care about love and not about nationality." Besides, she argues, mixed marriages produce genetically stronger children. Even a 59-year-old man who spoke Yiddish to his wife, grew up in a religious home, and said he observed all the holidays "in as traditional a way as possible," admitted to being uneasy about mixed marriages but could not oppose them because, after all, "among Russians and Ukrainians there are good people too." In other words, the only reason not to marry non-Jews would be if the latter were not "good people." Some opined that the more intermarriage the better because it would reduce ethnic conflict.

In response to another question, every third respondent in 1997 said they would not care if their own children married non-Jews. Even among those who said one should choose a spouse of one's own nationality, fewer than half would be opposed to their own child marrying a non-Jew. As a teacher in Moscow said, "I would be happy if they [her children] would marry Jews. But if not, I wouldn't make a tragedy of it."[84] An elderly woman in Kiev reported, "All our children married Russians and I don't think it really matters. If you love someone you cannot start thinking about the fate of the Jewish people." In yet another measure of attitudes toward intermarriage, only one of five Russian respondents and slightly less than one of three in Ukraine thought it is "absolutely necessary" to marry a Jew to consider oneself a "real Jew." Only one in five believed that marriage to a Jew is a sine qua non for considering one a "genuine Jew," though one in three thought it desirable.

These attitudes may carry over when ex-Soviet Jews immigrate to the United States or Germany. In the words of one American born in the USSR, "Some of our parents approve of traditions being reclaimed; others disapprove the strictness of Torah observance. In fact, some Russian-Jewish parents feel more comfortable with having a Russian-speaking non-Jew than an American Jew as a daughter-in-law."[85]

People married to Jews, no matter their own ancestry, are most firmly committed to the idea that Jews should marry other Jews. Between 70–80 percent in that group believe it necessary for Jews to marry other Jews. Those who are fully Jewish and are married to Jews are twelve times as likely to oppose their children intermarrying as those married to non-Jews. It seems that once an intermarriage occurs, opposition to intermarriage in general weakens, and it will be more likely to occur in succeeding generations; after all, if one's parents have intermarried there would seem to be little reason for their children not to do so.

Attitudes toward ethnically mixed marriages vary clearly (and predictably) by age. The younger one is, the more inclined one is to say that it is not necessary for Jews to choose a Jewish spouse. Only some elderly people, especially in

---

[84] Zvi Gitelman, Valeriy Chervyakov and Vladimir Shapiro, "Natsional'noe samosoznanie rossi-iskikh evreev. Materialy sotsiologicheskogo issledovaniia 1997–1998," *Diaspory* 3 (2000), esp. 74–83.
[85] Sergey Kadinsky, "Russian Jews Here are Still Searching," *The Jewish Week* (NY), December 5, 2007.

Chernivtsi, unambiguously condemned intermarriage as leading to assimilation or because, as a 79-year-old woman put it, God did not mean for Jews to mix with other nations, just as "he didn't mean for, say, ducks to mix with cranes.... God wanted each species to preserve itself." Even among those over 60, only 57–58 percent in 1992 and 42–49 percent in 1997 believed that Jews should marry other Jews.[86] This is in line with the general trend between 1992 and 1997 toward greater acceptance of interethnic marriage and reflects the actual tendency of Jews to marry non-Jews. One does not know, of course, whether the change in attitudes toward intermarriage preceded its actual rise and facilitated it, or whether increased intermarriage is due less to attitudinal change and more to the shrinkage of the Jewish marriage market and the ongoing weakening of tradition.

Faced with the reality of intermarriage, people's attitudes have changed accordingly, as they have apparently in the United States and other countries. The decline in 1992–97 in the proportion of Russian and Ukrainian Jews affirming that Jews should marry each other may be due to the greater emigration of the endogamously married. Even among those advocating marriage only to Jews, a majority claimed they would *not* be upset were their children to marry non-Jews. Thus, the historic boundary setting Jews off from others is rapidly blurring.

One of every five of our respondents had a spouse with no Jewish ancestry at all, and another 2 percent were in marriages in which both spouses were of partially non-Jewish descent. Some candidly evaluated the role that ethnicity had played in their married life. A 30-year-old man in Ekaterinburg, married to a German woman, was ambivalent about mixed marriages. As he gets older, he said, he thinks it would be better if Jews married Jews and he would "not have minded if his wife were Jewish." Although he was only 36 years old, an activist in Jewish affairs in Kiev had been married three times – the first time to a Jew, the second to a Ukrainian with no Jewish ancestry, and the third to a woman with a paternal Jewish grandfather. He claimed that ethnicity played no role in any of his marriages and did not affect his own Jewish identity or activities.

As in Western countries, intermarriage was almost negligible among the ancestors of the very oldest age cohort among our respondents, but rose monotonically as one moves down in age, a trend found among all citizens of Ukraine to some degree.[87] Figures 10.1 and 10.2 show the ethnic origins of our respondents in the first and second interview waves.

---

[86] The question was worded, in Russian: *"Kak vy schitaete, evreiam sleduet vybrat' sebe suprugu(a) svoei natsional'nosti, drugoi natsional'nosti, ili eto ne imeet znacheniia?"*

[87] In annual national surveys in Ukraine taken between 1994 and 1998, about 80 percent of respondents reported that their parents were of the same nationality, but only 57 to 59 percent had spouses of the same nationality and 19 to 23 percent had spouses of another nationality (the others were not married or gave no response). N. Panina and E. Golovakha, *Tendencies in the Development of Ukrainian Society (1994–1998): Sociological Indicators* (Kyiv: Institute of Sociology, Ukrainian Academy of Sciences, 1999), 89.

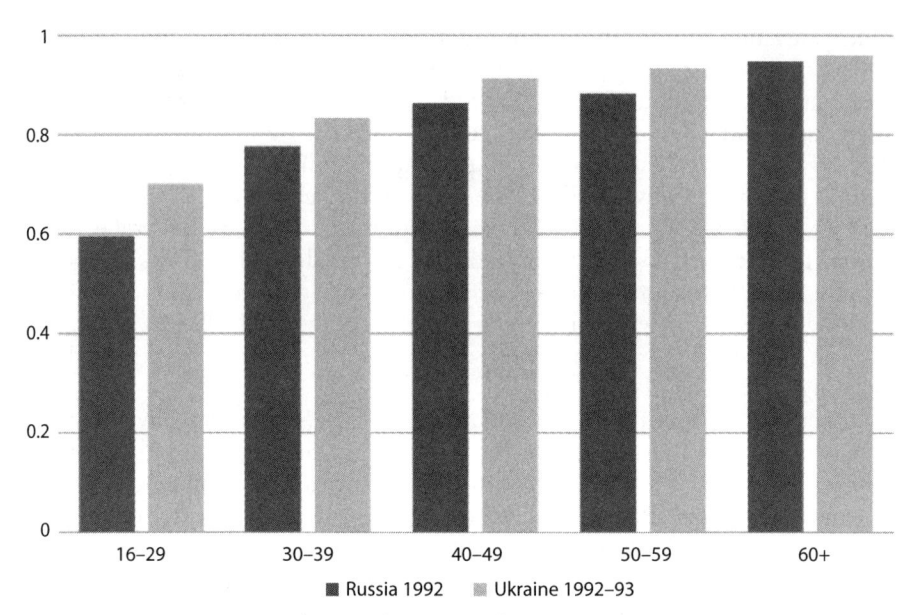

FIGURE 10.1. Proportion of respondents identifying as a pure Jew by age group.

In the first wave, the majority of respondents in both Russia and Ukraine have only Jewish antecedents, but among those under 40, there is a higher percentage of respondents with mixed ancestry. In every age group, there is a higher proportion of those fully Jewish in Ukraine than in Russia. This is probably due to the persistence of *shtetl* life in Ukraine and the fact that West Ukraine, where Jews had clung to tradition longer than their Soviet Ukrainian Jewish neighbors, was annexed from Poland as late as 1939.

The same differences by age can be seen in the second survey. For example, in the 1997 Russian sample, among those 70 or older, only one in twenty has some non-Jewish ancestors; in the next younger cohort (50–69 year olds), one in six has non-Jewish ancestors, and in the under-30 group, more than half do. Overall, comparing the earlier and later surveys, we find more respondents who have mixed ancestry in 1997, especially among those under 40. In the first survey, fully Jewish respondents made up 86 percent of the Russian and 90 percent of the Ukrainian samples, but five years later the proportion of full Jews had declined to 80 percent in Russia and 75 percent in Ukraine. Of full Jews in Russia in 1997, slightly more than half are married to full Jews; one-quarter are married to non-Jews. This means that the trend away from fully Jewish ancestry observed between 1992 and 1997 will accelerate.

Are Ethnically Mixed Marriages Really Less Happy?

As mentioned earlier, some Western Jews who oppose intermarriage argue that it might be morally unobjectionable but is undesirable on pragmatic grounds.

Ethnicity and Marriage

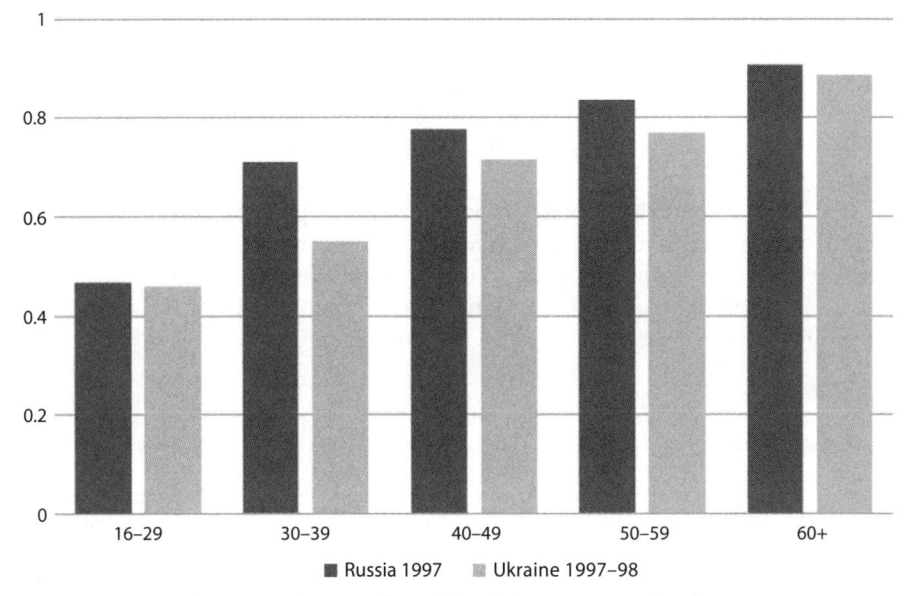

FIGURE 10.2. Proportion of respondents identifying as a pure Jew by age group.

Are interethnic marriages really more fragile than endogamous partnerships? That appears to be true in the United States, although research among other ethnic groups outside that country indicates this is not always the case.[88] Among American Jews, strikingly, "The divorce rate among mixed marriages is double that the rate among endogamous marriages,"[89] and many believe that religious differences play a role in causing those divorces.

Altshuler compared divorce rates among endogamous and exogamous (mixed) Jewish families in the USSR in the 1920s and 1930s. In the earlier decade the divorce rate was one-third higher among intermarried couples than among couples where both partners were Jewish. However, by the mid-1930s in Ukraine and Belorussia the divorce rate among mixed couples was slightly *lower* than that among homogeneous couples. Altshuler attributes the change to "the contraction of the cultural and mental gulf between the Jews and the surrounding population. In any case, there is no substantial proof that in the 1930s a mixed family was less stable than an endogamous Jewish family."[90] Mark Tolts observed that in 1988–89, there were 24.0 divorces per 1,000 married

---

[88] Research comparing Adygei-Adygei and Russian-Adygei marriages concludes that interethnic marriages are no more conflictual than ethnically homogeneous marriages. However, in marriages where there is some conflict, differences in ethnicity become another source of conflict. Delova, *Mezhetnicheskaia sem'ia v polikul'turnom sotsiume*, 47–48.
[89] Bruce Phillips, *Re-Examining Intermarriage*, 64.
[90] *Soviet Jewry on the Eve of the Holocaust*, 79.

Jewish females and 23.2 per 1,000 married Jewish males.[91] He notes that these rates are very similar for males and females, despite the fact that approximately twice as many Jewish men were currently married to non-Jewish women as were Jewish women to non-Jewish men.[92] However, our study shows that, as late as the 1990s, marriages of full Jews to non-Jews were *less* happy than endogamous marriages.[93]

In Western countries it may be impolitic, and perhaps futile, to inquire about spousal relations in mass surveys. In the Former Soviet Union, people are less reluctant to discuss such matters, so we asked some questions about relationships in families.[94] First, we inquired in some detail about the ethnicity of respondents' spouses; our findings are summarized in Figure 10.3.[95]

---

[91] M. S. Tolts and T.L. Kharkova, "Razvodimost'" (Divorce), in A. Ya. Kvasha et al., eds., *Narodonaselenie, Entsiklopedicheskii slovar'* (Moscow: Bol'shaya Russkaya entsiklopedia, 1990), 370.

[92] Mark Tolts, "The Interrelationship between Emigration and the Socio-Demographic Profile of Russian Jewry," in N. Lewin-Epstein, Y. Ro'I, and P. Ritterband, eds., *Russian Jews on Three Continents* (London: Frank Cass, 1997), 158 and 174, note 34. "At the same time, in 1988–1989, in the Russian Federation there were 17.1 divorces per 1,000 married Russian females, and 17.7 per 1,000 married Russian males. Thus, surprisingly the rates for Jews were not much higher than for Russians, despite the fact that the structure of Jews (most reside in big cities, etc.) should lead to a greater incidence of divorce. I think that above cited Russian data can not be seen as proof of a higher propensity to divorce in Jewish mixed marriage, especially for Jewish males. Russia is not America! Unfortunately, I do not know any other published Jewish divorce data for the FSU." Personal communication, October 28, 2010.

[93] In 1980–92, fieldwork and archival research were conducted among Mountain Jews (Kavkazskie Evreii) in Nal'chik, capital of the Kabardino-Balkar Autonomous Republic in the Caucasus. In the 1990s about 6,000 Mountain Jews lived in the republic, 98 percent in Nal'chik. From 1927–89, about 20 percent of the local Jews had married non-Jews (mostly Russians) or European, Bukharan, or Georgian Jews, with 41 percent in 1966 and 34 percent in 1989 marrying someone other than a Mountain Jew, the vast majority not being Jews at all. This was a far lower rate of interethnic marriage than among the overall population of Nal'chik and was understood as a result of the "significant role of ethnic preferences among Mountain Jews, connected with their preservation of some ethnocultural traditions" (60). Researchers found, as we have, that the children of interethnic marriages involving Jews were themselves more likely to marry people of other ethnicities. They also found that non-Jewish spouses often learned the Mountain-Jewish language ("Tat") and adopted "elements of the traditional national culture of their marriage partners" (65).

Of 713 divorces involving Mountain Jews in Nal'chik between 1943 and 1989, 71 percent involved endogamous marriages and 29 percent involved marriages between a Mountain Jew and a non-Jew (except in two cases where the spouse was a different kind of Jew). Curiously, the researchers comment on differences in age and social standing as possible causes of divorce but do not mention ethnicity, although 16 percent of divorces in 1980–89 were between partners of different nationality. See Iu. I. Murzakhanov, *Soveremennaia semi'ia u gorskikh evreev Kabardino-Balkarii* (Moscow, 1994).

[94] In 1992, 56 percent of our respondents in Russia were married and 57 percent in Ukraine (n = 724 and 1,145). In 1997, the proportions declined somewhat to 49.8 and 53 percent, respectively (n = 647 and 1,060).

[95] We distinguish among "purely Jewish" marriages, where both spouses have only Jewish parents; "predominantly Jewish" marriages, which mean one of the following: two partially Jewish spouses, or one partially Jewish and one non-Jewish spouse, or one partially Jewish and one

Ethnicity and Marriage

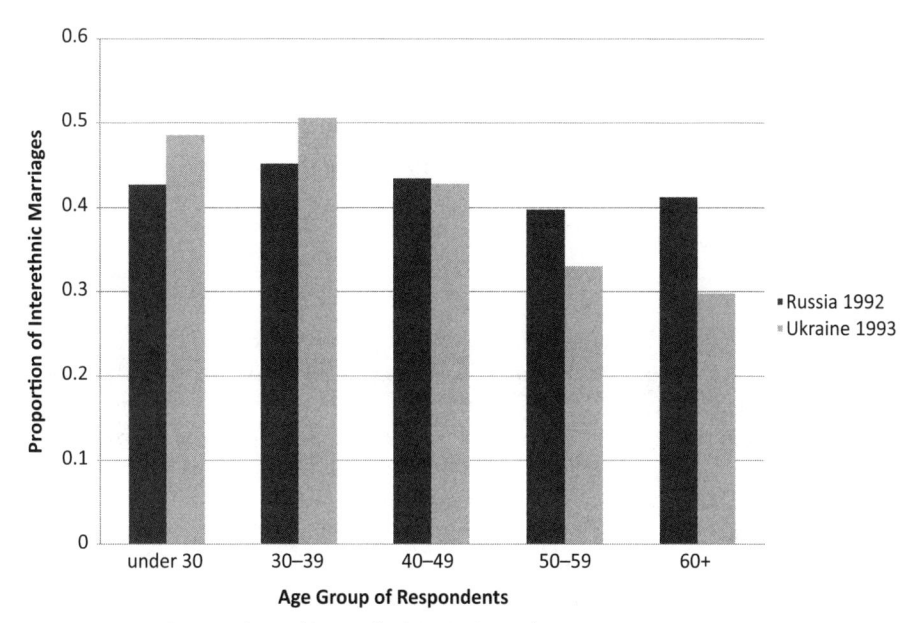

FIGURE 10.3. Proportion of interethnic marriages by age group.

Surprisingly, although older respondents have more uniformly Jewish ancestry than younger ones, in Russia they have not married Jews to a greater extent, unless our results mask a substantial number of second marriages of people, mostly men, who were married the first time to Jews, but not the second time. (In the United States, there is a much higher rate of intermarriage among remarriages than in first marriages – 40 percent vs. 14 percent.[96]) In both survey years there is a remarkably even distribution among all ages of people married to fully, partly and non-Jewish spouses.[97] However, in Ukraine the oldest age group is considerably more likely to be married to fully Jewish spouses, though the proportion declined from 70 to 52 percent between the surveys, again perhaps because of second marriages or because the in-married were more likely to emigrate. By 1997 in Ukraine, among those under 40, only one of four or five was married to a spouse whose antecedents were fully Jewish. About one-quarter of married respondents had completely *non*-Jewish spouses in the early 1990s; by the end of the decade, more than one-third of Russian respondents and 41 percent of Ukrainian respondents were married to non-Jews. In the latter period, in both countries one in five was married to someone with

with Jewish ancestry that is less than one quarter; and "inter-ethnic" marriages, which mean two partially Jewish spouses, or one partially Jewish and one non-Jewish spouse, or one partially Jewish and one with no more than one Jewish grandparent, or a "pure Jew" married to a non-Jew.

[96] Kosmin et al., *Intermarriage, Divorce and Remarriage among American Jews*, 9.
[97] The one anomaly is that in 1997, 60 percent (38 of 63) of marriages in the youngest cohort were to Jews, whereas in the other age groups, 40 to 45 percent were married to Jews.

TABLE 10.3. *Interethnic Marriage and Reported Marriage Happiness (percent)*

Spouse type	Russia 1992	Russia 1997	Ukraine 1992–93	Ukraine 1997–98
Jewish	84.6	88.8	85.3	90.9
Partially Jewish	82.8	90.3	78.0	87.7
Non-Jewish	71.8	82.2	75.9	84.7
N	1,300	1,314	2,000	1,984

mostly, but not entirely, Jewish ancestry. The proportion of those in interethnic marriages is the same in all cohorts in Russia. In Ukraine, though the oldest cohort is least likely to be married to non-Jews, the overall proportion of people married to non-Jews is about the same as in Russia because among those under 50 intermarriage rates are *higher* than in Russia even in the early 1990s, and the gap increased at the end of the decade.

Barriers to intermarriage seem to have fallen more quickly in Ukraine, which is surprising because generally Jewish tradition has survived more there than in Russia. Perhaps the proportionally greater emigration from Ukraine has shrunk the marriage market even more than in Russia (the Jewish population is less than half of that of Russia). In any case, the younger the person, the greater the propensity to marry a non-Jew, except men over 60, who when marrying a second time, seem to marry non-Jews to a far greater extent than they did when they originally married.[98]

Ethnicity and Marital Happiness

Are those married to Jews any happier in their marriages than those who are not? We asked our respondents, "In general, do you consider your marriage to be happy or unhappy?" We also asked seven specific questions regarding the degree of agreement between spouses on such issues as culture, politics, Jewish matters, the future of the children, and "marital life." Of course, the happiness of a marriage depends on many things other than agreement between spouses on important issues, but we hesitated to inquire about more personal issues and believe that agreement on these issues may be generally necessary, if not sufficient, for a happy marriage. About four of five married respondents characterized their marriages as happy, but those who have Jewish spouses were somewhat more likely to do so than those whose spouses have no Jewish background. This is true in both years, as Table 10.3 makes clear. The differences in the happiness of the marriages are modest, but consistent and clear. For some reason, irrespective of the spouse's ethnicity, respondents were more likely to

---

[98] It is not clear why this should be so. There are many available Jewish widows and other singles. Perhaps when Jewish men marry for the second time, they are less concerned about the Jewish continuity of their families. The Jewishness of children is no longer a consideration. This is a more likely explanation for mixed second marriages in the West, but in the FSU, where people are less reluctant to enter into mixed marriages and the impact on the Jewishness of the family seems to be a minor consideration, this explanation would not hold much water. The propensity

Ethnicity and Marriage

report happier marriages in 1997 than in 1992.[99] The differences between 1992 and 1997 were largest for those respondents who have spouses who are not purely Jewish.

At first blush, it seems that ethnically similar spouses share higher levels of marriage satisfaction. If there is a causal relationship, it seems likely to run from ethnic similarity to increased marriage happiness. However, despite the relatively straightforward logic of causality, we still need to control for a variety of other variables that might influence marital accord. We tested three specifications of the hypothesis that ethnic commonality between spouses creates happier marriages:

1. High levels of ethnic similarity will lead to marriages that are generally happier than marriages with ethnically different spouses.
2. As ethnic similarity within marriages increases, levels of marital accord will increase generally across all issues.
3. As ethnic similarity within marriages increases, levels of marital accord will increase most especially on issues of ethnic import (e.g., religion) in comparison to general issues.

Dependent Variables

To evaluate these three hypotheses, we need dependent variables that measure marriage satisfaction and marital accord. We measured marital satisfaction by asking individuals if their marriages were happy, unhappy, or if they were not sure. We coded responses as a 0–2 scale, with "unhappy" as "0," "don't know" as "1," and "happy" as "2."

The second set of dependent variables is a bit more complex. First, we measured responses to seven questions asking individuals to rate their compatibility on a number of issues in their marriage on the same 0–2 scale as earlier. As mentioned earlier, those issues include views of spirituality, cultural interests, "Jewish problems" (or "issues"), political viewpoints, goals for their children, family life, and views of Jewish culture. We generated additive scales based on the responses to test the proposition that ethnic similarity leads to greater marriage accord specifically on ethnic issues. The "ethnic" questions on spirituality, cultural interests, "Jewish problems," and Jewish culture created an 8-point scale of ethnic accord, whereas the more generic questions having to do with political views, goals for children, and family life formed a 6-point scale of secular accord. Because these questions were only asked in the 1992/93 waves of the survey, we could test only Hypotheses 2 and 3 for the earlier Russian and Ukrainian surveys.

---

of Jewish widowers (and perhaps the divorced) to marry non-Jews to a greater extent than in first marriages awaits a better explanation.

[99] In 1992/93, in Russia 81 percent and Ukraine 82 percent reported "happy marriages;" by 1997, the percentages had risen to 87 and 88, respectively.

Independent Variables

Our explanatory variable measures the ethnicity of the respondent's spouse on a scale of 0–2, with "0" indicating no Jewish ancestry and "2" indicating full Jewish ancestry. Limiting the tested sample to individuals of full Jewish ethnicity allows us to employ this variable as a measure of the ethnic distance between spouses. We expect this "spouse" variable to have a positive relationship with all dependent variables. However, in accordance with Hypotheses 2 and 3, we expect it to have a more pronounced positive relationship with the ethnic accord scale than with the one measuring general accord.

Control Variables

The point of estimating a regression is to parse out the influences of other factors that might contribute to marital happiness and to avoid contaminating the effects of ethnicity on marital happiness. We controlled for four potential confounding variables: age, gender, education, and economic well-being. First, more elderly married people have possibly been married longer and perhaps are more likely to express high satisfaction in their marriage, so we included an age variable that records the age of an individual in years. Gender is a dichotomous variable with females as "0". Education is measured in five levels of schooling. Economic well-being is a rather difficult issue to measure in the FSU because of the hidden nature of social class. The Soviet command economy dictated wages, which on the surface tended to be much less stratified than those in the West. However, the economic situations of individuals did vary, with not much regard to their official salaries. To get around this problem, we asked participants to discuss how well off they felt materially, ranging from not being able to buy routine necessities to being able to take expensive vacations often. That should capture variations in economic well-being both under the Soviet system and the somewhat more Westernized economic systems of the post-USSR period.

Method

Although none of the scales of the dependent variables we used are strictly continuous, because of the relatively large number of ordinal categories for the scales of ethnic accord and secular accord, it is acceptable to use ordinary least squares (OLS) regression to test Hypotheses 2 and 3. However, because the marriage "happiness" scale has only three ordinal categories, OLS becomes more problematic. Therefore we substituted an ordinal probit, specifically designed to deal with such limited-value dependent variables, to test Hypothesis 1.

Results

Tables 10.4 and 10.5 show the results of Hypothesis 1. As we see, the ethnicity of the spouse has a strong positive relationship with marriage happiness in all four surveys. But what does this mean substantively? Because probit equations are more complicated than their OLS counterparts, we cannot directly infer effect size through the coefficients. However, by holding other variables

Ethnicity and Marriage

TABLE 10.4. *Relationship between Marital Happiness and Spouse Ethnicity (for pure Jews)*

	Russia 1992	Ukraine 1992/93	Russia 1997	Ukraine 1997/98
Spousal ethnicity	.225 (.066)	.156 (.052)	.168 (.074)	.142 (.062)
Gender	.235 (.116)	.178 (.091)	.044 (.142)	.120 (.116)
Well-being	.154 (.072)	.042 (.052)	.161 (.070)	.190 (.068)
Education	−.075 (.062)	−.043 (.037)	.026 (.064)	−.077 (.050)
Age	.003 (.004)	.007 (.003)	.007 (.005)	.007 (.005)
Cut-point 1	−1.251 (.445)	−.972 (.272)	−.750 (.454)	−1.288 (.353)
Cut-point 2	−.284 (.440)	−.337 (.269)	.053 (.449)	−.574 (.347)
Pseudo R-squared	.029	.017	.027	.023
N	649	1,065	550	840

constant, we can show the predicted probability that a respondent with particular characteristics will have a happy marriage. As is standard statistical practice, we hold all variables except spousal ethnicity to their median values. In the 1992 Russia survey, this is a 55-year-old man with a university education, able to meet his daily expenses. We find that he has a 73 percent chance of being in a happy marriage with a spouse who has no Jewish ancestry and an 86 percent predicted probability of being in a happy marriage with a spouse of completely Jewish ancestry.[100] For a median female respondent in Russia 1992 wave, the predicted chance of being in a happy marriage is lower, but the overall pattern is the same. She has a 65 percent chance of being in a happy marriage with a spouse who has no Jewish ancestry and an 80 percent predicted probability of being in a happy marriage with a spouse of exclusively Jewish ancestry.[101] The results for the other surveys are not quite of the same magnitude, because of higher overall levels of marriage satisfaction in general, yet the substantive import exists.

Table 10.6 shows results regarding our second and third hypotheses. The first column under each country employs the scale of ethnic accord as the dependent variable, whereas the second column uses the secular accord index. The results clearly support Hypothesis 2: full ("pure") Jews who have spouses of a similar ethnic background tend to score higher in all areas of marital accord, as values for spouse's ethnicity correlate highly with both types of the marriage accord variable in both Russia and Ukraine.

Does Hypothesis 3 – that the ethnic similarity of spouses will have a particular effect on ethnic issues in a marriage – hold? Usually in regression analysis,

---

[100] The 95 percent confidence intervals for the 73.1 percent estimate run from 65.8 to 80.5 percent, whereas the interval around the 85.7 percent estimate goes from 81.6 to 89.8 percent. Therefore the difference is statistically significant at the .05 level.

[101] The respective 95 percent confidence intervals here run from 55.0 to 74.8 percent, and 74.3 to 85.3 percent. Thus the difference is not statistically significant at the .05 level. However, the overlap is very small.

TABLE 10.5. *Relationship between Spouse Ethnicity and Marital Accord (for Pure Jews)*

	Russia 1992		Ukraine 1992/93	
	Ethnic Accord	Secular Accord	Ethnic Accord	Secular Accord
Spousal ethnicity	.904 (.107)	.336 (.068)	.718 (.083)	.210 (.060)
Gender	.262 (.181)	.109 (.115)	.152 (.138)	.060 (.100)
Well-being	.164 (.106)	.062 (.068)	−.076 (.081)	.013 (.059)
Education	.031 (.089)	.086 (.057)	.004 (.540)	−.015 (.039)
Age	.031 (.007)	.007 (.004)	.015 (.005)	.009 (.004)
Constant	2.975 (.662)	3.467 (.424)	4.276 (.412)	4.084 (.300)
Adjusted R-squared	.1131	.038	.088	.017
N	649	649	1,065	1,065

we compare the impact of different independent variables on the same dependent variable. Here, we reverse that logic and use an unorthodox tactic to test Hypothesis 3 – measuring the impact of the same set of independent variables on two distinct dependent variables. We predict that the ethnic similarity of spouses is more important to predicting accord on ethnic (Jewish) issues than on general marital issues. Therefore, our variable of measuring spousal similarity should have a larger relationship with our scale of ethnic (Jewish) accord than with the scale of secular (general) accord.

This analysis reveals that two factors support Hypothesis 3.[102] However, substantively speaking, it is a stronger predictor of ethnic marriage accord in both the Russian and Ukrainian examples. Simple multiplication of the coefficients shows that the spouses with identical pure Jewish backgrounds will score 1.8 points higher on the ethnic accord scale than their ethnically different counterparts in Russia (22.5 percent of the 8-point scale) and 1.4 points in the Ukraine (17.5 percent of the 8-point scale). In comparison, spouses with identical pure Jewish backgrounds will score only 0.67 points higher on the ethnic accord scale than their ethnically different counterparts in Russia (11.1 percent of a 6-point scale), and 0.4 points in the Ukrainian survey (6.7 percent of the 6-point scale).

Second, the magnitude of the adjusted R-squared value, which shows the total amount of variation in the data that the right-side variables in a regression account for, is roughly three times as great for the regression using the ethnic accord scale as the dependent variable than for the regression employing the secular marriage accord in Russia (.118 to .038) and five times as great in Ukraine (.088 to .017). Formal tests performed to compare the magnitudes of the spousal variables after pairing the two equations in seemingly unrelated regression are significant at the .0001 level (chi-squared statistics: 35.51 for

---

[102] "Spousal ethnicity" is significant at the .001 levels under all regression estimations.

Ethnicity and Marriage

TABLE 10.6. *Spouse Ethnicity and Marital Accord (for Pure Jews)*

	Russia 1992		Ukraine 1992/93	
	Ethnic Accord	Secular Accord	Ethnic Accord	Secular Accord
Spousal ethnicity	.904 (.107)	.336 (.068)	.718 (.083)	.210 (.060)
Gender	.262 (.181)	.109 (.115)	.152 (.138)	.060 (.100)
Well-being	.164 (.106)	.062 (.068)	−.076 (.081)	.013 (.059)
Education	.031 (.089)	.086 (.057)	.004 (.540)	−.015 (.039)
Age	.031 (.007)	.007 (.004)	.015 (.005)	.009 (.004)
Constant	2.975 (.662)	3.467 (.424)	4.276 (.412)	4.084 (.300)
Adjusted R-squared	.1131	.038	.088	.017
N	649	649	1,065	1,065

Russia and 53.11 for the Ukraine). Thus, the ethnic accord variable has a statistically distinct coefficient from the secular accord variable.[103] In other words, **issues involving Jewishness are more contentious that other issues in marriages between Jews and non-Jews**, even in Russia and Ukraine where people were taught to believe that ethnicity does not matter and certainly should not be a source of contention. It turns out that **ethnicity matters in marriage**, as it does in so many other areas.

Conclusion

Marriage of Jews to non-Jews has been a theological, sociological, psychological, and even political issue in many places and times. Traditional Jews have regarded it as anathema, Soviet authorities saw it as "progressive," and, as we have seen, many Jews (and some non-Jews) are deeply ambivalent about it. Marriage may be an intensely personal, private matter, but it has profound consequences for the Jewish collectivity now and in the future. Some argue that Jews who marry non-Jews ensure the future of a demographically challenged diasporic minority by compensating for the lack of natural increase and by diversifying and thereby strengthening the gene pool. Yet the evidence from several countries shows that, unless the non-Jewish spouse converts to Judaism, there is little chance that the offspring of such marriages will be Jewish in any meaningful or even nominal way. Moreover, not a few conversions are pro forma and do not change the values or behaviors of the formerly non-Jewish partner. Rationalizations for intermarriage abound, but it clearly is not "good for the Jews." In Russia and Ukraine, where conversions to Judaism are very rare, it is even less so.

---

[103] According to Table 10.1, it appears that women are more likely to view their marriages as unhappy than men are. However, this phenomenon fades in the second wave of surveys.

11

Politics, Affect, Affiliation, and Alienation

In 2004, when Ukrainians launched their "Orange Revolution" in protest against a rigged presidential election, many anticipated a breakthrough toward a stable democracy in a state that had come into being only in 1991, as well as a clear reorientation from Russia toward the West, specifically, the European Union. However, by 2010, Ukraine had reverted to a more conservative and Russian-oriented government. Russians had a somewhat parallel experience. The 1990s were the most democratic era in their history. But Vladimir Putin's rise to Russia's presidency in 2000 initiated significant retreats from democracy toward more authoritarian politics. The euphoria of reformist, competitive politics has dissipated in Russia and Ukraine.

However, in the 1990s, citizens of Russia and Ukraine took a lively interest in politics, which suddenly became meaningful, arousing a sense of political efficacy among peoples long accustomed to being the objects, not the subjects, of politics. People were free to determine both individually and communally the meaning or cultural content of their identities and how they should relate to the states in which they live. Throughout the decade peoples and states in the former Soviet Union were redefining themselves in the wake of the simultaneous collapse of the supranational ideology of communism and of the Soviet state. The leaders of Estonia, Latvia, and most Central Asian states constructed their countries largely as ethnic states whose purpose is to serve the interests of the dominant ethnic group. In such states other peoples are tolerated but not given equal access to positions of leadership in politics and economic and social life. In contrast, Russia and Ukraine, whatever their failures to institutionalize democratic politics, became civic states in which the ties of citizens to the state are political, economic, and territorial, not ethnic.[1] In predominantly ethnic states, Jews and other non-autochthonous peoples are relegated to the political sidelines, but in civic states they should be equal players and have to define

---

[1] This is despite the fact that the Russian Federation has ethnic regions and republics.

their relationship to the state. In the 1990s nonterritorial peoples – Jews, Poles, Germans, and even Russians in the "near abroad" (former Soviet republics) – were also considering how they should relate to co-ethnics abroad and whether to stay in their native land or emigrate to their putative homelands. As we shall see, Russian Jews identified more with the Russian state than Ukrainian Jews did with their state.

Jews and the State

Historically, diaspora Jews have related to the states in which they lived in several ways. Some rulers protected them in return for their provision of economic services. Ruler and ruled were linked in a specific exchange relationship, and Jews' allegiance was primarily to the ruler rather than to an abstract state. They lived *pod zamczem* (under the castle) in Krakow, Lublin, Bratislava, and elsewhere. When the inhabitant of the castle changed Jews sometimes had to renegotiate their contract with the new ruler. Such a relationship implied a sojourner status. Once protection was removed Jews were likely to move on. A modern variant of this is found among a minority of English Jews, who are willing to tolerate their exclusion from sectors of the polity, economy, and society because they regard themselves as living in a *malchus shel chesed*, a benevolent kingdom that has granted them the right of residence. The state itself belongs to the English and Jews can only aspire to be British – that is, to have a civic identity – but they can never attain the privileged ethnic identity. Unlike in countries of immigration, in England there is an established ethnic group that, some Jews feel, has the right to dominate.

A second type of sojourner is the Jew who resides in a country to which he or she has no deep and permanent loyalties. This is true of many *haredim* (ultra-Orthodox) in Belgium, England, Switzerland, the United States, and even in Israel, and of some non-*haredi* Holocaust survivors and other immigrants. Citizenship is a flag of convenience, and some people hold several passports. The sojourner stance toward the state may explain in part why these Jews sometimes flout local laws.

A third type is the citizen whose loyalty is conditional on receiving what he or she defines as proper or fair treatment by the state. This type of citizen relates to the state pragmatically, with little sentiment involved. Again, we observe this relationship among some Jews, especially in Ukraine. Others may be citizens whose loyalty is unconditional, assumed both by the state and themselves, and no different from non-Jewish citizens in this respect. Still others might be "super-patriots" intent on proving to state authorities that they are reliable and without conflicting loyalties. Lenin, among others, noted that the most fanatical nationalists are often not ethnically members of the group whose cause they espouse; for example, Stalin in the USSR, and perhaps even Adolf Hitler, an Austrian. Vladimir Volfovich Zhirinovsky in Russia today and Samu Stern, leader of the Neolog community in Budapest in the 1930s,[2] are different kinds of Jewish examples of this phenomenon. During World War I, a Hungarian Jew wrote,

> I can say that I never belonged to any religion, I don't belong to the community and I don't feel for the members of my race, [but] I am greatly pleased when a Jew acts well in the face of death. Does not cry, does not flee from it. Every time I find someone who is likely to be a member of my faith [sic!] in the list of our fallen soldiers, I am really happy for him. These fallen proclaim that we are Hungarians and that our genuine attachment to the motherland is stronger than faith, stronger than death.[3]

Finally, Jews famously have been rebels aiming to reform, reshape, or destroy a state they view as oppressive or unjust; for example, Trotsky, Rosa Luxemburg and other Jewish radicals.

Needless to say, Jews in a single country, let alone the world, may distribute themselves across this spectrum of relationships, though in some countries and times one type or another may predominate. These are fluid and permeable categories, and the same individual may move among them, as might entire groups of Jews.

Jews in Russia and Ukraine, who together constitute the second or third largest diaspora Jewish population, chose among these alternatives in the 1990s and continue to do so. Jews' collective memories of historical relations with Russian and Ukrainian states, peoples, and cultures might have influenced their choices. After discussing these choices, I present an empirically based analysis of Russian and Ukrainian Jewish attitudes and behaviors. However, the major focus of this chapter is on how Jews relate to the burgeoning Jewish institutions and organizations in their localities and to their respective states, and what are the connections between these two.

One can imagine five patterns of relationships between Jews and the Russian and Ukrainian (or other) states:

1. Jews see their ethnicity as a fact with few behavioral or attitudinal implications and relate to the state no differently from non-Jews; they relate very little to Jewish public life.
2. Jews strongly identify with the state and participate in it actively (vote, run for office, lobby, follow political events), but also take part in Jewish communal life, seeing one as complementing the other.
3. Because they are overwhelmingly urban and relatively well educated, Jews participate more actively in the state than the average citizen but not much in Jewish communal life.

---

[2] In 1938, Stern, head of the Neolog Jewish community of Pest, wrote, "The homeland must be loved even when it does not bestow upon us the totality of its love. God must be worshipped even when he reduces us to dust.... We worship our earthly god, our homeland, whatever our fate may be in this homeland." Quoted in Ezra Mendelsohn, *The Jews of East Central Europe between the World Wars* (Bloomington: Indiana University Press, 1983), 123.

[3] Sandor Brody, "Zsidokrol," *Feher Konyv*. (1915), 67–86, translated in Guy Miron and Anna Szalai, *Yehudim al parshat derachim* (Ramat Gan, Israel: Bar Ilan University Press, 2008), 93.

4. Jews identify primarily with the Jewish community and live their public lives within it, passively participating in state activities only to the extent demanded (paying taxes, serving in the military, obeying the law).
5. Jews are alienated from their state and perhaps even from the majority populations, if not from the majority cultures, and either live their lives as much as possible apart from the state and its politics or seek to emigrate.

The Historical Evolution of Jewish Stances toward Russia and Ukraine

Jews were barred from the Russian Empire until the end of the eighteenth century when the tsars' imperial appetite swallowed much of Poland and with it a huge Jewish population.[4] To control the "damage" caused by the sudden influx of Jews, the Pale of Settlement was established, confining Jews to the fifteen westernmost provinces of the empire. Its boundaries were firmly fixed in 1835 in a statute that imposed other disabilities on Jews. The Pale was not abolished until 1915 – and then only because during World War I the Russian government feared that Jews would collaborate with the invading central powers. Jews were generally forbidden to own and work the land in a country where four of every five inhabitants earned their living from agriculture. The Russian government periodically expelled Jews from the villages and from the two capitals of St. Petersburg and Moscow, and restricted their access to higher education and the professions by the *numerus clausus*. Under Tsar Nikolai I (1825–55) Jewish boys were subject to a twenty-five-year term of military service preceded by as much as a decade of pre-military training in special districts, or cantons, a system designed to wean them away from Judaism and the Jewish community.[5] In addition, Jews were subject to pogroms that the regime generally tolerated, if not initiated.[6]

---

[4] See John Klier, *Russia Gathers Her Jews: The Origins of the Jewish Question in Russia, 1772–1825* (DeKalb, IL: Northern Illinois University Press, 1985) and Heinz-Dietrich Lowe, *The Tsars and the Jews: Reform, Reaction and Anti-Semitism in Imperial Russia, 1772–1917* (Chur: Harwood, 1993).

[5] See, among others, Klier, *Imperial Russia's Jewish Question 1855–1881* (Cambridge: Cambridge University Press, 1995); Michael Stanislawski, *Tsar Nicholas I and the Jews: The Transformation of Jewish Society in Russia, 1825–1855* (Philadelphia: Jewish Publication Society of America, 1983); and Salo Baron, *The Russian Jew under Tsar and Soviets* (New York: Macmillan, 1964). Older works include Louis Greenberg, *The Jews in Russia: The Struggle for Emancipation*. 2 vols. (New Haven: Yale University Press, 1944–51) and Simon Dubnow, *History of the Jews in Russia and Poland*, 3 vols. (Philadelphia: Jewish Publication Society, 1916–20). Some contemporary researchers have taken a more benign view of tsarist policies. See, for example, Yohanan Petrovsky-Shtern, *Jews in the Russian Army, 1827–1917* (New York: Cambridge University Press, 2009) and Eugene Avrutin, *Jews and the Imperial State: Identification Politics in Tsarist Russia* (Ithaca: Cornell University Press, 2010). They argue that whatever the intent of the tsars, some of their policies resulted in the integration of Jews into Russian society.

[6] See I. Michael Aronson, *Troubled Waters: The Origins of the 1881 Anti-Jewish Pogroms in Russia* (Pittsburgh: University of Pittsburgh Press, 1990); John Klier and Shlomo Lambrozo, eds., *Pogroms: Anti-Jewish Violence in Modern Russian History* (Cambridge: Cambridge University Press, 1991); Stephen Berke, *Year of Crisis, Year of Hope* (Westport, CT: Greenwood

Jews reacted to these policies by "exit voice, and loyalty," to use Albert Hirschman's terms. Throughout the nineteenth century Jews migrated to other parts of Europe, to the Americas, and elsewhere, as discussed in Chapter 3. From 1881 to 1912, 1,889,000 Russian Jews left their homeland.[7] Russian Jews made up more than 70 percent of the Jewish immigrants to the United States in that period. In 1881–1910, Jews made up 48.3 percent of all immigrants coming from Russia to the United States.[8]

The "voice" option was exercised by people who sought to reform or revolutionize Russia. Some *maskilim* and the wealthy intelligentsia of St. Petersburg joined Russian liberals and reformers in attempts to lead the Russian system toward constitutional monarchy or democracy.[9] Others judged that reform was hopeless or even undesirable and rebelled against the system. Many were interested primarily in curing all of Russia's ills, not those of the Jews specifically, although the Bund and other movements explicitly addressed Jewish problems and offered radical solutions to them.[10]

"Loyalty" is perhaps a not entirely accurate label for the largest group of Jews, the apolitical people who neither opposed nor attempted to change the tsarist regime but sought to live within the cocoons of Jewish communities, limiting their contacts with the regime and the larger society to a minimum.

All segments of Jewish society welcomed the fall of tsarism in February–March 1917, but few sympathized with the more radical elements who seized power in October–November of that year.[11] A census taken of the Bolshevik party membership in 1922 revealed that fewer than a thousand Jewish members

---

Press, 1985); and Elias Tsherikover, *Di ukrainer pogromen in yor 1919* (New York: YIVO Institute, 1956) and his *Antisemitizm un pogromen in ukraine 1917–1918* (Berlin: Mizrekh-Yidishn historishn arkhiv, 1923).

[7] On modern Jewish migration, see Mark Wischnitzer, *To Dwell in Safety* (Philadelphia: Jewish Publication Society, 1948) and Ronald Sanders, *Shores of Refuge* (New York: Henry Holt, 1988).

[8] D. S. Pasmanik, *Sud'by evreiskago naroda* (Moscow: Safrut, 1917), 145. See also Samuel Joseph, *Jewish Immigration to the United States* (New York: Columbia University Studies in History, Economics and Public Law, 1914) Vol. LIX, No. 4, 101.

[9] See Christoph Gassenschmidt, *Jewish Liberal Politics in Tsarist Russia 1900–14* (Houndmills: Macmillan 1995) and Benjamin Nathans, *Beyond the Pale: The Jewish Encounter with Late Imperial Russia* (Los Angeles: University of California Press, 2002).

[10] See, *inter alia*, Eli Lederhandler, *The Road to Modern Jewish Politics* (Oxford: Oxford University Press, 1991); Jonathan Frankel, *Prophecy and Politics: Socialism, Nationalism and the Russian Jews, 1862–1917* (Cambridge: Cambridge University Press, 1981); Henry Jack Tobias, *The Jewish Bund in Russia from its Origins to 1905* (Stanford: Stanford University Press, 1972); Erich Haberer, *Jews and Revolution in Nineteenth Century Russia* (Cambridge: Cambridge University Press, 1995); and Yitzhak Maor, *She'elat hayehudim batenuah haliberalit vehamehapchanit berusiya* (Jerusalem: Mosad Bialik, 1964).

[11] Oleg Budnitskii has shown that some Jews sympathized with the Whites during the Russian Civil War and that the picture of Jews siding decisively with the Bolsheviks is overdrawn. See *Rossiiskie evrei mezhdu krasnymi i belymi, 1917–1920* (Moscow: Rosspen, 2005).

had joined the party before 1917.[12] The myth of Judaeo-Bolshevism, used later with devastating consequences in Poland, Ukraine, and, especially, Germany, was based on the presence of people of Jewish origins in the higher echelons of the Bolshevik regime and on the post-1918 rush by Jews into governmental posts abandoned by tsarist officialdom. Aided by the British government's Balfour Declaration in November 1917, which promised support for a "Jewish national homeland," the Zionists emerged as the most popular Jewish party, but the Bolsheviks suppressed their movement. By 1921, the Bund and other Jewish socialist parties had split into pro- and anti-Bolshevik factions, their leftist factions absorbed as individuals by the Communist/Bolshevik Party and the others suppressed.[13]

Many Jews became supporters of the Soviet government, if not of the Communist Party, "*lo meahavat Mordechai elah misin'at Haman*," not because they were ideologically convinced Marxist-Leninists but because the anti-Semitism of the White opponents of Bolshevism and of Ukrainian nationalists left them no domestic political alternative. Moreover, the Soviet regime, like the Provisional Government before it, abandoned all the tsarist restrictions on Jews and other second-class citizens. Jews seized new opportunities in higher education, the military and police, government, industry, and even agriculture. Many were bankrupted by the economic policies of War Communism, because they were petty traders, small merchants, and other "capitalists," but they gained some respite during the New Economic Policy that lasted until 1928.

Often, political cleavages were congruent with generational lines. Many of the older generation remained in the *shtetlakh*, clinging to their traditional way of life. They had no sympathy for the godless Bolsheviks, but large numbers of young people were drawn to the cities and to industry. As they moved, they changed their clothes, foods, language, and values. They became increasingly acculturated to Russian and, to a lesser extent, Ukrainian culture. Only the introduction of internal passports in 1931–32, in which one's nationality was registered, prevented mass assimilation (loss of identity).

In the 1920s – the era of *korenizatsiia* or "rooting" of Bolshevism among non-Russians – the Jewish Sections of the Communist Party (*Evsektsii*) tried to create a Soviet secular Yiddish culture to replace traditional Jewish and Zionist culture. After 1930, when the *Evsektsii* were abolished, the state withdrew its support from this effort. In any case, this effort had fallen between two stools. Those who embraced Soviet ideals and culture saw no need to do it in Yiddish, when Russian was clearly the dominant culture and the vehicle to success. Traditionalists or Zionists regarded the militantly antireligious, anti-Hebrew, and anti-Zionist "Evseks" as traitors and their culture as ersatz. Other Jewish and non-Jewish communists looked askance at the Evseks as "latecomers to

---

[12] For details, see Zvi Gitelman, *Jewish Nationality and Soviet Politics* (Princeton: Princeton University Press, 1972).

[13] The one very minor exception was the Jewish Communist Party – Poalei Zion – which survived until 1928.

the Revolution," because most had been members of non-Bolshevik Jewish parties before 1919. By the 1930s many of them were regarded as enemies of the people – and paid the price.

In that decade the gargantuan reconstruction of the economy commanded by Stalin generated enormous enthusiasm, especially among younger people. Perhaps this support made the purges politically possible. In the course of the first and second Five-Year Plans, urbanization and movement from the former Pale areas to the Russian republic accelerated. *Korenizatsiia*, encouraging the development of non-Russian cultures, was replaced by "proletarian internationalism," which in practice meant Russianization. Coming into close contact with non-Jews and having abandoned traditional strictures, an unprecedented proportion of Jews married non-Jews. The abandonment of religion and Yiddish, the disappearance of Jewish parties and ideologies, and the suppression of Hebrew put Jews firmly on the Soviet road to *sliianie*, the ultimate fusion of nationalities and the disappearance of ethnicity. Jews' enthusiasm for the Soviet enterprise probably peaked during this period and in the first years of World War II.

This enthusiasm was dampened in the 1940s by the grassroots anti-Semitism that appeared not only in the German-occupied territories but also in those to which Jews had been evacuated. Then the government, which had once combated anti-Semitism, began to shift its policy. By 1944 Jews in military service noticed that they were not receiving the awards and promotions given their non-Jewish comrades-in-arms.[14] As they liberated the occupied territories, Jewish soldiers were appalled to discover the extent of collaboration with the Nazis, especially in Ukraine and the Baltic states. Soviet authorities were embarrassed by this collaboration and were intent on punishing the collaborators. Already in 1943, Soviet authorities tried to disguise the fact that Jews were singled out by the Nazis for mass murder.[15]

Disillusionment accelerated immediately after the war when returning Jews, servicemen and evacuees, confronted hostile occupants of their former apartments and jobs and were denied admission to institutions of higher education. The process was completed by the dissolution of the Jewish Anti-Fascist Committee; closure of all Yiddish cultural institutions in 1948 and the arrest of leading Jewish cultural and political figures; the "anti-cosmopolitan" campaign of 1949 and the purge of Jews from high- and middle-level positions in all walks of life; the execution of nearly two dozen Jewish cultural leaders in 1952; and the "discovery" of the "Doctors' Plot" in early 1953. From that

---

[14] Based on reading several hundred oral histories of Soviet Jewish war veterans that I have been collecting in the United States, Russia, and Israel.
[15] A vivid example can be found in John Garrard and Carol Garrard, *The Bones of Berdichev: The Life and Fate of Vasily Grossman* (New York: Free Press, 1996), 182. See also Zvi Gitelman, ed., *Bitter Legacy: Confronting the Holocaust in the Soviet Union* (Bloomington: Indiana University Press, 1997).

point, Jews were regarded again as lesser quality citizens at best and pariahs or traitors at worst. They reciprocated by abandoning the enthusiasm many once had for the regime and the system.

Nikita Khrushchev's denunciation of Stalin at the Twentieth Party Congress in February 1956 notably did not include a critique of his predecessor's anti-Semitic policies. Yiddish culture was not revived, although a few symbolic gestures were made in this direction, largely to ward off foreign criticism.[16] The removal of Lazar Kaganovich from the Politburo in 1957 marked the end of a significant Jewish presence in the highest organs of the party.[17] Individual Jews could attain high positions and state awards in some fields, especially science, medicine, and technology, but "sensitive" areas such as the military, politics, the police, foreign service, and journalism were increasingly closed to them.

Little wonder that in the 1960s and 1970s Jews were disproportionately represented in the dissident movement and that some began to advocate emigration from the USSR. During the 1980s some were enthusiastic about Mikhail Gorbachev's innovative policies of glasnost and perestroika and attempted to use them to revive organized, public Jewish life. But by the end of the Soviet period most Jews had become alienated from politics, if not from the country and its system. Ironically, it was the weakening and ultimate collapse of the system that caused a million Jews to emigrate between 1989 and 1998. As the reins of government loosened in the late 1980s, anti-Semitism raised its head, the price paid for the freer expression allowed by glasnost; perestroika allowed the formation of anti-Semitic movements. Jews feared anarchy of the sort that had permitted pogroms in 1918–21 and in 1941 in the Baltic and West Ukraine, so many emigrated. Those who remained watched warily in 1991 as the former Soviet republics became independent. Would independence lead to greater freedom or more open anti-Semitism? Would Jews become full-fledged citizens of the new states, or would they continue to be regarded as outsiders, perhaps now on the basis of their Russian culture, which was alien in all but Russia itself and Belarus?

Continuing a trend begun about 1988 in the Soviet Union, local and national Jewish organizations, most of them "cultural associations," began to form in the newly independent states. In the early 1990s it appeared that Jews would be able not only to live as equals in the successor states but also to build their own communities. How would Jews act politically in the new conditions, and how would their communities relate to the larger states?

---

[16] Beginning in 1959, a few Yiddish books were published each year. In 1961 the Yiddish journal *Sovetish haimland* began to appear, at first in an edition of 25,000. Not a single Yiddish school was reopened and only amateur theaters were permitted. A prayer book was published in an edition of 3,000, but restrictions on religious practice remained largely in place.

[17] Kaganovich was removed not because he was Jewish but because he disagreed with Khrushchev's policies, especially de-stalinization.

Jewish Public Life in Russia and Ukraine

There have been three radical and positive changes for Jews in all the successor states of the Soviet Union: none of the fifteen states pursues anti-Semitic policies; emigration is unfettered; and Jews are free and even encouraged to reconstruct communal, cultural, and religious institutions. Of course, mass emigration vitiates attempts to reconstruct Jewish life, especially because the young and most Jewishly conscious are overrepresented in the emigration. Nevertheless, Jewish communal life has been reborn in Russia and Ukraine. In the 1990s, there were more than two dozen all-day Jewish schools, several dozen Jewish newspapers, and hundreds of local Jewish organizations in the two states, none of which existed before 1988. At the height of perestroika, in the spring of 1989, 185 representatives of 48 cultural organizations in 27 locales met and decided to form a national Jewish umbrella organization that could represent the Jews of the USSR to the government (see Chapter 7). By December, about 750 delegates of some 250 Jewish cultural associations met in a festive and exciting atmosphere in Moscow and established the Va'ad, or Confederation of Jewish Communities and Organizations.[18] The second congress of the Va'ad in January 1991 saw close to 400 organizations, from 86 localities, represented. However, the breakup of the Soviet Union eleven months later led to the splintering of the Va'ad. Just as the Baltic republics led the break-away movement from the USSR, so did the Baltic Jewish organizations hasten to dissociate themselves from the Moscow-based Va'ad. Thereafter, in most of the successor states national organizations were formed, though in some republics there were none and, in others, several.

As emigration and economic decline continued, organizations shifted their attention somewhat from politics and education to social welfare. According to Joseph Zissels, president of the Va'ad of Ukraine, at the end of the 1990s in that country there were 16 day schools, around 80 Sunday schools, 11 kindergartens, several yeshivas, around 150 *ulpanim* (Hebrew study courses), a Jewish university, and two colleges with 20,000 participants.[19] There were about seventy Orthodox and fifteen Reform communities served by eighteen Orthodox rabbis. Four "umbrella" organizations claimed to unite around 300 local Jewish organizations. According to a Jewish activist in Ukraine, in the mid-to-late 1990s the grassroots Jewish organizations became overshadowed by umbrella organizations financed by Ukrainian Jewish businessmen: "As a result, a good part of what remained of Jewish community life... depended completely on the financing of a few individuals. In turn, their positions in... Jewish organizations provided these individuals with increased civic status and

---

[18] The name echoes the *Va'ad Arba Aratsot*, Council of Four Lands, the regional governing body of Russian-Polish-Lithuanian Jewry of the sixteenth to eighteenth centuries.
[19] "The Jewish Community of Ukraine: Its Status and Perspectives," in Miriam Weiner, ed., *Jewish Roots in Ukraine and Moldova* (New York: YIVO Institute and Routes to Roots Foundation, 1999), 75.

political visibility."[20] An example is the "All-Ukrainian Jewish Congress, with the Ukrainian-Israeli businessman Vadim Rabinovich as its president," which "originally came from the common initiative of a group of Jewish businessmen and the Kiev Center of the Tse'irei-Habad movement."[21]

Jewish communal life was heavily subsidized by foreign Jewish organizations. The most active were the American Jewish Joint Distribution Committee (the Joint), the Israeli *Lishkat hakesher* (Liaison Office) and Jewish Agency (*Sochnut*), and religious movements: the Chabad and Karlin-Stolin Hasidic movements and the World Union for Progressive Judaism. Because the Israelis' goal was to encourage immigration to Israel, they were not initially interested in developing Jewish communal life in the FSU except insofar as it promoted aliyah. However, by the twenty-first century, the *Sochnut* realized that the reservoir of potential immigrants had been largely drained, and it became more accommodating of communal rebuilding efforts.[22] None of the other organizations opposed aliyah or emigration to the United States. They saw their roles as serving the needs of the remaining population or, in the case of the religious organizations, creating such needs if they did not exist. The activities of these organizations were and are greatly appreciated, but raised issues of paternalism. Some local activists and organizations became identified as "clients" of one foreign agency or another. However, as Russian and Ukrainian Jews began to amass wealth, local Jews established and funded Jewish communal organizations. In January 1996 the Russian Jewish Congress (RJC) was established by wealthy Jewish bankers and businessmen to fund educational, welfare, and anti-defamation activities.

To what extent did Jews identify with or participate in the emergent Jewish communities? Were they the focus of their political and social activities and aspirations? Because the Jewish population changed so rapidly and because communal activism was often a prelude to emigration, the answers to these questions change constantly. Part of our field research aimed to discover how Jews relate to the communal institutions and to the two states. We found that about one of every three respondents had participated either actively or passively in Jewish communal activities and events during the previous year. The first survey was taken in a period of unprecedented politicization, when the ethnicity of Russian and Ukrainian Jews could be freely expressed. This resulted

---

[20] Aleksandr Burakovskiy, "Key Characteristics and Transformation of Jewish-Ukrainian Relations during the Period of Ukraine's Independence: 1991–2008," *Nationalism and Ethnic Politics* 15 (2009), 115.

[21] Vladimir (Ze'ev) Khanin, "Institutionalization of the Post-Communist Jewish Movement: Organizational Structures, Ruling Elites, and Political Conflicts," *Jewish Political Studies Review* 14, 1–2 (Spring 2002), 7. Rabinovich has been consistently denied an entry visa to the United States because of his alleged ties to criminal organizations in Ukraine.

[22] By 2010, the head of the Jewish Agency, Soviet-born Natan Sharansky, publicly announced that its goal should be redefined as building Jewish identity and commitment in the diaspora. Gal Beckerman and Jane Eisner, "A Funding Clash Forces Choices: Food or Identity?" *Forward*, May 7, 2010, 1.

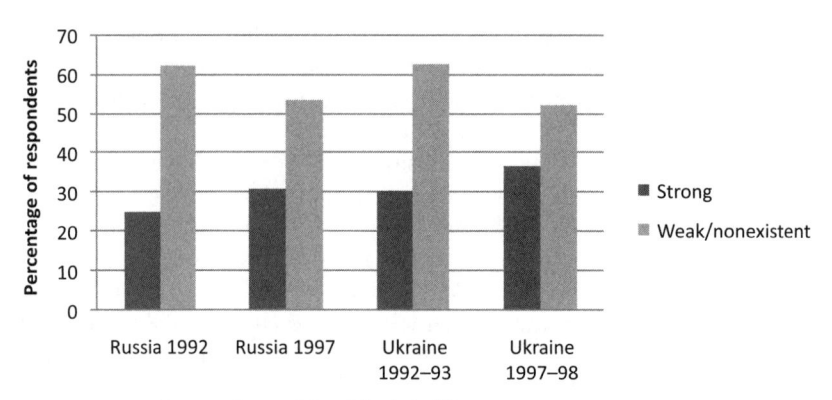

FIGURE 11.1. Perceptions of Jewish civic life.

in the astonishingly rapid formation of Jewish communal and cultural organizations, some with a political agenda. However, over the five years between the surveys, interest in politics declined significantly in both Russia and Ukraine, as manifested in lower voter turnouts in successive parliamentary and presidential elections. In an atmosphere of growing cynicism and disillusion with politics, one might have expected either that the interest of the average Jew in national organizations would have waned or that, as disillusion with *national* politics grew, people would turn their attention to more *local or parochial* concerns. If people regarded national politics as corrupt and hopeless, they might seek outlets in more modest arenas such as ethnic politics and activities. This shift seemed to occur, although to a very modest degree. In Ukraine and in Russia respondents saw Jewish national life as somewhat more active in 1997 than in 1992 (see Figure 11.1).

As ethnicity became more salient in post-Soviet life – the wars in Chechnya, assertiveness by Tatars, and more militant Russian nationalism ensured that – and as interest in politics declined, ethnic organizations may have become more attractive and acquired social importance. Moreover, as their welfare services became widely known, the organizations attracted more people. Most respondents (two-thirds in Russia and three-quarters in Ukraine) were aware of the existence of at least one Jewish organization. This awareness rose modestly in the five-year interval. We found no differences between men and women in their awareness of Jewish organizations nor were there differences by education. The key explanatory variable is age. In Russia those completely unaware of Jewish organizations were concentrated in the older age group.

We found significant differences among the cities in the proportion of activists in their Jewish populations. As we saw in Chapter 7, the smaller the city and its Jewish population, the higher the proportion of activists. One might observe that in smaller communities there are greater opportunities for office holding. Yet, one should not dismiss the possibility that there is a greater sense of efficacy in smaller populations, as the political science literature suggests.[23] Once again we find gender differences inconsequential and age a powerful explanatory variable. Significantly, the youngest cohort in Russia had the largest proportion of activists (17.3%). The relation between age and Jewish activism in Ukraine only partially resembled that in Russia. In the youngest group, one-third of whom were students, the level of activism (16.4%) was only about 1.2 times higher than among all Ukrainian Jews. As in Russia, activism declined sharply in the next cohort – it was three times less frequent among the 30–39 year olds than among the younger group. However, in contrast to Russia, in the rest of the age categories the level of activism intensified. The two oldest groups displayed more activism than the youngest cohort. Among the oldest, every fourth person was an activist, perhaps because many retirees were among them. Contrary to what one might suppose, we discovered that in both countries *the oldest and youngest people are the most active in Jewish public life.* The middle generations seem to be preoccupied with earning a living, raising families, and caring for elderly parents. It may also be that the oldest cohort, socialized in the 1930s and the early 1940s, when there was little stigma attached to Jewishness, found it easier to be active than the middle generations, socialized in the 1950s, 60s, and 70s when Jews were marginalized. The reforms of the 1980s and the collapse of the USSR removed the stigma from Jewishness, making it easier for young people to identify as Jews.

"Pure Jews" (those with two Jewish parents) in both Russia and Ukraine were more active in Jewish public life than part-Jews. The ethnicity of one's spouse also influenced activism. The intermarried, especially those whose spouses had no Jewish background at all, were less active than those married to Jews. Similarly, those whose self-described national consciousness or identity is "primarily Jewish" were more likely to be active in Jewish life than those who perceived their identity as being "both Jewish and not Jewish," and they were twice as active as those who felt themselves to be predominantly not Jewish. Among Ukrainian Jews these differences were nearly twice as great.

Finally, there is a clear connection between Jewish activism and plans for emigration. Here lies the great paradox of post-Soviet Jewry, discussed in Chapter 7: *the more definitely one intends to emigrate, the higher one's level of local Jewish activism.* Thus, in Russia the proportion of activists among those resolutely decided on emigration "in the near future" was more than twice as great as among those who had absolutely no intention of leaving.

---

[23] Some of the literature on participation is Lester Milbrath, *Political Participation* (Chicago: Rand McNally, 1965); Sidney Verba and Norman Nie, *Participation in America* (New York: Harper and Row, 1972); Verba, Nie and Jae-On Kim, *The Modes of Democratic Participation: A Cross-National Comparison*, Vol. 2 (Beverly Hills: Sage Comparative Politics Series, 1971); and Robert Putnam, *Making Democracy Work: Civic Traditions in Modern Italy* (Princeton: Princeton University Press, 1993).

The passive participants, those who attend Jewish events occasionally, comprised about 30 percent of our sample in both years of the survey. The proportion of "clients," people who depend on Jewish organizations for food, supplements to their pension, and other assistance, was only between one-fifth and one-sixth, but it grew substantially over the five years.

Do these levels of knowledge and participation point to an active, viable national Jewish community in Russia and Ukraine? The answer is "not yet." There are well-established local communities, but it seems that the future of public Jewish life in Russia and Ukraine still hangs in the balance. It will take perhaps a decade or more to tell whether sustainable, self-perpetuating local and national Jewish communities will emerge or whether in these countries there will be only small cohesive publics functioning as organized communities. In any case, it is clear that Jewish communities are not powerful or attractive enough to be the focus of loyalty and activity for most Jews. The communities cannot be regarded as alternatives to the states, able to divert the energies, talents, resources, and loyalties of Jews away from national structures.

There is a parallel between the slow development of Jewish communities and the formation of political parties in postcommunist states such as Poland, Bulgaria, and Romania. Political parties there have not developed strong social bases and loyal constituencies, they are perceived as elite-dominated, and there has been little turnover among party leaders. Similarly, Jewish communal organizations have not engendered strong loyalties, nor has the first generation of leadership yielded to a new one.

Jews as Political Actors in Russia and Ukraine

Because of their small numbers – about 259,000 in the Russian Federation and 103,700 in Ukraine according to post-Soviet censuses – Jews cannot form effective voting blocs. Their high levels of urbanization and education, general success in the post-Soviet economies, and support from abroad give them potential influence, if not power, but most Jews are not interested in constituting themselves as a political entity. No Jewish parties have emerged since 1991, in contrast to the flowering of such groups before, during, and shortly after the Russian Revolution of 1917. No Jewish community in the FSU has "formed a 'sectarian' political structure in order to get official recognition in government."[24] Jewish organizational leaders seem to have seen national and Jewish politics as mutually exclusive.

Our respondents clearly indicated a preference to be seen publicly as citizens of their states rather than as ethnic Jews. Interviewed in 1997, just before the Russian Federation abolished the fifth line on the internal passport identifying ethnicity, many respondents disapproved of having nationality inscribed in their passports. Only 43 percent of respondents in Russia said they would

---

[24] Khanin, "Institutionalization," 9.

voluntarily enter "Jew" into their passports were they to have a choice. Roughly half preferred to have no nationality registration at all.

Jews' desire to avoid ethnic registration and identification contrasts with the resistance in some ethnic republics of the Russian Federation to the elimination of the "fifth line." The political and intellectual elites of these republics opposed its elimination and were able to mobilize significant public support. They argued that their peoples were vulnerable to assimilation into the Russian people. The titular ethnicity of the republic is smaller than the Russian population in at least twelve of the twenty-one ethnically titled federal units, and they reasoned that official registration would help maintain ethnic consciousness and slow the tide of Russianization.[25] It is quite understandable how the different historical experiences of Jews from those of Tatars, Bashkirs, Tuvins, Yakuts, and others in their territorial homelands yielded such a different position. The difference between Jews and others is best explained by the fact that all these other nationalities were politically subordinated to the dominant Russians in the Soviet period, and peoples such as Chechens and Balkars suffered at least as much as Jews; having territorial bases recognized as federal units allows them to promote "their own" ahead of Russians and others to positions of influence and power. In contrast, Jews lacked an historical homeland in Imperial Russia and the USSR, Birobidzhan notwithstanding.

Political Involvement of Russian Jews

How do Jews in Russia and Ukraine relate as individual citizens to their respective states? Valeriy Tishkov, the Russian minister for nationalities under President Boris Yeltsin, cautions that it would be unreasonable to expect citizens of the states that emerged from the shattered Soviet Union to develop deep attachments to those states in the first few years after independence. This is especially true of "nontitular" groups, such as Russians in the Baltic states, who went from being part of a dominant nationality to a disadvantaged minority in states determined to distance themselves from everything Russian. In Russia itself, the notion of a civic "Rossiiskii" nation supplanting or even complementing an ethnic "Russkii" nation has not really taken hold.[26]

After their experience with the Soviet, Russian-dominated state in the 70 years before it fell apart, how strong is Jews' attachment to its successor, the Russian Federation? A striking novelty of post-Soviet Russian politics was the sudden, meteoric rise of individual Jews to positions of power. After about a half-century with no Jews in such positions, President Boris Yeltsin's governments included Jews or half-Jews such as Boris Nemtsov, deputy prime minister; Alexander Livshitz, minister of finance and deputy prime minister; Yakov

---

[25] Sven Gunnar Simonsen, "Between Minority Rights and Civil Liberties: Russia's Discourse over 'Nationality' Registration and the Internal Passport," *Nationalities Papers* 33, 2 (June 2005), 214–18.

[26] Valeriy Tishkov, *Rekviem po etnosu* (Moscow: Nauka, 2003), 166–67.

Urinson, minister for economics; and Sergei Kirienko, prime minister before the economic crash of August 17, 1998. Several Jewish or part-Jewish deputies also served in the Duma or parliament. Interestingly, all the Jewish ministers were replaced by non-Jews when Yeltsin replaced Kirienko with Evgenii Primakov, who is reported to be of Jewish origin. It is not clear whether they lost their positions because they were prominently identified with the market economy and privatization, because Yeltsin was attempting to form a more popular government and the presence of so many Jews had been criticized by communists and nationalists, or whether both motivations coincided.

The sudden rise of so many Jews to high places may have several explanations: (1) they were untainted by association with the Soviet regime; (2) as we see later, Jews are completely identified with the liberal reformer/free-market end of the political spectrum and are highly educated, so a disproportionate number of them would likely be among activists and "technocrats"; (3) perhaps Jews were seizing opportunities that had been denied them in the Soviet regime, ironically just as they had done after the fall of the tsarist regime; or (4) several of the prominent Jewish politicians may have had personal connections to Yeltsin, to each other, and to prominent Jewish businessmen who were major supporters of Yeltsin. Whatever the explanation may be, the Jews are gone in the Putin and Putin-Medvedev administrations.

A variety of factors work against the political mobilization of Jews, including their small numbers, the very high proportion of Jewish elderly, and their fear of presenting too high a political profile. In addition, lobbies are not very effective in the Duma because power rests so heavily in the presidency, and Jews have little leverage because they are strongly identified with one end of the political spectrum: reformers and democrats can take them for granted, and conservatives would not take them seriously as potential supporters. Interest groups have been generally weak in Russia and are highly fractionated, poorly organized, and not very skilled in political maneuvering.[27]

Despite these obstacles there have been some attempts at aggregating and representing Jewish interests. In 1995 a coalition was formed of national minorities in Russia. Known as KNOR (*Kongress natsional'nykh ob'edinenii Rossii*), it included representatives from Jewish, Korean, Polish, Ukrainian, and other ethnic organizations and ran in the Duma elections in association with the Russia's Choice (*Vybor Rossii*) party. That party held 16 percent of Duma seats after the 1993 elections, but in the 1995 elections failed to cross the 5 percent threshold to get into the Duma.[28] Still, in 1996 the Duma passed a law whereby the state recognized representative bodies of national minorities and granted them national-cultural autonomy. The Jewish representative body is ENKA (*Evreiskaya natsional'no-kulturnaya avtonomiya*) and includes representatives of the Va'ad, Russian Jewish Congress, and KEROR, an

---

[27] See, for example, Stephen Crowley, *Hot Coal, Cold Steel: Russian and Ukrainian Workers from the End of the Soviet Union to the Post-Communist Transformations* (Ann Arbor: University of Michigan Press, 1997).
[28] Thomas Remington, *Politics in Russia* (New York: Longman, 1999), 153, 162.

TABLE 11.1. *Russian Jewish Voter Intentions vs. National Voter Intentions** *(percent)*

Party	Jews 1997	VTsIOM General Survey 1998*
Communists	1.1	23
Our Home is Russia	9.0	2
Liberal Democrats**	0	6
Russia's Democratic Choice	30.9	?+
Yabloko***	33.5	14
National Republicans	1.9	?
Other parties	1.8	5
For no party	16.6	40
Don't know	5.2	11
N	1,317	1,600

* Conducted by VTsIOM (All-Russian Center for Research on Public Opinion), January 1998, n=1,600. Results published in *VTsIOMetr*, 1998, vyp. 1, p. 3.
** Party led by Vladimir Volfovich Zhirinovsky, who, despite his Jewish father, is a radical Russian nationalist and was widely perceived as anti-Semitic.
*** Party led by the late Yegor Gaidar, in charge of Yeltsin's first privatization program and widely blamed for the dislocations it caused.
+ The VTsIOM survey uses the category "democrats," which could apply to several parties and individuals.

association of Orthodox and Reform religious communities. However, the government has provided no funding for national-cultural autonomy, and ENKA seems to be dormant.[29]

What were the political preferences and outlooks of ordinary Jews in the immediate post-Soviet decade? In 1997/98 we asked respondents for whom they would vote in parliamentary elections. It is instructive to compare their preferences to a January 1998 national survey of voters in the Russian Federation, conducted by the All-Russian Center for Research on Public Opinion (see Table 11.1).

The VTsIOM survey results show that the political profile of the Jewish respondents was dramatically different from that of Russians overall and from the national vote in parliamentary elections. In the 1999 election, the Communist Party got more votes among the general public and more seats in the Duma than any other party, although according to our survey only 1 percent of the Jewish sample would have voted for them. Among 16–29 year old Jews, *not a single one* would have voted for the Communists. Of course, one could hardly expect much Jewish support for the Communist Party, not only because of its association with the Soviet era but also because its constituency is the least educated and the elderly. In contrast, the two reformist or liberal parties, Yabloko (Apple) and Russia's Democratic Choice, would have gotten nearly two-thirds of the Jewish vote, but received only 14 percent of the national

[29] For some instances of ethnic political mobilization in Russia, see Elise Giuliano, *Constructing Grievance: Ethnic Nationalism in Russia's Republics* (Ithaca: Cornell University Press, 2011).

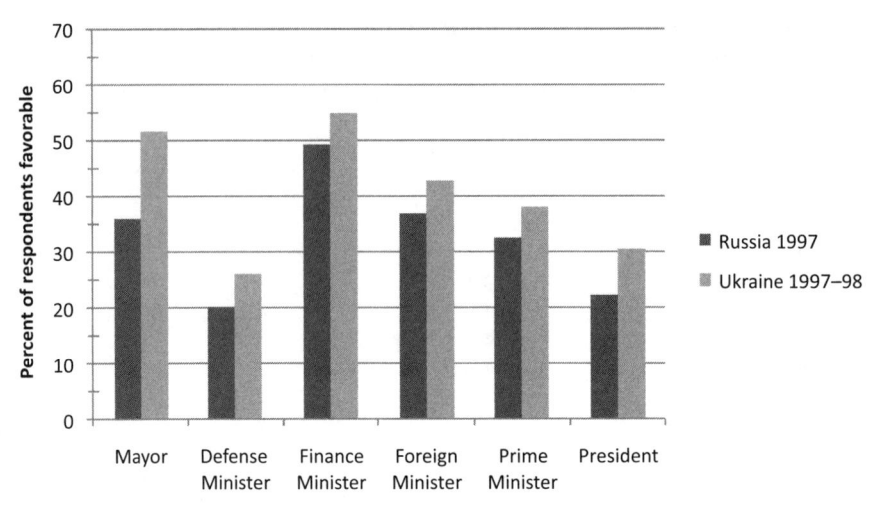

FIGURE 11.2. Jewish perceptions of a Jew holding office.

vote. Jews would not support nationalist parties because of the long-standing association between Russian nationalism and anti-Semitism.

Finally, Jews' higher level of political engagement than that of the overall population is striking. Whereas in 1998 fully 40 percent of the population said they had no preference for any party, only 17 percent of the Jews did so. In the December 1995 parliamentary elections, 35 percent of eligible voters did not show up at the polls. Jews may have a higher level of political engagement because they are completely urbanized and are mostly highly educated, traits associated with politicization, but perhaps Jews perceived greater dangers than others in remaining passive and felt they had to ensure that democratic forces were supported.

Attitudes toward Jews in Politics

Perhaps the most revealing question we posed is how respondents felt about the prospects of Jews holding high governmental positions. This uncovered deep-seated Jewish anxieties and revealed profound differences between Russian and Ukrainian Jews (see Figure 11.2).

Russian and Ukrainian Jews are more receptive to having a Jew as finance minister or foreign minister, no doubt because these are positions in which Jews have been prominent and supposedly excelled. As noted, in the Yeltsin years there were Jewish ministers with financial portfolios and even serving as prime ministers. Significantly, my Russian colleague, Valery Chervyakov, interpreted these data as showing that the tendency to keep a low profile, developed over centuries of persecution, is no longer dominant among Russian Jews because the prospect of having Jews in high places aroused no more negative than positive reactions. His view is supported by an analysis of the data by age: as one moves from the youngest to the oldest groups, there is increasing reluctance to have a Jewish president. Thus, among the youngest group, 30 percent were opposed to having a Jewish president, compared to 55 percent among the oldest respondents. The same relationship obtains in regard to all the other offices, in both Russia and Ukraine. Yet, as an American Jew, I interpret these results differently – as a reflection of Jewish insecurity, albeit diminished in the post-Soviet generation. If in a conservative society such as Great Britain, where anti-Semitism is not unknown, Malcolm Rifkind can be defense minister and David Miliband foreign secretary and his brother Edward leader of the Labour Party, and the United States can have a Cohen as secretary of defense, not to speak of Henry Kissinger and Madeleine Albright[30] as secretaries of state (foreign minister), why should Russian Jews be so hesitant about Jews filling parallel positions in their country? There are three possibilities. Either they fear that Jews in such posts would arouse anti-Semitism, or they feel that "these are not the right places" for Jews, or both. After the Bolshevik Revolution, Jews quipped, "The Trotskys made the revolution, but the Bronshtains will pay for it." (Leon Trotsky's real name was Lev Davidovich Bronshtain.) Indeed, after the fall of communism, nationalist groups blamed Jews for the Bolshevik Revolution, for murdering the tsar and his family, and for setting into motion all the horrors of communism.

It is striking that Jews expressed the greatest skepticism regarding Jews serving as the president and defense minister. There are several possible explanations for this finding. Perhaps as the central authority, the president would be the target of the greatest criticism. Or, because there has never been a Jewish head of state in Russia it is not "natural" for a Jew to be president. Third, there may be a feeling that the president should be of the titular nationality, just as first secretaries of the Communist Party in the Soviet republics were. After all, the country is the *Russian* (albeit *Rossiyskaia Federatsiya* and not *Russkaia*) Federation, and others may still perceive non-Russians as sojourners rather than as "owners." In fact, many citizens of the Russian Federation, over 80 percent of whom are ethnic Russians, believe that their leader should be a Russian. According to one poll, 45 percent were opposed to having someone who is not an ethnic Russian as president versus only 9 percent in favor.[31] National surveys in Russia make it clear that much of the population is unwilling to have Jews occupy positions of power,[32] and Jews are no doubt

---

[30] William Cohen's mother was not Jewish nor does he consider himself a Jew. The story of Madeleine Albright's discovery of her Jewish origins is well known.

[31] Thirty percent were indifferent and 16 percent could not decide. Ethnic Russians were the most opposed to a non-Russian president. About one-third of Ukrainians, Belarusians, and members of "Muslim" nationalities living in the Russian Federation favor a non-Russian president, but 24 percent of Ukrainians and Belarusians and 8 percent of Muslims oppose one. These data were supplied to Valery Chervyakov by Franz Sheregi of the Russian Independent Institute of Social and National Problems and the Center for Social Prognosis and Marketing.

[32] Lev Gudkov reports that in a survey by VTsIOM, in its time reputed to be the most reliable polling organization in Russia, 64 percent of respondents (year not specified) said that it is

aware of this attitude and react to it by shying away from political power. In 1997, whereas only 9 percent of a national sample in Russia thought that one's nationality should be taken into account in admission to higher education, 43 percent thought that should be done when accepting people into security services, the army, and police, and 53 percent thought so regarding people who take leading positions in government.[33]

Interestingly, Turkish Jews seem to feel the same way as Russian Jews. As a small minority in a Muslim country, where they have been treated far better than in other Muslim countries, they still prefer to keep a low profile. As one Turkish Jewish immigrant in Israel put it, "Jews could become deputies, but nothing more. They also can't serve as chief [of the] general staff, and this is very understandable. Turkey's chief of general staff should be a Muslim Turk, because Turkey is a Muslim country. This is the normal way in my opinion. For example, a Muslim Arab can't become Israel's chief of general staff. I believe that the majority should rule."[34]

According to Lev Gudkov, a prominent Russian survey researcher, few citizens of the Russian Federation "would consider it desirable to prohibit or limit engagement in business inside Russia for: Muslims −4%; Jews −3%; those not of the Russian Orthodox faith −2%." However, in 1992, 29 percent supported "the need to restrict any 'non-Russians' from either access to influential positions in the government leadership or participation in the political institutions of the regime," a number that increased to 34 percent in 1997 – although in both cases, a plurality believed no such restrictions were necessary. Sixty percent supported restrictions on directors and managers of large businesses. These restrictions were not primarily focused on Jews. In a 2000 survey of 1,600 people, only 3 percent of respondents said they favored restrictions on Jews owning businesses and 8 percent supported limitations on Jews in high levels in government. In contrast, 14 and 15 percent, respectively, supported restrictions on individuals from the Caucasus. Gudkov observes,

> The fact that a candidate for Deputy (for example, to the State Duma) is not ethnically Russian would prevent 29 per cent of respondents from supporting that person, or would force them to vote against that person. This statistic, however, reflects the most general and undifferentiated ethnic prejudices: in relation to people of different ethnic or religious affiliation, such attitudes can vary significantly. Thus, 21% would vote against such a candidate only if he were Muslim; 14%, if he were Jewish; 6%, if he were an atheist.[35]

---

undesirable that the president of Russia be a Jew. Lev Gudkov, "Antisemitizm v possovetskoi Rossii," in Galina Vitkovskaya and Alexei Malashenko, eds, *Neterpimost' v Rossii* (Moscow: Carnegie Foundation, 1999), 77.

[33] Ibid., 86.

[34] Quoted in Sule Toktas, "Citizenship and Migration from Turkey to Israel: A Comparative Study on [sic] Turkish Jews in Israel," *East European Quarterly* XLI, 2 (June 2007), 137.

[35] Lev Gudkov, "Attitudes towards Jews in Post-Soviet Russia and the Problem of Anti-Semitism," paper presented at a conference honoring Prof. Mordechai Altshuler, Leonid Nevzlin Research Center for Russian and East European Jewry, Hebrew University, December 2003, 22.

Politics, Affect, Affiliation, and Alienation

TABLE 11.2. *Attitudes of Pure Jews and Part-Jews toward the Prospect of a Jewish President (percent)*

Attitude	Russia 1997		Ukraine 1997–98	
	Pure Jew	Part-Jew	Pure Jew	Part-Jew
Positive	22.1	22.8	26.9	42.0
Indifferent	20.6	43.2	24.1	31.6
Negative	51.3	29.2	44.4	22.5
Don't know	6.0	4.8	4.7	4.7
N	1,059	250	1,493	490

Gudkov therefore concludes,

> Jews have ceased to be the object of any particular aggression, hostility or fearing mass consciousness, despite all the significant mass alienation from them. For the overwhelming majority of the population, they are not perceived as a threat to basic traditional values. (The only exception is the *lumpen*ized groups of the most extreme nationalists, together with some of the intelligentsia and the self-perpetuating state bureaucracy who have developed an inferiority complex due to lack of professional competitiveness.) In this respect, far greater significance as threats to Russia's future is attributed to: Islamic extremists (39% fear them), "Caucasus" nationals (32%), "tycoons" (22%), and even to the sinister nature of "Russians themselves" (21%), as well as to Russian and non-Russian nationalists (15%).[36]

There is a significant difference between pure and part-Jews in their attitudes toward Jews holding political office. Pure Jews are about twice as disinclined as part-Jews, on average, to want to see Jews in high governmental posts. It is not that part-Jews are more inclined to want Jews in high posts, but they are more inclined to be indifferent to the possibility. This can be seen in Table 11.2, which shows results for both Russia and Ukraine.

One way to interpret this finding is that a mixed ethnic background inclines people to be less sensitive to Jewish ethnicity and its possible consequences and perhaps less concerned about ethnicity in general. Another interpretation is that people of mixed backgrounds are highly aware of ethnicity because they may frequently ask themselves what their ethnic identity "truly" is; however, they are less likely to encounter anti-Semitism because they are more likely to have non-Jewish family names, official identities, and perhaps appearances.[37]

---

[36] Ibid.
[37] My friends and colleagues, Dr. Valery Chervyakov and Professor Vladimir Shapiro, both of the Jewish Research Center, Institute of Sociology, Russian Academy of Sciences, differ on the interpretation of these findings. Chervyakov proposes the first hypothesis and Shapiro the second. In the absence of further evidence, the matter must rest here for the while.

In sum, although Russian Jews expressed some insecurity about having Jews in prominent political positions, they were politically aware, intended to participate in politics, and had a distinct – and minority – political profile. They were engaged in the political life of their country both psychologically and as holders of government positions. With the recent retreat from competitive, meaningful politics, they are probably less engaged, as is the rest of the population.

Ukrainian Jews: Apathy and Alienation

In stark contrast, even in the first decade of Ukrainian independence Ukrainian Jews placed themselves at a considerable distance from the political life of their country. Asked "if elections were held for the legislature (Supreme Rada) in the near future, for whom would you vote," 70 percent (!) said they would not vote for anyone [50%] or did not know for whom they would vote [20%], and 20 percent did not answer. Among the two youngest groups (16–39 years old), four of five would not have voted or did not respond; only one in five Russian Jews responded in this way. Among Ukrainian Jews the older one is, the more likely he or she was to express a partisan preference, although even among the most "engaged" group – those over 70 – three of five would not have voted for anyone or did not respond to the question. The same relationship between age and willingness to vote held when respondents were asked for whom they would vote as president. The incumbent, Leonid Kuchma, was supported by more people than any other politician, although only 9 percent said they would vote for him. (In 1995, 37 percent of a national sample said they felt positive about Kuchma; by 1998 only 12 percent felt this way, and only 10 percent expressed trust in him.[38]) The next closest candidates, for whom only 7 percent each of the Jewish sample would have voted, were Volodymyr Lanovyi, a liberal, reformist, market-oriented economist, and Oleksandr Moroz, head of the Socialist Party of Ukraine and speaker of parliament from 1994–98. Thus, a small minority of Ukrainian respondents favored about equally the leader of the party in power, an advocate of greater marketization, and the head of a party advocating a mixed but state-regulated economy.[39] Perhaps the more difficult economic situation in Ukraine best explains this support for economic reform: "The economic difficulties that Ukraine continues to experience ... have been felt most directly and forcefully by ordinary citizens.... According to a nationwide survey conducted at the end of 1995, people's standard of living was seen by 72 percent of respondents as Ukraine's most important problem. Almost 85 percent were dissatisfied to one degree or another with the overall situation in

---

[38] N. Panina and E. Golovakha, *Tendencies in the Development of Ukrainian Society (1994–1998): Sociological Indicators* (Kyiv: Institute of Sociology, Ukrainian Academy of Sciences, 1999), 72.

[39] Seventeen percent of all respondents would not vote in elections to the Duma. Among the two youngest cohorts the percentages are 19 and 21.

the country."⁴⁰ Moreover, Jewish attitudes were not very different from those of other Ukrainian citizens, at least before the Orange Revolution of November 2004. Between 1995 and 1998, about two-thirds of citizens said they distrusted political parties, and only small minorities said that there were political parties or movements that "deserved power."⁴¹ Political parties were the least trusted among more than twenty people and institutions that were rated.⁴² One analyst, writing in 2002, commented that for Ukrainians "the dream of a dignified democratic existence continues to be a dream deferred, reinforcing an atomized society where 89% of the population considers its government corrupt and, hence, not concerned with the well-being of the country's long-suffering people."⁴³

Between 1994 and 1998, roughly corresponding to the years of our survey, fewer than 10 percent of respondents in national surveys said they were "very interested" in politics, and 27 to 30 percent declared that they were totally uninterested (the rest were "somewhat interested").⁴⁴ Moreover, a majority of respondents each year expressed distrust in the government, and about one-third could not say whether they trusted or distrusted the government.

As in Russia, the Jewish voting profile was radically different from the general Ukrainian distribution of the vote. One main difference is that, whereas 71 percent of the Ukrainian electorate participated in the 1998 elections, about the same proportion of Jews said they would *not* vote for anyone or would not answer the question. The highest proportions saying they would vote "for no one" were in Lviv and Chernivtsi in West Ukraine. Jews in Lviv are generally Russophones and quite skittish about Ukrainian nationalism. Perhaps their lack of interest in voting reflects a more general distance from Ukrainian affairs.

The second difference between Jews and others is that the Communist Party enjoyed about five times as much support among the general public than among Jews. As in Russia, Jews expressed almost no support for the communists. Table 11.3 shows how Jews said they would vote compared to the distribution of party representation in the Supreme Rada (February 1997)⁴⁵ and in the 1998 parliamentary elections. It should be noted that we did not include in our questionnaire all parties represented in the Rada.

---

[40] Roman Solchanyk, "The Post-Soviet Transition in Ukraine: Prospects for Stability," in Taras Kuzio, ed., *Contemporary Ukraine: Dynamics of Post-Soviet Transformation* (Armonk, NY: M. E. Sharpe, 1998), 21.

[41] Based on representative samples of the adult population of Ukraine, using quota samples to ensure the proper distribution of sex, age and educational levels, with about 1,800 respondents each year. Panina and Golovakha, *Tendencies in the Development of Ukrainian Society*, 50.

[42] Ibid., 62.

[43] Ilya Prizel, ""Ukraine's Hollow Decade," *East European Politics and Societies* 16, 2 (Spring 2002), 385.

[44] Information kindly provided by Dr. Roman Solchanyk.

[45] Calculated from the number of seats held in the Rada by the parties as reported in ibid., 26.

TABLE 11.3. *Ukrainian Jewish Voter Intentions vs. National Vote Outcomes (percent)*

Party	Jews in 1997–98 Survey	1998 Rada Election Party List Results
Democrats	5.7	3.5
Communists	4.8	17.4
Interregional Reform	6.5	0.6 (Party for Regional Revival?)
Ukrainian People's Party (Rukh)	2.9	6.6
Socialists	6.4	6.0
Other parties	3.2	26.7
No party	50.1	32.9
Don't know/ no answer	19.9	N/A
N	1,984	37,540,092

Some would be surprised that Ukrainian Jews were more willing than Russian Jews to have Jews serve in high government offices, as seen in Figure 11.2. After all, the popular perception among Jews is that Ukraine has been a hotbed of anti-Semitism. If our explanation for Russian Jews' reluctance to see a Jewish president is correct, then Ukrainian Jews should be that much more fearful that such a person might be a magnet for popular anti-Semitism. What may explain the differences between Russian and Ukrainian Jews is a feeling among Jews that Ukrainians, never having had a state, are less capable of managing one than Russians or Jews. If only for the sake of managing a country properly, Jews should hold key political posts. A Jewish woman in Lviv observed, "Ukraine isn't yet mature, but is trying to be independent; it's not working out very well.... It's like a boy who wants to be an adult, plays adult games, but doesn't know how to."[46] Another woman in the same city supported Ukrainian independence, but was not sure what Ukrainians want: "They themselves don't know what they want.... What are we building? I can't say I'm for or against it. It doesn't interest me."[47]

For every single political post there is more support in Ukraine than in Russia for a Jewish incumbent. Still, even in Ukraine in only two instances did a bare majority favor a Jew holding the office. Perhaps the majority support for a Jewish mayor derives from the fact that Odessa and Vinnitsa have had Jewish mayors but no major Russian city has. We see that in both countries, in addition to the mayoral position, the finance ministry and ministry of foreign

---

[46] Interview conducted by Jeremy Shine, University of Michigan, 1997, Ukraine. "Jewish Identity, Community and Citizenship in Ukraine," unpublished paper, 17.
[47] Ibid., 17, 22. Following the 2010 elections, when the Orange Revolution was put to rest, many Ukrainians, in Ukraine and elsewhere, expressed similar opinions. See, for example, Alexander Motyl, "End of Ukraine and Future of Eurasia," *Kyiv Post*, May 7, 2010.

affairs are the offices deemed most appropriate for Jews and the presidency and defense ministry least appropriate.

Why are Jews in Ukraine so much more disaffected from politics than their co-ethnics in Russia? In addition to the fact that at the time of our surveys, the Ukrainian population in general was highly skeptical of political institutions and politics, two kinds of explanation suggest themselves. One derives from history and traditional Jewish attitudes; the other is that the economic and political situation in Ukraine disillusioned Jews about the new state. Their Ukrainian compatriots can take comfort in Ukrainian independence, but Jews have less of a stake in that and, perhaps like ethnic Russians, will formulate their relationship to Ukraine as one of exchange. Should the state fail economically, politically, or socially, Jews will remain skeptical about the worth of an independent Ukraine. As Roman Solchanyk observes, "The generally weak support for independent statehood in eastern Ukraine does not preclude a sense of Ukrainian identity... [but] is motivated primarily by social and economic factors rather than ethnic and linguistic considerations."[48] This may apply to Jews in all parts of Ukraine.

Briefly, the historical-cultural argument for Jewish indifference to Ukrainian politics is that Jews came even later than Ukrainians to seeing Ukraine as an entity distinct from Poland, the Austro-Hungarian Empire, or Russia/Soviet Union. The very term "Ukraine" was absent from the Jewish geographical imagination. It does not appear, for example, in regional styles of prayer (*nusach*) nor in the works of the Ukrainian-born Yiddish writer, Sholem Aleichem, who makes liberal use of Ukrainian characters and language but does not refer to "Ukraine" as such.[49] To the extent Ukraine was "imagined," it was associated with anti-Semitism and pogroms over a 300-year period, beginning with Bohdan Khmel'nytsky and the Haidamak uprisings in the seventeenth century and continuing through the 1880s, 1905–6, the Russian civil war of 1918–21, attacks on Jews in West Ukraine in 1939–41, and large-scale collaboration with the Nazis by Ukrainians. Whereas Jews see Khmel'nytsky in a very bad light, a national survey in Ukraine found him to be the individual people most wanted to appear on banknotes in Ukraine when a new currency was introduced in 1996.[50]

Unlike in Russia, Ukrainian Jews normally use a language other than the state language. As they have done in most areas in which multiple cultures coexisted, Jews tended to adopt the languages of the rulers of Ukraine – Polish and Russian – rather than the language and culture of the subservient people.

---

[48] Solchanyk, "The Post-Soviet Transition in Ukraine," 33.
[49] Jewish prayer books (siddurim) of the nineteenth century refer to "*minhag* [custom or style] *Poilin, Liteh ve-Raisin*" (the latter roughly today's Belarus) or "*ve-Zamut*" (a region in Lithuania), but never to "*minhag Ukraineh*."
[50] Andrew Wilson, "Elements of a Theory of Ukrainian Ethno-National Identities," *Nations and Nationalism* 8, 1 (2002), 47.

When those people then gained power, Jews paid a price. More than a century ago a journal that spoke for the Ukrainian national movement editorialized,

> The Jews have kept themselves apart while living among the South Russian [Ukrainian] population; they have nothing in common with our people, and do not take a single step toward rapprochement with them; on the contrary, they often act against the spirit and needs of our people. For a nation (*natsiia*) nothing can be more harmful than the existence in its midst of different nationalities (*narodnosti*) which keep off to one side and are apathetic to its fate or – still worse – endeavor to subjugate it to their power or influence.[51]

Jews today are a largely Russian-speaking group – only 2 percent claimed Ukrainian as their native language in the 1989 census – although many have a facility in Ukrainian. The language issue is especially sensitive because it is a crucial component of Ukrainian identity; the Ukrainian language was harshly repressed under the Poles and imperial Russians and more subtly undermined by the Soviets. Although 66 percent of inhabitants of Ukraine listed Ukrainian as their mother tongue [*ridna mova/rodnoi iazyk*] in 1989, there may be a significant difference between "mother tongue" and the language one uses most often. Surveys in Ukraine that ask about "language of convenience" or "of everyday preference" reveal that "Ukrainophone Ukrainians make up a minority of the population (approximately 40 percent), while ethnic Russians account for 20 to 21 percent [nearly all of them are Russophone] and Russophone Ukrainians a massive 33 to 34 percent."[52] In annual national surveys between 1994 and 1998, about 62 percent declared Ukrainian to be their mother tongue, but only 32 to 38 percent said they spoke only Ukrainian at home and about the same proportion reported they spoke only Russian. Nearly the same proportions said they spoke "one or two languages, depending on the circumstances."[53] Declarations of language preference "could be considered as a political position and declaring Ukrainian as native could imply support for the country or for a Ukrainian identity rather than the reality."[54]

Just because only about 2 percent of Ukrainian Jews declare Ukrainian as their mother tongue, one should not infer that Jews are hostile to the language or culture. Polese and Wylegala make a convincing case that "[l]anguage does not define the nation but attitude toward the language does.... thus the use of Odessa [Russian] instead of Odesa [Ukrainian] and Lvov [Russian] instead of Lviv [Ukrainian] is not necessarily a sign of a negative attitude towards a

---

[51] Osnova, November 11, 1861, quoted in John Klier, *Imperial Russia's Jewish Question 1855–1881* (Cambridge: Cambridge University Press, 1995) 109.
[52] Mykola Riabchouk, "Civil Society and Nation Building in Ukraine," in Kuzio, *Contemporary Ukraine*, 89. Riabchouk points out that "language of everyday preference" may also lead to underreporting of Ukrainian as a language used because of the greater social prestige of Russian in public discourse.
[53] Panina and Golovakha, *Tendencies in the Development of Ukrainian Society*, 89.
[54] Abel Polese and Anna Wylegala. "Odessa and Lvov or Odesa and Lviv: How Important is a Letter? Reflections on the 'Other' in Two Ukrainian Cities," *Nationalities Papers* 36, 5 (November 2008), 790. They cite works by Dominique Arel and O. Shevel.

Ukrainian identity."[55] In any case, Ukraine launched a policy of Ukrainization that is regarded skeptically, if not with hostility, by some Jews. In the 1990s, majorities of those surveyed expressed the opinion that Russian should be an official language of Ukraine.[56]

Rebecca Golbert, who studied Ukrainian Jewish youth, asked them, "How do Jews fit into the Ukrainian nation-building project? She concludes that "Jewish linguistic behaviors reflect strategies of social and cultural accommodation and survival, not linguistic and cultural affinity with the Ukrainian nation and national culture."[57] Her respondents told Golbert that they would not vote in the 1998 parliamentary elections and when Ukrainian Independence Day was mentioned, it was "an occasion to unleash a flow of criticism against the state, its political and economic deficiencies, and levels of corruption."[58] Yet, Golbert argues, these same people "feel intimately tied to Ukrainian soil, the entity Ukraine, its mixed population, its local and regional entities and the local fabric of Ukrainian Jewish memory."[59] She sees a picture "of a community sharing a strong sense of belonging to Ukraine in a depoliticized and denationalized form."[60]

The historical arguments about Jewish distance from Ukraine are somewhat speculative. We cannot be certain of the existence, content, and power of collective memory. Moreover, the Russian-Jewish relationship has not been much more benign than the Ukrainian-Jewish one, so the differences between Jewish attitudes toward the Russian and Ukrainian states could not be explained wholly on the basis of history. There is a widespread impression in the West that independent Ukraine has been plagued by inefficiency, corruption, and political thuggery. Steven Kotkin has drawn a very dismal picture indeed: the government "embezzles colossal sums of money that it launders abroad, manipulates voting outcomes, forcibly expropriates businesses, destroys even the pathetically semi-independent media, methodically blackmails and frames critics or rivals, covers up criminal acts committed by itself and those whom it favors" and decapitates its enemies.[61] Moreover, "Ukraine did not inherit a uniform national identity."[62] One scholar asserts that "Ukraine remains an amorphous society with a weak sense of national identity" and that "the

---

[55] Ibid., 791.
[56] Ibid., 77.
[57] Rebecca Golbert, "Constructing Self: Ukrainian Jewish Youth in the Making," unpublished doctoral dissertation, St. Cross College, University of Oxford, 2001, 309.
[58] Ibid.
[59] Ibid., 310–11.
[60] Ibid., 315.
[61] The reference is to the journalist Georgiy Gongadze who had written exposes of the regime and whose decapitated body was found. A defecting presidential bodyguard brought out tapes that purported to show President Kuchma ordering Gongadze's murder and violent measures against political opponents. Steven Kotkin, "Trashcanistan," *The New Republic*, April 15, 2002, 32.
[62] Taras Kuzio, "Identity and Nation-Building in Ukraine," *Ethnicities* 1,3 (December 2001), 358.

TABLE 11.4. *Percentage of Jews Identifying Country as "the Motherland"* [**Rodina**]

	Russian Jews	Ukrainian Jews
Russia	77.6	3.3
Ukraine	0.5	54.6
USSR	1.5	20.2
Israel	10.3	12.6
Other	5.6	3.1
No answer	4.4	6.3
Total N	1,314	1,984

Ukrainian *cives* is as yet unable to rest on any stable cultural core or develop any powerful transcendent idea."[63]

We do have two tangible indicators of contemporary Jewish distancing from Ukraine. One is the significantly larger emigration of Jews from Ukraine than from Russia. From 1970 through 1997, more than 422,000 Jews emigrated from Ukraine, in comparison to 308,500 from Russia,[64] despite the fact that the Jewish population in Russia was larger. We cannot determine with certainty the cause of the greater Ukrainian migration but perhaps migration indicates less attachment to Ukraine than to Russia because this phenomenon predates the dissolution of the USSR by about twenty years. Because the economic situation in the Russian and Ukrainian Soviet republics was roughly comparable, one cannot argue that the larger Ukrainian migration then was driven by a poorer Ukrainian economy or even by harsher rule. However, Vladimir Shapiro suggests that greater anti-Semitism in Ukraine, particularly of the official and ideological variety, may account for the larger volume of emigration.[65]

The second indicator of greater Jewish distancing from Ukraine comes from our survey. We asked respondents to name their "Motherland [*rodina*] with a capital 'M'" (see Table 11.4). Only 55 percent of Ukrainian Jews identify Ukraine as their "Motherland," in contrast to 78 percent of Russian Jews who call their motherland Russia. About equal proportions of respondents in both successor states were born in the USSR, so the difference between the less than 2 percent in Russia who name the USSR as their birthplace and the 20 percent in Ukraine who do so is dramatic. The response "Russia" rather than "USSR" is understandable because many people, before and after 1991, equated the two. The Russian Federation sees itself as the major successor of the USSR and is perceived thus by its citizens. At the end of the 1980s, in a survey "among various peoples of the Soviet Union," almost 70 percent of ethnic Russian respondents "considered the entire Soviet Union their homeland

---

[63] Wilson, "Elements of a Theory of Ukrainian Ethno-National Identities," 31.
[64] See Chapter 9, note 32.
[65] Personal communication, December 28, 1998.

[*rodina*]. And even after the 'parade of sovereignties' [when Soviet republics declared themselves sovereign, if not independent] and armed ethnic conflicts, surveys conducted... in December 1990 showed that in most republics, from 70 to 80 percent of Russians considered themselves, first of all, citizens of the USSR."[66]

So why do only a bare majority of Ukrainian Jews identify Ukraine as their homeland, when most were born when Ukraine was known as the *Ukrainian Soviet Socialist Republic* and Ukraine is not seen as the USSR's major successor? Their responses may indicate that, like the Russians whom they have adopted as their cultural models, it was the Soviet state as a whole, not its Ukrainian component, that was most salient for them. Identifying with the USSR may also be an expression of nostalgia not for a country that no longer exists, but for the economic security it appeared to provide. In the 1994 poll referred to earlier, in West Ukraine 27 percent said they identified with the former Soviet Union, rather than with Ukraine. Solchanyk interprets this as due to their association of the Soviet Union "with economic and social stability."[67] In a 1997 national survey, "up to 30 per cent still consider[ed] Soviet as *some* part of their identity."[68]

Many Jews have a pragmatic and unsentimental attitude toward Ukraine. As long as it provides even less material satisfaction and social security than the USSR, they will not claim it as their homeland. The "Israel" response clearly signals a distancing from Ukraine and an assertion that Jews do not belong there but in Israel. Those with a weak emotional attachment to independent Ukraine or who are skeptical about Ukrainians' ability to conduct affairs of state cannot be expected to pay much attention to Ukrainian politics. This may explain many of our respondents' attitudes.

However, indifference to Ukrainian politics should not be taken as indifference to the country or its culture. A woman in Donetsk explained that she is a "Ukrainian Jew" who understands Ukrainian and who "belongs to this state.... I feel for it. I live here. That is, all the same I worry about Ukraine. How can you live in this country and not think about her...? But I am a Jew all the same."[69] Even a woman in Lviv who planned to emigrate to Israel said, "I love Ukraine very much.... An interesting culture. An interesting, beautiful language, beautiful music.... I love Ukraine. I love my city very much, I love

---

[66] V. A. Turaev, *Etnopolitologiia* (Moscow: Ladomir, 2001), 29, n13.
[67] Solchanyk, "The Post-Soviet Transition," 31. Valeri Khmelko and Andrew Wilson acknowledge that "[t]he most common explanation of the growing gap between east and west (Ukraine) is that the serious fall in the standard of living in Ukraine (and Russia's comparatively better economic performance)... left those with an underdeveloped national consciousness disillusioned with the idea of Ukrainian independence they had supported back in December 1991." However, they conclude that cultural rather than material factors explain the diminished enthusiasm for Ukrainian independence. "Regionalism and Ethnic and Linguistic Cleavages in Ukraine," in Kuzio, *Contemporary Ukraine*, 71.
[68] Wilson, "Elements of a Theory of Ukrainian Ethno-National Identities," 37.
[69] Shine, "Jewish Identity, Community and Citizenship in Ukraine," 10.

Ukraine madly.... It's very hard for me to part with her."[70] For another citizen of Ukraine, the issue is complicated. Ethnically, he asserted, "your origins don't allow you to be more than one thing." He loved both Russian [he does not mention Ukrainian] and Jewish cultures, "but how to be [Russian and Jewish] simultaneously? I don't know." As a citizen of Ukraine, with family roots there going back centuries, he insisted that he is as Ukrainian as ethnic Ukrainians. Moreover, "I consider the Israeli army to be 'ours,' but I also consider 'ours' the army of the country in which I live and in which I served. I would hate, really hate, to fight in a war between these two armies, because I would not know on which side of the barricades to stand. And one cannot stand on both sides!"[71]

These remarks make clear that the relationships between Jews and Ukraine are varied and complex. Much depends on the state continuing to accommodate ethnic interests and, more difficult to accomplish, climbing out of the economic morass it has been in since independence. By the same token, should the Russian Federation come to be led by elements hostile to Jews and its economy deteriorate drastically, the relationship of Russian Jews to their state may change profoundly. However, for the foreseeable future Jews in Ukraine will be both an ethnic and cultural minority, generally perceived as part of a somewhat alien Russophone community, whereas in Russia they are an ethnic minority but in the cultural mainstream.

Conclusion

Jews in the Russian Federation and in independent Ukraine relate differently to their respective polities. There seems to be a higher proportion of "sojourners" among Ukrainian Jews than among Russian Jews. Whereas Russian Jews are fully integrated into the dominant culture, Ukrainian Jews share with Russians in Ukraine a language that fell out of political favor. Russian Jews were at one point very prominent at the highest levels of politics and the economy, whereas Ukrainian Jews have been practically absent from high government positions[72] and less prominent in the economy. Russian Jews are much more engaged in their country's politics, although their political profile is heavily skewed toward the liberal and democratic end of a spectrum increasingly dominated by authoritarians. Ukrainian Jews simply lack a political profile, except that they are much less supportive than the general population of the Communist Party and, of course, of Ukrainian nationalists.

Neither in the 1990s nor in the following decade have Jewish communities and institutions emerged as alternative arenas for public life. The communities

---

[70] Ibid., 11.
[71] Interview at the Institute of Contemporary Jewry, Hebrew University of Jerusalem. I am grateful to Professor Dov Levin and Ms. Riki Garti for making the interview available to me.
[72] The exception is former Prime Minister Zvihailsky who fled to Israel after criminal charges were pressed against him but who returned to Ukraine with parliamentary immunity.

are not organized and powerful enough to be effective lobbies vis-à-vis the government, nor have they so far attracted large proportions of the Jewish population to take active roles in them. Migration in the 1990s vitiated efforts to establish and develop Jewish communal life. Israel's policy of taking in Jewish immigrants unconditionally and post-Soviet policies of free emigration made a sojourner posture reasonable and viable for Russian and Ukrainian Jews. They are not disloyal to their states; they do not work against them or on behalf of any foreign states, but many adopt a conditional and exchange relationship with their native countries. Should the latter not provide security, equality, and a satisfactory standard of living, Jews are (thus far) free to exercise the emigration option. They have done this more frequently in Ukraine, possibly because of their collective historical experience but more likely because of the less satisfactory economic situation in Ukraine and their greater distance from the dominant culture and people. Thus, whereas Russian Jews fall more into the first and third patterns of relationship to the state described at the beginning of this chapter (Jewishness has no impact on political behavior; Jews participate more than others in politics but not much in Jewish communal life), Ukrainian Jews tend more toward the fifth pattern (living apart from politics and even emigrating). Few fit the third or fourth patterns, participating enthusiastically in both the political and Jewish arenas or concentrating their public lives within the Jewish community. Nevertheless, there is a distinct Jewish political profile in both Russia and Ukraine, one that resembles those in other countries. Jews are more liberal politically than the population as a whole; although they might not consciously act politically as a group, in the aggregate, their attitudes and behaviors mark them as a distinct group.

In both states there are people who fall into all five patterns delineated earlier, and their proportions easily shift over time. For example, in our 1992/93 interviews greater proportions in Russia and, especially, Ukraine, declared their intention to emigrate than in 1997/98 – and this could change again. Particularly in Ukraine, Jews appear to relate to the state on an exchange basis rather than being totally and uncritically committed to it, come what may, as Jews elsewhere have been. Jews in Russia and Ukraine will no doubt continue to negotiate their relationships with these unstable, troubled, but potentially prosperous and powerful states.

Conclusion

"No one has been able to define Jew, and in essence this defiance of definition is the central meaning of Jewish consciousness which is inescapable.... Being a Jew is the consciousness of being a Jew, and the Jewish identity, with or without religion, with or without history, is the significant fact."[1]

Ethnicity has proved more persistent than many predicted, but more malleable than many assumed. In many parts of the world self-conscious ethnic groups persist despite urbanization, industrialization, cultural homogenization, and, in some cases, deliberate attempts by states or other groups to diminish or eliminate them. At the same time, perhaps as part of their survival strategy, ethnic groups have redefined themselves and changed both their cultures and the boundaries separating them from others. Bosnians, for example, have been trying since the early 1990s to separate their language from Croatian and Serbian by inserting Turkish and Arabic elements that highlight the connection with Islam, a religion that Croatians and Serbians do not share. Jews struggle with the nature of the boundaries that separate them from others, the rules of admission to the Jewish "people," and the contradiction between Orthodox definitions of being Jewish and the Jewish state's rules of admission to citizenship. Canadians wrestle with how much linguistic and cultural diversity can be encompassed while remaining Canadian. Russians who used to differentiate between Soviet citizenship (a civic concept) and Russian nationality (ethnicity) now try to draw a distinction between *Rossiiskii* (of the Russian Federation, civic identity) and *Russkii* (Russian ethnicity). Turks and others continue to deny the legitimacy of a Kurdish national identity, whereas Israelis have conceded the existence of a Palestinian people. Germans, who for centuries emphasized lineage and bloodlines as defining *Deutschtum*, recognize that their country has a significant number of non-German immigrants and are more prepared to grant citizenship, if not ethnic status, to those immigrants.

---

[1] Karl Shapiro, *Poems of a Jew* (New York: Random House, 1958), ix.

Conclusion

Japanese, long criticized for their insularity and refusal to grant citizenship to descendants of non-Japanese immigrants, are reconsidering traditional practices.

The Soviet experiment of nearly a century was plagued by contradictions between ideology and practice, principle and policy. Marxist-Leninist ideology advocated the abolition of religion and ethnicity and predicted they would not survive the capitalist epoch. Yet the urge to know as much as possible about the citizenry in order to control it led the Soviet state to identify each citizen by a near-immutable ethnicity ("nationality"), unintentionally preserving consciousness of one's ethnic heritage even if it was emptied of cultural content. Some groups, particularly in Central Asia, even gained a national consciousness once Soviet authorities granted them nominal sovereignty in their own invented republics. Doctrines of "proletarian internationalism," "friendship of the peoples," and "fraternal relations among nationalities" were countermanded both by lingering ethnic prejudices and by Stalinist policies, some persisting after his death, that discriminated at one time or other against some nationalities – Ukrainians, Poles, Germans, Crimean Tatars, Chechens, and Jews, among others. Members of those groups could not lose their identities even if they wished to, in spite of the doctrines of *sblizhenie* and *sliianie*, rapprochement and mutual fusion.

The Soviet experiment was not without its successes. It gave non-Russians, who by 1989 constituted about half the population, a degree of equality few had enjoyed before the Revolution and afforded them unprecedented educational, vocational, and economic opportunities. By the end of the Soviet period, overt ethnic discrimination had become socially and politically "incorrect," and huge numbers of previously uneducated and impoverished people had gained an education, a reasonable standard of living, and influential positions in many hierarchies in Soviet society. Central Asian, Siberian, and, to some extent, Caucasian peoples benefited in these respects from Soviet practices.

The balance sheet of the Soviet experience shows that the regime uprooted institutionalized religion almost entirely, but was less successful in doing the same to belief. Russian Orthodoxy was left in institutionally far better condition than Judaism or Islam at the end of the Soviet period. However, in the decade after the fall of communism, Jews received a great deal of external assistance in reclaiming houses of worship and restoring the means by which to acquire religious knowledge. The Soviets created a firm sense among Jews that they were part of an ethnic group or nationality, but weakened the belief that Jews were a nation and subverted the idea that they were linked inextricably to a tribal religion. As a result, our research has demonstrated that many post-Soviet Jews have a deep sense of ethnic identity, but are unsure whether they share it with people to whom they are not culturally related. Some are also unsure about the connection between Judaism and Jewish ethnicity, which is very widely acknowledged by Jews outside the FSU. Most post-Soviet Jews are uncertain of what being Jewish means and implies. Jews elsewhere may understand "being

Jewish" differently, and act on their understandings in different ways, but they share some clearly defined conceptions.

In important ways, American and Russian-speaking Jews adopted different understandings of Jewishness because of their respective environments. American Jews seem to have sensed that ethnicity was not a valued category in American society, whereas religion is. The pressure to become American that was felt in the "melting pot" resulted in Jews abandoning former languages and customs and following the Yankee model. As a highly "churched" society in which no public figure dare declare him- or herself an atheist, America accepted Jews as a religious, not an ethnic group. In the USSR, by contrast, no faith was considered legitimate, but ethnic identity was imposed on all. Being Jewish became an ethnicity with no connection to religion.

Yet the Soviet regime destroyed thick Jewish culture in all its expressions – religious, Hebraic, and even Yiddish secular. Because of its rigid adherence to Stalinist definitions of a nation and a somewhat mechanical understanding of ethnicity, it could not imagine that a "thin culture" could survive, although this possibility was debated by some Soviet academics in the late 1960s. As one put it, "Even while losing the mother tongue and even cultural characteristics, national consciousness is often preserved (Russianized Germans and Jews, Tatarified Bashkirs)."[2] Jews had a thick culture before the 1930s – a "complex whole which includes knowledge, belief, art, law, morals, custom, and any other capabilities and habits acquired by... a member of society."[3] Thick culture "matters," is "fundamental" and holistic, precedes both behavior and institutions, and is externally bounded and "internally homogeneous."[4] Thin culture, which is different from no culture at all, does not always explain behavior and thought. Although "partly rooted in the past [it is] also substantially conditioned by recent and contemporary experience.... Ethnic identities are as much self-chosen or psychologically primed as they are primordial. They are acquired through a lifetime's learning process in which more proximate experiences frequently dominate." Institutions and behavior shape thin culture as much as it shapes them. Thin culture is "relatively unbounded and diverse... heterogeneous and ambivalence," but also dynamic. Different values are in tension and even contradiction. Therefore, it is best measured on the individual level, as we have done. "Although changes in individual attitudes can appear random and non-rational, processes at the group-level are remarkably well behaved."[5]

---

[2] I. S. Gurvich, "Some Problems of Ethnic Development of Peoples in the USSR," *Sovetskaia etnografiia* 5, (1966), 63.
[3] Edward Tylor, *Primitive Culture* (London, 1871), quoted in William Mishler and Detlef Pollack, "On Culture, Thick and Thin: Toward a Neo-Cultural Synthesis," in Detlef Pollack, Jorg Jacobs, Olaf Muller, and Gert Pickel, eds., *Political Culture in Post-Communist Europe* (London: Ashgate, 2003), 239.
[4] Ibid., 239–40.
[5] Ibid., 242–43.

A very small minority of Soviet Jews managed to preserve a thick culture after World War II; a larger minority lost any kind of Jewish culture; and most Jews, like those we interviewed, retained a thin culture that they redefined in light of changing circumstances. In this they were not unique. Jews outside the FSU have done the same, though they have generally retained more of the thick culture. Within the Former Soviet Union, other nationalities have also undergone similar transformations. In Siberia, for example, Yupik knowledge transmission "now proceeds via creation of a new cultural blend that could be labeled mixed culture.... The original... symbolic and ritual meanings are packaged in new combinations with secular interpretations based on contemporary environmental discourse, modern views... and/or new ideologies of ethnic revival."[6]

These are broad generalizations about entire groups that are composed of individuals who can choose the intensity, if not always the nature, of their ethnic identities and commitments.[7] As Aviel Roshwald notes,

> It may be... useful to think of ethnic identity as falling along a gradient within any given population. At one end... are those who subsume all issues under the rubric of ethnicity and engage with utmost passion in debates about... the rights and interests of the ethnic group.... At the other end... are those with mixed or multiple identities and those who embrace the possibility of assimilation into another ethno-national culture. Most people probably fall somewhere between these two extremes. And, to be sure, the overall distribution of attitudes shifts and changes over time.[8]

This is a fair characterization of Jews in Russia and Ukraine in the 1990s.

On the basis of her fieldwork in provincial Russian cities, Elena Nosenko-Shtein has drawn up this typology of Jews: (1) Traditional Jewish self-identification – mostly people age 65 and over who speak Yiddish and remember traditions; most are not religious but go to a synagogue as a kind of Jewish "club"; (2) "Internationalist" self-identification – people indifferent to their Jewishness who usually identify as Jews only when confronted by anti-Semitism; most never participate in any form of Jewish life; (3) People who often call themselves "Russian Jews"; they try "to be Jews" by taking part in Jewish life but consider Russian culture their dominant culture; and (4) "Newly Jewish," mostly young people who became involved in Jewish life in the late 1980s and 1990s; for some, this became a kind of "ethnic business."[9]

Soviet Jewish thin culture was partly derived from the thick culture that preceded it and partly from conditions created by the Soviet system. Survivals

---

[6] Igor Krupnik and Nikolay Vakhtin, "Indigenous Knowledge in Modern Culture: Siberian Yupik Ecological Legacy in Transition," *Arctic Anthropology* 34, 1, (1997), 248–49.
[7] On the measurement of ethnic identity, see Rawi Abdelal, Yoshiko Herrera, Alastair Ian Johnston, and Rose McDermott, *Measuring Identity* (New York: Cambridge University Press, 2009).
[8] Review of Rogers Brubaker, *Ethnicity without Groups, Nationalities Papers* 36, 1 (March 2008), 174.
[9] Personal communication, fall 2007.

from the thick culture included shards of languages, traces of holiday observances, memories of ways of life and practices, and a feeling that Jews were, at the least, different – "not Russians/Ukrainians." Jews constitute "communities of memory."[10] They tell stories that contain "conceptions of character, what a good person is like," but also

> painful stories of shared suffering that sometimes create deeper identities than success.... People growing up in communities of memory not only hear the stories that tell how the community came to be, what its hopes and fears are, and how its ideals are exemplified in outstanding men and women; they also participate in the practices – ritual, aesthetic, ethical – that define the community as a way of life. We call these "practices of commitment" for they define the patterns of loyalty and obligation that keep the community alive.[11]

In 1921, a Hungarian Jew wrote, "A person cannot have a family tree of two thousand years without... that putting its stamp on him. I carry with me the heritage of my ancient forebears... as a bundle on my shoulder... and even the marks of the nails on my palms. Addresses are engraved in my brain; faint traces of neural paths." The Bible teaches Jews to "remember that you were slaves in Egypt" and that "you should love the stranger for you were a stranger in Egypt.... Such things cannot but leave an imprint on the collective life of people. Many things have happened since then to Jews, but whatever happens to them – after periods of forgetting, long or short – Jews will remember that we were slaves in Egypt (and in other places as well)."[12]

Soviet Jews heard some of the group's "stories," but did not participate in the practices. For most of them, state-imposed identity and those stories were enough to generate identity. Post-Soviet Jews, by contrast, hear the stories, not just of their families and friends but also of Jews more generally. They can also participate in the practices and perhaps through that may be able not only to "keep the community alive" but also to revive it.

Soviet Jews were a "category" (i.e., they were quite precisely defined by the Soviet state), but even without that they were a community of memory and a community of fate. However, until the 1990s they did not have institutions, activities, or organizations. They had no formal means of communicating; there were no Jewish newspapers, bulletins, radio and television programs, or even books. Soviet Jews were widely scattered geographically, and although they were very highly urbanized, they did not usually live in Jewish neighborhoods after World War II. They could not even share publicly the memory of their common catastrophe, the Shoah. There were very few monuments, no museums (of living or past Soviet or world Jewry),[13] no sermons and speeches, and few

---

[10] Robert Bellah, Richard Madsen, William Sullivan, Ann Swidler and Steven Tipton, *Habits of the Heart* (New York: Harper and Row, 1985), 153.
[11] Ibid., 154.
[12] Lajos Biro, *A zsidok utja* (Vienna, 1921) translated into Hebrew as "Netiv hayehudim," in Guy Miron and Anna Szalai, *Yehudim al parshat derachim* (Ramat Gan, Israel: Bar Ilan University Press, 2008), 155–56.
[13] Before the 1950s such museums existed in Georgia and Lithuania, and perhaps elsewhere.

books, movies, or documentaries on the Shoah[14]; there were no associations of survivors or of survivors' children, no Holocaust studies in universities, and, most telling perhaps, no acknowledgment of their special fate by the government or, for the most part, by society. In contrast to the United States, where Jewish World War II veterans, both individually and organizationally, are dying out but Holocaust memorialization groups are legion, in the FSU there are more veterans groups than victims groups. Far more books have been published on the role of Jews in the war than on the systematic murder of Jews. Many focus on localities or regions; very few deal with the Holocaust in the USSR as a whole.[15]

Yet, probably every Jew in the FSU knows what happened to Jews during World War II, if only because information was passed on within families and social circles. Even in Soviet times there were silent understandings that a community of memory and a community of fate would have. Significantly, among the very first "dissident" activities of the 1960s were cleanups, mainly by young people, of wartime killing sites such as Rumbuli in Latvia. Jews were also deeply aware of the "black years" and of the ongoing disabilities of being a Jew in the USSR. These shared memories and fates cut across class, education, gender, and, for the most part, geographical lines. They created invisible, "latent communities" that were activated by perestroika and post-Soviet activities, some generated by foreigners but mostly not.

Other memories bound them as well – of parental and grandparental religious practices, of phrases and sayings in Yiddish, of foods, stories, and family legends. Jewish jokes were so important that they became part of the Soviet urban cultural repertoire. In extensive interviews with hundreds of Soviet Jews, we found a great deal of nostalgic warmth expressed for grandparents, whom Soviet propaganda would have depicted as "backward elements." Today's educated professionals at one time might have disdained or been embarrassed by their sometimes illiterate, often poor parents and grandparents, but when looking back they generally are not. Perhaps this reflects a tendency to paint the past in rosier colors than it might warrant, but the uniformly positive feelings sustain communities of memory.

As we have seen, there are also many negative associations with Jewishness, often beginning with childhood. Curiously and perhaps significantly, it is my impression that the phrases of Yiddish that are remembered and invoked are usually negative – *az och un vey; ganev, shiker, gevalt*.[16] A friend who grew up in Minsk recalls that her father, born in 1912, would say "*'mach shmay vezichray*" [may his name and memory be erased] every time he saw a picture

---

[14] See Zvi Gitelman, *Bitter Legacy: Confronting the Holocaust in the USSR* (Bloomington, IN: Indiana University Press, 1997), ch. 2.

[15] Exceptions include three books written or edited by Ilya Al'tman: *Zhertvy nenavisti: Kholokost v SSSR, 1941–45 gg.* (Moscow: Fond 'Kovcheg,' 2002); *Kholokost i evreiskoe soprotivlenie na okupirovannoi territorii SSSR* (Moscow: Fond 'kholokost,' 2002 [a school text]); and Al'tman, ed., *Kholokost, soprotivlenie, vozrozhdenie* (Moscow-Jerusalem: Fond 'kholokost,' 2000).

[16] Alack and alas; thief; drunkard; raise a cry!

of a communist leader.[17] Positive memories, mostly held by older people, are often of food or music. They are sometimes vivid and are part of the positive aura with which the memories of grandparents are suffused. In the post-Soviet decade new "memories" or associations were created as Jews participated in communal celebrations and "relearned" Jewish traditions, including words, phrases, foods, rituals, and ceremonies. The close personal connection many post-Soviet Jews have with Israel, through relatives and friends, is a new element in Jewish consciousness in Russia and Ukraine.[18]

There were several major tenets of Soviet Jewish civil religion. First, there was respect for the past. Young enthusiasts in the prewar era may have denounce d Stalinism, but after the Holocaust, the obvious "errors" of Stalinism and the inadequacies of the system were appreciated, and the lost cultures of the past were no longer condemned. The second tenet was consciousness of the Holocaust, which brought home the realization that whatever one's subjective attitude toward one's Jewishness, there was an inescapable bond with other Jews. Identification with Israel, another major tenet, existed before 1948, was heightened in 1967, and then reinforced by the mass emigration of friends, acquaintances, and relatives. For many, though less so in the 1990s, there was a sense of being discriminated against: the shared burden of the *piataia grafa*, the fifth (nationality) line in the internal passport, was widely understood and not always questioned. For example, "Of course, he was not accepted to that faculty, you know, so he had to go to another one." "They already had a Jewish worker so, of course..." Another tenet was a sense of being alien in the USSR and even in some post-Soviet states (certainly in Central Asia if you are Ashkenazi and felt by Russophone Jews today in the Baltics and in Ukraine). Finally, Jewish civic religion was based on several "folk beliefs" such as that Jews drink less, work harder, are smarter, strive for higher education, appreciate the finer things in life, and treat their wives and children better.

Ironically, the Soviet system helped create a thin Jewish culture by allowing Jews mobility so that urbanism and education, instead of the practice of Judaism, became markers of being Jewish. Jews began to realize that these assets could facilitate mobility beyond the borders of the USSR. Along with the profound alienation from the state and even society felt by many, this realization has driven about half the Jews of the FSU of 1970 to emigrate.

Prospects

Soviet Jews were cut off from their co-ethnics for decades. Once they emigrated, they had an enormous impact on Israel and on the Jewish populations of Germany and the United States. By the same token, their departure from Russia, Ukraine, and other former Soviet republics raises questions about the viability of communal Jewish life there. At present, one of every five Israeli Jews is from

---

[17] A corruption of "*yimach shmo vezichro*," pronounced in Litvish Yiddish.
[18] Many have noted the intense interest in Israel displayed by Jewish émigrés in Germany and the United States, as well as by those who have not left the FSU.

the FSU. The largest single immigration to Israel has come from the state that consistently opposed Zionism and whose ideologues did so even before the Revolution. From the late 1980s to the early 1990s, about 13,000 scientists, 80,000 engineers and technicians, and 16,000 in the medical profession came to Israel. In 1989–92 the number of engineers in Israel more than doubled, and the number of physicians rose more than 70 percent. The high-tech revolution in Israel and its continued economic success in the face of the worldwide economic crisis would not have been possible without the labor force of technologically oriented, innovative, hard-working Russian immigrants. The impact of the immigrants on music, art, and sports in Israel has also been unparalleled. Many Israeli competitors in the Olympics were trained in the USSR. Small cities and towns formed full-fledged orchestras to accommodate the many Soviet performers who arrived.

The largely secular Jewishness of the Soviet immigrants is more easily accommodated in Israel than elsewhere because the state is identified as "Jewish," whereas in most other places "Jewish" is identified with religion. Soviet and post-Soviet immigrants could not only become formal citizens of Israel, but by adopting the dominant language, calendar, celebrations, commemorations, and holidays of Israel, all associated with Jewish culture, they also connected easily with contemporary, nonreligious Jewish culture. Becoming Israeli is the most viable way of being a committed secular Jew.

The more than 300,000 non-Jews who have come from the FSU as part of Jewish families or descendants of Jews are accepted as *Israelis* (defined by the Law of Return) but not as *Jews* (defined in Israel by halakha). Continuing the Ottoman tradition, religious authorities in Israel administer matters of personal status, now largely confined to marriage, divorce, and burial. This leaves hundreds of thousands of non-Jewish former Soviet Israelis in limbo. Because conversion to Judaism has increasingly come under the control of ultra-Orthodox (*haredi*) authorities who have imposed a very strict interpretation of Jewish law on the conversion procedure, only a small number of immigrants have converted to Judaism, which would bring their Israeli and Jewish identities into comfortable alignment. Instead the majority of non-Jewish immigrants have become part of the non-Arab, non-Jewish minority of Israelis.

Soviet Jewish immigration increased the Jewish population of Germany about tenfold (to about 200,000) until 2005 when more restrictive immigration policies were adopted. Ironically, the immigration includes more than a few Jews who were last in Germany in 1945 in the Soviet armed forces. German Jewish communities define Jews according to halakhic criteria and so "Law of Return" Jews[19] do not qualify as members of the communities and are ineligible for certain benefits.

---

[19] In the vernacular of Russian-speaking Jews there is actually now a category of "*khokashvutnye evreii*" [Jews according to the Law of Return but not according to halakha]. The term is a compound of two Hebrew words – *khok hashvut* [Law of Return] and a Russian adjectival suffix [*nye*].

In the United States, the Russian-speaking immigration, numbering between 350,000–500,000, is the largest Jewish immigration since before World War I. It has not drawn much attention from a community that otherwise studies itself intensively,[20] perhaps because so many who came from the FSU have "made it" in America, using their technological skills, higher education, and urban experience to move rapidly up the social and economic ladders and from old Jewish neighborhoods where they were initially resettled to middle-class and upper middle-class suburbs. American Jewry is so decentralized that issues of Jewish status of the immigrants have been dealt with locally, if at all, and probably in quite different ways.

The emigration benefited the receiving Jewish communities and countries, but it weakened attempts to reconstruct Jewish commitments and communities in the FSU. Younger people are generally overrepresented in migrations; this one is no exception. The Jewish population of the FSU had tilted toward the older cohorts well before the emigration began – the result of the Holocaust, other losses during the war, and a low birth rate. Emigration accelerated this trend. The lack of young people means that there is less energy and talent available for Jewish communal reconstruction. It also means a further, and steep, decline in the Jewish population, a prospect made more certain by the high rate of intermarriage. As noted earlier, by 1988, 48 percent of Soviet Jewish women and 58 percent of Jewish men who married did so with non-Jews.[21] In the Russian Republic, the rates were even higher. In 1989, Jewish deaths in the USSR exceeded births by about 3:1–4:1 in the RSFSR – and the ratio has widened since.[22]

Which of these diametrically opposed trends will prevail: Jewish re-identification or Jewish assimilation through out-marriage? The answer has profound implications for policy. Should investments be made in a Jewish population that may have no future? Can such investments strengthen the trend to re-identification and slow assimilation? The most likely future scenario is that, as in other Jewish communities, both trends will coexist. Post-Soviet Jewry may not be as differentiated and heterogeneous as, say, American Jewry, if only because the denominationalism and hyper-organization of American Jewish life are thus far absent in the FSU. Yet neither are all the Jews of the FSU cut from the same cloth. As we have seen, they differ significantly by age, place of residence, and gender, and within these categories people have different aspirations.

---

[20] There are no national studies of the economic, vocational, linguistic, and social histories of the post-1970s Soviet and post-Soviet immigrants in the United States nor of their Jewish identities and commitments.
[21] Mark Tolts, "Jewish Marriages in the USSR: A Demographic Analysis," *East European Jewish Affairs* 22, 2 (1992), 8.
[22] Mark Tolts, "Trends in Soviet Jewish Demography since the Second World War," in Yaacov Ro'i, ed., *Jews and Jewish Life in Russia and the Soviet Union* (London: Frank Cass, 1995), 366.

Conclusion

Some scholars and Jewish community activists bemoan the fractionation of world and Israeli Jewry along several fault lines, probably as their predecessors have long done. For example, David Vital wrote, "The nature and structure of contemporary Jewry is profoundly fractured and dysfunctional."[23] He asked whether the Jews are still a nation and suggested that the Jews of Israel and those in the rest of the world will constitute two separate Jewish peoples:

> The Jewish world – beaten by assimilation on the one hand and by destruction and threats of further punishment on the other – is now coming apart. Where there was once a single, if certainly a scattered and far from monolithic people – indeed a nation – there is now a sort of archipelago of discrete islands composed of rather shaky communities of all qualities, shapes and sizes, in which the Island of Israel, as it were, is fated increasingly to be in a class by itself.... In sum, the old unity of Jewry [where?! when?!–ZG]... lies shattered today, almost beyond repair.[24]

Vital may have exaggerated fractionation and compared it to an imagined earlier unity, but this study has demonstrated how dramatically post-Soviet Jews differ from both historic Jewry and contemporary norms and assumptions. In post-Soviet Jewry, the connection between Judaism and Jewishness is tenuous, no thick culture survived the Soviet experience, and there is no set of consensual norms, practices, or behaviors that can constitute the foundations of an organized community. Those norms and behaviors transplanted from Israel, North America, or Europe have not taken root, nor should they have been expected to, at least not in the first post-Soviet decade. Moreover, the uncertain ethnicity of FSU Jews challenges conventional ideas of Jewishness, making for some awkward confrontations with Jews in the host countries.

Has the attempt to resurrect Jewish public life in Russia and Ukraine succeeded according to the following criteria?

1. Having a national representative body effectively representing common Jewish interests and lobbying on their behalf.
2. Institutional religious revival – wider public observance of holidays, attendance at religious services, rabbis taken seriously as guides to thought and behavior, more learning of precepts and classical Jewish texts.
3. Linguistic revival (Yiddish and/or Hebrew) and some readership and writing in those languages.
4. Cultural revival – music, art, dance, and literature though not necessarily in Jewish languages.
5. Affiliation by individuals with Jewish organizations and institutions.
6. Pride in manifesting or exhibiting that affiliation.
7. Higher rates of endogamous marriage.

---

[23] David Vital, *The Future of the Jews* (Cambridge: Harvard University Press, 1990), 41.
[24] Ibid., 147–48.

8. Growth of fund-raising and self-supporting welfare institutions; financial autonomy from the state and from foreign organizations.
9. Diminished emigration (though Israelis and Zionists would argue the opposite).

There is no country in which Jews can claim to have achieved all of these criteria. Therefore they should be construed as goals,[25] and communities can be compared on the degree to which they have moved toward them. Post-Soviet Jewry has had little time to create Jewish institutions and organizations. It is disadvantaged by the deliberate destruction of Jewish culture and organized religion by the Soviet system, a process essentially completed by 1950.

Vi es kristelt zich, azay idelt zich – as with the Gentiles so with the Jews. For all that has been written about the period of transition in the former communist states, the endpoints of the transitions – "democracy," "Europe" – is usually vague. How to get there is even less well defined. The actors involved in these processes of transition generally do not share visions of a common future – if they have any visions at all beyond self-interest – and do not trust each other, a vital ingredient of any stable system in which power must be shared.[26] Foreign models are sometimes invoked, but nationalism and a poor understanding of those models and how to adapt them to local circumstances make them irrelevant in practice. Among Jews, the lack of clear goals and the absence of well-formulated ideologies of Jewishness on the communal level are paralleled on the individual level. Unlike their ancestors of three and more generations ago, Jews in Russia and Ukraine have not defined their Jewishness ideologically and have not formed political and social movements. Most define and formulate their Jewish identities ad hoc, with no aspirations or values to shape them. Being Jewish is a fact, not a program, just as is the case for many Western Jews.

The weakness of civil society in Russia and Ukraine, the authoritarian bent of Russian governments since 2000, and the instability and ineffectiveness of successive Ukrainian governments have not been conducive to the development of authoritative national Jewish organizations; their development has also been hampered by personal and institutional rivalries and the pursuit of individual interests within Jewish communities. As in the larger arenas, Jewish collectives in Russia and Ukraine suffer from opportunistic, unstable leadership at the national level, which lacks ideology and seems committed primarily to self-promotion. One indicator of this problem, and a source of weakness, is the rapid turnover in the leadership of the Russian Jewish Congress (RJC). Some leaders have left the country (Vladimir Gusinsky, Leonid Nevzlin), others have

---

[25] I am well aware that some believe that noninstitutionalized and artistic expressions of Jewishness are the wave of the future among younger diaspora Jews, and some foundations have poured large sums into subsidizing what they construe as "Jewish expression." The rapid demise of many publications, online or not, groups, and activities of this "cutting edge" has shown it to be rather dull. What is hip today is gone tomorrow.
[26] As of this writing, the same may be said of the Arab Spring of 2011.

quit (Evgenii Satanovsky), and still others have used it as a vehicle to move up and out (Viacheslav Moshe Kantor became president of the European Jewish Congress). It is not easy to construct Jewish communities de novo, but the skeletal "buildings" thrown up are unfinished and sometimes occupied largely by "professional Jews." Of course, similar tendencies are observed in Western Jewish communities where ideologues and spiritual leaders have been replaced by wealthy people, many of whom lack Jewish knowledge or ideology. The disappearance of some organizations – for example, the American Jewish Congress, which closed in 2010 – is compensated for, in a sense, by the rise of new types of organizations with different agendas. This countercurrent is not yet observable in Russia and Ukraine.[27]

There has not been a genuine "religious revival" in Russia or Ukraine in the 1990s or later. Religious institutions, mainly those of the Chabad-Lubavitch and Karlin-Stolin Hasidic and the Progressive/Reform movements, have small groups of adherents. Having failed to "return" many Jews to religion, Chabad has been acting as a parallel welfare institution to the Joint Distribution Committee and local Jewish welfare organizations.[28] The alliance between Vladimir Putin and Chabad,[29] continued by President Dmitri Medvedev, and Chabad's willingness to go it alone on the local and national levels do not sit well with many Russian Jews who favor a more democratic government. In Ukraine Chabad is weaker, though it did have more influence when Viktor Yushchenko was president (2005–10). The Karlin-Stolin group has managed to hold on to important posts, and the Reform/Progressive movement has at least two rabbis functioning in Ukraine. Modern Orthodoxy, Conservative Judaism, and Reconstructionism have not displayed sustained interest or invested in developing communities in Russia or Ukraine.

This is not to say that individual Jews have not become religious, but it seems that the Hasidic movements encourage them to emigrate, which is perhaps a sign that the movements themselves have little faith in the future of Judaism in Russia and Ukraine. Synagogues have become somewhat like their counterparts

---

[27] Among the organizations that have either disappeared or have weakened considerably are fraternal or social organizations such as B'nai Brith. Some women's organizations, such as Hadassah, have seen a decline and aging of their membership, partly because women who used to spend a great deal of time in voluntary activities are now in the workforce.

[28] Chabad claims of "membership" cannot be taken seriously. In Odessa, when a local Chabad rabbi told me that there were 10,000 members of Chabad there, I elicited his admission that anyone who had at any time been on their mailing list was included – regardless of whether the person had emigrated, died or ever expressed any interest in Chabad. The same kinds of patently absurd claims are made in my local community.

[29] Was this to prevent Jewish self-organization or was it the unintended consequence of Putin going after the "oligarchs," who included the then-president of the Russian Jewish Congress, Vladimir Gusinsky? For Chabad, the alliance has meant the backing of the state in its attempt to dominate, if not completely control, Jewish religious life. Nevertheless, the long-standing dispute between Chabad and the Russian Federation about the disposition of part of the library of Rabbi Yosef Yitzhak Schneerson, who was forced to leave the USSR without his library, has not been resolved.

in the West: they are places of gathering not just for prayer, most of which is done pro forma, but also for socializing, intellectual activities, celebration, and commemoration.

FSU Jewish schools are often thought of as second-rate educationally and face the challenges of a shrinking population base and the complex issue of the Jewish status of their students.[30] There is some serious Jewish scholarship going on, as evidenced in the annual meetings of Sefer, a remarkably strong association of those studying a wide range of Jewish subjects on the postsecondary level, and the publication *Tirosh*, a journal featuring articles by mostly younger Jewish students and scholars. In light of the intellectual traditions and aspirations of Soviet Jewry, these are natural, organic developments. Hebrew and Yiddish have largely disappeared as languages of daily use everywhere in the diaspora, but in the FSU a fair number of people are making serious efforts to revive them – in the case of Hebrew largely for pragmatic reasons (immigration to Israel, study and research in Judaica) and, as regards Yiddish, out of a realization that it was in the recent past the mother tongue of millions of Soviet Jews.

Perhaps the most popular expressions of Jewishness are in the arts. Concerts of Jewish music, including cantorial – and hence nominally religious – material, were well attended in the 1990s. Jewish music groups – choirs and instrumental ensembles – sprang up everywhere. This was to be expected, given the strong musical traditions of the USSR and its Jews and the easy accessibility of music to both performers and listeners. Moreover, it demands no knowledge of classic Jewish texts and no religious commitment.

In many Western countries, Jewish communal success and strength are measured by affiliation and philanthropy, which are easy to quantify and are publicly visible. A strong Jewish community is thought to be one where a high proportion of self-identified Jews belong to Jewish organizations and are involved in a Jewish institution such as a school or study group and which supports itself by raising funds for its own communal needs and for national and international Jewish causes. In the USSR there was not even a single Jewish organization. Because all organizations were controlled by the state, "joiners" were usually considered toadies or opportunists. The state assumed responsibility for and control over all philanthropic functions. Therefore joining and giving were not natural or learned behaviors for Soviet citizens, including Jews. A decade proved insufficient to resocialize most FSU Jews to these behaviors.

As we argued in Chapter 10, it is increasingly unlikely that Jews will marry other Jews in Russia and Ukraine. The marriage market has shrunk drastically because of emigration and a low birth rate, and the stricture against marriage to non-Jews, once a key element of the boundary of Jewishness, is not widely observed. Emigration has slowed considerably and the reservoir

---

[30] See Zvi Gitelman, "Do Jewish Schools Make a Difference in the Former Soviet Union?" *East European Jewish Affairs* 37, 4 (December 2007), 377–98. Revised in Alex Pomson, ed., *Jewish Day Schools, Jewish Communities: A Reconsideration* (Oxford: Littman Library, 2009).

of potential emigrants is probably largely drained, although economic downturns, political instability, and a revival of anti-Semitism may cause it to fill again.

Yet, much that happened in the 1990s augurs well for a renewal of Jewish public life and stronger individual Jewish identities based on positive affirmations of the value of being Jewish, rather than on anti-Semitism. Russian and Ukrainian Jews have gained domestic and international recognition as ethno-religious communities. In many places, synagogues and other communal properties seized by the Soviet authorities were returned to the re-formed Jewish communities. Post-Soviet Jewry attracted external support and gained state recognition. Russian and Ukrainian Jews are increasingly visible in international Jewish organizations, and Jews from the FSU are active in Israeli politics and Jewish communal activities in the United States, Canada, and Germany. There are weaknesses in the Jewish educational networks, but one must remember that in 1987 there was not a single Jewish school of any kind – religious, secular, Hebrew, or Yiddish – anywhere from the Baltic to the Sea of Japan. There were no Jewish textbooks, trained teachers, or school buildings. Largely by their own efforts, scholars, teachers, and students have attained levels of international respectability, though not yet leadership, in two decades. The intellectual traditions and commitments, as well as the high levels of interest in Jewish subjects in Russia and Ukraine, bode well for the further development of Jewish education and scholarship. The twenty-year-old ties with world Jewry and Israel can only strengthen Jewish learning, communal initiatives, and cultural redevelopment.

Finally, unlike in the Soviet era, Jews are not threatened by governmental anti-Semitism. If only because Russia, Ukraine, and other successor states have aspirations to join "Europe," contemporary governments can be expected to try to hold grassroots anti-Semitism in check.

Larger Perspectives

We observed in Chapter 4 that the Jewish identity of Russian and Ukrainian Jews is stronger than many would suppose, but is problematic because it was the product of a Soviet environment that no longer exists. In the USSR, state-imposed identity and governmental anti-Semitism combined with grassroots anti-Semitism to maintain boundaries between Jews and others long after Jewish content had largely disappeared from Jewish ethnicity. Today Russia and Ukraine do not impose an official ethnic identity, and no successor state to the USSR pursues anti-Semitic policies. Popular anti-Semitism, which may wax and wane, may be the last barrier to assimilation.

As noted, in the first post-Soviet decade only a minority began to participate in public Jewish activities, educate their children Jewishly, and explore Jewish traditions and cultures. The revival of Jewish life has been vitiated by the mass emigration. Ironically, return migrants from Israel – there is no reliable information on their numbers – and part-time residents in Israel who spend the rest of the time in the FSU have become a source of Jewish knowledge and a link to the Jewish state and diaspora Jewish communities.

This is but one aspect of the globalization of Russian-speaking Jewry. There are about four times as many Jewish speakers of Russian *outside* the borders of the FSU as within them. A shared language and history, family and friendship ties, and business relations link the half-million Jews in the FSU to the more than a million who left it. Modern technology, especially the Internet, has created a virtual community where influences and ideas flow in several directions. It seems likely that, at least for a generation, Jews in the FSU will be increasingly exposed to the new ideas, commitments, and practices of their compatriots abroad. In the United States, some young people born in the FSU but raised mostly in America call themselves the "1.5 generation." They have graduated from American institutions of higher education; many are making successful careers in the professions, the sciences, and business. Yet, they seem to associate (and marry) disproportionately with other Russian speakers, sometimes speaking Russian among themselves. They are bicultural in a very broad sense, but it is likely that in their children's generation American culture will dominate.

This is not unprecedented in Jewish history. Before World War II, Jewish immigrants from Europe, the Americas, and Palestine communicated with their friends and relatives (mostly in Yiddish) who remained in "the old country." Newspapers in New York featured writers from Warsaw and Jerusalem, and vice versa. "American" Yiddish movies were made in Poland, and Yiddish-speaking entertainers, artists, and musicians toured South Africa, Western Europe, the Americas, and Palestine. The "greeners" were American citizens, but their way of life was distinct from that of "real Americans."

However, the war destroyed much of European Jewry and severed family ties. The Iron Curtain made even cultural and friendship connections very dangerous to Soviet Jews. At the same time, acculturation to local languages and cultures weakened the incentives of the émigrés to maintain their old ties. Even without those catastrophic events, it is likely that over several generations the personal ties of Jews who shared common origins and culture would have weakened as family connections grew more distant and cultures evolved in the sending and receiving countries. The same is likely to happen among Russian-speaking Jews. Yet, for the émigré generation and many of their children, connections will remain, visits will be exchanged, culture will be absorbed, and influences will flow. If Russian-speaking Jews in Israel and elsewhere will come closer to what have become normative modes of expressing Jewishness, the "export" of those modes to the FSU will be facilitated. At the same time, non-FSU Jews will be even more challenged to rethink their conceptions and the boundaries of Jewishness to which they have become accustomed.

The conceptions of being Jewish held by the great majority of Russian and Ukrainian Jews are so different from those prevailing in the rest of the diaspora and in Israel that sensitive questions of mutual recognition inevitably arise. The criteria for admission to the "Jewish club" are neither uniform nor are they shared by a significant portion of post-Soviet Jewry. In Chapter 4, we discussed these criteria and the choices that gatekeepers have in developing membership rules. Too flexible a set of rules could mean including "Jews for Jesus," "Messianic Jews," or "Hebrew Christians," which would run against the historical grain. However, if rules become so restrictive as to deny admission to many who seem to have a strong case for membership, they may form their own, competing "Jewish club," or they may turn away from the gates and seek membership elsewhere. For example, in postcommunist Warsaw and Prague people who self-identify as Jews but are not accepted as such by the *kehilla* (the community that operates under Orthodox rules) have formed their own congregations or communities, "Beit Warszawa" and "Beit Praha," respectively.

Diaspora Jewish organizations and the State of Israel seem to assume that these boundary issues can and must be resolved. One analyst of boundary issues in Jewish history asserts, "The complexity of our reality must be matched by the complexity of our boundary policies.... Jewish collective life will not survive without a shared boundary policy."[31] The logic is compelling, but historical precedent, diversity of beliefs and practices among Jews, and the absence of a consensual, authoritative decision-making body among them militate against a "shared boundary policy." More likely, Jews will continue to recognize each other as members of the group for certain purposes, such as self-defense or aiding those in need, and to draw lines of exclusion for other purposes, such as marriage and religious rituals. Tensions will ebb and flow, some groups will change their policies, and others will not. The only force likely to bring all together will be a common danger rather than the common good. FSU Jews will confront the boundary issue if they emigrate, but not very much in Russia or Ukraine.

As discussed in Chapter 4, constructing a secular Jewish identity is challenging. However, there are many instances of religious rituals that have been transformed into an ethnic culture. For example, not all nominal Christians participate in a religious service, but on Christmas most have a decorated tree, exchange gifts, and gather around a family dinner. Muslims in Central Asia observe rituals that originate in Islam, but have become associated with being Uzbek, Tajik, Kazakh, Turkmen, or Kirghiz. Among American Jews, empirical evidence suggests that, "many Conservative Jews still practice religious rituals not out of a religious belief so much as to affirm their Jewish identity.... Some Conservative American Jews maintain their Jewish identity by carrying out a few but conspicuous symbolic and episodic behaviors, such as the bar or bat mitzvah of their children."[32]

Just as Christmas has been secularized, so have Jewish holidays. Few people are opposed to Christmas's message of "peace on earth and good will toward all men," and few would reject a celebration of liberation from slavery, as Passover

---

[31] Donniel Hartman, *The Boundaries of Judaism* (London: Continuum, 2007), 180.
[32] Jack Wertheimer, ed., *Jews in the Center: Conservative Synagogues and Their Members* (New Brunswick: Rutgers University Press, 2000), 264.

is understood. Militantly secular kibbutzim in Israel celebrate Passover and write their own *haggadot* to rid them of theistic elements and emphasize the formation of the Jewish people, social justice, and other values they held dear.[33] There are *haggadot* rewritten in conformity with the beliefs of those who describe themselves in the United States as "cultural, secular and humanistic Jews."[34] Although not all Jewish rituals can be "ethnicized" and divorced from their religious origins, many can, serving as the symbols, traditions, and customs that every ethnic group maintains as defining characteristics. However, they have far less normative power, once they are stripped of supernatural authority and the concept of *mitzvah* as commanded obligation is ignored. Therefore it is up to members of the ethnic group to choose, individually, whether to maintain, ignore, or reject its cultural practices. This decision-making power may empower the individual, but it weakens the collective.

Jewish minorities all over the world have acculturated to majority cultures, and even in the only country in which they form a majority, Israeli Jews have adopted Western modes of dress, foods, music, and leisure-time activities. There are isolated enclaves in New York, London, Montreal, Antwerp, Paris, and elsewhere that have not acculturated to the majority culture and where the Yiddish language, for example, is spoken as a community vernacular. All these are Orthodox or ultra-Orthodox communities where Jewish rituals are widely observed.

Perhaps at the other end of the spectrum of preservation-to-acculturation are Jews in the Former Soviet Union: they are highly acculturated – most often to Russian culture – and live their lives predominantly in the majority culture and milieu and only occasionally in their Jewish equivalents. Communal activists and employees are a partial exception, but they too speak non-Jewish languages and most observe Jewish rituals and customs only from time to time. Almost a century ago, a Hungarian Jew asked, "What is Jewishness after all?... Jews all over the world... cannot find a consensual answer to this and, in fact, each Jew has his own answer. Nevertheless, gradually western Jewry (Europe and America) is evolving a consensual answer and in the near future the Jewish masses of Poland and Russia will embark on the path of western Jewry. In essence, this is the historic path of the Jews."[35]

In the Former Soviet Union this has *not* been the path of the Jews. Because religious forms were unacceptable, they did not serve the same purpose as in the United States or Britain. Secular, socialist, Soviet forms devised by the *Evsektsii* were seen as ersatz. They never replaced Judaism-based symbols and rituals. Nevertheless, secular Jewish identity in the Soviet Union was powerful because it was maintained by a combination of official designation,

---

[33] Now that many kibbutzim have abandoned socialism and few are any longer militantly atheist, their *haggadot* have become "collectibles."
[34] See Peter Schweitzer, *The Liberated Haggadah* (2003). This publication lists sixteen other *haggadot* appropriate for "non-theistic Jews."
[35] Lajos Biro, *A zsidok utja*, 147–48.

anti-Semitism – whether state generated or at the grassroots – and a feeling of apartness, especially after the 1930s. Today, as we have seen, some of these elements of identity are gone. Will "the Jewish masses of... Russia [and Ukraine] embark on the path of Western Jewry" and adopt and adapt Judaism into Jewishness that is not dependent on religious faith? If so, we can expect substantial changes in the meanings and importance of Jewish observances, such as have occurred in the United States where Hanukkah, a minor holiday, is more widely observed than Shavuot, a major one, and feasting is taken more seriously than fasting. As elsewhere, in the absence of authoritative norm setters and because of diverse practices and beliefs, there will be no single consensual way of expressing Jewishness in the FSU.

Already in the 1990s, as we have seen, Russian and Ukrainian Jews' conceptions of Jewishness were inconsistent and diverse. This is not surprising. As noted earlier, there are often logical inconsistencies in people's attitudes, let alone between attitudes and behaviors.[36] Moreover, in the FSU, where there was no Jewish education that would promote norms based on classic and common premises but only informal socialization to understandings of Jewishness, there is bound to be lack of uniformity or consensus. Informal socialization was carried out in the family, within peer groups, and as a result of life experiences. Because there was a fair degree of variance in all three, as well as regional variations, people were bound to form quite different conceptions of Jewishness – what it is, how it is acquired, and how it is transmitted. These conceptions might not have much in common with conceptions across space (those held by other Jews) and across time (those held historically).

The interesting question becomes what new understandings will emerge. Is thin culture or "symbolic ethnicity" transferable across generations? As Bethamie Horowitz asks about American Jews, "If the nature of contemporary American Jewish identity is that it is constructed, discovered and created, how does discovery and invention of personal meaning relate to the transmissibility of identity across generations?"[37] How far can something that is already thin be stretched across generations before it breaks entirely? In other words, can Jewishness survive without Judaism or in the absence of an intense, multifaceted secular Jewish culture that features uniquely Jewish language, art, music, food, and dress?

Calvin Goldscheider has argued that American Jews have become distinctive in social class and are concentrated in certain occupations. Therefore, they are linked to "institutions, networks, families, neighbourhoods and political interests," and this is "a powerful basis of ethnic continuity."[38] This may be

[36] See. For example, Philip Converse, "The Nature of Belief Systems in Mass Publics," in David Apter, ed., *Ideology and Discontent* (New York: Free Press of Glencoe, 1964), 206–61.
[37] Bethamie Horowitz, "Connections and Journeys: Shifting Identities among American Jews," *Contemporary Jewry* 19 (1998).
[38] Calvin Goldscheider, "Modernization: Ethnicity and the post-War Jewish World," in Robert Wistrich, ed., *Terms of Survival: The Jewish World since 1945* (London: Routledge, 1995), 136.

even more relevant to post-Soviet Jews who have little thick culture as their nexus. Yet are these kinds of ties ethnic or social? Is it more important to the highly educated professional to associate with others of his or her education level and cultural tastes than with co-ethnics of a quite different social class and with different cultural preferences and values? It is precisely because increasing proportions of American Jews come into close contact with people of similar social and economic standing that the rates of marriage across ethnic lines have escalated and the proportion of progeny identifying as Jews, let alone acting as such, has declined. Perceptions of cultural and social commonality are not the same as feelings of ethnic consanguinity. Ethnic and social markers are distinct.

Broader Horizons

Many scholars revel in averring that ethnicity is pliable, with frequently changing boundaries and content; by contrast, ethnic and national leaders often proclaim that ethnic groups are "ancient" and stable. The Israeli statesman Abba Eban once pointed out that the Jews are a people who have never adopted a different religion, reside in large numbers in their ancient ancestral homeland, speak the language spoken by their ancestors, and read texts that are thousands of years old. Steven Whitfield similarly argues that Jewish history "can serve as a warning that the case for contingency and plasticity can be pushed too far.... The recent scholarly emphasis on social construction obscures the determinacy that governs social persistence.... Practices that may not be rituals and values that may not be invested with theological meaning, plus Judaism, add up to a culture."[39] This may be an apt characterization of the Jewish culture that evolved among FSU Jews – practices and values specific to the group but not deriving from religious conviction or consciousness of an ethnic culture.

Can we learn anything more generally about ethnicity from the study of post-Soviet Jewry and other groups in the 1990s? One powerful testimony to the persistence of ethnicity are the emigration patterns of Soviet nonterritorial ethnic groups, such as Jews, Koreans, Germans, and Poles. Israel and Germany encouraged their respective co-ethnics to "return home," though (South) Koreans did not. Territorial groups such as Russians and Ukrainians became free to emigrate, as they had not been from about 1924 to the late 1980s, but unless individual émigrés had desirable skills or close relatives in the potential countries of immigration, the doors of most Western countries were closed to FSU citizens. Millions of Jews and Germans emigrated because they wanted to leave an oppressive political system, a failing economic one, and a place where they had suffered ethnic discrimination and to migrate to more democratic and more economically promising countries. Their choices of Israel and Germany may have been pragmatic – these countries would admit them, they would enjoy some cultural advantages in them, other co-ethnics would

---

[39] Stephen J. Whitfield, "Enigmas of Modern Jewish Identity," *Jewish Social Studies* 8, 2–3 (Winter–Spring 2002), 166.

follow — but we cannot dismiss the possibility that cultural and sentimental ties pulled them to Israel and Germany, even though by the 1970s Jews and Germans were far removed from their original cultures and kinfolk. By that time large proportions of each group had married people of other nationalities and many were of multiethnic descent. Many had chosen the non-German or non-Jewish nationality of a parent, but retained some attachments to family and even to the greatly extended family, the ethnic group. Of course, others had lost or cut those ties. Yet in light of strong government-inspired and social pressures to lose their German or Jewish ethnicity, and strong personal incentives to do so, that millions retained such attachments, in whatever degree, testifies to the persistent power of ethnicity, for all that it is "constructed," "situational," and "instrumental."

Ethnicity has been found to be sustainable among other groups. For example, many third- and fourth-generation Armenians born in America do not know Armenian, nor eat Armenian food on a regular basis, nor marry Armenians, but they still "feel Armenian."[40] Ethnic consciousness survives among many groups. As one writer put it,

> On being with some other Finn, "I do not have to explain myself; because we are both Finns, he will know." And, at the level of the group rather than of the individual, "All of us are Finns and we all basically understand each other." This idea of ethnicity as a sense of being a group is not simply a group label. It is not the same as a sense of all having gone to General Sherman Elementary School together. It is founded on Weber's notion of imputed common descent and is reinforced by the power of kinship.[41]

It is not true that "[a] minority cannot endure except at the cost of fanatic conviction and rigorous practice."[42]

Do mutual recognition and thin culture suffice to advance an ethnic cause or motivate one to defend perceived common interests, associate largely with the group and marry within it, and preserve and promote its culture? We return to the intensity with which ethnic identities are held, the commitments they evoke, and how they affect one's life. The persistence of ethnic feelings in the USSR is impressive in light of all the forces, "natural" and man-made, that were aligned against it. Perhaps equally impressive is the ability of a powerful, ambitious,

---

[40] Miri Song, *Choosing Ethnic Identity* (Cambridge: Polity Press, 2003), 9, paraphrasing Anny Bakalian, *Armenian-Americans: From Being to Feeling Armenian* (New Brunswick, NJ: Transaction, 1993). Significantly, "being" and "feeling" are the contrastive terms used by Elena Nosenko-Shtein in her study of post-Soviet Jews, *Byt' ili chuvstvovat'?:osnovnye aspekty formirovaniia evreĭskoĭ samoidentifikatsii u potomkov smeshannykh brakov v sovremennoĭ Rossii* [To Be or to Feel? Basic Aspects of the Formation of Jewish Self-Identification among Children of Mixed Marriages in Contemporary Russia] (Moscow: Russian Academy of Sciences, 2004).

[41] Paul R. Spickard, *Mixed Blood: Intermarriage and Ethnic Identity in Twentieth-Century America* (Madison: University of Wisconsin Press, 1989), 15.

[42] A. Causse, *Du groupe ethnique a la communaute religieuse: Le probleme sociologique de la religion d'Israel* (Paris: Librairie Felix Alcan, 1937), 235.

and all-encompassing state to redefine the content and value of ethnicity. Millions did assimilate – that is, changed their ethnicity – either instrumentally to gain some advantage or as a result of a genuine change in self-perception. Large numbers of people maintained a dual or even more complicated ethnic consciousness – for example, they thought of themselves as both Russian and Ukrainian – but official Soviet classifications forced them to declare only one ethnicity and be identified as such. Just as the Soviet regime was less successful in eradicating belief in a supernatural power than it was in destroying knowledge of religions, it seems to have been less successful in cutting the emotional, nonrational ties of individuals to ethnic groups than it was in either stripping ethnicity of its cultural content or reshaping it significantly. Traditions were lost, languages forgotten, customs abandoned, literatures and the arts made inaccessible, and national histories ignored or reshaped according to ideological criteria.

Those who emigrated bore with them the localized, Sovietized conceptions and practices developed over the decades, but their descendants are likely to adopt the norms and cultures of their co-ethnics in the countries of immigration. Immigrants to Israel will act and think increasingly like Israelis; Germans who resettle in Germany will lose their "Soviet Germanness" over time. Although traces of Soviet-style ethnicity will probably remain, just as they have among previous generations of migrants, in the main, those who leave the FSU will come closer to the understandings of ethnic culture as defined in their host countries. This should be easier for German émigrés than for Jews, because in Israel and the Jewish diaspora the link between religion and ethnicity remains fairly strong, although it had been largely broken by the Soviets.

Just as some Westerners wrongly believed that the fall of communism meant an almost automatic transition to democracy and capitalism (the two are often confused), so did some assume that cultural vacuums and psychological uncertainties created by Soviet policies would be filled and resolved as people rushed to embrace "authentic" cultures and proudly reassert their allegiance to their nominal ethnicities. The assumption underlying that mistaken belief was that the "ethnics" had resisted Soviet assimilation, if not acculturation, and were eager to embrace that which others assumed had been forcibly taken away from them.

The assumptions were wrong. They assumed that democracy and capitalism were universally normative. They did not take into account how isolation from alternative economic and political forms or expressions of ethnic cultures could restrict people's imaginations. They also underestimated the ability of a determined, ambitious, if insecure, state to shape people's thinking and behavior. The Soviet experiment can be judged a failure, because the system did not last a century, but it did reshape the outlooks, beliefs, and behaviors of millions. Those who judge Soviet and post-Soviet Jewry as assimilated or lost to the Jewish people caricature reality. As with all other ethnic groups elsewhere, some Russian-speaking Jews will reduce or abandon their affiliations, others will intensify them, and the majority will probably incorporate them into the wide spectrum of associations, interests, and practices available in the developed world. The salience of ethnicity varies with how it is situated. In some settings, people hide their ethnicity or it is irrelevant; in others the very same people display it prominently; in most settings ethnicity is consciously felt but not important. In the FSU it is likely that Jewishness will be a secondary, tertiary, or even more remote driving force of most Jews' thinking and behavior, as it is among most of the world's Jews. Those whose professions or leisure activities involve them heavily in Jewish affairs will be the exception, as they are now. In the absence of valued, vibrant communal institutions and a thick culture, there are relatively few occasions to display Jewishness more prominently than others of the "nested identities" we all have.

This does not mean that Jewish culture will be irrelevant or inconsequential to the majority. Today it is largely up to the individual and not at all up to the state to determine the location of ethnicity in the hierarchy of a person's identities. Just as there are opera fans who attend several performances a year and pay heavily for the privilege, and just as some spend some time outside the opera reading and thinking about it, so too will Jewish culture, however expressed, continue to entertain, fascinate, attract, and engage. Yet like opera, it will not determine much behavior nor serve as a guide to life for most Russian and Ukrainian Jews.[43] Ethnic groups defined by borders alone give the individual only a feeling, a sense of belonging to an entity. This sense of belonging, or "identity," will likely be regarded by most as a biological accident that has no bearing on thinking and behavior. There may be no positive reason to want to identify with that entity, and there may be strong reasons not to do so, as was the case for some Soviet peoples, including Jews. Ethnicity may become only a "cross to bear."

Among Jews and some other Soviet ethnic groups, feelings of belonging, even if unwanted and resented, sufficed to keep ethnic consciousness alive. After the end of communism, the contentious issue became what cultural content would inform that consciousness. Content can be dictated by the state or urged by external actors, but, as in the 1990s in Russia and Ukraine, it is often up to individuals to choose that content. Eliezer Ben-Rafael has observed, "In many cases

[43] "A Jewishness based on identity rather than an assumed way of life complicates matters for Jewish survival, but, at the same time, seems to be the only way to achieve Jewish survival in our times. The question remains as to whether even that is enough.... Speaking social scientifically, it does not seem likely that it will be a successful project. It requires too much voluntary effort on the part of a population that essentially is becoming more ignorant of what being Jewish all about, generation by generation if not even more quickly. In addition, it must be achieved in the face of horrendous [sic] competition which, precisely because it seems so open and welcoming, is so dangerous to the success of the project, imposing its norms and ways on the Jewish people in the name of freedom, choice, and democracy, very real values in their own right. At the same time, however, Jews have confounded social scientists or their predecessors for many centuries. Hence, as long as the effort is made, no final verdict can be registered." Daniel Elazar, "Jewish Religious, Ethnic, and National Identities: Convergences and Conflicts," in Steven M. Cohen and Gabriel Horenczyk, eds., *National Variations in Jewish Identity* (Albany: SUNY Press, 1999), 41.

of Western societies, Jews evolve in environments [of] marked individualism and weak density of community life. Jewish identity is then firstly grounded in self-understandings that may fluctuate from milieu to milieu or from individual to individual."[44] When aggregated, the preferences of individuals become the empirically defining characteristics of the ethnic group, though they continue to be contested, itself a sign of the vitality of the group. Tensions between historic norms and beliefs, on one hand, and contemporary understandings and practices, on the other, engender both disharmony and creativity. This has been true of the Jewish people for several millennia and is likely to be true for as long as they exist.

---

[44] "Russian-Speaking Jews in Germany," paper prepared for a conference on "The Russian-Speaking Jewish Diaspora," Davis Center for Russian Studies, Harvard University, November 2011.

Appendix A: The Evolution of a Survey
Methods and Sample

Two colleagues in Moscow, Dr. Valery Chervyakov and Professor Vladimir Shapiro, and I conducted a survey of 3,300 Jews in three Russian and five Ukrainian cities in 1992/93,[1] followed by a survey of the same number (not the same people) in 1997/98 in the same cities: in Russia – Moscow, St. Petersburg, and Ekaterinburg; and in Ukraine – Kiev, Kharkiv, Lviv, Chernivtsi, and Odessa. Because of the geographical and cultural diversity of these cities and the fact that they include more than half the Jewish population, we are confident that the survey represents the broad cultural and geographical spectrum of Russian and Ukrainian Jewry.

Face-to-face interviews were conducted in respondents' homes by interviewers of Jewish origin trained specifically for this project. Interviews generally lasted between one and one-and-a-half hours. The 1992/93 survey was replicated in expanded form during 1997/98 in the same three Russian cities and five Ukrainian cities. The same kind of sample was constructed in each of the survey years, and the majority of questions were phrased exactly the same way in both waves of the survey, assuring a high degree of comparability. However, the number of questions in the second wave is about 25 percent higher than in the first because we went into greater detail on some issues and added several areas of inquiry.

---

[1] Some of the findings of the first phase are reported in Z. Gitelman, V. Chervyakov, and V. Shapiro, "Iudaizm v natsional'nom samosoznanii rossiskikh evreev," *Vestnik Evreiskogo Universiteta v Moskve*, 3 (7) 1994. Revised and expanded English version is "Religion and Ethnicity: Judaism in the Ethnic Consciousness of Contemporary Russian Jews," *Ethnic and Racial Studies*, 20, 2 (April 1997); Zvi Gitelman, "The Reconstruction of Community and Jewish Identity in Russia," *East European Jewish Affairs*, 24, 1 (1994); Zvi Gitelman, "Language, Ethnicity, and the Reconstruction of Jewish Identities in Post-Soviet Russia and Ukraine," paper delivered at the Annual Meeting of the American Association for the Advancement of Slavic Studies, November 1996; Chervyakov, Gitelman and Shapiro, "The Ethnicity of Russian and Ukrainian Jews," *East European Jewish Affairs*, 31 2 (2001); idem,"Natsional'noe samosoznanie rossiiskikh evreev," *Diaspory*, No. 3, 2000, and nos. 1 and 2, 2001.

In Russia we conducted the survey in Moscow and St. Petersburg (Leningrad) because they have the largest concentrations of Russian Jews, and in Ekaterinburg (Sverdlovsk, in Soviet times), an industrial city in the Urals with a population then of about 10,000 Jews, the fifth largest in Russia, which we regard as fairly typical of provincial Russian Jewish communities. More than half (53.2%) of the Jewish urban population of Russia – about 99 percent of Russian Jews are classified as urban – lives in these three cities. Moscow had the largest number of Jews in 1989 (175,000), and St. Petersburg the second largest (102,400).

Our Ukrainian research sites were Kiev, the capital and home to the largest Ukrainian Jewish population; Odessa, a historically "Jewish" city with a distinct character; Kharkiv (Kharkov), an industrial city in East Ukraine where Russians are concentrated and where Russian culture prevails, even among ethnic Ukrainians; Lviv (Lvov, Lwow, Lemberg) in West Ukraine, the center of Ukrainian nationalism where Ukrainian culture dominates; and Chernivtsi (Chernovtsy, Cernauti, Czernowitz), which, like Lviv, was annexed to the USSR only in 1939–40. Slightly more than half (50.6%) of the Jewish urban population of Ukraine lives in these five cities.[2]

Jews were enumerated in the 1989 census, as in earlier censuses, according to their own declaration of nationality, which did not have to be confirmed by any documentation. We believe that nearly all who declared themselves Jewish in the census were registered as such in their passports. The great majority of such people have two Jewish parents.[3] It is reasonable to assume that there is an indeterminate but fairly large number of people who have one Jewish parent or, certainly, some Jewish grandparents, but who did not identify themselves as Jews to the census-taker. Should they emigrate to Israel, they may qualify for automatic citizenship under the definitions of Jewish status in the Law of Return [*khok hashvut*], but they would not be considered Jewish for purposes of marriage. For example, a person with a paternal Jewish grandfather or a fully Jewish father, but whose mother is not Jewish, is not considered Jewish according to halakha (Jewish law) and therefore cannot be married to another Jew in a Jewish religious ceremony (Reform Judaism, which would allow such a marriage, is not recognized as authoritative in Israel). A Jewish religious ceremony is the only kind of marriage permitted in Israel, which, following Ottoman precedent, does not recognize civil marriage (unless contracted outside Israel). Yet this same person would qualify as a Jew according to the Law of Return that was consciously adopted as the mirror image of the Nazi Nuremburg race laws of 1935. Under those laws, if a person had three or more Jewish grandparents, he or she was classified as a Jew, even if his or her mother

---

[2] In 1989, 100,000 were living in Kiev, 65,000 in Odessa, and 48,000 in Kharkiv. Chernivtsi and Lviv had substantially smaller populations, 16,000 and 13,000, respectively.

[3] Most people who had just one Jewish parent would choose to register themselves as being of the non-Jewish parent's nationality, especially if that parent were Russian or Ukrainian, which is most often the case in Russia and Ukraine.

Appendix A: The Evolution of a Survey

was not Jewish and the person was a Christian by faith.[4] The Law of Return admits immigrants to Israel as Jews as long as they have or had a single Jewish grandparent.

We interviewed 1,300 people in Russia[5] – 500 each in Moscow and St. Petersburg and 300 in Ekaterinburg; and 2,000 in Ukraine – 500 each in Kiev and Kharkiv, 400 in Odessa, and 300 each in Chernivtsi and Lviv, which are smaller than the other Ukrainian cities. Respondents had to be at least 16 years old, but there was no upper age limit. In 1992/93, our sample replicated very closely the gender and age distribution of the Jewish population over 16 years of age in each city. Because of the lack of updated information, in the second wave we structured the local samples according to the 1989 age-gender distributions. The only important change from 1989 is the dramatic aging of the Jewish population due to the very unfavorable ratio of births to deaths and the emigration of younger people who were overrepresented among the 464,000 Jews who emigrated in 1989–91.[6]

Absent a list of Jewish residents of each city, we created the sample by a "snowball" technique. First, in each city we created a group or panel of several dozen Jewish men and women of different ages and socioeconomic status. We did not interview them but asked them to name several of their relatives, friends, and acquaintances whom they considered Jewish. Then we asked these friends and relatives for their agreement to be interviewed and asked them to identify, in turn, *their* friends and relatives who might be interviewed. Only one member of each family could be interviewed. The panels informed us of the gender, age, type of employment, and professional background of potential respondents. This allowed us to adjust the sample structure constantly to conform to the parameters of the overall Jewish population over age 16 in each city. As can be seen in Tables A.1 and A.2, the age and gender structure of the Russian and Ukrainian samples conforms very closely to the profile of the Jewish population in general.

In addition to the mass surveys, in 1998 we interviewed in depth eight people in each of the eight cities. The sixty-four interviews were designed to probe more deeply into the survey findings. We wanted to understand some of the meanings and nuances that lay behind the responses to our survey questions, even the open-ended questions that allowed respondents to state their understandings in their own words. Interviewees for the more extensive discussions were chosen to represent a broad spectrum of types in each city: men and women, young and old, active Jews and passive ones, and people of different political generations and different professions.

---

[4] A person with two Jewish grandparents was classified as a Mischlinge, one of mixed race.
[5] Actually, there are 1,317 people in the Russian sample but this did not affect the structure of the sample.
[6] Emigration data taken from publications of National Conference on Soviet Jewry; Jewish Agency for Israel; and HIAS.

TABLE A.1. *Distribution of Jewish Urban Population of Russia, 16 and Older, 1989 Census and 1994 Microcensus, and Distribution of our Sample by Age and Gender (percent)*

Age	1989 Census Russia	1989 Census Selected Cities (Moscow, St. Petersburg, Ekaterinburg)	Microcensus 1994 Russia	Survey Sample in Moscow, St. Petersburg, Ekaterinburg 1992–93	Survey Sample in Moscow, St. Petersburg, Ekaterinburg 1997–98
Men					
16–19	3.0	3.0	2.9	2.9	2.6
20–29	9.9	9.3	7.9	9.3	9.2
30–39	14.7	13.1	11.8	14.0	13.4
40–49	16.6	16.7	17.7	16.2	16.7
50–59	21.7	22.2	20.6	22.3	22.5
60 and older	34.1	35.7	39.1	35.3	35.6
Women					
16–19	2.6	2.5	2.6	2.6	2.5
20–29	7.9	7.3	6.5	7.0	7.1
30–39	11.9	10.5	9.5	10.9	10.5
40–49	13.6	13.5	14.6	13.2	13.2
50–59	18.1	17.7	17.3	18.7	18.0
60 and older	45.9	48.5	49.5	47.6	48.7

One standard variable used in social science analyses, level of education, was not useful in this study. The great majority of Russian and Ukrainian Jews have some form of postsecondary education, and as in the United States, the Jewish proletariat of the 1920s–1940s, is gone. It was also difficult to get at another standard variable, income. Soviet society was highly egalitarian, at least nominally. Wages and salaries ranged relatively little, and status was conferred less by wealth than by education, residence, political connections, and profession. Moreover, in the years of our interviews, currencies and their worth changed radically and often. Ukraine went from using the Soviet ruble to "kupony" to the "hryvnia," and the Russian ruble that succeeded the Soviet one underwent several devaluations and transformations. Instead of asking about income in numbers, we therefore asked about the purchasing power of people's incomes, as follows:

"What level of well-being does your present income provide for you and your family?

1. We live from salary payment to salary payment, often have to borrow money to buy the most essential goods, and can save nothing.
2. We have enough money for everyday needs, but even buying clothes is difficult for us: we have to make economies or to borrow money for these purposes.

Appendix A: The Evolution of a Survey

TABLE A2. *Distribution of Jewish Urban Population of Ukraine, 16 and Older, 1989 Census and Distribution of our Sample by Age and Gender (percent)*

	1989 Census		Survey Sample in Kiev, Odessa, Kharkiv, Lviv, and Chernivtsi	
Age	Ukraine	Selected Cities (Kiev, Odessa, Kharkiv, Lviv, Chernivtsi)	1992–93	1997–98
Men				
16–19	3.6	3.6	3.7	3.3
20–29	10.5	10.7	10.5	10.9
30–39	15.9	15.7	16.0	16.2
40–49	15.5	16.0	16.0	16.1
50–59	21.3	21.1	20.5	20.4
60 and older	33.2	32.9	33.3	33.1
Women				
16–19	2.9	3.0	3.0	3.3
20–29	8.4	8.7	8.8	8.3
30–39	12.4	11.9	12.5	12.5
40–49	13.0	13.2	13.2	12.9
50–59	18.5	18.1	17.7	17.6
60 and older	44.8	45.1	44.8	45.4

3. We have enough money for most of our expenses, we can even save some, but it is enough for buying expensive goods, and we have either to use credit or to borrow money.
4. Buying most goods is not a problem for us. But we cannot buy a car or spend money on an expensive vacation trip.
5. We can make some expensive purchases, that is, we have enough money for buying a car, expensive furniture, a country villa, in a word, not deny ourselves anything.

Finally, our analyses rely heavily on years of experience living among or observing Soviet and post-Soviet Jews. Because we focus on culturally and politically conditioned meanings and conceptions, we feel it is a great advantage to be able to approach our subject not as an abstract issue examined from afar but with an appreciation for the specifics of the environments in which it has played out.

Appendix B: Index of Jewishness

The questions used to construct the Ukraine 1997 "Jewishness index" are as follows. Indices for the other three samples used the same questions (except for those that were either not asked in 1992/93 or that were specific to Ukraine), and the results should be considered comparable.

1. By what nationality are you registered in your passport?
    1 Jewish (go to question 3)
    2 Other (ask which one; go to question 3)
    3 I have a new-type passport, nationality is not an entry
2. What nationality do you feel you belong to now?
    1 I feel myself a Jew
    2 I feel myself a person of another nationality (ask which one)
    3 I do not feel I belong to any particular nationality
    4 Other (write in answer)
3. During your life, were you more often proud or ashamed to be a Jew?
    1 More often proud
    2 More often ashamed
    3 Both equally
    4 Neither
    5 Other (write in answer)
    9 Difficult to answer
4. To which of the residents of our city do you feel closer spiritually and culturally: Ukrainians, Russians, or Jews?
    1 Ukrainians
    2 Russians
    3 Jews
    4 Both Jews and Ukrainians, but not Russians
    5 Both Jews and Russians, but not Ukrainians
    6 Both Russians and Ukrainians, but not Jews
    7 All of them equally close

Appendix B: Index of Jewishness

      8 All of them equally distant
      9 Difficult to answer
  5. To whom do you feel closer to spiritually: the Ukrainians of this city, the Russians of this city, or Jews in Russia?
      1 The Ukrainians of this city
      2 The Russians of this city
      3 Jews of Russia
      4 Both Jews in Russia and Ukrainians in this city are close, but not Russians
      5 Both Jews in Russia and Russians in this city are close, but not Ukrainians
      6 Both Russians and Ukrainians in this city are close, but not Jews in Russia
      7 All of them equally close
      8 All of them equally distant
      9 Difficult to answer
  6. Who are more close to you spiritually: the Ukrainians of this city, the Russians of this city, or Georgian Jews?
      1 The Ukrainians of this city
      2 The Russians of this city
      3 Georgian Jews
      4 Both Georgian Jews and Ukrainian in this city are close, but not Russians
      5 Both Georgian Jews and Russians in this city are close, but not Ukrainians
      6 Both Russians and Ukrainians in this city are close, but not Georgian Jews
      7 All of them equally close
      8 All of them equally distant
      9 Difficult to answer
12. If you could be born anew, would you like to be born a Jew or non-Jew?
      1 A Jew
      2 Non-Jew
      9 Not sure, do not know
13. Is your national self-consciousness mostly Jewish/mostly non-Jewish/both?
      1. Mostly Jewish
      2. Both (for example, Ukrainian or Russian)
      3. Mostly non-Jewish
      4. Neither one nor the other
      5. Other (write in answer)
      9. Do not know
15. In your view, is there much/little/nothing typical Jewish in you?
      1. Much

2. Little
3. Nothing
9. Do not know

16. Irrespective of cliches, how would you describe your ethnic identity? Which is most important to you? Choose only one answer.
    1. Ukrainian
    2. Russian
    3. Jew (by religion)
    4. Jew (by ethnicity)
    5. Ukrainian Jew
    6. Russian Jew
    7. Israeli
    8. Cosmopolitan ("*kosmopolit*")
    9. Citizen of the world
    10. Other (write in answer)
    11. Don't know

30. What nation's traditions and customs are closest to you?
    1. Jewish
    2. Other nation (write in answer)
    3. Both Jewish and other equally (write which one)
    4. Other (write in answer)
    9. Don't know

31. What nation's culture, art, and literature are closest to you?
    1. Jewish
    2. Other nation (write in answer)
    3. Both Jewish and other equally (write which one)
    4. Other (write in answer)
    9. Don't know

32. What nation's history is closest to you?
    1. Jewish
    2. Other nation (write in answer)
    3. Both Jewish and other equally (write which one)
    4. Other (write in answer)
    9. Don't know

174. In your opinion, is it necessary for Jews to choose a spouse of the same nationality or does it not matter?
    1. Choose a spouse of the same nationality
    2. Choose a spouse of another nationality
    3. It does not matter
    9. Do not know

175. Generally speaking, is your home primarily Jewish, Ukrainian, or Russian in its spirit and way of life?
    1. Primarily Jewish
    2. Primarily Ukrainian
    3. Primarily Russian

Appendix B: Index of Jewishness

       4. Primarily Jewish and Ukrainian, but not Russian
       5. Primarily Jewish and Russian, but not Ukrainian
       6. Primarily Russian and Ukrainian, but not Jewish
       7. All of these to the same degree
       8. Our home has no national/ethnic character at all
       9. Do not know

196. How would you react if your child were to marry a non-Jew?
       1. Positively
       2. Makes no difference
       3. Negatively
       4. Other
       9. Don't know/no answer

In your view, what is absolutely necessary, what is desirable, and what is unimportant for one to consider oneself a genuine Jew? [1 = Necessary; 2 = Desirable; 3 = Makes no difference; 9 = Difficult to answer]

197. To demonstrate openly one's belonging to the Jewish people, and 17 other items
198. Which of the above mentioned items is the most important in order to consider someone a genuine Jew?

    Score 1 if respondent answered "To demonstrate openly one's belonging to the Jewish people," Score 0 if other answer given. Do the same for the other items.

199. Can you or can you not call yourself a real Jew?
       1. Unhesitatingly, yes
       2. Yes, but with some reservations
       3. I think, no
       9. Do not know

Index

Page numbers followed by letters *f* and *t* indicate figures and tables, respectively.

Abkhazians, 26, 45, 98
acculturation: vs. assimilation, 12–13; definition of, 42; of post-Soviet Jews, 118, 342; of Soviet Jews, 12–13, 161
activism, of post-Soviet Jews, 170, 172*f*, 177–78, 305–8, 306*f*; categories of, 189–93; by city, 180–81, 180*t*; community size and, 190, 306–7; and emigration, 193–94, 305, 307; factors influencing, 178–81, 306–7; friendship patterns and, 170, 172*f*, 181–82
Adygei people, 279*n*68, 287*n*88
Afghanistan, Soviet invasion of, 94, 204, 241, 243
age: and attitudes toward interethnic marriage, 284–85; and attitudes toward Jews in politics, 313; and awareness of Jewish identity, 164, 215, 218–19; and awareness of Jewish organizations, 188, 189, 306; and conception of Jewishness, 116, 216–20, 329; and emigration decisions, 194, 253, 255–56, 255*f*, 263*f*, 334; and experience of anti-Semitism, 16, 196; and friendship patterns, 167, 172; and interethnic marriage, 289–90, 289*f*; and Jewish activism, 190–91, 192, 307; and political participation, 316; and pure Jewish ancestry, 285–86, 286*f*, 287*f*; Russian Jewish population distribution by, 352*t*; and sensitivity to anti-Semitism, 221, 222–23; and survey findings, 6; Ukrainian Jewish population distribution by, 353*t*

Albright, Madeleine, 313, 313*n*30
alienation, of Soviet Jews, 78, 93–94, 204, 303, 332; and emigration, 230, 244
All-Ukrainian Jewish Congress, 189*t*, 305
Altshuler, Mordechai, 278, 279, 287
am (term), 59, 59*n*63, 70
American Jewish Congress, 337
American Jewish Joint Distribution Committee (the Joint), 160, 186, 305, 337; persecution of Soviet Jews linked to, 92; respondents' knowledge of, 188*t*, 189, 189*t*
American Jews: decentralized communities of, 334; friendship patterns among, 167–68; and interethnic marriage, 274–77, 281, 283, 284, 287; Judaism as expression of ethnicity among, 116, 134; in leadership positions, 313; post-Soviet Jews compared to, 334; "privatization" of religion among, 110–11; public expression of Jewishness by, 111; religion and identity of, 115; religious observance by, 144, 144*n*96, 147, 151*n*119; secularization of, 135, 135*n*66; self-conceptions of, 68–69, 121, 328; as social class, 343; Soviet Jews compared to, 15; support for Soviet Jewish emigration, 246; taboo on practicing other faiths, 113; ties to Israel, 237, 238
Amish, 122–23
Anderson, Benedict, 27, 46, 57
Andropov, Yuri, 242
Anti-Defamation League, 160

359

anti-Semitism: age and sensitivity to, 221, 222–23; early Soviet efforts to curb, 201; and emigration, 230, 247, 249, 250, 256, 322; and endogamous marriage, 279; and Jewish identity, 16, 54n38, 159–60, 164, 195–96, 213–14, 221–23, 222f, 232–33; memories of encounters with, 223–26; modern European, 197; perestroika and, 303; physical appearance and, 220–21; in post-Soviet era, 104, 114, 204–13, 222–26, 222f, 230–32, 231f, 233, 339; Russian Orthodox Church and, 199, 206–7, 223; and Soviet Jews' self-understanding, 121; in Soviet Union, 78, 161, 201–4; under Stalin, 201–2; theological vs. racial, 127; in tsarist Russia, 198–99, 299; World War II and, 11–12, 302

Anti-Zionist Committee of the Soviet Public, 176n1

Arendt, Hannah, 55, 198

Armenians: clashes with Azeris, 45, 97; emigration by, 183, 239, 243; ethnic consciousness of, 345; as nation, 58; Russian attitudes toward, 206

Armstrong, John, 79

arts, expression of Jewishness in, 165, 336n25, 338

assimilation: vs. acculturation, 12–13, 161; Bund's views on, 58; definition of, 42; emancipation and, 72; in post-Soviet era, 339; as solution to Jewish problem, doubts about, 76; of Soviet Jews, assumptions regarding, 8, 12, 346–47; of Soviet Jews, factors preventing, 8, 121, 301; Stalin on, 88; state policy of, 42

atheism: in post-Soviet era, 131, 132t, 153, 153t, 154; in Soviet Union, 128–31, 136, 142–43

Austria: Jews in, 76; Toleration Edict in, 126

Azeris: clashes with Armenians, 45, 97; status in Soviet Union, 79, 206

Babel, Isaac, 11, 152, 195

Baltic states: collaboration with Nazis, 302; declarations of independence, 7; demonstrations for sovereignty, 97; nationalism in, 24; post-Soviet, ethnic policies of, 98. See also Estonia; Latvia; Lithuania

Baron, Salo, 63

Belarusians: national consciousness of, 24, 84n18; in post-Soviet era, 7n6, 98–99

belonging, feelings of: Jewish identity and, 14, 15, 105, 109–10; religion and, 126; and synagogue attendance, 116

belonging, markers of, 21

Ben-Rafael, Eliezer, 347–48

ben Zakai, Rabbi Yohanan, 61–62

Betar (Zionist organization), 154

Biro, Lajos, 195, 342

Bleich, Yaakov, 138

B'nai Brith, 167, 337n27

B'nai Zion, 167

Bolshevik Revolution (Revolution of 1917), Jews at time of, 3, 10–11, 168, 200, 308, 313

Bolsheviks: association of Jews with, 300–301, 313; attacks on religion, 128–30; classification of Jews by, 2, 77, 127; vs. Zionists, 301

Borotbist party, 81

Bosnians, 122, 122n12, 326; emergence as nation, 8; ethnic consciousness of, 40

Bragin, Abram, 89

Brass, Paul, 25

Brezhnev, Leonid, 93, 160, 242

Britain: assimilationist policies of, 43; Church of England in, 124; definition of Jew in, 69; secularization of, 6

British Jews: attitudes toward intermarriage, 281; friendship patterns among, 163, 167; religious observance by, 147–48; as sojourners, 297; ties to Israel, 237

Bromley, Yuri, 20n4

Brubaker, Rogers, 39

Brym, Robert, 154, 205–6, 207, 223n101, 241, 283

Buber, Martin, 147

Budnitskii, Oleg, 300n11

Bund (Jewish Labor Bund), 3, 9n9, 74–75; founding of, 74; on Jewish nationalism, 58; on religion, 129; split of, 301; views of, 9–10, 26, 129

Canada: accommodationist strategies in, 42; ethnic diversity in, 40–41, 326

Catholicism: and ethnicity, 99; and identity, 124n19, 124n20, 125; on intermarriage, 267. See also Ukrainian Catholic Church

Caucasus: attitudes toward peoples of, 158, 207, 210, 224, 232, 314; ethnic riots in, 3–4; Jews of, 20, 170, 288n93; in post-Soviet era, 104, 158; Soviet policies in, 81, 85, 327; Stalin on, 26. See also Armenians; Azeris; Chechens; Georgia

Index

Central Asia, 158; attitudes toward peoples of, 158, 207; ethnic policies of post-Soviet states in, 98, 296; Jews in, 20, 131, 143, 159, 170, 174; persistence of clans in, 159; Soviet policies and national consciousness in, 327. *See also* Uzbekistan

Chabad-Lubavitch movement, 137, 138, 138*n*77, 305, 337; membership claims of, 337*n*28; Putin and, 138*n*80, 184–85, 205, 337, 337*n*29; respondents' knowledge of, 188*t*, 189*t*; welfare services by, 186

Chechens, 158, 209, 209*n*65; attitudes toward, 208*f*, 232

Chervyakov, Valeriy, 4, 5, 6, 312, 316*n*37, 349

children: of interethnic marriage, 149, 215, 266, 266*n*4, 273–74, 273*n*34, 274*n*39, 278, 281; of non-Jewish mothers, 119–20. *See also* home, childhood

Christianity: and Judaism, blurring of boundaries between, 152; post-Soviet Jews and, 153–54, 153*t*; as universal religion, 123. *See also* Catholicism;; conversion to Christianity; Russian Orthodox Church

citizenship: changes in, and changes in ethnic identity, 43–44; diverse laws on, 42–43; Soviet, vs. ethnicity, 3, 11, 45

civic states, vs. ethnic states, 296–97

civil war. *See* Russian civil war

class: American Jews as, 343; definitions of, 19–20; vs. ethnicity/religion, 30; vs. nation, 77

Clinton, Chelsea, 265, 275

Cohen, Shaye, 61, 270

Cohen, Steven M., 68, 69, 266*n*4

Cohen, William, 313, 313*n*30

Cold War, repression of Soviet Jews during, 90–95

Communist Party, Jewish Sections of (*Evsektsii*), 129, 301–2

Connor, Walker, 26

Conservative (Masorti) Judaism, 137; on intermarriage, 281

constructivism, 54; on identity/ethnicity, 25, 30; on Jewishness, 50–51

conversion to Christianity: emancipation and, 72; intermarriage and, 272; and Jewish identity, 49, 53, 154; personal experience of, 203; post-Soviet Jews' views on, 113, 154–55; Russian attitudes toward, 63; Spanish Jews and, 162; in tsarist Russia, 127

conversion to Judaism: immigration to Israel and, 333; intermarriage and, 295; and Jewish identity, 22, 48, 108–9, 155–56; and kinship, 60

Cooper, Frederick, 39

"cosmopolitanism," Soviet campaign against, 30, 91, 168, 201, 302

Crimean Jews, 77, 88

Crimean Tatars, 94, 211, 327

culture: changes in, break-up of states and, 1; Jewish, future of, 343, 347–48; Russian, Jews and, 12, 168–69, 175; thick vs. thin, 22–23, 328–30

Czechoslovakia: failure to create super-ethnic loyalty in, 35, 166; Soviet-led invasion of, 93; split-up of, 2, 41

Daniel, Brother, 67, 67*n*101, 113, 266

Daniel, Yuli, 93

democracy: conditions necessary for, 97; decoupling of religion and ethnicity in, 126; "ethnic," 135*n*67

Democratic Choice party, 311*t*, 312

descent: and Jewish identity, 14, 15, 110, 155, 162; pure Jewish, age of respondent and, 285–86, 286*f*, 287*f*

Despres, Leo, 33*n*60

Deutsch, Karl, 36

dietary laws (kashrut), observance in post-Soviet era, 103, 104*t*, 107, 156*n*135

Disraeli, Benjamin, 53

dissident movement, in Soviet Union: emergence of, 94; and Jewish assertiveness, 169; Jews in, 94, 241, 303, 331

Doctors' Plot, 143*n*94, 201–2, 302

Draitser, Emil, 203, 217

Dubnow, Simon, 75, 199

Duch, Raymond, 205

Eastern Europe: shifts and dislocations in 20th century, 1–2; Zionist movement in, 74. *See also specific countries*

Eban, Abba, 344

education: and emigration decisions, 254, 258, 259*f*, 260, 261, 263*t*; impact on religiosity, 130–31; and Jewish identity, 332; of post-Soviet Jews, 352; religious, in post-Soviet era, 148–49; religious, Soviet prohibition on, 129. *See also* schools, Jewish

education tax, emigration and, 240, 242

Ehrenburg, Ilya, 92

Einstein, Albert, 11

Elizabeth (Tzarina of Russia), 197
emancipation of Jews, 63; responses to, 72–73
Emerson, Rupert, 27, 60
emigration, of Russian-speaking Jews, 242–44, 243f, 260; in late 19th–early 20th century, 90, 199–200, 300; in 1970s, 94–95, 204, 239–40, 244, 245, 332; in 1980s, restrictions on, 95; in 1990s, 246–47, 249, 249n32, 260, 303; activism as prelude to, 193–94, 305, 307; anti-Semitism and, 230, 247, 249, 250, 256, 322; decline in 21st century, 244, 247, 254–55, 338–39; demographic factors and, 253–54; destination countries for, choice of, 257–60, 259f, 264, 264t, 344–45; factors influencing, 116–17, 230, 249–57, 255f, 260–61, 263t; and interethnic marriage, 279, 280, 290; Jewishness and, 249, 250–53, 255f, 256–57, 258, 259f, 260; motivations for, 244–47, 261, 344; perestroika and, 13, 95, 204; in post-Soviet era, 2, 100, 101, 183, 193–94, 304; shifts in Soviet policy on, 241–42; Soviet control over, 235, 240; from Ukraine, 248–49, 249n32, 322; U.S.-Soviet relations and, 241, 242; and viability of Jewish community in FSU, 234–35, 261, 304, 332, 334. *See also specific destination countries*
Endelman, Todd, 63n81, 65, 162
Engels, Friedrich, 7
ENKA *(Evreiskaya natsional'no-kulturnaya avtonomiya)*, 310–11
entrepreneurs, ethnic and religious, 50, 182–83; modern technology and, 35–36; in post-Soviet era, 13, 98, 137–38
Estonia, post-Soviet: as ethnic state, 135n67, 296; Russian language speakers in, 43–44. *See also* Baltic states
ethnic diversity, challenges associated with, 165–66
ethnic group(s): creation and destruction of, 8, 29–30, 50; family compared to, 4, 36–37; Jews as, 67, 68, 70; in post-Soviet era, 4, 45; redefining boundaries of, 326; shared content and boundaries of, 21; Soviet/Marxist vision of, 3, 6, 11; Soviet policies on, 7; tribal religions and attributes of, 58. *See also* ethnic relations; *natsional'nost'*
ethnicity: biological basis of, 165; concept of, 19, 65; constructivist perspective on, 25, 30; definitions of, 19–21, 20n4; disappearance of, predictions regarding, 3, 6, 19, 30–31, 30–34, 97; early Soviet policies on, 81–82; environment and salience of, 347; and identity, 3; instrumentalist perspective on, 23–25; and Jewish identity, 9–10, 77, 108, 139, 140, 147; Lenin's theory of, 7, 30–31, 77, 81–82; liberalism on, 31–33; malleability of, 326, 344; modernization and, 34–36; persistence of, 9, 34–38, 326, 344–45; political identity and, 43–44; post-Soviet states' policies on, 98–99; primordialist perspective on, 23–25, 28, 32, 38, 328; as product of interaction, 30; reconstitution in post-Soviet era, 7; in Soviet era, 29, 345–46; "symbolic," 23. *See also* ethnic group(s); ethnicity and religion; ethnic relations; interethnic marriage
ethnicity and religion: fusion of, 47, 60–61, 69, 122–23, 124–26; separation of, 13, 115, 127, 155, 162, 335; spectrum of relationships between, 122–26
ethnic relations, in Soviet Union, 3–4, 160–61; conflicts of late 1980s, 3, 97; in early years, 11; *sblizhenie* (rapprochement), 31, 96–97, 160, 278; *sliianie* (fusion), 31, 97, 160, 278–79, 302
ethnic states, vs. civic states, 135n67, 296–97
ethnie: definition of, 20, 67; Jews as, 67; and nation, 57n48. *See also* ethnic group(s); ethnicity
Europe: ethnicity vs. religious identification in, 126; medieval, Jewish identity in, 62; parameters of identity in, 3; secularization of, 6, 126. *See also* Eastern Europe; West European Jews; *specific countries*
Evsektsii (Jewish Sections of Communist Party), 129, 301–2

family: and emigration decisions, 245, 250–51; ethnic group compared to, 4, 36–37; Jewish, distinctive characteristics of, 112–13; and Jewish activism, 179, 181; and Jewish identity, 69, 164–65. *See also* children; kinship; mothers
Federation of Jewish Communities of Russia (FEOR), 138n80, 184–85
Feingold, Henry, 117
Feuchtwanger, Leon, 226
foods, Jewish: holiday, 142, 146; and Jewish consciousness, 165. *See also* dietary laws (kashrut)
food taboos: functions of, 21, 125; as thick culture, 22

Index

France: assimilationist policies of, 43; terms for Jews in, 71
fraternal orders, Jewish, 167, 337n27
Free Sons of Israel, 167
Freud, Sigmund, 46
Friedgut, Ted, 185
Friedlaender, Israel, 65
"friendship of the peoples," Soviet ideal of, 3, 168. *See also* internationalism
friendships: and Jewish identity, 163, 164, 167–68; of post-Soviet Jews, 169, 170–73, 172*f*; of Soviet Jews, 163, 169
Frost, Robert, 37
Frumkin, Esther, 89

Gagauz, 98
Gaidar, Yegor, 311*t*
Gallup, George, 147
Geertz, Clifford, 23, 34
Gellner, Ernest, 27
gender: and activism of post-Soviet Jews, 179, 180; and emigration decisions, 254, 263*t*; and friendship patterns, 172, 172*n*35; and interethnic marriage, 280, 280*n*71; Russian Jewish population distribution by, 352*t*; and survey findings, 5–6; and synagogue attendance, 179*n*12; Ukrainian Jewish population distribution by, 353*t*. *See also* women
Georgia: Jewish population in, 108, 131, 143, 143*n*94, 174, 245; Ossetian and Abkhaz separatism and, 26, 45, 98
Germans, in Soviet territories, 26; emigration in 1970s, 239; in post-Soviet era, 98, 99, 123, 183; during World War II, 84, 85
Germany: choice as immigration destination, 344–45; citizenship laws in, 42–43; Jewish communities in, assistance to, 120; Soviet Jewish immigration to, 2, 183, 193, 243, 244, 247, 257, 260, 333
Gezerd (organization), 89, 176*n*1
Gibson, James, 205
Giffords, Gabrielle, 268
Gildin, Chaim, 278
glasnost, 95. *See also* perestroika
Glazer, Nathan, 38, 68
globalization: and nationalism, paradox of, 158; of Russian-speaking Jewry, 339–44
Goebbels, Joseph, 63*n*81
Goering, Hermann, 63*n*81
Golbert, Rebecca, 114*n*24, 321
Goldscheider, Calvin, 343
Goldschmidt, Pinchas, 184

Goldstein, Eric, 64*n*83
Goldstein, Moritz, 197
Golovakha, E. I., 211
Gorbachev, Mikhail: and collapse of Soviet Union, 97; emigration under, 13, 95, 204, 241; Jewish support for, 303; and perestroika, 4, 95, 184, 204
goy (term), 59, 59*n*63
Grosby, Steven, 59, 59*n*65
Gruen, Erich, 252*n*37
Guberman, Igor, 234
Gudkov, Lev, 210, 282, 314–15
Gusinsky, Vladimir, 184, 336, 337*n*29

Ha-Am, Ahad (Asher Ginzburg), 74
Hadassah, 337*n*27
halakha (Rabbinic Jewish law): on apostate Jews, 266; on Jewish identity, 14, 22, 108–9, 120, 281, 333; on marriage, 350; on women's obligations, 179*n*12
Ha-Levi, Yehudah, 28*n*43, 47, 48
Hanania, Rabbi, 252*n*37
Hanukkah: in post-Soviet era, 144*t*, 145, 146; traditional foods for, 142; in United States, 146*n*99, 275–76
Hapsburg Empire, Jews in, 76
Harkavy, Alexander, 70
Hasidim, 152*n*121; in post-Soviet era, 137, 152. *See also* Chabad-Lubavitch movement; Karlin-Stolin movement
Hattam, Victoria, 65
Hayes, Christine, 268*n*7, 268*n*10
Hebrew (language): and Jewish identity, 15; secular literature in, 3; speakers of, 22; suppression in Soviet era, 12; terminology in, 59, 59*n*63, 70
Hebrew (term), and conceptions of Jewishness, 61, 71
Hebrew Christians, 266, 341
Heine, Heinrich, 53, 72
Heller, Agnes, 37
Herberg, Will, 147
Herskovits, Melville, 46
Herzl, Theodor, 28, 58, 74
Hesed societies, 192, 194
Hillel, 186, 188*t*, 189, 189*t*
Hinduism, 122
Hirsch, Samson Raphael, 73
Hirschman, Albert, 300
Hitler, Adolf, 65, 297
Hobsbawm, E. J., 28, 57
Hochman, Genya, 142
Hoffman, Eva, 37

holiday observances: intermarriage and, 275–76; and Jewish consciousness, 165; in post-Soviet era, 143–46, 144t; secularization of, 275–76, 341–42; in Soviet era, 141–43; in United States, 275–76, 343

Holocaust, 227–29; in American media of 1950s, 227n106; and Jewish consciousness, 229, 229n114; memory of, in post-Soviet era, 331, 332; remembrance of, and Jewish identity, 103–4, 104t, 196; and Soviet Jews' self-perception, 121; and state of Israel, creation of, 235, 236

home, childhood: and Jewish activism, 179, 181; and Jewish identity, 164–65

Horowitz, Bethamie, 343

Hungary, Jews in, 76, 115–16, 120, 237, 271, 298

identity: choice of, 155; constructivist perspective on, 25, 30; critique of category of, 38–39; definitions of, 8, 38, 99; ethnicity and, 3; group and, 8, 41; individuation and, 41–42; inertia in, 44; instrumentalist perspective on, 23–25; multiplicity of, 39–40, 119; primordialist perspective on, 23–25, 28, 32, 38, 109, 169, 328; religion and, 3, 39, 124–25; shifts in, 39–40, 42–43; social scientists on, 2–3. *See also* Jewish identity

immigration: and identity outcomes, 42; state policies on, 42–43. *See also* emigration, of Russian-speaking Jews; *specific destination countries*

income: and emigration decisions, 253–54, 258, 259f, 260, 261; measuring in survey, 352–53

Independent Order of Sons of Abraham, 167

individualism: and identity, 41–42; and intermarriage, 276; religious, 68–69; and secularization, 126

instrumentalist perspective: vs. constructivist perspective, 25; on ethnicity, 23–25

interethnic marriage: age and, 289–90, 289f; American Jews and, 274–77, 281, 283, 284, 287; arguments against, 272–74, 286–87; attitudes toward, in post-Soviet era, 281–85; children of, 149, 215, 266, 266n4, 273–74, 273n34, 274n39, 278, 281; consequences for Jewish collectivity, 295, 334; diverse views on, 265–66; divorce rates for, 287–88; evolution of Jewish views on, 266–68; and holiday observances, 275–76; and Jewish activism, 307; in Jewish history, 268–72; and marital happiness, 288, 290–95, 290t, 293–295t; opposition to, 267, 281–82; post-Soviet Jews and, 113, 279–81, 285; Reform Judaism on, 119–20, 120n2, 268n7, 274–75; among remarriages, 289, 290, 290n98; secularization and, 272–77; Soviet Jews and, 96, 131, 277–79, 302; in Soviet Union, 3

internationalism, Soviet, 11, 217, 302; contradictions in doctrine of, 80, 302, 327; vs. Jewish assertiveness, 169; shift away from, 83, 201

interviews: factors influencing responses in, 5–6; methodology used in, 5, 349, 351–53; number of participants in, 4, 351; types of, 351

Iranian Jews, in Los Angeles, 166n23

Isaacs, Harold, 36

Islam: on intermarriage, 267, 267n6; in Soviet era, 81; as universal religion, 123

Israel: assimilationist policies of, 43; establishment of state of, 235–36; ethnic/religious entrepreneurs from, 182; identification with, 57, 135, 332; Judaism in, 135–36; Law of Return in, 120, 350–51; marriage in, 350; as motherland for post-Soviet Jews, 322t, 323; organizations active in FSU, 305; post-Soviet Jews' attitudes toward, 238–39; question of Jewish identity in, 55; Reform Judaism in, 350; Soviet hostility toward, 93, 202–3, 237–38, 242–43; Western Jews' disillusionment with, 239, 240

Israel, immigration of Russian-speaking Jews to, 12, 242–44, 340; in 1970s, 94–95, 204, 239–40; in 1990s, 246–47; decline in 21st century, 244, 245–46, 247; emotional attachment and, 261; factors influencing choice of, 258–60, 259f, 264, 264t, 344–45; impact of, 332–33; objective connections and, 250–52, 256, 259, 259f, 263t; in post-Soviet era, 2, 98, 100, 101, 193–94, 234–35; and return migration, 339–40; subjective connections and, 252–53, 256–57, 259, 259f, 263t

Israelites, evolution into nation, 56–64, 59n63

Japan, citizenship laws in, 43, 327

Jenkins, Richard, 41, 196n2

Jewish Agency for Israel *(Sochnut)*, 183, 186, 305; respondents' knowledge of, 188t, 189, 189t

Index

Jewish Anti-Fascist Committee, 91, 176n1, 236, 302
Jewish Communist Party, 301n13
Jewish Council on Public Affairs, 182n15
Jewish Cultural Associations, 184
Jewish identity (Jewishness): and activism, 307; age and awareness of, 164, 215, 218–19; anti-Semitism and, 16, 54n38, 159–60, 164, 195–96, 213–14, 221–23, 222f, 232–33; artistic expressions of, 165, 336n25, 338; awareness of, emotions associated with, 215–20; biological basis of, post-Soviet Jews on, 108–9; constructivist perspective on, 50–51; continuity and change in meanings of, 49–52; conversion to Christianity and, 49, 53, 154; conversion to Judaism and, 22, 48, 108–9, 155–56; definition of, real-world consequences of, 55, 69; definitions of, 21–22, 47–52, 70–71, 326; definitive characteristics of, 10, 14–16, 41, 53–54; descent and, 14, 15, 110, 155, 162; different conceptions of, 71–72, 119–20; in emancipation era, 63; and emigration decisions, 249, 250–53, 255f, 256–57, 258, 259f, 260, 263t; ethnicity and, 9–10, 77, 108, 139, 140, 147; as feeling, 103, 109–10, 112; feeling of belonging and, 14, 15, 105, 109–10; formation of, factors influencing, 9, 11, 159–60, 164–65, 216–19, 222f, 223; friendships and, 163, 164, 167–68; fusion of religion and ethnicity in, 47, 60–61, 69, 122–23, 124–26; future of, 347–48; halakha (Rabbinic Jewish law) on, 14, 22, 108–9, 120, 281, 333; historical evolution of, 55–64; Holocaust and, 229, 229n114; index of, 354–57; insecurities associated with, 15–16; vs. internationalism of early Soviet era, 11; vs. Judaism, separation in post-Soviet era, 127, 155, 162, 335; Judaism and, 9, 16, 22, 53, 60–62, 66, 68–69; language and, 10, 14, 15, 61, 75, 162; matrilineal basis of, 14, 22, 48, 164, 267n7; multiplicity of, 52, 118; negative factors in formation of, 9, 11, 216, 217, 218–19; Nuremberg Laws on, 21–22, 55, 350–51; persistence of, 9, 161; policy implications of study of, 120; positive factors in formation of, 222f, 223; postmodernists on, 49, 50; post-Soviet Jews' understanding of, 14–16, 103–13, 104t, 139–41, 327–28; pride and, 15, 103, 104t, 109, 220; primordialist perspective on, 109; private and public manifestations of, 110–12; secular, post-Soviet Jews and, 105–8; self-understanding and, 348; shifting meanings of, 9–10; Soviet definition of, 2, 14; of Soviet Jews, 8–9, 121–22, 159–60, 162–64, 330–32; traditionalists on, 49–50; traits associated with, 112–13
Jewish Labor Bund. *See* Bund
Jewish organizations (in Russia and Ukraine): ability to deal with anti-Semitism, 232; awareness of, among post-Soviet Jews, 186–89, 187–189t, 306; categories of involvement with, 189–93; clients of, 192–93, 194, 308; future of, 232, 308; perestroika and appearance of, 13, 184; and politics, 308; in post-Soviet era, 173, 177–78, 186, 303, 304–5, 306, 336–37; in Soviet Union, 176, 176n1; and welfare services, 186, 192–93, 194, 304, 306, 337. *See also* activism; *specific organizations*
Jews: Bolshevik perspective on, 2, 14, 77; difficulty in categorizing, 46–47; as ethnic group, 67, 68, 70; founding myths of, 70; geographical concentration of, 119; global community of, prospects for, 340–44; identity issues in post-Soviet era, 99; as nation, 29, 56–64, 59n63, 67–68, 70, 73, 87–88, 108, 173–75; as nationality (*natsional'nost'*), 2, 14, 77, 87, 88–90, 104, 108, 127; in post-Soviet era, 101–2; as race, 55, 64–67; religiosity of, questioning of, 146–47; Russian-speaking, globalization of, 339–40; and state, relationship to, 252n37, 297–303; terms used for, 71–72. *See also* American Jews; British Jews; Jewish identity; post-Soviet Jews; Russian Jews; Soviet Jews; Ukrainian Jews
Jews for Jesus, 50, 53, 114, 154, 266, 341
the Joint. *See* American Jewish Joint Distribution Committee
Judaism: Bolsheviks' attacks on, 129–30; and Christianity, blurring of boundaries between, 152; denominations of, popularity in FSU, 151–52; among diaspora Jews vs. Jewish state, 53n35; ethnic and communal dimensions of, 55–56; and ethnicity, fusion of, 47, 60–61, 69, 122–23, 124–26; on intermarriage, 267–70; in Israel, 135–36; and Jewish identity, 9, 16, 22, 53, 60–62, 66, 68–69; Jewish identity divorced from, 13, 127, 155, 162, 335; Khazars and, 125, 125n26; Khrushchev's campaign against, 93; as nonproselytizing religion, 61;

Judaism: Bolsheviks' attacks on (*cont.*)
   portability of, 62; in post-Soviet era, 105–8, 136–40, 149–52, 151*t*, 153*t*, 155; in post-Soviet Jews' understanding of Jewishness, 103, 104*t*, 105–7, 140; separation from Jewishness, in post-Soviet era, 127, 155; in Soviet Union, 130–31, 136; and traditions, 136, 140; as tribal religion, 55–56, 61, 148; Zionism in relation to, 73–74. *See also* conversion to Judaism; *specific denominations*

kabbalah, 148
Kaganovich, Lazar, 303, 303*n*17
Kalinin, Mikhail, 89–90
Kallen, Horace, 105*n*4
Kantor, Viacheslav Moshe, 337
Karimov, Islam, 136
Karlin-Stolin Hasidic movement, 137, 305, 337; in post-Soviet Ukraine, 138
kashrut (dietary laws), observance in post-Soviet era, 103, 104*t*, 107, 156*n*135
Katz, Jacob, 47
Kautsky, Karl, 127*n*33
Kazakhstan, ethnic riots in, 3, 97
Khazars, 125, 125*n*26
Khmel'nytsky, Bohdan, 141*n*88, 319
Khrushchev, Nikita, 93, 131, 303
Khvylovyi, Mykola, 81
kinship: ethnicity as extension of, 4, 36–37, 165; and Jewish collective consciousness, 69; in Soviet era, 159. *See also* family
Kirienko, Sergei, 310
Kirill, Metropolitan, 133
Kishinev pogrom, 198–99
Kissinger, Henry, 313
Klier, John, 198, 199*n*18
KNOR (*Kongress natsional'nykh ob'edinenii Rossii*), 310
Komzet (organization), 89
Kondratenko, Nikolai, 204
Koreans: in Former Soviet Union, 98; in Soviet Union, during World War II, 84, 85
korenizatsiia (rooting), policy of, 81, 301–2
Kornblatt, Judith Deutsch, 154
Kosmin, Barry, 265*n*4
Kotkin, Steven, 321
Kozlov, V. I., 87*n*29
Krausz, Michael, 50–51, 52
Kravchuk, Leonid, 100, 232
Kuchma, Leonid, 100, 138, 232, 316, 321*n*61
Kurds: Stalin's definition of nation and, 26, 326; Turks' view of, 29

Kymlicka, Will, 32

Laitin, David, 24*n*21, 43
landsmanshaftn (organizations), 167
language(s): and ethnicity, 20*n*4, 21; Jewish, in FSU, 338; Jewish, speakers of, 8, 10, 12, 12*n*13, 22, 56; and Jewish identity, 10, 14, 15, 61, 75, 162; and nationhood, 26; non-Russian, in Soviet era, 31; Russian Jews and, 12; Soviet policies on, 85, 96–97; terms for Jews in, 71; as thick culture, 22; Ukrainian Jews and, 319–21
Lanovyi, Volodymyr, 316
Latvia: as ethnic state, 135*n*67, 296; Jews in, 245, 280. *See also* Baltic states
Lazar, Berl, 138*n*80, 184
League of Militant Atheists, 130
League of the Godless, 129
Lenin, Vladimir Ilyich, 3, 7, 58; on assimilation of Jews, 8; on ethnicity, 7, 30–31, 77, 81–82; on Jews as nation, 87, 127*n*33
Lerner, Daniel, 33
Levayev, Levi, 138*n*80
Levin, Bernard, 53
Liebman, Charles, 51, 69
Lishkat hakesher (Liaison Office), Israel, 305
Lithuania: emigration from, 245, 246; ethnicity and religion in, 99; Jews in, 117, 139, 185, 245, 280; shifts and dislocations in 20th century, 1. *See also* Baltic states
Lithuanians: in dissident movement, 94; persistent identity of, 42*n*105
Livshitz, Alexander, 309
Locke, John, 60
Lueger, Karl, 63
Lukashenko, Alexander, 99
Lustick, Ian, 54, 119
Lustiger, Cardinal Jean-Marie, 49, 67, 266
Luxemburg, Rosa, 30, 30*n*47, 298

Maimonides, 48–49, 113
Markowitz, Fran, 15, 100, 110, 111
marriage, endogamous: anti-Semitism and, 279; halakha on, 350; and Jewish activism, 181. *See also* interethnic marriage
Marx, Karl, 11; on demise of ethnicity, 30–31; on nations, 6, 7; on religion, 128; on social class, 19
Masorti Judaism. *See* Conservative Judaism
Mayer, Egon, 121
McKinney, William, 111
Medem, Vladimir, 203

Index

Medvedev, Dmitrii, 185, 210, 310, 337
Meir, Golda, 29
memory: and Jewish identity, 103–4, 330; Soviet Jews as community of, 330–32
Mendels, Doron, 59
Messianic Judaism, 50, 57, 266, 266n5, 341
Meyer, Alfred G., 197
Meyer, Michael, 47
Mezvinsky, Marc, 265, 275
Mikhalkov, Sergei, 85
Mikhoels, Solomon, 90–91
Miliband, David, 313
Miliband, Edward, 313
Mill, John Stuart, 31
Milosevic, Slobodan, 24
Mitnagdim, 152, 152n121
modernization: concept of, 33–34; and ethnicity, 34–36; and Jewish identity, challenges to, 63–64
Modern Orthodox Judaism, 137
Moldova: creation of, 7; post-Soviet, 98; Transdniestrian Republic in, 45, 98
Moldovans, identity issues of, 22n12, 30
Montagu, Ashley, 66
Moroz, Oleksandr, 316
motherland, post-Soviet Jews on, 322–23, 322t
mothers: Jewish, characteristics of, 112; and Jewish identity, 14, 22, 48, 164, 267n7; non-Jewish, status of children of, 119–20; and traditions/holiday observances, 142–43, 216
Motyl, Alexander, 24n21, 39
Mountain Jews, 108, 174, 288n93
Moynihan, Daniel Patrick, 38, 68
music, and Jewish identity, 165, 338

Nagorno-Karabakh, 45, 97
narod: use of term, 87n29. *See also* Russian people *(Russkii narod)*; Soviet people *(Sovetskii narod)*
narodnost': Soviet Jews as, 77, 89; use of term, 87
nation(s): artificial, Jews as, 67–68; Bolshevik view of, 77; communication patterns and, 36; definitions of, 25–27, 45n113, 58, 60n66; Jews as, 29, 56–64, 59n63, 67–68, 70, 73, 87–88, 108; Soviet rejection of, 87–88, 108, 127n33, 173–75; modernist vs. perennialist perspective on, 27–28, 57, 57n48; origins of, theories of, 27, 30; political implications of membership in, 55; real vs. invented, 28–29; Russian term for, 87, 87n29; Stalin's definition of, 26, 88

nationalism: in Baltic states, 24; in era of globalization, paradox of, 158; ethnicity and, 38, 297; Jewish, 28, 58, 73; in post-Soviet era, 96, 98; Russian, 79, 85–86, 201; and shift in meaning of Jewishness, 9–10; Stalin's, 297; and violence, 6–7, 19
nationality. *See natsional'nost'*
natsiia (nation), use of term, 87, 87n29
natsional'nost' (nationality, ethnic group), in Soviet Union: definition of, 45n113; government role in creation of, 83–84, 84n18; Jews as, 2, 14, 77, 87, 88–90, 104, 108, 127; nonterritorial minorities, 7, 84–85; passports indicating, 80, 83, 108, 121, 161, 197, 301, 308–9; vs. Soviet citizenship, 3, 11, 45; state policies on, 7, 31, 79–87, 96–97; use of term, 87, 87n29
Nazis: identity cards under, 197; on Jews as race, 55; Nuremberg Laws of, 21–22, 55, 350–51; Russian and Ukrainian collaborators of, 9, 85, 302, 319. *See also* Holocaust
Nemtsov, Boris, 309
Nevzlin, Leonid, 336
New Age religions, 148
Nikolai I (Tsar of Russia), 299
Nosenko-Shtein, Elena, 329
Nuremberg Laws, 21–22, 55, 350–51

Oistrakh, David, 11
Orange Revolution, Ukraine, 96, 100
Orthodox Christianity. *See* Russian Orthodox Church; Ukrainian Orthodox Church
Orthodox Judaism: emancipation and origins of, 73; on intermarriage, 281; post-Soviet Jews and, 107, 150, 152
Ossetians, 26, 45, 98

Palatnik, Raisa, 92
Pale of Settlement, 62, 168, 174n39, 198, 299
Palestinians: emergence as nation, 8, 28; Hebrew spoken by, 22; national consciousness of, Zionism and, 30
Pamyat' (organization), 104
Panina, N. V., 211
Passover: and Jewish consciousness, 165; observance in post-Soviet era, 144t, 145, 145n98; secularization of, 341–42
passports, Soviet, 80, 83, 108, 121, 161, 197, 301, 308–9
perestroika, 4, 95; and anti-Semitism, 303; and emigration, 13, 95, 204, 241; Jewish organizations during, 13, 184

Petliura, Semen, 224
pogroms: during Russian civil war, 200; in Russian Empire, 198–99, 299; in Ukraine, 141*n*88, 319
Poles: Catholicism and identity of, 124*n*19, 125; identity issues in post-Soviet era, 99; nationalist mobilization of, 21; religion and ethnicity in identity of, 123; in Soviet Union, during World War II, 84, 85
political identity, impact on ethnic identity, 43–44
politics, in post-Soviet era, 100–101; attitudes toward Jews being in, 312–16, 312*f*, 315*t*, 318–19; participation of Jews in, 309–12, 311*t*, 316–19, 318*t*, 324
postmodernists, 54; on malleability of Jewishness, 49, 50
post-Soviet Jews: acculturation of, 118, 342; activism among, 170, 172*f*, 177–78, 305–8, 306*f*; American Jews compared to, 334; anti-Semitism and, 104, 114, 204–13, 222–26, 222*f*, 230–32, 231*f*, 233; attitudes toward conversion to Christianity, 113, 154–55; attitudes toward Israel, 238–39; attitudes toward Jews in politics, 312–16, 312*f*, 315*t*; awareness of Jewish organizations, 186–89, 187–189*t*; education of, 352; emigration and viability of Jewish community in FSU, 234–35, 261, 304, 332, 334; ethnicity vs. religion in self-identification of, 108, 139, 140, 147; friendship patterns among, 169, 170–73, 172*f*; immigration to Israel, 2, 98, 100, 101, 193–94, 234–35; intermarriage among, 113, 279–81, 285; Jewish organizations and, 173, 177–78; Judaism and, 105–8, 136–40, 149–52, 151*t*, 153*t*; meaning of Jewishness to, 14–16, 103–13, 104*t*, 139–41, 327–28; motherland identified by, 322, 322*t*, 323; as nationality, 104; political participation of, 309–12, 311*t*, 316–19, 318*t*; problematic aspects of Jewish identity of, 113–18; propensity to emigrate, 254, 255*f*, 256; public vs. private display of Jewishness by, 101–2, 112; relationship to state, 298–99, 303, 305–8, 309; religiosity of, 148, 156–57; religious preferences of, 153–54, 153*t*; ritual observance by, 149–51, 151*t*; secularization of, 105–8, 106*t*, 115–16, 117; separation of religion and ethnicity by, 127, 155; traditions and, 140–41, 143–46, 144*t*; uncertain future of, 114–15, 193, 194, 196, 261, 308, 334–35; unique characteristics of, 127, 157, 173, 335, 338, 340–41; urbanization of, 352*t*; voting preferences of, 311–12, 311*t*. *See also* emigration, of Russian-speaking Jews; Russian Jews; Ukrainian Jews

Primakov, Evgenii, 310
primordialist perspective: on ethnicity, 23–25, 28, 32, 38, 328; on Jewish identity, 109, 169; on Jewish nationalism, 38, 58
privatization, of religion, 110–11, 148
Progressive Judaism. *See* Reform Judaism
proletarian internationalism. *See* internationalism, Soviet
Purim, observance in post-Soviet era, 144*t*, 145, 146
Putin, Vladimir, 96, 100, 134, 210, 296; administration of, 310; and Chabad-Lubavitch movement, 138*n*80, 184–85, 205, 337, 337*n*29
Putnam, Robert, 165–66

Rabbinic Jewish law. *See* halakha
rabbis: Chabad, 185; in FSU, 137
Rabinovich, Vadim, 305
race: as biological category, 66–67; Jews as, 55, 64–67; as socially constructed category, 65*n*90, 67
rapprochement. *See* sblizhenie
rebels, Jews as, 298, 300
Reform (Progressive) Judaism, 72–73; on intermarriage, 119–20, 120*n*2, 268*n*7, 274–75; in Israel, 350; and term Hebrew, 71
"refuseniks," plight of, 240
Reines, Rabbi Yitzhak Yaacov, 73*n*125
religion(s): Bolshevik attacks on, 128–30; definition of, 19; and identity, 3, 39, 124–25; ignorance about, in FSU, 132, 156; individualism in, 68–69; and Jewish identity, 9, 16, 22, 53, 60–62, 66, 68–69; Jewish identity divorced from, 13, 127, 155, 162, 335; in post-Soviet era, 96, 131–34, 132*t*, 136–39, 147, 149–50, 153–54, 153*t*, 156–57; privatization of, 110–11, 148; resurgence of, 6; ritual observance vs. belief, 149–50; Soviet suppression of, 3, 77, 93, 131, 156, 202, 327; in Soviet Union, 80–81; tribal, 55–56, 58, 61, 122–23, 148; universal, 122–24; Zionism in relation to, 73–74. *See also* atheism; ethnicity and religion; *specific religions*
religious organizations, in post-Soviet era, 140, 143

Index

Revolution of 1917. *See* Bolshevik Revolution
Rifkind, Malcolm, 313
Roma, 14
Roof, Wade Clark, 111
Rosh Hashanah, observance in post-Soviet era, 144*t*, 145
Roshwald, Aviel, 329
Rosman, Moshe, 47, 52
Rossiiskii narod (term), 87*n*29, 99, 326
Rufeisen, Oswald. *See* Daniel, Brother
Rusinek, Alla, 203
Russia: Jewish population in, 248, 248*t*. *See also* Russia, post-Soviet; Russian Jews; Russian people; Soviet Union; tsarist Russia
Russia, post-Soviet, 100; anti-Semitism in, 204–10, 223; attitudes toward different ethnic groups in, 208*f*; attitudes toward intermarriage in, 281–83, 282*t*, 283*t*; ethnicity in, 42, 99, 296; politics in, 296; religion in, 100, 106–7, 106*t*, 337
Russian civil war (1917–21): Jewish allegiances during, 300*n*11; pogroms during, 200
Russian culture: and post-Soviet Jews, 175; and Soviet Jews, 12, 168–69
Russian Jewish Congress (RJC), 184, 305; turnover in leadership of, 336–37
Russian Jews, post-Soviet: activism of, 307; ancestry of, 286, 286*f*, 287*f*; attitudes toward Jews in politics, 312, 312*f*, 315*t*; awareness of Jewish organizations, 186–89, 187*t*, 188*t*; communal life of, 304, 335–36; immigrants to U.S., 249*n*32; Jewish identity of, 339; meaning of Jewishness to, 14–16; political involvement of, 309–12, 324; population distribution by age and gender, 352*t*; population of, 193, 248*t*, 308; relationship to state, 298–99, 325; religiosity among, 151, 151*t*; voting preferences of, 311–12, 311*t*
Russian nationalism: and anti-Semitism, 201; in Soviet era, 79; during World War II, 85–86
Russian Orthodox Church (ROC): and anti-Semitism, 199, 206–7, 223; in post-Soviet era, 99, 133–34, 136, 150; Russian ethnicity identified with, 133; in Soviet era, 80, 327; Stalin and, 86; in tsarist Russia, 128
Russian people *(Russkii narod)*: in post-Soviet era, 99, 326; preferential status in Soviet Union, 82, 83, 85–87, 90, 201
Russia's Choice *(Vybor Rossii)* party, 310
Rusyns, 29
Ryvkina, Rozalina, 154, 171*n*34, 178*n*11, 179, 224, 231, 283

Sabbath observance: in Georgian communities, 143*n*94; in post-Soviet era, 103, 104*t*, 142, 150–51; in United States, 151*n*119
Safran, Gabriella, 63, 198
Salitan, Laurie, 241
Sarna, Jonathan, 155
Sartre, Jean-Paul, 196, 213
Satanovsky, Evgenii, 337
sblizhenie (rapprochement) of nationalities, 31, 96–97, 160; interethnic marriage and, 278
Scherer, John, 242*n*18
Schindler, Alexander, 120*n*2
Schnapper, Dominique, 32, 71
Schneerson, Menachem Mendel, 138
Schneerson, Yosef Yitzhak, 138*n*78, 337*n*29
Scholem, Gershom, 57*n*53, 163
schools, Jewish: in post-Soviet era, 137, 139, 148–49, 185, 304, 338, 339; in Soviet Union, 16, 80; in tsarist Russia, 73*n*125
Schopflin, George, 76
Schreiber, Rabbi Moshe, 73
secularization, process of: in Europe, 6, 126; in Soviet Union, 130–31, 277
secularization of Jews: American, 135, 135*n*66; factors responsible for, 117; and holiday observances, 275–76, 341–42; and intermarriage, 272–77; post-Soviet, 105–8, 106*t*, 115–16, 117; and shift in meaning of Jewishness, 9–10; Soviet, 3, 130–31, 342–43
Sefer (association), 338
selbsthass (self-hatred), among minorities, 214
Shaevich, Adolf, 184
Shaked, Gershon, 136
Shapiro, Vladimir, 4, 5, 6, 144, 148, 283*n*83, 316*n*37, 322, 349
Sharansky, Natan, 305*n*22
Shavuot, 142, 343
Shcherbakov, Alexander, 92
Sherman, C. Bezalel, 68
Shils, Edward, 38, 56
Shternshis, Anna, 150, 153*n*122, 278*n*56, 279
Shumsky, Oleksander, 81
Sikhs, 122, 122*n*10
Sinyavsky, Andrei, 93
Skrypnik, Mykola, 81
Slezkine, Yuri, 84
sliianie (fusion) of nationalities, 31, 97, 160, 302; interethnic marriage and, 278–79

Slovaks, 123
Smith, Anthony D., 20, 27, 35, 57n48, 58, 60
Sochnut. See Jewish Agency for Israel
Social-Democratic Labor Party (Russia), 26, 75
socialism: and atheism, 128; nations' disappearance under, 77; as solution to "Jewish problem," 74, 76
social scientists: on anachronism of ethnicity, 33; on ethnicity and nationalism, 38; on identity, 2–3
Solchanyk, Roman, 319, 323
South African Jews, 167
Soviet Jews: acculturation of, 12–13, 161; alienation of, 78, 93–94, 204, 230, 244, 303, 332; anti-Semitism and, 78, 161, 201–4; assimilation of, 8, 12, 121, 301, 346–47; as community of memory, 330–32; confusion about categorization of, 88–89; connections to West, as liability, 90, 91, 92; in early Soviet era, 79, 199–200, 210; emigration of, in 1970s, 94–95, 204, 239–40; emigration of, Western Jews' support for, 240–41; friendships among, 163, 169; holiday observances by, 141–43; immigrants in Brooklyn, New York, 15, 110; impact of state policies on, 77–78; intermarriage among, 96, 131, 277–79, 302; Israeli state and, 236–38; Jewish identity of, 8–9, 121–22, 159–60, 162–64, 330–32; *korenizatsiia* (rooting) policy toward, 81, 301–2; in leadership posts, 79, 92, 210; as *narodnost'*, 77, 89; as *natsional'nost'*, 2, 14, 77, 87, 88–90, 104, 108, 127; persecution after World War II, 11–12; population of, 95–96, 248t; postrevolutionary generation of, 10–11; privatization and individualization of faith among, 111–12; relationship to state, 301–3; repression during Cold War, 90–95; Russian culture and, 12, 168–69; secularization of, 3, 130–31, 342–43; socialization to Jewishness, 162–64; thick vs. thin culture of, 78; unique experience/characteristics of, 10–12, 113–14, 127; vocational profile of, 163; during World War II, 95, 227. *See also* emigration, of Russian-speaking Jews
Soviet people *(Sovetskii narod)*, 82; collapse of ideal of, 4; as fundamentally new people, 160; Russian people's status within, 82, 83, 85–87, 90; use of term, 87n29
Soviet Union: anti-Semitism in, 78, 161, 201–4; atheism in, 128–31, 136; dissident movement in, 94; ethnicity in, 29, 345–46; ethno-territorial federalism in, 84; language policies in, 85, 96–97; as motherland for post-Soviet Jews, 322–23, 322t; nationality policies in, 7, 31, 79–87, 83–84, 84n18; religion in, suppression of, 3, 77, 80–81, 93, 131, 156, 202, 327; "second economy" in, 176–77; secularization in, 130–31, 277; social engineering experiment of, 3–4, 159, 327. *See also* ethnic relations, in Soviet Union; Soviet Jews; Soviet people; Soviet Union, collapse of
Soviet Union, collapse of, 4, 97; causes of, 31, 97, 98; ethnicity after, 4, 45, 161; identities after, 40, 99; Jewish emigration after, 2, 100, 101, 183; nations and nationalities after, 158–59; religion after, 96, 131–34, 132t, 136–39, 147–50
Speiser, E. A., 62
Stalin, Joseph: anti-Semitism under, 201–2; definition of nation, 26, 88; and group vs. individual rights, 84; on Jews and disappearance of nations, 77, 88; nationalism of, 297; and preferential status of Russian people, 85, 86; and Russian Orthodox Church, 86; shifts in policies of, 82–83; World War II policies of, 85–86
state, diaspora Jews' relationship to, 252n37, 297–98; in post-Soviet era, 298–99, 303, 305–8, 309, 320–25; in Soviet era, 301–3; in tsarist Russia, 299–300
statehood: nationhood as prerequisite for, 29; territory and, 29, 74; Zionism and, 74
Stein, Sarah Abrevaya, 50
Stern, Samu, 297, 298n2
Steyn, Juliet, 50
Strauss, Leo, 195
Sultan-Galiev, Mirza, 81
Suny, Ronald, 84, 115n25
synagogue: feelings of belonging and attendance of, 116; gender and attendance of, 179n12; in post-Soviet era, 337, 339

Tenenbaum, Joseph, 56, 65n90
territory: and ethnicity, 21; and identity, 39; and Jewish identity, 2, 22, 62, 62n74; and nationhood, 26, 45n113; and statehood, 29, 74
thick culture, Jewish, 328; destruction under Soviet rule, 78, 328; vs. thin culture, 22–23; transferability across generations, 343
thin culture, Jewish, 328; Soviet system and creation of, 332; survival under Soviet rule, 78, 328–29, 330; vs. thick culture, 22–23

Index

Tirosh (journal), 338
Tishkov, Valeriy, 20, 20*n*5, 23, 27, 59*n*63, 84, 201
Tito, Josip Broz, 40
Tolts, Mark, 279, 281, 287
traditions, Jewish: and Jewish consciousness, 165, 341; Judaism and, 136, 140; in post-Soviet era, 140–41, 143–46, 144*t*; in Soviet era, 141–43, 162. *See also* holiday observances
tribal religion(s), 122–23; and ethnic group, survival of, 125; Judaism as, 55–56, 61, 148; and nation, 58
Trotsky, Leon, 298, 313
tsarist Russia: anti-Semitism in, 198–99, 299; Jewish population in, 58, 87, 127, 168, 248, 248*t*; Jews' relationship to state in, 300; Orthodox Church in, 128; Zionism in, 58
Tshernovitz, Khaim, 73*n*125
Tudjman, Franjo, 24
Turkey: Jews in, 314; Kurds in, 326; modernization in, 33–34

Ukraine: anti-Semitism and pogroms in, 141*n*88, 319; emigration from, 248–49; famine of 1932–33 in, 85; Jewish population in, 248, 248*t*. *See also* Ukraine, post-Soviet; Ukrainians
Ukraine, post-Soviet, 100–101; anti-Semitism in, 210–13, 223; attitudes toward ethnic groups in, 212*t*; as civic state, 296; East vs. West, 323, 323*n*67; ethnic policies of, 42, 99, 232; Jewish organizations in, 185, 304–5; Judaism in, 138; Orange Revolution in, 96, 100, 296; politics in, 296; religion in, 106, 106*t*, 107, 134, 337. *See also* Ukrainian Jews
Ukrainian Catholic Church (Uniate): in post-Soviet era, 134; in Soviet era, 80
Ukrainian Jews, post-Soviet: activism of, 190–91, 307; ancestry of, 286, 286*f*, 287*f*; attitudes toward Jews in politics, 312, 312*f*, 315*t*; awareness of Jewish organizations, 186–89, 187*t*, 189*t*; communal life of, 304, 335–36; cultural and religious freedom of, 96; emigration of, 248–49, 249*n*32, 322; friendship patterns among, 170, 175; holiday observance among, 145; intermarriage among, 280, 283–84, 289–90; Jewish identity of, 14–16, 339; language issues for, 319–21; political involvement of, 316–19, 324; population distribution by age and gender, 353*t*; population of, 193, 308; relationship to state, 298–99, 320–24, 325; religiosity among, 149, 151, 151*t*; sense of kinship among, 108, 109; as sojourners, 324; voting preferences of, 316, 317, 318*t*
Ukrainian Orthodox Church, in post-Soviet era, 134
Ukrainians: collaboration with Nazis, 302, 319; in dissident movement, 94; emergence as nation, 8, 28; ethnic consciousness of, 24; nationalist mobilization of, 21; Russian attitudes toward, 29, 208*f*; West vs. East, ethnic consciousness of, 29–30. *See also* West Ukrainians
Union of American Hebrew Congregations (Union for Reform Judaism), 71
United States: acceptance of Jews in, 167; assimilationist policies of, 43; Civil Rights Act in, 69; definition of Jew in, 69; ethnic diversity and reduced social solidarity in, 165–66; ethnic diversity and survival of, 40–41; ethnic identities in, 37; evangelicals in, 125–26; immigration of Russian-speaking Jews to, 2, 183, 193, 243, 243*n*22, 244, 245–46, 247, 252, 257, 259, 260, 300, 334, 340; Jewish holidays in, 146*n*99, 275–76, 343; privatization of religion in, 110–11, 148; relations with Soviet Union, and Soviet immigration policies, 241, 242; religion and ethnicity in, 124, 124*n*24; religiosity in, 6, 156, 156*n*133; Soviet Jews in Brooklyn, New York, 15, 110; terms for Jews in, 71. *See also* American Jews
universal religions, 122–24
urbanization: impact on religiosity, 130–31; and Jewish identity, 332; of Russian Jews, 352*t*; of Ukrainian Jews, 353*t*
Urinson, Boris, 309–10
Uvarov, Count S. S., 128
Uzbekistan, religion in, 136
Uzbeks: identity issues in post-Soviet era, 99; Russian attitudes toward, 208*f*

Va'ad: establishment of, 13, 184, 304; founding congress of, 4; respondents' knowledge of, 186, 188*t*, 189*t*
Van Den Berghe, Pierre, 25, 37, 165
Van Evera, Stephen, 34
Varshney, Ashutosh, 24, 25, 45*n*113
violence: and hardening of ethnic identities, 33, 35; nationalism and, 6–7, 19
Vital, David, 335
Vladimir (Grand prince of Kiev), 125

Vlasov, Andrey, 85
Voroshilov, Marshall Kliment, 236
voting preferences: of Russian Jews, 311–12, 311t; of Ukrainian Jews, 316, 317, 318t

Waters, Mary, 37
Webber, Jonathan, 52, 54, 118
Weber, Max, 26
Weinreich, Uriel, 70–71
welfare services, Jewish organizations and, 186, 192–93, 194, 304, 306, 337
Werblowsky, R. J. Zwi, 157
Western Jews: arguments against intermarriage, 286–87; community leadership among, 337; disillusionment with Israel, 239, 240; evolution of identity of, 342, 343; support for Soviet Jewish immigration, 240–41. *See also* American Jews; British Jews; West European Jews
West European Jews: after emancipation, 197; on Jewish identity, 109; social segregation in 19th and 20th centuries, 162–63; ties to Israel, 237, 238
West Ukrainians: attitudes toward different ethnic groups, 212; ethnic consciousness of, 24, 29–30, 99, 158; identification with Soviet Union, 323; religion of, 134; Soviet policies on, 79. *See also* Zapadniki
Whitfield, Stephen, 41, 344
Wilson, Andrew, 323n67
women: Jewish organizations for, 337n27; in Soviet era, 280n71; synagogue attendance by, 179n12; and traditions/holiday observances, 141–43, 216. *See also* gender; mothers
World Union for Progressive Judaism, 305
World War II: and anti-Semitism, 11–12, 302; Jews in Soviet armed forces in, 228, 228n110; Russian nationalism during, 85–86; Soviet Jews as victims in, 95, 227; Soviet losses in, 227; Soviet nationalities suspected of disloyalty during, 84–85. *See also* Holocaust

Yabloko party, 311t, 312
Yahadut/Yahadus (term), 70
Yanukovich, Victor, 101
Yeltsin, Boris, 100, 133, 204, 206, 210; Jews in government of, 309–10
Yiddish culture, Soviet, 11, 200, 301; remnants of, 331; suppression of, 91, 201, 302; "thaw" and, 93; before World War II, 340
Yiddishism, 75–76, 115
Yiddishkayt (term), 70–72
Yoffie, Rabbi Eric, 120n2
Yom Kippur, observance in post-Soviet era, 144t, 145, 145n98
Yugoslavia: failure to create super-ethnic loyalty in, 29, 35, 40, 166; fracturing of, 2, 40, 41; nationalism and violence in, 19. *See also* Bosnians
Yupiks, 329
Yushchenko, Viktor, 101, 138, 337

Zapadniki (Westerners): emigration by, 245; influence of, 145; and knowledge of Judaism, 131
Zhdanov, Andrei, 92
Zhirinovsky, Vladimir, 208, 297; party led by, 311t
Zhitlovsky, Chaim, 75
Zionism, 3, 9, 235–36; Bolshevik suppression of, 301; and immigration, 244–45, 256; on Jews as nation, 127n33; Jews in Russian Empire and, 58; Judaism in relation to, 73–74; origins of, 58, 73; and Palestinian national consciousness, 30; post-Soviet Jews' attitudes toward, 238; "primordial" Jewish nationalism and, 28; Reform Judaism's opposition to, 72–73; as response to emancipation, 73; Soviet opposition to, 93, 202, 203, 237, 242; traditional ethno-religious fusion and, 76
Zissels, Joseph, 304
Zvi, Sabbatai, 57